Computer Concepts with QuickBASIC

SHELLY
CASHMAN
SERIES™

Computer Concepts with QuickBASIC

GLORIA A. WAGGONER and JAMES S. QUASNEY

boyd & fraser

boyd & fraser publishing company

A Division of South-Western Publishing Company
Boston, MA 02116

Developed by Susan Solomon Communications
Manufactured in the United States of America

ISBN 0-87835-764-5

1 2 3 4 5 6 W 5 4 3 2 1

CONTENTS IN BRIEF

PREFACE xiii

RESEARCH AND PHOTO ACKNOWLEDGMENTS xvi

CHAPTER 1 AN INTRODUCTION TO COMPUTERS 1.1

CHAPTER 2 MICROCOMPUTER APPLICATIONS: USER TOOLS 2.1

CHAPTER 3 PROCESSING DATA INTO INFORMATION 3.1

CHAPTER 4 INPUT TO THE COMPUTER 4.1

CHAPTER 5 THE PROCESSOR UNIT 5.1

CHAPTER 6 OUTPUT FROM THE COMPUTER 6.1

CHAPTER 7 AUXILIARY STORAGE 7.1

CHAPTER 8 FILE ORGANIZATION AND DATABASES 8.1

CHAPTER 9 DATA COMMUNICATIONS 9.1

CHAPTER 10 OPERATING SYSTEMS AND SYSTEM SOFTWARE 10.1

CHAPTER 11 COMMERCIAL APPLICATION SOFTWARE 11.1

CHAPTER 12 THE INFORMATION SYSTEM DEVELOPMENT LIFE CYCLE 12.1

CHAPTER 13 PROGRAM DEVELOPMENT 13.1

CHAPTER 14 CAREER OPPORTUNITIES IN THE AGE OF INFORMATION PROCESSING 14.1

CHAPTER 15 TRENDS AND ISSUES IN THE INFORMATION AGE 15.1

INTRODUCTION TO DOS DOS 1

PROGRAMMING IN QuickBASIC QB 1

INDEX I.2

CONTENTS

CHAPTER 1 AN INTRODUCTION TO COMPUTERS 1.1

OBJECTIVES 1.2
WHAT IS A COMPUTER? 1.3
WHAT DOES A COMPUTER DO? 1.3
WHY IS A COMPUTER SO POWERFUL? 1.4
HOW DOES A COMPUTER KNOW WHAT TO DO? 1.4
INFORMATION PROCESSING: A BUSINESS APPLICATION 1.4
THE INFORMATION PROCESSING CYCLE 1.6
WHAT ARE THE COMPONENTS OF A COMPUTER? 1.6
CATEGORIES OF COMPUTERS 1.8
COMPUTER SOFTWARE 1.9
WHAT ARE THE ELEMENTS OF AN INFORMATION SYSTEM? 1.15
A TOUR OF AN INFORMATION SYSTEMS DEPARTMENT 1.16
SUMMARY OF AN INTRODUCTION TO COMPUTERS 1.21
CHAPTER SUMMARY 1.21
KEY TERMS 1.23
REVIEW QUESTIONS 1.23
CONTROVERSIAL ISSUES 1.24
RESEARCH PROJECTS 1.24

THE EVOLUTION OF THE COMPUTER INDUSTRY 1.25

CHAPTER 2 MICROCOMPUTER APPLICATIONS: USER TOOLS 2.1

OBJECTIVES 2.2
AN INTRODUCTION TO GENERAL MICROCOMPUTER APPLICATIONS 2.2
THE FOUR MOST COMMON GENERAL APPLICATIONS 2.4
WORD PROCESSING SOFTWARE: A DOCUMENT PRODUCTIVITY TOOL 2.4
ELECTRONIC SPREADSHEET SOFTWARE: A NUMBER PRODUCTIVITY TOOL 2.9
DATABASE SOFTWARE: A DATA MANAGEMENT TOOL 2.12
GRAPHICS SOFTWARE: A DATA PRESENTATION TOOL 2.14
OTHER POPULAR MICROCOMPUTER APPLICATIONS 2.16
INTEGRATED SOFTWARE 2.17
GUIDELINES FOR PURCHASING MICROCOMPUTER APPLICATIONS SOFTWARE 2.18
LEARNING AIDS AND SUPPORT TOOLS FOR APPLICATION USERS 2.19
TIPS FOR USING MICROCOMPUTER APPLICATIONS 2.20
CHAPTER SUMMARY 2.23
KEY TERMS 2.23
REVIEW QUESTIONS 2.24
CONTROVERSIAL ISSUES 2.24
RESEARCH PROJECTS 2.24

CHAPTER 3 PROCESSING DATA INTO INFORMATION 3.1

OBJECTIVES 3.2
OVERVIEW OF THE INFORMATION PROCESSING CYCLE 3.2
WHAT IS DATA AND HOW IS IT ORGANIZED? 3.4
DATA MANAGEMENT 3.5
HOW THE INFORMATION PROCESSING CYCLE WORKS 3.7
METHODS OF PROCESSING DATA INTO INFORMATION 3.14
QUALITIES OF INFORMATION 3.20
SUMMARY OF PROCESSING DATA INTO INFORMATION 3.21
CHAPTER SUMMARY 3.21
KEY TERMS 3.23
REVIEW QUESTIONS 3.23
CONTROVERSIAL ISSUES 3.23
RESEARCH PROJECTS 3.24

CHAPTER 4 INPUT TO THE COMPUTER 4.1

OBJECTIVES 4.2
WHAT IS INPUT? 4.3
THE KEYBOARD 4.4
TERMINALS 4.5
OTHER INPUT DEVICES 4.7
INPUT DEVICES DESIGNED FOR SPECIFIC PURPOSES 4.10
USER INTERFACES 4.15
EVOLUTION OF USER INTERFACE SOFTWARE 4.15
GRAPHICS 4.20
FEATURES OF A USER INTERFACE 4.21
DATA ENTRY FOR INTERACTIVE AND BATCH PROCESSING 4.22
AN EXAMPLE OF ONLINE DATA ENTRY 4.24
DATA ENTRY PROCEDURES 4.28
ERGONOMICS 4.31
SUMMARY OF INPUT TO THE COMPUTER 4.32
CHAPTER SUMMARY 4.32
KEY TERMS 4.33
REVIEW QUESTIONS 4.34
CONTROVERSIAL ISSUES 4.34
RESEARCH PROJECTS 4.34

CHAPTER 5 THE PROCESSOR UNIT 5.1

OBJECTIVES 5.2
WHAT IS THE PROCESSOR UNIT? 5.2
HOW PROGRAMS AND DATA ARE REPRESENTED IN MEMORY 5.4
PARITY 5.7
NUMBER SYSTEMS 5.7
HOW THE PROCESSOR UNIT EXECUTES PROGRAMS AND MANIPULATES DATA 5.10
PROCESSOR SPEEDS 5.11
ARCHITECTURE OF PROCESSOR UNITS 5.13
TYPES OF MEMORY 5.14
SUMMARY 5.16
CHAPTER SUMMARY 5.20
KEY TERMS 5.21
REVIEW QUESTIONS 5.21
CONTROVERSIAL ISSUES 5.22
RESEARCH PROJECTS 5.22

MAKING A CHIP 5.17

CHAPTER 6 OUTPUT FROM THE COMPUTER 6.1

OBJECTIVES 6.2
WHAT IS OUTPUT? 6.2
COMMON TYPES OF OUTPUT 6.2
PRINTERS 6.6
PRINTERS FOR SMALL AND MEDIUM COMPUTERS 6.8
PRINTERS FOR LARGE COMPUTERS 6.13
SCREENS 6.14
OTHER OUTPUT DEVICES 6.19
SUMMARY OF OUTPUT TO THE COMPUTER 6.22
CHAPTER SUMMARY 6.22
KEY TERMS 6.24
REVIEW QUESTIONS 6.24
CONTROVERSIAL ISSUES 6.25
RESEARCH PROJECTS 6.25

CHAPTER 7 AUXILIARY STORAGE 7.1

OBJECTIVES 7.2
WHAT IS AUXILIARY STORAGE? 7.2
AUXILIARY STORAGE FOR PERSONAL COMPUTERS 7.4
AUXILIARY STORAGE FOR MEDIUM AND LARGE COMPUTERS 7.12
OTHER FORMS OF AUXILIARY STORAGE 7.17
SUMMARY OF AUXILIARY STORAGE 7.19
CHAPTER SUMMARY 7.19
KEY TERMS 7.21
REVIEW QUESTIONS 7.21
CONTROVERSIAL ISSUES 7.21
RESEARCH PROJECTS 7.22

CHAPTER 8 FILE ORGANIZATION AND DATABASES 8.1

OBJECTIVES 8.2
WHAT IS A FILE? 8.3
TYPES OF FILE ORGANIZATION 8.3
HOW IS DATA IN FILES MAINTAINED? 8.7
DATABASES: A BETTER WAY TO MANAGE DATA AND INFORMATION 8.11
WHAT IS A DATABASE? 8.11
WHY USE A DATABASE? 8.11
TYPES OF DATABASE ORGANIZATION 8.13
DATABASE MANAGEMENT SYSTEMS 8.15
QUERY LANGUAGES: ACCESS TO THE DATABASE 8.15
DATABASE ADMINISTRATION 8.17
MANAGING DATA ON A PERSONAL COMPUTER 8.18
SUMMARY OF DATABASES 8.18
CHAPTER SUMMARY 8.18
KEY TERMS 8.20
REVIEW QUESTIONS 8.20
CONTROVERSIAL ISSUES 8.20
RESEARCH PROJECTS 8.20

CHAPTER 9 DATA COMMUNICATIONS 9.1

OBJECTIVES 9.2
WHAT IS DATA COMMUNICATIONS? 9.2
COMMUNICATION CHANNELS 9.3
LINE CONFIGURATIONS 9.6
CHARACTERISTICS OF COMMUNICATION CHANNELS 9.9
COMMUNICATION EQUIPMENT 9.12
COMMUNICATION SOFTWARE 9.14
COMMUNICATION NETWORKS 9.14
NETWORK CONFIGURATIONS 9.16
THE PERSONAL COMPUTER AND DATA COMMUNICATIONS 9.17
SUMMARY OF DATA COMMUNICATIONS 9.18
CHAPTER SUMMARY 9.18
KEY TERMS 9.20
REVIEW QUESTIONS 9.20
CONTROVERSIAL ISSUES 9.20

CHAPTER 10 OPERATING SYSTEMS AND SYSTEM SOFTWARE 10.1

OBJECTIVES 10.2
WHAT IS SYSTEM SOFTWARE? 10.2
WHAT IS AN OPERATING SYSTEM? 10.3
LOADING AN OPERATING SYSTEM 10.3
TYPES OF OPERATING SYSTEMS 10.4
FUNCTIONS OF OPERATING SYSTEMS 10.5
POPULAR OPERATING SYSTEMS 10.10
UNIX 10.10
MS-DOS 10.10
OS/2 10.11
SUMMARY OF OPERATING SYSTEMS AND SYSTEM SOFTWARE 10.12
CHAPTER SUMMARY 10.12
KEY TERMS 10.13
REVIEW QUESTIONS 10.13
CONTROVERSIAL ISSUE 10.13
RESEARCH PROJECT 10.13

CHAPTER 11 COMMERCIAL APPLICATION SOFTWARE 11.1

OBJECTIVES 11.2
WHAT IS COMMERCIAL APPLICATION SOFTWARE? 11.2
GENERAL APPLICATION SOFTWARE 11.3
FUNCTIONAL APPLICATION SOFTWARE 11.5
THE DECISION TO MAKE OR BUY APPLICATION SOFTWARE 11.6
HOW TO ACQUIRE COMMERCIAL APPLICATION SOFTWARE 11.7
SUMMARY OF COMMERCIAL APPLICATION SOFTWARE? 11.11
CHAPTER SUMMARY 11.11
KEY TERMS 11.12
REVIEW QUESTIONS 11.12
CONTROVERSIAL ISSUES 11.12
RESEARCH PROJECTS 11.12

CHAPTER 12 THE INFORMATION SYSTEM DEVELOPMENT LIFE CYCLE 12.1

OBJECTIVES 12.2
WHAT IS AN INFORMATION SYSTEM? 12.2
TYPES OF INFORMATION SYSTEMS 12.3
WHAT IS THE INFORMATION SYSTEM DEVELOPMENT LIFE CYCLE? 12.5
PHASE 1—ANALYSIS 12.6
PHASE 1—ANALYSIS AT SUTHERLAND 12.10
PHASE 2—DESIGN 12.11
PHASE 2—DESIGN AT SUTHERLAND 12.15
PHASE 3—DEVELOPMENT 12.16
PHASE 3—DEVELOPMENT AT SUTHERLAND 12.16
PHASE 4—IMPLEMENTATION 12.16
PHASE 4—IMPLEMENTATION AT SUTHERLAND 12.17
PHASE 5—MAINTENANCE 12.18
PHASE 5—MAINTENANCE AT SUTHERLAND 12.19
SUMMARY OF THE INFORMATION SYSTEM DEVELOPMENT LIFE CYCLE 12.19
CHAPTER SUMMARY 12.20
KEY TERMS 12.21
REVIEW QUESTIONS 12.21
CONTROVERSIAL ISSUES 12.21
RESEARCH PROJECTS 12.22

CHAPTER 13 PROGRAM DEVELOPMENT 13.1

OBJECTIVES 13.2
WHAT IS A COMPUTER PROGRAM? 13.2
WHAT IS PROGRAM DEVELOPMENT? 13.3
STEP 1—REVIEW OF PROGRAM SPECIFICATIONS 13.3
STEP 2—PROGRAM DESIGN 13.4
STEP 3—PROGRAM CODING 13.9
STEP 4—PROGRAM TESTING 13.9
STEP 5—FINALIZING PROGRAM DOCUMENTATION 13.10
PROGRAM MAINTENANCE 13.11
SUMMARY OF PROGRAM DEVELOPMENT 13.11
WHAT IS A PROGRAMMING LANGUAGE? 13.11
CATEGORIES OF PROGRAMMING LANGUAGES 13.11
PROGRAMMING LANGUAGES USED TODAY 13.15
APPLICATION GENERATORS 13.18
HOW TO CHOOSE A PROGRAMMING LANGUAGE 13.19
SUMMARY OF PROGRAMMING LANGUAGES 13.19
CHAPTER SUMMARY 13.20
KEY TERMS 13.21
REVIEW QUESTIONS 13.21
CONTROVERSIAL ISSUE 13.22
RESEARCH PROJECT 13.22

CHAPTER 14 CAREER OPPORTUNITIES IN THE AGE OF INFORMATION PROCESSING 14.1

OBJECTIVES 14.2
THE INFORMATION PROCESSING INDUSTRY 14.2
WHAT ARE THE CAREER OPPORTUNITIES IN INFORMATION PROCESSING? 14.4
COMPENSATION AND GROWTH TRENDS FOR INFORMATION PROCESSING CAREERS 14.6
PREPARING FOR A CAREER IN INFORMATION PROCESSING 14.7
CAREER DEVELOPMENT IN THE INFORMATION PROCESSING INDUSTRY 14.8
SUMMARY OF COMPUTER CAREER OPPORTUNITIES 14.10
CHAPTER SUMMARY 14.10
KEY TERMS 14.11
REVIEW QUESTIONS 14.11
CONTROVERSIAL ISSUE 14.11
RESEARCH PROJECT 14.11

CHAPTER 15 TRENDS AND ISSUES IN THE INFORMATION AGE 15.1

OBJECTIVES 15.2
INFORMATION SYSTEMS IN BUSINESS 15.2
BRINGING THE INFORMATION AGE HOME 15.7
SOCIAL ISSUES 15.12
SUMMARY OF TRENDS AND ISSUES IN THE INFORMATION AGE 15.15
CHAPTER SUMMARY 15.16
KEY TERMS 15.16
REVIEW QUESTIONS 15.16

Computer Concepts INDEX I.1

INTRODUCTION TO DOS DOS 1

OBJECTIVES DOS 2
INTRODUCTION DOS 2
USING THE DISK OPERATING SYSTEM (DOS) DOS 3
ENTERING DISK OPERATING SYSTEM (DOS) COMMANDS DOS 6
DIRECTORY COMMAND (DIR) DOS 7
FORMATTING A DISKETTE DOS 9
CLS COMMAND DOS 13
MANAGING DATA AND PROGRAM FILES ON DISKS DOS 13
COPY COMMAND DOS 14
RENAME COMMAND DOS 19
ERASE AND DEL COMMANDS DOS 21
USING DIRECTORIES AND SUBDIRECTORIES DOS 21
LOADING A PROGRAM DOS 26
SUMMARY DOS 27
STUDENT ASSIGNMENTS DOS 28

Introduction to DOS INDEX DOS 32

Programming in QuickBASIC

PROJECT 1 AN INTRODUCTION TO PROGRAMMING IN QuickBASIC QB 1

THE PROGRAMMING PROCESS QB 1
SAMPLE PROGRAM 1 — PATIENT LISTING QB 2
THE DATA STATEMENT QB 5
THE CLS, PRINT, AND END STATEMENTS QB 6
VARIABLES QB 7
THE READ STATEMENT QB 7
THE DO WHILE AND LOOP STATEMENTS QB 8
TRY IT YOURSELF EXERCISES QB 11
THE QB OPERATING ENVIRONMENT QB 12

EXECUTING PROGRAMS AND HARD-COPY OUTPUT QB 17
SAVING, LOADING, AND ERASING PROGRAMS QB 20
THE QB ADVISOR ON-LINE HELP SYSTEM QB 22
TRY IT YOURSELF EXERCISES QB 23
STUDENT ASSIGNMENTS QB 23

PROJECT 2 BASIC ARITHMETIC OPERATIONS AND ACCUMULATING TOTALS QB 25

THE LET STATEMENT QB 25
SAMPLE PROGRAM 2 — AUTO EXPENSE REPORT QB 27
REPORT EDITING QB 33
PRINTING A REPORT ON THE PRINTER QB 38
TRY IT YOURSELF EXERCISES QB 39
STUDENT ASSIGNMENTS QB 40

PROJECT 3 DECISIONS QB 42

THE IF STATEMENT QB 42
CODING IF-THEN-ELSE STRUCTURES QB 44
SAMPLE PROGRAM 3 — VIDEO RENTAL REPORT QB 47
LOGICAL OPERATORS QB 51
THE SELECT CASE STATEMENT QB 54
TRY IT YOURSELF EXERCISES QB 56
STUDENT ASSIGNMENTS QB 59

PROJECT 4 INTERACTIVE PROGRAMMING, FOR LOOPS, AND AN INTRODUCTION TO THE TOP-DOWN APPROACH QB 62

THE INPUT STATEMENT QB 62
THE BEEP AND LOCATE STATEMENTS QB 64
EDITING DATA ENTERED THROUGH THE KEYBOARD QB 65
SAMPLE PROGRAM 4 — ITEM COST REPORT QB 66
THE FOR AND NEXT STATEMENTS QB 68
AN INTRODUCTION TO THE TOP-DOWN APPROACH QB 72
THE GOSUB AND RETURN STATEMENTS QB 73
TRY IT YOURSELF EXERCISES QB 77
STUDENT ASSIGNMENTS QB 80

PROJECT 5 SEQUENTIAL FILE PROCESSING QB 83

FILE ORGANIZATION QB 83
CREATING A SEQUENTIAL DATA FILE QB 83
SAMPLE PROGRAM 5A — CREATING A SEQUENTIAL DATA FILE QB 85
READING DATA FROM A SEQUENTIAL DATA FILE QB 91
SAMPLE PROGRAM 5B — PROCESSING A SEQUENTIAL DATA FILE QB 92
TRY IT YOURSELF EXERCISES QB 96
STUDENT ASSIGNMENTS QB 97

PROJECT 6 ARRAYS AND FUNCTIONS QB 99

ARRAYS QB 99
THE DIM STATEMENT QB 100
SAMPLE PROGRAM 6 — CUSTOMER ACCOUNT TABLE LOOKUP QB 101
FUNCTIONS QB 108
TRY IT YOURSELF EXERCISES QB 112
STUDENT ASSIGNMENTS QB 113

APPENDIX QuickBASIC DEBUGGING TECHNIQUES QB 115

EXAMINING VALUES THROUGH THE IMMEDIATE WINDOW QB 115
EXECUTING ONE STATEMENT AT A TIME QB 115
BREAKPOINTS QB 116
TRACING QB 116
SET NEXT STATEMENT QB 116
RECORDING QB 117
WATCH VARIABLES AND WATCHPOINTS QB 117

QuickBASIC INDEX QB 118

QuickBASIC Reference Card R.1

PREFACE

Computer Concepts with QuickBASIC is designed for a course combining fundamental computer concepts with DOS and Microsoft QuickBASIC programming. This book incorporates salient material from, and is based upon the methodology and pedagogy of, earlier works by Gary B. Shelly and Thomas J. Cashman.

The user's point of view is emphasized in fifteen concepts chapters and is reinforced by two appendices — an *Introduction to DOS* and six projects in *Programming in QuickBASIC*. Neither the chapters nor the appendices require any previous experience with computers and neither assumes mathematics beyond the high school freshman level.

ORGANIZATION OF THE TEXTBOOK

The Concepts Chapters

We include fifteen chapters that cover a full range of computer and processing concepts. The concept of the information system is introduced in Chapter 1 and used throughout the text. The six elements of an information system—equipment, software, data, personnel, users, and procedures—are introduced in this chapter; subsequent chapters relate back to one or more of these six elements. The impact of microcomputers is addressed throughout the textbook. Chapter 2 presents a unique overview of the four most commonly used microcomputer applications—word processing, spreadsheet, database, and graphics. Chapter 3 discusses data—how it is organized in fields, records, files, and databases and how it is processed into information. The chapter also defines and describes the information processing cycle—input, process, output, and storage. Each of these operations is discussed in the next four chapters (Chapters 4–7).

Chapter 8 discusses file and database organization and emphasizes the significance and the advantages of relational database systems. Data communications, including networking, is discussed in Chapter 9.

Chapters 10 through 13 cover concepts relating to software, software acquisition, and software development: operating systems and systems software (Chapter 10), commercial applications software (Chapter 11), the information systems development life cycle (Chapter 12), and program development and popular programming languages (Chapter 13).

The concluding chapters point out career opportunities in the field of information processing (Chapter 14) and discuss some of the trends and issues in the information age (Chapter 15).

An Introduction to DOS

To use a computer effectively, students need a practical knowledge of operating systems. The *Introduction to DOS* appendix, therefore, presents the most commonly used DOS commands such as formatting a diskette, copying, and renaming and deleting files.

Programming in QuickBASIC

Six projects introduce students to fundamental programming concepts and Microsoft QuickBASIC. These projects present the essentials of QuickBASIC and acquaint students with structured and top-down programming techniques. In each project a problem is presented and then, step by step, *thoroughly* solved with a QuickBASIC program. Each project includes one or more sets of Try It Yourself Exercises, paper-and-pencil practice exercises to help students master the concepts presented. Also included are

Student Programming Assignments. These field-tested assignments contain instructions, sample input data, and sample output results. The Appendix, QuickBASIC Debugging Techniques, follows the projects and demonstrates how to use the immediate window, stepping one statement at a time, breakpoints, tracing, recording, and watchpoints to debug programs. Finally, a reference card lists all statements, functions, and features of QuickBASIC.

SUPPLEMENTS TO ACCOMPANY COMPUTER CONCEPTS AND INTRODUCTION TO DOS

Instructor's Guide and Answer Manual

This manual contains Lesson Plans and Answers and Solutions. The Lesson Plans include: chapter or project objectives, chapter or project overviews, chapter or project outlines that are annotated with textbook page numbers on which the outlined material is covered, notes, teaching tips, additional activities, and a key for using the Transparency Masters. Complete answers and solutions for all exercises, projects, controversial issues, and Student Assignments are included.

Test Bank

This book contains test questions with answers and is a hard-copy version of MicroSWAT III (see below). It is comprised of three types of questions—true/false, multiple-choice, and fill-in.

MicroSWAT III

This easy-to-use, computerized test-generating system is available free to adopters of this textbook. MicroSWAT III is menu-driven and allows the creation of custom testing documents plus answer keys. It includes all of the questions from the Test Bank including true/false, multiple-choice, and fill-in. It will run on the IBM PC, IBM PS/2, or compatible systems with two diskette drives or a hard disk.

Transparency Masters

A Transparency Master is available for *every* line drawing and screen shot.

HyperGraphics

HyperGraphics is an instructional delivery system; it is software that presents the content of *Computer Concepts* and *Introduction to DOS* by using graphics, color, animation, and interactivity. It is a state-of-the-art, computer-based teaching and learning environment that enhances classroom instruction and promotes interactive learning and self-study.

ClassNotes and Study Guide

The *ClassNotes and Study Guide* provides a chance for students to review and study independently. If used with HyperGraphics, this supplement relieves students from laborious and tedious notetaking responsibilities, freeing them to concentrate on the instruction.

SUPPLEMENT TO ACCOMPANY PROGRAMMING IN QuickBASIC

The Instructor's Materials supplement includes the following:

- Lesson Plans with lecture outlines and notes
- Answers/solutions to all Try It Yourself Exercises and Student Assignments
- Test questions with answer key
- Transparency Masters for every figure
- Instructor's Diskette containing the files used in *Introduction to DOS*, and answers/solutions to all Try It Yourself Exercises and Student Assignments. This is included in both 3 1/2" and 5 1/4" formats.

ACKNOWLEDGMENTS

Our thanks to the many talented individuals who contributed to the quality of this book. Special thanks to Bill Waggoner, John Maniotes, Diane Larson, Pat Donegan, Anne Craig, Ginny Harvey, Jeanne Huntington, Ken Russo, Becky Herrington, Susan Solomon, and Tom Walker.

RESEARCH AND PHOTO ACKNOWLEDGMENTS

The following organizations donated materials used for research and photographs in this book. We thank them.

3Com Corp.; 3M Company; ACCO International, Inc.; Accurex Corp.; Acme Visible Records; ADAC Laboratories; Adage, Inc.; Addisk, Inc.; Adobe Systems, Inc.; Advanced Computer Communications; Advanced Matrix Technology, Inc.; Agricultural Software Consultants; Aim Technology; Aldus Corp.; All Easy Software Corp.; Allied Corp.; Amdahl Corp.; Amdek Corp.; American Laser Systems, Inc.; American Software; AMP, Inc.; Analog Devices; Anderson Jacobsen; Apollo Computer, Inc.; Apple Computer, Inc.; Applicon, Inc.; Applied Data Research, Inc.; Armor Systems, Inc.; Ashton-Tate; Ask Computer Systems, Inc.; AST Research, Inc.; AT&T Bell Laboratories; Atchison, Topeka and Santa Fe Railway Co.; Atek Information Services, Inc.; Auto-Trol Technology Corp.; Autodesk, Inc.; Automated Insurance Resource Systems, Inc.; Aydin Corp.; BancTec, Inc.; Bank of America; BASF Corp. Information Systems; Bates Manufacturing Co.; BBN Software Products; BDT Products, Inc.; Beagle Bros.; Beehive International; Bell & Howell Co.; Bishop Graphic, Inc.; BR Intec Corp.; Broderbund Software, Inc.; Brother International Corp.; Bruning Computer Graphics; Buttonware, Inc.; CADAM, Inc.; Cadlogic Systems Corp.; Caere Corp.; CalComp; Camwil, Inc.; Canon USA, Inc.; Century Analysis, Inc.; Chrislin Industries, Inc.; Chromatics, Inc.; Chrysler Motors, Inc.; Cincinnati Milacron, Inc.; Cincom Systems, Inc.; Cipher Data Products, Inc.; Claris Corp.; Cognotronics Corp.; Coin Financial Systems, Inc.; Cole, Layer, Trumble Co.; Command Technology Corp.; Compaq Computer Corp.; CompuScan, Inc.; Computer Associates; Computer Methods Corp.; Computer Museum, Boston; Computer Power Products; Computer Power, Inc.; Computer Support Group; ComputerEdge Magazine; ComputerLand; Computervision Corp.; Control Applications; Control Data Corp.; Convergent Technologies, Inc.; Corning Glass Works; CPT Corp.; Cray Research, Inc.; Cullinet Software; Cummins-Allison Corp.; Cylix Communications Corporation; Dartmouth College News Service; Data General Corp.; Datacopy Corp.; Datagram Corp.; Datapoint Corp.; Dataproducts Corp.; Daytronic Corp.; DBX; Delco Associates, Inc.; Dest Corp.; Develcon, Inc.; Diebold, Inc.; Digital Equipment Corp.; Dorf & Stanton Communications, Inc.; Drexler Technology Corp.; Eastman Kodak Company; ElectroCom Automation, Inc.; Electrohome Ltd.; Electronic Arts; Electronic Form Systems; Emerson Electric Co.; Emulex Corp.; Engineered Data Products; Epson America, Inc.; Esprit Systems, Inc.; Evans & Sutherland; Everex Systems, Inc.; Eye Communication Systems, Inc.; Fellowes Manufacturing Co.; Firestone Tire & Rubber Co.; Forney Engineering Co.; Fortune Systems Corp.; Fujitsu of America, Inc.; Gandalf Technologies, Inc.; General Electric Co.; General Meters Corp.; General Motors Corp.; General Robotics Corp.; GenRad, Inc.; Geber Systems Technology, Inc.; Gould, Inc.; GRiD Systems Corp.; Harris Corp.; Harris/3M; Haworth, Inc.; Hayes Microcomputer Products, Inc.; HEI, Inc.; Heidelberg West; Hercules Computer Technology; Hewlett-Packard Co.; Hitachi America Ltd.; Honeywell Bull, Inc.; Hughes Aircraft Co.; Hunt Manufacturing Co.; ICS Computer Products; Imunelec, Inc.; Index Technology; Industrial Data Terminals Corp.; Information Builders; Information Design, Inc.; Infotron Systems Corp.; InfoWorld Publishing, Inc.; Intecolor Corp.; Integrated Marketing Corp.; Integrated Software Systems Corp.; Intel Corp.; Interface Group, Inc.; Intermec Corp.; Internal Revenue Service; International Business Machines Corp.; International Mailing Systems; International Power Machines; Intertec Diversified Systems, Inc.; Ioline Corp.; ITT Information Systems; Jax International; Jet Propulsion Laboratory/California Institute of Technology; John Fluke Manufacturing Co., Inc.; Kao Corp. of America; Kaypro Corp.; Krueger, Inc.; Kurta Corp.; L/F Technologies, Inc.; Lear Siegler, Inc.; Liberty Electronics; Lockheed Corp.; Logical Business Machines; Logitech, Inc.; Lotus Development Corp.; LXE Division of Electromagnetic Sciences, Inc.; Management Science America, Inc.; Maxell Corp. of America; Maxtor Corp.; MBI, Inc.; McDonnell Douglas Computer Systems, Inc.; MDS Qantel, Inc.; Mead Data Central; Memorex Corp.; Mentor Graphics Corp.; Message Processing Systems, Inc.; MICOM Systems, Inc.; Micro Display Systems, Inc.; Microcomputer Accessories, Inc.; Micrografx, Inc.; Micron Technology, Inc.; MicroPro International Corp.; Microsoft Corp.; Microtek; Mini-Computer Business Applications, Inc.; Minolta Corp.; Modular Computer Systems, Inc.; Moore Business Forms, Inc.; Motorola, Inc.; Mountain Computer, Inc.; MSI Data Corp.; NASA; National Semiconductor Corp.; NCR Corp.; NEC America, Inc.; NEC Home Electronics; NEC Information Systems, Inc.; Neuron Data, Inc.; Norman Magnetics, Inc.; Norsk Data; Northern Telecom, Inc.; Novation, Inc.; Okidata; Olivetti USA; Oracle Corp.; Packard Bell; Panafax Corp.; Panasonic Industrial Co.; Panel Concepts, Inc.; Paperback Software; Paradyne Corp.; Penril DataComm; Perception Technology; Pertec Peripherals Corp.; Photo & Sound Co.; Pitney Bowes; Plus Development Corp.; Polaroid Corp.; Prentice Corp.; Princeton Graphics Systems; Princeton University; Printronix; Promethus Products, Inc.; Pyramid Technology; Quadram Corp.; Quality Micro Systems; Questronics, Inc.; Quicksoft, Inc.; Racal-Milgo; Racal-Vadic; Radio Shack, A Division of Tandy Corp.; RB Graphic Supply Co.; RCA; Reliance Plastics & Packaging Division; Ring King Visibles, Inc.; Rockwell International; Royal Seating Corp.; Sato Corp.; Schlage Electronics; Scientific Atlanta; Scientific Calculations, Inc.; Scotland Rack, Ltd.; Seagate Technology; Shaffstall Corp.; Sharp Electronics Corp.; Siecor Corp. of America; Siemens Information Systems, Inc.; Silicon Graphics; Sony Corp. of America; Soricon Corp.; Spectra Physics; Spectragraphics Corp.; SRI International; STB Systems, Inc.; Steelcase, Inc.; Storage Technology Corp.; Summagraphics Corp.; Sun Microsystems, Inc.; Sunol Systems; Symbolics, Inc.; Synergistics, Inc.; Syntrex, Inc.; T/Maker Co.; TAB Products Co.; Talaris Systems, Inc.; Tallgrass Technologies; Tandem Computers, Inc.; Tandon Corp.; Tangent Technologies; TDA, Inc.; Tecmar, Inc.; Telematics; Telenet Communications Corp.; Telenova, Inc.; TeleVideo Systems, Inc.; Telex Communications, Inc.; Telex Computer Products, Inc.; Teltone Corp.; Texas Instruments, Inc.; Thomson Information Systems Corp.; Thunderware, Inc.; Toor Furniture Corp.; Topaz, Inc.; TOPS, a division of Sun Microsystems, Inc.; Toshiba America, Inc.; Totec Co. Ltd.; U.S. Department of the Navy; U.S. Postal Service; UIS, Inc.; Ungermann-Bass, Inc.; Unisys Corp.; Universal Data Systems; Varityper; Ven-Tel, Inc.; Vermont Microsystems; Versatec; Verticom, Inc.; Video-7, Inc.; Viking; Votan; Voxtron Systems, Inc.; Wandel & Goltermann, Inc.; Wang Laboratories, Inc.; Weber Marking Systems, Inc.; Western Digital Corp.; Western Graphtec, Inc.; Westinghouse Furniture Systems; WordPerfect Corp.; Wyse Technology; Xerox Corp.; Xtra Business Systems; Z-Soft Corp.; Zehntel, Inc.; Zenith Data Systems; Ziff-Davis Publishing Co.

CHAPTER 1

An Introduction to Computers

CHAPTER 1

An Introduction to Computers

OBJECTIVES

- Explain what a computer is and how it processes data to produce information.
- Identify the four operations of the information processing cycle: input, process, output, and storage.
- Explain how the operations of the information processing cycle are performed by computer hardware and software.
- Identify the major categories of computers.
- Describe the six elements of an information system: equipment, software, data, personnel, users and procedures.
- Identify the qualities of information.
- Describe the evolution of the computer industry.

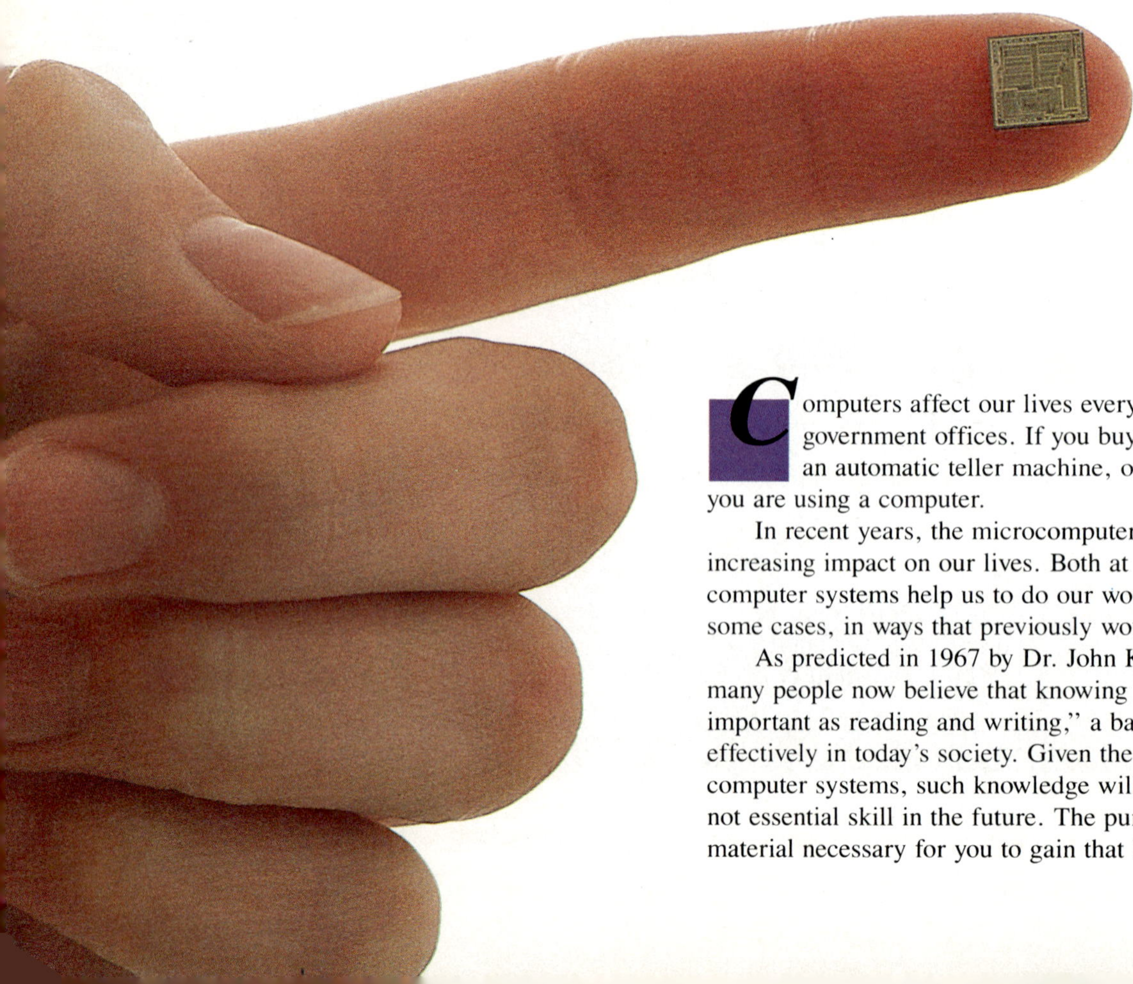

FIGURE 1-1
This microcomputer chip contains the electronic circuits that perform the operations of a computer.

Computers affect our lives every day: in businesses, schools, and government offices. If you buy groceries at a supermarket, use an automatic teller machine, or place a long-distance phone call, you are using a computer.

In recent years, the microcomputer or personal computer has had an increasing impact on our lives. Both at home and at work, these desktop computer systems help us to do our work faster, more accurately, and in some cases, in ways that previously would not have been possible.

As predicted in 1967 by Dr. John Kemeny of Dartmouth College, many people now believe that knowing how to use a computer is "as important as reading and writing," a basic skill necessary to function effectively in today's society. Given the increasing use and availability of computer systems, such knowledge will continue to be an important if not essential skill in the future. The purpose of this book is to present the material necessary for you to gain that knowledge.

WHAT IS A COMPUTER?

The most obvious question related to understanding computers and their impact on our lives is, "What is a computer?" A **computer** is an electronic device, operating under the control of instructions stored in its own memory unit, that can accept data (input), process data arithmetically and logically, produce output from the processing, and store the results for future use. This definition of a computer encompasses devices of many different sizes and capabilities. While a microcomputer chip such as the one shown in Figure 1-1 may fulfill the definition of a computer, the term is generally used to describe a collection of devices that function together to process data. An example of the devices that make up a computer is shown in Figure 1-2.

WHAT DOES A COMPUTER DO?

Whether they are small or large, computers are capable of performing four general operations. These operations comprise the **information processing cycle**. They are input, process, output, and storage. Collectively, these operations describe the storage capabilities of a computer and the procedures that a computer performs in order to process data into information.

Data is required for all computer processing. It refers to the raw facts, including numbers and words, given to a computer during the input operation. In the processing phase, the computer manipulates the data in a predetermined manner to create information. **Information** refers to data that has been processed into a form that has meaning and is useful. The production of information by processing data on a computer is called **information processing**, or sometimes **electronic data processing**. During the output operation, the information that has been created is put into some form, such as a printed report, that people can use. The information can also be stored in an electronic format for future use.

The people who either use the computer directly or utilize the information it provides are called **computer users**, **end users**, or sometimes just simply **users**. Figure 1-3 shows a computer user and demonstrates how the four operations of the information processing cycle can take place on a personal computer. (1) The computer user inputs data by pressing the keys on the keyboard. (2) The data is then processed or manipulated by the unit called the processor.

FIGURE 1-3
The use of this personal computer illustrates the four operations of the information processing cycle: input, process, output, and storage. ▼

FIGURE 1-2
The devices that comprise a microcomputer. ▶

(3) The output or results from the processing are displayed on the screen or printed on the printer, providing information to the user. (4) Finally, the output may be stored on a disk for future reference.

WHY IS A COMPUTER SO POWERFUL?

The input, process, output, and storage operations that a computer performs may seem very basic and simple. However, the computer's power derives from its ability to perform these operations very quickly, accurately, and reliably. In a computer, operations occur through the use of electronic circuits contained on small chips as shown in Figure 1-4. When data flows along these circuits it travels at close to the speed of light. This allows processing to be accomplished in billionths of a second. The electronic circuits in modern computers are very reliable and seldom fail.

Storage capability is another reason why computers are so powerful. They can store enormous amounts of data and keep that data readily available for processing. This capability combined with the factors of speed, accuracy, and reliability are why a computer is considered to be such a powerful tool for information processing.

HOW DOES A COMPUTER KNOW WHAT TO DO?

For a computer to perform the operations in the information processing cycle, it must be given a detailed set of instructions or steps that tell it exactly what to do. These instructions can be called a **computer program**, **program instructions**, or **software**.

Before the information processing cycle for a specific job begins, the computer program corresponding to that job is stored in the computer. Once it is stored, the computer can begin to process data by executing the program's first instruction. The computer proceeds to execute one program instruction after another until the job is complete.

FIGURE 1-4
Inside a computer are boards containing the chips and other electronic components that process data in billionths of a second.

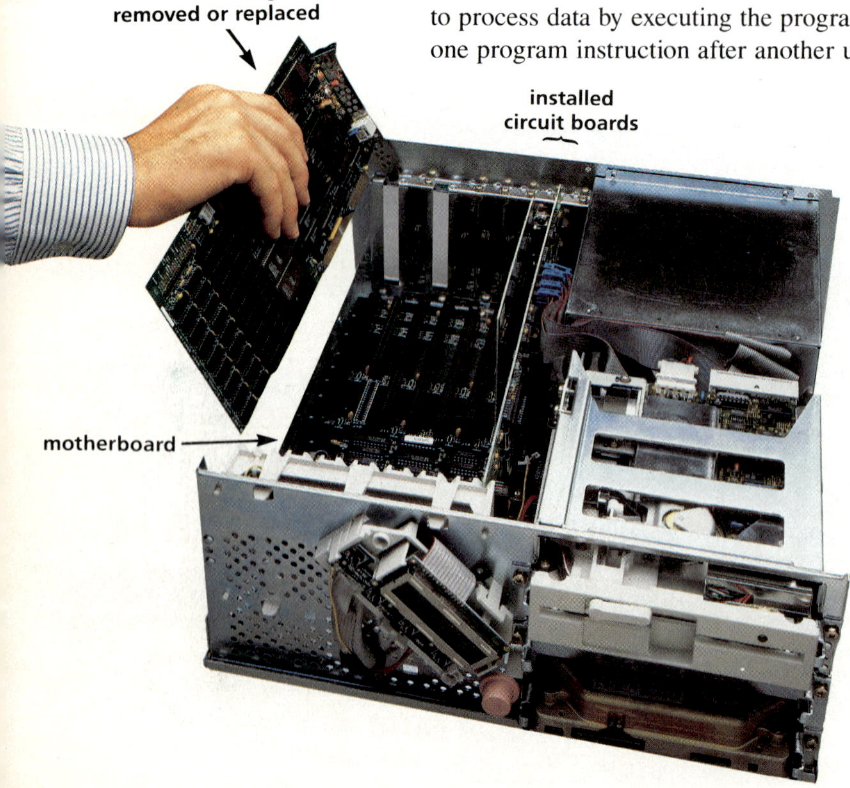

INFORMATION PROCESSING: A BUSINESS APPLICATION

The example in Figure 1-5 illustrates the use of a computer to produce varied information from data contained on a sales invoice. Once the appropriate computer program has been loaded into the computer, processing occurs as follows:

1. The computer user enters data on the sales invoice into the computer.
2. The data entered into the computer is processed to create information.

3. Output from the processing is generated in three forms:
   a. A bar chart illustrates the daily sales, using a different color to represent each day of the week.
   b. A monthly sales report shows the monthly sales. The report displays the total sales for each week, together with the total sales for the month.
   c. The screen displays the name of the salesperson who generated the most sales during the month. In this example, Joan Rice had total sales of $1,250.00, which was the highest for the month.
4. The data entered and information created are stored for future use.

A key point of this example is that several different forms of information can be produced from a single set of data. Without the computer's ability to manipulate the data, the information produced would be difficult, costly, and time consuming to obtain.

FIGURE 1-5
The data contained on the sales invoices is entered into the computer. After the data is processed, information in the form of a graph, a report, and a screen display is produced.

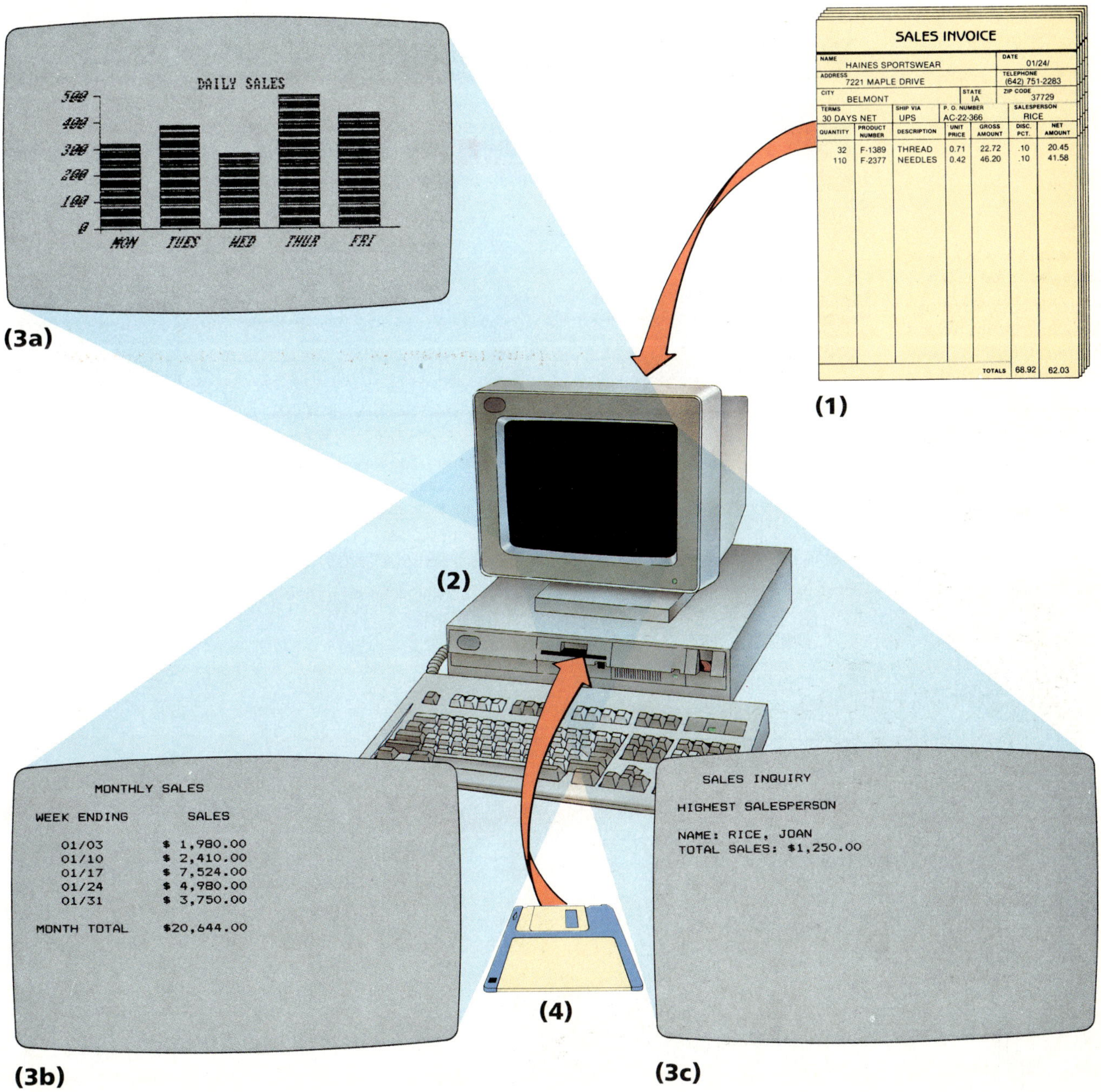

THE INFORMATION PROCESSING CYCLE

Your understanding of the information processing cycle introduced in this chapter is fundamental to understanding computers and how they process data into information. To review, the information processing cycle consists of four operations. They are: input, process, output, storage.

The first three of these operations, **input**, **process**, and **output**, describe the procedures that a computer performs in order to process data into information. The fourth operation, **storage**, describes a computer's electronic storage capability. As you learn more about computers you will see that these four operations apply to both the computer equipment and the computer software. The equipment or devices of a computer are classified according to the operations that they perform. Computer software is made up of instructions that describe how the operations are to be performed.

WHAT ARE THE COMPONENTS OF A COMPUTER?

Processing data on a computer is performed by specific equipment that is often referred to as computer **hardware** (Figure 1-6). This equipment consists of: input devices, processor unit, output devices, auxiliary storage units.

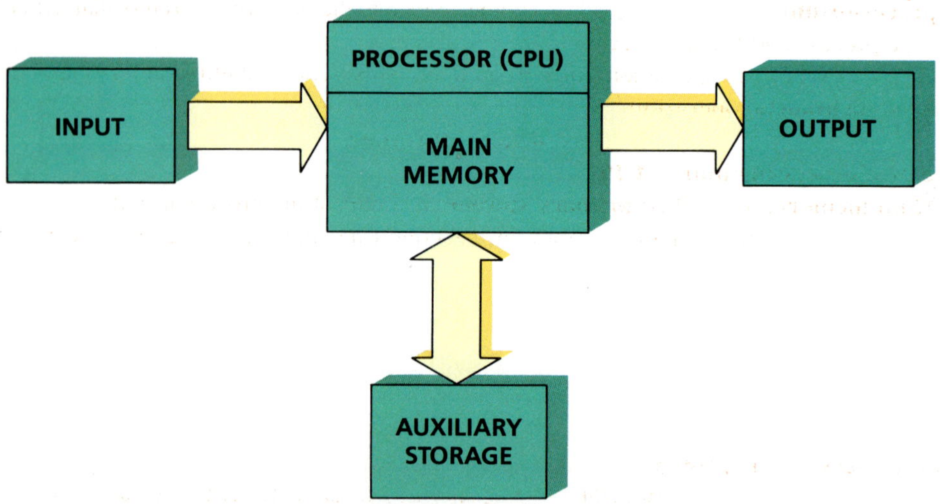

FIGURE 1-6
A computer is composed of input devices through which data is entered into the computer; the processor that processes data stored in main memory; output devices on which the results of the processing are made available; and auxiliary storage units that store data for future processing.

Input Devices

Input devices are used to enter data into a computer. A common input device is the **keyboard** (Figure 1-7a). As the data is entered or **keyed**, it is displayed on a screen and stored in the computer.

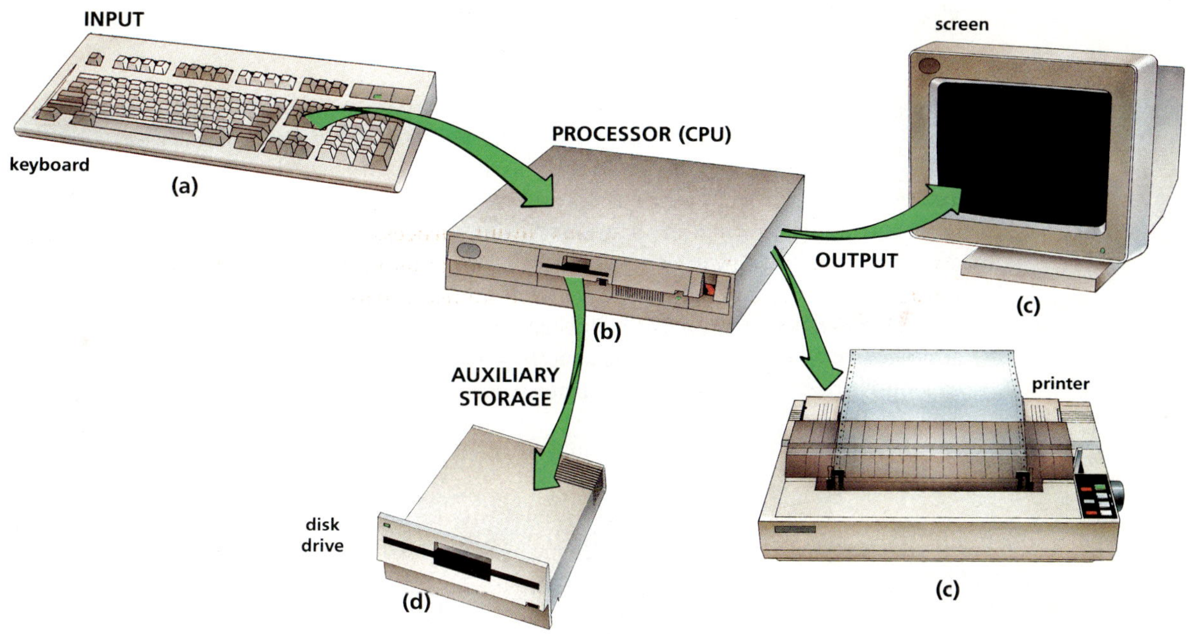

FIGURE 1-7
This figure illustrates the components of a computer that perform the four operations of the information processing cycle.

Processor Unit

The **processor unit** (Figure 1-7b) of a computer contains the electronic circuits that actually cause the processing of data to occur. All arithmetic and logical data processing takes place in the processor. Numeric calculations such as addition, subtraction, multiplication, and division are called **arithmetic operations**. Comparisons of data to see if one value is greater than, equal to, or less than another are called **logical operations**. The processor is sometimes called the **central processing unit** or **CPU**.

Main memory, also called **primary storage**, is a part of the processor unit. Main memory electronically stores data and program instructions when they are being processed.

Output Devices

Output from a computer can be presented in many forms. Where the computer is used for business applications or business-related personal applications, the two most commonly used **output devices** are the **printer** and the computer **screen** (Figure 1-7c). Other frequently used names for the screen are the **monitor** or the **CRT**, which stands for **cathode ray tube**.

Auxiliary Storage Units

Auxiliary storage units store instructions and data when they are not being used by the processor unit. A common auxiliary storage device on personal computers is a disk drive (Figure 1-7d), which stores data as magnetic spots on a small plastic disk called a **diskette** or **floppy disk**. Another auxiliary storage device is called a **hard disk drive**. Hard disk drives contain nonremovable metal disks and provide larger storage capacities than floppy disk drives.

Each computer component plays an important role. The processing unit is where the actual processing of data occurs. The input devices, output devices, and auxiliary storage units that surround the processing unit are sometimes referred to as **peripheral devices**.

CATEGORIES OF COMPUTERS

Figure 1-8 shows the following four major categories of computers: microcomputers, minicomputers, mainframe computers, and supercomputers.

Computers are generally classified according to their size, speed, processing capabilities, and price. However, because of rapid changes in technology, firm definitions of these categories do not exist. This year's speed, performance, and price classification of a mainframe might fit next year's classification of a minicomputer. Even though they are not firmly defined, the categories are frequently referred to and should be generally understood.

Microcomputers (Figure 1-8a), also called **personal computers** or **micros**, are the small desktop-size systems that have become so widely used in recent years. These machines are generally priced under $10,000. This category also includes laptop, portable, and supermicro computers.

FIGURE 1-8
(a) Microcomputers are small desktop-sized computers. These machines have become so widely used that they are sometimes called ''desktop appliances.''

(b) Minicomputers can perform many of the functions of a mainframe computer, but on a smaller scale.

(c) Mainframe computers are large, powerful machines that can handle many users concurrently and process large volumes of data.

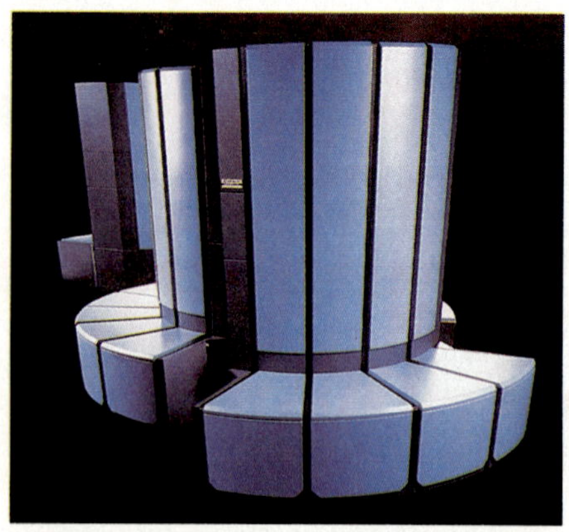

(d) Supercomputers are the most powerful and expensive computers.

Minicomputers (Figure 1-8b) are more powerful than microcomputers and can support a number of users performing different tasks. Originally developed to perform specific tasks such as engineering calculations, their use grew rapidly as their performance and capabilities increased. These systems can cost from approximately $25,000 up to several hundred thousand dollars. The most powerful "minis" are called superminicomputers.

Mainframe computers (Figure 1-8c) are large systems that can handle numerous users, store large amounts of data, and process transactions at a very high rate. Mainframes usually require a specialized environment including separate air conditioning and electrical power. Raised flooring is often built to accommodate the many cables connecting the system components underneath. The price range for mainframes is from several hundred thousand dollars to several million dollars.

Supercomputers (Figure 1-8d) are the most powerful category of computers and, accordingly, the most expensive. The ability of these systems to process hundreds of millions of instructions per second is used for such applications as weather forecasting, space exploration, and other jobs requiring long, complex calculations. These machines cost several million dollars.

COMPUTER SOFTWARE

As previously mentioned, a computer is directed by a series of instructions called a computer program (see Figure 1-9), which specifies the sequence of operations to be performed. To do this, the program must be stored in the main memory of the computer. Computer programs are commonly referred to as **computer software**.

COMPUTER PROGRAM LISTING

```
100 REM TELLIST              SEPTEMBER 22            SHELLY/CASHMAN
110                                                             REM
120 REM THIS PROGRAM DISPLAYS THE NAME, TELEPHONE AREA CODE
130 REM AND PHONE NUMBER OF INDIVIDUALS.
140                                                             REM
150 REM VARIABLE NAMES:
160 REM    A.....AREA CODE
170 REM    T$....TELEPHONE NUMBER
180 REM    N$....NAME
190                                                             REM
200 REM ***** DATA TO BE PROCESSED *****
210                                                             REM
220 DATA 714, "749-2138", "SAM HORN"
230 DATA 213, "663-1271", "SUE NUNN"
240 DATA 212, "999-1193", "BOB PELE"
250 DATA 312, "979-4418", "ANN SITZ"
260 DATA 999, "999-9999", "END OF FILE"
270                                                             REM
280 REM ***** PROCESSING *****
290                                                             REM
300 READ A, T$, N$
310                                                             REM
320 WHILE N$<> "END OF FILE"
330   PRINT N$, A, T$
340   READ A, T$, N$
350 WEND
360                                                             REM
370 PRINT " "
380 PRINT "END OF TELEPHONE LISTING"
390 END
```

FIGURE 1-9
A computer program contains instructions that specify the sequence of operations to be performed. This program is written in a language called BASIC. It allows the user to generate a telephone directory of names, area codes, and telephone numbers.

Many instructions can be used to direct a computer to perform a specific task. For example, some instructions allow data to be entered from a keyboard and stored in main computer memory; some instructions allow data in main memory to be used in calculations, such as adding a series of numbers to obtain a total; some instructions compare two values stored in main memory and direct the computer to perform alternative operations based on the results of the comparison; and some instructions direct the computer to print a report, display information on the screen, draw a color graph on a screen, or store data on a disk.

Computer programs are written by people with specialized training. They determine the instructions necessary to process the data and place the instructions in the correct sequence so that the desired results will occur. Complex programs may require hundreds or even thousands of program instructions.

Computer software is the key to productive use of computers. Without the proper software, a computer cannot perform the desired tasks. With the correct software, a computer can become a valuable tool.

Application Software Packages

Most end users do not write their own programs. In large corporations, the information processing department develops programs for unique company applications. In addition, programs required for common business and personal applications can be purchased from software vendors or stores that sell computer products (Figure 1-10). Purchased programs are often referred to as **application software packages** or simply **software packages**.

Microcomputer Applications Software Packages

Personal computer users often use application software packages. The four most commonly used packages, shown in Figure 1-11, are: word processing software, electronic spreadsheet software, computer graphics software, and database software.

FIGURE 1-10
Many programs commonly required for business and personal applications can be purchased from computer stores.

FIGURE 1-11
Commonly used microcomputer applications software packages.

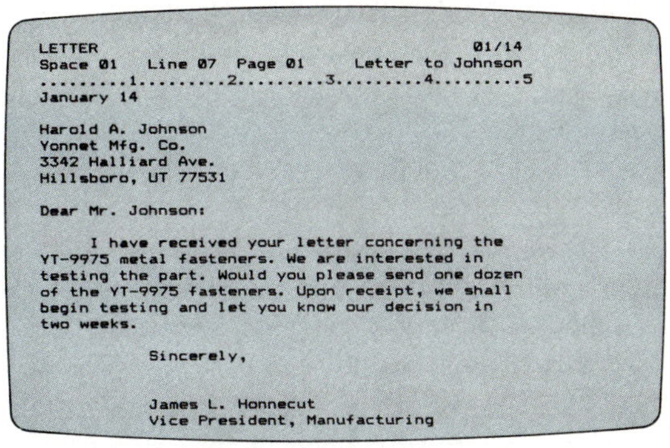

(a) word processing

(a) **Word processing** is used to write letters, memos, and other documents. As the user keys in words and letters, they display on the screen. The user can easily add, delete, and change any text entered until the document is exactly as desired. When the text is correct, the user can save the document on auxiliary storage and can also print it on a printer.

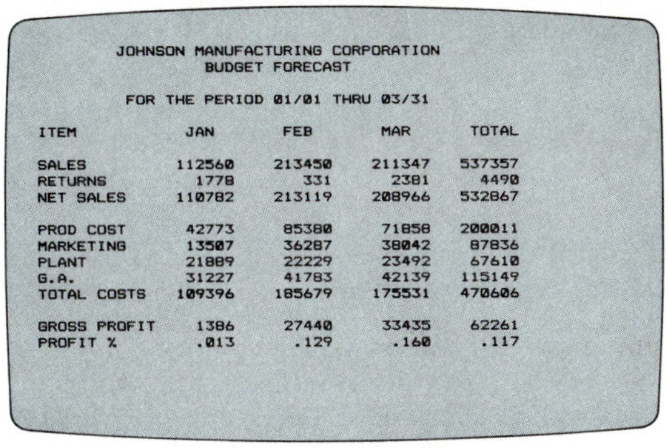

(b) electronic spreadsheet

(b) **Electronic spreadsheet** software is frequently used by people who work with numbers. The user enters the data and the formulas to be used on the data; then the program applies the formulas to the data and calculates the results. A powerful feature of electronic spreadsheet software is the ability to ask "what if" questions by changing the data and quickly recalculating the new results. For example, the user could direct the software to recalculate the profits based on a percentage increase in sales and a percentage decrease in costs.

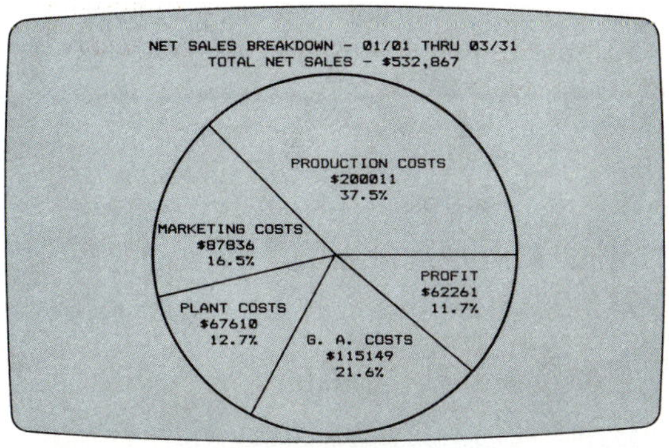

(c) computer graphics

(c) **Computer graphics** software provides the ability to transform a series of numeric values into graphic form for easier analysis and interpretation. In this example, the cost values from the electronic spreadsheet have been transformed into a pie chart. The chart makes it easier to see the various cost elements. Using graphics software, these graphs can be produced in seconds instead of the days that were required for a graphic artist to hand draw each graph.

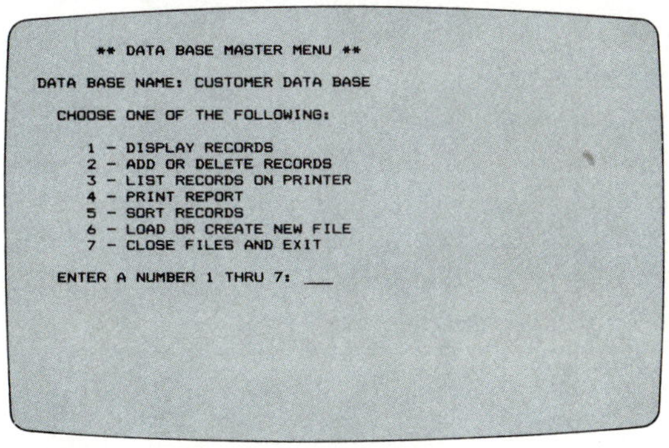

(d) database

(d) **Database** software allows the user to enter, retrieve, and update data in an organized and efficient manner. This screen shows a menu created with a database package. A menu is a list of processes that can be selected by the user and then performed by the program. The user chooses the number corresponding to the processing desired. In this example, the user can display records from the database, add or delete records, list and print data on a printer, sort records, and perform other database maintenance functions.

Word processing software (Figure 1-11a) is used to create and print documents that would otherwise be prepared on a typewriter. A key advantage of word processing software is its ability to make changes easily in documents, such as correcting spelling, changing margins, and adding, deleting, or relocating entire paragraphs. These changes would be difficult and time consuming to make on a typewriter. Once created, the documents can be printed quickly and accurately.

Electronic spreadsheet software (Figure 1-11b) allows the user to add, subtract, and perform user-defined calculations on rows and columns of numbers. These numbers can be changed and the **spreadsheet** quickly recalculates the new results. Electronic spreadsheet software eliminates the tedious recalculations required with manual methods.

Graphics software (Figure 1-11c) converts numbers and text into graphic output that visually conveys the relationships of the data. Some graphics software allows the use of color to further enhance the visual presentation. Line, bar, and pie charts are the most frequent forms of graphics output. Spreadsheet information is frequently converted into a graphic form, such as these charts. In fact, graphics capabilities are included in many spreadsheet packages.

Database software (Figure 1-11d) allows the user to enter, retrieve, and update data in an organized and efficient manner. These software packages have flexible inquiry and reporting capabilities that allow users to access the data in different ways.

A Typical Application: Budget Spreadsheet

Electronic spreadsheets are one of the most widely used software applications. In the following example, a user develops a budget spreadsheet for the first quarter of a year. The user enters the revenues and the costs for the first three months of the year. Then the spreadsheet program calculates the total revenues and total costs, the profit for each month (calculated by subtracting costs from revenues), and the profit percentage (obtained by dividing the profit by the revenues). In addition, the spreadsheet program calculates the total profit and the total profit percentage.

The diagrams in Figures 1-12, 1-13, and 1-14 show the steps that occur in order to obtain the spreadsheet output. A more complete description of these steps follows.

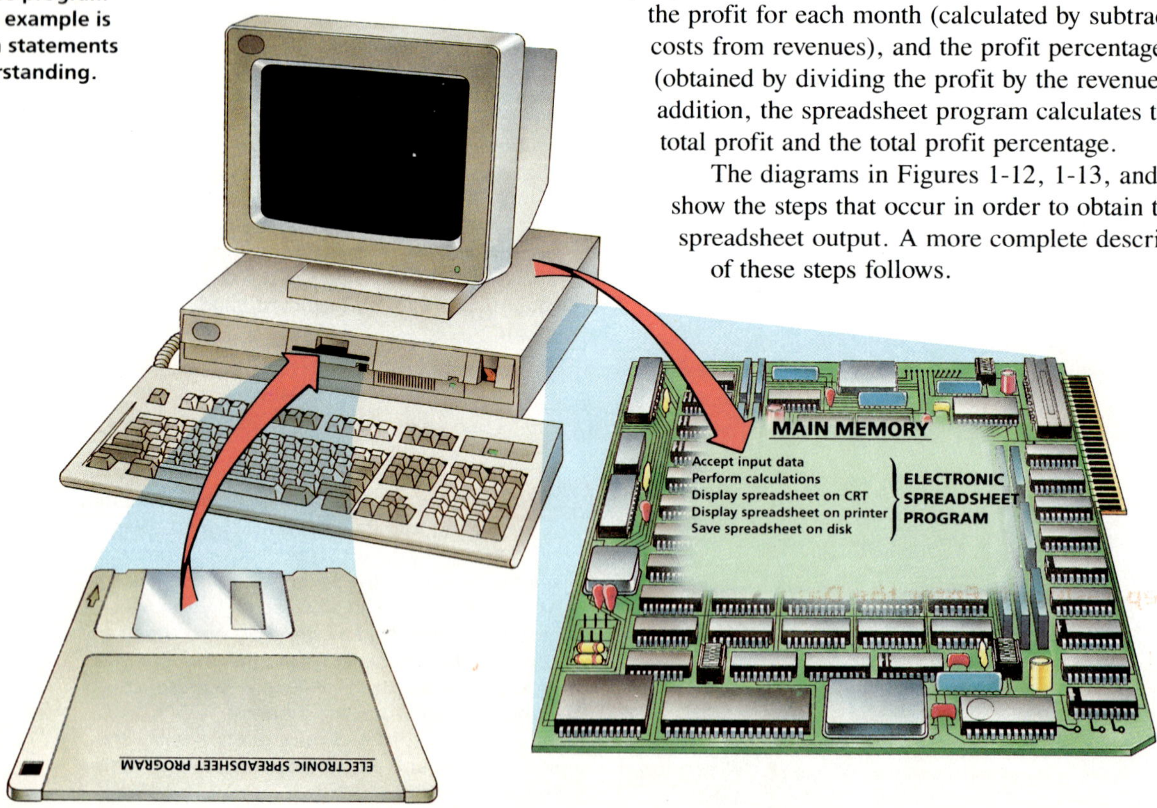

FIGURE 1-12
After the floppy disk is inserted in the disk drive, the spreadsheet program is copied into main memory. The program illustrated in this example is shown as English statements for ease of understanding.

Loading the Program For processing to occur, a computer program must first be stored in the main memory of the computer. The process of getting the program into memory is called loading the program. The spreadsheet program in this example is stored on a floppy disk. To load the program into the main memory of the computer, a copy of the spreadsheet program is transferred from the floppy disk into main memory.

In Figure 1-12, the floppy disk on which the program is stored is inserted into the floppy disk drive. The user then issues the command to load the program from the floppy disk into main memory. After the program is loaded into main memory, the user directs the computer to begin executing the program.

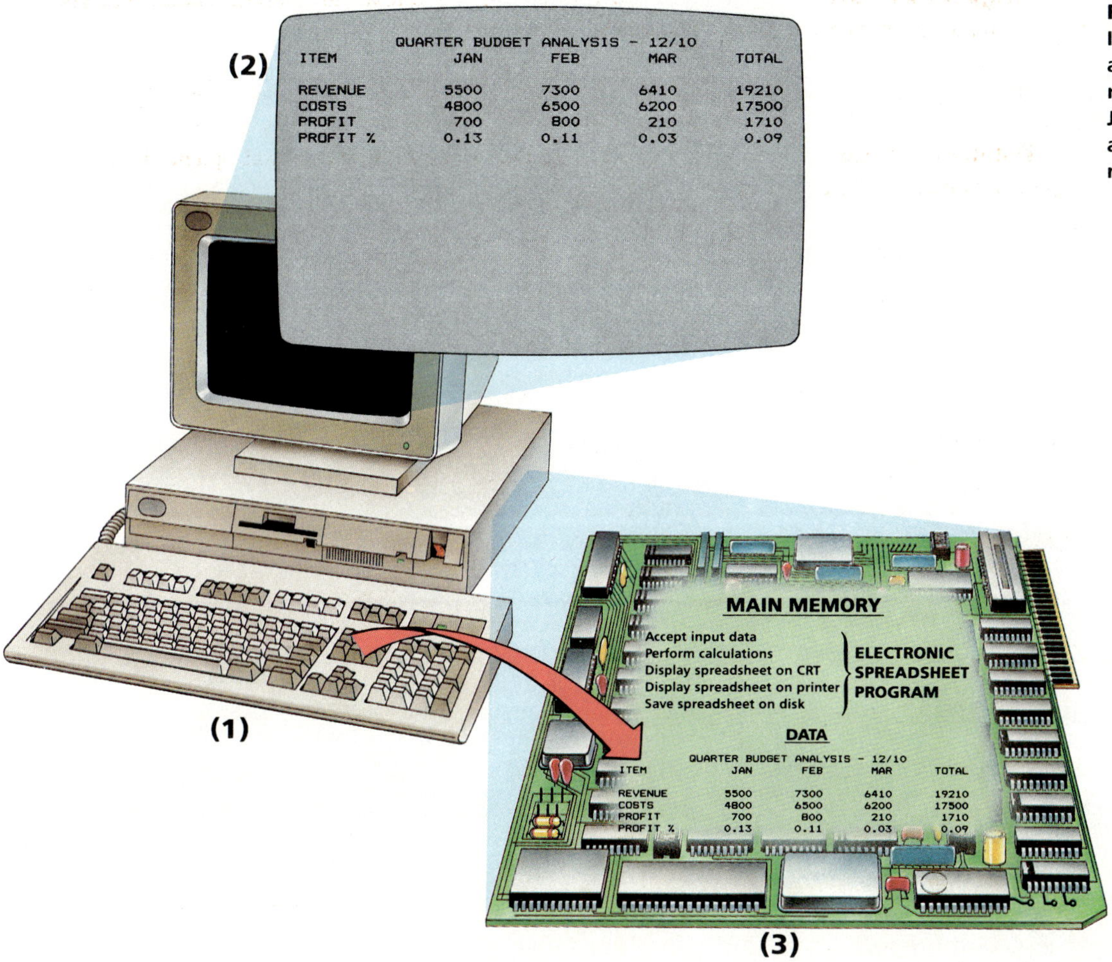

FIGURE 1-13
In this example, the user enters a report heading, column and row headings, the revenues for January, February, and March, and the costs for the three months.

Step 1—Input: Enter the Data The first step in the program is to input the data (Figure 1-13). This is accomplished by using a keyboard. As the data is entered on the keyboard (1), it is displayed on the screen (2) and stored in main memory (3).

The data for this application consists of not only the numbers on which calculations are to be performed, but also some words indicating the contents of each of the columns and rows on the screen.

Step 2—Process: Perform the Calculations As Figure 1-14 shows, the user has entered the data (1) and the program will direct the processor to perform the required calculations (2). In this example, the program calculates the profit for each month, the total revenue, costs, and profit for the quarter, the profit percent for each month, and the total profit percent.

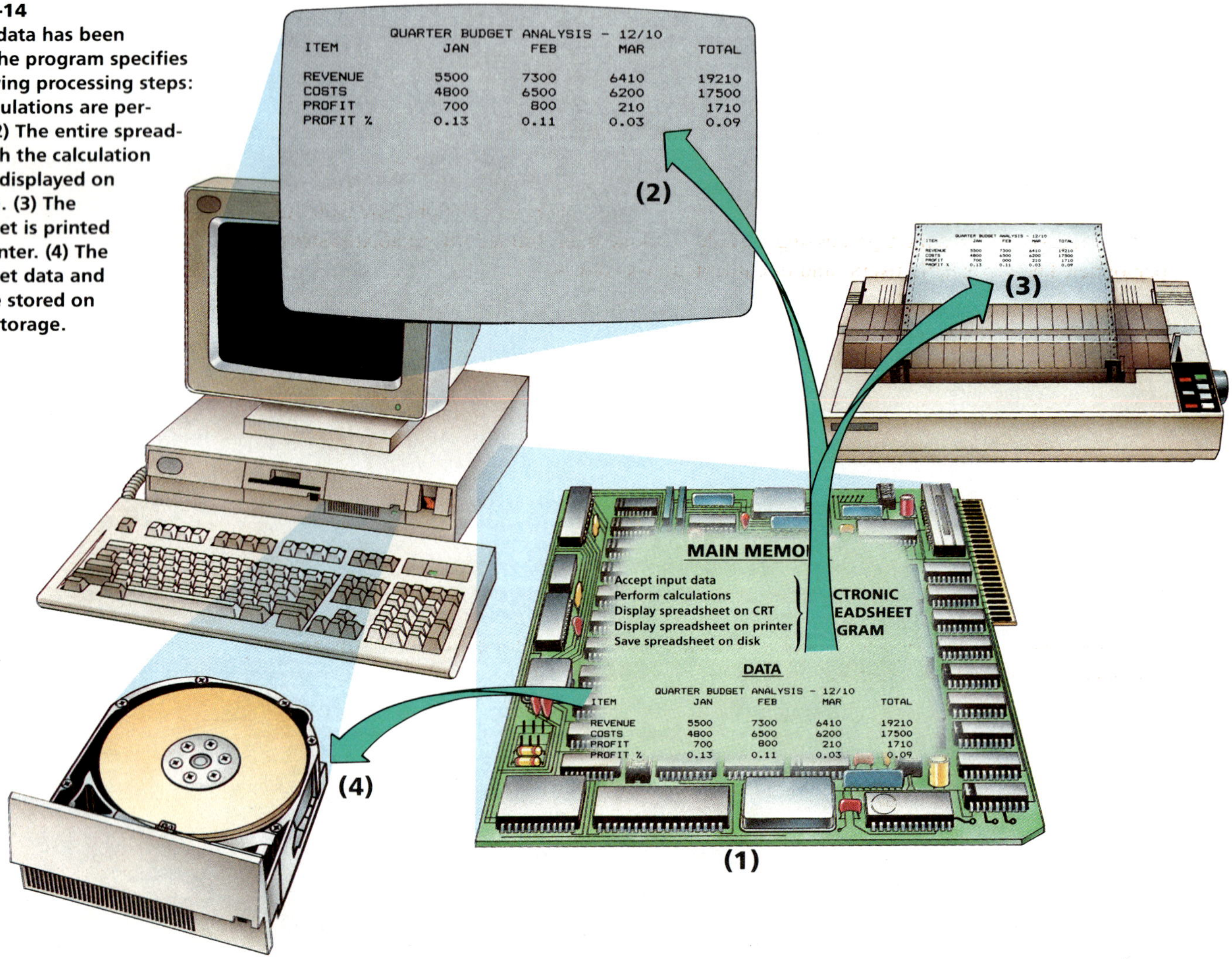

FIGURE 1-14
After the data has been entered, the program specifies the following processing steps: (1) All calculations are performed. (2) The entire spreadsheet, with the calculation results, is displayed on the screen. (3) The spreadsheet is printed on the printer. (4) The spreadsheet data and results are stored on auxiliary storage.

The preceding operations illustrate the calculating ability of computers. Whenever any calculations are performed on data, the data must be stored in main memory. The results of the calculations are also stored in main memory. If desired, the program can issue instructions to store the results on an auxiliary storage device, such as a hard or floppy disk.

Step 3—Output: Display the Results After the calculations have been completed, the program specifies that the spreadsheet, with the results of the calculations, is to be displayed on the screen. The program also specifies that the results are to be printed on the printer (3). When this instruction is executed, the spreadsheet is printed on paper so that the results of the processing can be used by someone other than the computer user.

Step 4—Storage: Save the Program and Data The spreadsheet is also stored on a disk, in this example a hard disk, so that at a later time it can be retrieved and utilized again (4).

WHAT ARE THE ELEMENTS OF AN INFORMATION SYSTEM?

Obtaining useful and timely information from computer processing requires more than just the equipment and software described so far. Other elements required for successful information processing include accurate data, trained information systems personnel, knowledgeable users, and documented procedures.

The equipment must be reliable and capable of handling the expected work load. The software must have been carefully developed and tested, and the data entered to be processed must be accurate. If the data is incorrect, the resulting information produced from it will be incorrect. Properly trained data processing personnel are required to run most medium and large computer systems. Users are sometimes overlooked as an important element of an information system, but with expanding computer use, users are taking increasing responsibility for the successful operation of information systems. This includes responsibility for the accuracy of both input and output information. In addition, users are taking a more active role in the development of computer applications. They work closely with information systems department personnel in the development of computer applications that relate to their areas of expertise. Finally, all information processing applications should have documented procedures covering not only the computer operations but any other related procedures as well.

To summarize, the six elements of an information system are: equipment, software, data, personnel, users, and procedures.

Figure 1-15 shows an example of each of the elements. The following section illustrates the elements as they occur in a large multiuser computer environment.

FIGURE 1-15
An information system requires (1) computer equipment; (2) software, which runs the equipment; (3) data, which the computer manipulates; people, including both (4) computer personnel who manage the equipment and (5) users who use the information that the equipment produces; and finally (6) procedures, which help the entire system run efficiently.

A TOUR OF AN INFORMATION SYSTEMS DEPARTMENT

Many organizations use computers that concurrently process requests from more than one user. For example, one or more accounts receivable clerks could be entering cash receipts at the same time that one or more accounts payable clerks are entering invoices. Such systems are usually referred to as **multiuser computers**. Multiuser computers are generally under the control of a separate department of the company called the **information systems department**, the **data processing department**, or sometimes just the **computer department**.

The discussion that follows illustrates the elements of an information system by touring a typical information systems department.

Equipment

We identified the hardware components of a computer system as input devices, processor, output devices, and auxiliary storage. These general classifications apply to the multiuser computer system discussed in this example.

Input Devices The primary input device on a multiuser system is a terminal (Figure 1-16). A **terminal** is a device consisting of a keyboard and a screen, which is connected through a communication line or cable to a computer.

FIGURE 1-16
A terminal contains a keyboard and a screen. The screen displays the data entered via the keyboard. ▼

Processor The processor unit of a multiuser computer (Figure 1-17) allocates computer resources to the programs that are being processed. Modern computer processors are so fast that they can usually handle numerous users and still provide very quick response time.

Output Devices The most commonly used output devices for a multiuser computer are a printer (Figure 1-18) and a terminal (Figure 1-19). When large volumes of printed output must be produced, high-speed printers are used. The terminal can display both text material and graphics in either monochrome or color.

◀ FIGURE 1-17
This mainframe computer processes data for numerous users. Such a computer is usually placed in a room designed specifically for the machine. Special air conditioning, humidity control, electrical wiring, and flooring are required for many of these installations.

Auxiliary Storage The two major types of auxiliary storage for a multiuser computer are magnetic disk and magnetic tape.

Magnetic disk is the most widely used auxiliary storage on multiuser computers. When using magnetic disk, data is recorded on an oxide-coated metal platter (the disk) as a series of magnetic spots. Disk drives can store data on either removable disks or fixed disks. **Removable disks** refer to disk packs that can be taken out of the disk drive. In Figure 1-20, the blue containers for the removable disk packs can be seen sitting on the disk drives. **Fixed disk** drives utilize nonremovable disk packs enclosed in sealed units that prevent contamination of the disk surface.

Magnetic tape (Figure 1-21) stores data as magnetic spots on one-quarter to one-half-inch tape on cassettes or reels. On systems with disk drives, tape is most often used to store data that does not have to be accessed frequently. Another common use of tape is for backup storage. The contents of the disk drives are regularly copied to tape to protect against data loss such as in the case of disk drive failure.

◄ **FIGURE 1-18**
High-speed printers are necessary to print the large volume of reports generated by a multiuser computer system.

FIGURE 1-19
A terminal is both an input and an output device. In this picture, the user is viewing a color graphics display. ▼

◄ **FIGURE 1-20**
Removable disk packs are mounted on the disk drives in this picture. The multiple disk drives shown here are common in large computer installations.

FIGURE 1-21
This photo shows a magnetic tape drive that uses reels of half-inch tape. Tape is often used to back up the data stored on disk drives. ▼

When a disk pack or tape is not in use, it is stored in a **data library** (Figure 1-22). These disk packs and tapes must be catalogued so that when they are required, they can be located quickly and taken to the computer room for use.

FIGURE 1-22
The data library stores disk packs and tapes when they are not in use.

Software

The information systems department keeps its software on either disks or tapes. Once the disk or tape containing the software is mounted on the disk or tape drive, the processor can run the software by reading it into main memory and executing the program instructions. Depending on the amount of disk storage available and how frequently a program is used, some software applications are always available for processing. An example would be order processing software that enters orders into the computer while the sales clerk is on the phone with the customer. Because a phone call can come in at any time, this software application must always be available for processing.

Data

Data exists throughout an organization and comes to the information systems department in many forms. Often data is in the form of **source documents**, which are original documents such as sales invoices. Sometimes there are no source documents. Then data can be entered directly into the system by users or it can be entered by machines that read special codes or labels. In all cases, the accuracy of the data is important because it will affect the usefulness of the resulting information.

Personnel

In order to implement applications on a computer, the information systems department usually employs people who have specialized training in computers and information processing. These employees may include data entry personnel to prepare and enter data into the computer; computer operators to run the computer; programmers to write specialized programs; systems analysts to design the software applications; a database administrator to control and manage data; and management to oversee the use of the computer.

Data Entry Personnel **Data entry personnel** (Figure 1-23) are responsible for entering large volumes of data into the computer system. Data is usually entered on terminals from source documents.

Computer Operators The **computer operator** is responsible for a number of different tasks. When the computer is running, messages are displayed on the **operator's console** (Figure 1-24) indicating the status of the system. For example, a message may indicate that a special form, such as a check, must be placed in a printer. The operator responds to these messages in order to keep the computer running. In many instances, more than one operator is required to run a large computer.

FIGURE 1-23
Data entry personnel specialize in entering large amounts of data from source documents.

Computer Programmers **Computer programmers** design, write, test, and implement specialized programs that process data on a computer. The design specifications from the systems analyst tell the programmer what processing needs to be accomplished. It is the programmer's job to develop the specific programs of computer instructions that process the data and create the required information. The analyst specifies "what" is to be done; the programmer decides "how" to do it.

FIGURE 1-24
The console allows the computer operator to monitor the processing.

Systems Analysts **Systems analysts** are called upon to review current or proposed applications within a company to determine if the applications should be implemented using a computer. Applications are considered for computer implementation if, among other things, productivity can be increased or more timely information can be generated to aid in the management of the company. If an application is to be "computerized," the analyst studies the application to identify the data used, how the data is processed, and other aspects of the application that are pertinent to the new system. The analyst then designs the new system by defining the data required for the computer application, developing the manner in which the data will be processed in the new system, and specifying the associated activities and procedures necessary to implement the application using the computer. Analysts work closely with both the people who will be using and benefiting from the new system and the programmers in the information systems department who will be writing the computer programs (Figure 1-25).

Database Administrator An important function within the information systems department is the management of data. In many companies, this task is the responsibility of the **database administrator**. Among other things, the database administrator must develop procedures to ensure that correct data is entered into the system, that confidential company data is not lost or stolen, that access to company data is restricted to those who need the data, and that data is available when needed. This function is very important to most companies where billions of pieces of data are processed on the computer, and the loss or misappropriation of that data could be detrimental to business.

Information Systems Department Management Management within an information systems department is found at varying levels, depending on the size and complexity of the department. Most information systems departments have operations management, systems management, programming management, and a manager of the entire department. The **systems manager** oversees the activities in the systems analysis and design area of the department. The **programming manager** is in charge of all programmers within the department. Each of the previously mentioned managers may also have **project managers** within their area. The **operations manager** oversees the operational aspects of the department, including the scheduling, maintenance, and operation of the equipment. The information systems department manager is in charge of the entire department and may have the title **vice president of information systems** or **chief information officer**.

FIGURE 1-25
Programmers, analysts, and users all work closely in developing new computer applications.

Users

Users interact with the information systems department in several ways. They are often the first to request that a specific application be computerized. When a systems analyst is assigned to study the application, the analyst will rely on the users' knowledge of the requirements to determine if computerization is feasible. Once an application is implemented, users usually maintain an ongoing relationship with the information systems department. They may request special reports or processing and make suggestions about improving the application.

Procedures

Written procedures are an important part of any information system. Procedures should be documented for all steps in the processing cycle, including those steps that are not computerized. Accurate, up-to-date procedures minimize processing errors, reduce training time for new employees, and serve as a guide for future changes to the application.

Summary of the Tour of an Information Systems Department

During the tour of the information systems department we have seen the six elements of an information system: equipment, software, data, personnel, users, and procedures. Each of these elements directly affects an organization's ability to successfully process data into useful information.

SUMMARY OF AN INTRODUCTION TO COMPUTERS

This chapter presented a broad introduction to concepts and terminology that are related to computers. You now have an understanding of what a computer is, how it processes data into information, and which elements are necessary for a successful information system. The following photo essay is a time line that shows the evolution of modern computers.

CHAPTER SUMMARY

1. A **computer** is an electronic device, operating under the control of instructions stored in its own memory unit, that can accept data (input), process data arithmetically and logically, produce output from the processing, and store the results for future use.
2. A computer can perform **input**, **process**, **output**, and **storage** operations. These operations are called the **information processing cycle**.
3. **Data** refers to the raw facts, including numbers and words, that are processed on a computer.
4. **Information** is data that has been processed into a form that has meaning and is useful.
5. The production of information by processing data on a computer is called **information processing**.
6. **Computer users** are the people who either directly use the computer or utilize the information it provides.
7. A computer is a powerful tool because it is reliable and can process data quickly and accurately.
8. A **computer program** is a detailed set of instructions that tells the computer exactly what to do.

9. Computer processing can produce many different forms of information from a single set of data.
10. Processing data on a computer is performed by computer equipment including input devices, the processor unit, output devices, and auxiliary storage units. Computer equipment is often referred to as **hardware**.
11. **Input devices** are used to enter data into a computer.
12. The **processor unit** contains the electronic circuits that cause processing to take place.
13. **Arithmetic operations** are numeric calculations such as addition, subtraction, multiplication and division that take place in the processor.
14. **Logical operations** are comparisons of data in the processor to see if one value is greater than, equal to, or less than another value.
15. The processor is sometimes called the **central processing unit (CPU)**.
16. **Main memory** consists of components that electronically store data and program instructions.
17. **Output devices** are used to print or display data and information.
18. **Auxiliary storage units** are used to store program instructions and data when they are not being used in the main memory of the computer.
19. The four major categories of computers are microcomputers, minicomputers, mainframes, and supercomputers.
20. Types of **microcomputers** include laptop, portable, desktop, and supermicro computers.
21. **Minicomputers** address the needs of users who want more processing power than a microcomputer but do not need the power of a mainframe. Minicomputers can support a number of users performing different tasks.
22. **Mainframe** computers are large systems that can handle numerous users, store large amounts of data, and process transactions at a very high rate.
23. **Supercomputers**, the most powerful and expensive category of computers, can process hundreds of millions of instructions per second and perform long, complex calculations.
24. **Computer software** is another name for computer programs.
25. A computer program must first be loaded into main memory before it can be executed.
26. Programs purchased from computer stores or software vendors are called **application software packages**.
27. Four commonly used personal computer software packages are word processing, electronic spreadsheet, graphics, and database software.
28. **Word processing software** is used to create and print documents.
29. **Electronic spreadsheet software** performs calculations on rows and columns of numeric data based on formulas entered by the user.
30. **Graphics software** provides the ability to transform numbers and text into a graphic format.
31. **Database software** allows the user to enter, retrieve, and update data efficiently.
32. The elements of an information system are equipment, software, data, personnel, users and procedures.
33. **Multiuser computers** can concurrently process requests from more than one user.
34. A **terminal**, consisting of a keyboard and screen, is the most commonly used input device for a large computer.
35. Modern computer processors are so fast that they can usually handle numerous users and still provide very quick response time.
36. The most commonly used output devices for large computers are terminals and high-speed printers.
37. Auxiliary storage devices used on a large computer include **magnetic disk** and **magnetic tape**.
38. A **data library** stores disk packs and tapes when they are not in use.
39. Data can be entered directly into the computer by users or by machines.
40. **Source documents** are original documents, such as sales invoices, from which data can be entered.
41. **Data entry personnel** prepare and enter data into the computer.
42. **Computer operators** run the computer equipment and monitor processing operations.
43. **Computer programmers** design, write, test, and implement programs that process data on a computer.
44. **Systems analysts** review and design computer applications. Analysts work closely with users and programmers.
45. A **database administrator** is responsible for managing a company's data.
46. Management within an information systems department includes a **systems manager**, **programming manager**, **operations manager**, and a department manager, sometimes called the **vice president of information systems** or **chief information officer**.
47. **Users** play an important role in the development of computer applications.
48. Procedures should be documented for all steps in the processing cycle, including those steps that are not computerized.

KEY TERMS

Application software packages *1.10*
Arithmetic operations *1.7*
Auxiliary storage units *1.7*
Cathode ray tube (CRT) *1.7*
Central processing unit (CPU) *1.7*
Chief information officer *1.20*
Computer *1.3*
Computer department *1.16*
Computer operator *1.19*
Computer program *1.4*
Computer programmers *1.19*
Computer software *1.9*
Computer users *1.3*
CPU (central processing unit) *1.7*
CRT (cathode ray tube) *1.7*
Data *1.3*
Data entry personnel *1.19*
Data library *1.18*
Data processing department *1.16*
Database administrator *1.20*
Database software *1.12*
Diskette *1.7*
Electronic data processing *1.3*
Electronic spreadsheet software *1.12*
End users *1.3*
Fixed disk *1.17*
Floppy disk *1.7*
Graphics software *1.12*
Hard disk drive *1.7*
Hardware *1.6*
Information *1.3*
Information processing *1.3*
Information processing cycle *1.3*
Information systems department *1.16*
Input *1.6*
Input devices *1.6*
Keyboard *1.6*
Keyed *1.6*
Logical operations *1.7*
Magnetic disk *1.17*
Magnetic tape *1.17*
Main memory *1.7*
Mainframe *1.9*
Micro *1.8*
Microcomputers *1.8*
Minicomputer *1.9*
Monitor *1.7*
Multiuser computers *1.16*
Operations manager *1.20*
Operator's console *1.19*
Output *1.6*
Output devices *1.7*
Peripheral devices *1.7*
Personal computers *1.8*
Primary storage *1.7*
Printer *1.7*
Process *1.6*
Processor unit *1.7*
Program instructions *1.4*
Programming manager *1.20*
Project managers *1.20*
Removable disks *1.17*
Screen *1.7*
Software *1.4*
Software packages *1.10*
Source documents *1.18*
Spreadsheet *1.12*
Storage *1.6*
Supercomputers *1.9*
Systems analysts *1.20*
Systems manager *1.20*
Terminal *1.16*
Users *1.3*
Vice president of information systems *1.20*
Word processing software *1.12*

REVIEW QUESTIONS

1. What is the definition of a computer?
2. Identify the four operations a computer can perform, and explain operation.
3. What is data? What is information? How is information derived from data?
4. What is the information processing cycle?
5. What are the four specific hardware units found on a computer? Describe each of them.
6. What is the difference between main memory and auxiliary storage? Why are both necessary?
7. What is computer software? Why is it critical to the operation of a computer?
8. Identify the four software packages most often used with personal computers.
9. Describe the processing of a typical application on a personal computer.
10. What are the six elements of an information system?
11. Identify some of the differences among microcomputers, minicomputers, mainframe computers, and supercomputers.
12. Who are some of the personnel who work in an information systems department?
13. What is the role of a systems analyst? How does that position differ from the job of a computer programmer?
14. What is the user's role in an information system?
15. List the key developments in the evolution of the modern computer.

CONTROVERSIAL ISSUES

1. When Dr. Kemeny made his prediction in 1967 that learning how to use a computer would be as important as learning how to read and write, few people had access to computers. Since that time, millions of computers have been sold. Do you feel that it is necessary for all students to study computers and their uses? If so, at what grade levels: elementary school, high school, or college?
2. Some people believe that the computer is replacing people in the workforce. Based on what you have learned about computers in Chapter 1, do you think this is a valid statement, or do you think that computers help people do a better job?
3. You learned in this chapter that accurate data is required in order to provide meaningful information. What are some of the consequences if management decisions are based on incorrect data? What obligation does management have to ensure that decisions are based on correct data?

RESEARCH PROJECTS

1. Write or call a manufacturer of a mini or mainframe computer (IBM, Honeywell, DEC, HP, etc.) and ask for a brochure describing one of their popular models. Prepare a report for your class based on what you learned.
2. Prepare a report for your class describing the use of computers at your school. You may focus on a single department or prepare a general report about computer use throughout the school.
3. Prepare a detailed report on an individual who made a contribution to the history of the computer industry.

The Evolution of the Computer Industry

The electronic computer industry began about fifty years ago. This time line summarizes the major events in the evolution of the computer industry.

During the years 1943 to 1946, Dr. John W. Mauchly and J. Presper Eckert, Jr., completed the ENIAC (Electronic Numerical Integrator and Computer), the first large-scale electronic digital computer. The ENIAC weighed thirty tons, contained 18,000 vacuum tubes, and occupied a thirty by fifty foot space.

In 1952, the public awareness of computers increased when the UNIVAC I correctly predicted that Dwight D. Eisenhower would win the presidential election after analyzing only 5% of the tallied vote.

1930 1937 1940 1945 1950 1952

Dr. John V. Atanasoff and his assistant, Clifford Berry, designed and began to build the first electronic digital computer during the winter of 1937-38. Their machine, the Atanasoff-Berry-Computer or ABC, provided the foundation for the next advances in electronic digital computers.

Dr. John von Neumann is credited with writing a report in 1945 describing a number of new hardware concepts and how to use stored programs. This brilliant breakthrough laid the foundation for the digital computers that have been built since then.

In 1951-52, after much discussion, IBM made the decision to add computers to their line of business equipment products. This led IBM to become a dominant force in the computer industry.

In 1952, Dr. Grace Hopper, a mathematician and commodore in the U.S. Navy, wrote a paper describing how to program a computer with symbolic notation instead of the detailed machine language that had been used.

FORTRAN (FORmula TRANslator) was introduced in 1957. This programming language proved that efficient, easy-to-use computer languages could be developed. FORTRAN is still in use.

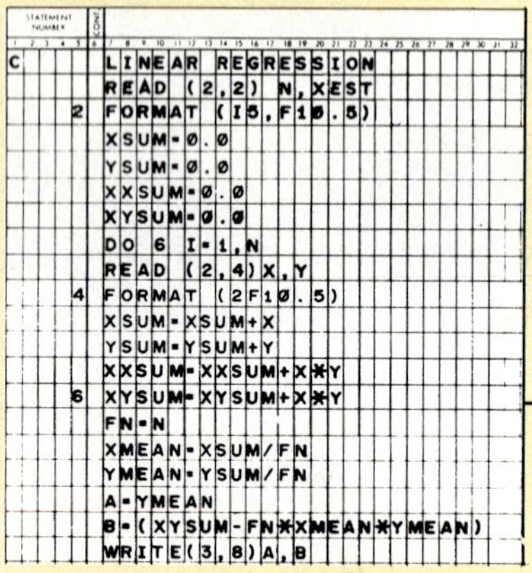

```
C     LINEAR REGRESSION
      READ (2,2) N,XEST
    2 FORMAT (I5,F1Ø.5)
      XSUM=Ø.Ø
      YSUM=Ø.Ø
      XXSUM=Ø.Ø
      XYSUM=Ø.Ø
      DO 6 I=1,N
      READ (2,4)X,Y
    4 FORMAT (2F1Ø.5)
      XSUM=XSUM+X
      YSUM=YSUM+Y
      XXSUM=XXSUM+X*Y
    6 XYSUM=XYSUM+X*Y
      FN=N
      XMEAN=XSUM/FN
      YMEAN=YSUM/FN
      A=YMEAN
      B=(XYSUM-FN*XMEAN*YMEAN)
      WRITE(3,8)A,B
```

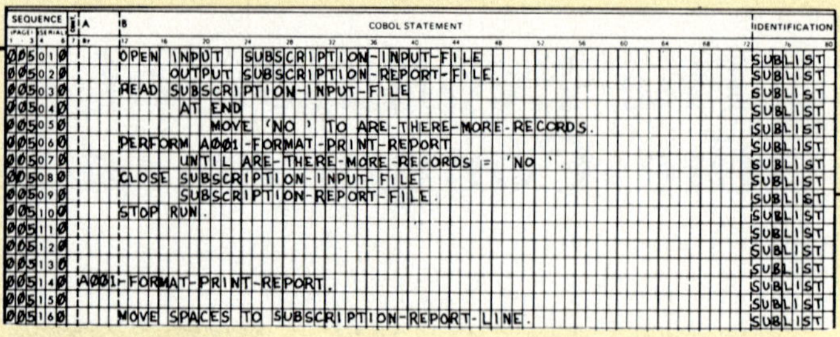

```
SEQUENCE  A   B                                                  IDENTIFICATION
ØØ5Ø1Ø        OPEN INPUT  SUBSCRIPTION-INPUT-FILE                    SUBLIST
ØØ5Ø2Ø             OUTPUT SUBSCRIPTION-REPORT-FILE.                  SUBLIST
ØØ5Ø3Ø        READ SUBSCRIPTION-INPUT-FILE                           SUBLIST
ØØ5Ø4Ø              AT END                                           SUBLIST
ØØ5Ø5Ø                 MOVE 'NO ' TO ARE-THERE-MORE-RECORDS.         SUBLIST
ØØ5Ø6Ø        PERFORM AØØ1-FORMAT-PRINT-REPORT                       SUBLIST
ØØ5Ø7Ø              UNTIL ARE-THERE-MORE-RECORDS = 'NO '.            SUBLIST
ØØ5Ø8Ø        CLOSE SUBSCRIPTION-INPUT-FILE                          SUBLIST
ØØ5Ø9Ø              SUBSCRIPTION-REPORT-FILE.                        SUBLIST
ØØ51ØØ        STOP RUN.                                              SUBLIST
ØØ511Ø                                                               SUBLIST
ØØ512Ø                                                               SUBLIST
ØØ513Ø                                                               SUBLIST
ØØ514Ø    AØØ1-FORMAT-PRINT-REPORT.                                  SUBLIST
ØØ515Ø                                                               SUBLIST
ØØ516Ø        MOVE SPACES TO SUBSCRIPTION-REPORT-LINE.               SUBLIST
```

Dr. Hopper became instrumental in developing high-level languages such as COBOL, a business applications language that was introduced in 1960. COBOL uses English-like phrases and can be run on most brands of computers, making it one of the most widely used languages in the world.

By 1959, over 200 programming languages had been created.

1952 | 1955 | 1957 | 1958 | 1959 | 1960

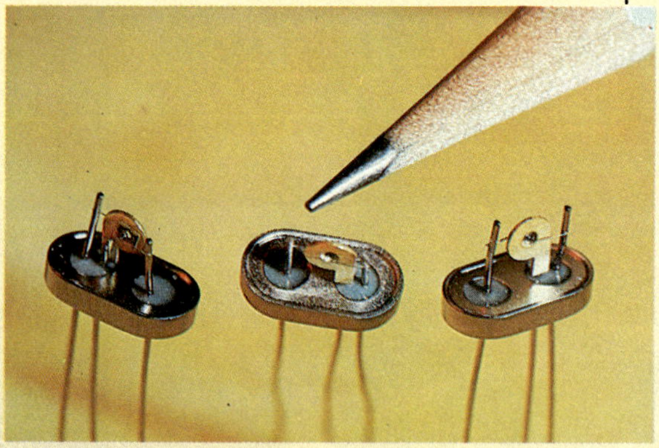

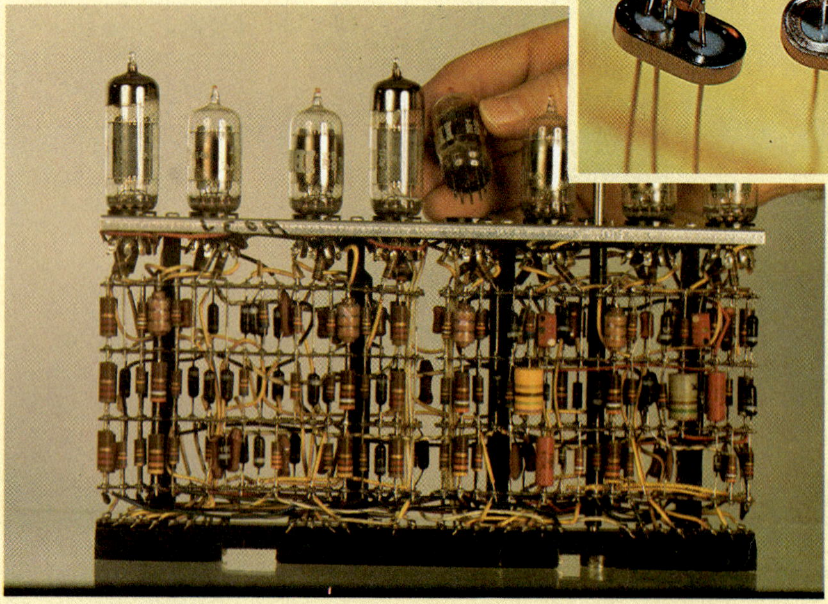

In 1958, computers built with transistors (above) marked the beginning of the second generation of computer hardware. Previous computers built with vacuum tubes (left) are called first-generation machines.

Third-generation computers were introduced in 1964. Their controlling circuitry is stored on chips. The family of IBM System/360 computers were the first third-generation machines.

Dr. Ted Hoff of Intel Corporation is credited with developing the first microprocessor or microprogrammable computer chip, the Intel 4004, in 1969.

1964 1965 1968 1969

From 1958 to 1964, it is estimated, the number of computers in the U.S. grew from 2,500 to 18,000.

In 1965, Dr. John Kemeny of Dartmouth led the development of the BASIC programming language. BASIC is the most commonly used language on microcomputers. More people know how to program in BASIC than any other language.

Digital Equipment Corporation (DEC) introduced the first minicomputer in 1965.

The 1960s saw the birth of the software industry. In 1968, Computer Science Corporation became the first software company to be listed on the New York Stock Exchange.

In 1969, under pressure from the industry, IBM announced that some of its software would be priced separately from the computer hardware. This "unbundling" opened up the industry to emerging software firms.

Fourth-generation computers emerged in 1970. These machines were built with chips that utilized LSI (large-scale integration). The chips used in 1965 could contain as many as 1,000 circuits. By 1970, the LSI chip could contain as many as 15,000.

The VisiCalc spreadsheet program written by Dan Bricklin and Bob Frankston was introduced in 1979. This product was originally written to run on Apple II computers. Together, VisiCalc and Apple II computers became rapidly successful in the business community. Most people consider VisiCalc to be the single most important reason why microcomputers gained acceptance in the business world.

1970 1975 1980

The MITS, Inc., Altair computer was the first commercially successful microcomputer. It sold in kit form for less than $500.

In 1976, Steve Jobs and Steve Wozniak built the first Apple computer.

In 1980, IBM offered Bill Gates, the founder of Microsoft Corporation, the opportunity to develop the operating system for the soon-to-be-announced IBM personal computer. Microsoft developed MS-DOS, the product that helped them achieve tremendous growth and success.

The Lotus 1-2-3 integrated software package, developed by Mitch Kapor, was introduced in 1983. It combined spreadsheet, graphics, and database programs in one package.

1981 1982 1983 1985

It is estimated that 313,000 microcomputers were sold in 1981. In 1982, the number jumped to 3,275,000.

The IBM PC was introduced in 1981, signaling IBM's entrance in the microcomputer marketplace. The IBM PC quickly garnered the largest share of the personal computer market and became the personal computer most often used in business.

The IBM Application System 400, introduced in 1988, made a significant impact on the minicomputer and mainframe market, allowing users to expand their computing capabilities more easily.

1987 1988 1990

Several microcomputers utilizing the powerful Intel 80386 microprocessor were introduced in 1987. These machines can handle processing that previously only large systems could perform.

OS/2, an IBM microcomputer operating system, will enable microcomputers to be as powerful as many of today's minicomputers. Further, it will allow microcomputers to become multiuser systems, that is, multiple keyboards and screens can be attached to the same computer.

The computer industry will continue to evolve as improved technology and innovation lead to a variety of new computer applications.

CHAPTER 2

Microcomputer Applications: User Tools

CHAPTER 2

Microcomputer Applications: User Tools

OBJECTIVES

- Identify the four most widely used general microcomputer software applications.
- Describe how each of the four applications can help users.
- Explain the key features of each of the four major microcomputer applications.
- Describe the key features of data communications and desktop publishing software.
- Explain integrated software and its advantages.
- List and describe five guidelines for purchasing software application packages.
- Discuss tips for using each of the four major microcomputer applications.

Computer literate is a term you might have heard used to describe people who have an understanding of computers and how they are used in our modern world. Today, understanding the common applications used on microcomputers is often considered a part of being computer literate. In fact, a knowledge of these applications is now considered by many educators and employers to be more important than a knowledge of programming. Because of this, we place an introduction to microcomputer applications focusing on the four most widely used applications early in this book. Learning the features of each application will help you understand how microcomputers are used by people in our modern world and provide a foundation to help you learn.

AN INTRODUCTION TO GENERAL MICROCOMPUTER APPLICATIONS

The applications discussed in this chapter are sometimes referred to as **general microcomputer applications**. This software is called "general" because it is useful to a broad range of users. Word processing is a good example of a general application. Regardless of the type of business a company does, word processing can be used as a tool to help employees generate documents.

An important advantage of general applications is that you don't need any special technical skills or ability to use them. These programs are designed to be **user friendly**, in other words, easy to use. You do not need detailed computer instructions as you would if you were programming. Instead, you operate the software through simple commands. **Commands** are the instructions that you use to operate the software. For example, when you are finished using an application and you want to save your work, you issue an instruction called a "save" command. To use this command you might type SAVE WORKFILE. The word SAVE is the command and WORKFILE is the name under which your work will be stored.

User interfaces (Figure 2-1) are methods and techniques that make using an application simpler. They include function keys, screen prompts, menus, and icons. The **function keys** that are included on computer keyboards are a type of user interface. Pressing a function key in an applications program is a shortcut that takes the place of entering a command. The software defines exactly what the function key causes to happen. If you used a function key to perform the SAVE command described above, pressing one key instead of several could generate the entire command SAVE WORKFILE.

FIGURE 2-1
User interfaces.

(a) Function keys are programmed to execute commonly used instructions.

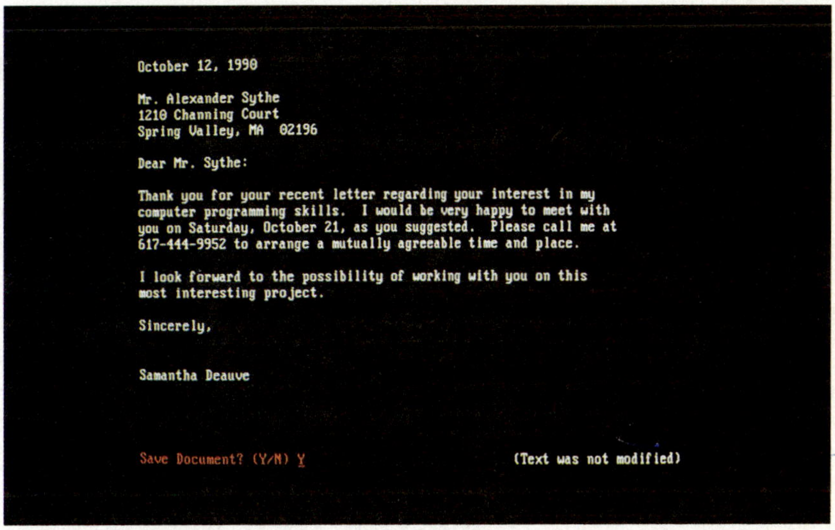

(b) Screen prompts, such as the red question in the lower left of this screen, indicate that the software is waiting for the user to respond.

(c) Menus offer a list of possible processing selections.

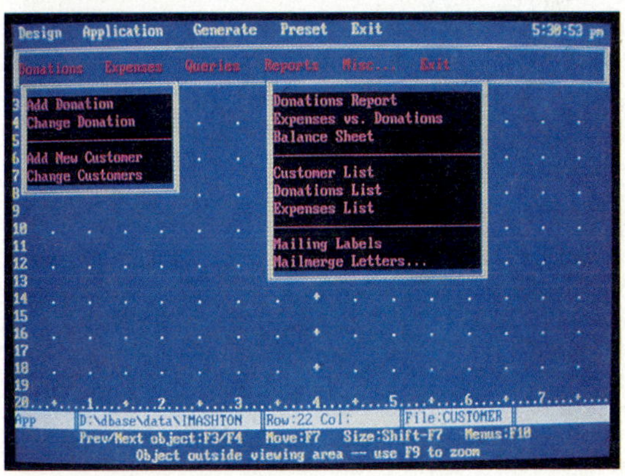

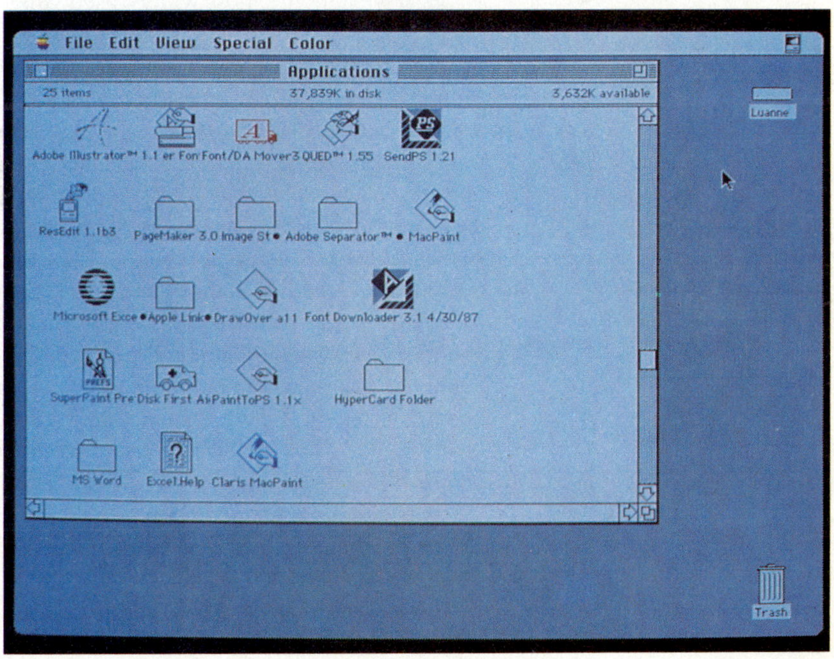

(d) Icons are symbols that represent a computer activity.

Screen **prompts** are the messages that the program displays to help you while you are using an application. **Menus**, a special kind of screen prompt, are used in applications to provide a list of processing options. You make a selection from the menu by pressing the number or letter key that corresponds with the desired option. **Icons** refer to pictures instead of words that are displayed on the screen to show you various program options.

These are some of the features included in general applications packages that help to make them user friendly. These aids minimize the need for technical computer knowledge when you are using general applications packages.

THE FOUR MOST COMMON GENERAL APPLICATIONS

While there are many kinds of general applications available, four software applications packages are the most widely used. They are:

1. word processing software
2. electronic spreadsheet software
3. database software
4. graphics software

Although we will discuss these four applications on microcomputers, they are actually available on computers of all sizes. The concepts you will learn about each application package on microcomputers will also apply if you are working on a larger system.

WORD PROCESSING SOFTWARE: A DOCUMENT PRODUCTIVITY TOOL

Probably the most widely used general application is word processing. If you need to create **documents**, such as letters or memos, you can increase your productivity by learning to use this software tool. Some of the popular packages used today include WordPerfect, WordStar, and Microsoft Word. This section discusses using a word processor to create a document.

Word processing software is used to prepare documents electronically (Figure 2-2). It allows you to enter text on the computer keyboard in the same manner as documents are created on a typewriter. As you enter the characters, they are displayed on the screen and stored in the computer's main memory. Because this is an electronic format, it is easy to **edit** the document by making changes and corrections to the text. Errors may be corrected and words, sentences, paragraphs, or pages may be added or deleted. When the document is complete, you enter a command and have the computer send the document to the printer. The document's format is also under your control. You can specify the margins, define the page length, and select the print style. The document can be printed as many times as you like. Each copy is an original and looks the same as the other copies. The computer's storage capability allows you to store your documents so that they can be used again. It is an efficient way to file documents because many documents can fit on one disk. If you wish, previously stored documents can be combined to make new documents, and you do not have to reenter the text as you would on a typewriter.

The value of word processing is that it reduces the time required to prepare and produce written documents. Any editing you wish to do in the document is easy because the software allows you to make changes quickly and efficiently. In addition, the tedious task of typing a final draft is eliminated.

FIGURE 2-2
Word processing using a computer is faster, more accurate, and less tedious than using a typewriter.

Most word processing packages include additional support features such as spelling checkers, a thesaurus, and some limited grammar checking.

Spelling Checkers

Spelling checker software allows you to check individual words or the entire document for correct spelling. To check individual words, you position the cursor at the start of the word and press a key defined by the software to indicate that the spelling is to be checked. The word in the text will then be checked against an electronic dictionary stored on a disk that is part of the spelling checker software. Some spelling checker dictionaries contain over 100,000 words. Spelling checkers, however, cannot detect incorrect grammar or word usage.

When the entire document is checked for spelling, each word is compared against entries in the dictionary. If an exact match is not found, the word is highlighted. A menu is then superimposed on the screen, giving you a list of similar words that may be the correct spelling. You may select one of the words displayed on the menu, edit the highlighted word, leave the word unchanged, or add the word to the dictionary. Many users customize their software dictionaries by adding company, street, city, and personal names to the dictionary so that the software can check the correct spelling of those words.

Thesaurus

Thesaurus software allows you to look up synonyms for words in a document while you are using your word processor. Using a thesaurus is similar to using a spelling checker. When you want to look up a synonym for a word, you place the cursor on the word that you want to check, enter a command through the keyboard, and the thesaurus software displays a menu of possible synonyms. If you find a word you want to use, you select the desired word from the list and the software automatically incorporates it in the document by replacing the previous word.

Grammar Checkers

Grammar checker software can be used to check for certain grammar, writing style, and sentence structure errors. These programs can check documents for excessive usage of a word or phrase and can identify sentences that are too long. They can also show you words that have been repeated such as "and and" or words used out of context such as "four example."

A Word Processing Example

Figures 2-3 through 2-10 illustrate the following word processing example. Let's say the vice president of sales of a company wants to send a memo announcing a meeting of all sales personnel. She remembers that last month she sent a similar memo to just the sales managers. Thus, the first thing she does is load last month's memo into main memory so it will appear on the screen (Figure 2-3). This memo might be stored on a hard disk or on a floppy diskette.

FIGURE 2-3
Last month's memo that will be changed for this month's meeting.

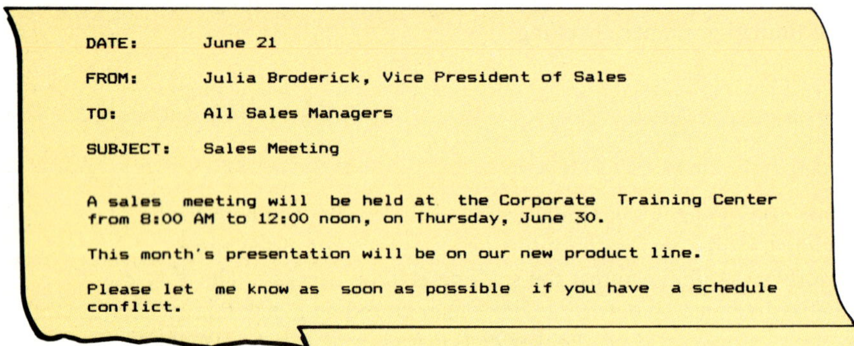

DATE: June 21

FROM: Julia Broderick, Vice President of Sales

TO: All Sales Managers

SUBJECT: Sales Meeting

A sales meeting will be held at the Corporate Training Center from 8:00 AM to 12:00 noon, on Thursday, June 30.

This month's presentation will be on our new product line.

Please let me know as soon as possible if you have a schedule conflict.

FIGURE 2-4 ▶
The shaded areas indicate text to be deleted.

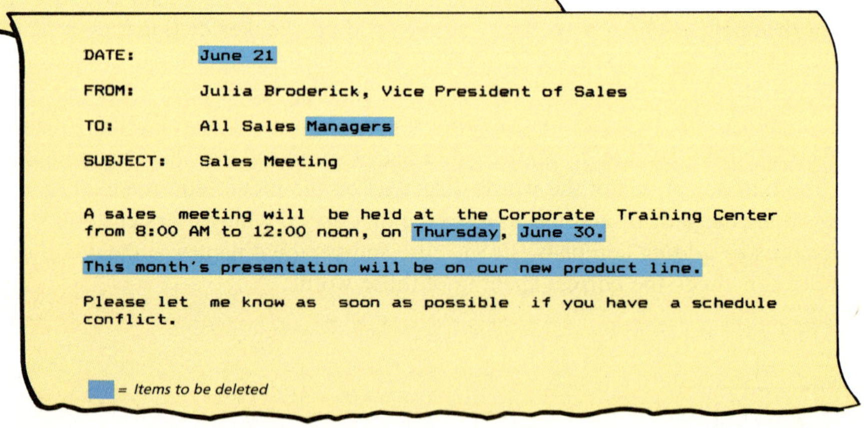

DATE: June 21

FROM: Julia Broderick, Vice President of Sales

TO: All Sales Managers

SUBJECT: Sales Meeting

A sales meeting will be held at the Corporate Training Center from 8:00 AM to 12:00 noon, on Thursday, June 30.

This month's presentation will be on our new product line.

Please let me know as soon as possible if you have a schedule conflict.

Word processing changes are usually of three types: to **insert** data, **delete** data, or **move** data. Often it makes sense to do your insertions and deletions at the same time; as you edit your document, you delete the existing word or phrase and insert the new one. **Replace** is a combination of the delete and insert commands. With replace, you can scan a document for a single or multiple occurrence of a word or phrase and replace it with another or delete it entirely. Figure 2-4 shows the document with the text to be deleted. Figure 2-5 shows the document after the new text has been inserted.

The **move** command allows you to either cut (remove) or copy a sentence, paragraph, page, or block of text. In our example, the VP of sales, Julia Broderick, decided she wanted to move the existing paragraph 3 in front of the existing paragraph 2 (Figure 2-6). First she would highlight or somehow signify the text to be moved. Next she would indicate that she wants to "cut" and not "copy" the marked text. With a **cut**, you are removing text from an area. With a **copy**, the word processor makes a copy of the marked text but leaves the marked text where it was. After you perform either the cut or the copy, the word processor needs to know where you want to place or **paste** the text. This is usually done by moving the cursor to the point where you want the moved text to begin. You then give a command to execute the move. Figure 2-7 shows the cut text "pasted" into a position that now makes it the second paragraph.

After the text changes are made, Julia runs a spelling checker. The spelling checker matches each word in the document against its spelling dictionary and discovers an unrecognized word: "personel." Figure 2-8 shows how a spelling checker might present two alternatives for the correct spelling of the word. Julia merely has to enter the letter B and the word processor will change "personel" to "personnel" (Figure 2-9).

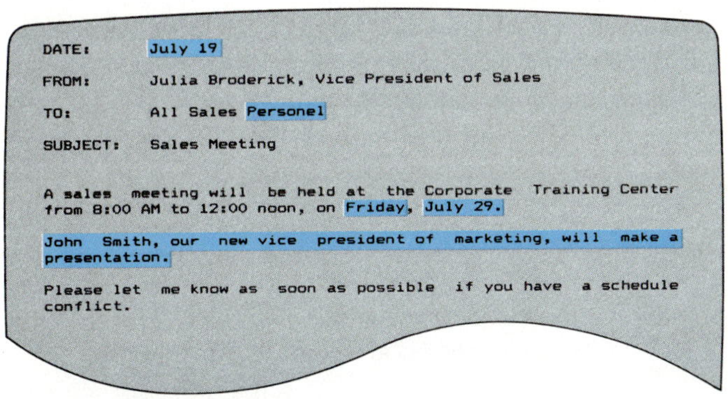

= *Inserted information*

▲
FIGURE 2-5
The shading on the computer screen shows the new text inserted into last month's memo.

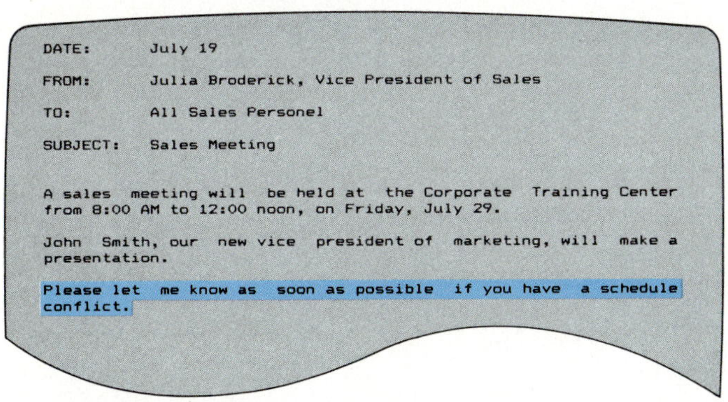

= *Block to be moved to second paragraph*

▲
FIGURE 2-6
The shading shows the text to be moved from third to second paragraph.

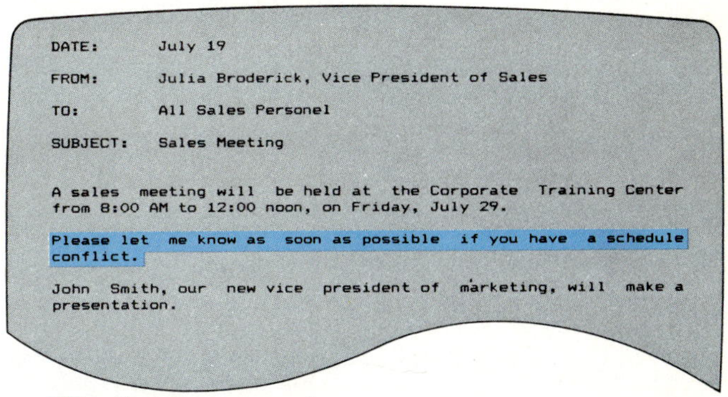

= *Block that was moved*

▲
FIGURE 2-7
Memo after third paragraph was moved to second paragraph.

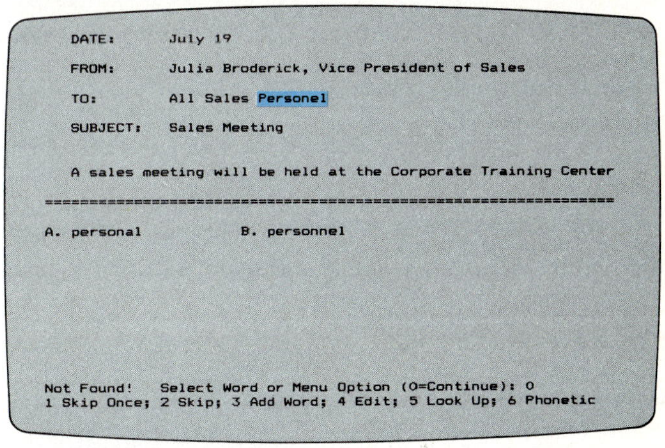

= *Block that was moved*

▲
FIGURE 2-8
Spelling checker highlighting unrecognized word and showing two possible spellings.

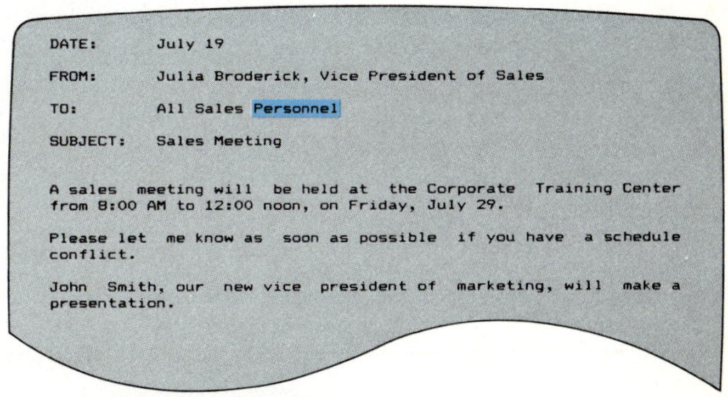

= *Correctly spelled word*

▲
FIGURE 2-9
Correct spelling of "personnel" inserted into text by spelling checker.

Before printing the memo, Julia reviews its format. She decides that the document is too wide and increases the margins. Figure 2-10 shows the document with the wider, 1 1/2-inch, margins.

FIGURE 2-10
Memo after margins are changed.

DATE: July 19

FROM: Julia Broderick, Vice President of Sales

TO: All Sales Personnel

SUBJECT: Sales Meeting

A sales meeting will be held at the Corporate Training Center from 8:00 AM to 12:00 noon, on Friday, July 29.

Please let me know as soon as possible if you have a schedule conflict.

John Smith, our new vice president of marketing, will make a presentation.

Now that the text and format are correct, Julia will save the document before printing it in case a system or power failure occurs during printing. Once saved, the document can be printed as often as necessary and is available for use or modification at a later date.

Word processing software is a productivity tool that allows you to create, edit, format, print, and store documents. Each of the many word processing packages available may have slightly different capabilities, but most have the features summarized in Figure 2-11.

FIGURE 2-11
Common features of word processing software.

WORD PROCESSING FEATURES	
INSERTION AND MOVING	**SEARCH AND REPLACE**
Insert character	Search and replace word
Insert word	Search and replace character strings
Insert line	**PRINTING**
Move sentences	Set top and bottom margins
Move paragraphs	Set left and right margins
Move blocks	Set tab stops
Merge text	Print columns
DELETE FEATURES	Single, double, triple space control
Delete character	Variable space control within text
Delete word	Right justify
Delete sentence	Center lines
Delete paragraph	Subscripts
Delete entire text	Superscripts
SCREEN CONTROL	Underline
Scroll up and down by line	Boldface
Scroll by page	Condensed print
Word wrap	Enlarged print
Uppercase and lowercase display	Special type fonts
Underline display	Proportional spacing
Screen display according to defined format	Headers
Bold display	Footers
Superscript display	Page numbering
Subscript display	Print any page from file

FIGURE 2-12
The electronic spreadsheet on the right still uses the row and column format of the manual spreadsheet on the left.

ELECTRONIC SPREADSHEET SOFTWARE: A NUMBER PRODUCTIVITY TOOL

Electronic spreadsheet software allows you to organize numeric data in a worksheet or table format called an **electronic spreadsheet** or **spreadsheet**. Manual methods have long been used to organize numeric data in this manner (Figure 2-12). You will see that the data in an electronic spreadsheet is organized in the same manner as it is in a manual spreadsheet, one that is done by hand. Within a spreadsheet, data is organized horizontally in **rows** and vertically in **columns**. The intersection where a row and column meet is called a **cell** (Figure 2-13).

Cells may contain three types of data: labels (text), values (numbers), and formulas. The text, or **labels** as they are sometimes called, are used to identify the data and to document the worksheet. Good spreadsheets are well documented and contain descriptive titles. The rest of the cells in a spreadsheet may appear to contain numbers or **values**. However, some of the cells actually contain formulas. The **formulas** perform calculations on the data in the spreadsheet and display the resulting value in the cell containing the formula.

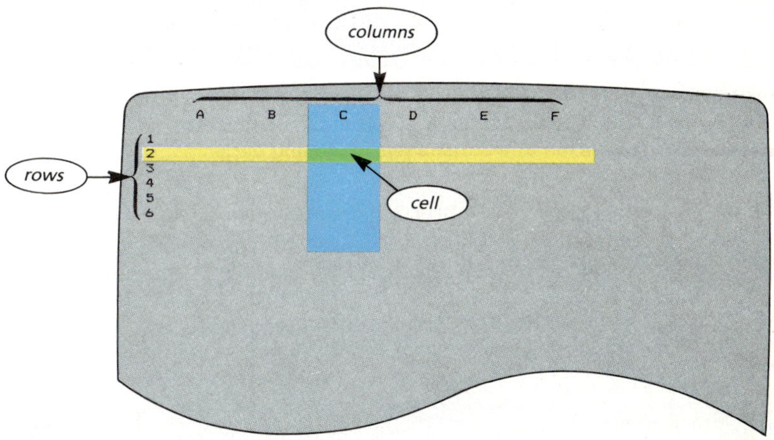

FIGURE 2-13
In a spreadsheet, rows refer to the horizontal lines of data and columns refer to the vertical lines of data. Note that rows are identified by numbers and columns are identified by letters. The intersection of a row and column is called a cell. The highlighted cell is the cursor. You can move the cursor by pressing the arrow keys on the keyboard.

In a manual spreadsheet, each of the totals would have to be calculated by hand. In an electronic spreadsheet, the user enters a formula into a cell. Then the result for that cell is calculated and displayed automatically. Once a formula is entered into a cell, it can be copied to any other cell that requires a similar formula. As the formula is copied, the formula calculations are performed automatically.

One of the most powerful features of the electronic spreadsheet occurs when the data in a spreadsheet changes. To appreciate the capabilities of spreadsheet software, let's discuss how a change is handled in a manual system. When a value in a manual spreadsheet changes, it must be erased and a new value written into the cell. All cells that contain formulas referring to the value that changed must also be erased, recalculated, and the result reentered. For example, the row totals and column totals would be updated to reflect changes to any values within their areas. In large manual spreadsheets, accurately posting changes and updating the values affected can be time consuming. But posting changes on an electronic spreadsheet is easy. You change data in a cell by simply typing in the new value. All other values that are affected are updated *automatically*. While the updating happens very quickly, if you watch the screen closely you can sometimes see the values change. As row and column totals are updated, the changes are said to *ripple* through the spreadsheet.

An electronic spreadsheet's ability to recalculate when data is changed makes it a valuable tool for management personnel. This capability allows managers to perform "what if" testing by changing the numbers in a spreadsheet (Figure 2-14). The resulting values that are calculated by the spreadsheet software provide management with valuable decision support information based on the alternatives tested.

To illustrate this powerful tool, we will show you how to develop the spreadsheet that was used as an example in Chapter 1. You may remember that the completed spreadsheet contains revenues, costs, profit, and profit percentage for three months and the totals for the three months. By following Figures 2-15 through 2-19, you can see that the first step in creating the spreadsheet is to enter the labels or titles. These should be short but descriptive, to help you organize the layout of the data in your spreadsheet. The next step is to enter the data or numbers in the body of the spreadsheet, and finally the formulas. At this point you can give commands to print the spreadsheet and to store it on a disk.

An electronic spreadsheet is a productivity tool that organizes and performs calculations on numeric data. Spreadsheets are one of the most popular software applications. They have been adapted to a wide range of business and nonbusiness applications. Some of the popular packages used today are Lotus 1-2-3, Excel, SuperCalc, and VP-Planner. Most of the packages available will have the features shown in Figure 2-20.

FIGURE 2-14
The "what if" testing capability of electronic spreadsheets is a powerful tool used to aid managers in making decisions.

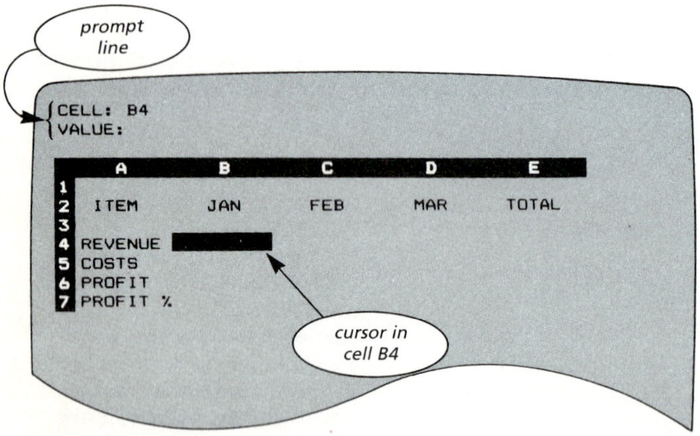

FIGURE 2-15
Labels identify rows and columns in a spreadsheet. The prompt line at the top left of the screen has two parts: CELL, which identifies the column and row being referenced; and VALUE, which identifies the value in the cell. The cursor, is located in cell B4, the intersection of column B and row 4. No value has been entered into B4.

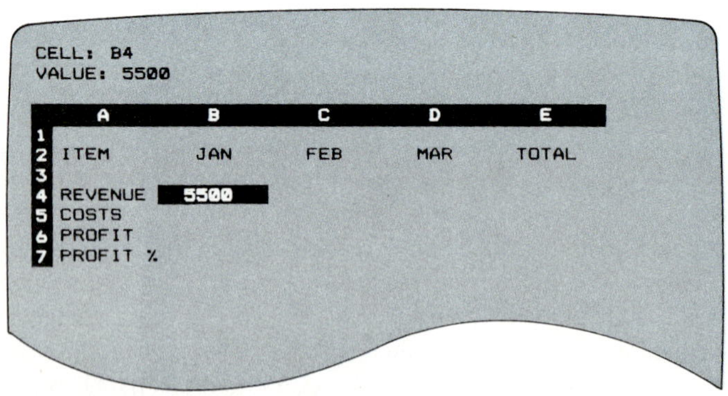

FIGURE 2-16
The value 5500 is entered and stored at cell B4. Note the entries in the display at the top left corner of the screen, identifying which value (in this case a number) has been entered into which cell.

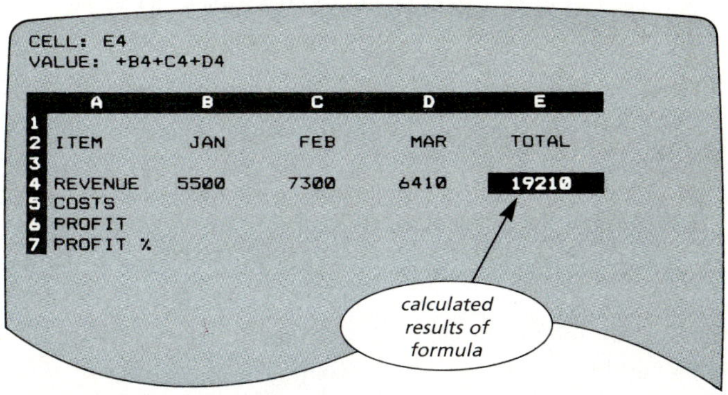

FIGURE 2-17
The arrow keys are used to move the cursor to cells in the spreadsheet. The values 7300 and 6410 are entered in cells C4 and D4. A formula is entered in cell E4. The formula specifies that the content of cell E4 is to be the sum of the values in cells B4, C4, and D4. The spreadsheet itself displays the numeric sum. The prompt line at the top of the screen, however, shows the formula used to calculate the value.

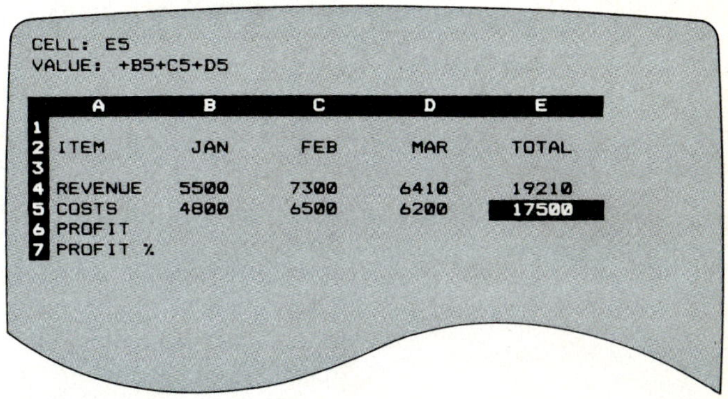

FIGURE 2-18
The formula required for cell E5 is similar to the one entered for cell E4; it totals the amounts in the three previous columns. When we copy the formula from E4 into E5, the software automatically changes the cell references from B4, C4, and D4 to B5, C5, and D5.

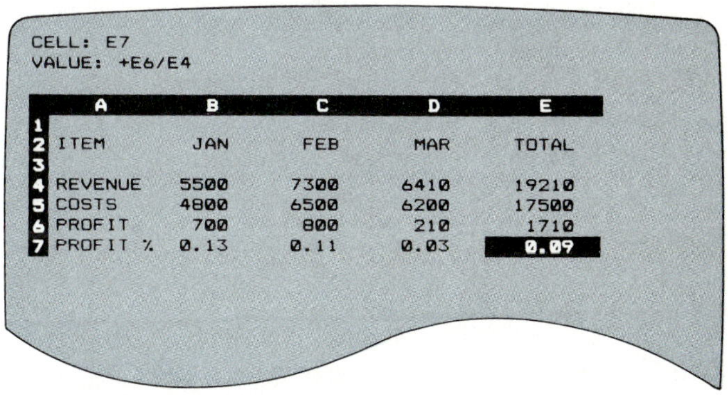

FIGURE 2-19
This screen shows the completed spreadsheet. The value in cell E7 is derived from the formula illustrated on the prompt line, which specifies that the value in cell E6 is to be divided by the value in cell E4. (The slash character indicates division.) Since the value in E6 is the total profit and the value in E4 is the total revenue, the result of the division operation is the profit percentage.

SPREADSHEET FEATURES	
WORKSHEET Global format Insert column Insert row Delete column Delete row Set up titles Set up windows **RANGE** Format range of data Erase cells **COPY** Copy from cells Copy to cells	**MOVE** Move from cells Move to cells **FILE** Save Retrieve Erase List **PRINT** Set up margins Define header Define footer Specify range to print Define page length Condensed print

FIGURE 2-20
Common features of spreadsheet software

DATABASE SOFTWARE: A DATA MANAGEMENT TOOL

Database software allows you to create electronic files on your computer and to retrieve, manipulate, and update the data you store in the files. Just as in a manual system, a **file** is a collection of related data. For example, a file might consist of customer's names and addresses. In a manual system (Figure 2-21), the data might be recorded on paper and stored in a filing cabinet. On the computer, the data will be stored in an electronic format on an auxiliary storage device such as a disk. Another term that is used to reference data is record. A **record** is a collection of related facts or data items. In our name and address file example, all the information that relates to one person would be considered a record. Each of the facts or data items within a record is called a **field**.

Sometimes the word database is used interchangeably with the word file. However, the term **database** usually refers to a collection of data that is organized in multiple files. Understanding the difference between the terms file and database will help you to understand the difference between file management software and database software. In general, **file management software** allows you to work with one file at a time, while database software allows you to work with multiple files.

The screens in Figures 2-22 through 2-26 present the development of a personal checking account file and inquiry system using a file management system. The file management main menu (Figure 2-22) presents 5 choices: to create a file, enter data, update the file, display data, and terminate the processing of the file management system. To begin, you would select option 1, CREATE FILE.

When you select option 1, the FILE MANAGEMENT CREATE FILE information shown in Figure 2-23 is displayed. A prompt asks you to enter a file name, the name under which the file being created will be stored on disk. In this example, you would enter the name CHECKING.

You are then asked to enter descriptions for each field in the records to be stored in the file. A field description consists of a field name, the type of data to be stored in the field (A for alphanumeric, N for numeric data), and the number of characters in the field. In a numeric field, if digits are to appear to the right of the decimal point, you must specify the number of digits to the right. Thus, for the amount field, the designation 6.2 means there are six numeric digits in the field with two of those digits to the right of the decimal point.

Once you have defined the fields in the records, you enter data into the records. Therefore, you would choose main menu entry 2, ENTER DATA and Figure 2-24 would appear. The file management system prompts you to enter data for each record by typing the data to be stored in the field. Thus, after the field name NUMBER, you enter the check number. You complete each field in the same manner, and continue to enter data until all data is entered for the checking account file.

After the file has been defined and data has been stored in it, you can use the file to produce information. Therefore you would choose option 4, DISPLAY DATA, from the main menu. You are then asked to enter the commands that specify what should be displayed and how the data should be processed prior to being displayed. As Figure 2-25 shows, you stated that the data should be sorted on the field called NUMBER, and that all fields in the record should be displayed.

FIGURE 2-21
An electronic database is similar to a manual system; related data items are stored in files.

In Figure 2-26, you direct the system to display only those records where the class is equal to UTILITY and to print a total for the field AMOUNT. As a result, the report shows only those records for which the classification is UTILITY. The values in the amount field are totalled and printed after all records have been processed.

In addition to creating, retrieving, and storing data, most database and file management software provide for the manipulation of the data. This includes sorting the data in ascending or descending sequence by specifying a few simple English-like commands. Figure 2-27 lists some features of popular database software, such as dBASE III PLUS.

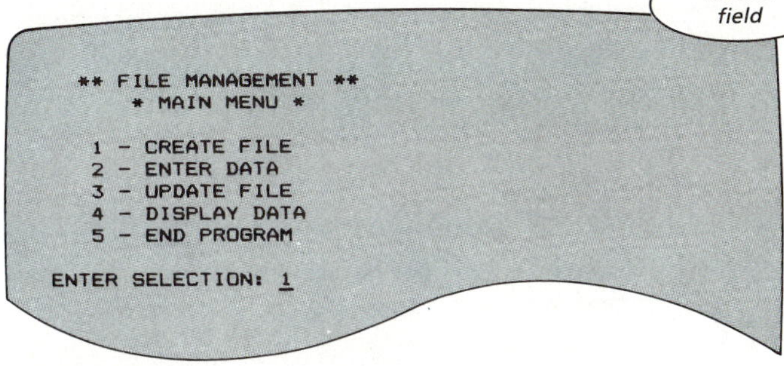

FIGURE 2-22
A typical main menu of file management software.

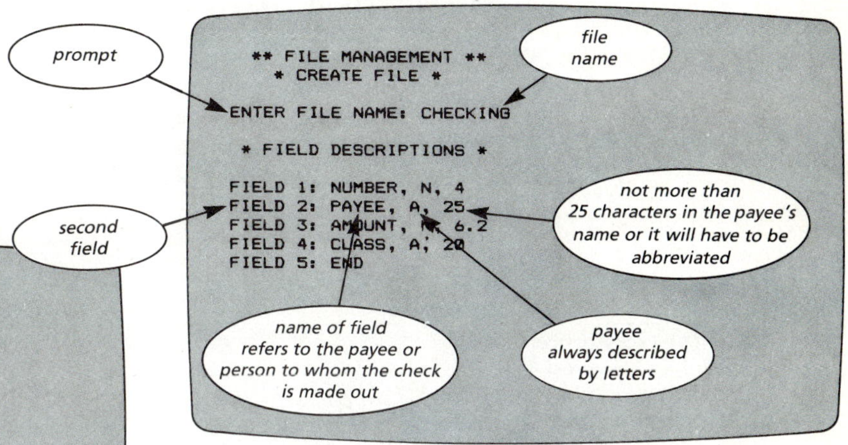

FIGURE 2-23
CREATE FILE screen showing definition of fields for records in the CHECKING file.

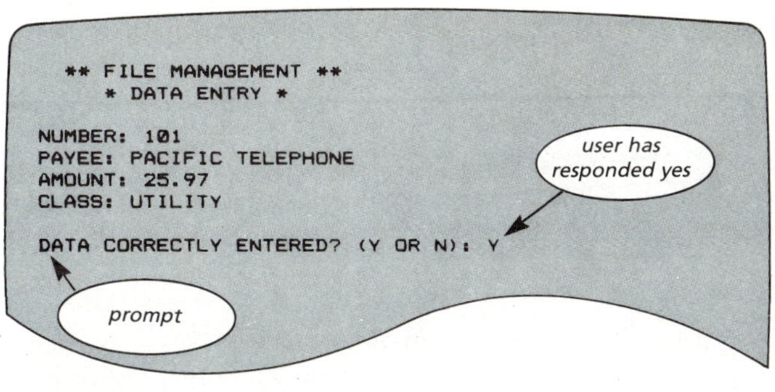

FIGURE 2-24
Data entry screen.

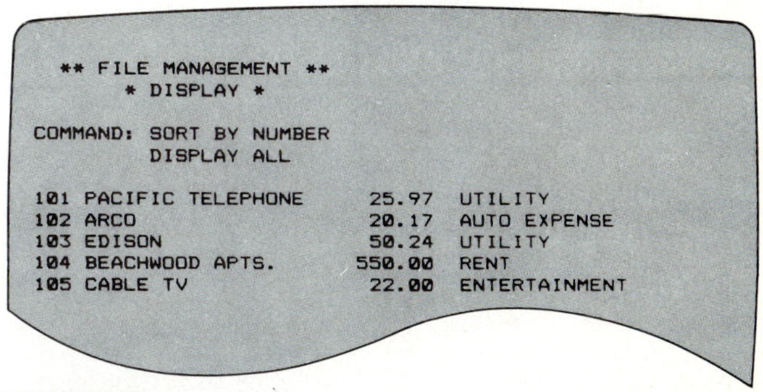

FIGURE 2-25
Display of all records sorted by record number.

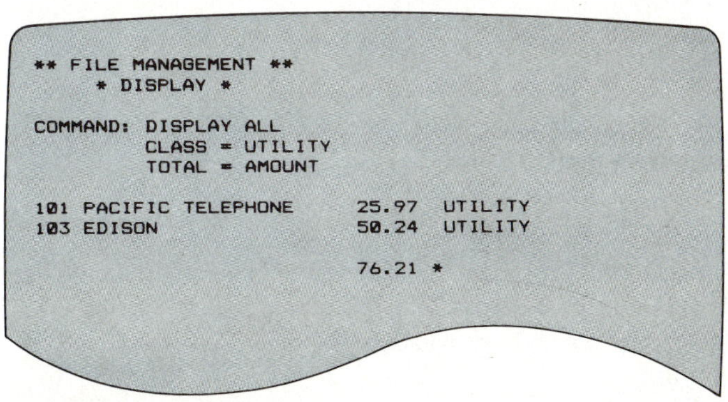

FIGURE 2-26
Display of only the UTILITY class records with a total calculated on the amount.

DATABASE FEATURES	
OPERATIONS Create database Copy data Delete data Sort data **EDITING** Display data Update data	**ARITHMETIC** Compute the average Count the records Sum data fields **OUTPUT** Retrieve data Produce a report

FIGURE 2-27
Common features of database software.

Note again that when using this microcomputer application, you do not need to have any special technical knowledge. Database software and file managers are general application tools that are designed to help you easily and efficiently manage data electronically.

GRAPHICS SOFTWARE: A DATA PRESENTATION TOOL

Information presented in the form of a graph or a chart is commonly referred to as **graphics**. Studies have shown that information presented in graphic form can be understood much faster than information presented in writing. Three common forms of graphics are **pie charts**, **bar charts**, and **line diagrams** (Figure 2-28).

FIGURE 2-28

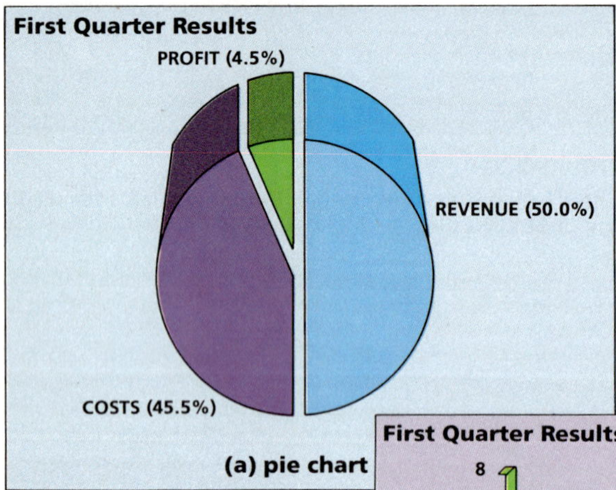

(a) Pie charts, so called because they look like pies cut into pieces, are particularly effective for showing the relationship of parts to a whole.

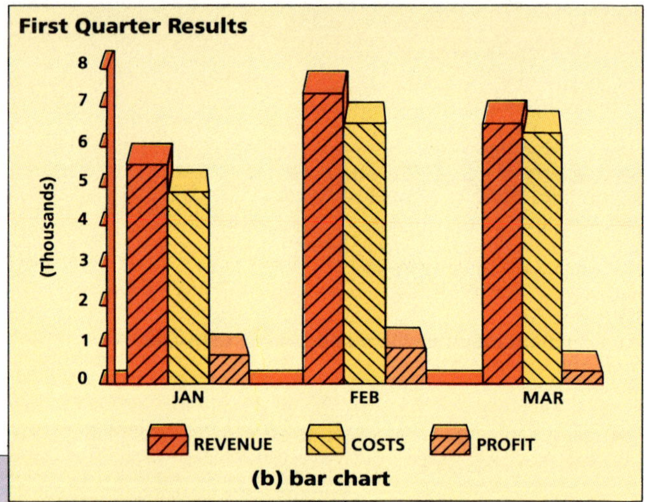

(b) Bar charts display blocks or bars to show relationships among data clearly and precisely.

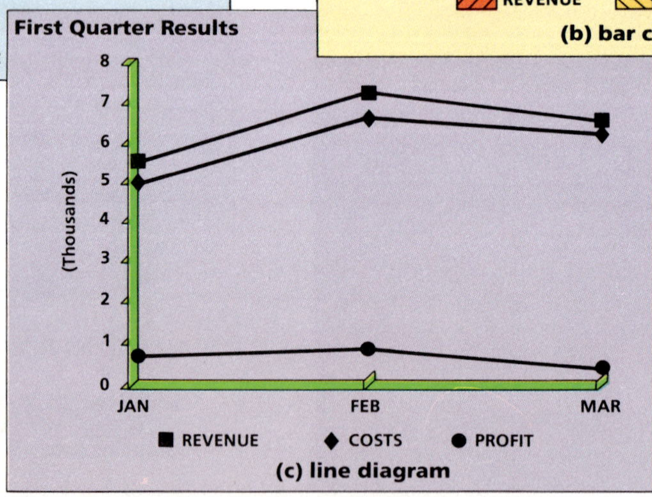

(c) Line diagrams are particularly effective for showing movement or a change in the condition of the data.

Today, there are many software packages of different capabilities that can create graphics, including most spreadsheet packages. The graphics capabilities of these packages can be grouped into two categories: analytical graphics and presentation graphics. Both kinds can transform numeric data into graphic form.

Analytical graphics is widely used by management personnel when reviewing information and when communicating information to others within their organization (Figure 2-29).

For example, a production manager who is planning a meeting with the president of the company may use color graphics to depict the expenditures of the production department. This graphic display would have more impact and lead to better understanding than would a printed column of production figures.

As its name implies, **presentation graphics** goes beyond analytical graphics by offering the user a wide choice of presentation effects. These include three-dimensional displays, background patterns, multiple text fonts, and image libraries that contain illustrations of factories, people, coins, dollar signs and other symbols that can be incorporated into the graphic (Figure 2-30). Figure 2-31 shows an example of presentation graphics projected in front of an audience and one of the devices that can be used to project presentation graphics.

To create graphics on your computer, you must follow the directions that apply to your graphics software package. Most packages will prompt you to enter the data the graph will represent, and then ask you to select the type of graph you would like. After entering the data, you can select several different graphic forms to see which one will best convey your message. When you decide on a graph, you can print it and also store it for future reference.

Using graphics software as a presentation tool allows you to efficiently create professional-quality graphics that can help you communicate information more effectively.

▲ **FIGURE 2-29**
Color can enhance the presentation of graphic information.

FIGURE 2-30
An example of presentation graphics.▼

◄ **FIGURE 2-31**
Presentation graphics can be an effective way to communicate information to a large group. Presenters can use devices such as the computer projection device shown. When this device is connected to a microcomputer and placed over a standard projector, it can project everything on the microcomputer screen onto a large screen.

OTHER POPULAR MICROCOMPUTER APPLICATIONS

The four applications discussed so far, word processing, spreadsheet, database, and graphics, are the most widely used microcomputer applications. Two other packages that are finding increasing use are data communications and desktop publishing.

Data Communications

Data communications software is used to transmit data from one computer to another. It gives users access to online databases such as stock prices and airline schedules, and services such as home banking and shopping.

Microcomputer data communications software often involves using a telephone line connected to special communication equipment either inside or attached to the computer. Similar equipment must be present at the other computer that will be accessed. The data communications software is used to dial the other system and establish the communication connection. Once the connection is established, the user enters commands and responses that control the transmission of data from one computer to the other.

Desktop Publishing

Desktop publishing software allows the user to combine text and graphics to produce high-quality printed documents. Desktop publishing systems go far beyond the capabilities of typical word processing systems by providing many different type sizes and styles and the ability to merge charts, pictures, and illustrations with the text. Numerous special effects such as borders and backgrounds can also be used to enhance the appearance of a document. Businesses of all sizes are increasingly using desktop publishing systems to produce better-looking brochures and communications and to control the production of work that previously could only be done by graphic artists. Figure 2-32 is an example of a document produced on a desktop publishing system.

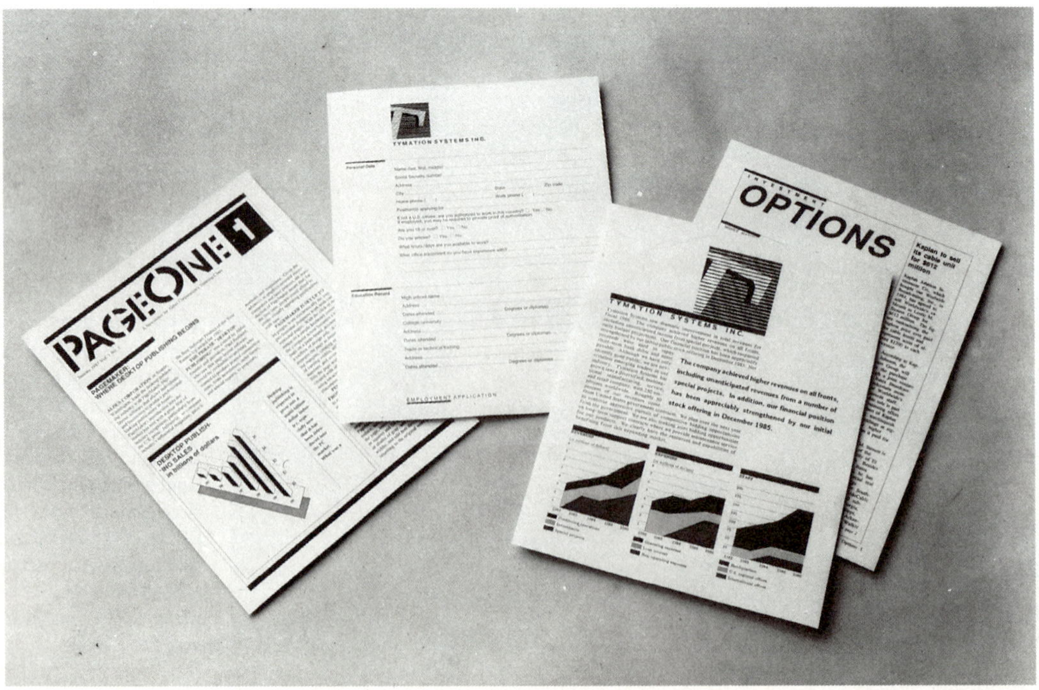

FIGURE 2-32
High-quality printed documents can be produced with desktop publishing software.

INTEGRATED SOFTWARE

Software packages such as electronic spreadsheet and word processing are generally used independently of each other. But what if you wanted to place information from a spreadsheet into a word processing document? The spreadsheet data would have to be reentered in the word processing document. This would be time consuming and errors could be introduced as you reentered the data. The inability of separate programs to communicate with one another and use a common set of data has been overcome through the use of integrated software.

Integrated software refers to packages that combine applications such as word processing, electronic spreadsheet, database, graphics, and data communications into a single, easy-to-use set of programs. Application packages that are included in integrated packages are designed to have a consistent command structure; that is, common commands such as those used to SAVE or LOAD files are the same for all the applications in the package. Besides the consistent presentation, a key feature of integrated packages is their ability to pass data quickly and easily from one application to another. For example, revenue and cost information from a database on daily sales could be quickly loaded into a spreadsheet. The spreadsheet could be used to calculate gross profits. Once the calculations are completed, all or a portion of the spreadsheet data can be passed to the graphics program to create pie, bar, line, or other graphs. Finally, the graphic (or the spreadsheet) can be transferred to a word processing document. A possible disadvantage of an integrated package is that individual integrated programs may not have all the features that are available in nonintegrated packages.

Integrated programs frequently use windows. A **window** is a rectangular portion of the screen that is used to display information. Windows can display help information about the commands of the program you are using or, with integrated packages, they can actually display data from another application. Many programs today can display multiple windows on the screen (Figure 2-33) and allow the user to move from one application window to another. Although they are called "windows" because of their ability to "see" into another part of the program, many people consider windows to be more like multiple sheets of paper on top of a desk. The papers can be shuffled, placed side by side, or moved entirely off the desk until needed again.

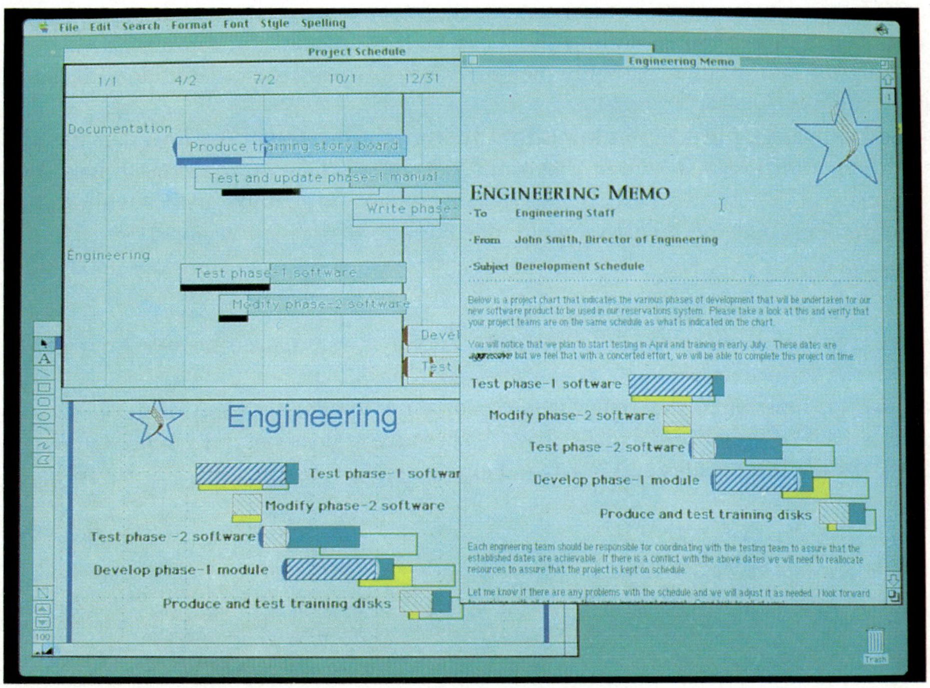

FIGURE 2-33
Windows on the Macintosh computer let you see several applications at one time. In this example the user can plan projects using project management software (top left), pictorially present the plan using graphics software (bottom left), and write about the plan using word processing software (right).

GUIDELINES FOR PURCHASING MICROCOMPUTER APPLICATIONS SOFTWARE

Whenever you purchase applications software (Figure 2-34), you should make sure that the software will meet your needs. Do this by following these five steps:

FIGURE 2-34
Shop carefully for software, evaluating the available packages and suppliers. Many people spend more on software than they do on their computer equipment.

1. **Verify that the software performs the task you desire.** In some cases, software that is supposed to perform particular functions either does not perform the functions or performs them in a manner that will be unacceptable to you. The best method of verifying that the software performs satisfactorily is to try it out prior to purchase. Many computer stores and software vendors will allow you to try software to see if it meets your needs before you purchase it. Some software developers even have special demonstration versions that allow you to try package features on a limited-use basis.
2. **Verify that the software will run on your computer.** The best way to verify this is to run the software on a computer that is the same as yours. Such factors as the number of disk drives, whether the software can run on a computer without a hard disk, main memory requirements, and graphics capabilities or requirements must be evaluated before you buy. For example, it would be unwise to purchase a package that is incompatible with your printer or one with graphics capabilities that your computer cannot handle.
3. **Make sure that the software is adequately documented.** The written material that accompanies the software is known as **documentation**. Even the best software may be unusable if the documentation does not clearly and completely describe what the software does, how it does it, how to recover from errors, and how to back up data.
4. **Purchase the software from a reputable store, distributor, or vendor.** Regardless of the care taken, software often contains errors. A reputable store or vendor will do everything possible to correct those errors. Admittedly, it can be hard to check on a company's reputation. Asking for references is probably the best method if you are not familiar with the prospective supplier.
5. **Obtain the best value, but keep in mind that that might not mean the lowest price.** Different stores or distributors will sell the same software package for different prices. Be sure to compare prices, but also ask about product support. Sometimes a store will offer training on products that you buy from them; other vendors provide no support or training. Also, some vendors offer telephone service so that you can call to ask questions about the software.

If you keep these factors in mind when buying application software packages, you are likely to be pleased with the software you buy.

A good place to look when shopping for microcomputer applications software is in computer magazines such as *InforWorld* and *PC World*. These magazines regularly review applications packages and publish articles and charts to help you choose the package best suited to your needs.

LEARNING AIDS AND SUPPORT TOOLS FOR APPLICATION USERS

Learning to use an application software package involves time and practice. Fortunately, several support tools are available to help you: tutorials, online help, trade books, and keyboard templates (Figure 2-35).

Tutorials are step-by-step instructions using real examples that show you how to use an application. Some tutorials are written manuals, but more and more, tutorials are in the software form, allowing you to use your computer to learn about a package.

Online help refers to additional instructions that are available within the application. In most packages, a function key or special combination of keys are reserved for the help feature. When you are using an application and have a question, pressing the designated "help" key will temporarily overlay your work on the screen with information on how to use the package. When you are finished using the help feature, pressing another key allows you to return to your work.

The documentation that accompanies software packages is frequently organized as reference material. This makes it very useful once you know how to use a package but difficult to

FIGURE 2-35
This figure shows four ways to learn application software packages.

Software **tutorials** help you learn an application while using the actual software on your computer.

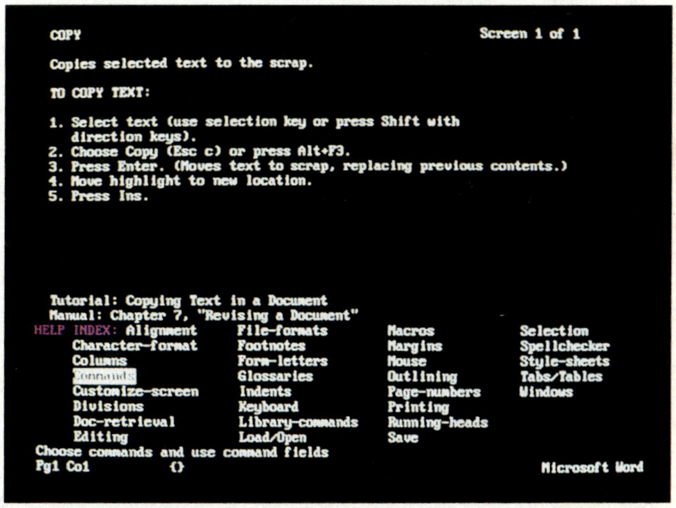

Online help gives you assistance without your having to leave the application.

Many **trade books** are available for the popular software applications.

Keyboard templates give you quick reference to software commands.

use when you are first learning it. For this reason, many **trade books** are available to help users learn to use the features of microcomputer application packages. These books can usually be found where software is sold and are frequently carried in regular bookstores.

Keyboard templates are plastic sheets that fit around a portion of your keyboard. The keyboard commands to select the various features of the application programs are printed on the template. Having these prompts readily available is helpful for both beginners and experienced users.

TIPS FOR USING MICROCOMPUTER APPLICATIONS

The following tips are listed under specific applications. Some of them will make sense now and will be useful to new users. Others may not be clear now but will be useful as you increase your proficiency with each application. Using this section for reference will help you develop good techniques as you learn microcomputer applications. Remember, it may take up to twenty hours or more of use before you become familiar with a package's capabilities. Don't expect to be an "instant expert."

Tips for Using Word Processing

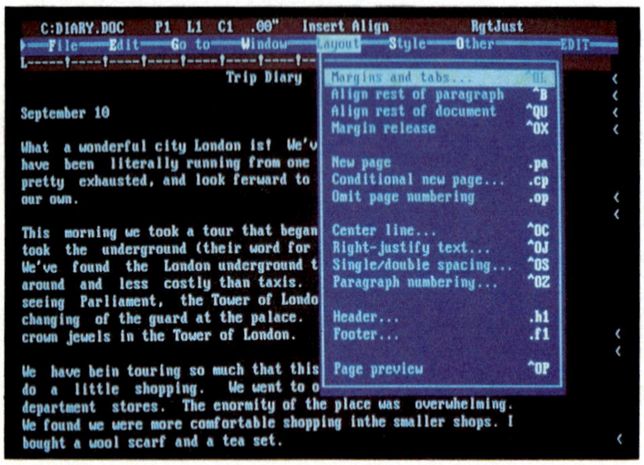

1. **Learn how to move the cursor.** Some people only learn the simplest methods of moving around inside a document: one character at a time sideways, and one line at a time up or down. But most word processors have a number of methods to move faster, such as a word at a time, to the end of a line, to the end of a sentence, to the top or bottom of the screen, to the top or bottom of a page, to a specific page, etc. Learn these movement commands and you'll save yourself a lot of editing time.
2. **Think about how your document "looks" as well as what it "says."** The use of underlining, boldface, indentation, borders, titles, and other stylistic features can enhance your document and help get your message across. After you get your words right, review your document one more time just to improve the visual presentation.
3. **Use a spelling checker.** Even if you're a champion speller, you still probably make a typo every once in a while. Get in the habit of running the spelling checker on all documents you create after every time you've added text.
4. **File your document under a meaningful name.** The main reason for a meaningful name is so you can recognize the document at a later date. If possible, place the name on the document itself. You've probably noticed document name or number references on letters from attorneys, accountants, and others who generate large volumes of correspondence.
5. **Create document templates for frequently used documents.** A **document template** is a document with the title, headings, footings, spacing, and other features that you want to have in frequently generated documents. The template usually contains everything except the text of the document. An example would be an interoffice memo template that contains the title (Interoffice Memorandum) and the TO:, FROM:, SUBJECT:, and DATE: headings. Using a document template reduces the time to prepare a document and results in a consistent format.

6. **When working on a document, save it frequently.** Nothing is more frustrating than entering a large amount of text and then losing it because of a system or power failure or an accidental mistake. Get in the habit of saving your document frequently, say every ten minutes or so, to minimize any data loss.

Tips for Using Electronic Spreadsheets

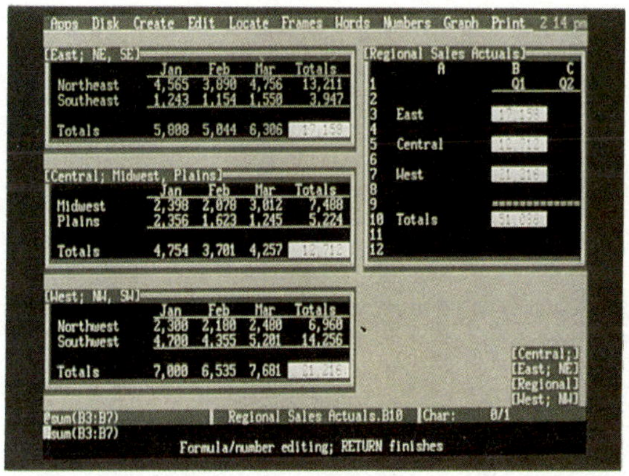

1. **State your assumptions explicitly in the upper portion of your spreadsheet. Assumptions** are data elements such as the unit selling price or an interest rate that are used in spreadsheet calculations. Instead of placing these items in formulas, put them in a separate cell and reference the cell in your formula. This not only makes your calculations more obvious but makes subsequent changes and "what if" testing easier.
2. **Use range names for key cells.** Rather than referring to the cell that contains the unit price assumption by its cell number, use the option to give that cell a name, such as PRICE. Using named cells minimizes reference errors and makes your formulas more meaningful.
3. **Use meaningful names for your row and column descriptions.** Give some thought to the text you use to label rows and columns, especially if your spreadsheet will be used by others. A few extra characters can go a long way to helping someone understand the data being presented.
4. **Leave room for expansion.** Even the best designed spreadsheets can grow as you add additional data elements, rows, or columns. Anticipate the areas of your spreadsheet that may expand and structure them accordingly by providing blank rows and columns.
5. **Highlight your results.** Remember that your spreadsheet is also a visual document. If the main purpose of the spreadsheet is to calculate a single number such as net profit, try to highlight the result by using underlines, asterisks, or white space to set it apart from the other data.
6. **Document your spreadsheet in your spreadsheet.** A description of the spreadsheet and the assumptions helps other users understand the spreadsheet's purpose and can help you if you haven't worked with it for a while.

Tips for Using Database Software

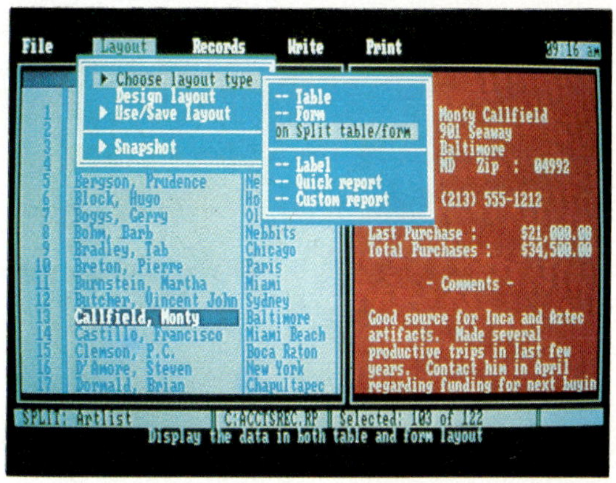

1. **Before you start, take time to design your file.** Although data elements can be added later, it's desirable to have all necessary elements provided for at the beginning.
2. **Use meaningful names for the files and data fields.** Meaningful names are a good practice for all applications but especially in a database, where it's likely that you'll be working with multiple files and a large number of data fields.
3. **Avoid the use of significant identification numbers (IDs).** A significant ID is the identifying field or key field of a record in which two or more data elements are combined, thus building "significance" into the ID. An example would be an inventory parts file ID in which the ID is the part number plus a code indicating the part type. The problem with significant ID schemes is that they grow increasingly more

complicated and eventually break down; sooner or later you'll encounter an item that won't fit the scheme. Avoid this confusion by establishing separate fields for each data item.

4. **Have the system generate IDs whenever possible.** This tip is closely related to the last tip discussing significant IDs. Obviously the system shouldn't generate the ID for files where the ID is something like a social security number. But when the ID is merely an identifier to be used to distinguish between the records, such as a transaction number, have the system generate it.
5. **Create an index file if you frequently access a file by something other than the file ID field.** Let's say you have an employee file that you normally access by its ID, the employee number. Occasionally, however, you need to access records by employee name. You could sort the file by name each time but a faster way would be to create and maintain an index to the file based on employee name.

Tips for Using Graphics

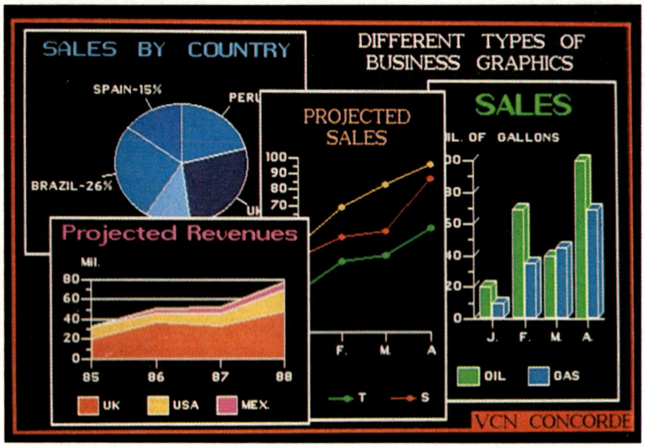

1. **Keep in mind that a graphic is a visual presentation.** Before you start, give some thought to the arrangement ("composition") of the information to be presented.
2. **Don't try to present too much information.** If you do, you'll wind up with a cluttered look that will make the information difficult to understand.
3. **Choose the most appropriate type of graphic.**
   a. Bar charts show the relationship between variables such as the amount of sales (variable 1) for each month (variable 2).
   b. Pie charts are excellent for showing the relationship between individual variables (the pie slices) and the total of all variables (the whole pie). The effectiveness of pie charts is lessened if some of the variables are too small in relation to the others (resulting in pie slices too thin) or if there are too many variables.
   c. Line diagrams link a set of variables with a connecting line and are excellent for showing a trend as indicated by a rising or falling line.
4. **Use words sparingly.** Use text to title the graphic and identify the variables but don't overdo the use of words. If you have a choice of type styles, choose one that's simple and easy to read. Leave space around text so that it will stand out and can be easily read.
5. **Use colors carefully.** If you have a choice of colors, choose them carefully. The right colors can enhance the presentation while the wrong ones can confuse and distract. Lighter colors should be on top of darker, "heavier" colors.
6. **Be consistent.** If you're making a series of graphics, the type style, graphic size, headings, borders, use of colors, etc., should be the same for all items.
7. **Projected graphics should be simple.** If your graphic is going to be projected in front of an audience, you can't display as much information as you can if the graphic is going to be read by an individual. Remember, the audience can't see the projected graphic as well as someone holding a printed copy and they will only have a limited amount of time to look at it.

CHAPTER SUMMARY

1. **Computer literate** is a term used to describe people who have an understanding of computers and how they are used in our modern world.
2. Software that is useful to a broad range of users is sometimes referred to as **general microcomputer applications software**.
3. The four most widely used microcomputer software applications are word processing, electronic spreadsheet, database, and graphics.
4. **Word processing software** is used to prepare documents electronically.
5. Additional support features for a word processing application can include a spelling checker, thesaurus, and grammar checker.
6. **Spelling checker software** allows you to check individual words or an entire document for correct spelling.
7. **Thesaurus software** allows you to look up synonyms for words in a document while you are using your word processor.
8. **Grammar checker software** identifies possible grammar, writing style, and sentence structure errors.
9. Word processing software is a document productivity tool that allows you to create, edit, format, print, and store documents.
10. **Electronic spreadsheet software** allows you to organize numeric data in a worksheet or table format.
11. A spreadsheet is composed of **rows** and **columns**. Each intersection of a row and column is a **cell**.
12. A spreadsheet cell can contain one of the following: a **label**, a **value**, or a **formula**.
13. The "what if" capability of electronic spreadsheet software is a powerful tool that is widely used by management personnel for decision support information.
14. **Database software** and **file management software** are used to organize, retrieve, manipulate, and update data that is stored in files.
15. In general, database software can work with data that is stored in multiple files. File management software is designed to work with one data file at a time.
16. Information presented in the form of a graph or a chart is commonly referred to as **graphics**. Three popular graphics used to present information include **pie, bar, and line charts**.
17. **Data communications software** allows you to transmit data from one computer to another.
18. **Desktop publishing software** can combine text and graphics to produce high-quality printed documents.
19. **Integrated software** packages combine several applications in one package and allow data to be shared between the applications.
20. When you purchase software, you should perform the following steps: (1) Verify that the software performs the task desired. (2) Verify that the software runs on your computer. (3) Make sure the software documentation is adequate. (4) Purchase the software from a reputable store, distributor, or vendor. (5) Obtain the best value.
21. Aids such as tutorials, online help, trade books, and keyboard templates are useful in learning and using microcomputer applications.

KEY TERMS

Analytical graphics *2.14*
Assumptions *2.21*
Bar chart *2.14*
Cell *2.9*
Columns *2.9*
Commands *2.2*
Computer literate *2.2*
Copy *2.7*
Cut *2.7*
Database *2.12*
Database software *2.12*
Data communications software *2.16*
Delete *2.6*
Desktop publishing software *2.16*
Document *2.4*
Document template *2.20*
Edit *2.4*
Electronic spreadsheet *2.9*
Electronic spreadsheet software *2.9*
Field *2.12*
File *2.12*
File management software *2.12*
Formula *2.9*
Function keys *2.3*
General microcomputer applications *2.2*
Grammar checker software *2.6*
Graphics *2.14*
Icons *2.4*
Insert *2.6*
Integrated software *2.17*

Keyboard templates *2.20*
Labels *2.9*
Line diagram *2.14*
Menus *2.4*
Move *2.6*
Online help *2.19*
Paste *2.7*
Pie chart *2.14*
Presentation graphics *2.15*
Prompts *2.4*
Record *2.12*
Replace *2.6*
Rows *2.9*
Spelling checker software *2.5*
Spreadsheet *2.9*
Thesaurus software *2.5*
Trade books *2.20*
Tutorials *2.19*
User friendly *2.2*
User interfaces *2.3*
Values *2.9*
Windows *2.17*
Word processing software *2.4*

REVIEW QUESTIONS

1. Define the term computer literate.
2. What is general microcomputer applications software?
3. List the four most widely used microcomputer application packages and describe how each application helps users.
4. What is a spelling checker? Describe a typical procedure when a misspelled word is found.
5. Explain how management personnel use the "what if" capability of electronic spreadsheets. Why is this capability useful for decision support?
6. What is the difference between database software and file management software?
7. List the three most commonly used charts. Draw an example of each.
8. Describe the advantage of using integrated software. What is a possible disadvantage? What are windows and how are they used in integrated software packages?
9. List the five steps that should be performed when purchasing software. Describe each of them.
10. List and describe four learning aids that can help you use general microcomputer application packages.

CONTROVERSIAL ISSUES

1. Some organizations insist that their employees use an integrated package so that data can be easily transferred between users. Other organizations let their users make individual decisions on which package they want to use for a particular application. Discuss the advantages and disadvantages of both policies.
2. Spreadsheets are increasingly used to support and justify management decisions. Sometimes these spreadsheets are very complex and are based on hundreds of calculations and assumptions. Discuss the responsibility of the person presenting the spreadsheet to document and explain the assumptions used by the spreadsheet.

RESEARCH PROJECTS

1. Interview a person who uses a word processing package on a regular basis. Write a report on the types of documents he or she prepares. Include the person's comments on the different word processing features.
2. Find someone who has developed an electronic spreadsheet no larger than a single page. Make a manual (hand-prepared) copy of the spreadsheet. Change one value in each data row and record the time it takes you to recalculate the spreadsheet totals. Report your findings.
3. Assume that you have decided to use a database package to record all the things you own. Define the fields that would make up your database record.

CHAPTER 3

Processing Data Into Information

CHAPTER 3

Processing Data Into Information

OBJECTIVES

- Explain the four operations of the information processing cycle: input, process, output, and storage.
- Define data and explain the terms used to organize data in an information processing system: field, record, file, database.
- Discuss data management and explain why it is needed.
- Explain arithmetic and logical processing.
- Describe interactive processing and batch processing.
- List and explain the qualities of information.

The information processing cycle is basic to all computers, large or small. It is important that you understand this cycle, for much of your success in understanding computers and what they do depends on having an understanding or "feeling" for the movement of data as it flows through the information processing cycle and becomes information. This chapter discusses the information processing cycle, examines the nature of data—how it is organized for processing on a computer and how it is managed—and describes the qualities of information. Reading this chapter will give you a more detailed understanding of the input, processing, output, and storage operations that a computer performs to process data into information.

Also, this chapter summarizes the general types of processing that computers perform and discusses interactive and batch processing methods. Each processing method has advantages and is appropriate for certain types of applications. Business examples demonstrate the use of each processing method.

OVERVIEW OF THE INFORMATION PROCESSING CYCLE

As seen in Chapter 1, the **information processing cycle** consists of four operations: input, processing, output, and storage. Regardless of the size and type of computer, these operations are used to process data into a meaningful form called information.

The operations in the information processing cycle are carried out through the combined use of computer equipment, also called computer hardware, and computer software. The computer software, or programs, contain instructions that direct the computer equipment to perform the tasks necessary to process data into information.

The diagram in Figure 3-1 illustrates some of the various devices used in conjunction with computer software to carry out the information processing cycle. Input devices are used to enter both the computer programs and the data into main memory. The primary input devices are keyboards on microcomputers and terminals on larger machines. Disk drives and tape drives can also be used to input data that has been stored on these auxiliary storage devices. The function of the input devices is to place into the main memory of the computer the program that is to be executed and the data that is to be processed. Both the program that is to control the processing and the data that is to be processed must be in main memory for processing to occur. Once the computer program is stored in main memory, the person using the computer gives a command to start the program. The processor executes each instruction in the program. These instructions direct the computer to perform the input, processing, output, and storage operations that will process the data into information.

The primary output devices on computers are printers and screens. The format of a report on a printer or a screen is under the control of the program stored in main memory. The program will format the data to be printed or displayed and then issue the commands that cause the output to occur.

Auxiliary storage devices, also called secondary storage devices, commonly used with computers are magnetic disk and magnetic tape. The programs and data not being used by the computer are stored on auxiliary storage until they are needed. Then they are loaded from auxiliary storage into main memory.

Note that some input and output devices can be used for more than one type of operation in the information processing cycle. For example, disk and tape units are used as auxiliary storage devices to store data, but when a disk or tape is receiving data from the main memory of the computer, it is operating as an output device. This process is described as writing or sending data to the auxiliary storage. When data is copied from disk or tape to the main memory of the computer, the disk or tape is operating as an input device. This process is described as reading data into the main memory of the computer. Terminals are also used as both input and output devices. Thus, to understand what is occurring in the information processing cycle, it is important for you to focus on the type of operation being performed rather than the device that is being used.

As we have discussed, the purpose of an information processing system is to process data into information. Data is the prime ingredient in this cycle. Without data, the computer hardware and software have nothing to manipulate. Because data is such an important part of the information cycle, it is important for you to understand what data is, how it is organized, and how it is managed.

FIGURE 3-1
A computer consists of input devices, the processor, output devices, and auxiliary storage units. This equipment or hardware is used to perform the operations of the information processing cycle.

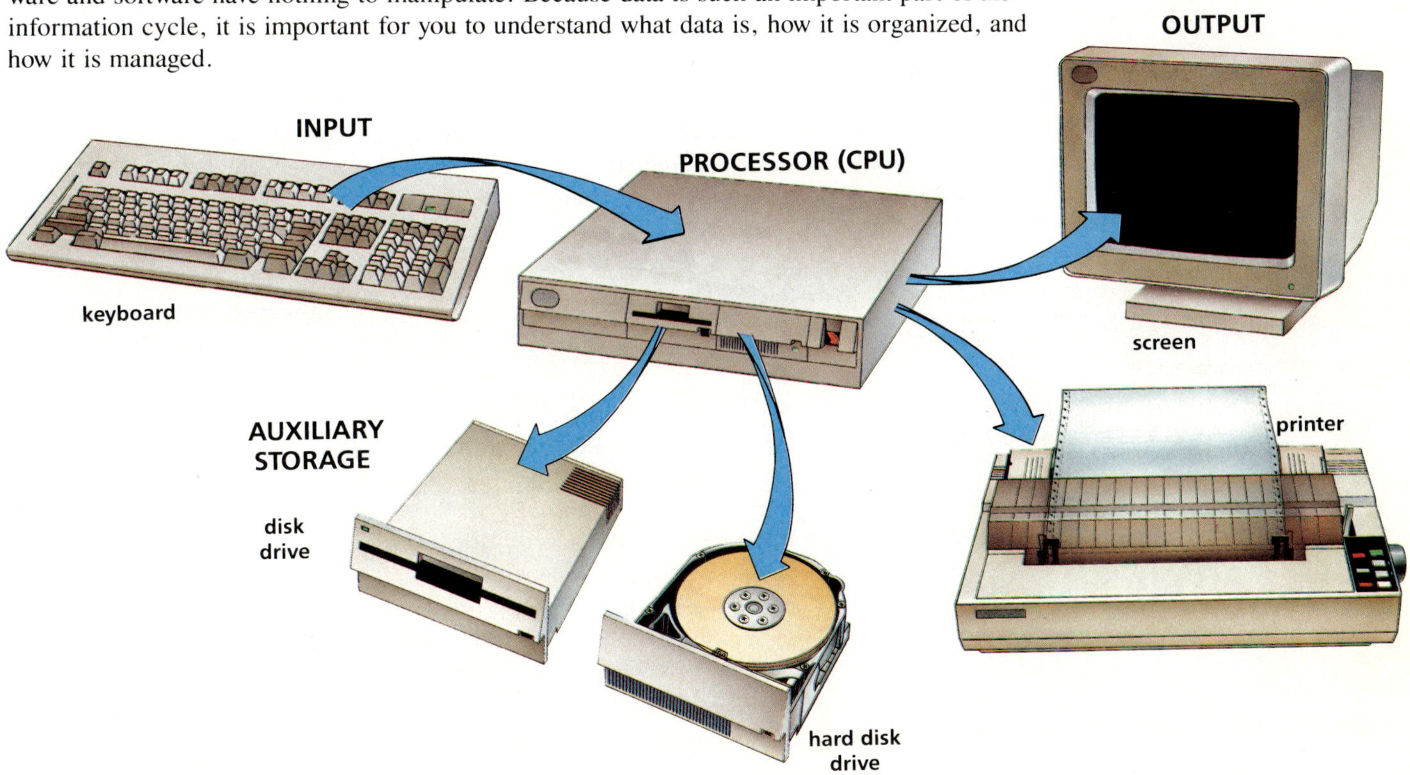

WHAT IS DATA AND HOW IS IT ORGANIZED?

Data is the raw facts, including numbers and words, that a computer receives during the input operation and processes to produce information. For example, in a monthly sales application (Figure 3-2), the value 01/31, identifying a month and day, is data. In a payroll application (Figure 3-3), the social security number 332-98-8776 is data. The name HAYNES is data.

Data is comprised of **characters**. These characters are classified as **alphabetic** (A–Z), **numeric** (0–9) or **special** (all characters other than A–Z and 0–9, such as , ? / ! % & : ;). The raw facts that we refer to as data are made up of a combination of these three kinds of characters. In the previous example, the date 01/31 is made up of the numeric characters 0 1 3 and the special character /. The social security number contains numeric characters and the special character -. The name Haynes contains only alphabetic characters.

Each fact or unique piece of data is referred to as a **data item**, **data field**, or just a **field**. Fields are classified by the characters that they contain. For example, a field that contains only alphabetic characters, such as the name field containing Haynes, is called an **alphabetic field**. A field that contains numeric characters is called a **numeric field**. Numeric fields may also contain some special characters that are commonly used with numbers, such as a decimal point (.) and the plus (+) and minus (–) signs. Even with the plus sign (+) and decimal point (.) the number +500.00 is still called a numeric field. Fields that contain a combination of character types, such as the date 01/31 (numeric and special characters), are called **alphanumeric** fields. Even though the word "alphanumeric" implies only alphabetic and numeric characters, it also includes fields that contain special characters. The term alphanumeric is used to describe all fields that do not fall into the alphabetic or numeric classifications.

A field is normally most meaningful when combined with related fields. To illustrate, the month and day 01/31 by itself is not as useful as when it is related to monthly sales (Figure 3-2). Also, the social security number 332-98-8776 is more useful when it is related to the name HAYNES and to the paycheck amount $327.00 (Figure 3-3). Because related fields are more meaningful if they are together, fields are organized into groups called records.

A **record** is a collection of related fields. Each record normally corresponds to a specific unit of information. For example, a record that could be used to produce the payroll report in Figure 3-3 is illustrated in Figure 3-4. The fields in the record are the social security number, employee name, and paycheck amount. This example shows that the data in each record is used to produce a line on the payroll report. The first record contains all the data concerning the employee named Haynes. The second record contains all the data concerning the employee named Johnston. Each subsequent record contains all the data for a given employee. Thus, you can see how related data items are grouped together to form a record.

PAYROLL REGISTER

SOCIAL SECURITY	EMPLOYEE NAME	PAYCHECK AMOUNT
332-98-8776	HAYNES	$327.00
776-09-9731	JOHNSTON	$265.45
751-07-3452	RADCLIFFE	$289.67

◄ **FIGURE 3-3**
The social security number becomes more meaningful when it is related to an employee name and pay rate.

MONTHLY SALES

MONTH END	MONTH SALES
01/31	$55,273.61
02/28	$61,177.84
03/31	$77,143.56
TOTAL	$193,595.01

◄ **FIGURE 3-2**
By itself the month ending date, 01/31, is not as useful as when it is related to the monthly sales amount.

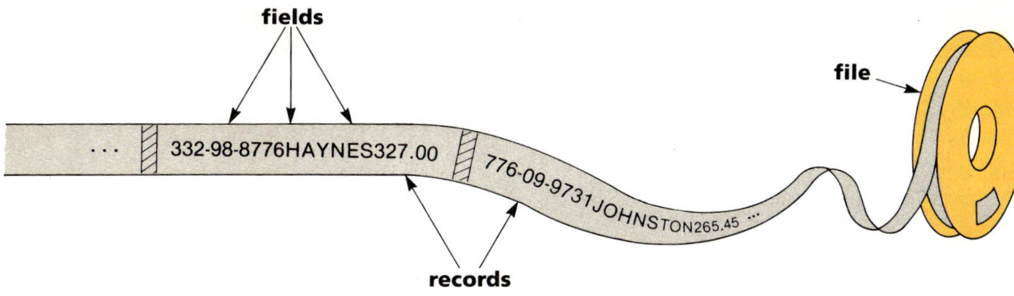

FIGURE 3-4
The records of this payroll file are sequentially stored on magnetic tape. The file contains the social security number, name, and paycheck amount for all employees.

A collection of records is called a **file**. The payroll file in Figure 3-4, for example, contains all the records required to produce the payroll register report. Files are stored on some medium, such as magnetic tape or magnetic disk. Records on tape are usually arranged in a **sequential** manner. This means that the records in the file are arranged in some sequence such as employee number order or product number order. In the payroll file, for example, records could be arranged alphabetically by employee name or numerically by employee number. The field that is used to arrange the records in a specific order is called the **key field**. The records in files stored on disk can be arranged sequentially or randomly. In a **random** file, records are not arranged in any sequence or specific order.

Data is frequently organized in a **database**. As we discussed in Chapter 2, a database provides an efficient way to establish a relationship between data items and implies that a relationship has been established between multiple files. Data that has been organized in a database can be efficiently manipulated and retrieved by a computer.

Summary of Data Organization

In this section we have defined data as the raw facts that are processed by a computer system. We have also defined the terms used to describe how data is organized. We have seen that the smallest elements of data are alphabetic, numeric, and special characters and that these characters are used to build the fields, records, files, and databases that are manipulated by an information system to create information.

DATA MANAGEMENT

For data to be useful in the processing cycle, it must have certain attributes such as accuracy. **Data management** refers to techniques, methods, and procedures that are used to manage these attributes and provide for the security and maintenance of data. The purpose of data management is to ensure that data required for an application will be available in the correct form and at the proper time for processing.

To illustrate data management, we use an example of a credit checking bureau (Figure 3-5). A summary of the application follows:

1. Data entered into the database of the credit bureau is acquired from numerous sources such as banks and stores. The data relates to people's credit ratings and includes facts such as income, history of paying debts, bankruptcies, and certain personal information.
2. The database is stored on auxiliary storage.

FIGURE 3-5
Data management is concerned with the attributes, security, and maintenance of data. If well managed, data will be available to users when they want it and in a form they can use to create information.

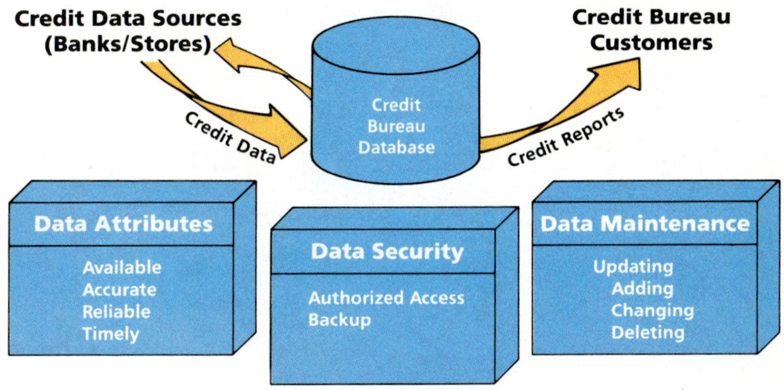

3. Customers of the credit bureau can call the bureau and request an individual's credit rating. The credit bureau employee uses a terminal to retrieve information concerning the credit rating from the database and gives the caller a brief credit history of the person in question. The system also generates a record that causes a complete credit history to be printed that night. The report will be mailed to the customer the following day.

Data Attributes

One attribute of data is that it must be *available*. In the credit bureau application, it would not be possible to implement the system if banks, stores, and other organizations were not willing to provide information about account holders. Therefore, prior to implementing an application on a computer, there must be assurance that the data required will be available.

Another important attribute of data in this application or any other is its integrity. **Data integrity** affects the confidence a user has in processing that data. The three primary elements of data integrity are: (1) data accuracy, (2) reliable data entry, and (3) timeliness.

For a user to have confidence in the information provided by a computer system, he or she first must be confident that the data used to create the information is *accurate*. This means that the source of the data is reliable and the data is correctly reported. For example, if someone incorrectly reports to the credit bureau that an individual did not pay a bill and this information becomes part of the database, a responsible customer could be denied credit unjustly. Users must be confident that the people and organizations providing data to the credit bureau provide accurate data.

A second element of data integrity is *reliable data entry*. Data entered for processing must be entered correctly. In the credit bureau example, if a bank reports that the balance on a credit card account is $200.00, but the balance is incorrectly entered as $20,000.00, the information generated would be invalid.

The third element of data integrity is timeliness. *Timeliness* means that data to be processed has not lost its usefulness or accuracy because time has passed. For example, assume that two years ago a salary of $15,000.00 was entered for an individual. Today, that data is not timely because two years have passed and the person may be earning either less or more.

Data integrity is critical. Before an application is implemented on a computer, all the criteria for valid data must be defined and checks for valid data should be placed in the programs.

Data Security

Data management also includes managing data security. **Data security** refers to protecting data to keep it from being misused or lost. This is an important issue because misuse or loss of data can have serious consequences. In the credit bureau example, a person's credit rating and history of financial transactions are confidential. People do not want their credit information made available to unauthorized organizations. Therefore, the credit bureau must develop systems and procedures that allow only authorized personnel to access the data stored in the database. In addition, if the data in the database should be tampered with or lost, the credit bureau must have some method for recovering the correct data. Therefore, data in an information system is periodically copied or backed up. **Backup** refers to making copies of data files so that if data is lost or destroyed, a timely recovery can be made and processing can continue.

Data Maintenance

Data maintenance, another aspect of data management, refers to the procedures used to maintain data accuracy by keeping data current. These procedures are called **updating** and include **adding** new data, such as creating a record for a new person to include in the credit bureau database; **changing** existing information, such as posting a change of address to an existing record; and **deleting** obsolete information, such as removing inactive records after some designated period of time.

Summary of Data Management

Management of data is critical if an application is to be successfully processed on a computer. Data management includes managing data attributes, data security, and data maintenance. If inadequate attention is given to managing data, the information processing system will not perform as intended and the output will have little value.

HOW THE INFORMATION PROCESSING CYCLE WORKS

Now that you have learned about data, and how it is organized and managed, we can discuss the input, process, output and storage operations of the information processing cycle and show the role that data plays in each of the four operations.

Input Operations

Input operations transfer data from an input device to main memory. We have already identified many input devices—including keyboards, terminals, magnetic disk, and magnetic tape. There are many other specialized types of input devices. Some of these devices can interpret special bar codes on products, numbers on checks, and handwritten characters. Some input devices even understand the human voice.

Regardless of the input device used, the principle is the same: data entered from the input device is electronically stored in main memory. Once in main computer memory, the data can be processed under the control of a computer program.

Figure 3-6 on the next page shows the input operation required to build employee files on a personal computer. Such files are common to all companies. The user enters, or inputs, the employee's name and social security number into the main memory by pressing the appropriate keys on the keyboard.

The steps involved in entering the data into main memory and forming the employee identification number are as follows:

1. A computer program is stored in main memory. When the program begins to process, it displays a message on the screen directing the user to enter the employee's name. When the user types the name on the keyboard of the computer, the name is stored in the NAME field in main memory.
2. The program then displays a message requesting that the user enter the employee's social security number. As the digits in the social security number are entered, they are stored in main memory in a SOCIAL SECURITY field that has been defined by the program. After both the name and the social security number have been entered and stored in main memory, the input operations are complete.

FIGURE 3-6
In this example of an input operation, the software directs the user to enter the employee's name and social security number. When the user enters this data on the keyboard, the data is electronically stored in main computer memory. The program then builds the employee number by moving the first letter of the last name and the last four digits of the social security number to the EMPLOYEE NUMBER field.

Important points illustrated by this portion of the example are: (1) Operations that occur on a computer are under the control of a program stored in the main memory of the computer. (2) The data entered from the input device (in this example, a keyboard) is electronically stored in main computer memory.

The input operation is important, because data must first be entered into main computer memory before it can be processed.

Processing Operations

Processing operations define how the data will be manipulated into a usable form. In the employee file example, the user wants to process data in order to build an employee identification number. The employee identification number consists of the first letter of the employee's last name and the last four digits of the social security number.

The processing operations are directed by instructions within the program. These instructions specify that the first letter of the last name and the last digits of the social security number are to be moved to the EMPLOYEE NUMBER field that has been defined by the program.

When data is moved from one location to another in main memory, the data in the sending location is copied or duplicated to the receiving location. Thus, in Figure 3-6, when the first letter of the last name is moved to the EMPLOYEE NUMBER field, the last name in the NAME field is not affected. Similarly, when the last four digits of the social security number are moved to the EMPLOYEE NUMBER field, the social security number in that field is not affected. The data is now located in both the sending and receiving memory locations.

As shown in the previous example, moving data from one location to another in main memory is considered a processing operation. Two other types of processing that are performed with computers include arithmetic and logical processing. The next two sections discuss these operations.

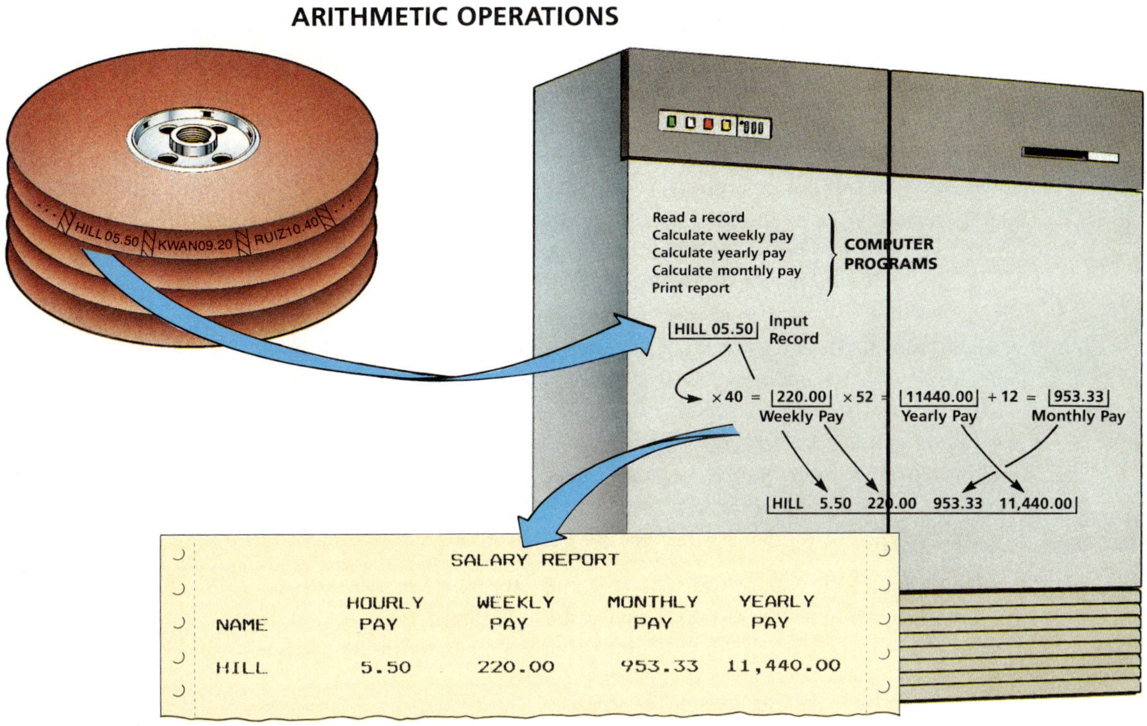

FIGURE 3-7
In this example of arithmetic processing, the program first reads an input record containing an employee name and hourly pay rate. The program then calculates the weekly, monthly, and yearly pay. The results of the calculations are printed in the salary report.

Arithmetic Operations Business and scientific applications frequently require that **arithmetic operations** such as addition, subtraction, multiplication, and division be performed. On many computers, millions of arithmetic operations can be performed in one second. The ability to perform arithmetic operations rapidly and accurately is an important characteristic of all computers.

To illustrate the arithmetic capabilities of the computer, Figure 3-7 shows an application developed to determine a person's weekly, monthly, and yearly pay, based on hourly pay.

The first program instruction reads a record from the disk into main memory. The record contains the employee name and the hourly pay rate. These two data fields are contained in each employee's record. The file stored on disk contains a record for each of the employees.

When the record is read into main memory, program instructions direct that the weekly, yearly, and monthly pay are to be calculated. The weekly pay is determined by multiplying the hourly rate times 40 hours. The yearly pay is obtained by multiplying the weekly rate by 52 weeks. The monthly pay is calculated by dividing the yearly pay by 12. Note that when the yearly and monthly pay are calculated, answers from the previous calculations are used. Any numeric data stored in main memory, including results of previous calculations, can be used in arithmetic operations. After the calculations are completed, instructions in the program describe the output operations that will print a report.

In Figure 3-7, the first record in the file for the employee Hill has been processed. The file contains subsequent records for Kwan, Ruiz, and others. The same operations that were performed to calculate the weekly, yearly, and monthly pay for Hill are required for each subsequent employee. Thus, the program instructions will be repeated for each employee record. The computer will input the data from each record one at a time and then repeat the instructions "Read a Record, Calculate Weekly Pay, Calculate Yearly Pay, Calculate Monthly Pay, Print Report" for each record so long as there are more records in the file to be processed.

The ability to repeat the instructions in a program is very important because it allows a computer to process any number of records with a single set of instructions. It is similar to the method you would use if you were computing the weekly pay for each employee by hand. You would compute the weekly pay for each employee one at a time and write the result in the report. You would follow the same steps for each employee. In a similar manner, the computer processes one employee, or record, at a time and repeats the same steps, or instructions, for each employee.

Important points illustrated by this example are: (1) The program stored in main memory can perform arithmetic operations on numeric data. (2) Answers derived from arithmetic operations can be used in other calculations and can also be used as output from a program. (3) The computer is processing one record at a time. (4) One set of program instructions can be repeated any number of times.

Logical Operations The **logical operations** are the computer's ability to *compare* data stored in main memory. All computers have instructions that can compare numeric, alphabetic, and special characters. Based on the results of the comparison, different types of processing can be performed. It is this logical ability of computers that allows them to compute overtime pay, play games such as chess, perform medical diagnoses, make hotel reservations, and perform any other task that is based on comparing data.

Three types of logical operations are performed by computer programs. They are:

1. Comparing to determine if two values are *equal to* each other.
2. Comparing to determine if one value is *greater than* another value.
3. Comparing to determine if one value is *less than* another value.

Each of these logical operations is explained in the following paragraphs.

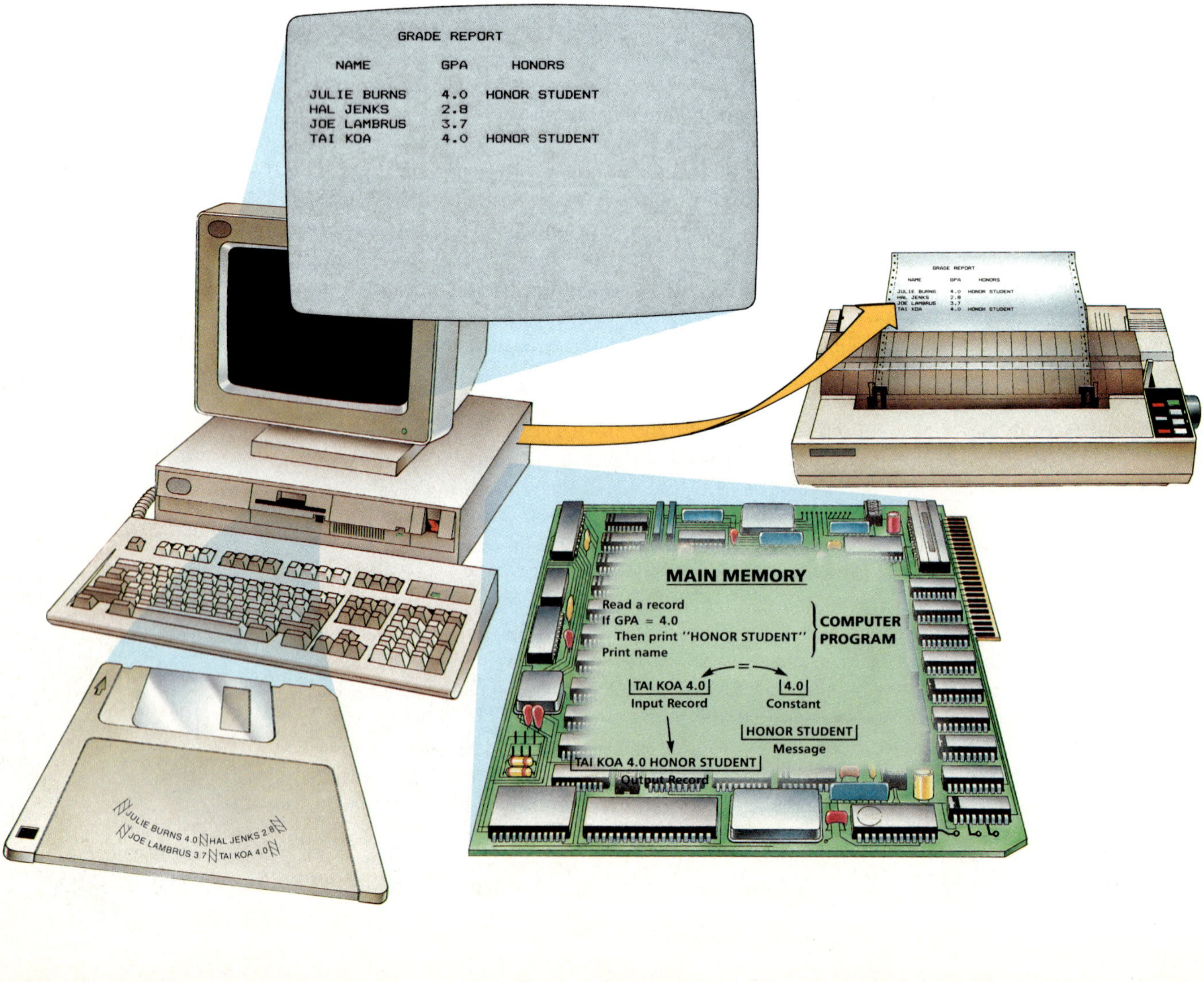

FIGURE 3-8
The program that creates the grade report uses the computer's ability to compare values. It compares a student's GPA (grade point average) to the value 4.0. If the GPA is equal to 4.0, the message HONOR STUDENT is printed on the report, along with the student's name and grade point average. If the comparison is not equal, no message is printed.

The example in Figure 3-8 illustrates the computer's ability to compare two values to determine if they are equal. This example shows a program whose function is to create a grade report. In order to make this report, an input record containing the student's name and grade point average is read. The grade point average is then compared to the value 4.0. If the grade point average is equal to 4.0, the message HONOR STUDENT is printed on the report. If the grade point average is not equal to 4.0, the message is not printed on the report.

When comparing two values, the program will specify what processing should occur when the condition tested is true and when it is false. In this example, when the condition is true (the grade point average is equal to 4.0), the processing is to print the message on the report together with the student name and average. When the condition is false (the grade point average is not equal to 4.0), the processing is not to print the message. Note that when comparing for an equal condition, the program essentially compares for an unequal condition as well.

A second type of comparison is to determine if one value is greater than another value. In the example in Figure 3-9, a database menu is displayed and the user is asked to enter a choice specifying which of the five functions is to be performed. The user should enter a value from 1 to 5. If, however, the value entered is greater than 5, an entry error has been made and the user is directed by the program to reenter the menu choice. How does the program cause the processing to occur? The program stored in main memory first displays the menu on the screen for the user. It then accepts the menu choice that the user enters. Next, the value entered by the user is compared to the value 5. If the choice entered by the user is greater than 5, the program displays the message, "Please reenter a value from 1 to 5." If the value entered by the user is not greater than five, processing will continue with another comparison to determine if the value is from 1 to 5.

FIGURE 3-9
When the user enters a menu choice, the program compares the value entered to 5, the number of valid selections. If the value entered is greater than 5, an error message is displayed and the user must reenter the choice. In this example, the user entered the value 6, the program displayed an error message, and the user was asked to reenter the choice.

The third type of comparison that is commonly performed on a computer is to determine if one value is less than another value. To illustrate this, the example in Figure 3-9 continues in Figure 3-10 on the next page, to check if the menu choice entered by the user is less than 1. If so, the user has entered an invalid value. The program will display an error message asking the user to reenter the choice and then will accept the new choice. If the value entered by the user is not less than 1, the program will continue with its processing.

An important point to note in each of the three comparison operations is that the program must specify the different types of processing that the computer is to perform. In other words, the program must specify what to do for both true and false comparison conditions. The ability of a computer to compare data and then select one of two processing paths is a simple but powerful feature that is used in programs of all levels of complexity.

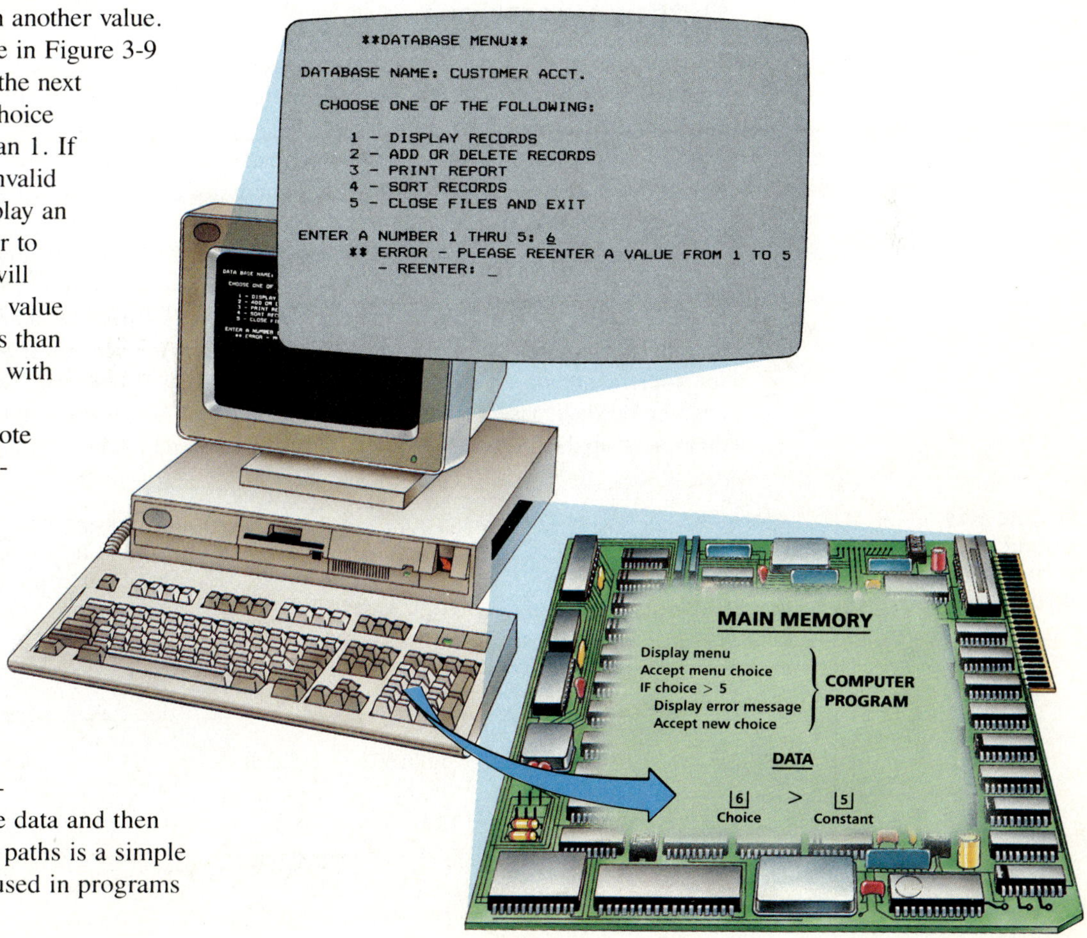

FIGURE 3-10
The value entered by the user is compared to the value 1. Because the value entered is less than 1, an error message is displayed and the user was asked to reenter a choice.

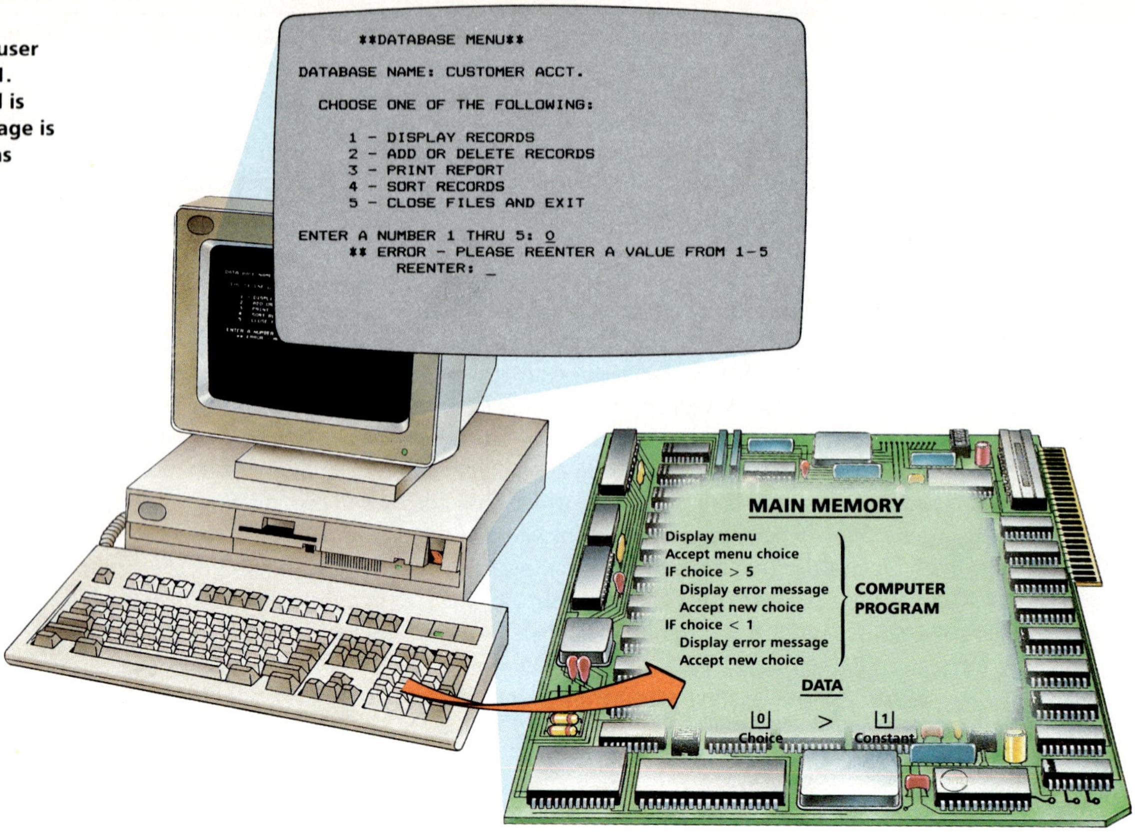

Output Operations

The purpose of the input operations is to provide data and of the processing operations is to produce information. **Output operations** refer to the operations that take the information produced and put it in a form that can be used by a person or a machine. Reports are a common form of output that are often used by business people. Reports may be printed on the printer or displayed on a screen (Figure 3-11). There are many other types of output, including graphics and sound.

The type of output produced by an application depends on several factors. Some of these factors include the intended use of the output, the speed with which output delivery must take place (i.e., does the user need it right now or can it wait until later), and whether the output is to be permanently kept or used only at the moment. Whenever an application is designed for implementation on a computer, the format of the output and the way it will be presented must be defined. Users work closely with information processing personnel during the development of applications to define the best method and format of presentation.

FIGURE 3-11
Output information may be printed on a report or displayed on a screen.

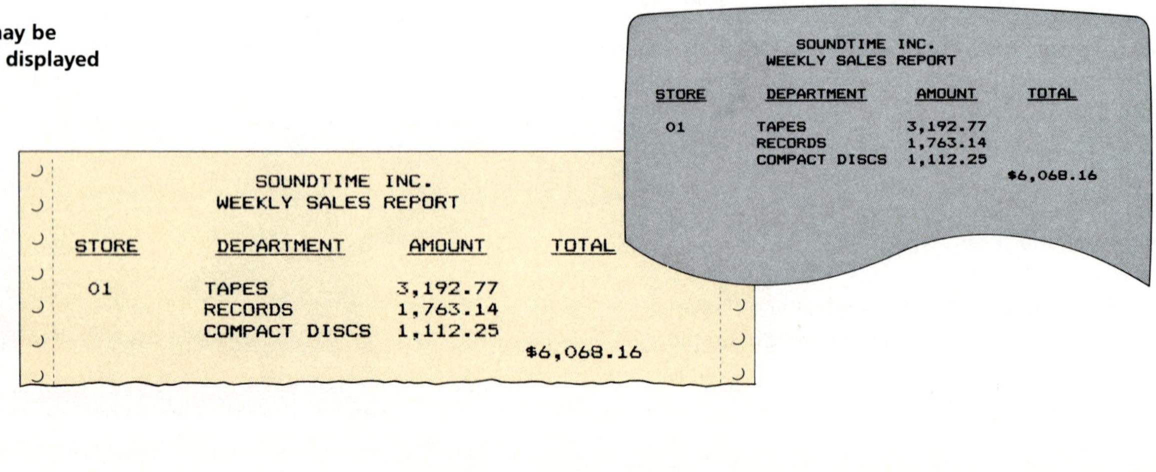

Storage Operations

The first three operations of the information processing cycle, input, process, and output, describe the procedures that a computer performs in order to process data into information. The fourth operation, storage, refers to the electronic storage capability of a computer. To be more specific, **storage operations** refer to the transfer of programs, data, and information from main memory to an auxiliary storage device such as magnetic disk and magnetic tape (Figure 3-12 on the next page). Storage operations allow programs, data, and information that are not currently needed in main memory to be saved in an electronic format for future use. Programs and data are usually stored in this manner. Sometimes information, or the result of processing, is stored on auxiliary storage. An example of information storage would be storing on disk or tape a copy of a report that is to be printed at a later time.

Summary of the Information Processing Cycle

As you have seen, the information processing cycle consists of input, processing, output, and storage operations. These operations are controlled by a computer program. When a program begins to execute, it first directs the input operation by specifying how the data that is to be processed should be entered into main memory. Both the program directing the processing and the data to be processed must be in main memory for processing to occur. Next, the computer program directs the processing operation. Processing consists of arithmetic and logical operations and includes moving data from one location to another in main memory. As the program continues executing, it directs the output operation. This phase of the information processing cycle organizes the information produced into some form that can be used by people or other machines. Finally, program instructions direct the storage operation. Programs, data, and information that may be needed for future use are stored on auxiliary storage devices for subsequent retrieval.

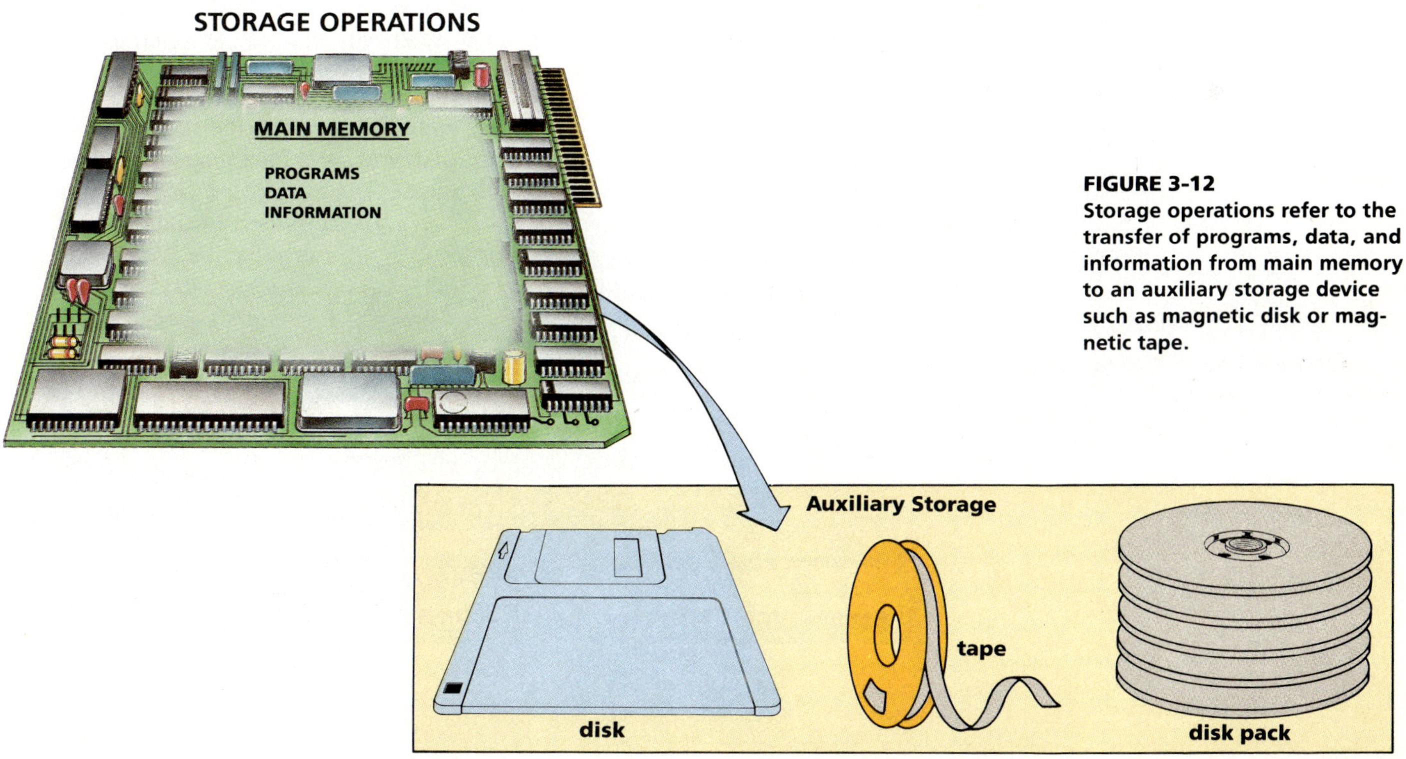

FIGURE 3-12
Storage operations refer to the transfer of programs, data, and information from main memory to an auxiliary storage device such as magnetic disk or magnetic tape.

METHODS OF PROCESSING DATA INTO INFORMATION

The information processing cycle is usually implemented on a computer in one of two ways. These two methods are called interactive processing and batch processing. **Interactive processing** means that data is processed upon entry and output is produced immediately. In **batch processing**, data is collected and at some later time, all the data that has been gathered is processed as a group or "batch." Examples of these methods are given in the following sections.

Interactive Processing

The example in Figure 3-13 illustrates interactive processing. The program used in a bank accepts a beginning year, a yearly deposit amount, and an interest rate. It then calculates and displays the annual value of the savings account. This program is interactive because after the user enters the year, deposit amount, and interest rate, the program immediately performs the calculations and produces output for the user. This example illustrates the use of a personal computer for interactive processing. But large computers, such as minicomputers and mainframes, can also be used for interactive processing.

One type of interactive processing is called transaction processing. In **transaction processing**, the computer user enters all the data pertaining to a complete transaction. After all the data is entered, the program performs the processing required for that particular transaction.

The example in Figure 3-14 illustrates transaction processing as it could be used in a car rental agency. When a car is returned, the rental clerk enters on the terminal all the data required to prepare the final auto rental agreement. The program immediately retrieves the car's record from the disk (based on the license number), performs the necessary calculations, and writes the final rental agreement on the printer. The clerk then gives a copy to the customer. In addition to printing the final rental agreement, the program changes the car's record on disk by placing the ending mileage in the record. After this processing is done, the entire auto rental transaction is completed.

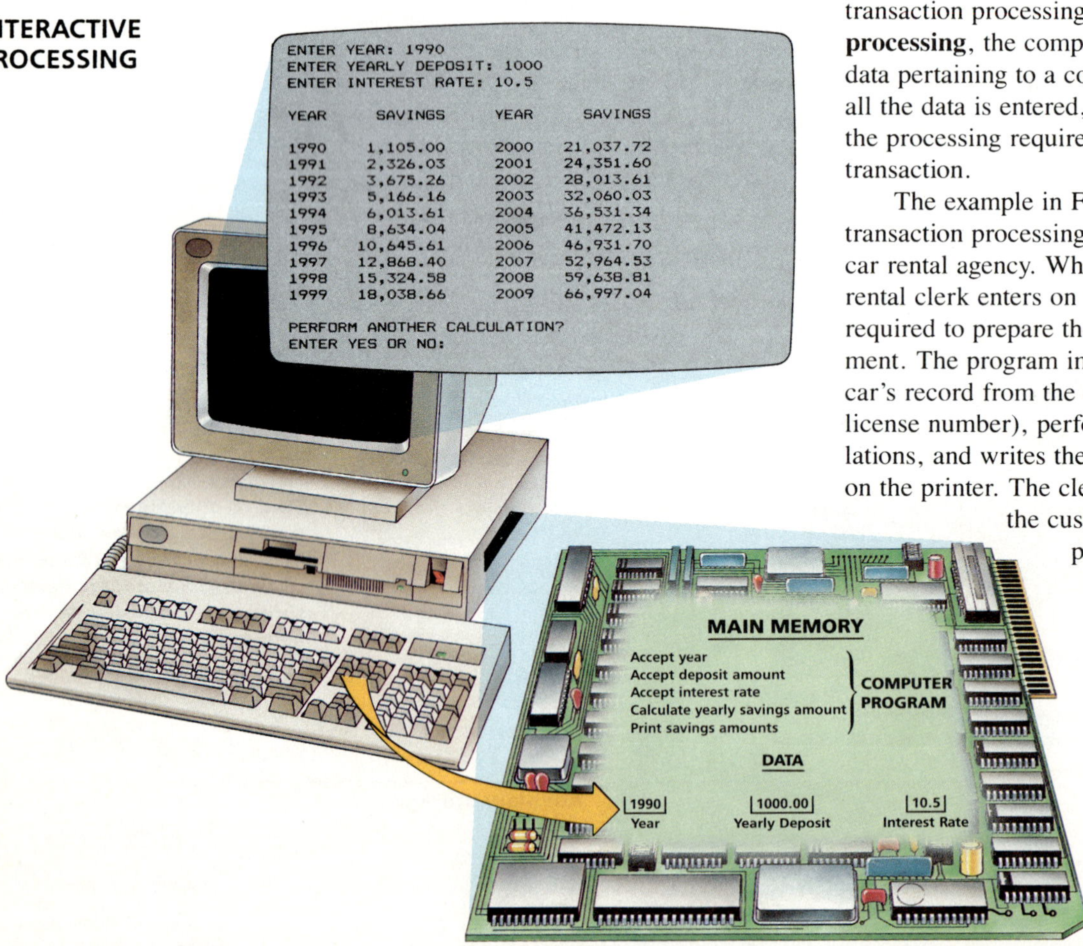

FIGURE 3-13
This is an example of interactive processing to calculate the value of a savings account. After the user enters the beginning year, yearly deposit amount, and the interest rate, the program calculates and displays what the value of the account would be for the next 20 years.

INTERACTIVE PROCESSING

Note that the entire transaction was completed immediately after the user entered the input data. The key to understanding interactive processing is to realize that as soon as the required input data has been entered, the program performs the processing and generates output.

TRANSACTION PROCESSING

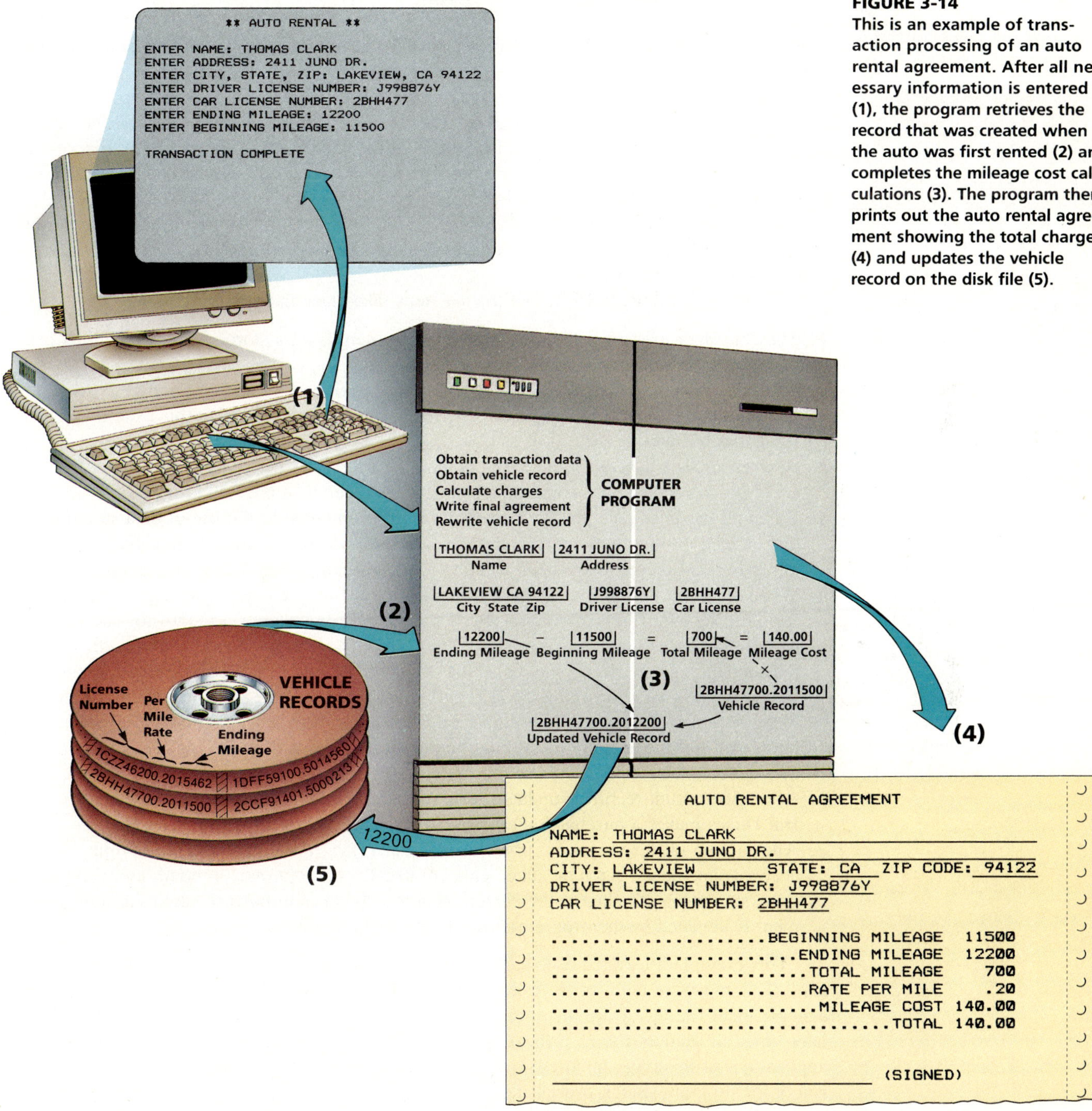

After the updated record is rewritten, the ending mileage (12200) would be in the record. This is not shown in the record stored on disk.

FIGURE 3-14
This is an example of transaction processing of an auto rental agreement. After all necessary information is entered (1), the program retrieves the record that was created when the auto was first rented (2) and completes the mileage cost calculations (3). The program then prints out the auto rental agreement showing the total charges (4) and updates the vehicle record on the disk file (5).

Batch Processing

Batch processing was used extensively when computers were first used in business. In many cases, source documents containing the data to be processed were brought to a central location where the data was punched on cards or placed on magnetic tape. All the data, in one single group or batch, was then read into the computer for processing. Many of the early applications implemented on computers, such as payroll or billing operations, were best processed in a batch environment.

Today, interactive processing is the most prominent method of processing because it provides immediate results and keeps data current. However, batch processing is still the best way to implement some applications. Applications that require periodic processing of a large number of records are good possibilities for batch processing. Payroll applications that create paychecks periodically, such as every other week, normally operate using a batch method of processing. Other users of batch processing include utility companies, which must send out thousands of bills each month, and credit card companies, which process thousands of charges and payments each month.

As shown in Figure 3-15, the following steps take place in batch processing.

1. The consumer uses a credit card to purchase an item from a store. A sales receipt is produced and becomes the source document.
2. The sales receipt is transmitted to the data entry section of the information systems department at the bank or company processing the credit card purchase. In this example, it is the First Federal Bank.
3. At a terminal, a data entry clerk enters the data from the sales receipt into a disk file. Several data entry personnel could be entering sales receipts at the same time.
4. When all the sales receipts for a given day have been entered, the file of data stored on disk is read into main memory and processed one record at a time. This is batch processing, where all records have been batched into one input file and then processed together.
5. When the input record is read from the batch input file, the corresponding customer record from the account file is also retrieved. The account file contains a record for each cardholder. The record contains the account number, the cardholder's name and address, and the account balance. In the example, the customer's name is Hal Dukes, the address is 613 Acorn Drive, Plain, Wyoming 83742, and the account balance prior to processing the purchase record is $265.40. When the account record is retrieved, it is updated to reflect the latest status of the account by adding the purchase amount from the input record to the account balance found in the account record.
6. After the account record is updated, it is rewritten in the account file. Thus, the next time Hal Dukes makes a purchase, the new balance, $309.39, will be in his account record.
7. After all the sales receipts are processed, another program might be run to prepare the account statements. Account statements are usually sent out once a month and contain the previous statement balance, the current charges, the current balance, the minimum payment (calculated by the program), and the payment due date.

This example illustrated each step that could occur when a purchase is made with a credit card. The important point of the example is that the input records are all batched together into a single input file. They are then processed as a group, updating the account file. At some later time, all account file records are processed as a batch to provide account statements. In applications of this type, hundreds or even thousands of records would be processed in one run of the program. Batch processing is the most appropriate method for processing this application because it provides the information when it is needed and it is cheaper than interactive processing.

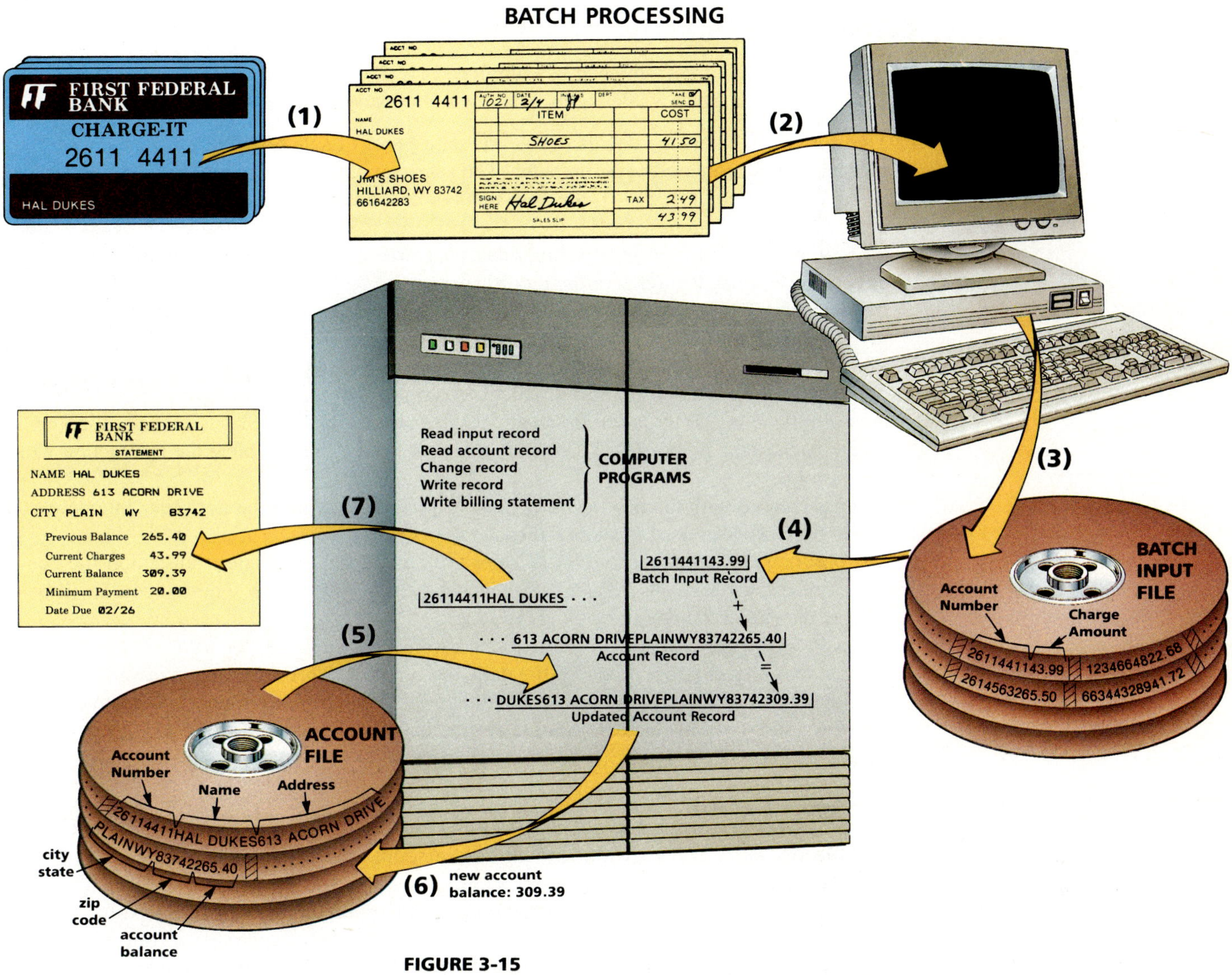

FIGURE 3-15
In this example of batch processing, a customer uses a credit card to make a purchase (1). A copy of the sales receipt is entered into the computer system (2) and recorded in a batch input file with charges for other customers (3). At the end of the day, when all charges have been entered into the file, the file is read by a program (4) and processed in a batch mode to update customer account balances stored on another file (5). New account balance amounts are written on the account file (6). At a later time, another program is run to produce customer account statements (7).

Combined Interactive and Batch Processing

Interactive and batch processing can be combined in a single application. This is illustrated in Figure 3-16, which shows a sales transaction in a retail store. The following steps occur:

1. The store clerk enters the details of the sale on a **point of sale terminal**, a special cash register that is connected to a computer. The sales data includes the department number where the sale took place (14), the item number of the item purchased (A437), and the quantity of items purchased (01).
2. As soon as the sales information (input data) is stored in main memory, the program directs the computer to retrieve the record corresponding to the item number (A437) from the item file. The record retrieved contains the item number (A437), the quantity of the item in inventory (0527), and the unit price for the item (14.95).
3. The program reduces the quantity in the item record (527) by the quantity purchased (1), giving the new inventory quantity (526). It also multiplies the quantity purchased (1) by the unit price (14.95) to determine the total sales amount (14.95). The total sales amount is sent back to the point of sale terminal, where the clerk can complete the transaction with the customer.
4. The item record with the new quantity (526) is written back into the item file. Interactive processing has been used in steps 1 through 4.
5. The program also adds a record to the sales transaction file. The sales transaction file contains a record for each sale that is made during the day at the store. These records will be used at the end of the day in batch processing.
6. After the store is closed and all transactions have been completed, the sales transaction file is input to a program that produces the daily sales report. This report contains the department and sales amount for each sale, the total dollar sales amount for each department of the store, and the total sales in the store for the day. Batch processing has been used in steps 5 and 6.

This application illustrates both interactive processing and batch processing of data generated from a single transaction. When the sales clerk enters the sale on the point of sale terminal and the program responds with the total sales amount, interactive processing has occurred. As soon as the data was entered, the program processed the data by performing the calculations, updating the item file, and producing output on the point of sale terminal. At the same time, input data for batch processing was created when the program wrote a record in the sales transaction file. When these transactions were used to produce the daily sales report, batch processing occurred. All the transaction records were batched together to be processed at one time. It would make little sense to produce the daily sales report until all the sales transactions for the day had been completed. Thus, batch processing is the appropriate method to use to prepare the daily sales report. Because each sale must be processed as it occurs, interactive processing is the appropriate method for the sales and item record processing.

Summary of Processing Methods

Interactive and batch processing are the two main methods for processing data on a computer. Generally, most processing that is performed on personal computers is interactive processing. On larger computers, the trend is toward more interactive processing, although batch processing is still appropriate for some applications. In addition, some processing involves a combination of both interactive and batch processing.

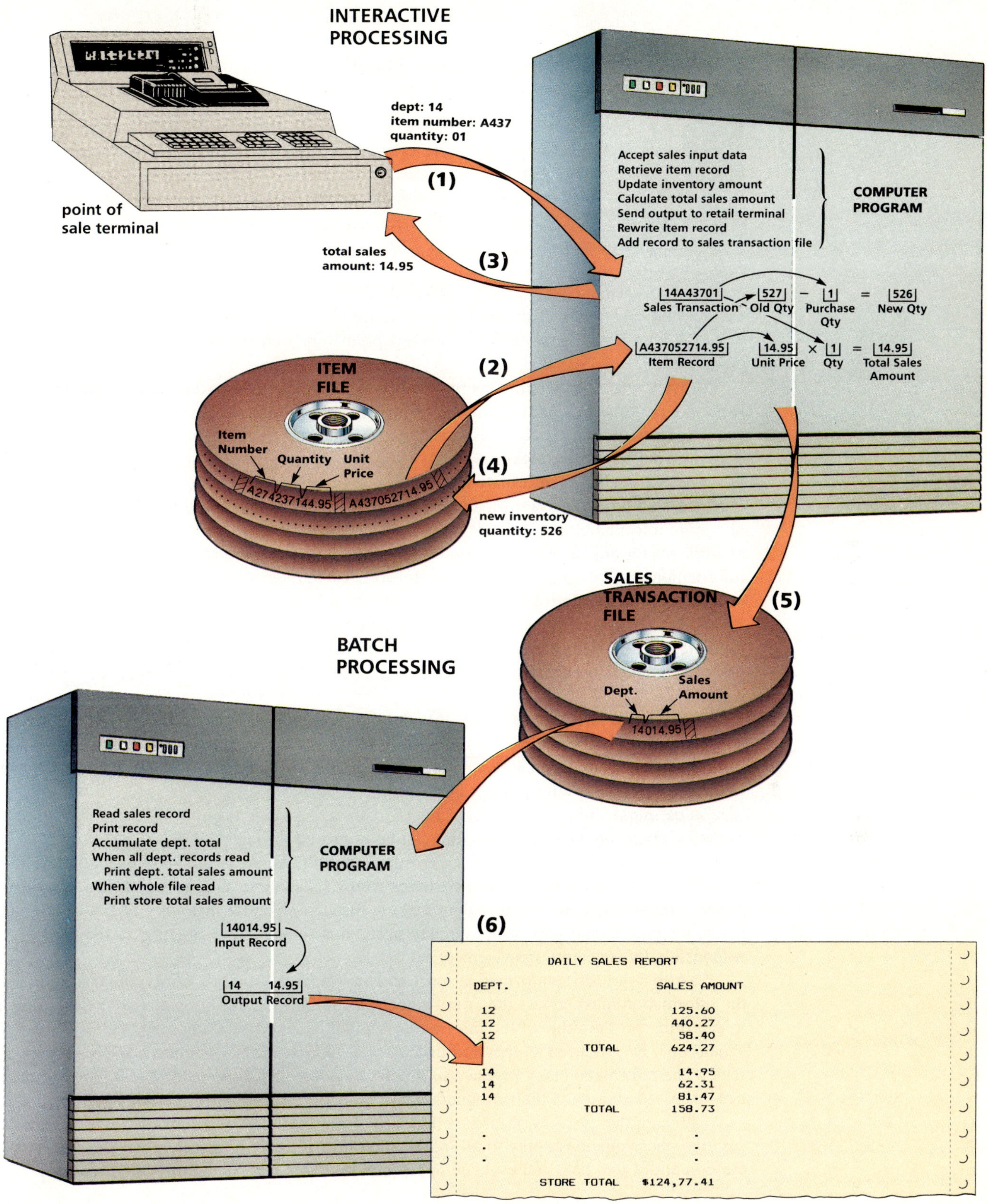

FIGURE 3-16
This example illustrates both interactive and batch processing resulting from a single sales transaction. The inventory balance is updated interactively but the sales report is prepared by batch processing at the end of the day.

QUALITIES OF INFORMATION

As we have discussed, the purpose of processing data is to create information. Just as data should have certain characteristics, so too should information. These characteristics are often called the "qualities of information." Terms used to describe these qualities include the following: accurate, verifiable, timely, organized, meaningful, useful, and cost effective.

Although it may seem obvious, the first quality of information is that it should be *accurate*. Inaccurate information is often worse than no information at all. As you may recall, accuracy was also a characteristic of data. And although accurate data does not guarantee accurate information, it is impossible to produce accurate information from erroneous data. The computer jargon term **GIGO** states this point very well; it stands for "Garbage In, Garbage Out."

Closely related to accuracy is the quality of information being *verifiable*. This means that if necessary, the user can confirm the information. For example, before relying on the amounts in a summary report, an accountant would want to know that the totals could be supported by details of transactions.

Another quality of information is that it must be *timely*. Although most information loses its value with time, some information, such as trends, becomes more valuable as time passes and more information is obtained. The important point here is that the timeliness must be appropriate for any decisions that will be made based on the information. Up-to-the-minute information may be required for some decisions while older information may be satisfactory or more appropriate for others.

To be of the most value, information should be *organized* to suit users' requirements. For example, a sales representative assigned to sell only to companies in a specific area would prefer to have a prospect list organized by zip code rather than a list that was only in alphabetical order.

Meaningful information means that the information is relevant to the person who receives it. Much information is only meaningful to specific individuals or groups within an organization. Extraneous and unnecessary information should be eliminated and the "audience" of the information should always be kept in mind.

To be *useful*, information should result in an action being taken or specifically not taken, as the case may be. Often, this quality can be improved through **exception reporting**, which focuses only on the information that exceeds certain limits. An example of exception reporting would be an inventory report showing items whose balance on hand is less than a predetermined minimum quantity. Rather than looking through an entire inventory report to find such items, the exception report would quickly bring these items to the attention of the persons responsible for inventory management.

Last, but not least, information must be *cost effective*. In other words, the cost to produce the information must be less than the "value" of the information. This can sometimes be hard to determine. If the value of the information cannot be determined, perhaps the information should only be produced as required instead of regularly. Many organizations periodically review the information they produce in reports to determine if the reports still have the qualities discussed above and their production cost can still be justified or possibly reduced.

Although the qualities of information have been discussed in conjunction with computer systems, these qualities apply to all information regardless of how it is produced. Knowing these qualities will help you evaluate the information you receive and provide every day.

SUMMARY OF PROCESSING DATA INTO INFORMATION

The concepts presented in this chapter concerning data, the information processing cycle, interactive and batch processing, and the qualities of information apply to all information processing systems. By now you have developed an understanding and a "feeling" for the way a computer processes data into information. Your increased understanding should help you to feel more comfortable with computers and how they can be used.

CHAPTER SUMMARY

1. The **information processing cycle** consists of input, processing, output, and storage operations.
2. Regardless of the size and type of computer, the information processing cycle is used to process data into information.
3. The operations in the information processing cycle are carried out through the combined use of computer equipment, also called computer hardware, and computer software.
4. Computer software, or programs, contain the instructions that direct the computer equipment to perform the four types of operations.
5. The primary input devices are keyboards on microcomputers and terminals on larger machines.
6. Input devices are used to enter both computer programs and data into main memory.
7. Both the program that is to control the processing and the data to be processed must be in main memory for processing to occur.
8. Program instructions are executed by the processor.
9. The primary output devices on computers are printers and screens.
10. Auxiliary storage devices commonly used with computers are magnetic tape and magnetic disk.
11. Some devices are used for more than one purpose in the information processing cycle. For example, disks can be used for both input and output.
12. Data is the prime ingredient of an information processing system.
13. **Data** is defined as raw facts and consists of the numbers and words that a computer receives and processes to produce information.
14. Data is composed of **characters**. These include **alphabetic** (A–Z), **numeric** (0–9), and **special** characters, such as ( ) * & % # @ , .
15. Individual facts are referred to as **data items**, **data fields**, or **fields**.
16. Fields may be classified as **numeric**, **alphabetic**, or **alphanumeric**.
17. A field is often more useful when it is combined with other related fields.
18. A **record** is a collection of related fields.
19. A collection of related records is called a **file**.
20. Files are stored on some medium, such as magnetic tape or magnetic disk.
21. In a **sequential** file, records are arranged in alphabetical or numerical order by a **key field**.
22. The records in a **random** file are not arranged in any sequence or order.
23. A **database** provides an efficient way to establish a relationship between data items and implies that a relationship has been established between multiple files.
24. Data is organized into fields, records, files, and databases for processing on a computer.
25. **Data management** refers to techniques and procedures that ensure that the data required for an application will be available in the correct form and at the proper time for processing.
26. Data management includes the management of data attributes, data security, and data maintenance.
27. Data attributes include data availability and data integrity.
28. Data that is required for input must be available.
29. **Data integrity** determines the confidence a user can have in the processing of that data. The three elements of data integrity are data accuracy, reliable data entry, and timeliness.

30. Accurate data depends on a reliable source.
31. Reliable data entry must occur for the information generated to be valid.
32. Timeliness means that data has not lost its usefulness or accuracy because time has passed.
33. **Data security** is an important issue because misuse or loss of data can have serious consequences.
34. **Backup** procedures provide for maintaining copies of data so that in the event of loss data can be recovered.
35. **Data maintenance** refers to **updating** data. This includes **adding**, **changing** and **deleting** data in order to keep it current.
36. **Input operations** cause the data that is to be processed to be stored in main memory.
37. Once data is stored in main memory, it can be processed under the control of a computer program.
38. **Processing operations** define how the data will be manipulated into a usable form.
39. When data is moved from one location in memory to another, it is not destroyed but is duplicated in the new location.
40. Two main types of processing operations include arithmetic and logical processing of data.
41. Many computers are able to perform millions of **arithmetic operations** in one second, including addition, subtraction, multiplication, and division.
42. The results of arithmetic operations can be used in subsequent arithmetic operations, moved to other locations in main memory, and used for output.
43. **Logical operations** allow a computer to compare two data fields to determine if one is **equal to**, **greater than**, or **less than** the other.
44. Logical operations are performed on a computer by the execution of program instructions that direct the computer to compare data fields that are currently stored in main memory.
45. The result of a logical operation determines which of the processing paths of a program will be performed.
46. The ability of a computer to compare data and then select one of two processing paths is a powerful feature that is used in programs of all levels of complexity.
47. The process of repeating the instructions in a program allows a single set of program instructions to process any number of records.
48. **Output operations** take the information produced and put it in a form that can be used by a person or a machine. A common form of output are reports that are displayed on the screen or printed on the printer.
49. **Storage operations** refer to the transfer of programs, data, and information from main memory to an auxiliary storage device such as magnetic disk and magnetic tape.
50. The two methods used for processing data on a computer are interactive processing and batch processing.
51. **Interactive processing** means that data is processed upon entry and output is produced immediately.
52. **Transaction processing** is a type of interactive processing in which the user enters all the data pertaining to a complete transaction and the program immediately performs all the processing required for that particular transaction.
53. In **batch processing**, data is collected and at some later time, all the data that has been gathered is processed as a group or batch.
54. Batch and interactive processing can be combined in a single application.
55. The terms used to describe the qualities of information include accurate, verifiable, timely, organized, meaningful, useful, and cost effective.
56. **GIGO** is an acronym that stands for "Garbage In, Garbage Out."

KEY TERMS

Adding (data) *3.7*
Alphabetic (characters) *3.4*
Alphabetic field *3.4*
Alphanumeric field *3.4*
Arithmetic operations *3.9*
Backup *3.6*
Batch processing *3.14*
Changing (data) *3.7*
Characters *3.4*
Data *3.4*
Database *3.5*
Data field *3.4*
Data integrity *3.6*
Data item *3.4*
Data maintenance *3.7*
Data management *3.5*
Data security *3.6*
Deleting (data) *3.7*
Exception reporting *3.20*
Field *3.4*
File *3.5*
GIGO *3.20*
Information processing cycle *3.2*
Input operations *3.7*
Interactive processing *3.14*
Key field *3.5*
Logical operations *3.10*
Meaningful *3.20*
Numeric (characters) *3.4*
Numeric field *3.4*
Output operations *3.12*
Point of sale terminal *3.18*
Processing operations *3.8*
Random *3.5*
Record *3.4*
Sequential *3.5*
Special (characters) *3.4*
Storage operations *3.13*
Transaction processing *3.14*
Updating *3.7*

REVIEW QUESTIONS

1. What are the four elements of the information processing cycle? What types and sizes of computers can be used to implement the information processing cycle?
2. What is the definition of data? What terms are used to describe how data is organized for processing?
3. Why is data management important?
4. What is data integrity? What are the three elements of data integrity?
5. What is meant by data security? How does it relate to the privacy of an individual?
6. What is the input operation on a computer? What happens when the input operation takes place?
7. Why is the ability to repeat instructions in a program important?
8. Name three logical operations that can be performed on data.
9. Describe the purpose of the output operations. What is the most common form of output used by people?
10. Why are storage operations necessary? What are the primary devices used for auxiliary storage?
11. What is interactive processing? Give an example.
12. What is transaction processing?
13. What is batch processing? When is its use appropriate?
14. Is it possible to have batch processing and interactive processing in the same application? Why wouldn't just one processing method be used?
15. Describe the qualities of information.

CONTROVERSIAL ISSUES

1. In this chapter, we noted that computers can perform millions of arithmetic operations in a single second. Some people claim that much greater speed is needed for computers so that applications such as weather prediction and space flight simulation can be accurately performed within a reasonable time period. These people think research money should be spent to find ways to develop faster computers. Other people argue that computers process data fast enough and that research money should be spent in other areas, such as developing privacy safeguards. Take a side in this debate and defend your position.

2. Software is currently available that lets medical patients inform a computer of their symptoms by answering a series of questions. The program then compares the answers to symptoms retrieved from auxiliary storage. When equal conditions are found, a possible diagnosis will be given and, perhaps, a treatment suggested. Is the computer doing the same type of "thinking" that a doctor does when analyzing symptoms? Take a position and defend it.
3. In the past few years, some have advocated that all applications placed on a computer should use the interactive processing method. These people state that such features as the inherent delays when processing data in a batch method make batch processing obsolete. Other experts dispute this, saying that for some applications, batch is the best means for processing data. Take a position on this disagreement and defend your position.

RESEARCH PROJECTS

1. A banking application was described in this chapter. Visit a bank or savings and loan in your area. Determine the techniques they use to enter a new customer, make changes in account records for deposits and withdrawals, and close an account. Write a report for your class.
2. Obtain a manual for a programming language such as BASIC or COBOL. List and describe all the instructions that are used to compare data and the comparisons they can make. Include in your report the rules for comparing numeric data to numeric data and alphabetic data to alphabetic data.

CHAPTER 4

Input to the Computer

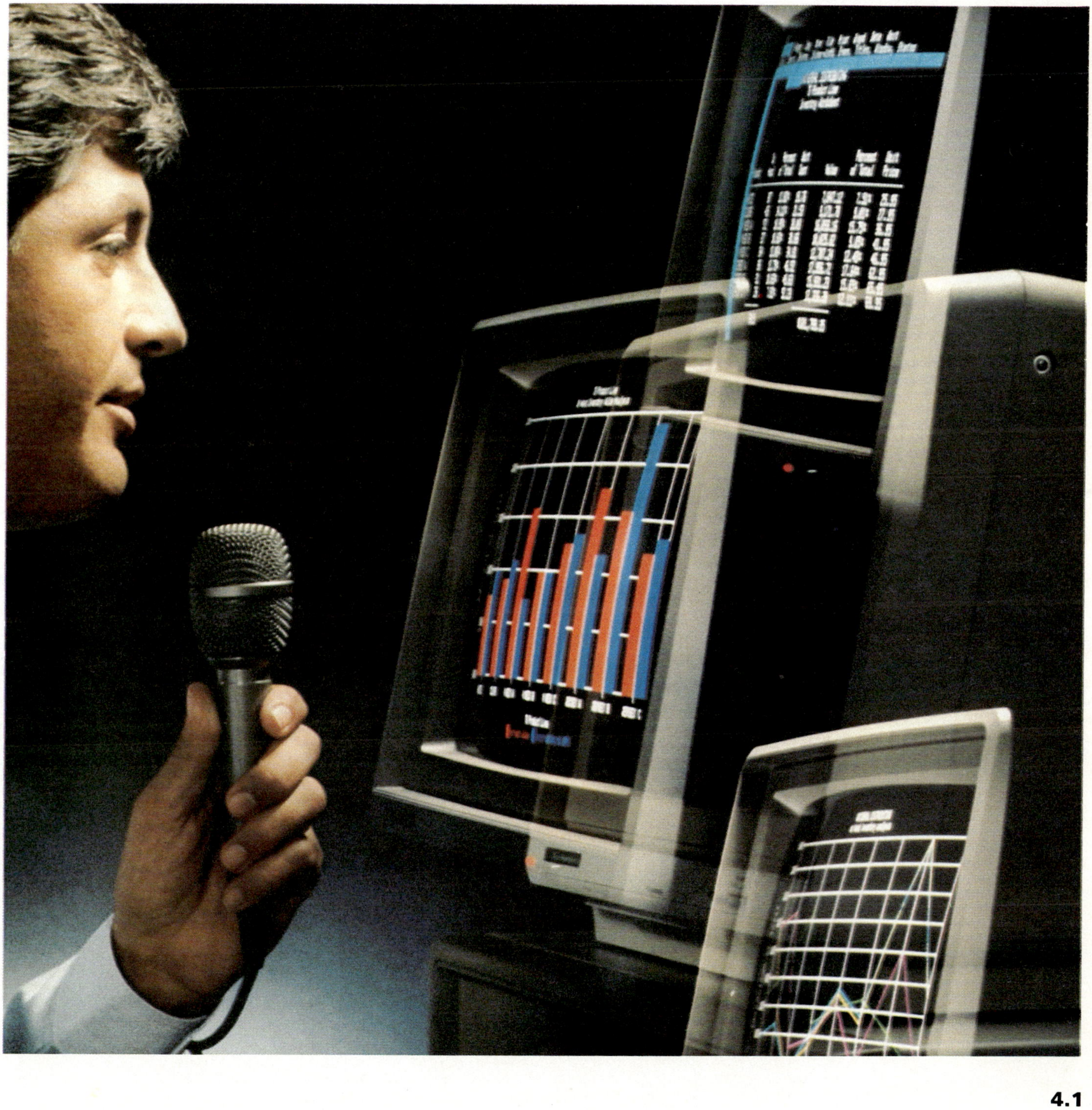

CHAPTER 4

Input to the Computer

OBJECTIVES

- Define the four types of input and how the computer uses each type.
- Describe the standard features of keyboards and explain how to use the cursor control and function keys.
- Identify the two types of terminals and how to use each type.
- Describe several input devices other than the keyboard and terminal.
- Define user interface and explain how it has evolved.
- Define the term menu and describe various forms of menus.
- Discuss some of the features that should be included in a good user interface.
- Discuss the differences between interactive and batch processing data entry.
- Describe online and offline data entry and the uses for each.
- List and explain the systems and procedures associated with data entry.
- Explain the term ergonomics and describe some of the changes that have occurred in equipment design.

In the information processing cycle, the input operation must take place before any data can be processed and any information produced. Without valid input data, a computer is not capable of producing any useful information.

When they were first utilized for business applications, nearly all computers used punched cards as input. The data was recorded on cards using a device called a keypunch. A keypunch is a machine that contains a keyboard and a punching mechanism. As the operator presses the keys, holes representing numbers, letters of the alphabet, or special characters are punched into the card. The cards are then collected together and read into main memory by a card reader.

Today, punched cards are not as often used as input to a computer. In addition, the user has more choices concerning the type of input device or devices to be used for an application. This chapter examines some of the devices used for input, the ways that both hardware and software are designed to make input operations easier for the user, and the various methods of entering data into the computer.

WHAT IS INPUT?

Input refers to the process of entering programs, commands, user responses, and data into main memory. Input can also refer to the media (e.g., tapes, cards, documents, etc.) that contain these input types. These four types of input are used by a computer in the following ways:

- **Programs** are the sets of instructions that direct the computer to perform the necessary operations to process data into information. The program that is loaded and stored in main memory determines the processing that the computer will perform. When a program is first entered into a computer it is input by way of a keyboard. Once the program has been entered and stored on auxiliary storage, it can be transferred to main memory by a command.
- **Commands** are key words and phrases that the user inputs to direct the computer to perform certain activities. For example, if you wanted to use a payroll program, you might issue a command such as LOAD "PAYROLL" to load the program named PAYROLL into main memory from auxiliary storage. To begin the execution of the program you would enter another command such as RUN (Figure 4-1).
- **User responses** refer to the data that a user inputs in response to a question or message from the software. Usually these messages display on a screen and the user responds through a keyboard. One of the most common responses is to answer "Yes" or "No" to a question. Based on the answer, the computer program will perform specific actions. For example, in a spreadsheet program, typing the letter Y in response to the message "Do you want to save this file?" will result in the spreadsheet file being saved (written) to the auxiliary storage device.
- **Data** is raw facts; it is the source from which information is produced. It must be entered and stored in main computer memory for processing to occur. For example, data entered from sales orders can be processed by a computer program to produce sales reports useful to management. Data is the most common type of input.

Regardless of the type, input will be entered through some kind of input device. The next section of this chapter discusses the various types of available input devices.

FIGURE 4-1
In this example, the computer user first entered a command to load the program called "PAYROLL" and then issued the command RUN, which will cause the program to be executed.

THE KEYBOARD

Keyboards are the most commonly used input devices. Users input data to a computer by pressing the keys on the keyboard. Keyboards are connected to other devices, such as a personal computer or a terminal, that have screens. As the user enters data on the keyboard, it displays on the screen.

The keyboards used for computer input are very similar to the keyboards used on the familiar office machine, the typewriter (Figure 4-2). They contain numbers, letters of the alphabet, and some special characters. In addition, many computer keyboards are equipped with a special **numeric keypad** on the right-hand side of the keyboard. These numeric keys are arranged in an adding machine or calculator format and aid the user with data entry.

FIGURE 4-2
The IBM PS/Model 30 keyboard shown in the picture contains a numeric keypad, cursor control keys, and function keys. The keys on the numeric keypad are arranged in the same order as the keys on an adding machine or a calculator. This arrangement allows those skilled in entering numbers to input numeric data at a much faster rate than if the number keys were across the top of the keyboard as they are on a typewriter. The four cursor control keys are identified by up ↑, down ↓, left ←, and right → arrows. When the user presses one of these keys, the cursor moves one position in the direction indicated by the arrow. Function keys are used for specific commands that are either programmed by the user or determined by the application software. Function keys can be located in different places, but on most keyboards they are either on the left side or along the top.

Keyboards also contain keys that can be used to position the cursor on the screen. A **cursor** is a symbol, such as a highlighted rectangle or an underline character, that indicates where on the screen the next character entered will be displayed. The keys that move the cursor are called **arrow keys** or **cursor control keys**. When pressed, the keys move the cursor in the direction where the arrow points. Cursor control keys have an up arrow, a down arrow, a left arrow, and a right arrow. When you press any of these keys, the cursor moves one space in the direction specified by the arrow. In addition, many keyboards contain other cursor control keys such as the HOME key, which when pressed sends the cursor to the upper left position of the screen or document.

Some computer keyboards also contain keys that are used to alter or edit the text displayed on the screen. For example, the INSERT and DELETE keys allow characters to be inserted into or deleted from data that appears on the screen.

Function keys are keys that can be programmed to accomplish certain tasks that will assist the user. For example, a function key might be programmed for use as a help key when a terminal is used for word processing. Whenever the key is pressed, messages will appear that give instructions pertaining to the word processor. Another use of function keys is to save keystrokes. Sometimes several keystrokes are required to accomplish a certain task, for example, printing a document. Some application software packages are written so that the user can either enter the individual keystrokes or press a function key and obtain the same result.

The disadvantage of using a keyboard as an input device is that training is required to use it efficiently. Users who do not know how to type are at a disadvantage because of the time they spend looking for the appropriate keys. While there are other input devices that are appropriate in some situations, users should be encouraged to develop their keyboard skills.

TERMINALS

Terminals, sometimes called **display terminals** or **video display terminals (VDTs)**, consist of a keyboard and a screen. They fall into two basic categories: dumb terminals and intelligent terminals (sometimes called programmable terminals). We explain the features of each type in the following paragraphs. Figure 4-3 shows an example of each type of terminal.

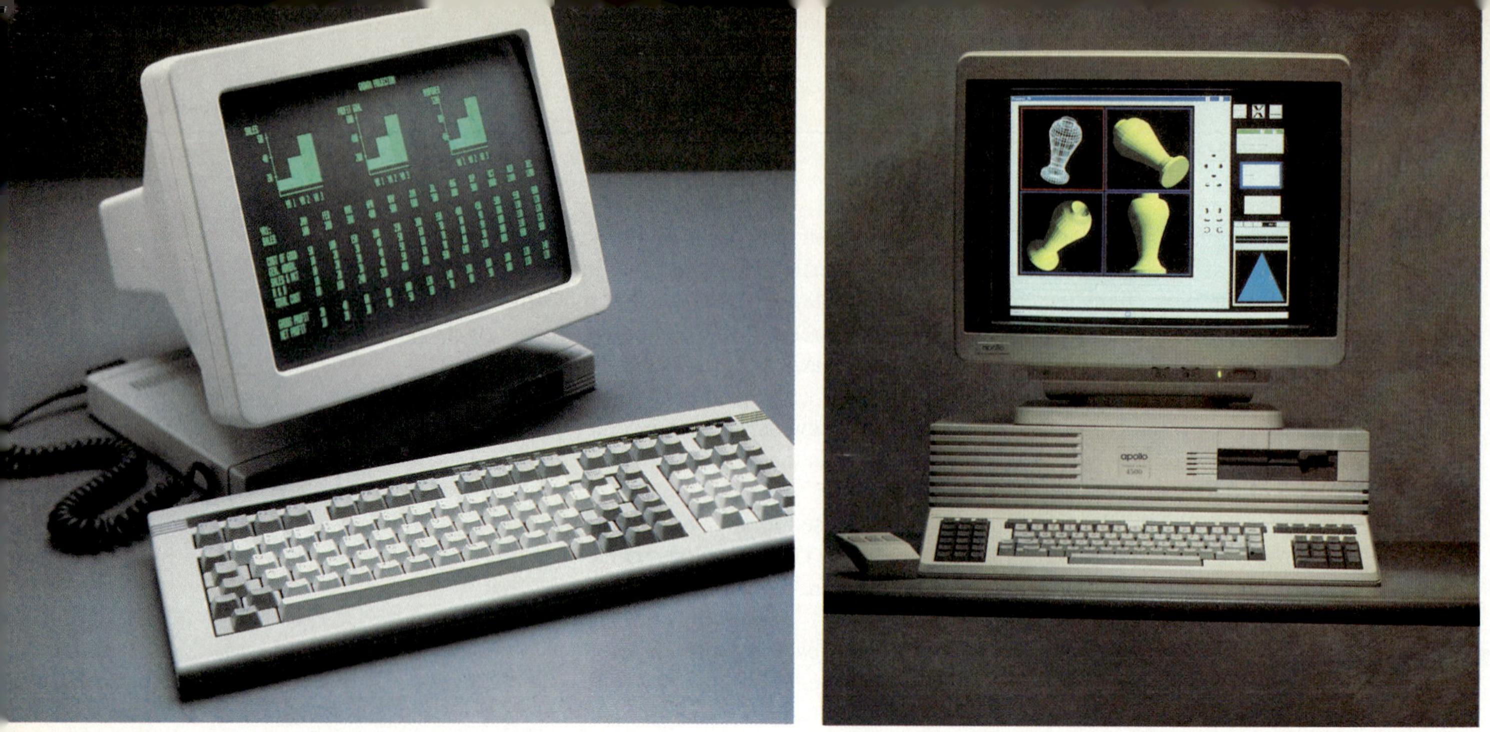

FIGURE 4-3
Terminals can be classified into two broad categories: dumb terminals and intelligent terminals. From appearance alone, it is often difficult to tell in which category a terminal belongs. In these photos the dumb terminal on the left lacks a CPU.

Dumb Terminals

A **dumb terminal** consists of a keyboard and a display screen that can be used to enter and transmit data to or receive and display data from a computer to which it is connected. A dumb terminal has no independent processing capability or auxiliary storage and cannot function as a stand-alone device.

Intelligent Terminals

Intelligent terminals are terminals whose processing capabilities are built in. These terminals are also known as **programmable terminals** because they can be programmed by the user to perform many basic tasks, including both arithmetic and logic operations. Personal computers are frequently used as intelligent terminals (Figure 4-4).

Intelligent terminals often contain not only the keyboard and screen associated with other terminals, but also are supported with disk drives and printers, so they can perform limited processing tasks when not communicating directly with the central computer. In some instances, when the user enters data, the data will be checked for errors and some type of report will be produced. In addition, the valid data that is entered will be stored on the disk connected to the terminal. After the data has been entered and stored on disk, it will be transmitted over communication lines to the central computer. This operation is sometimes called **uploading**, because the data is loaded from the smaller terminal "up" to the bigger main computer. Uploading is used most often when the data entered is to be processed in a batch processing mode.

As the amount of processing power that is incorporated into intelligent terminals increases, more processing can occur at the site of the terminal prior to sending the data to the central computer. This means that the large minicomputer or mainframe at the central site can perform the main processing and serve multiple users faster, rather than having to use its resources to perform tasks that can be performed by the intelligent terminal.

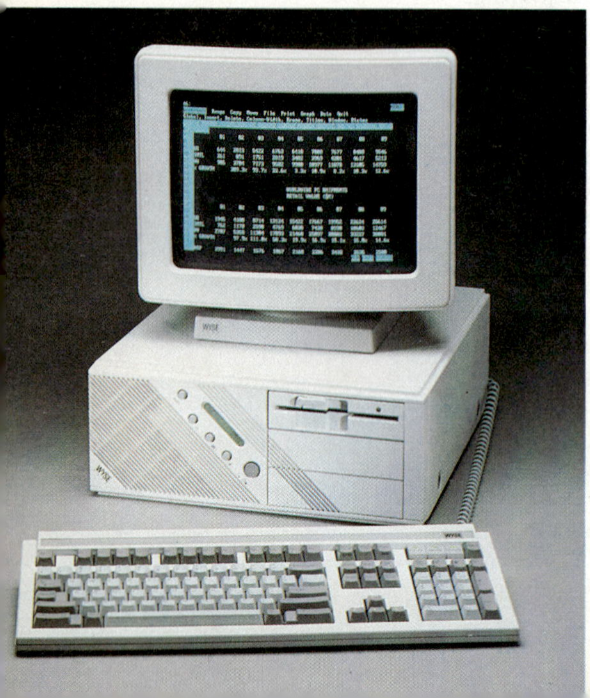

FIGURE 4-4
This WYSE pc 286 personal computer can function as both a stand-alone computer or as a terminal when it is connected to another computer system.

Special Purpose Terminals

Terminals are found in virtually every environment that generates data for processing on a computer. While many are standard terminals like those previously described, others are designed to perform specific jobs and contain features uniquely designed for use in a particular industry.

The terminal shown in Figure 4-5 is called a point of sale terminal. **Point of sale terminals** allow data to be entered at the time and place where the transaction with a customer occurs, such as in fast-food restaurants or hotels, for example. Point of sale terminals serve as input to either minicomputers located at the place of business or larger computers located elsewhere. The data entered is used to maintain sales records, update inventory, make automatic calculations such as sales tax, verify credit, and perform other activities associated with the sales transactions and critical to running the business. Point of sale terminals are designed to be easy to operate, requiring little technical knowledge.

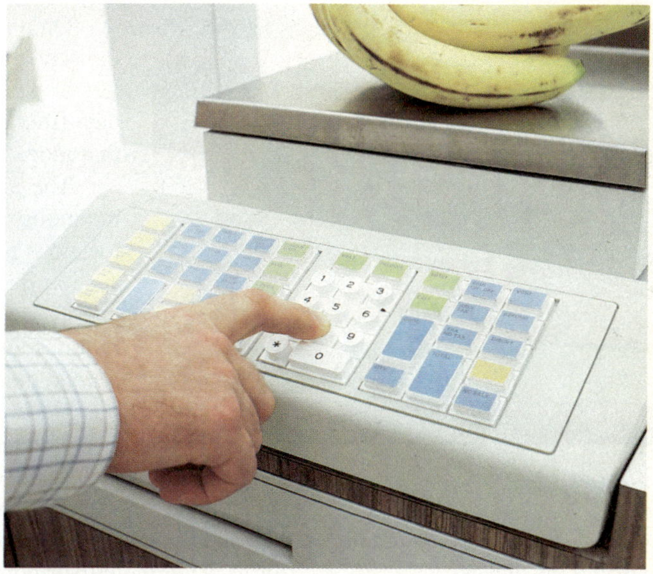

FIGURE 4-5
This point of sale terminal is specially designed for grocery store item entry. The checker can press separate keys to process the prices of produce, meat, and other items.

OTHER INPUT DEVICES

Besides keyboards and terminals, there is an increasing variety of other input devices. This section describes some of the devices used for general purpose applications.

The Mouse

The mouse, initially designed by Xerox, is a unique device used with personal computers and some computer terminals. A **mouse** is a small, lightweight device that easily fits in the palm of your hand. You move it across a flat surface such as a desktop (Figure 4-6) to control the movement of the cursor on a screen. The mouse is attached to the computer by a cable. On the bottom of the mouse are one or more wheels or balls. As the mouse moves across the flat surface, the computer electronically senses the movement of the wheels. The movement of the cursor on the screen corresponds to the movement of the mouse (Figure 4-7). When you move the mouse left on the surface of the table or desk, the cursor moves left on the screen. When you move the mouse right, the cursor moves right, and so on.

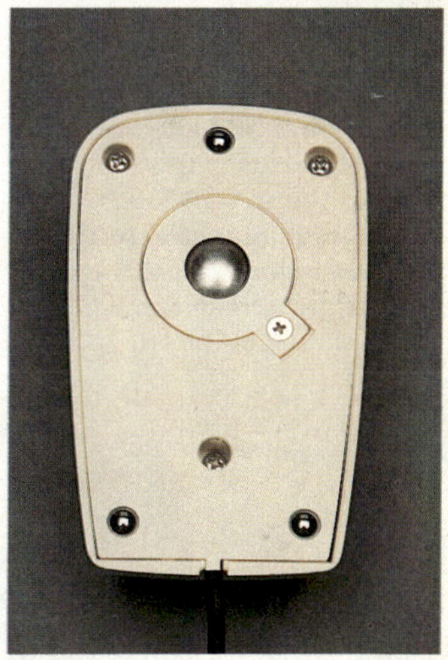

FIGURE 4-6 ▶
The mouse can be moved to control the cursor on the screen. Press the button at the top of the mouse to make selections or perform functions, depending on the software being used. The ball on the underside of the mouse moves as the user pushes the mouse around on a hard, flat surface. The movement of the ball causes the cursor to move correspondingly on the screen.

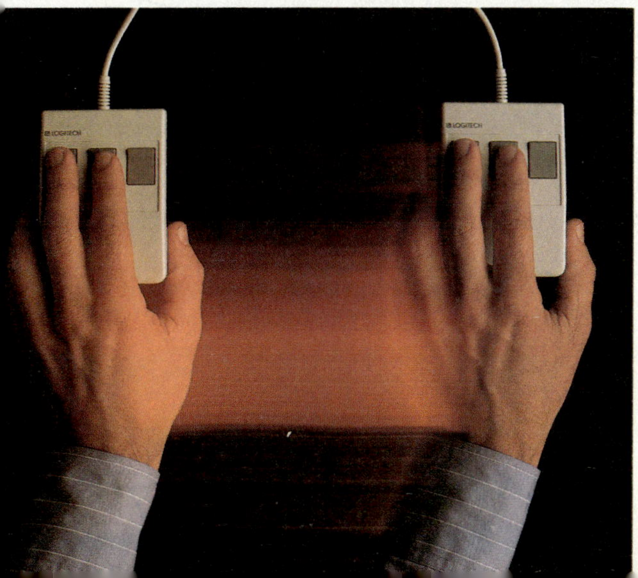

◀ FIGURE 4-7
This drawing illustrates using a mouse. The index finger, which rests on the top of the mouse, acts as a pointer to guide the movement of the mouse and the related movement of the cursor on the screen.

FIGURE 4-8
Notice that some amount of clear desk space is required for moving the mouse.

On top of the mouse are one or more buttons. By moving the cursor on the screen and pressing the buttons, you can make menu choices, choose letters or words in a word processing application for addition or deletion, move data from one point on the screen to another, and perform many other actions that move and rearrange information displayed on the screen.

The primary advantage of a mouse is that it is easy to use. Proponents of the mouse say that with a little practice, a person can use a mouse to point to locations on the screen just as easily as using a finger. For some applications such as desktop publishing, a mouse is indispensable.

There are two major disadvantages of the mouse. The first is that it requires empty desk space where it can be moved about (Figure 4-8). The second disadvantage is that the user must remove a hand from the keyboard and place it on the mouse whenever the cursor is to be moved or a command is to be given. Some keyboard experts have noted that taking hands from the keyboard slows the effective data entry speed considerably. Thus, some people have said the mouse is not an effective tool in those environments where keying must be performed rapidly, such as in word processing applications. Others, however, say that using a mouse is far superior to using the cursor control keys on a keyboard.

Touch Screens

Touch screens allow users to merely touch areas of the screen to enter data. They let the user interact with a computer by the touch of a finger, rather than typing on a keyboard or moving a mouse. The user enters data by touching words or numbers, or locations identified on the screen (Figure 4-9).

Several electronic techniques change a touch on the screen into electronic impulses that can be interpreted by the computer software. One of the most common techniques utilizes beams of infrared light, that are projected across the surface of the screen. A finger or other utensil touching the screen interrupts the beams, generating an electronic signal. This signal identifies the location on the screen where the touch occurred. The software interprets the signal and performs the required function.

Touch screens are not used to enter large amounts of data. They are used, however, for applications in which the user must issue a command to the software to perform a particular task or must choose from a list of options to be performed.

There are both advantages and disadvantages of touch screens. A significant advantage is that they are very "natural" to use; that is, people are used to pointing to things. With touch screens, they can point to indicate the processing they want performed by the computer. In addition, touch screens are usually easy for the user to learn. As quickly as pointing a finger, the user's request is processed. Finally, touch screens allow absolute cursor movement; that is, the user can point a finger at the location where the cursor is to appear and it will. This can be considerably faster than repeatedly pressing arrow keys to move the cursor from one location on the screen to another.

Two major complaints are lodged against touch screens. First, the resolution of the touching area is not precise. Thus, while a user can point to a box or a fairly large area on the screen and the electronics can determine the location of the touch, it is difficult to point to a single character in a word processing application, for example, and indicate that the character should be deleted. In cases such as these, a keyboard is easier to use. A second complaint is that after a period of reaching for the screen, the user's arm may become tired.

FIGURE 4-9
Touch screens allow the user to make choices and execute commands by actually touching areas of the screen. Touch screens require special software that determines where the user touched the screen and what action should be taken.

Graphic Input Devices

Graphic input devices are used to translate graphic input data, such as photos or drawings, into a form that can be processed on a computer. Three major devices that are used for graphic input are light pens, digitizers, and graphics tablets. A **light pen** is used by touching it on the display screen to create or modify graphics (Figure 4-10). A **digitizer** converts points, lines, and curves from a sketch, drawing, or photograph to digital impulses and transmits them to a computer (Figures 4-11 and 4-12). A **graphics tablet** works in a manner similar to a digitizer, but it also contains unique characters and commands that can be automatically generated by the person using the tablet (Figure 4-13).

FIGURE 4-10
Placing the light pen at a point on the screen activates a sensing device within the pen. The activated pen transmits the location of the light to the computer, where the program can perform the desired tasks. ▼

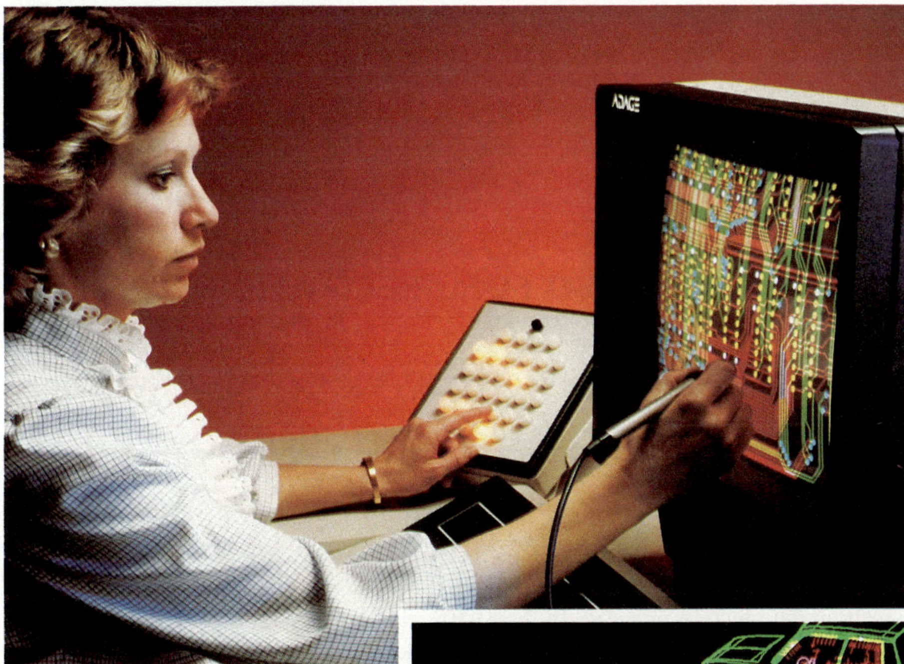

FIGURE 4-11
The device in this aerospace engineer's hand reads and translates the coordinates on the printed wiring board layout into coordinates that can be stored in the computer and later used to reproduce the drawing on a screen or a printer. ▼

FIGURE 4-12
Digitizers are used in business to create original art or to trace and reproduce existing art quickly and accurately. ▼

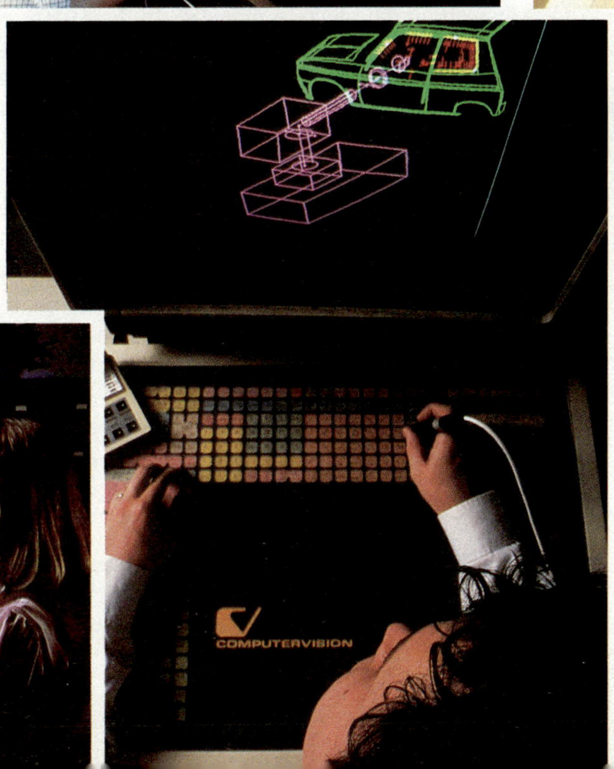

◄ FIGURE 4-13
The graphics tablet in this picture is used by an automotive design engineer for the development and definition of a car body. The stylus, held in the engineer's right hand, is used to input commands by touching specific sections of the tablet.

FIGURE 4-14
This manager has just used his voice input system to request that sales data be presented in a bar graph. Often such systems have to be "trained" to recognize a particular user's voice.

Voice Input

One of the more exciting developments is the use of voice input, sometimes referred to as voice or speech recognition. As the name implies, **voice input** allows the user to enter data and issue commands to the computer with spoken words (Figure 4-14).

Most systems require the user to "train" the system first by speaking the words that will be used a number of times. As the words are spoken, they are digitized by the system; that is, they are broken down into digital components that the computer can recognize. After each word has been spoken several times, the system has developed a digital pattern for the word that can be stored on auxiliary storage. When the user later speaks a word to the system to request a particular action, the system compares the word to words that were previously entered and that it can "understand." When it finds a match, the software performs the activity associated with the word. For example, in voice-controlled word processing systems, spoken words can be used to control such functions as single and double spacing, choosing type styles, and centering text.

The major advantage of voice input is that the user does not have to key, move, or touch anything in order to enter data into the computer. It is expected that voice input will be a significant factor in the years to come.

INPUT DEVICES DESIGNED FOR SPECIFIC PURPOSES

Some input devices have been designed to perform specific tasks. Here we illustrate a few of these devices.

Magnetic Ink Character Recognition

Magnetic ink character recognition or **MICR** is a type of machine-readable data. This type of data is read into the computer by input devices called **MICR readers**. MICR is found almost exclusively in the banking industry. In the 1950s, the industry chose MICR as the method to be used to encode and read the billions of checks written each year.

When MICR is used, special characters encoded on checks identify such items as the bank number and the account number. When a check is processed, the amount is also encoded on it by a bank operator. The items are encoded in special MICR characters (Figure 4-15) using a special ink that can be magnetized during processing. MICR readers interpret the electronic signals generated from the magnetized characters so checks can be sorted and processed to prepare bank statements for customers. MICR devices can process over 1,000 checks per minute (Figure 4-16). MICR also is used in utility companies, credit card companies, and other industries that must process large volumes of data.

FIGURE 4-15
The characters at the bottom of a check can be read by MICR devices. All the banks in the United States and in many foreign countries use these codes for checks.

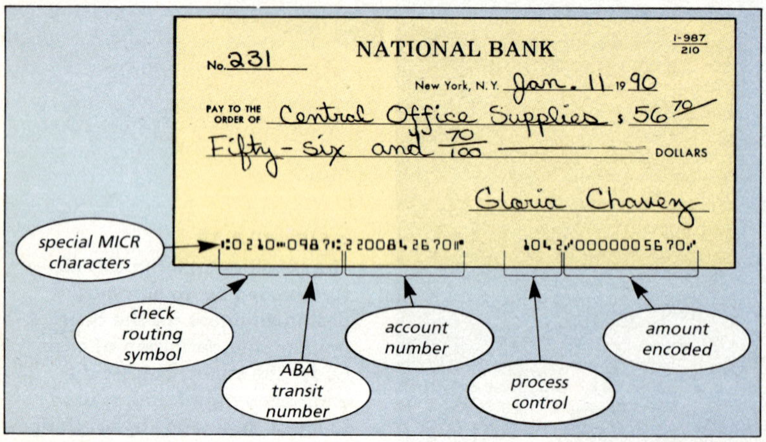

Scanners

Scanners include a variety of devices that "read" printed codes, characters, or images and convert them into a form that can be processed by the computer. This section describes several different types of scanning devices.

Optical Character Readers **Optical character recognition (OCR)** devices are scanners that read typewritten, computer-printed, and in some cases hand-printed characters from ordinary documents. OCR devices range from large machines that can automatically read thousands of documents per minute to hand-held wands (Figure 4-17).

An OCR device scans the shape of a character on a document, compares it with a predefined shape stored in its memory, and converts the character read into a corresponding bit pattern for storing in main memory. The standard OCR typeface, called OCR-A, is illustrated in Figure 4-18 on the next page. The characters can be read easily by both humans and machines. OCR-B is a set of standard characters widely used in Europe and Japan.

FIGURE 4-16 ▲
This MICR reader-sorter can process up to 1,200 documents per minute. After the documents are read, they are sorted into the vertical bins shown in the top center portion of the machine. This device can be connected directly to a computer to allow the documents to be processed as they are read.

◀ FIGURE 4-17
This hand-held optical character recognition device is being used to read a typed document. Such wands can be used for both interactive and batch data entry.

FIGURE 4-18
In the full OCR-A standard character set shown above. Characters such as B and 8, S and 5, and zero and the letter O are designed so the reading device can easily distinguish between them.

FIGURE 4-19
These hand-printed characters can be read by some types of OCR devices. The two small dots in each square identify where certain portions of each numeric digit must be placed.

Some optical character readers can read hand-printed characters. Building a machine able to read and interpret hand-printed characters is a challenging task even in this era of high technology. The characters must be carefully printed according to a strict set of rules regarding their shapes. The example in Figure 4-19 illustrates the shape of hand-printed characters that can be read with an OCR device.

The most widespread application for OCR devices is for reading turn-around documents prepared by computer printers. A **turn-around document** is designed to be returned to the organization that originally issued it. When the document is returned ("turned around"), the data on it is read by an OCR device. For example, many utility bills, department store bills, insurance premium statements, and so on request that the consumer return the statement with a payment (Figure 4-20). The statement is printed with characters that can be read by OCR devices. When the customer returns it, the machine reads it to give proper credit for the payment received. Some OCR devices, such as the one shown in Figure 4-20, are small enough to fit on top of a desk.

Optical Mark Readers An **Optical mark reader (OMR)** is a scanning device that can read carefully placed pencil marks on specially designed documents. The pencil marks on the form usually indicate responses to questions and can be read and interpreted by a computer program. Optical mark readers are frequently used to score tests.

FIGURE 4-20
In this picture, utility company payment receipts are being read by an OCR device. These receipts are examples of turn-around documents because they were designed to be returned to the utility with the customer's payment.

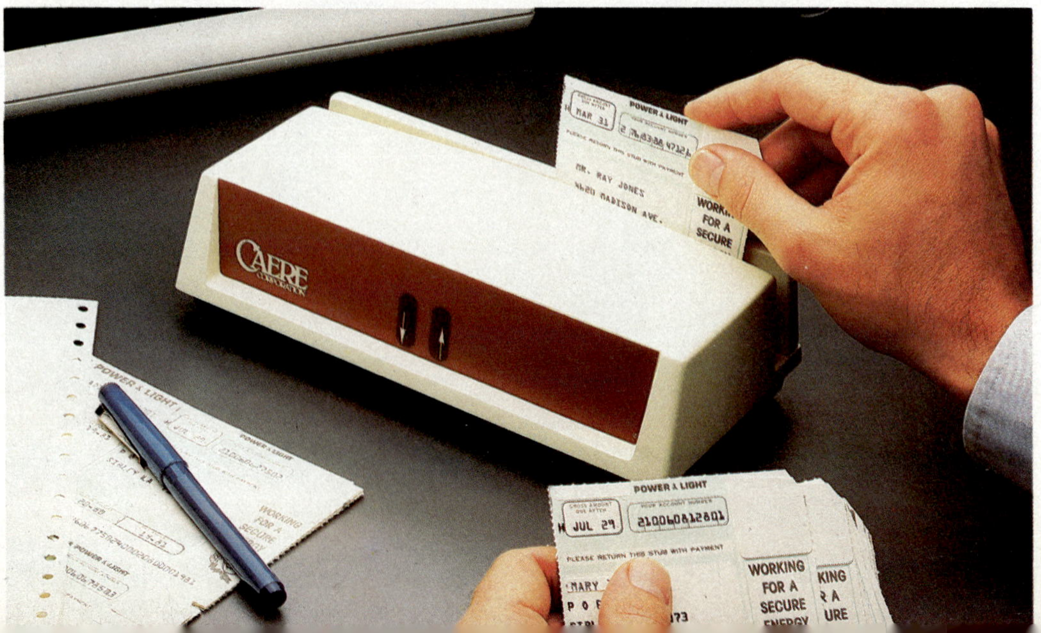

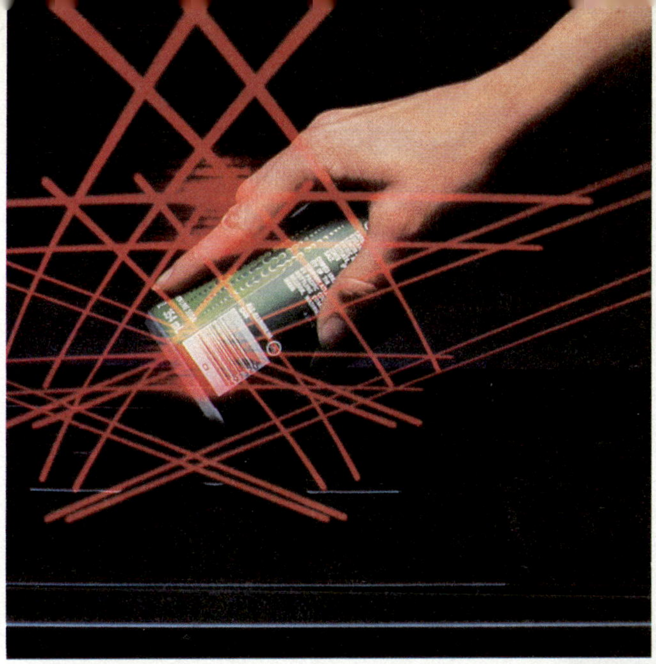

FIGURE 4-21
Most modern grocery stores use optical scanning devices such as the one shown here. A laser beam, emitted from the opening on the counter, reads the bar code on the product package. Most retail products have the Universal Product Code (UPC) imprinted somewhere on the label or package. The UPC code uniquely identifies both the manufacturer and the product. The scanning device is connected to a computer system that uses the UPC code to look up the price of the product and add the price into the total sale. A keyboard above the scanner is used to code the numbers for items such as fruit, which do not have UPC labels.

Laser Scanners A scanning device often used by modern grocery stores at checkout counters is a **laser scanner** (Figure 4-21). These devices use a laser beam to scan and read the special bar code printed on the products.

Page Scanners A **page scanner** is a type of scanner that can convert an entire page of printed material into the individual characters and words that can be processed by a word processing program. Other types of scanners can convert images such as photos and art work for eventual use with desktop publishing systems (Figure 4-22).

Image Processing As we've previously discussed, much of the information input to the computer is taken from source documents. Usually, only a portion of the information on the source document is input. But sometimes the entire source document is needed for data, such as a signature or a drawing. In these situations, organizations often implement image processing systems. **Image processing systems** use software and special equipment, including scanners, to input and store an actual image of the source document. These systems are like giant electronic filing cabinets that allow users to rapidly access and review exact reproductions of the original documents (Figure 4-23).

FIGURE 4-22
The scanner at the left can input text, graphics, or photographs for use in word processing or desktop publishing applications.

FIGURE 4-23
Image processing systems record and store an exact copy of a document. These systems are often used by insurance companies that may need to refer to any of hundreds of thousands of documents.

Data Collection Devices

Data entry is not confined to office environments or restricted to dedicated data entry personnel. **Data collection devices** are designed and used for obtaining data at the site where the transaction or event being reported takes place. For example, in Figure 4-24 a man is taking inventory in a warehouse. Rather than write down the number and type of items and then enter this data, he uses a portable data collection device to record the inventory count in the device's memory. After he takes the inventory, the data can be transmitted to a computer for processing.

Unlike most terminals, data collection equipment is designed to be used in environments where heat, humidity, and cleanliness are difficult or impossible to control (Figure 4-25). In addition, data collection devices are often used by people whose primary task is not to enter the data. Entering the data is only a small portion of their job duties. Therefore, the terminals must be easy to operate in any environment.

Using data collection devices can provide important advantages over alternative methods of input preparation. Because the data is entered as it is collected, clerical costs and transcription errors are reduced or eliminated. If the data collection devices are directly connected to the computer, the data is immediately available for processing.

Data collection devices range from portable devices that can be carried throughout a store or factory (such as in Figure 4-24) to sophisticated terminal systems with multiple input stations that feed directly into a central computer. These devices will continue to improve and find increased use in data entry applications.

FIGURE 4-24
This portable data collection device is being used to take an inventory in a warehouse. The data is stored in memory and can later be transferred to a computer system for processing.

Figure 4-26 summarizes the most commonly used input devices. While each device has advantages and disadvantages, each is appropriate for specific applications. Several of these devices incorporate a user interface to be more efficient.

FIGURE 4-25
This photograph illustrates a data collection terminal that has been designed to accommodate the user. Data collection devices should be simple and quick to operate, so that entering the data does not interfere with the main job of the person using the terminal.

DEVICE	DESCRIPTION
Keyboard	Most commonly used input device. Special keys may include numeric keypad, cursor control keys, and function keys.
Terminal	Video display terminals are dumb or intelligent.
Mouse	Small input device used to move the cursor on a screen and select options.
Touch screens	User interacts with the computer by touching the screen.
Graphic input	Light pens, digitizers, and graphics tablets translate graphic data into a form that can be processed by a computer.
Voice input	User enters data and issues commands with spoken words.
MICR reader	Used primarily in banking to read the magnetic ink characters printed on checks.
Scanner	A variety of devices that read printed codes, characters, or images.
Data collection	Used to input data where it is generated.

FIGURE 4-26 This table summarizes some of the more common data input devices.

USER INTERFACES

With the widespread use of terminals and personal computers, input operations are performed by many types of users whose computer knowledge and experience varies greatly. Some users have a limited knowledge of computers and others have many years of experience. In addition, some users interact with computers daily, while others use them only occasionally. Information systems need to provide all users with a means of interacting with the computer efficiently. This is done through user interfaces.

A **user interface** is the combination of hardware and software that allows a user to communicate with a computer system. Through a user interface, users are able to input values that will: (1) respond to messages presented by the computer; (2) control the computer; and (3) request information from the computer. Thus, a user interface provides the means for communication between an information system and the user.

Both the hardware and software working together form a user interface. A terminal is an example of hardware that is frequently part of a user interface. The screen on the terminal displays messages to the user. The devices used for responding to the messages and controlling the computer include the keyboard, the mouse, and other types of input devices. The software associated with an interface are the programs. These programs determine the messages that are given to the user, the manner in which the user can respond, and the actions that will take place based on the user's responses.

EVOLUTION OF USER INTERFACE SOFTWARE

In most instances, the software determines the quality of the user interface. To help you understand user interfaces we examine how user interface software has evolved and where the user interface software technology is today.

When computers were first used for business processing, users did not interact with the computer. Programmers and computer operators were the only people allowed to control the computer processing. While some programmers were also users (for example, scientists who wrote programs so they could use the results in their own work), there was generally little need to worry about the interface with nontechnical users. All that was required was a means for technicians such as operators and programmers, who were familiar with the computer and its operations, to communicate with the software.

In addition, during the early years of computer usage, computers executed programs much more slowly than they do today and memory was very expensive. Therefore, when software was developed, the ease of using a program was secondary to the fact that software had to execute quickly and use as little memory as possible. This dictated that commands and messages be as brief as possible.

When terminals first became available and gave users direct access to the central computer, most software was still difficult to use. Frequently, users had to learn detailed commands to direct the computer to perform the desired tasks. These commands normally consisted of special characters, words, and cryptic abbreviations that made them difficult to learn and remember. Infrequent users often had to retrain themselves each time they wanted to use the machine.

The example in Figure 4-27 illustrates a typical procedure and commands that a user might have used in the 1960s to communicate with the computer. First, users had to "log on" to the computer by identifying themselves. The software would determine if the person was an authorized user and if access to the computer should be allowed. While this is still common today, the procedures for logging on are much easier now than in earlier years. Note that the user had to begin the message with a single slash (/) followed by the word LOGON. This entry was followed immediately by a comma, open quotation marks, a name, and closed quotation marks. A comma was entered next and then the date. This format and spacing had to be followed exactly. A missing comma, quotation mark, slash, or even any one of these in the wrong position would cause the software to issue an error message. Thus, the user needed to know not only the data to be entered, but also the exact format to be followed.

The example in Figure 4-27 shows the additional lines that were required. The entry /T.1 means that terminal 1 was being used. The next entry designated the program to be executed, and the last entry informed the software that the user had entered all the commands. When the /END command was entered, the software would begin performing the processing requested by the user.

FIGURE 4-27
The entries illustrated here represent the type of commands that were required when users first began to have access to computers. Spacing and punctuation also had to be correct for the commands to be accepted. Understandably, many users found it difficult and frustrating to use the computer.

The entries illustrated in this example were acceptable for computer specialists, but such commands were not easy for the general user to master. Both users and computer professionals recognized that there was considerable room for improvement in the software that communicated with users.

The following sections discuss some of the user interface techniques that have been developed, such as prompts and menus, and how they have improved communication between the user and the computer.

Prompts

One of the first steps in improving user interface software was to display prompts on the screen. A **prompt** is a message to the user that displays on the screen and provides helpful information or instructions regarding some entry to be made or action to be taken.

The example in Figure 4-28 illustrates the use of prompts. On the first line, the prompt ENTER LAST NAME: appears on the screen. This message tells the user to enter his or her last name.

After the user enters his or her last name, a second prompt displays. This prompt, ENTER DATE (MM/DD/YY), indicates not only what is to be entered but also the exact format it should have. MM/DD/YY means to enter the date as a two-digit month number followed by a slash (/), a two-digit day number followed by a slash, and a two-digit year number. Thus, the entry 04/05/90 is valid, but 4/5/90 is not.

To help ensure that the user inputs valid data, the software should use **data editing**, the ability to check the data for proper format and acceptable values. When data is entered incorrectly, a message should be displayed so that the user becomes aware of the error and can reenter the data. The example in Figure 4-29 illustrates what might occur when the data is not entered in the correct format. Note that an error message displays and requests the user to reenter the date.

Prompts, combined with data editing, were a great stride forward in developing user interfaces. Today, prompts are widely used to assist users in entering valid input and communicating with computer systems.

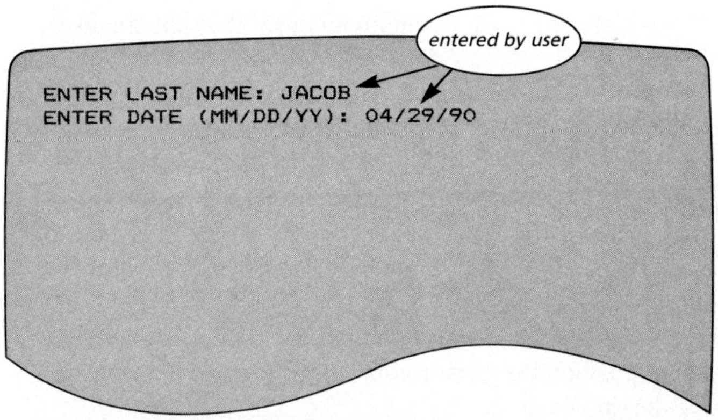

FIGURE 4-28
Prompts aid the user in entering data. They can tell the user what data to enter as well as the required format (as shown for the date entry). Prompts were one of the first types of interfaces designed to assist the user in utilizing the computer.

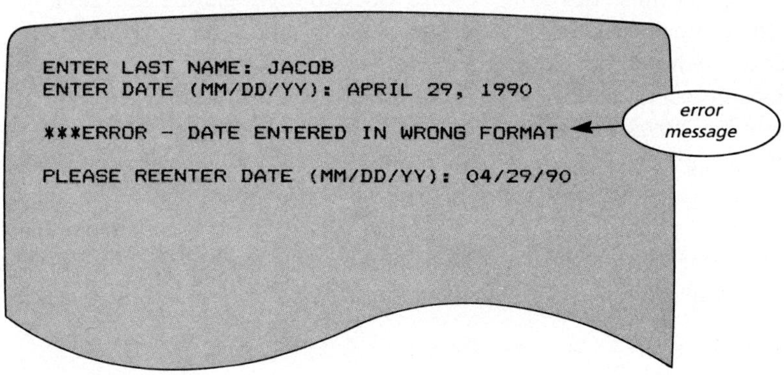

FIGURE 4-29
The software used for this screen checks the date entered and gives an error message if the date is entered in the wrong format.

Menus

As user interfaces continued to develop, people who wrote software recognized that much of the data entry users required was involved with choosing alternatives. For example, the user might have to choose which of four software programs to execute, which of five documents to use during word processing, or which function to perform in an electronic spreadsheet application. To allow the user to make an easy choice from various alternatives, menus were developed.

A **menu** is a display on a screen that allows a user to make a selection from multiple alternatives. A menu generally consists of three parts (Figure 4-30): a title, the selections, and a prompt. The title identifies the menu and orients the user to the choices that can be made. The selections consist of both a means for identifying the choices and the words that describe them. The prompt asks the user to enter one of the selections.

The screens in Figure 4-31 illustrate several ways in which a user can choose word processing from menus.

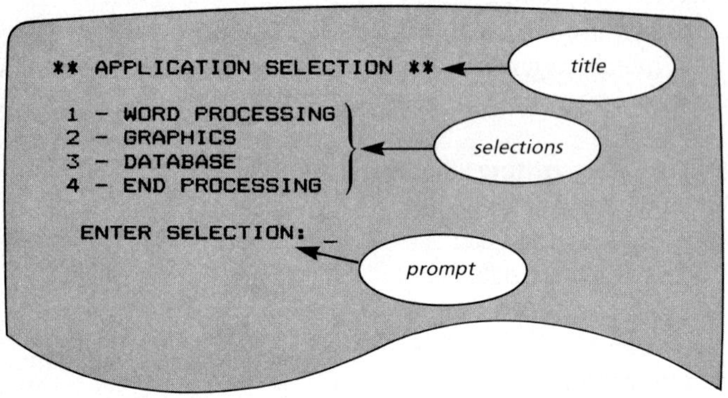

FIGURE 4-30
A menu consists of a title, the selections that can be made, and a prompt for the user to make an entry.

Sequential Number In Example 1, each of the selections is identified by a number. The user enters the numbers 1, 2, 3, or 4 to select the desired processing operation. Entering a 1 means that the word processing program will be retrieved from auxiliary storage and brought into main memory for execution. Entering a 2 executes the graphics program, and entering a 3, the database program. Menus should always contain an entry that lets the user exit. In Example 1, this is entry 4.

Alphabetic Selection In Example 2 letters of the alphabet identify the various processing options. The user makes a selection by entering the letter next to the processing description. Sometimes the letters used are simply A, B, C, and D but the person who designed this menu chose to make the letters significant. Thus, entering W will select word processing; entering G selects graphics; D, database; and E ends the processing.

Cursor Positioning Example 3 illustrates a menu in which the choice is made by using the arrow or cursor control keys to position the cursor adjacent to the desired selection. Then the Enter key is pressed to make the choice.

Reverse Video Example 4 illustrates using reverse video to highlight the selection. **Reverse video** means that the normal screen display pattern, such as amber on black, is reversed to highlight and draw attention to a certain character, word, or section of the screen. In the example, the directions instruct the user to move the reverse video from one selection to another by pressing the space bar. Pressing the space bar once moves the reverse video from the word processing option to graphics; pressing it again highlights the database option. If the space bar was pressed when reverse video was highlighting the end processing option, the reverse video would move to word processing. This is called **wraparound**. It is a shortcut that allows users to go quickly from the bottom to the top or from the top to the bottom of a menu. To make a selection in reverse video, the user highlights the desired procedure and presses the Return key.

Icon Selection In Example 5, the same reverse video method is used to highlight the choices, but the choices are also identified by graphic images or icons. An **icon** is a pictorial representation of a function to be performed on the computer. Pressing the space bar highlights each of the words under the graphic in reverse video. Pressing the Return key executes the chosen function.

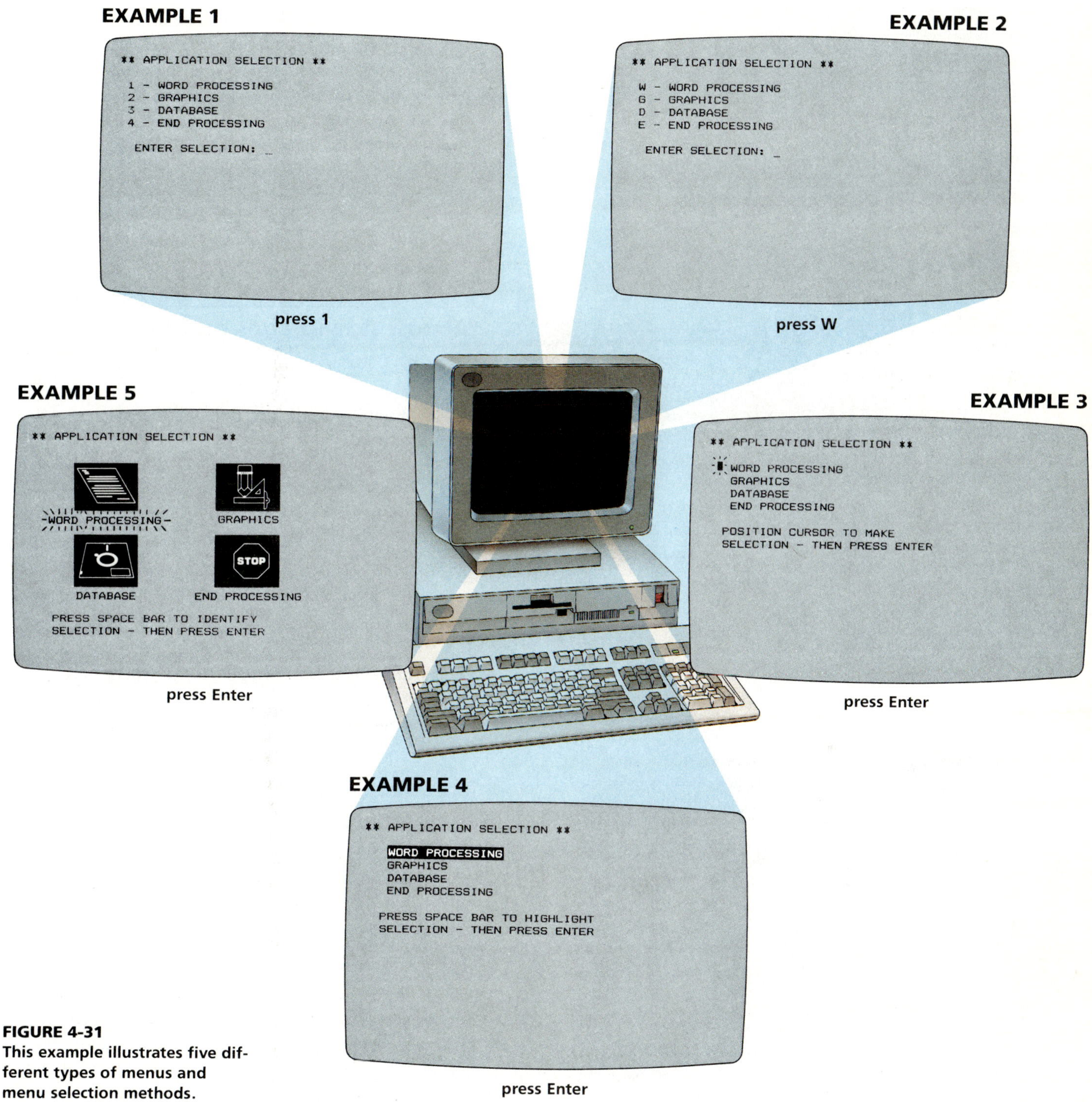

FIGURE 4-31
This example illustrates five different types of menus and menu selection methods.

From these examples, it is clear that a variety of methods can be used to identify and choose the selections in a menu.

Submenus

Some applications require the use of several related menus. Menus that further define the operations that can be performed are called **submenus**.

The example in Figure 4-32 illustrates the main menu from Example 1 in Figure 4-31,

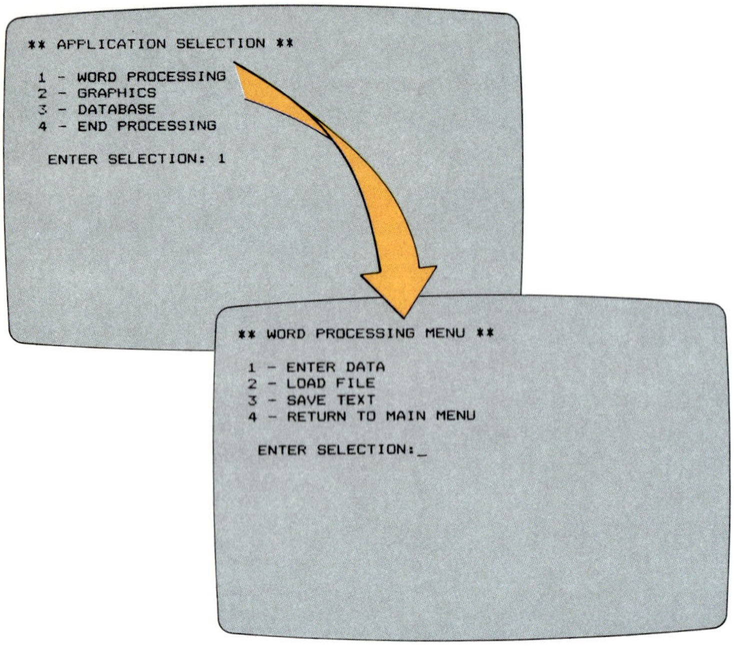

FIGURE 4-32
A submenu is used when additional selections can be made within an application. In this example, the submenu displays additional word processing selections.

which allows the user to select word processing, graphics, or database. When the word processing function is selected, a submenu appears. This submenu contains more detailed functions. Depending on the submenu selection, additional menus could be displayed. For example, if the user selected option 1, enter data, from the submenu shown in Figure 4-32, a third menu could appear that would display selections relative to margin settings, page length, and other word processing functions.

Menus: Advantages and Disadvantages

Menus are a type of user interface that is used with all sizes and types of computers. There are both advantages and disadvantages to menus. Some of the advantages are:

1. The user does not have to remember special commands. He or she merely chooses a selection from a list of possible operations or functions.
2. The user can become productive with a minimum of training. Instead of having to learn a lot of technical computer information, he or she merely needs to understand the application and the results of choosing a particular option from the menu.
3. The user is guided through the application because only the options that are available are presented.

The disadvantage most often associated with menus, according to some experienced users, is that they can be slow and restrictive. For example, the menus illustrated in Figure 4-32 are good for the novice or infrequent computer user because they take him or her step-by-step through the possible operations that can be performed. The experienced user, however, knows what processing is required. Therefore, he or she may prefer to enter a few quick commands and immediately begin work instead of having to view and respond to two or more menus.

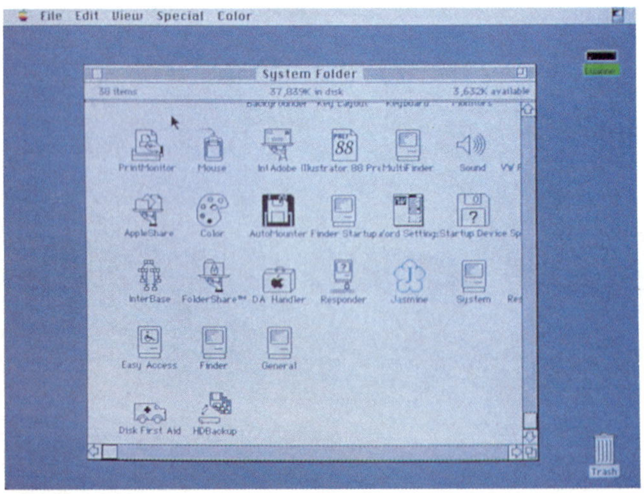

FIGURE 4-33
This screen illustrates icons representing functions or data that the user can select. In the upper right corner, for example, the icon of a speaker refers to the turning off or turning on of sounds the computer can make to signal errors and other messages to the user. Icons allow the user to quickly identify the processing options available.

GRAPHICS

Graphics can play an important role in aiding the user to effectively interact with a computer. For example, in Figure 4-33, the user's option to choose color is represented by the icon (picture) of an artist's palette. An icon representing functions to be performed on a computer is helpful because people not familiar with computer terminology can still use the machine.

FEATURES OF A USER INTERFACE

The following list identifies some features that should be included in a good user interface.

1. System responses to the user—**System responses** are those messages and actions taken by the computer when a user enters data into the computer. In a well-designed system, the user receives a response for every action taken. A response can be shown in two ways. First, a message can be displayed that tells the user something is happening. For example, when a large program is being loaded into main memory from auxiliary storage, the message "Program Loading" would appear on the screen. A second type of feedback occurs when the screen changes based on an entry by the user. For example, in Figure 4-32, when the user chose selection 1 from the main menu, a submenu immediately displayed on the screen. This action told the user that the data had been accepted by the computer and was being operated on. Without a response from the computer, the user does not know if the input was accepted. A response from the system avoids user confusion.

   A second issue with respect to user response is response time. **Response time** is the elapsed time between the instant a user enters data and the instant the computer responds. A common guideline for response time is that it should never be greater than two seconds. When the activity requested by the user will require more than two seconds for the computer to accomplish, a message such as "Processing—Please Wait" should be displayed.
2. Screen design—The design of the messages and pictures that appear on the screen can have a significant impact on the usability of the system. The most important rule is to keep the screen uncluttered and simple. Each message and each action that a user must take should be clear and easily understood. All messages, menus, and prompts within a system should follow a consistent format. This reduces the time needed for users to learn how to use a system and increases ease of use for experienced users.
3. User responses—In general, the simpler the entry required from the user, the better the user interface. Users are seldom skilled typists. Thus, if the user does not have to enter a large number of characters, data entry will be faster and fewer errors will occur.
4. Error recovery—Because errors are inevitable, it should be as easy as possible for a user to recover from one. Whenever the user makes an error, three user interface activities should take place: (1) the user should be alerted that an error has been made; (2) the error should be identified as specifically as possible; and (3) the user should be told how to recover from the error. In general, error recovery can take place in three ways: (1) the user can reenter the data that caused the error; (2) the user can "back up" to a previous operation; or (3) the user can exit from the operation where the error was made.
5. Control and security—Many multiuser computer systems require users to "sign on" to the computer by entering an identification, such as a name or account number followed by a password. A **password** is a value, such as a word or number, which identifies the user. Unless the user enters the password, the computer will not allow access to the machine. These procedures help to ensure that only authorized users obtain access to the computer.

The systems and procedures listed on the previous page should be kept in mind by computer professionals when designing and developing user interfaces, and by users when they are evaluating software or hardware for purchase.

The question that must be asked when designing or deciding on a user interface is, Who will be using it and what is their level of computer experience? A good user interface must be appropriate for the people who are going to be using it.

DATA ENTRY FOR INTERACTIVE AND BATCH PROCESSING

As discussed in Chapter 3, computer applications use either interactive or batch processing methods to process data into information. The methods used to enter data for interactive and batch processing differ. We explain them in the following paragraphs.

Data Entry for Interactive Processing

Data entered in the interactive processing mode generates immediate output. In most interactive data entry, the person entering the data is communicating directly with the computer that will process the data. Therefore, data entry for interactive processing is said to be **online data entry**, meaning that the device from which the data is being entered is connected directly to the computer.

FIGURE 4-34
In this example of data entry for interactive processing, the data is entered by a terminal operator in the order entry department. The output generated, a picking slip, is printed in the warehouse. In addition, a record of the order is stored on disk.

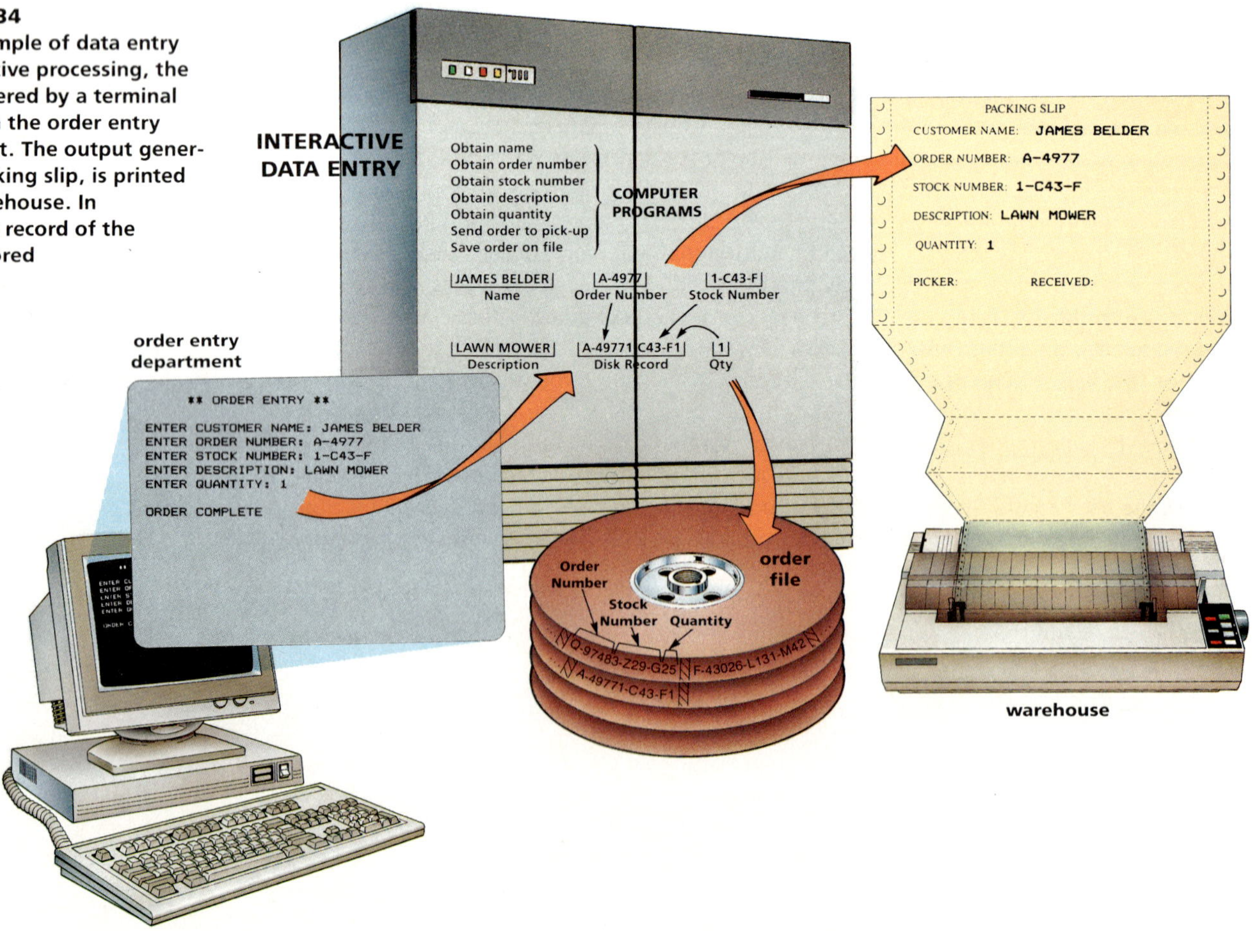

The output generated from interactive data entry processing is not always produced at the location where the data was entered. In Figure 4-34, for example, the data is entered from a terminal located in the order entry department. The data entered concerns a purchase by a customer. After the data is entered, a picking slip is printed in the warehouse. The worker in the warehouse would then retrieve the item purchased (in this case, a lawn mower) and package it for shipping. The terminal operator in the order entry department never sees the output generated, yet this is interactive processing because the data entered is processed immediately.

The person entering the order in the order entry department may enter hundreds of such orders each day. When large amounts of data are entered by a terminal operator whose only job is to enter the data, the data entry function is said to be **production data entry**.

Data Entry for Batch Processing

When data is entered for processing in the batch processing mode, it is stored on a storage medium (usually tape or disk) for processing at a later time. Data for batch processing can be entered in either an online or offline manner. As noted previously, online data entry means that the device from which the data is being entered is connected directly to the computer that will process it (Figure 4-35).

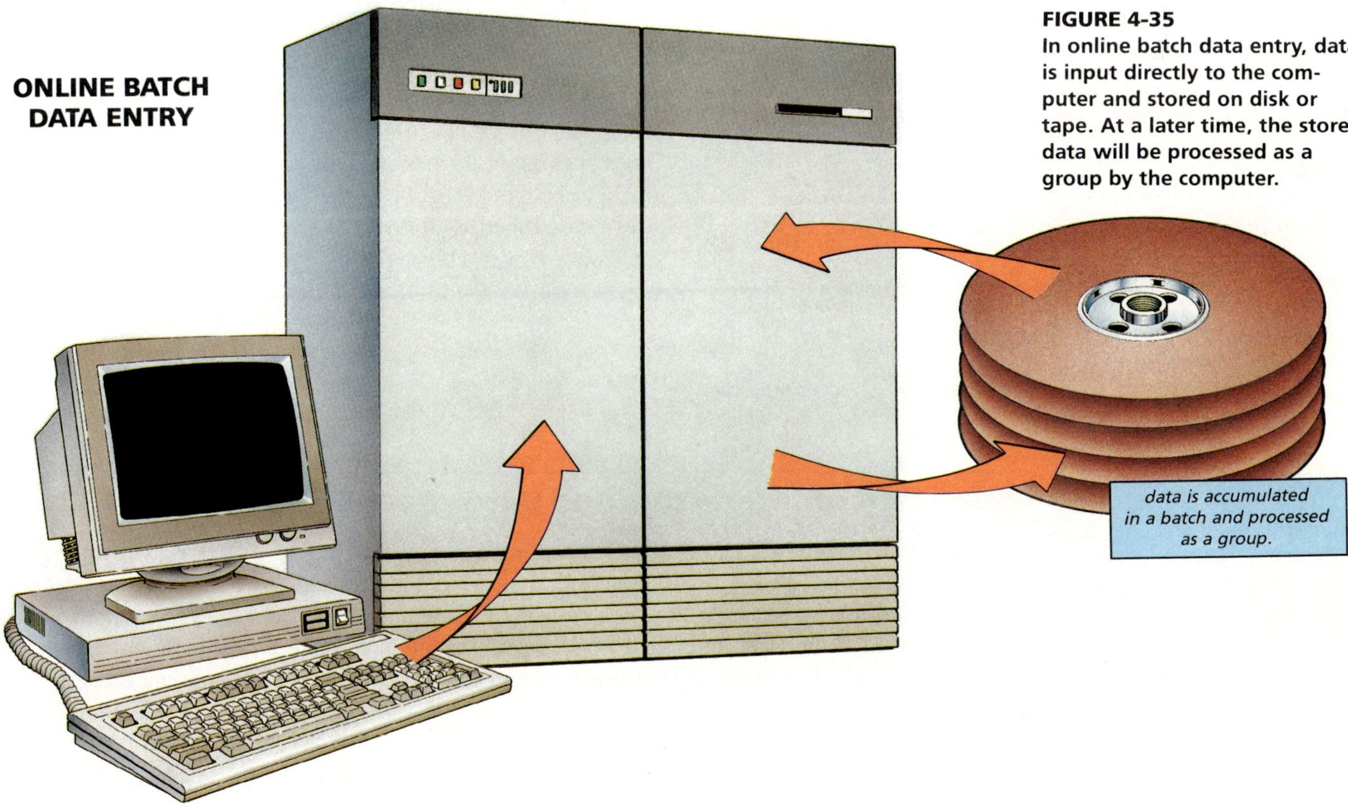

FIGURE 4-35
In online batch data entry, data is input directly to the computer and stored on disk or tape. At a later time, the stored data will be processed as a group by the computer.

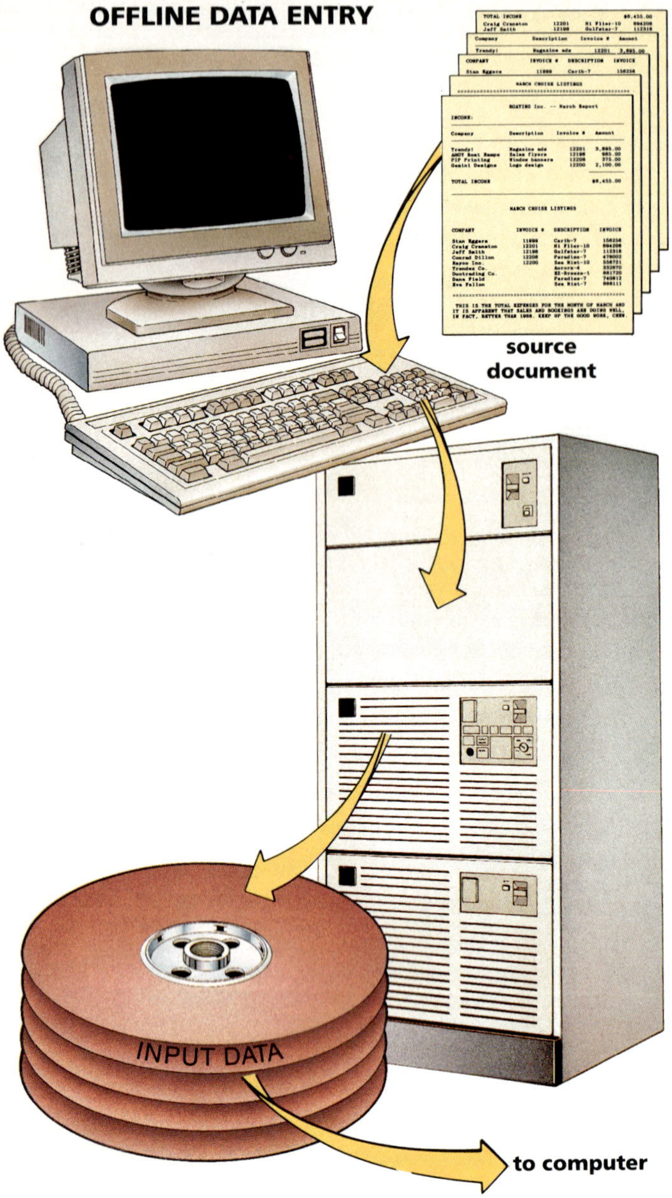

FIGURE 4-36
In offline data entry, the data is input to a computer other than the one that will eventually process it. Often computers used for offline data entry are dedicated to data input functions and perform little if any processing. The data entered is later transferred to another computer for processing.

Offline data entry means that the device from which the data is being entered is not connected to the computer that will process it (Figure 4-36). Instead, the data is entered using a dedicated computer or other device devoted to the data entry function. This computer or special device accepts the input data and stores it on disk or tape. At a later time, the disk or tape can be transported to the site where the data will be entered for processing in a batch mode to produce information. An example of such a system is the key-to-disk shared processor system shown in Figure 4-37.

When offline data entry is used, source documents must be accumulated prior to entering the data. For example, in a payroll application, timecards for hourly employees would be the source documents from which the hours worked would be entered by the data entry operators.

In many applications, controls are established to ensure that data is entered and processed accurately. In a credit card payment application, for example, payments are usually divided into batches for processing. The payments for each batch are added manually and recorded prior to data entry. When the payment batches are processed on the computer, the total amount of the payments calculated by the computer for each batch is compared to the total determined from the manual addition performed prior to data entry. If the totals are the same, it is evidence that the data was input to the computer accurately. If the totals are not the same, however, then further checking must be performed to determine if the data was entered incorrectly or if the manually determined batch total was wrong. This technique of balancing to a predetermined total is called a **batch control**.

Summary of Interactive and Batch Data Entry

Entering data to produce information can take place online or offline. Online data entry is always used for interactive processing and often for batch processing as well. Offline data entry is used for batch processing. When using offline data entry, source documents from which the data is obtained must be gathered prior to the data being entered. Regardless of the processing method, producing information often requires a large amount of data entry.

AN EXAMPLE OF ONLINE DATA ENTRY

Many types of devices can be used to enter data but by far the most common device is the terminal. We illustrate using terminals for online data entry with an order entry example. Order entry is the process followed when an order is received from a customer. An order entry application usually proceeds in the following manner:

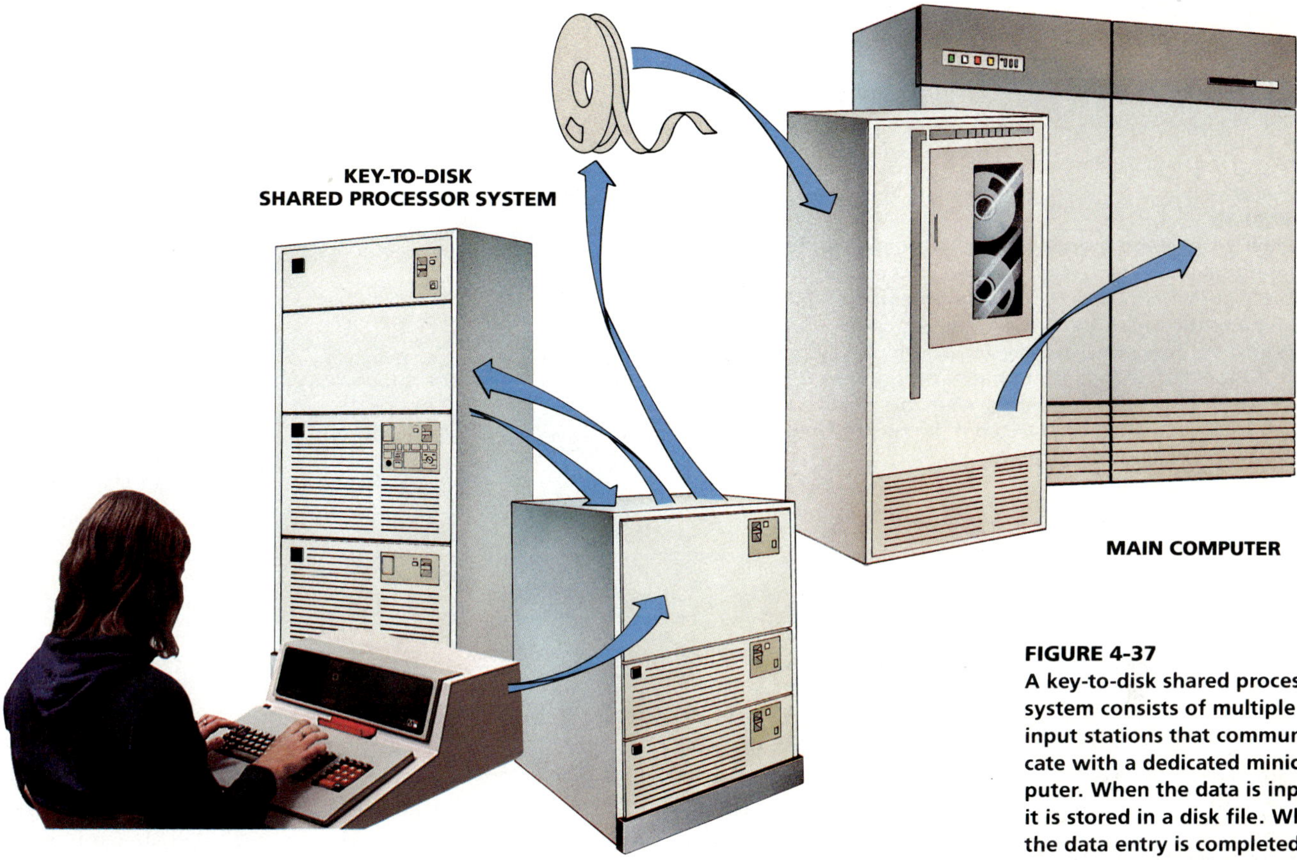

FIGURE 4-37
A key-to-disk shared processor system consists of multiple input stations that communicate with a dedicated minicomputer. When the data is input, it is stored in a disk file. When the data entry is completed, the disk file is output to tape. The tape is then physically transferred to another computer that will process the data.

1. The order is received from the customer, either through the mail or over the telephone, and the data concerning the customer and the order is entered into the computer by the data entry operator.
2. When the order is entered, the order entry program performs a credit check by retrieving credit data from a credit file stored on disk. The order is stored in the open order disk file so that a record of it is retained.
3. In addition, when the order is entered, the order entry program controlling the data entry operation determines if the item ordered is in inventory by reading a record from an inventory file or database. If the item ordered is in inventory, a picking slip is printed in the warehouse. A picking slip alerts warehouse personnel that an order has been received and specifies who the customer is and what items are to be shipped. Then, or at a later time, the warehouse personnel retrieve the item and package it for shipping. When the item is shipped, they will enter that information into the computer. Then the record for the order will be removed from the open order file and placed in the shipped file.
4. If the item ordered is not in the warehouse inventory, the order record will be placed in the backorder file and the customer will be notified that the item is not available. A backorder is an order for an item that is not currently in inventory. The order will be held until the item is available, at which time the order will be filled.

The following sections explain the data entry procedure that could be followed by a person entering orders using an online entry system.

Order Entry Menu

The data entry process for the sample order entry system begins with the Order Entry menu (Figure 4-38). In this example, the function to be performed is entering orders. Therefore, the data entry operator enters the value 1 to choose the option ENTER ORDERS.

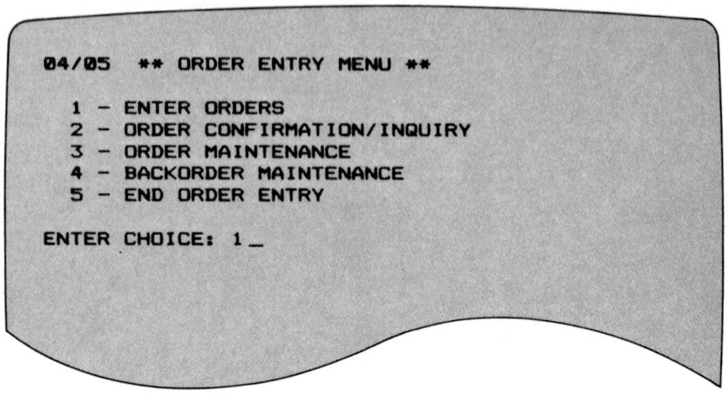

FIGURE 4-38
The Order Entry menu specifies the options available for processing sales orders. Option 1 allows orders to be entered. Option 2 provides for order confirmations and inquiries into the order file. Option 3 allows certain changes to be made to orders, such as revising the ship to address. Option 4 provides for changes to backorders, orders for products that were not in inventory when the order was entered. Option 5 would be selected if the user wanted to end the order processing function.

Enter Orders

The following six steps are illustrated in Figure 4-39.

In Step 1, when the data entry operator chooses option 1 on the main menu, the first of two screens required to enter orders displays. The screen contains colors to designate different types of information. The blue characters are either headings or prompts that identify the fields to be processed. Each area where data will be displayed or entered is shown in reverse video. The white areas indicate fields that must be entered by the data entry operator. The red areas will contain fixed data based on the operator's entries. These fixed areas cannot be changed by the data entry operator. The yellow areas indicate **default values**, data that will be automatically displayed but which can be changed by the operator if needed.

In Step 2, the operator enters the data for the first field, the customer number. Here the value AE-1073 is the number for the customer ordering items. Note that instead of reverse video when the data is entered, the actual characters display in the same color as the reverse video; that is, the customer number displays in white because the reverse video was in white. The process of entering the data is shown in Figure 4-40 on the next page, where the first character (A) has been entered. The character is white but the rest of the input area on the screen where data has not yet been entered retains the reverse video. This technique is commonly used on terminals where reverse video identifies input fields.

Step 3 shows what the screen would look like after the operator enters the customer number. The order number is generated by the order entry computer program. It displays in red because the terminal operator cannot reference or change the order number. The bill to data also displays in red because it will not be changed. The bill to data, which is the name of the company and the address to which the bill for the items will be sent, was obtained from a customer file based on the customer number that was entered. The ship to data identifies the place to which the items will be sent. The company name displays in red because it will not be changed. The ship to address, however, displays reversed on a yellow background because the data is default data. It is used in data entry so that the operator does not have to spend time entering data that normally does not change. In this case, the address shown is the same as the bill to address because most of the time, items ordered by Hinkle Ltd. are shipped to the same address. This is the default address, so the operator would merely press the Enter key and continue to the next field. In this example, however, the ship to address is to be changed. Therefore, the operator must key in the new ship to address. Step 4 shows how the new ship to address displays.

FIGURE 4-39
These six steps show how data would be entered in the first screen of a sample order entry application.

STEP 1

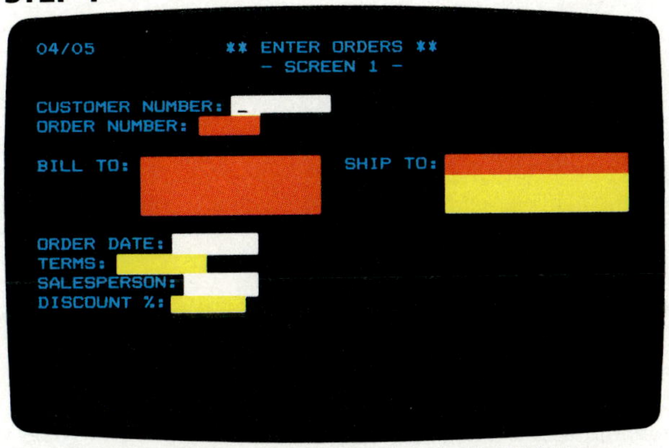

Step 1: Each field is identified by color. The blue fields are titles and prompts. The red fields will contain data that cannot be changed. The white fields must be entered by the operator. The yellow fields are default fields.

STEP 2

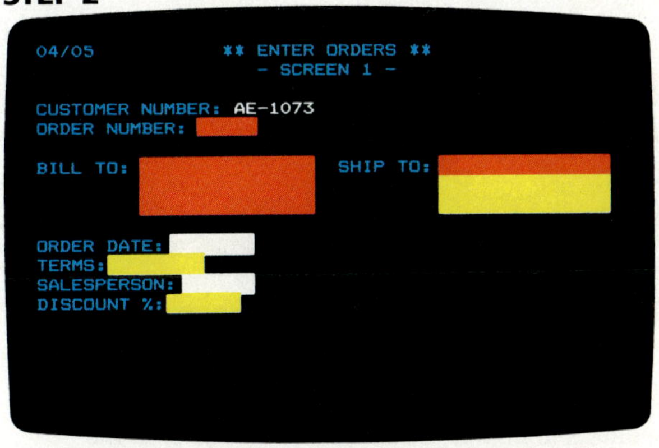

Step 2: In this step, the data entry operator has entered the customer number. The customer number is displayed in white letters because the operator had to enter the data. The operator would then press the Enter key to continue.

STEP 3

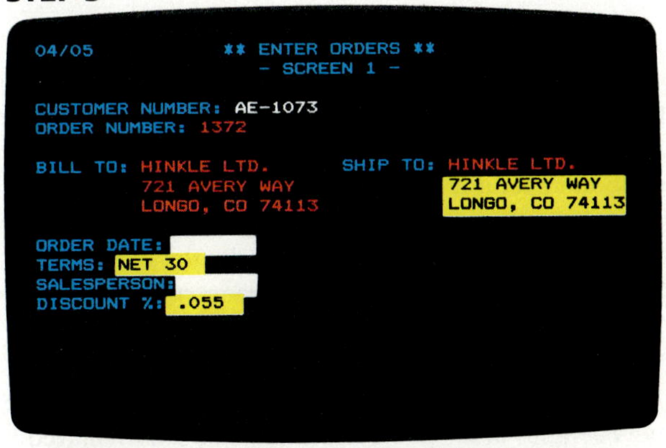

Step 3: Data retrieved from a customer file based on the customer number is displayed on the screen. The cursor is placed on the ship to address. The operator can enter data here if it is different from the default values.

STEP 4

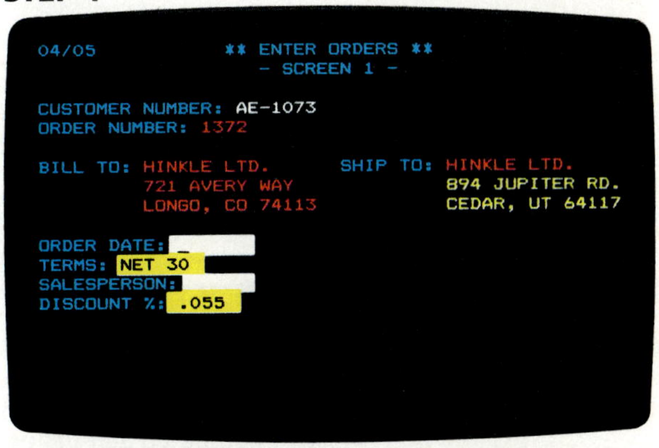

Step 4: The order date must be entered by the operator. Therefore, it is displayed in white. The default values in the ship to field have been changed to yellow characters because they have now been entered.

STEP 5

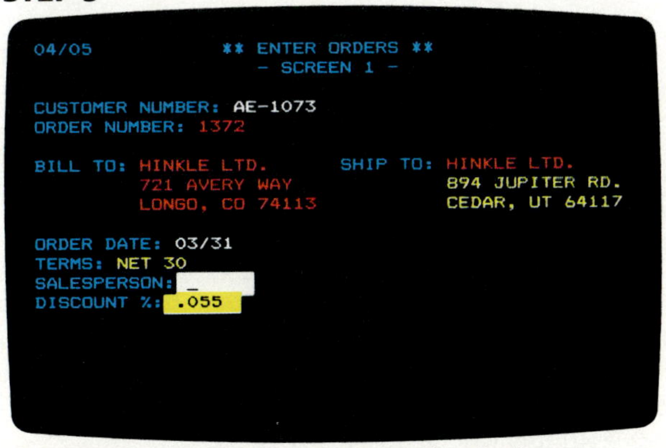

Step 5: The salesperson must be entered by the data entry operator. The default value in the terms field specified net 30. The operator accepted the default value by pressing the Enter key instead of entering new data.

STEP 6

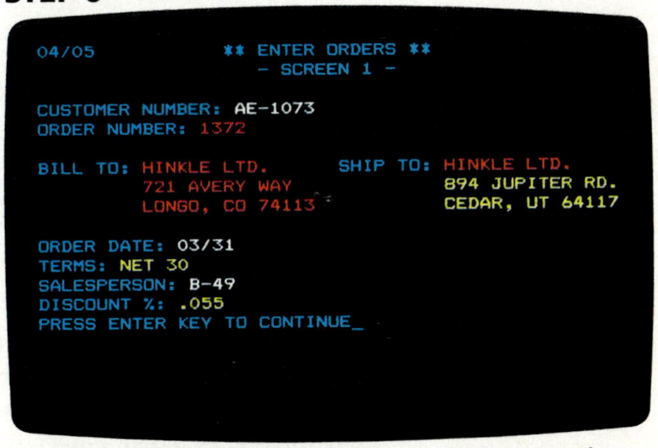

Step 6: After the data entry operation for the first screen has been completed, all data is displayed as color characters on a black screen. The reverse video is not necessary because no data remains to be entered.

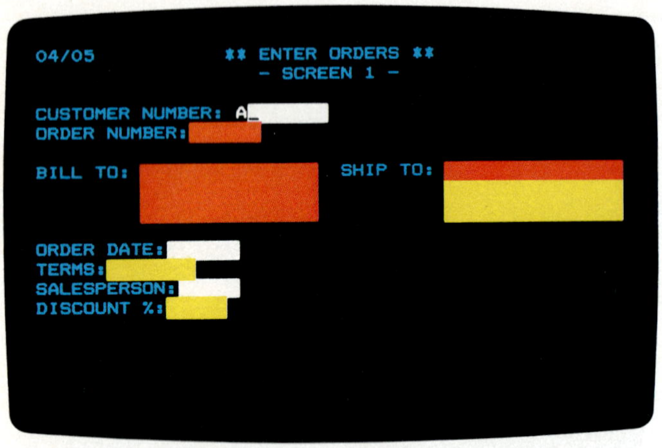

FIGURE 4-40
When a value is entered in a reverse video field, the normal technique is to display the character in the color of the reverse video field and to remove the reverse video field for that character. Here, the letter A has been entered into a white field; therefore, the letter is displayed in white on a black background.

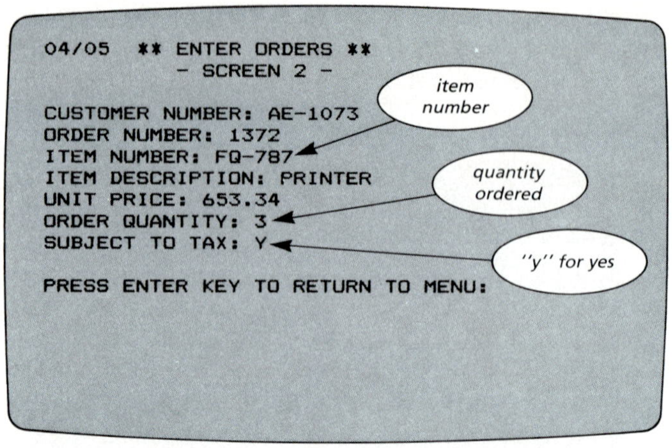

FIGURE 4-41
On the second order entry screen, the operator enters the item number and the quantity ordered. The program uses the item number to look up and display the item description and the unit price. The subject to tax default value is Y, but the operator can change it.

Next, the controlling program places the cursor at the order date field (Step 5) and the operator enters the order date (03/31). The order date field is white because the operator must always enter the order date.

In Step 5, by pressing the Enter key, the operator has accepted the default terms that the program displayed. The salesperson data, however, must be entered by the operator because it is in white. The default value for the discount percent is also accepted by the operator.

Step 6 shows how the screen would look after all data entry has been completed for the first order entry screen.

Next, the operator presses the Enter key to display the second screen required for the order entry operation (Figure 4-41). On this screen, the operator must enter the number of the item purchased and the order quantity. The item description and unit price are displayed by the order entry program. The single default value on this screen is the subject to tax field. Here, the operator can change the Y (signifying yes to the question, Is this purchase subject to tax?) to N. In this example, the default value was accepted. After entering all the data, the operator can press the Enter key to return to the main menu (Figure 4-38) and enter another order.

This example is a composite of many different order entry systems and illustrates some of the features of these systems.

DATA ENTRY PROCEDURES

The procedures developed for the data entry function are important because accurate data must be entered into a computer to ensure data integrity. In addition, since users are interacting directly with the computer during the data entry function, procedures and documentation must be quite clear. The following issues must be addressed in order to implement a data entry application successfully:

1. Origination of data—Data entered for processing on a computer is generated from many sources throughout a company. It is important to identify which people and operations will generate the data so that appropriate procedures can be written to specify what data is to be gathered, how it is to be gathered, and who is to gather it.
2. Location of the data entry function—Data is generally entered either from the centralized data entry section of the information systems department or from various locations throughout an organization. The hardware, software and personnel needs vary depending upon which of these two locations is used. In a **centralized data entry** operation, the data is keyed by trained operators from source documents. When data is entered in the centralized data entry section, it is usually processed in a batch processing mode.

   Entering data from various locations in an organization is called **distributed data entry**. Quite often the data entry takes place at the site where the data is generated, for example, sales orders being entered by the sales department. Often, data entered using distributed data entry is processed in an interactive processing mode.
3. Timing requirements for acquiring the data—In some applications, the time of day or the day of the week when the data becomes available is important. For example, if all timecards for employees must be received by Monday at 4 p.m. for employees to be paid Friday, timing is important and must be identified in the documentation for the data entry.
4. Timing requirements for entering the data—The amount of time that can elapse between when the event being reported takes place and when the data about that event must be entered should be specified. In some applications, an event can occur but the data need not be entered until hours or even days later. For example, in the payroll application mentioned above, timecards are retrieved Monday at 4 p.m. These timecards record the workers' time for the previous week. The data may not be entered until Tuesday. Therefore, more than a week might elapse between when the event occurred and when the data about the event was entered.

   In most cases when entry time is not a critical factor, the data is recorded on source documents and given to data entry personnel in either a centralized or distributed location to enter. In other applications, however, the data must be entered as the event or transaction is occurring and at the location where it is occurring. This process is sometimes called **source data collection**. For example, when a retail sale is made using a point of sale terminal, the data must be entered at the moment the sale is made so that the sale can be completed with the customer. Therefore, it is important that the documentation for the data entry system specify the timing requirements for entering data.
5. Flow of the input data—The documentation must specify the flow of the data from the point where it originates to the point where it is entered for processing on the computer. Any handling required, any recording on source documents, and any changes in format from source to data entry must be documented.
6. Transaction volume—The amount of data entered for a given time period and location must be estimated. Any particularly high or low volumes may require special procedures.
7. Manner of entering the data—Based on many of the factors specified in items 1–6, the procedures must specify how the data is to be entered, identifying devices and methods. For example, it could be specified that data is to be entered from source documents using terminals in an online, centralized environment.
8. Editing and error handling—The documentation must specify the editing for the entered data and the steps to take if the data is not valid. Although different applications will have specific criteria for validating input data, there are a number of tests that are performed on input data before the data is processed in a computer. Some of these tests are:

   a. Tests for numeric or alphabetic data (Figure 4-42)—For example, in the United States a zip code must always be numeric. Therefore, the program performing the editing can check the values in the zip code field. If they are not numeric, the data is incorrect.

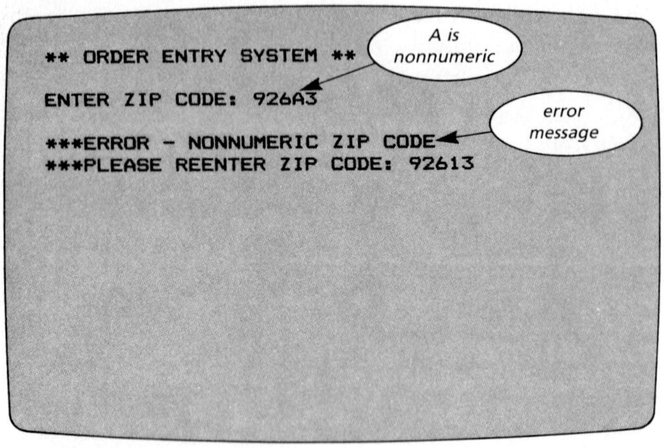

FIGURE 4-42
In this example, a nonnumeric zip code is entered and an error message displays. When a numeric zip code is entered, the data is accepted and no error message displays.

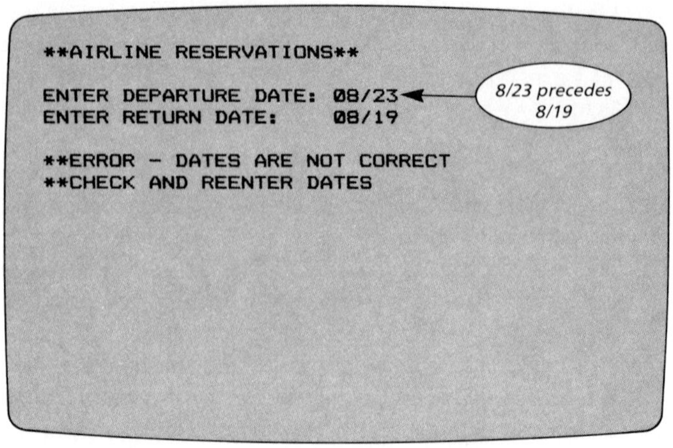

FIGURE 4-43
On this airline reservation screen, the user entered a return date earlier than the departure date and the system displayed an error message.

b. Tests for data reasonableness—A reasonableness check ensures that the data entered is within normal or accepted boundaries. For example, suppose no employee within a company is authorized to work more than 80 hours per week. If the value entered in the hours worked field is greater than 80, the value in the field would be indicated as a probable error.

c. Tests for data consistency—In some cases, data entered cannot, by itself, be found to be invalid. If, however, the data is examined in the context of other data entered for the same record or group of fields, discrepancies might be found. For example, in an airline reservation system, round-trip tickets are often purchased (Figure 4-43). If the terminal operator enters the date on which the passenger is leaving, the editing program can only check whether the date entered is valid. Similarly, when the return date is entered, the program can again make sure it is a valid date. In addition, however, the return date can be compared to the departure date. If the return date is earlier than the departure date, it is likely that an error has been made when entering one of the dates.

d. Tests for transcription and transposition errors—There is always a possibility that an operator will make an error when entering data. A **transcription error** occurs when an error is made in copying the values from a source document. For example, if the operator keys the customer number 7165 when the proper number is 7765, a transcription error has been made. A **transposition error** happens when the operator switches two numbers. Such an error has occurred when the number 7765 is entered as 7756.

9. Data controls and security—The controls and security that will be applied to the data must be defined. This includes what the controls and security measures are, how they are to be implemented, and what action is to be taken if the security of the data is compromised in any way.

10. Personnel requirements—Specifying personnel requirements includes defining who will gather the data, who will enter it, and how many people will be required to enter the data for the application. Personnel must be educated about gathering and entering the data. They must be trained in using the equipment and software, ensuring reliable data entry, entering the data according to specified procedures, and interpreting any output received from the computer during interactive processing.

ERGONOMICS

To be efficient when you are using a computer, it is important that you be comfortable. Being comfortable results in less fatigue, better accuracy, and higher input rates, factors that are important to all users, but particularly to data entry personnel. **Ergonomics** is the study of the design and arrangement of equipment so that people will interact with the equipment in a healthy, comfortable, and efficient manner. As related to computer equipment, ergonomics is concerned with such factors as the physical design of the keyboard, screens, and related hardware, and the manner in which people interact with these hardware devices.

The first computer terminals contained the keyboard and screen as a single unit. The screen frequently displayed white characters on a black background. Early studies found significant user dissatisfaction with the terminals. One study reported that 90% of the personnel who used these terminals complained of health problems, including eye fatigue, blurred vision, itching and burning eyes, and back problems. As a result of these studies, a number of design recommendations for terminals were made. These recommendations included the following:

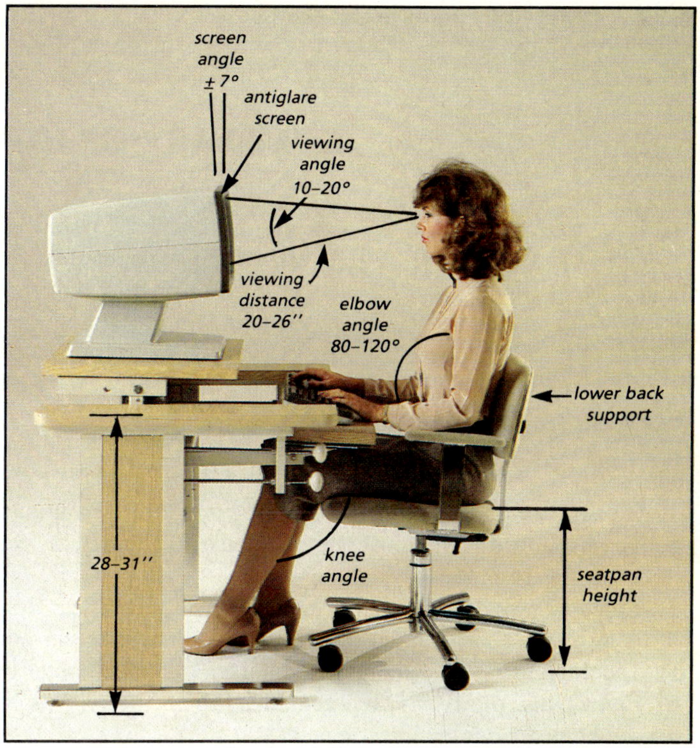

FIGURE 4-44
This illustration shows some of the ergonomic factors that should be considered when using a terminal for a long or repeated length of time.

1. Computer keyboards should be detached from the screen so that they can be positioned on a desk for the convenience and comfort of the user.
2. The screen should be movable, and the angle at which the user views the contents of the screen should be adjustable.
3. Amber or green text on a black background is preferable to black characters on a white background or white characters on a black background.
4. The screen should be of high quality to eliminate any flickering of the image and characters on the screen. The characters displayed on the screen should appear as solid as possible.
5. The images on the screen should be in sharp focus over the entire screen area.
6. The screen should have an antiglare coating. Screen glare has been a common complaint of many terminal users, and it is known that glare can be harmful to eyes. A flat screen, now used on some terminals, can also reduce glare.
7. Screens that will display multiple elements of information should use color to distinguish the different elements, thus cutting down on the strain of looking for and identifying information displayed on the screen.

Figure 4-44 illustrates some of the above recommendations. The keyboard is detachable, the visual display unit is adjustable, and the screen has an antiglare coating. The illustration also shows the use of a lower back support. Note the position of the user's body in relation to the terminal.

As more and more workers use terminals and personal computers, the importance of ergonomically designed equipment increases. Manufacturers are now aware of the importance of ergonomic design and, as a result, are designing and building terminals and personal computers that incorporate ergonomic design for the health and comfort of users.

SUMMARY OF INPUT TO THE COMPUTER

This chapter covered various aspects of input to the computer. We discussed the four types of input and how they are used, input devices, user interfaces, and data entry. After reading this chapter you should have a better overall understanding of computer input.

CHAPTER SUMMARY

1. **Input** refers to the process of entering programs, commands, user responses, and data into the computer memory.
2. The **keyboard** is the most commonly used input device. Special keys may include the **numeric keypads**, **cursor control keys**, and **function keys**.
3. **Video display terminals** fall into two basic categories: **dumb terminals** and **intelligent terminals**.
4. A **mouse** is a small input device used to control the movement of the cursor and to select options displayed on the screen.
5. **Touch screens** allow the user to interact with a computer by merely touching the screen.
6. **Light pens**, **digitizers**, and **graphics tablets** are graphic input devices used to translate graphic input data into a form that can be processed by the computer.
7. **Voice input** allows the user to enter data and issue commands to a computer with spoken words.
8. **Magnetic ink character recognition (MICR)** is a type of machine-readable data used almost exclusively in the banking industry.
9. **Scanners** are devices that read printed codes, characters, or images and convert them into a form that can be processed by the computer.
10. **Optical character recognition (OCR)** devices are scanners that read typewritten, computer-printed, and in some cases hand-printed characters from ordinary documents.
11. An **Optical mark reader** is a scanning device that can read carefully placed pencil marks on a specially designed form.
12. **Data collection devices** are designed and used for obtaining data at the site where the transaction or event being reported takes place.
13. A **user interface** is the combination of hardware and software that allows a user to communicate with a computer system.
14. User interfaces have evolved from technical commands to techniques such as prompts and menus.
15. A **prompt** is a message to the user that is displayed on the screen and provides information or instructions regarding some entry to be made or action to be taken.
16. **Data editing** is used to check input data for proper format and acceptable values. It helps to ensure that valid data is entered by the user.
17. A **menu** is a display on a screen that allows the user to select from multiple alternatives. There are several types of menu selection techniques including sequential and alphabetic selection, cursor positioning, reverse video, and icon selection.
18. An **icon** is a pictorial representation of a function to be performed on the computer.
19. Graphics can play an important role in aiding the user to interact effectively with a computer.
20. Features that relate to good interfaces include: system responses, screen design, user responses, error recovery, and control and security.
21. When a user enters data into a computer, the messages and action taken by the computer are referred to as **system responses**.
22. The elapsed time between the instant a user enters data and the instant the computer responds is called the **response time**.
23. Screen design should provide messages and pictures in an uncluttered, simple format.
24. All messages, menus, and prompts within a system should follow a consistent format.
25. Input will be faster and fewer errors will be made if the operator response or input from users is as simple as possible.
26. When user input errors occur, a good interface will tell the user, identify the error, and explain how to correct it.
27. **Passwords** are unique user identification codes that are used on multiuser systems to allow only authorized users access to the computer.

28. Data entry for interactive processing is said to be **online**, meaning that the device from which the data is being entered is connected directly to the computer.
29. Data entry for batch processing is said to be **offline**, meaning that the device from which the data is being entered is not connected to the computer that will process it.
30. In many applications, controls are established to ensure that the data entered is processed accurately. For example, balancing to a predetermined total is called a **batch control**.
31. The procedures developed for the data entry function are important because accurate data must be entered into a computer to ensure data integrity.
32. Within an organization, it is important to identify which people and operations will generate the data.
33. **Centralized data entry** is performed by trained operators from **source documents**.
34. **Distributed data entry** often takes place at the site where the data is generated and is input to the computer by a variety of users.
35. In most applications, timing requirements for acquiring and entering data are important and should be identified.
36. Data documentation should specify the flow of the data from the point where it originates to the point where it is entered for processing.
37. Transaction volume refers to the amount of data that must be entered for a given time period and a given location.
38. Data entry procedures should identify the devices and the methods for entering data.
39. Data editing and error handling procedures include a number of distinct tests that can be performed on the data prior to processing. Some of these are numeric and alphabetic testing, tests for reasonableness and consistency, and transcription and transposition tests.
40. **Transcription errors** refer to operator errors made at the time of input, such as entering 7165 instead of 7665.
41. **Transposition errors** refer to operator errors where two characters are switched, such as entering 7756 instead of 7765.
42. Data controls and security procedures should be defined.
43. Data entry procedures should specify the personnel requirements for both gathering and entering input data.
44. **Ergonomics** is the study of the design and arrangement of equipment so that people will interact with the equipment in a healthy, comfortable, and efficient manner.
45. Manufacturers are now designing equipment that incorporates ergonomic design features.

KEY TERMS

Arrow keys *4.5*
Batch control *4.24*
Centralized data entry *4.29*
Commands *4.3*
Cursor *4.5*
Cursor control keys *4.5*
Data *4.3*
Data collection devices *4.14*
Data editing *4.17*
Default values *4.26*
Digitizer *4.9*
Display terminals *4.5*
Distributed data entry *4.29*
Dumb terminals *4.6*
Ergonomics *4.31*
Function keys *4.5*
Graphic input devices *4.9*
Graphics tablet *4.9*
Icon *4.19*
Image processing system *4.13*
Input *4.3*
Intelligent terminals *4.6*
Keyboards *4.4*
Laser scanner *4.13*
Light pen *4.9*
Magnetic ink character recognition (MICR) *4.10*
Menu *4.18*
MICR readers *4.10*
Mouse *4.7*
Numeric keypad *4.4*
Offline data entry *4.24*
Online data entry *4.22*
Optical character recognition (OCR) *4.11*
Optical mark reader (OMR) *4.12*
Page scanner *4.13*
Password *4.21*
Point of sale terminal *4.7*
Production data entry *4.23*
Programmable terminals *4.6*
Programs *4.3*
Prompt *4.17*
Response time *4.21*
Reverse video *4.18*
Scanners *4.11*
Source data collection *4.29*
Submenus *4.20*
System responses *4.21*
Touch screens *4.8*
Transcription error *4.30*
Transposition error *4.30*
Turn-around document *4.12*
Uploading *4.6*
User interface *4.15*
User responses *4.3*
Video display terminals (VDTs) *4.5*
Voice input *4.10*
Wraparound *4.18*

REVIEW QUESTIONS

1. What are the four types of input and how are they used?
2. Describe the features available on a computer keyboard.
3. Name two types of display terminals. Describe each type.
4. Describe a mouse and list its advantages and disadvantages.
5. Describe three different types of graphic input devices.
6. What are data collection devices? How do they differ from other input devices?
7. What is a user interface? Why is it important?
8. Describe the evolution of user interface software.
9. What is a prompt? What are the attributes of a good prompt?
10. What is a menu? Describe the five types of menu selection.
11. What is an icon? Why is an icon used?
12. Name and briefly describe the five features that apply to good user interfaces.
13. What are the differences between data entry for interactive and for batch processing?
14. List ten procedures associated with data entry.
15. What is ergonomics? List and describe six ergonomic features that a terminal should have.

CONTROVERSIAL ISSUES

1. Manufacturers of computer hardware and software that use the mouse as an input device and icons on the screen claim that the majority of people who use computers will prefer this method. They claim that most people are not familiar with computers and the easier computers are to use, the more people who will use them. Some of their competitors claim that these devices are useful when people are learning to use a computer but that users quickly tire of the "cuteness" and prefer a device on which more productive work can be done. Which argument do you think is correct? Could they both be correct?
2. Proponents of touch screen technology claim that the touch screen is the answer to user interface problems because all a user must do is touch the screen to input data. Opponents claim it is much too limited as an input device. Take a position in this dispute.
3. The use of display terminals has increased significantly in recent years. With the increased use has come claims that using terminals is harmful to health. It has been claimed that long use of video display terminals has caused such problems as miscarriages and back ailments. Some unions have questioned the advisability of sitting in front of a terminal for eight hours. Terminal manufacturers have argued that ergonomically designed terminals present no danger to health. Research the arguments and take a position on this controversy.

RESEARCH PROJECTS

1. Visit a local computer store that sells a computer that uses a mouse and icons. Use the machine for a period of time and report back to your class concerning its good points and bad points.
2. Visit a retail or grocery store in your area and prepare a report on the point of sale terminals in use. Be sure to identify the type of terminal used, the manner in which data is entered, the computer to which the terminal is connected, and any problems or difficulties employees have had using the terminals.
3. Visit a local bank or retail store that has terminals communicating with a large computer. Ask a person at the establishment to show you how they interface with the computer. Pay particular attention to the screen formats, the data that the user must enter, and the response times. Prepare a report on your experiences for your class.
4. Bring a turn-around document that you have received in the mail and explain it to the class.
5. The data entry function has changed significantly during the history of business data processing. Research the history of the data entry function and prepare an oral or written report. Include in your report the hardware devices used, the manner in which data was entered, the location from which data was entered, and the different procedures used for data entry over the years.

CHAPTER 5

The Processor Unit

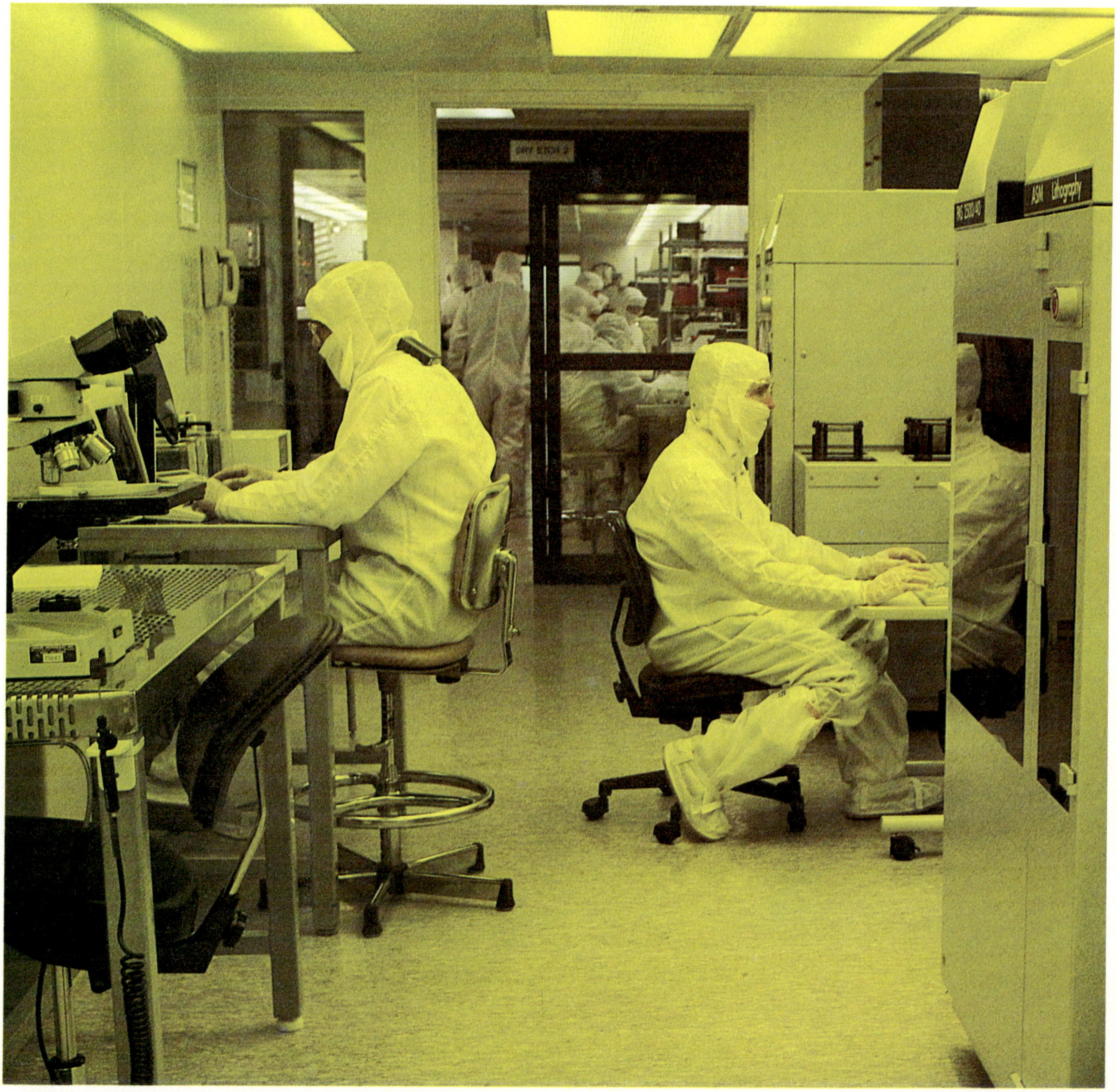

CHAPTER 5

The Processor Unit

OBJECTIVES

- Identify the components of the processor unit and describe their use.
- Define a bit and describe how a series of bits in a byte is used to represent characters.
- Discuss how the ASCII and EBCDIC codes represent characters.
- Describe why the binary and hexadecimal numbering systems are used with computer systems.
- List and describe the four steps in a machine cycle.
- Discuss the three primary factors that affect the speed of the processor unit.
- Describe the characteristics of RAM and ROM memory. List several other types of memory.
- Describe the process of manufacturing integrated circuits.

The information processing cycle consists of input, processing, output, and storage operations. When an input operation is completed and both a program and data are stored in main memory, processing operations can begin. During these operations, the processor unit executes, or performs, the program instructions and processes the data into information.

This chapter examines the components of the processor unit, describes how main memory stores programs and data, and discusses the sequence of operations that occurs when instructions are executed on a computer.

WHAT IS THE PROCESSOR UNIT?

While the term computer is used to describe the collection of devices that perform the information processing cycle, it is sometimes used more specifically to describe the processor unit. It is in the processor unit that the execution of computer programs and the manipulation of data takes place. The main components of the processor unit are the central processing unit or CPU and the main memory of the computer (Figure 5-1).

The Central Processing Unit

The central processing unit (CPU) contains the control unit and the arithmetic/logic unit. These two components work together using the program and data stored in main memory to perform the processing operations.

The control unit can be thought of as the "brain" of the computer. Just as the human brain controls the body, the control unit "controls" the computer. The **control unit** operates by repeating the following four operations: fetching, decoding, executing, and storing. **Fetching** means obtaining the next program instruction from main memory. **Decoding** is translating the program instruction into the commands that the computer can process. **Executing** refers to the actual processing of the computer commands, and **storing** takes place when the result of the instruction is written to main memory.

The second part of the CPU is the **arithmetic/logic unit**. This unit contains the electronic circuitry necessary to perform arithmetic and logical operations on data. Arithmetic operations include addition, subtraction, multiplication, and division. Logical operations consist of comparing one data item to another to determine if the first data item is greater than, equal to, or less than the other.

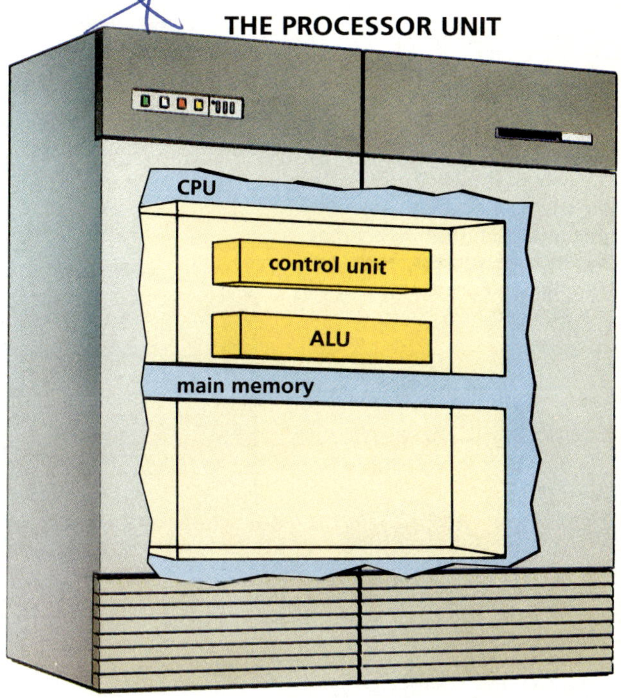

FIGURE 5-1
The processor unit of a computer contains two main components: the central processing unit (CPU), which includes the control unit and the arithmetic/logic unit, and main memory.

Main Memory

In addition to the CPU, **main memory** or **primary storage** is also contained in the processor unit of the computer. (Figure 5-2) Main memory stores three items: (1) the *operating system* or software that directs and coordinates the computer equipment; (2) an *application program* containing the instructions that will direct the work to be done; and (3) the *data* currently being processed by the application program. Data is stored in areas of main memory referred to as input and output areas. These areas receive and send data to the input and output devices. Another area of main memory called working storage is used to store any other data that is needed for processing.

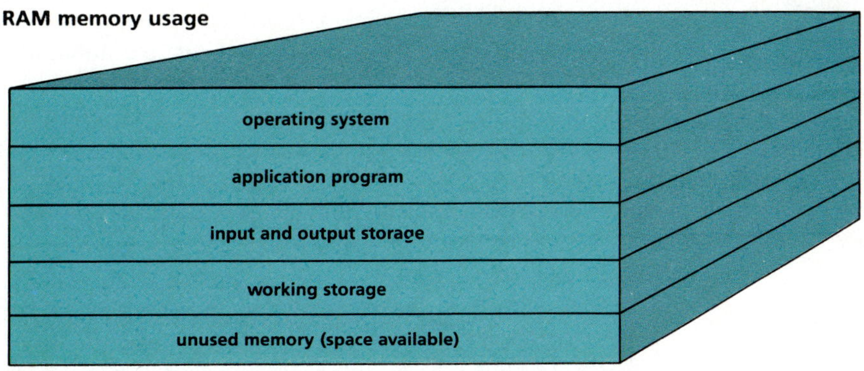

FIGURE 5-2
Main memory is used to store several types of data and programs. As program instructions are executed and new data and programs are input and output, the allocation of memory space changes.

Within main memory, each storage location is called a **byte**. Just as a house on a street has a unique address that indicates its location on the street, each byte in the main memory of a computer has an address that indicates its location in memory (Figure 5-3). The number that indicates the location of a byte in memory is called a **memory address**. Whenever the computer references a byte, it does so by using the memory address of that location.

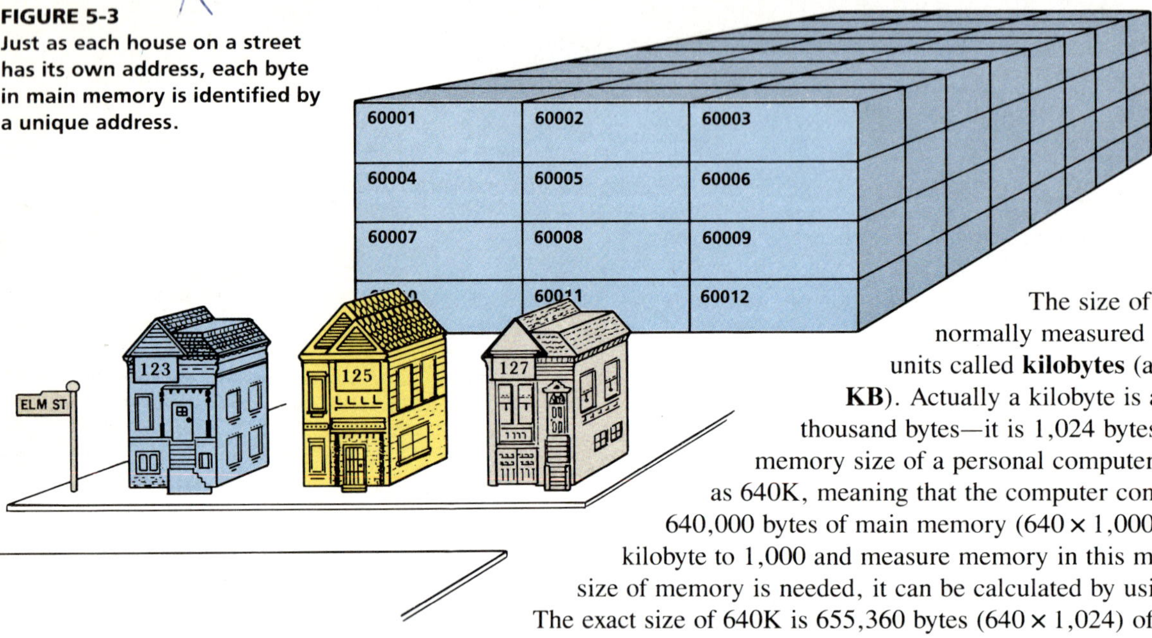

FIGURE 5-3
Just as each house on a street has its own address, each byte in main memory is identified by a unique address.

The size of main memory is normally measured in thousand-byte units called **kilobytes** (abbreviated as **K** or **KB**). Actually a kilobyte is a little larger than a thousand bytes—it is 1,024 bytes. For example, the memory size of a personal computer could be expressed as 640K, meaning that the computer contains approximately 640,000 bytes of main memory (640 × 1,000). Most users round kilobyte to 1,000 and measure memory in this manner. If the exact size of memory is needed, it can be calculated by using the value 1,024. The exact size of 640K is 655,360 bytes (640 × 1,024) of main memory.

Several other terms are used to describe memory size. When memory exceeds 1,000K or one million bytes, it is measured in **megabytes**, abbreviated **MB**. A billion bytes of memory, available on some large computers, is called a **gigabyte** or **GB**.

HOW PROGRAMS AND DATA ARE REPRESENTED IN MEMORY

Program instructions and data are made up of a combination of the three types of characters: alphabetic (A through Z), numeric (0 through 9) and special (all other characters). To understand how program instructions and data are stored in main memory, it is sometimes helpful to think of them as being stored character by character. Generally speaking, when we think of characters being stored in main memory, we think of one character being stored in one memory location or byte. Thus, the name TOM would take three memory locations or bytes because there are three letters in that name. The number $157.50 would take seven memory locations or bytes because there are seven characters (including the $ and .) in the number (Figure 5-4).

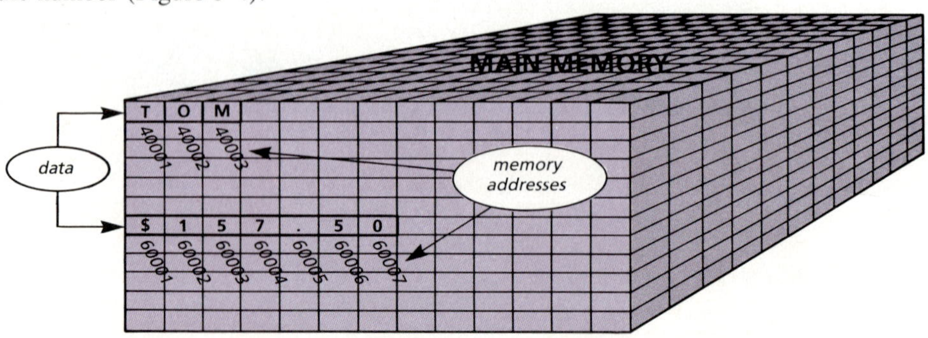

FIGURE 5-4
Each character (alphabetic, numeric, or special) usually requires one memory location (byte) for storage.

A byte contains eight bits. A **bit** is an element of a byte that can represent only two values. It can either be "off," represented in Figure 5-5 by an open circle, or "on," represented by a filled-in circle. Each alphabetic, numeric, and special character stored in the memory of the computer is represented by a combination of on and off bits. The computer can distinguish between characters because the combination of off and on bits assigned to each character is unique.

A mathematical way of representing the off and on conditions of a bit is to use 0 to represent off and 1 to represent on. The **binary** number system (base 2) represents quantities by using only the two symbols, 0 and 1. For this reason, binary is used to represent the electronic status of the bits inside the processing unit (Figure 5-5). The term bit was derived from the words *b*inary dig*it*.

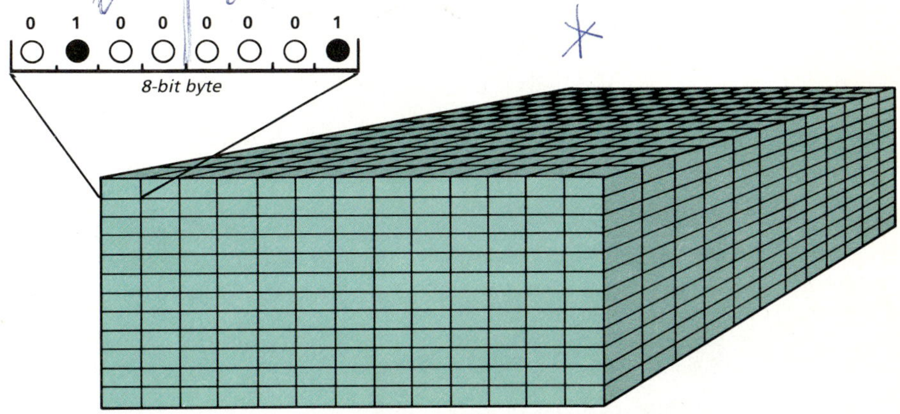

FIGURE 5-5
A graphic example of an eight-bit byte with two bits on and six bits off. The on bits (filled-in circles) are represented by the binary number 1 and the off bits (open circles) are represented by binary 0. (This combination of bits represents the letter A in ASCII code).

Two popular codes that use combinations of zeros and ones for representing characters in memory are the ASCII and EBCDIC codes. A chart summarizing these codes is shown in Figure 5-6. Notice how the combination of bits, represented in binary, is unique for each character.

SYMBOL	ASCII	EBCDIC	SYMBOL	ASCII	EBCDIC	SYMBOL	ASCII	EBCDIC
(space)	0100000	01000000	?	0111111	01101111	^	1011110	
!	0100001	01011010	@	1000000	01111100	_	1011111	
"	0100010	01111111	A	1000001	11000001	a	1100001	10000001
#	0100011	01111011	B	1000010	11000010	b	1100010	10000010
$	0100100	01011011	C	1000011	11000011	c	1100011	10000011
%	0100101	01101100	D	1000100	11000100	d	1100100	10000100
&	0100110	01010000	E	1000101	11000101	e	1100101	10000101
'	0100111	01111101	F	1000110	11000110	f	1100110	10000110
(	0101000	01001101	G	1000111	11000111	g	1100111	10000111
)	0101001	01011101	H	1001000	11001000	h	1101000	10001000
*	0101010	01011100	I	1001001	11001001	i	1101001	10001001
+	0101011	01001110	J	1001010	11010001	j	1101010	10010001
,	0101100	01101011	K	1001011	11010010	k	1101011	10010010
–	0101101	01100000	L	1001100	11010011	l	1101100	10010011
.	0101110	01001011	M	1001101	11010100	m	1101101	10010100
/	0101111	01100001	N	1001110	11010101	n	1101110	10010101
0	0110000	11110000	O	1001111	11010110	o	1101111	10010110
1	0110001	11110001	P	1010000	11010111	p	1110000	10010111
2	0110010	11110010	Q	1010001	11011000	q	1110001	10011000
3	0110011	11110011	R	1010010	11011001	r	1110010	10011001
4	0110100	11110100	S	1010011	11100010	s	1110011	10100010
5	0110101	11110101	T	1010100	11100011	t	1110100	10100011
6	0110110	11110110	U	1010101	11100100	u	1110101	10100100
7	0110111	11110111	V	1010110	11100101	v	1110110	10100101
8	0111000	11111000	W	1010111	11100110	w	1110111	10100110
9	0111001	11111001	X	1011000	11100111	x	1111000	10100111
:	0111010	01111010	Y	1011001	11101000	y	1111001	10101000
;	0111011	01011110	Z	1011010	11101001	z	1111010	10101001
<	0111100	01001100	[	1011011	01001010	{	1111011	
=	0111101	01111110	\	1011100		}	1111101	
>	0111110	01101110	]	1011101	01011010			

FIGURE 5-6
This chart shows alphabetic, numeric, and special characters as they are represented in the ASCII and EBCDIC codes. Note how each character is represented in binary using zeros and ones.

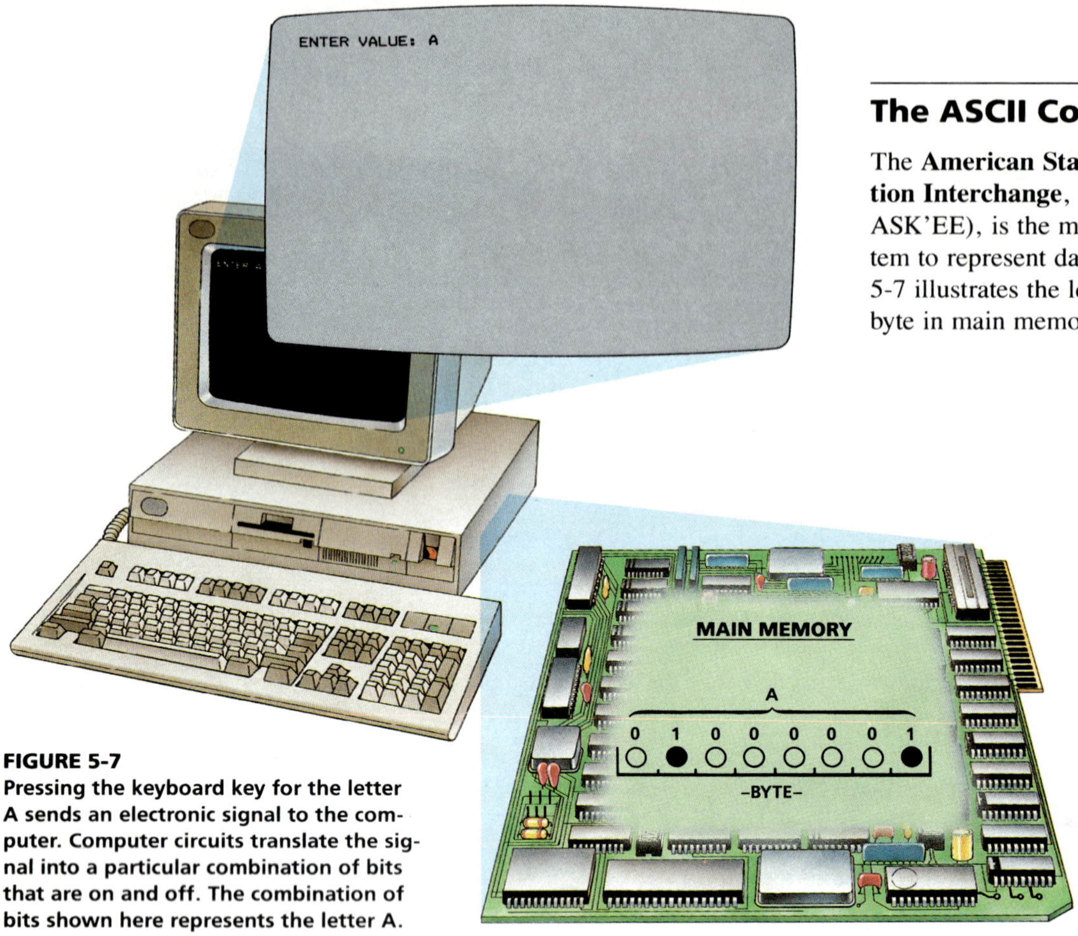

FIGURE 5-7
Pressing the keyboard key for the letter A sends an electronic signal to the computer. Computer circuits translate the signal into a particular combination of bits that are on and off. The combination of bits shown here represents the letter A.

The ASCII Code

The **American Standard Code for Information Interchange**, called **ASCII** (pronounced ASK'EE), is the most widely used coding system to represent data. The example in Figure 5-7 illustrates the letter A stored in an eight-bit byte in main memory using the ASCII code.

When you type the letter A on the keyboard, the electronic circuitry of the computer interprets the character and stores it in main memory as a series of on and off bits. In the example, the combination of bits that are on and off represent the letter A in the ASCII code. When the character is displayed on the screen or printed, the ASCII code is translated back into the alphabetic symbol A.

As you can see by looking at the chart in Figure 5-6, the ASCII code uses only the rightmost seven bits of the eight bits in a byte to represent characters. These seven bits provide 128 combinations, enough to represent all the standard characters including numeric, uppercase and lowercase alphabetic, and special.

The EBCDIC Code

The ASCII code is widely used on personal computers and many minicomputers. Another common coding scheme used primarily on mainframes is called the **Extended Binary Coded Decimal Interchange Code** or **EBCDIC** (pronounced "EB-SEE-DICK").

Binary Representation of Numbers

When the ASCII or EBCDIC codes are used, each character that is represented is stored in one byte of memory. Note, however, that there are other binary formats of data representation that allow multiple digits to be stored in one byte or memory location.

PARITY

Regardless of whether ASCII, EBCDIC, or other binary methods are used to represent characters in main memory, it is important that the characters be stored accurately. For each byte of memory, most computers have at least one extra bit, called a **parity bit**, that is used by the computer for error checking. A parity bit can detect if one of the bits in a byte has been inadvertently changed. Such an error could occur because of voltage fluctuations, static electricity, or a memory chip failure.

Computers are either odd or even parity machines. In computers with **odd parity**, the total number of "on" bits in the byte (including the parity bit) must be an odd number (Figure 5-8). In computers with **even parity**, the total number of on bits must be an even number. Parity is checked each time a memory location is used. When data is moved from one location to another in main memory, the parity bits of both the sending and receiving locations are compared to see if they are the same. If the system detects a difference or if the wrong number of bits is on (e.g., an even number in a system with odd parity), an error message displays. Some computers use multiple parity bits that enable them to detect and correct a single bit error and detect multiple bit errors.

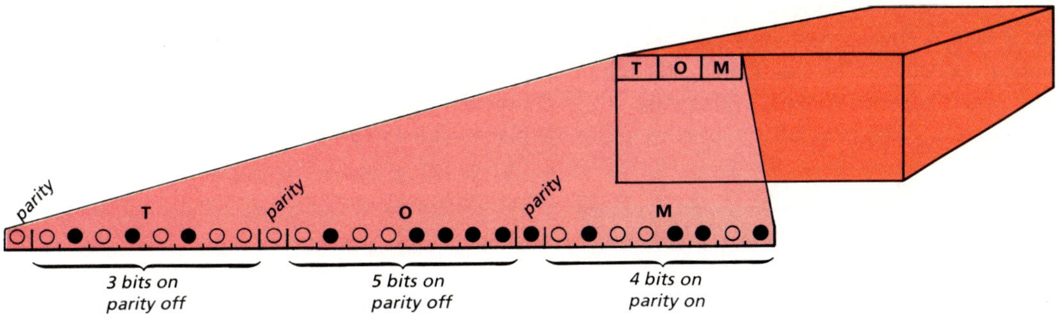

FIGURE 5-8
In a computer with odd parity, the parity bit is turned on or off in order to make the total number of on bits (including the parity bit) an odd number. Here, the letters T and O have an odd number of bits and the parity bit is left off. However, the number of bits for the letter M is even, so in order to achieve odd parity, the parity bit is turned on. Turning on the parity bit makes the total number of bits in the byte an odd number (five).

NUMBER SYSTEMS

This section describes the number systems that are used with computers. While thorough knowledge of this subject is required for technical computer personnel, a general understanding of number systems and how they relate to computers is all most users need.

As you have seen, the binary (base 2) number system is used to represent the electronic status of the bits in main memory. It is also used for other purposes, such as addressing the memory locations. Another number system that is commonly used with computers is **hexadecimal** (base 16). Figure 5-9 shows how the decimal values 0 through 15 are represented in binary and hexadecimal.

DECIMAL	BINARY	HEXADECIMAL
0	0000	0
1	0001	1
2	0010	2
3	0011	3
4	0100	4
5	0101	5
6	0110	6
7	0111	7
8	1000	8
9	1001	9
10	1010	A
11	1011	B
12	1100	C
13	1101	D
14	1110	E
15	1111	F

FIGURE 5-9
The chart shows the binary and hexadecimal representation of decimal numbers 0 through 15. Note how letters represent the numbers 10 through 15.

The mathematical principles that apply to the binary and hexadecimal number systems are the same as those that apply to the decimal number system. To help you better understand these principles we will start with the familiar decimal system, then progress to the binary and hexadecimal number systems.

The Decimal Number System

The decimal number system is a base 10 number system (note that "deci" means 10). The *base* of a number system indicates how many symbols are used in it. Decimal uses the 10 symbols 0 through 9. Each of the symbols in the number system has a value associated with it. For example, you know that 3 represents a quantity of three and 5 represents a quantity of five. The decimal number system is also a positional number system. This means that in a number such as 143, each position in the number has a value associated with it. When you look at the decimal number 143, you know that the 3 is in the ones, or units, position and represents three ones or (3 × 1); the 4 is in the tens position and represents four tens or (4 × 10); and the 1 is in the hundreds position and represents one hundred or (1 × 100). The number 143 is the sum of the values in each position of the number (100 + 40 + 3 = 143). Figure 5-10 is a power chart showing how the positional values (hundreds, tens, and units) for a number system can be calculated. Starting on the right and working to the left, we raise the base of the number system, in this case 10, to consecutive powers (10^2 10^1 10^0). These calculations are a mathematical way of computing the place values in a number system.

FIGURE 5-10
This chart shows the positional values in the decimal number 143.

power of 10	10^2	10^1	10^0
positional value	100	10	1
number	1	4	3

$$(1 \times 100) + (4 \times 10) + (3 \times 1) = 100 + 40 + 3 = 143$$

When you use number systems other than decimal, the same principles apply. The base of the number system indicates the number of symbols that are used and each position in a number system has a value associated with it. The positional value can be calculated by raising the base of the number system to consecutive powers.

The Binary Number System

As we have discussed, binary is a base 2 number system ("bi" means two), and the symbols that are used are 0 and 1. Just as each position in a decimal number has a place value associated with it, so does each position in a binary number. In binary, the place values are successive powers of two (such as 2^3 2^2 2^1 2^0) or (8 4 2 1). To construct a binary number, ones are placed in the positions where the corresponding values add up to the quantity that is to be represented and zeros are placed in the other positions. For example, the binary place values are (8 4 2 1) and the binary number 1001 has ones in the positions for the values 8 and 1 and zeros in the positions for 4 and 2. Therefore, the quantity represented by 1001 is 9 (8 + 0 + 0 + 1) (Figure 5-11).

power of 2	2^3	2^2	2^1	2^0
positional value	8	4	2	1
binary	1	0	0	1

$$(1 \times 8) + (0 \times 4) + (0 \times 2) + (1 \times 1) =$$
$$8 + 0 + 0 + 1 = 9$$

FIGURE 5-11
This chart shows how to convert the binary number 1001 to the decimal number 9. Each place in the binary number represents a successive power of 2.

The Hexadecimal Number System

Many computers use a base 16 number system called hexadecimal. The hexadecimal number system uses 16 symbols to represent values. These include the symbols 0 through 9 and A through F (Figure 5-9). The mathematical principles previously discussed also apply to hexadecimal (Figure 5-12).

power of 16	16^1	16^0
positional value	16	1
hexadecimal	A(10)	5

$$(10 \times 16) + (5 \times 1) =$$
$$160 + 5 = 165$$

FIGURE 5-12
This chart shows how the hexadecimal number A5 is converted into the decimal number 165. Note that the value 10 is substituted for the A during computations.

The primary reason why the hexadecimal number system is used with computers is because it can represent binary values in a more compact form and because the conversion between the binary and the hexadecimal number systems is very efficient. An eight-digit binary number can be represented by a two-digit hexadecimal number. For example, in the EBCDIC code (used by some computers to represent data), the decimal number 5 is represented as 11110101. This value can be represented in hexadecimal as F5.

One way to convert a binary number to a hexadecimal number is to divide the binary number (from right to left) into groups of four digits; calculate the value of each group; and then change any two-digit values (10 through 15) into the symbols A through F that are used in hexadecimal (Figure 5-13).

Summary of Number Systems

As mentioned at the beginning of the section on number systems, binary and hexadecimal are used primarily by technical computer personnel. For the general user, a complete understanding of numbering systems is not required. The concepts that you should remember about number systems are that binary is used for purposes such as representing the electronic status of the bits in main memory and also for memory addresses. Hexadecimal is used to represent binary in a more compact form.

positional value	8421	8421
binary	1111	0101
decimal	15	5
hexadecimal	F	5

FIGURE 5-13
This chart shows how the EBCDIC code 11110101 for the value 5 is converted into the hexadecimal value F5.

HOW THE PROCESSOR UNIT EXECUTES PROGRAMS AND MANIPULATES DATA

The program instructions that users write are usually in a form similar to English. Before these instructions can be executed, they must be translated by the computer into a form called machine language instructions. A **machine language instruction** is one that the electronic circuits in the CPU can interpret and convert into one or more of the commands in the computer's instruction set. The **instruction set** contains the commands such as add or move that the computer's circuits can directly perform. To help you understand how the processor unit works, let's look at an example of a machine language instruction.

Machine Language Instructions

A machine language instruction is usually composed of three parts: an operation code; values indicating the number of characters to be processed by the instruction; and the addresses in main memory of the data to be used in the execution of the instruction (Figure 5-14).

FIGURE 5-14
A machine language instruction consists of an operation code, the lengths of the fields to be processed, and the main memory addresses of the fields.

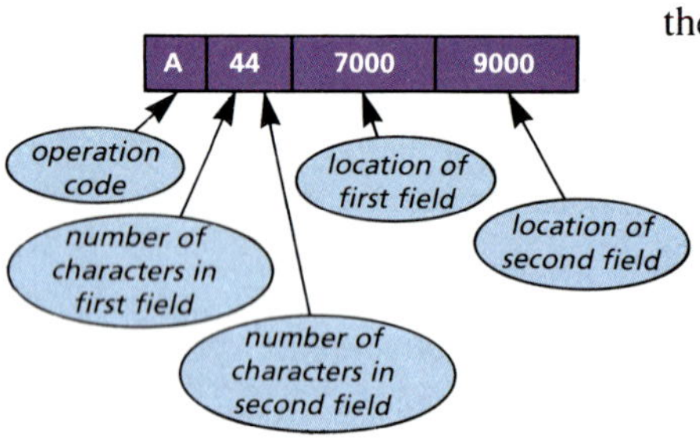

The **operation code** is a unique value that is typically stored in the first byte in the instruction. This unique value indicates what operation is to be performed. For example, the letter A stored as the operation code might indicate that an *add*ition operation is to occur. The letter M might mean that a *move* operation is to take place.

The number of characters to be processed is included in the machine language instruction so that the CPU will manipulate the proper number of bytes. For example, if a four-digit field were to be added to another four-digit field, the number of characters specified in the instruction for each field would be four.

The main memory addresses of the fields involved in the operation are also specified in the instruction. This specification of the main memory address enables the CPU to locate where in main memory the data to be processed is stored.

The illustration in Figure 5-15 shows the steps involved in executing a computer instruction. The instruction A44 7000 9000 indicates that the four-digit fields that begin in locations 7000 and 9000 are to be added together. When this instruction is executed, the following steps occur:

FIGURE 5-15
Executing a program instruction

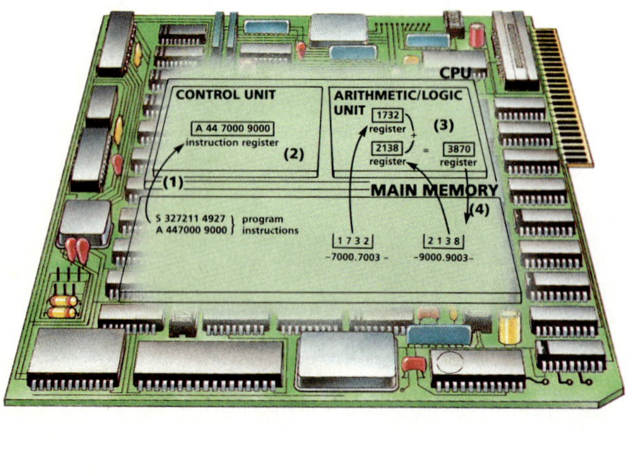

1. The instruction is fetched from main memory and placed in an instruction register. An **instruction register** is an area of memory within the control unit of the CPU that can store a single instruction at a time.
2. After the control unit decodes the instruction, it fetches the data specified at the two addresses in the instruction from main memory.
3. The arithmetic/logic unit executes the instruction by adding the two numbers.
4. The control unit then stores the result of the processing by moving the sum to main memory.

This basic sequence of fetch the instruction, decode the instruction, execute the instruction, and store the results is the way most computers process instructions.

The Machine Cycle

The four steps illustrated above, fetch, decode, execute, and store, are called the **machine cycle**. As shown in Figure 5-16, the machine cycle is made up of the instruction cycle and the execution cycle. The **instruction cycle** refers to the fetching of the next program instruction and the decoding of that instruction. The **execution cycle** includes the execution of the instruction and the storage of the processing results. When the computer is again ready to fetch the next program instruction, one machine cycle is completed.

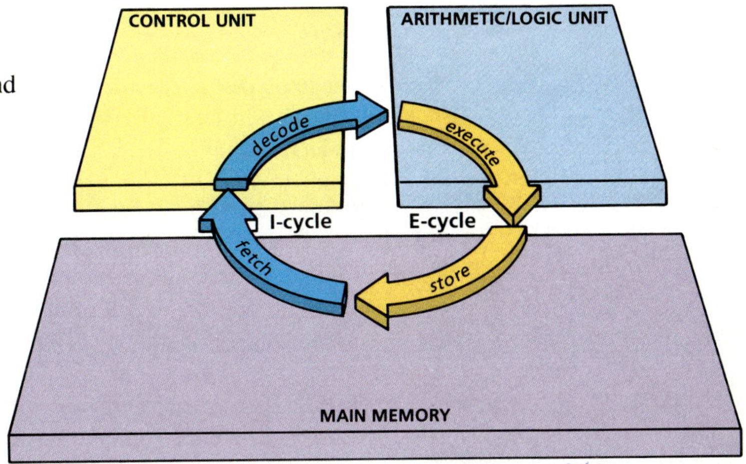

FIGURE 5-16
The machine cycle consists of four steps: fetching the next instruction, decoding the instruction, executing the instruction, and storing the result. Fetching and decoding are considered part of the instruction or I cycle. Executing and storing are considered part of the execution or E cycle.

PROCESSOR SPEEDS

Although the machine cycle may appear to be cumbersome and time consuming, computers can perform millions of machine cycles in one second. In fact, the processing speed of computers is often compared in **MIPS**—million instructions per second. A computer with a rating of 1 MIPS could process one million instructions per second. The most powerful personal computers today are rated at between 3 and 4 MIPS. Larger computers can process 75 to 100 MIPS and supercomputers are capable of over 200 MIPS.

The speed in which a computer can execute the machine cycle is influenced by three factors: the system clock, the buses, and the word size (Figure 5-17).

FACTOR	AFFECT ON SPEED
System clock	The clock generates electronic pulses used to synchronize processing. Faster clock speed results in more operations in a given amount of time.
Bus width	Bus width determines how much data can be transferred at any one time. A 32-bit bus can transfer twice as much data at one time as a 16-bit bus.
Word size	Word size is the number of bits that can be manipulated at any one time. A computer with a 32-bit word size can manipulate twice as much data at one time as a system with a 16-bit word size.

FIGURE 5-17
Factors affecting computer speed.

System Clock

The control unit utilizes the **system clock** to synchronize, or control the timing, of all computer operations. The system clock generates electronic pulses at a fixed rate, measured in **megahertz**. One megahertz equals one million pulses, or cycles, per second. The speed of the system clock varies among computers. Some personal computers can operate at speeds in excess of 30 megahertz.

Buses

As we explained, computers store and process data as a series of electronic bits. These bits are transferred internally within the circuitry of the computer along paths capable of transmitting electrical impulses. The bits must be transferred from input devices to memory, from memory to the CPU, from the CPU to memory, and from memory to output devices. Any path along which bits are transmitted is called a **bus** or **data bus**. Buses can transfer eight, 16, or 32 bits at a time. An eight-bit bus has eight lines and can transmit eight bits at a time. On a 16-bit bus, bits can be moved from place to place 16 bits at a time and on a 32-bit bus, bits are moved 32 bits at a time.

The larger the number of bits that are handled by a bus, the faster the computer can transfer data. For example, assume a number in memory occupies four eight-bit bytes. With an eight-bit bus four steps would be required to transfer the data from memory to the CPU because on the eight-bit data bus, the data in each eight-bit byte would be transferred in an individual step. A 16-bit bus has 16 lines in the data bus, so only two transfers would be necessary to move the data in four bytes. And on a 32-bit bus, the entire four bytes could be transferred at one time. The fewer number of transfer steps required, the faster the transfer of the data occurs.

Word Size

Another factor that affects the speed of a computer is the word size. The **word size** is the number of bits that the CPU can process at one time, as opposed to the bus size, which is the number of bits the computer can transmit at one time. Like data buses, the word size of a machine is measured in bit sizes. Processors can have eight-, 16-, 32-, or 64-bit word sizes. A processor with an eight-bit word size can manipulate eight bits at a time. If two four-digit numbers are to be added in the ALU of an eight-bit processor, it will take four operations because a separate operation will be required to add each of the four digits. With a 16-bit processor, the addition will take two operations and with a 32-bit processor, only one operation would be required to add the numbers together. Sometimes the word size of a computer is given in bytes instead of bits. For example, a word size of 16 bits may be expressed as a word size of two bytes because there are eight bits in a byte. The larger the word size of the processor, the faster the computer is able to process data.

In summary, the speed of a computer is influenced by the system clock, the size of the buses, and the word size. When you purchase a computer, the speed requirements you want should be based on your intended use of the computer. Eight-bit computers may be useful and fast enough for personal and educational applications. Sixteen-bit computers are widely used today for applications such as word processing, electronic spreadsheets, or database. Thirty-two-bit computers are considered very powerful and are useful for multiuser systems and applications that require complex and time-consuming calculations, such as graphics. A few personal computers, many minicomputers, and most mainframes are 32-bit computers. Most supercomputers are 64-bit computers.

ARCHITECTURE OF PROCESSOR UNITS

The processor unit of a computer can be designed and built in many different ways. For example, the processor for a personal computer may be housed on a single printed circuit board while a larger machine may require a number of circuit boards for the CPU, main memory, and the related electronic circuitry.

Microprocessors

The smallest processor, called a **microprocessor** (Figure 5-18), is a single integrated circuit that contains the CPU and sometimes memory. An **integrated circuit**, also called an **IC**, **chip**, or **microchip**, is a complete electronic circuit that has been etched on a small chip of nonconducting material such as silicon. Microcomputers are built using microprocessors for their CPU. Figure 5-19 lists some of the microprocessors commonly used in personal computers today.

FIGURE 5-18 ▶
The Intel 80386 microprocessor has a word size and bus width of 32 bits and can operate at between 16 and 32 megahertz.

FIGURE 5-19
A comparison of some of the more widely used microprocessor chips. ▼

MICROPROCESSOR	MANUFACTURER	WORD SIZE (BITS)	I/O BUS WIDTH (BITS)	CLOCK SPEED MHz)	MICROCOMPUTERS USING THIS CHIP
6502	MOS Technology	8	8	4	Apple IIe Atari 800
8088	Intel	16	8	8	IBM PC and XT HP 150 Compaq Portable
8086	Intel	16	16	8	Compaq Deskpro Many IBM compatibles
80286	Intel	16	16	8–12	IBM PC/AT IBM PS/2 model 50 Compaq Deskpro 286
68000	Motorola	32	16	12.5	Apple Macintosh SE and Commodore Amiga
68020	Motorola	32	32	12.5–32	Apple Macintosh II
80386	Intel	32	32	16–32	Compaq Deskpro 386 IBM PS/2 model 80

Coprocessors

One way computers can increase their productivity is through the use of a **coprocessor**, a special microprocessor chip or circuit board designed to perform a specific task. For example, math coprocessors are commonly added to computers to greatly speed up the processing of numeric calculations. Other types of coprocessors extend the capability of a computer by increasing the amount of software that will run on the computer.

Parallel Processing

Most computers contain one central processing unit (CPU) that processes a single instruction at a time. When one instruction is finished, the CPU begins execution of the next instruction, and so on until the program is completed. This method is known as **serial processing**. **Parallel processing** involves the use of multiple CPUs, each with their own memory. Parallel processors divide up a problem so that multiple CPUs can work on their assigned portion of the problem simultaneously. As you might expect, parallel processors require special software that can recognize how to divide up problems and bring the results back together again.

RISC Technology

As computers have evolved, more and more commands have been added to hardware instruction sets. In recent years, however, computer designers have reevaluated the need for so many instructions and have developed systems based on RISC technology. **RISC**, which stands for reduced instruction set computing (or computers), involves reducing the instructions to only those that are most frequently used. Without the burden of the occasionally used instructions, the most frequently used instructions operate faster and overall processing capability or *throughput* of the system is increased.

In summary, you can see that there are many different types of processor architecture that are used on computers. Regardless of the architecture used, the important concept to remember is that the processor units on all computers perform essentially the same functions.

FIGURE 5-20
This photograph illustrates 32 transistors on an NCR semiconductor chip that is used for computer memory. The transistors are enlarged 600 times their actual size.

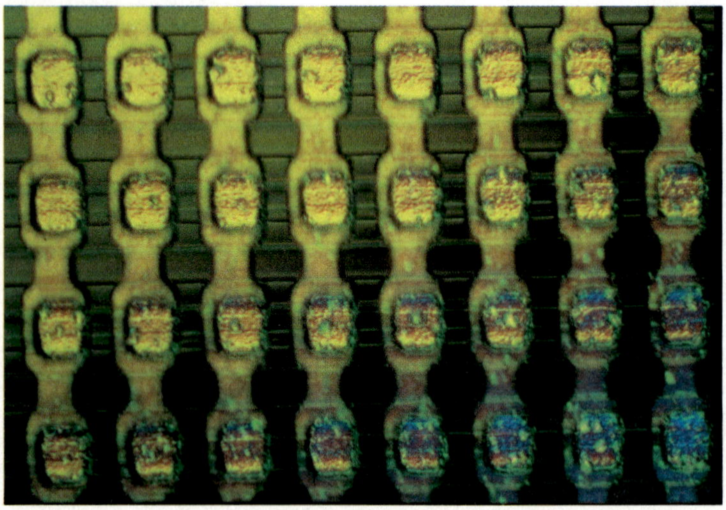

TYPES OF MEMORY

As we noted, electronic components are used to store data in computer memory. The actual materials and devices used for memory have changed throughout the years. The first device used for storing data was the vacuum tube. After the vacuum tube, core memory was used. **Core memory** consisted of small, ring-shaped pieces of material that could be magnetized, or polarized, in one of two directions. The polarity indicated whether the core was on or off. Today, semiconductor memory is used in virtually all computers (Figure 5-20). **Semiconductor memory** is an integrated circuit containing thousands of transistors. A **transistor** is an electronic component that can be either on or off and represents a bit in memory.

When core memory was used as main memory, the time required to access data stored in the memory was measured in **microseconds** (millionths of a second). Access to data stored in semiconductor memory is measured in **nanoseconds** (billionths of a second). In addition, the cost of semiconductor memory is just a fraction of the cost for core memory. Today you can buy 64K of semiconductor memory for about $30, whereas 64K of core memory once cost as much as $15,000. Figure 5-21 shows how the storage capacity of semiconductor memory has increased over recent years, while the cost of semiconductor memory has decreased. The trend is expected to continue. It has been predicted that by the end of the century it will be possible to store over a billion components on a chip.

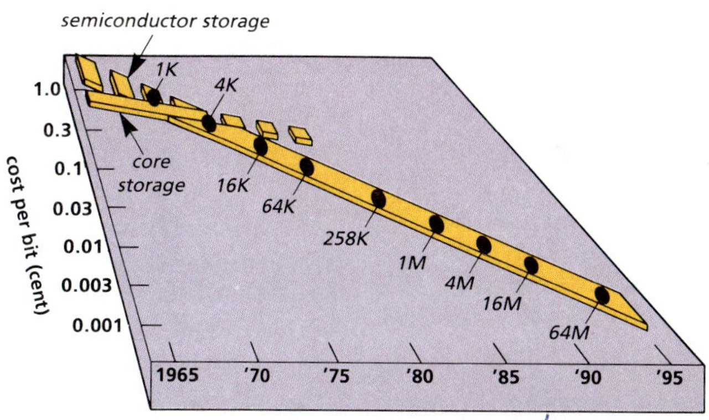

FIGURE 5-21
The chart shows the declining cost and increased storage capacity of semiconductor storage.

As you can see, semiconductor memory is compact, fast, and inexpensive. Several different types of semiconductor memory chips are used in computers. They are RAM, ROM, PROM, EPROM, and EEPROM chips.

RAM Memory

Random access memory, or **RAM**, is the name given to the integrated circuits or chips that are used for main memory. It is the type of memory that we have discussed so far in this chapter. Data and programs are transferred into and out of RAM and data stored in RAM is manipulated by computer program instructions.

There are two types of RAM memory chips: dynamic RAM and static RAM. **Dynamic RAM** chips are smaller and simpler in design than static RAM chips. With dynamic RAM the current or charge on the chip is periodically refreshed or regenerated by special regenerator circuits in order for the chip to retain the stored data. **Static RAM** chips are larger and more complicated than dynamic RAM and do not require the current to be periodically regenerated. The main memory of most computers uses dynamic RAM chips.

The example in Figure 5-22 illustrates the processing that could occur as a series of area codes are entered into RAM (computer memory) from a terminal. The first area code, 212, is entered from the keyboard and stored at memory locations 66000, 66001, and 66002. Once in memory, this field can be processed as required.

FIGURE 5-22
The instruction in the program specifies that the area code is to be read into adjacent memory locations beginning with location 66000. After the data is placed in these locations, it can be processed by the program. When the same instruction is executed the second time, the value 714 entered by the terminal operator is stored in locations 66000, 66001, and 66002, where it can be processed by the same instructions that processed area code 212.

When the instruction to read (input) data into memory from the keyboard is executed again, the second area code entered from the keyboard, area code 714, would replace the previous value (212) at locations 66000, 66001, and 66002 in memory. Area code 714 could then be processed by the same instructions that processed area code 212.

When data is moved from one location to another in main memory, the data at the receiving location is replaced by the new data. The data in the sending location remains intact. Data is not removed from one location and placed in another location. Instead, the data remains in the sending location and a copy of the data is transferred to and stored in the new location.

Another aspect of RAM memory is that it is said to be **volatile** because the programs and data stored in RAM are erased when the power to the computer is turned off. Auxiliary storage is used to store programs or data that may be needed for future use.

ROM Memory

ROM stands for **read only memory**. With ROM, data is permanently recorded in the memory when it is manufactured. ROM memory retains its contents even when the power is off. The data or programs that are stored in ROM can be read and used, but cannot be altered, hence the name "read only." ROM is used to store items such as the instruction set of the computer. In addition, many of the special purpose computers used in automobiles, appliances, and so on use small amounts of ROM to store instructions that will be executed repeatedly. Instructions that are stored in ROM memory are called **firmware** or **microcode**.

Other Types of Memory

PROM means **programmable read only memory**. PROM acts the same as ROM when it is part of the computer; that is, it can only be read and its contents cannot be altered. With PROM, however, the data or programs are not stored in the memory when they are manufactured. Instead, PROM can be loaded with specially selected data or programs prior to installing it in a computer. A variation of PROM is **EPROM** (pronounced "EE-PROM"), which means **erasable programmable read only memory**. In addition to being used in the same way as PROM, EPROM allows the user to erase the data stored in the memory and to store new data or programs in the memory. EPROM is erased through the use of special ultraviolet light devices that destroy the bit settings within the memory.

EEPROM (pronounced "double-E-PROM"), or **electronically erasable programmable read only memory**, allows the stored data or programs to be erased electrically. The advantage of EEPROM is that it does not have to be removed from the computer to be changed.

SUMMARY

In this chapter we examined various aspects of the processor unit including its components, how programs and data are stored, and how the processor executes program instructions to process data into information. While a detailed understanding of this material is not a prerequisite for computer literacy, understanding these principles will increase your overall comprehension of how processing occurs on a computer.

Making a Chip

A chip is made by building layers of electronic pathways and connections by using conducting and nonconducting materials on a surface of silicon. The combination of these materials into specific patterns forms microscopic electronic components such as transistors, diodes, and capacitors that make up the integrated chip circuit. The application of the materials to the silicon is done through a series of technically sophisticated chemical and photographic processes. The following photographs illustrate some of the manufacturing steps.

1

A chip begins with a design developed by an engineer using a computer aided circuit design program. Some circuits only take a month or two to design whereas others may take a year or more. The computer aided design system (1) allows the engineer to rearrange the design of the circuit pathways and then see them displayed on the screen. Most chips have at least four to six layers but some have up to fifteen. A separate design is required for each layer of the chip circuit. To better review the design, greatly enlarged printouts are prepared (2). After the design is finalized, a glass photo mask is prepared for each layer (3). To provide for mass production of the chips, the design is reduced to the actual size of the circuit, approximately 1/4-inch square, and duplicated over one hundred times on the surface of the photo mask. In a process similar to printing a picture from a negative, the photo mask will be used to project the circuit design onto the material used to make the chips.

2

3

Although other materials can be used, the most common raw material used to make chips is silicon crystals (4) that have been refined from quartz rocks. The silicon crystals are melted and "grown" into a cylinder, called an ingot, two to three feet long and six inches in diameter (5). After being smoothed, the silicon ingot is sliced into wafers four to six inches in diameter and 4/1000 of an inch thick. Much of the chip manufacturing process is performed in special laboratories called "clean rooms." Because even the smallest particle of dust can ruin a chip, rooms are kept 1000 times cleaner than a hospital operating room. People who work in these facilities must wear special protective clothing called "bunny suits" (6). After the wafer has been polished and sterilized, it is placed in a diffusion oven where the first layer of material is added to the wafer surface (7). These layers of materials will be etched away to form the circuits. Before etching, a soft, gelatin-like emulsion called photoresist is added to the wafer. During lithography (8), the photoresist is covered by a photo mask and exposed to ultraviolet light. The exposed photoresist becomes hard and the covered photoresist remains soft. The soft photoresist and some of the surface materials are etched away with chemicals or hot gases leaving what will become the circuit pathways. In some facilities, the etching process is done by a robot (9).

4

5

6

8

7

The process of adding material and photoresist to the wafer, exposing it to ultraviolet light, and etching away the unexposed surface, is repeated using a different photo mask for each layer of the circuit. After the circuits are tested on the wafer, they are cut into individual die by the use of a diamond saw (10) or a laser. The individual chip die (11), approximately 1/4-inch square, are packaged in a hard plastic case (12) that contains pins that connect the chip to a socket on a circuit board (13).

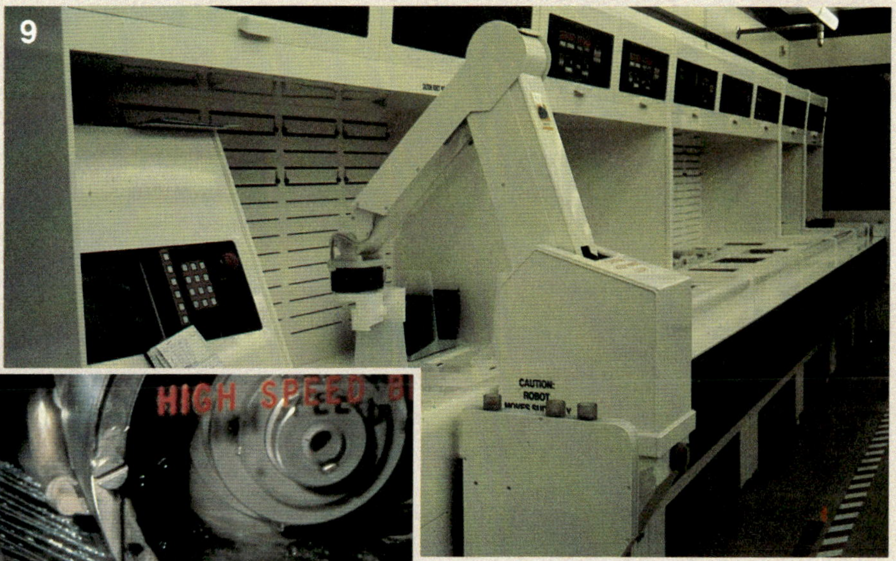

9

10

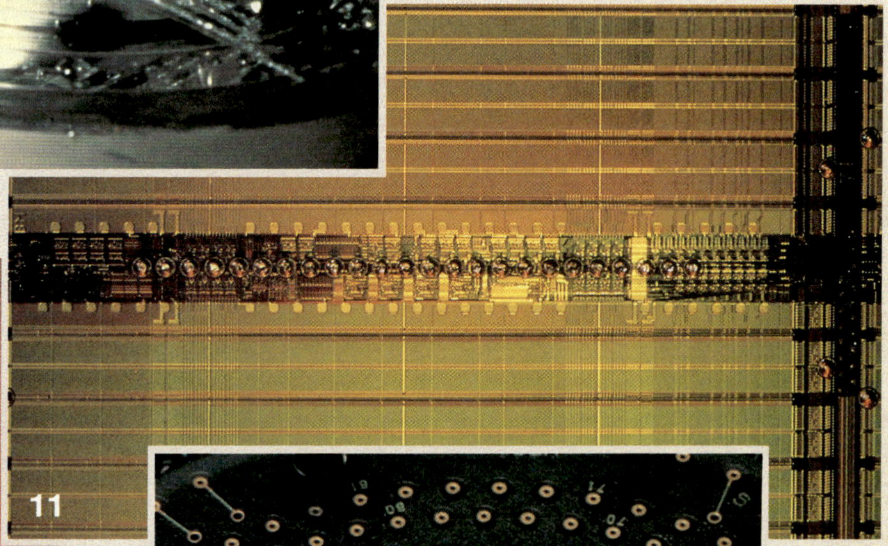
11

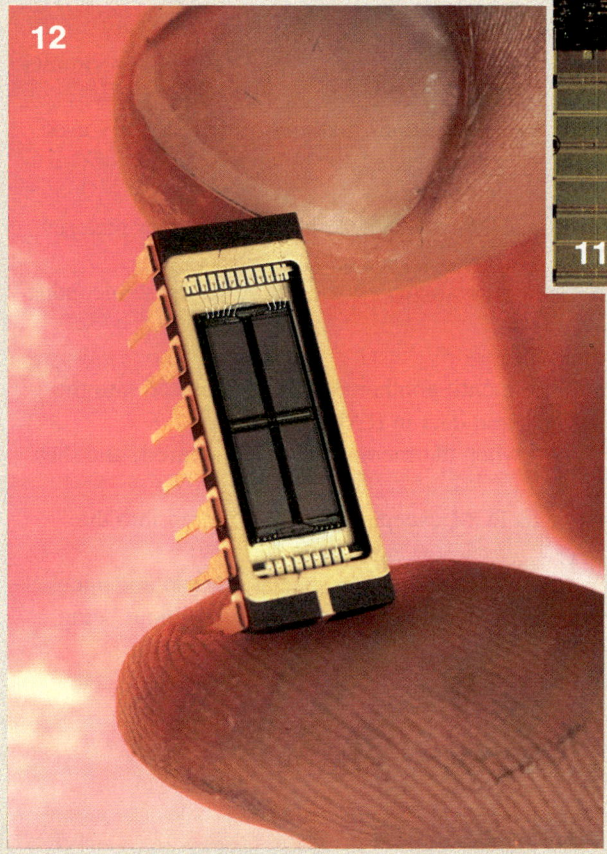
12

13

CHAPTER SUMMARY

1. The central processing unit and the main memory are contained in the processor unit.
2. The central processing unit or CPU contains the **control unit** and the **arithmetic/logic unit**. The control unit directs and coordinates all the activities on the computer. The arithmetic/logic unit performs arithmetic and logic operations.
3. The **main memory**, also called **primary storage** stores programs and data.
4. Each storage location in main memory is called a **byte** and is identified by a **memory address**.
5. The size of main memory is normally expressed in terms of **kilobytes** (approximately 1,000 bytes) of storage. A machine with 640K has approximately 640,000 memory locations.
6. A byte consists of eight **bits**. A bit can represent only two values—off and on.
7. When a letter is entered into main memory from a keyboard, the electronic circuitry interprets the character and stores the character in memory as a series of on and off bits. The computer can distinguish between characters because the combination of off and on bits assigned to each character is unique.
8. One of the most widely used codes to represent characters is the **American Standard Code for Information Interchange**, called the **ASCII code**.
9. A code used for mainframes is the **Extended Binary Coded Decimal Interchange Code (EBCDIC)**.
10. Most computers use **parity bits** for error checking.
11. The **binary** (base 2) number system is used by the computer for purposes such as memory addresses and representing the electronic status of the bits in main memory. **Hexadecimal** (base 16) is used to represent binary in a more compact form.
12. A **machine language instruction** can be decoded and executed by the CPU.
13. A machine language instruction is usually composed of an **operation code**; values indicating the number of characters to be processed; and main memory addresses of the data to be processed.
14. Steps in the **machine cycle** consist of: fetch the next instruction; decode the instruction; execute the instruction; store the results.
15. The speed of a computer is influenced by the system clock, the bus size, and the word size.
16. The **system clock** is used by the control unit to synchronize all computer operations.
17. A **bus** is any line that transmits bits between memory and the input/output devices, and between memory and the CPU.
18. The number of bits that the CPU can process at one time is called the **word size**.
19. Computers can be eight-bit, 16-bit, 32-bit, or 64-bit machines.
20. **Microprocessors** are used for the CPU in microcomputers.
21. **Coprocessors** can be used to enhance and expand the capabilities of a computer.
22. Parallel processors divide up a problem so that multiple CPUs can work on their assigned portion of the problem simultaneously.
23. **RISC** technology involves reducing a computer's instruction set to only those instructions that are most frequently used.
24. **Core memory** consisted of small, ring-shaped pieces of material that could be magnetized, or polarized, in one of two directions.
25. **Semiconductor memory** is now used in most computers. It consists of transistors etched into a semiconductor material such as silicon.
26. A **microsecond** is a millionth of a second. A **nanosecond** is a billionth of a second. Access to data stored in semiconductor memory is measured in nanoseconds.
27. **RAM**, which stands for **random access memory**, is used for main memory.
28. Once a character is stored at a location in RAM memory, it will remain there until another character is placed into the same location. When the electrical power supply is turned off, all programs and data in RAM are erased.
29. **ROM** stands for **read only memory**. Data or programs are stored in ROM when the memory is manufactured, and they cannot be altered.
30. **PROM** means **programmable read only memory**. PROM acts the same as ROM except data can be stored into the PROM memory prior to being installed in the computer.
31. **EPROM**, or **erasable programmable read only memory**, can be erased through the use of special ultraviolet devices.
32. **EEPROM** or **electronically erasable programmable read only memory**, can be electronically erased without being removed from the computer.

KEY TERMS

American Standard Code for Information Interchange (ASCII) *5.6*
Arithmetic/logic unit *5.3*
ASCII code *5.6*
Binary *5.5*
Bit *5.5*
Bus *5.12*
Byte *5.4*
Chip *5.13*
Control unit *5.3*
Coprocessor *5.14*
Core memory *5.14*
Data bus *5.12*
Decoding *5.3*
Dynamic RAM *5.15*
EBCDIC *5.6*
EEPROM *5.16*
Electronically erasable programmable read only memory (EEPROM) *5.16*
EPROM *5.16*
Erasable programmable read only memory (EPROM) *5.16*
Even parity *5.7*
Executing *5.3*
Execution cycle *5.11*
Extended Binary Coded Decimal Interchange Code (EBCDIC) *5.6*
Fetching *5.3*
Firmware *5.16*
GB *5.4*
Gigabyte (GB) *5.4*
Hexadecimal *5.7*
IC *5.13*
Instruction cycle *5.11*
Instruction register *5.10*
Instruction set *5.10*
Integrated circuit (IC) *5.13*
K *5.4*
KB *5.4*
Kilobyte (K or KB) *5.4*
Machine cycle *5.11*
Machine language instruction *5.10*
Main memory *5.3*
MB *5.4*
Megabyte (MB) *5.4*
Megahertz *5.11*
Memory address *5.4*
Microchip *5.13*
Microcode *5.16*
Microprocessor *5.13*
Microsecond *5.15*
MIPS *5.11*
Nanoseconds *5.15*
Odd parity *5.7*
Operation code *5.10*
Parallel processing *5.14*
Parity bit *5.7*
Primary storage *5.3*
Programmable read only memory (PROM) *5.16*
PROM *5.16*
RAM *5.15*
Random access memory (RAM) *5.15*
Read only memory (ROM) *5.16*
RISC (reduced instruction set computing) *5.14*
ROM *5.16*
Semiconductor memory *5.14*
Serial processing *5.14*
Static RAM *5.15*
Storing *5.3*
System clock *5.11*
Transistor *5.14*
Volatile *5.16*
Word size *5.12*

REVIEW QUESTIONS

1. Identify the two components of the central processing unit and describe the functions of each.
2. Define the terms bit and byte. Illustrate how the number 14 is represented in binary, hexadecimal, ASCII, and EBCDIC.
3. What does the letter K stand for when referring to main memory?
4. Describe how a group of characters entered into the computer as a field are stored in main memory. Draw a diagram to illustrate how the letters in your first name would be stored using the ASCII code. Begin at main memory address 45663.
5. What is parity and how is it used?
6. What are the two number systems that are used with computers? Why are they used?
7. What are the components of a machine language instruction? Describe the steps that occur in main memory and the CPU when two numbers are added together.
8. What are the three factors that influence the speed of a processor?
9. What is a microprocessor and how is it used?
10. Define each of the following terms: RAM, ROM, PROM, EPROM, EEPROM.
11. Describe the process of manufacturing integrated circuits.

CONTROVERSIAL ISSUES

1. The lower cost of producing electronic components outside the United States has caused many U.S. companies to become involved in offshore manufacturing. In addition, the importation of computer goods from foreign manufacturers has affected the computer industry in this country. Discuss whether restrictions should be placed on integrated circuits and other computer goods that are imported or manufactured offshore.
2. All microcomputers are not compatible. For example, unless special enhancements are made, software that is written for an IBM personal computer system will not run on an Apple Macintosh computer. Some people feel that industry standards should be set to eliminate the problems caused by incompatibility. Others feel that standards would restrict competition and product development. Write a paper to discuss your opinions on this topic.

RESEARCH PROJECTS

1. Many different types of devices and methods have been used for main memory. Research the history of main computer memory and prepare a report. Include information on the way the data was stored, the speed of the memory, any limitations of the method, the amount of memory that could be used, and the cost of the memory.
2. The semiconductor industry is very competitive. It develops both the microprocessors and the memory chips used in most computers today. Not only is the industry competitive in the United States, but significant competition is also generated by foreign manufacturers. Prepare a report on the industry as it is today, and include an analysis of its stance with respect to foreign competition.

CHAPTER 6

Output from the Computer

CHAPTER 6

Output from the Computer

OBJECTIVES

- Define the term output.
- List the common types of reports and graphs that are used for output.
- Describe the classifications of printers.
- List the types of printers used with personal computers and describe how they work.
- Discuss the quality of output obtainable from various types of printers.
- Describe printers used for large computers.
- Describe the types of screens available and list common screen features.
- List and describe other types of output devices used with computers.

Output is the way the computer communicates with the user; therefore it is important to know the many ways this communication can take place. This chapter discusses the types of output and the devices computers use to produce output.

WHAT IS OUTPUT?

Output is data that has been processed into a useful form called information that can be used by a person or a machine. Output that is used by a machine, such as a disk or tape file, is usually an intermediate result that eventually will be processed into output that can be used by people. Computer output exists in a variety of forms.

COMMON TYPES OF OUTPUT

The type of output generated from the computer depends on the needs of the user and the hardware and software that are used. The two most common types of output are reports and graphics. These types of output may be printed on a printer or displayed on a screen. Output that is printed is called **hard copy** and output that is displayed is called **soft copy** (Figure 6-1).

Reports

A **report** is data or information presented in an organized form. Most people think of reports as items printed on paper or displayed on a screen. But information printed on forms such as invoices or payroll checks can also be considered types of reports. One way to classify reports is by who uses them. An **internal report** is used by individuals in the performance of their jobs. For example, a daily sales report that is distributed to sales personnel is an internal report because it is used only by personnel *within* the organization. An **external report** is used outside the organization. Payroll checks that are printed and distributed to employees each week are external reports.

Reports may be classified by the way they present information. Three types of reports are common: detail reports, summary reports, and exception reports.

FIGURE 6-1
This photograph shows the same output in hard copy and soft copy form. An advantage of hard copy is that the user can write comments on it and route it to other users.

In a **detail report**, each line on the report usually corresponds to one input record that has been read and processed. Detail reports contain a great deal of information and can be quite lengthy. They are usually required by individuals who need access to the day-to-day information that reflects the operating status of the organization. For example, people in the sales department of a retail store should have access to the number of units sold of each product. The units sold report in Figure 6-2 contains a line for each item, which corresponds to each input record.

As the name implies, a **summary report** summarizes data. It contains totals for certain values found in the input records. The report illustrated in Figure 6-3 contains a summary of the units sold for each department. The information on the summary report consists of totals from the information contained in the detail report in Figure 6-2. Summary reports are most useful for individuals who do not require a detailed knowledge of each transaction. For example, detail reports contain more information than most managers have time to review. With a summary report, however, a manager can quickly review information in summarized form.

UNITS SOLD REPORT

DEPT.	DEPT NAME	ITEM	DESCRIPTION	QTY SOLD
10	MENS FURNISHINGS	105	T-SHIRT	3
10	MENS FURNISHINGS	109	SOCKS	127
12	SLEEPWEAR	199	ROBE	6
14	MENS ACCESSORIES	266	HAT	4

FIGURE 6-2
The data for this detail report was obtained from each input record that was read and processed. A line was printed for each record.

SALES BY DEPARTMENT

DEPT. NO.	DEPT. NAME	UNITS SOLD	SALES $
10	MENS FURNISHINGS	130	653.35
12	SLEEPWEAR	6	189.70
14	MENS ACCESSORIES	4	98.00

FIGURE 6-3
This summary report contains the sales for each department. The report can be prepared from the same data that prepared the report in Figure 6-2.

INVENTORY EXCEPTION REPORT

ITEM NO.	ITEM DESCRIPTION	QUANTITY ON HAND
105	T-SHIRT	24
125	SCARF	3
126	BELT	17

FIGURE 6-4
This exception report lists inventory items with a quantity of less than 25. They could have been selected from thousands of inventory records. Only these items met the user's "exception criteria."

An **exception report** contains information that is outside of "normal" user-specified values or conditions and thus is an "exception" to the majority of the data. For example, if an organization with an inventory wanted to have an on-hand quantity of more than 25 of every inventory item at all times, it would design an exception report to tell them if the amount of any inventory items fell below this level. An example of such a report is shown in Figure 6-4.

Exception reports help users to focus on situations that may require immediate decisions or specific actions. The advantage of exception reports is that they save time and money. In a large department store, for example, there may be over 100,000 inventory items. A detail report containing all inventory items could be longer than 2,000 pages. To search through the report to determine the items whose on-hand quantity was less than 25 would be a difficult and time-consuming task. The exception report, however, could extract these items, which might number 100–200, and place them on a two- to four-page report that could be prepared in just a few minutes.

Graphics

Another common type of output is computer graphics. In business, **computer graphics** are often used to assist in analyzing data. Computer graphics display information in the form of charts, graphs, or pictures so that the information can be understood easily and quickly (Figure 6-5). Facts contained in a lengthy report and data relationships that are difficult to understand in words can often be summarized in a single chart or graph.

In the past, graphics were not widely used in business because each time data was revised, a graphic artist would have to redraw the chart or graph. Today, relatively inexpensive graphics software makes it possible to redraw a chart, graph, or picture within seconds rather than the hours or days that were previously required. Many application software packages, such as spreadsheets, include graphics capabilities. As we discussed in Chapter 2, the three most popular types of charts and graphs are pie charts, bar charts, and line charts.

A **pie chart** is normally used to depict data that may be expressed as a percentage of a whole (Figure 6-6). Pie charts show easy visual comparisons of the relative size of each component within a whole, where the whole represents 100 percent. If used with a color output device, most graphics software allows each component to be displayed in a different color, lets text material be placed on the screen in various colors, and provides shading. Some graphics software even allows certain segments of the chart to be shown with a three-dimensional effect for emphasis.

SALES BY CATEGORY

HIGH SCHOOLS	2,500
COLLEGES	6,200
VO-TECHS	1,200
PRIVATE SCHOOLS	890

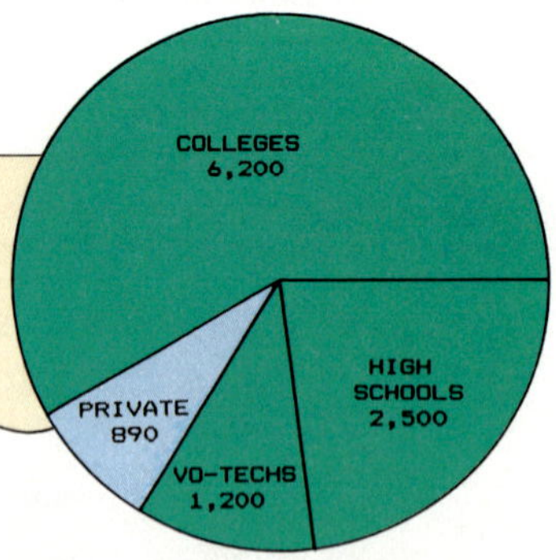

FIGURE 6-5
This small report lists sales of magazines by school category. With the addition of the pie chart graphic, however, the manager can easily see that colleges account for more than half the sales and that private schools represent a small percentage of the sales. Both the report and the graphic use the same information, but the graphic helps the manager to understand the information more quickly.

Bar charts are among the most versatile and popular types of display charts used for comparing data (Figure 6-7). Bar charts represent data by vertical or horizontal bars. They are useful for comparing data in which sizes or quantities vary and the amount of variance needs to be made clear. Graphics software can display bars of different colors, vertical or horizontal bars, and text material where required.

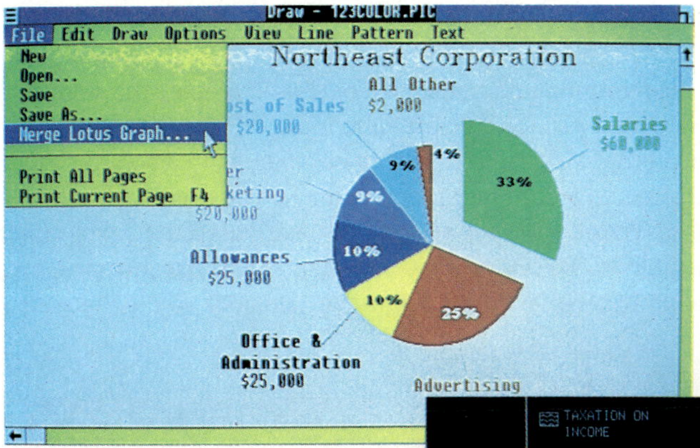

FIGURE 6-6
Pie charts show the relationship of a part to a whole. Color helps distinguish the individual parts of the chart. Some software packages allow repositioning of the pie segments for emphasis.

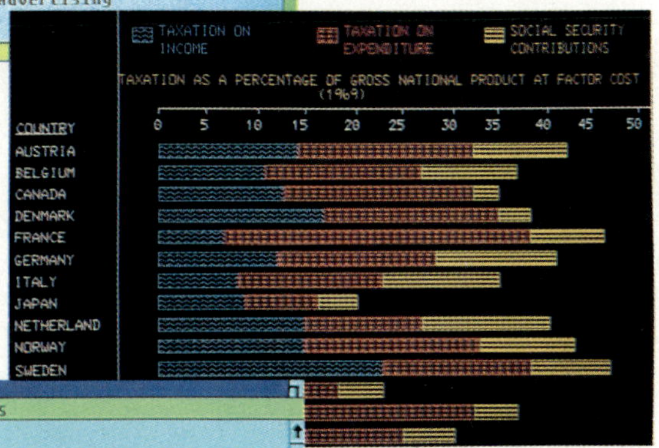

FIGURE 6-7
A bar chart (left) can have vertical or horizontal bars. The horizontal bars in this picture depict taxation as a percentage of the gross national product for different countries. The length of the bars represents the total taxation. The colors within the bars represent the different parts of the whole taxation amount.

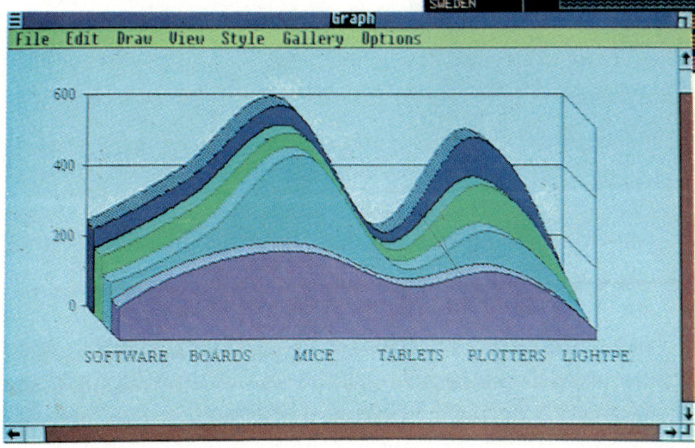

FIGURE 6-8
Line charts are excellent for showing changes over a period of time. The line chart in this picture is rendered using three dimensions and color to enhance the data's presentation.

Line charts may also be generated by graphics software. These charts represent data relationships by a continuous line across the chart (Figure 6-8). Line charts are particularly useful for showing a change in a value or quantity over a period of time.

From the examples of the various types of graphs and charts, you can see how computer graphics offers a powerful tool for the business user who must present data in a meaningful manner or for the manager who must review, analyze, and make decisions based on data relationships.

A variety of devices are used to produce the output created in the information processing cycle. The following paragraphs describe the most commonly used output devices.

PRINTERS

Printing requirements vary greatly among computer users. For example, the user of a personal computer generally uses a printer capable of printing 100 to 200 lines per minute. Users of mainframe computers, such as utility companies that send printed bills to hundreds of thousands of customers each month, need printers that are capable of printing thousands of lines per minute. These different needs have resulted in the development of printers with varying capabilities. Due to the many choices available and because printed output is so widely used, users must be familiar with the factors to consider when choosing a printer (Figure 6-9).

FIGURE 6-9
Factors that affect the choice of a printer

QUESTION	EXPLANATION
How much output will be produced?	Desktop printers are not designed for continuous use. High volume (more than several hundred pages a day) requires a heavy-duty printer.
Who will use the output?	Most organizations want external reports to be prepared on a high-quality printer.
Where will the output be produced?	If the output will be produced at the user's desk, a sound enclosure may be required to reduce the noise of some printers to an acceptable level.
Are multiple copies required?	Some printers cannot use multipart paper.

How Are Printers Classified?

Printers can be classified by how they transfer characters from the printer to the paper, either by impact or nonimpact, and by printer speed.

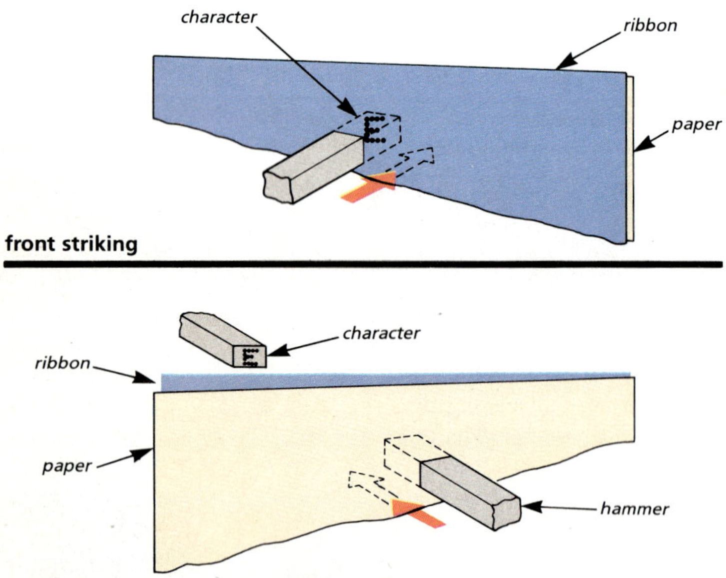

FIGURE 6-10
Impact printers operate in one of two ways: front striking or hammer striking.

Impact and Nonimpact **Impact printers** transfer the image onto paper by some type of printing mechanism striking the paper, ribbon, and character together. One technique is **front striking** in which the printing mechanism that forms the character strikes a ribbon against the paper from the front to form an image. This is similar to the method used on typewriters. The second technique utilizes a **hammer striking** device. The ribbon and paper are struck against the character from the back by a hammer to form the image on the paper (Figure 6-10).

A number of technologies are used to accomplish nonimpact printing. **Nonimpact printing** means that printing occurs without having a mechanism striking against a sheet of paper. For example, ink is sprayed against the paper or heat is used to transfer the character.

Each of these two methods of printing has its advantages and disadvantages. Impact printing can be noisy because the paper is struck when printing occurs. But because the paper is struck, carbon paper can be used to create multiple copies of a report, such as an invoice, that go to different people. Although nonimpact printers cannot create carbon copies, they are very quiet and are ideal for desktop applications where the normal requirements only call for a single printed copy.

Speed Another way to classify printers is by the speed at which they print. Printers can be classified as low speed, medium speed, high speed, and very high speed.

Low-speed printers print one character at a time. The rate of printing for low-speed printers is expressed in the number of characters that can be printed in one second. Low-speed printers can print from 15 to 600 characters per second.

Medium-speed and high-speed printers are called **line printers** because they can print multiple characters on a line at the same time. The rate of printing for these machines is stated in terms of the number of lines per minute that can be printed. **Medium-speed printers** can print from 300 to 600 lines per minute. Printers that can print from 600 to 3,000 lines per minute are classified as **high-speed printers**.

Very high-speed printers can print in excess of 3,000 lines per minute; some, more than 20,000 lines per minute. Very high-speed printers are often called **page printers** because they print an entire page at one time.

Printer Features

To decide which printer to choose for a particular job, it is important to know the different features that a printer might have. Common feature choices include carriage size, type of paper feed mechanism, and bidirectional printing capability.

Carriage Size Most printers are built with either a standard or wide carriage. A **standard carriage** printer can accommodate paper up to 8 1/2 inches wide. A **wide carriage** printer can accommodate paper up to 14 inches wide. Using a normal character size, most printers can print 80 characters per line on a standard carriage and 132 characters per line on a wide carriage.

Feed Mechanism The feed mechanism determines how the paper is moved through the printer. Two types of feed mechanisms are found on printers, tractor feed and friction feed. **Tractor feed mechanisms** transport continuous form paper through the printer by using sprockets, small protruding prongs of plastic or metal, which fit into holes on each side of the paper. The pages of **continuous form paper** are connected for continuous flow through the printer (Figure 6-11). Where it is necessary to feed single sheets of paper into the printer, **friction feed mechanisms** are used. As the name implies, paper is moved through friction feed printers by pressure on the paper and the carriage, as it is on a typewriter. As the carriage rotates, the paper is transported through the printer.

FIGURE 6-11
Each sheet of continuous form paper is connected with the next. A feed mechanism pulls the paper through the printer using the holes on each side of the form. Perforations between each page allow a printed report to be folded and may be used to separate each page.

Bidirectional Printing Some printers are designed to print in a **bidirectional** manner. That is, the print head, the device that contains the mechanism for transferring the character to the paper, can print as it moves from left to right, and from right to left. The printer does this by storing the next line to be printed in its memory and then printing the line forward or backward as needed. Bidirectional printing can almost double the number of characters that can be printed in a given period of time.

PRINTERS FOR SMALL AND MEDIUM COMPUTERS

The increased popularity and use of personal computers has resulted in the development of a large number of printers that vary significantly in speed, quality, and price. Some of these printers are also used on larger systems. The following paragraphs describe the print devices most commonly used on small and medium-size computers.

Dot Matrix Printers

Dot matrix printers are used extensively because they are versatile and relatively inexpensive. The Epson printer shown in Figure 6-12 is a well-known dot matrix printer that is used with personal computers. Figure 6-13 shows a popular Printronix printer that is frequently used with many medium-size computers.

A **dot matrix printer** is an impact printer. Its print head consists of a series of small tubes containing pins that, when pressed against a ribbon and paper, print small dots. The

FIGURE 6-12
The Epson FX-86e printer is a dot matrix printer.

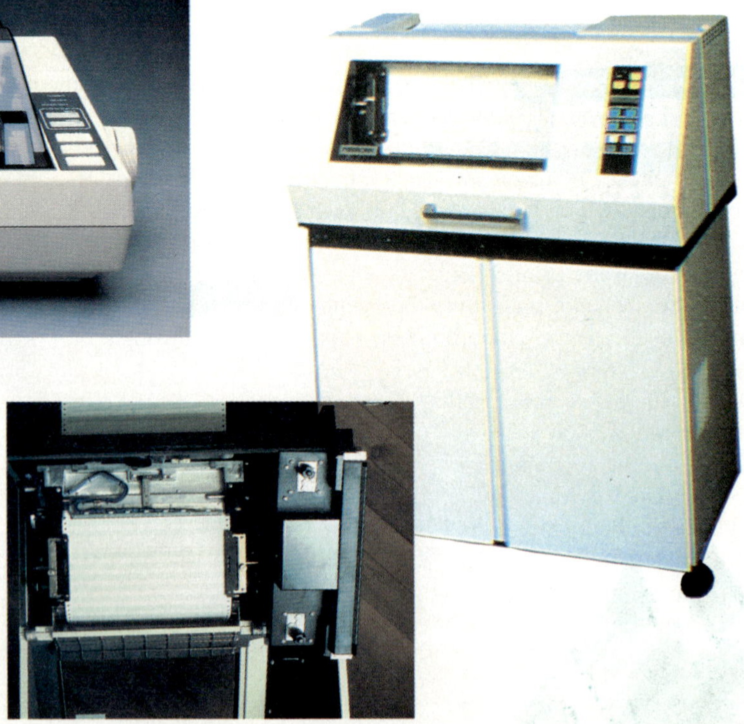

FIGURE 6-13
This line dot matrix printer can print up to 800 lines per minute and is used in many business applications. As shown in the photo with the printer cover open, print heads at each print position allow this device to print an entire line at one time.

combination of small dots printed closely together forms the character (Figure 6-14).

To print a character using a dot matrix printer, the character stored in main memory is sent to the printer's electronic circuitry. The printer circuitry activates the pins in the print head that correspond to the pattern of the character to be printed. The selected pins strike the ribbon and paper and print the character. Low-speed dot matrix printers utilize a movable print head that prints one character at a time. Medium- and high-speed dot matrix printers have print mechanisms at each print position and are able to print an entire line at one time.

Dot matrix printers can contain a varying number of pins, depending on the manufacturer and the printer model. Print heads consisting of nine and 24 pins are most common. Figure 6-15 illustrates the formation of the letter E using a nine-pin dot matrix printer.

A character produced by a dot matrix printer is made up of a series of dots. The quality of print produced is partly dependent on the number of pins used to form the character. A 24-pin print head produces better-looking characters than a nine-pin print head because the dots are closer together.

Several methods are used to improve the quality of dot matrix printers. On a nine-pin printer, one method is to print a line twice. Using this technique a line is printed, and then the print head is shifted very slightly and the line is printed again. This results in overlapping dots, which give the appearance of solid characters (Figure 6-16). The disadvantage, of course, is that the printing takes longer since each character is printed twice. Twenty-four-pin printers can produce the same print quality in a single pass.

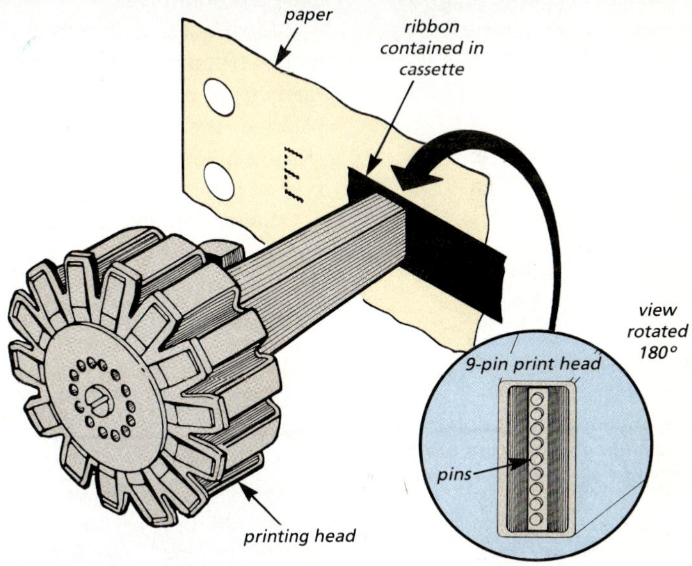

FIGURE 6-14
The print head for a dot matrix printer consists of a series of pins. When activated, the pins strike the ribbon that strikes the paper, creating a dot on the paper.

FIGURE 6-16
The letter E in this example is formed by overprinting, or printing the character twice. When it is printed the second time, the print head is slightly offset so that much of the space between the dots is filled in. This gives the character a better appearance and makes it easier to read.

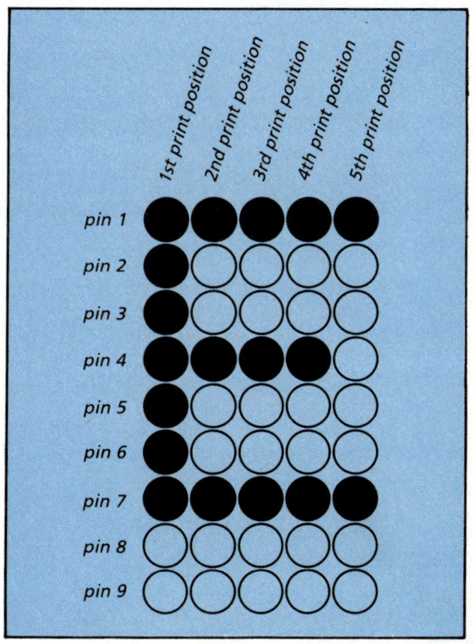

FIGURE 6-15
The letter E is formed with seven vertical and five horizontal dots. As the nine-pin print head moves from left to right, it fires one or more pins into the ribbon, which makes a dot on the paper. At print position 1, it fires pins 1 through 7. At print positions 2 through 4, it fires pins 1, 4, and 7. At print position 5, it fires pins 1 and 7. Pins 8 and 9 are used for lowercase characters such as p, q, y, g, and j that extend below the line.

FIGURE 6-17
Three type sizes are shown in this example—condensed, standard, and enlarged. All three are printed using normal and emphasized (also called "bold") print density.

Many dot matrix printers can also print characters in two or more sizes and densities. Typical sizes include condensed print, standard print, and enlarged print. In addition, each of the three print sizes can be printed with increased density or darkness, called bold print. Figure 6-17 illustrates condensed, condensed bold, standard, standard bold, enlarged, and enlarged bold print.

Most dot matrix printers have a graphics mode that enables them to print pictures and graphs (Figure 6-18). In graphics mode, the individual print head pins can be activated separately or in combination to form unique shapes or continuous lines. When special software packages are used, dot matrix printers can print in many different type styles and sizes (Figure 6-19). The flexibility of the dot matrix printer has resulted in widespread use of this type of printer by all types of computer users.

Some dot matrix printers can print in multiple colors using ribbons that contain the colors red, green, and blue. Color output is obtained by repeated printing and repositioning of the paper, print head, and ribbon. Such printers can be useful in printing graphs and charts, but output quality is not comparable to color produced by other types of printers.

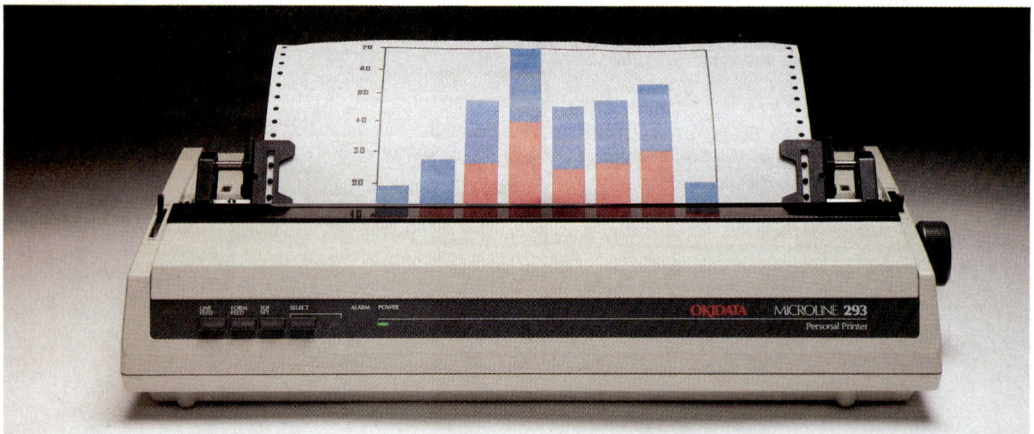

FIGURE 6-18
Many dot matrix printers are capable of producing colored output using special ribbons.

FIGURE 6-19
These letter styles illustrate the abilities of dot matrix printers to print graphics, depending on the software directing the printer.

Daisy Wheel Printers

When users require printed output of high quality, such as for business or legal correspondence, a letter-quality printer is often used. The term **letter quality** refers to the quality of the printed character that is suitable for formal or professional business letters. A letter-quality printed character is a fully formed, solid character like those made by typewriters. It is not made up of a combination of dots, as by a dot matrix printer.

The letter-quality printer most often used with personal computers is the daisy wheel printer (Figure 6-20). The **daisy wheel printer** is an impact printer. It consists of a type element containing raised characters that strike the paper through an inked ribbon.

The daisy wheel element somewhat resembles the structure of a flower, with many long, thin petals (Figure 6-21). Each "petal" has a raised character at the tip. When printing occurs, the type element (daisy wheel) rotates so that the character to be printed is in printing position. A hammer extends, striking the selected character against the ribbon and paper, printing the character. Because of the time required to rotate the daisy wheel, the daisy wheel printer is normally slower than a dot matrix printer; however, the print quality is higher. Printing speeds vary from 20 to 80 characters per second.

An additional feature of the daisy wheel printer is that the daisy wheel can be easily replaced. Daisy wheels come in a variety of sizes and fonts. A font, or typeface as they are sometimes called, is a complete set of characters in a particular style such as script, gothic, or roman. Therefore, whenever the user wishes to change fonts, he or she can remove one daisy wheel and put another wheel on the printer.

The disadvantage of a daisy wheel printer is that it is capable of printing only the characters that are on the wheel. It cannot, therefore, print graphic output.

FIGURE 6-20
A daisy wheel printer produces letter-quality output comparable to that produced by a typewriter. Either continuous form or single-sheet paper can be used with most daisy wheel printers.

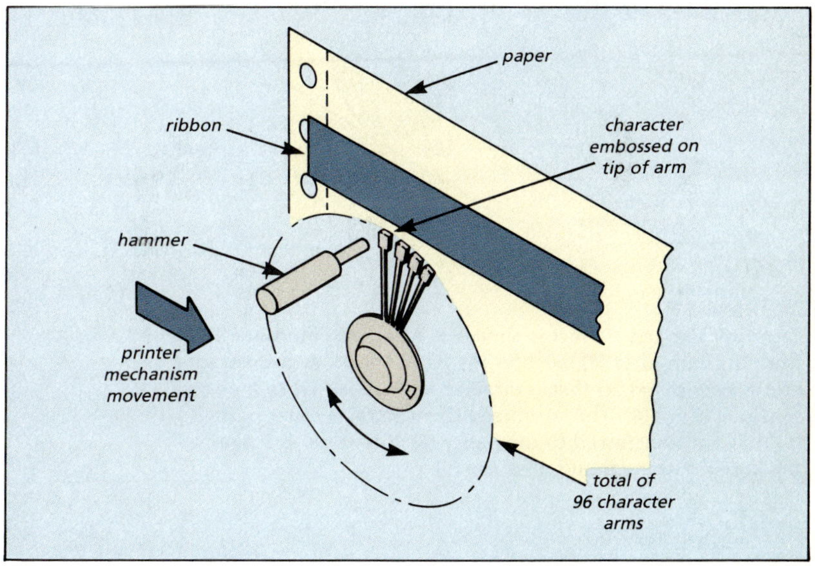

FIGURE 6-21
The daisy wheel print element consists of a number of arms, each with a character at the end. When the printer is running the wheel spins until the desired character is lined up with the hammer. The hammer then strikes against the ribbon and paper, printing the character.

FIGURE 6-22
A color ink jet printer by IBM.

Thermal Printers

Thermal printers use heat to produce fully formed characters, usually on special chemically treated paper. An advantage of thermal printers is that they are very quiet. Disadvantages are their need for special paper and their relatively slow printing speed. Thermal printers are not as commonly used as they once were.

Ink Jet Printers

A popular type of nonimpact printer is an **ink jet printer**. To form a character, an ink jet printer uses nozzles that spray ink onto the page. Ink jet printers produce relatively high-quality print and are very quiet because the paper is not struck as it is by dot matrix or daisy wheel printers. Disadvantages are that ink jet printers cannot produce multiple copies, and the ink sometimes smears on soft, porous paper. The ink jet printer in Figure 6-22 is designed for use with personal computers.

Laser Printers

The **laser printer** is a nonimpact printer that operates in a manner similar to a copying machine (Figure 6-23). The laser printer converts data from the computer into a laser beam that is directed by a mirror to a positively charged revolving drum. Each position on the drum touched by the laser beam becomes negatively charged and attracts the toner (powdered ink). The toner is transferred onto the paper and then fused to the paper by heat and pressure. The end result is a high-quality printed image. As shown in Figure 6-24, laser printers can produce a variety of output.

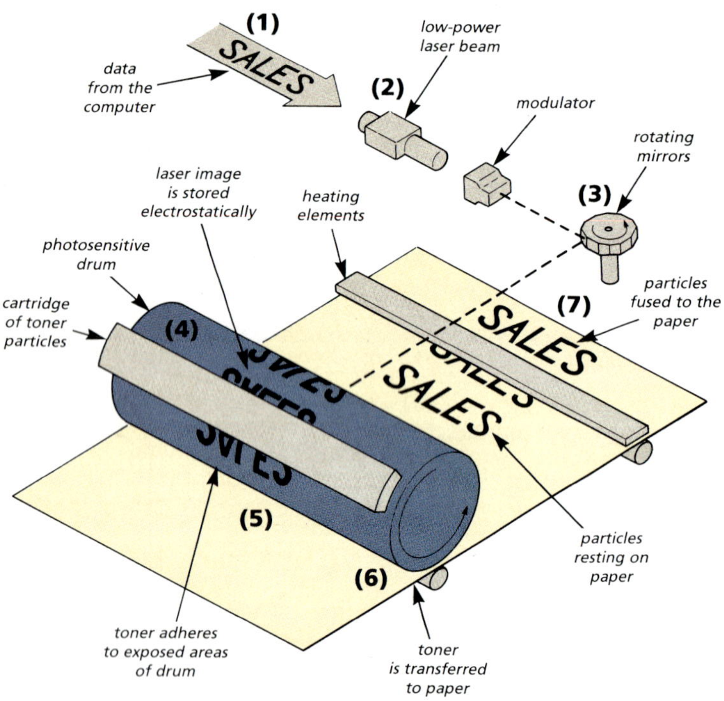

FIGURE 6-23
Laser printers use a process similar to a copying machine. Data from the computer (1), such as the word SALES, is converted into a laser beam (2) that is directed by a mirror (3) to a photosensitive drum (4). The sensitized drum attracts toner particles (5) that are transferred to the paper (6). The toner is fused to the paper with heat and pressure (7).

FIGURE 6-24
The output illustrated in this picture was produced by a laser printer. Note that the output contains a mixture of different sizes and styles of print.

PRINTERS FOR LARGE COMPUTERS

Minicomputers and mainframes are frequently used to process and print large volumes of data. As the demand for printing information from a computer increases, the use of higher speed printers is required. The three types of printers often used on large computers are chain printers, band printers, and high-speed laser printers.

Chain Printers

The **chain printer** is a widely used high-speed printer. It contains numbers, letters of the alphabet, and selected special characters on a rotating chain (Figure 6-25). The chain consists of a series of type slugs that contain the character set. The character set on the type slugs is repeated two or more times on the chain mechanism. The chain rotates at a very high speed. Each possible print position has a hammer that can fire against the back of the paper, forcing the paper and ribbon against the character on the chain. As the chain rotates, the hammer fires when the character to be printed is in the proper position.

The chain printer has proven to be very reliable. It produces good print quality at up to 3,000 lines per minute. The printers in the large computer installation in Figure 6-26 are chain printers.

Band Printers

Band printers, similar to chain printers, utilize a horizontal, rotating band containing characters. The characters are struck by hammers located behind the paper and a ribbon to create a line of print on the paper (Figure 6-27).

Interchangeable type bands can be used on band printers. The different type bands contain many different fonts or print styles. A band printer can produce up to six carbon copies, has good print quality, high reliability, and depending on the manufacturer and model of the printer, can print in the range of 300 to 2,000 lines per minute.

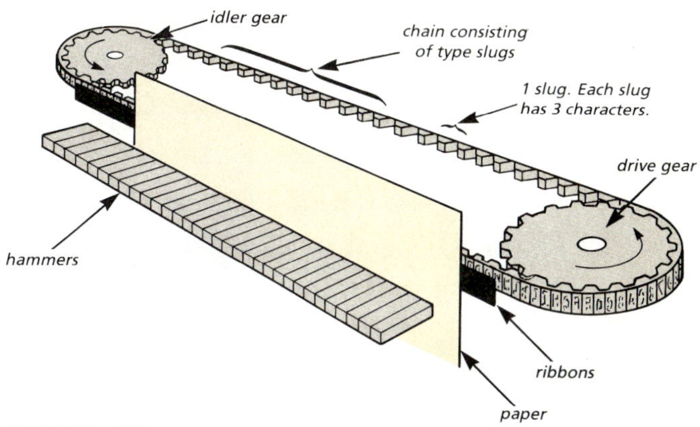

FIGURE 6-25
The chain printer contains a complete set of characters on several sections of a chain that rotates at a high, constant rate of speed. Print hammers are located at each horizontal print position. The paper and ribbon are placed between the hammers and the chain. As the chain rotates, the hammers fire when the proper characters are in front of their print positions.

FIGURE 6-26
These high-speed chain printers are used in a large computer installation to produce thousands of lines of printed output per minute.

FIGURE 6-27
A band printer uses a metal band that contains solid characters. Print hammers (shown inside the band) at each print location strike the paper and the ribbon, forcing them into the band to print the character.

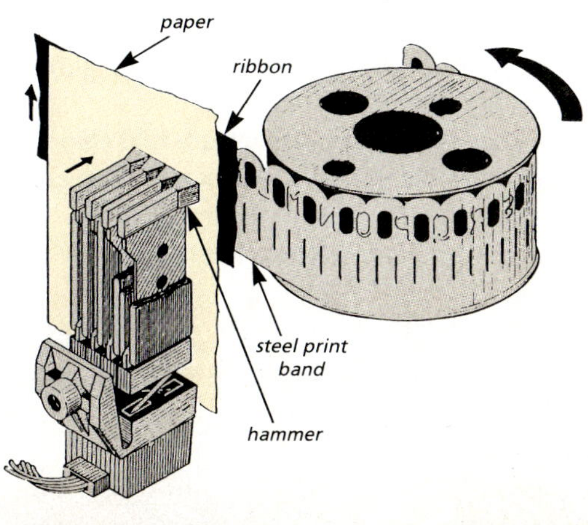

FIGURE 6-28
This laser printer can operate at speeds up to 70 pages per minute. As shown in the picture, high-speed printers often use tape drives that contain the data to be printed.

High-Speed Laser Printers

High-speed laser printers, also called **page printers**, can produce printed output at the rate of over 20,000 lines per minute, the equivalent of over 400 pages of 50 lines per page. As shown in Figure 6-28, these high-speed printers usually consist of a dedicated computer and tape drive to maximize the printing speed. When the device is printing, the paper moves so fast that it must be folded and stacked mechanically.

SCREENS

The **screen**, also called the monitor, CRT (cathode ray tube), or VDT (video display terminal), is another important output device. Screens are used on both personal computers and terminals to display many different types of output. For example, responses obtained from user inquiries to a database are frequently displayed on a screen. A screen can also be used to display electronic spreadsheets, electronic mail, and graphs of various types.

Screen Features

Size The most widely used screens are equivalent in size to a 12- to 15-inch television screen. Although there is no standard number of displayed characters, screens are usually designed to display 80 characters on a line with a maximum of 25 lines displayed at one time. The 25th line is often reserved for messages or system status reports, not for data. This provides for a maximum of 2,000 characters on the screen at once. Some terminals can display up to 132 characters on a single horizontal line. The more characters that are displayed on a line, the smaller the size of the characters. Therefore, an important consideration when selecting a terminal is the number of characters displayed on the screen at one time and the *resolution* (clarity) of the characters displayed.

FIGURE 6-29
Many users prefer amber or green characters rather than white characters.

Color Most of the early screens displayed white characters on a black background. Research has indicated, however, that other color combinations are easier on the eyes. Today, many screens display either green or amber characters on a black background (Figure 6-29).

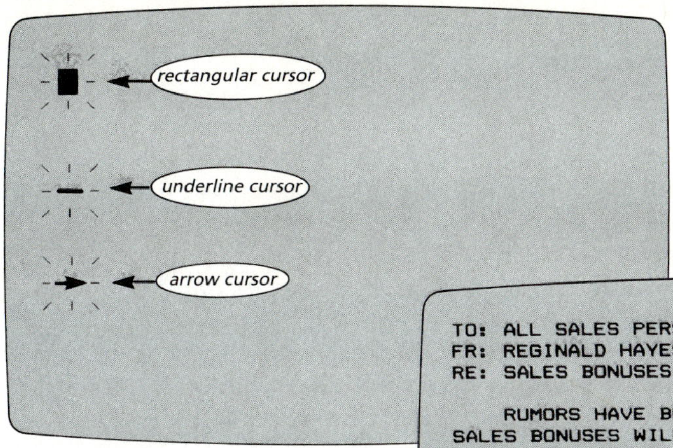

◄ **FIGURE 6-30**
Three types of cursors are shown in this illustration—a rectangular cursor, an underline cursor, and an arrow cursor. Often, cursors blink to be easily identified.

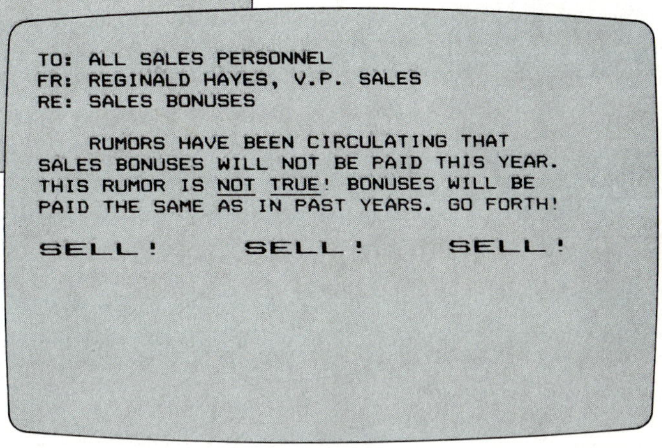

FIGURE 6-31►
The memo shown on the screen uses both underlining and double-size characters to emphasize portions of the message.

Cursor A **cursor** is a symbol that indicates where on the screen the next character entered will be displayed. It can also be used as a marker on a screen to identify the choices a user can make. Some of the symbols used to represent cursors are shown in Figure 6-30. Most cursors blink when they are displayed on the screen so the user can quickly find their location.

Scrolling **Scrolling** is a method of moving lines displayed on the screen up or down one line at a time. As a new line is added, for example, to the bottom of the screen, an existing one, from the top of the screen, is removed. The line removed from the screen remains in the computer's memory even though it is no longer displayed. When the screen is scrolled in the opposite direction (in this example, down), the line from the top that was removed reappears on the screen and the line at the bottom is removed.

Paging When **paging** is used, an entirely new "page" or screen of data can be displayed. This feature is useful in applications such as word processing when a user wants to use the screen to move quickly through pages of a long document.

Other Screen Features Screen features also include several options that can be used to emphasize displayed characters: reverse video, underlining, bold, blinking, and double size. **Reverse video** refers to the process of reversing the normal display on the screen. For example, it is possible to display a dark background with light characters or a light background with dark characters. Thus, if the normal screen had amber characters on a black background, reverse video shows black characters on an amber background. This feature permits single characters, whole words or lines, and even the entire screen to be reversed. The **underlining** feature allows characters, words, lines, or paragraphs to be underlined. Another feature used for emphasis is the ability to display some characters or words as bold. **Bold** means that characters are displayed at a greater brightness level than the surrounding text. The **blinking** feature makes characters or words on a screen blink, thus drawing attention to them. The **double size** feature means that certain characters or words are displayed at twice the size of normal characters and words. Figure 6-31 illustrates how underlining and double-size characters highlight data on the screen.

FIGURE 6-32
The high resolution of this plasma display allows the screen to display any combination of character fonts, line drawings, charts, sketches and letters.

Types of Screens

Several types of screens are used with computers. The most common types are monochrome screens, color screens, plasma screens, and LCD screens. Plasma and LCD screens, which do not use the conventional cathode ray tube technology, are sometimes called **flat panel display screens** because of their relatively flat screens.

Monochrome screens specially designed for use with personal computers or for use as computer terminals usually display a single color, such as white, green, or amber characters on a black background. The characters are displayed without flicker and with very good resolution. Some monochrome screens have graphics capabilities.

The use of **color screens** is increasing in business and science applications, because numerous studies have found that color enables the user to more easily read and understand the information displayed on the screen.

A **plasma screen** produces a bright, clear image with no flicker (Figure 6-32). The screens are flat, so that they can be installed on desks or walls, taking up very little space.

With the development of truly portable computers that could be conveniently carried by hand or in a briefcase came a need for an output display that was equally as portable. Although several technologies have been developed, **liquid crystal displays (LCD)** are used as the output display for a number of laptop computers (Figure 6-33). LCD displays are also used in watches, calculators, and other electronic devices.

FIGURE 6-33
The liquid crystal display (LCD) screen used with this portable computer can display numbers, letters, and special characters, and even has some graphics capabilities.

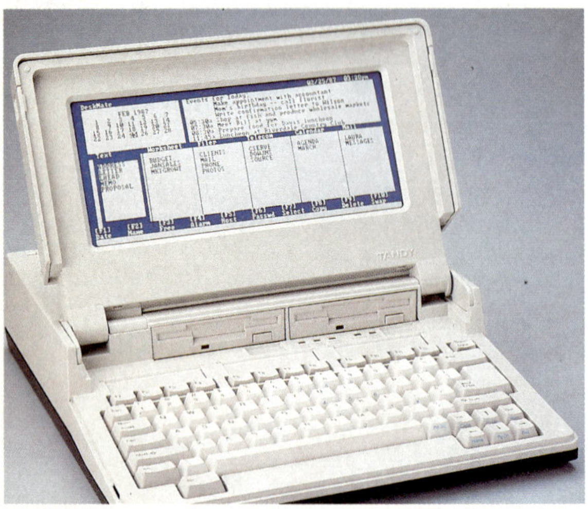

How Characters Are Displayed on a Screen

Most screens used with personal computers and terminals utilize cathode ray tube (CRT) technology. When these screens produce an image, the following steps occur (Figure 6-34):

1. The image to be displayed on the screen is sent electronically from the CPU to the cathode ray tube.
2. An electron gun generates an electron beam of varying intensity, depending on the electronic data received from the CPU.
3. The yoke, which generates an electromagnetic field, moves the electron beam horizontally across the **phosphor-coated screen**.
4. The electron beam causes the desired phosphors to emit light. The higher the intensity of the beam, the brighter the phosphor glows. It is the phosphor-emitted light that produces an image on the screen.

On most screens, the phosphors that emit the light causing the image on the screen do not stay lit very long. They must be *refreshed* by having the electron beam light them again. If the screen is not scanned enough times per second, the phosphors will begin to lose their light. When this occurs, it appears that the characters on the screen are flickering. To eliminate flicker, a scan rate of 60 times per second is normal when the screen is used for alphanumeric display.

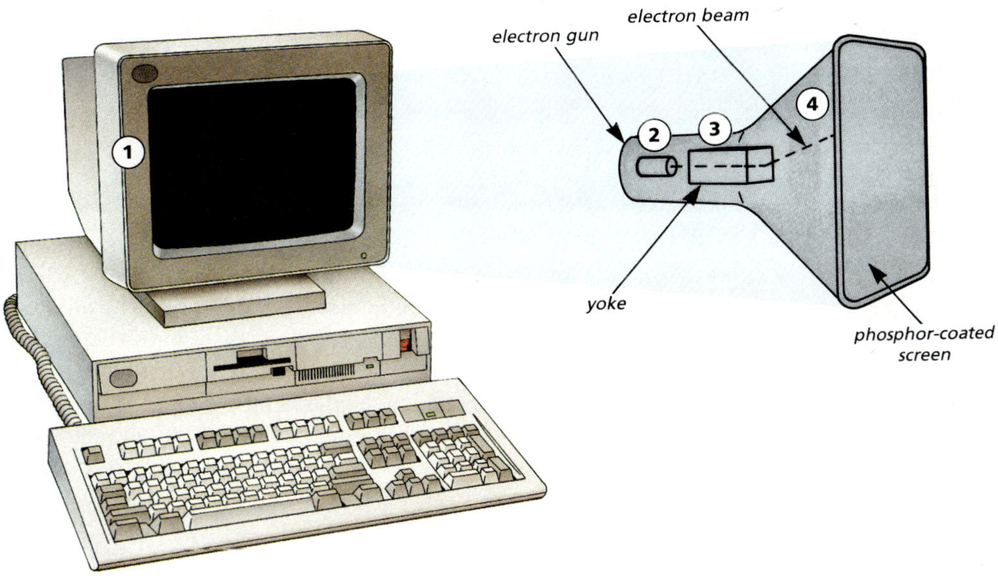

FIGURE 6-34
When an image is formed on a screen, the information to be displayed is sent to the screen (1). Then the electron gun (2) generates an electron beam. The yoke (3) directs the beam to a specific spot on the screen (4), where the phosphors struck by the electron beam begin to glow and form an image on the screen.

The brightness of the image on the screen depends on the intensity of the electron beam striking the phosphor, which in turn depends on the voltage applied to the beam. As the beam scans each phosphor dot, the intensity is varied precisely to turn each dot on or off.

Computer screens are divided into addressable locations. The manner of indicating the number of addressable locations varies with the type of screen. On a screen used primarily for characters and alphanumeric displays, the number of locations is usually identified by specifying the number of lines and the number of characters per line that can be displayed (sometimes called the character display addressing scheme).

Screens used for graphics are called **dot-addressable displays**, or sometimes **bit-mapped displays**. On these monitors, the number of addressable locations corresponds to the number of dots that can be illuminated. Each addressable dot that can be illuminated is called a **picture element** or **pixel** (Figure 6-35).

With dot-addressable displays, the resolution or clarity of the characters depends to a great extent on the number of pixels on the screen. The greater the number of pixels, the better the screen resolution. The number of pixels on a screen is determined through a combination of the software in the computer, the connection between the computer and the screen, and the screen itself. Some screens and computers operate in two or more resolution modes. For example, the IBM PS/2 series of personal computers, when operating in graphics mode, can use either medium or high resolution. In medium resolution, the screen contains 64,000 individual pixels arranged in 200 rows, each row containing 320 pixels. When high resolution is used, 480 rows can contain 640 pixels for a total of 307,200 distinct points.

Devices are currently available that offer very high-resolution graphics. The resolution of these devices is high enough to provide

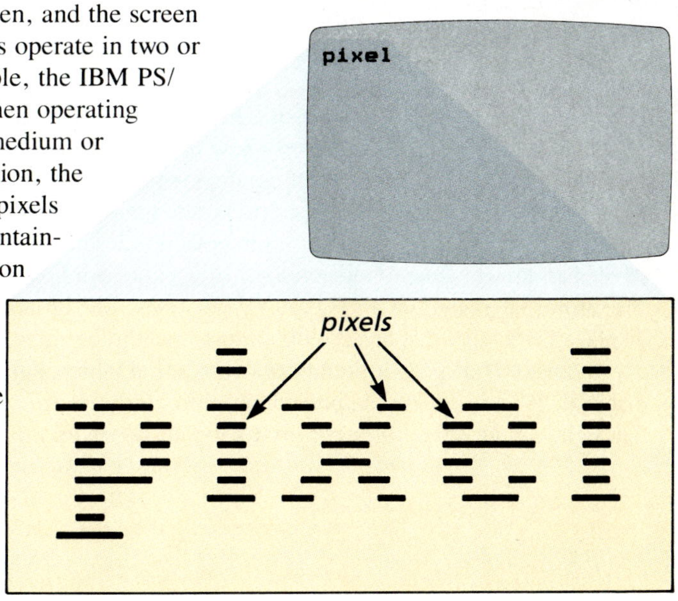

FIGURE 6-35
The word pixel shown in this drawing is made up of pixels as they would be displayed on a dot-addressable or bit-mapped screen. Each pixel is a small rectangular spot of light that appears on the screen at the point where it is activated by an electron beam. These pixels must be reactivated about 60 times per second to appear as a solid character without screen flicker.

FIGURE 6-36
The picture on the left shows how very high-resolution graphics can depict features such as shading, reflections, and highlights. The picture on the right shows how very high-resolution graphics can be used for simulation exercises; in this case, a flying situation. Through the use of the computer, this picture could be changed quickly to show the plane taking off and landing.

an image that is almost equivalent to the quality of a photograph (Figure 6-36). High-resolution graphics requires a great deal of storage, and it is more difficult electronically to maintain a steady image on the screen. In the past few years, however, there have been great improvements in picture resolutions. In addition, costs have been reduced so that high-resolution graphics are now widely used. Several graphics standards have been developed, including CGA (Color Graphics Adapter), EGA (Enhanced Graphics Adapter), and the latest standard from IBM called VGA (Video Graphics Array). Each standard provides for different numbers of pixels and colors.

How Color Is Produced Color is produced on a screen in several ways. Remember that on a monochrome screen, a single electron beam strikes the phosphor-coated screen, causing the chosen phosphor dot to light. If the characters are green on a black background, the phosphors emit a green light when activated. Similarly, if the characters are amber on black, the phosphors emit an amber light.

To show color on a screen, three phosphor dots are required for each pixel. These dots are red, blue, and green (Figure 6-37). The electron beam must turn on the desired color phosphors within the pixel to generate an image. In the simplest configuration, eight colors can be generated—no color (black), red only, blue only, green only, red and blue (magenta), red and green (yellow), blue and green (blue-green), and red, blue, and green together (white). By varying the intensity of the electron beam striking the phosphors, many more colors can be generated.

Two common types of color screens are composite video monitors and RGB monitors. Both monitors produce color images, and both monitors can be used for color graphics. A **composite video monitor** uses a single electron signal to turn on the color phosphors within the pixel. An **RGB monitor** uses three signals, one for each color, red, green, and blue, to turn on the required phosphors. The difference is that the RGB monitor produces a much clearer display with much better color and character resolution.

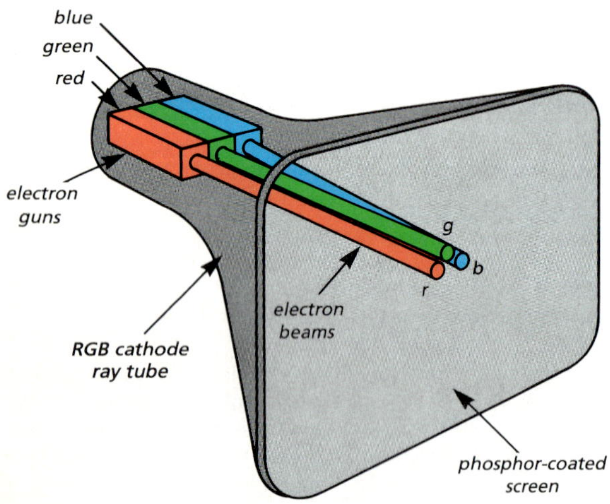

FIGURE 6-37
On color monitors, each pixel contains three phosphor dots: one red, one green, and one blue. These dots can be turned on individually or in combinations to display a wide range of colors.

How Flat Panel Displays Work Plasma screens use a relatively new display technology. A plasma screen consists of a grid of conductors sealed between two flat plates of glass. The space between the glass is filled with neon/argon gas. When the gas at an intersection in the grid is electronically excited, it creates an image. Each intersection of the grid of wires in a plasma screen is addressable. Therefore, characters in a variety of type styles, line drawings, charts, or even pictures can be displayed. Pictures displayed look almost like photographs.

In an LCD display, a liquid crystal material is deposited between two sheets of polarizing material. When a current is passed between crossing wires, the liquid crystals are aligned so that light cannot shine through, producing an image on the screen.

OTHER OUTPUT DEVICES

Although printers and display devices provide the large majority of computer output, other devices are available for particular uses and applications. These include plotters, computer output microfilm devices, and voice output devices.

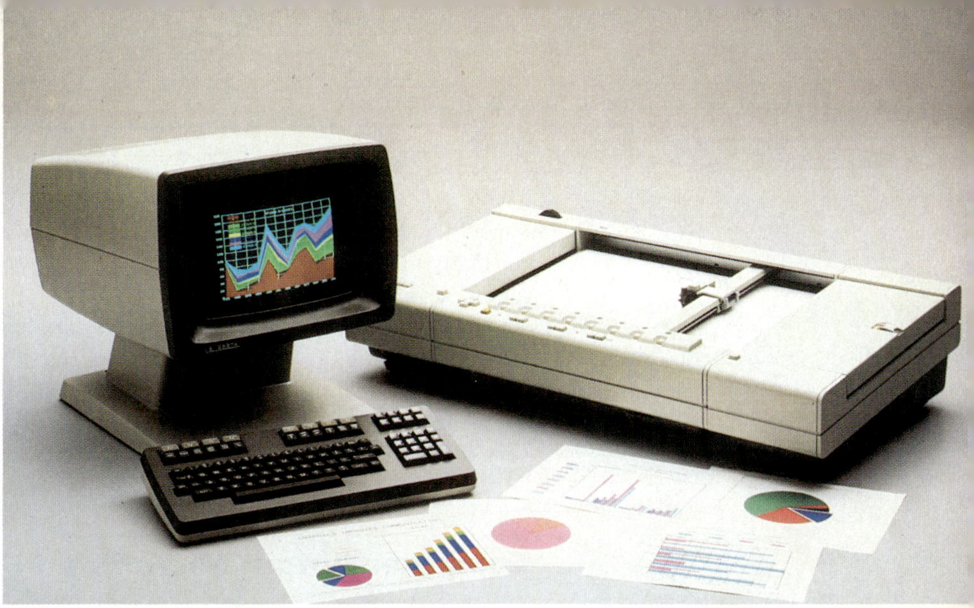

FIGURE 6-38
An example of a flatbed plotter.

Plotters

A **plotter** is an output device used to produce high-quality line drawings, such as building plans, charts, or circuit diagrams. These drawings can be quite large; some plotters are designed to handle paper up to 40 inches by 48 inches, much larger than would fit in a standard printer. The plotter can also draw numbers and letters to add text to the output. Plotters can be classified by the way they create the drawing. The two types are pen plotters and electrostatic plotters.

As the name implies, **pen plotters** create images on a sheet of paper by moving one or more pens over the surface of the paper or by moving the paper under the tip of the pens.

Two different kinds of pen plotters are flatbed plotters and drum plotters. When a **flatbed plotter** is used to plot or draw, the pen or pens are instructed by the software to move to the down position so the pen contacts the flat surface of the paper. Further instructions then direct the movement of the pens to create the image. Most flatbed plotters have one or more pens of varying colors or widths. The plotter illustrated in Figure 6-38 is a flatbed plotter that can create color drawings. Another kind of flatbed plotter holds the pen stationary and moves the paper under the pen.

A **drum plotter** uses a rotating drum or cylinder over which drawing pens are mounted. The pens can move to the left and right as the drum rotates, creating an image (Figure 6-39). An advantage of the drum plotter is that the length of the plot is virtually unlimited, since roll paper can be used. The width of the plot is limited by the width of the drum.

With an **electrostatic plotter**, the paper moves under a row of wires (called styli) that can be turned on to create an electrostatic charge on the paper. The paper then passes through a developer and the drawing emerges where the charged wires touched the

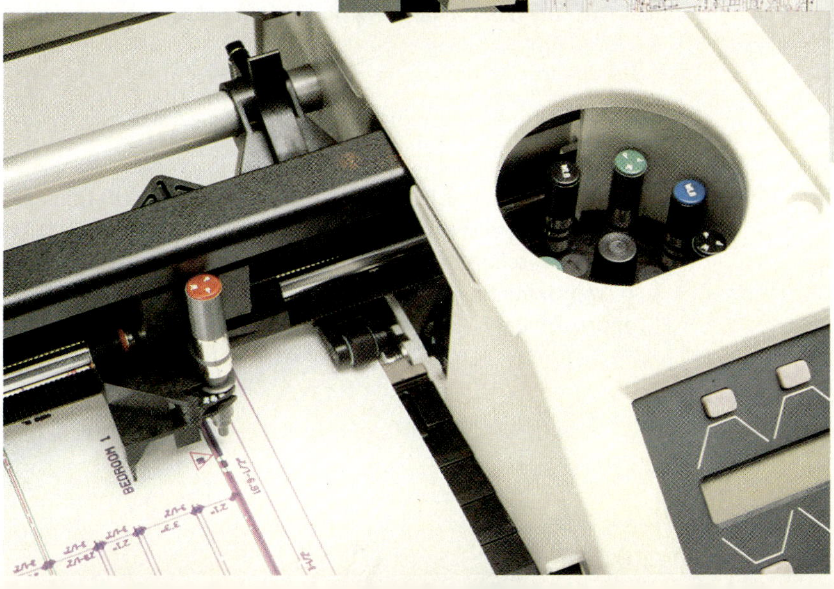

FIGURE 6-39
This drum plotter utilizes eight pens of different colors to create diagrams. As the paper moves forward and back, the pens move left and right and, under software control, draw where instructed.

paper. The electrostatic printer image is composed of a series of very small dots, resulting in relatively high-quality output. In addition, the speed of plotting is faster than with pen plotters.

Factors affecting the cost of a plotter are based on the resolution of the drawing and the speed of the plotting. Resolution is determined by the smallest movement a pen can make on the paper. Typical plotter movements may vary from .001 to .0005 inch. Plotting speeds of up to 36 inches per second are possible. Costs range from under $1,000 to over $100,000 for very high-speed plotters with extremely fine resolution.

Computer Output Microfilm

Computer output microfilm (COM) is an output technique that records output from a computer as microscopic images on roll or sheet film. The images stored on COM are the same as the images that would be printed on paper. The COM recording process reduces characters 24, 42, or 48 times smaller than would be produced on a printer. The information is then recorded on sheet film called **microfiche** or on 16mm, 35mm, or 105mm roll film.

The data to be recorded by the device can come directly from the computer (online) or from a magnetic tape that was previously produced by the computer (offline) (Figure 6-40). After the COM film is processed, the user can view it.

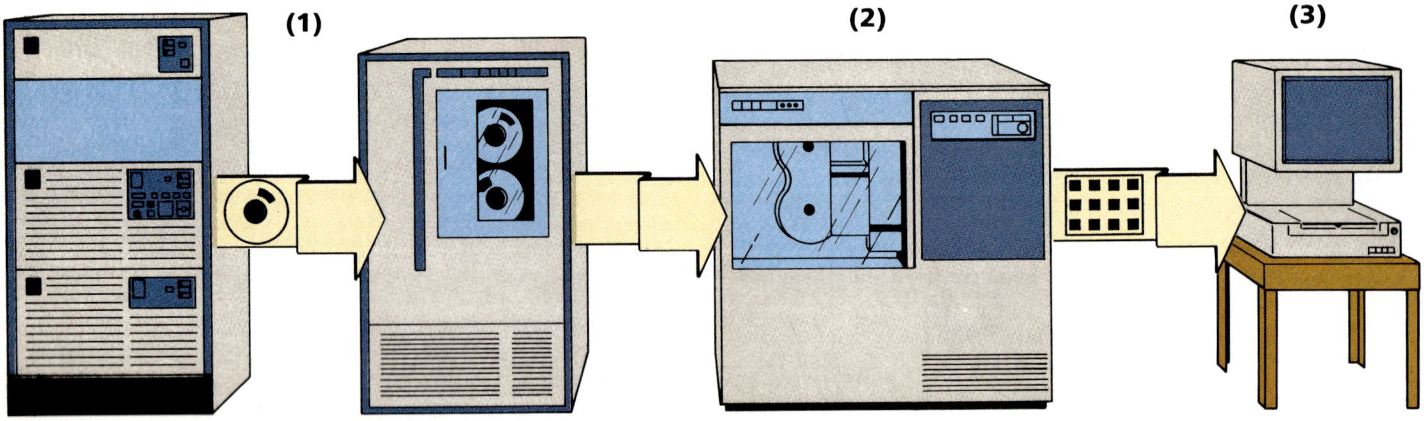

FIGURE 6-40
This drawing illustrates the computer output microfilm (COM) process. The computer generates printed images on an output tape that is transferred to the tape drive attached to the COM machine (1). The COM machine reads the tape and produces reduced images of the printed output on film (2); in this example, microfiche sheet film. Then the film can be viewed using special microfilm reader devices (3).

Microfilm has several advantages over printed reports or other storage media for certain applications. Some of these advantages are:

1. Data can be recorded on the film at up to 30,000 lines per minute—faster than all except very high-speed printers.
2. Costs for recording the data are lower. The cost of printing a three-part, 1,000-page report is approximately $28, whereas the cost of producing the same report on microfilm is approximately $3.

3. Less space is required to store microfilm than printed materials. A microfiche that weighs one ounce can store the equivalent of 10 pounds of paper.
4. Microfiche provides a less expensive way to store data. For example, the cost per million characters (megabyte) on a disk is approximately $20, while the cost per megabyte on microfilm is approximately $.65.

To access data stored on microfilm, a variety of readers are available. They utilize indexing techniques to provide a quick reference to the data. Some microfilm readers can perform automatic data lookup, called **computer-assisted retrieval**, under the control of an attached minicomputer. With the powerful indexing software and hardware now available for microfilm, a user can usually locate any piece of data in a 200,000,000-character database in less than 10 seconds, at a far lower cost per inquiry than using an online inquiry system consisting of a computer system that stores the data on a hard disk.

Voice Output

The other important means of generating output from a computer is voice output. **Voice output** consists of spoken words that are conveyed to the user from the computer. Thus, instead of reading words on a printed report or monitor, the user hears the words over earphones, the telephone, or other devices from which sound can be generated.

The data that produces voice output is usually created in one of two ways. First, a person can talk into a device that will encode the words in a digital pattern. For example, the words "The number is" can be spoken into a microphone, and the computer software can assign a digital pattern to the words. The digital data is then stored on a disk. At a later time, the data can be retrieved from the disk and translated back from digital data into voice, so that the person listening will actually hear the words.

A second type of voice generation is new but holds great promise. Called a **voice synthesizer**, it can transform words stored in main memory into speech. The words are analyzed by a program that examines the letters stored in memory and generates sounds for the letter combinations. The software can apply rules of intonation and stress to make it sound as though a person were speaking. The speech is then projected over speakers attached to the computer. computer.

You may have heard voice output used by the telephone company for giving number information. Automobile and vending machine manufacturers are also incorporating voice output into their products. The potential for this type of output is great and it will undoubtedly be used in many products and services in the future.

SUMMARY OF OUTPUT TO THE COMPUTER

The output step of the information processing cycle uses a variety of devices to provide users with information. Some of the devices that were discussed in this chapter, including printers and screens, are summarized in Figure 6-41.

FIGURE 6-41
This table summarizes some of the more common output devices

OUTPUT DEVICE	DESCRIPTION
Printers—Impact	
Dot matrix	Prints text and graphics using small dots.
Daisy wheel	Prints letter-quality documents—no graphics.
Chain	High-speed printer to 3,000 lines per minute—designed to print text.
Band	High-speed printer to 2,000 lines per minute—designed to print text.
Printers—Nonimpact	
Thermal	Uses heat to produce fully formed characters.
Ink jet	Sprays ink onto page to form text and graphic output—prints quietly.
Laser	Produces high-quality text and graphics.
High-speed laser	Can exceed 20,000 lines per minute.
Screens	
Monochrome	Displays white, green, or amber images on a black background.
Color	Uses multiple colors to enhance displayed information.
Plasma	A flat screen that produces bright, clear images with no flicker.
LCD	A flat screen used on many laptop computers.
Plotters	Produces hard copy graphic output.
COM	Records reduced-size information on sheet film called microfiche or on roll film.
Voice	Conveys information to the user from the computer in the form of speech.

CHAPTER SUMMARY

1. **Output** is data that has been processed into a useful form called information that can be used by a person or a machine.
2. An **external report** is used outside the organization.
3. An **internal report** is used within an organization by people performing their jobs.
4. The major consideration for internal reports is that they be clear and easy to use. For external reports, the quality of the printed output may be important.
5. In a **detail report**, each line on the report usually corresponds to one input record.
6. A **summary report** contains summarized data, consisting of totals from detailed input data.
7. An **exception report** contains information that will help users to focus on situations that may require immediate decisions or specific actions.
8. **Computer graphics** are used to present information so it can be quickly and easily understood.
9. A **pie chart** is normally used to depict data that can be expressed as a percentage of a whole.

10. A **bar chart**, is best used for comparing sizes or quantities.
11. **Line charts** are particularly useful when showing changes over a period of time.
12. Computer printers fall into two broad categories: impact printers and nonimpact printers.
13. **Impact printing** devices transfer the image onto paper by some type of printing mechanism striking the paper, ribbon, and character together.
14. Impact printers can be **front striking** or **hammer striking**.
15. A **nonimpact printer** creates an image without having characters strike against a sheet of paper.
16. Impact printing is noisy but multiple copies can be made.
17. Nonimpact printers are quiet and some print very fast.
18. Computer printers may be classified by the speed at which they print: low, medium, high, and very high speed.
19. The printing rate of **low-speed printers** is expressed as the number of characters that can be printed in one second.
20. The printing rate for **medium-speed printers** and **high-speed printers** is stated as the number of lines printed per minute.
21. Medium- and high-speed printers are sometimes called **line printers**.
22. **Very high-speed printers** are sometimes called **page printers**.
23. Features of printers include carriage size, type of paper feed mechanism, and bidirectional printing.
24. The pages of **continuous form paper** are connected for continuous flow through the printer.
25. **Tractor feed mechanisms** transport continuous form paper by using sprokets inserted into holes on the sides of the paper.
26. **Friction feed** mechanisms move paper through a printer by pressure between the paper and the carriage.
27. **Dot matrix printers** can print text and graphics and are used with more personal computers than any other type of printer.
28. Dot matrix printers have small pins that are contained in a print head. The pins strike the paper and ribbon to print a character.
29. Most dot matrix printers print **bidirectionally**, meaning the print head can print while moving in either direction.
30. The quality of a dot matrix printer is partly dependent on the number of pins used to form the character.
31. Most dot matrix printers can print condensed print, standard print, and enlarged print.
32. Some dot matrix printers can print in color.
33. A **letter-quality** printed character is a fully formed character that is easy to read.
34. The most widely used letter-quality printer for personal computers is the **daisy wheel printer**.
35. Speeds of a daisy wheel printer vary from 20 to 60 characters per second.
36. **Thermal printers** use heat to produce fully formed characters, usually on chemically treated paper.
37. An **ink jet printer** uses a nozzle to spray liquid ink drops onto the page. Some ink jet printers print in color.
38. **Chain printers** print up to 3,000 lines per minute.
39. **Band printers** have interchangeable bands with many different styles of fonts.
40. **Laser printer** are nonimpact printers that operate in a manner similar to a copying machine.
41. Types of screens include monochrome screens, color screens, plasma screens, and LCD screens.
42. **Monochrome** monitors usually display green, white, or amber characters on a black background.
43. **Color screens** are being used more because color enables the user to more easily read and understand the information displayed on the screen.
44. A **plasma** display can produce all kinds and sizes of type styles, charts, and drawings.
45. **Liquid crystal displays** use a polarizing material and liquid crystal to form images.
46. Most screens utilize cathode ray tube (CRT) technology.
47. To display color on a color monitor, three separate dots (red, blue, green) are turned on by an electron beam.
48. The two types of color monitors are: **composite video monitors** and **RGB monitors**.
49. A **computer plotter** is an output device that can create drawings, diagrams, and similar types of output.
50. **Computer output microfilm (COM)** is an output technique that records output from a computer as microscopic images on roll or sheet film.
51. COM offers the advantages of faster recording speed, lower costs of recording the data, less space required for storing the data, and lower costs of storing the data.
52. **Voice output** consists of spoken words that are conveyed to the computer user from the computer.
53. A **voice synthesizer** can transform words stored in main memory into human speech.

KEY TERMS

Band printers *6.13*
Bar charts *6.4*
Bidirectional *6.8*
Bit-mapped displays *6.17*
Blinking *6.15*
Bold *6.15*
Chain printer *6.13*
Color screens *6.16*
COM *6.20*
Composite video monitor *6.18*
Computer-assisted retrieval *6.21*
Computer graphics *6.4*
Computer output microfilm (COM) *6.20*
Continuous form paper *6.7*
Cursor *6.15*
Daisy wheel printer *6.11*
Detail report *6.3*
Dot-addressable displays *6.17*
Dot matrix printer *6.8*
Double size *6.15*
Drum plotter *6.19*
Electrostatic plotter *6.19*
Exception report *6.4*
External report *6.3*
Flatbed plotters *6.19*
Flat panel display screens *6.16*
Friction feed mechanisms *6.7*
Front striking *6.6*
Hammer striking *6.6*
Hard copy *6.2*
High-speed laser printers *6.14*
High-speed printers *6.7*
Impact printers *6.6*
Ink jet printer *6.12*
Internal report *6.3*
Laser printers *6.12*
LCD *6.16*
Letter quality *6.11*
Line charts *6.5*
Line printers *6.7*
Liquid crystal displays (LCD) *6.16*
Low-speed printers *6.7*
Medium-speed printers *6.7*
Microfiche *6.20*
Monochrome screens *6.16*
Nonimpact printing *6.6*
Output *6.2*
Page printers *6.7*
Paging *6.15*
Pen plotters *6.19*
Phosphor-coated screen *6.16*
Picture element *6.17*
Pie charts *6.4*
Pixel *6.17*
Plasma screen *6.16*
Plotter *6.19*
Report *6.3*
Reverse video *6.15*
RGB monitor *6.18*
Screen *6.14*
Scrolling *6.15*
Soft copy *6.2*
Standard carriage *6.7*
Summary report *6.3*
Thermal printers *6.12*
Tractor feed mechanisms *6.7*
Underlining *6.15*
Very high-speed printers *6.7*
Voice output *6.21*
Voice synthesizer *6.21*
Wide carriage *6.7*

REVIEW QUESTIONS

1. Name and describe three types of commonly used reports.
2. What are the advantages of displaying information in a graphic form? What are the disadvantages? What are the three most commonly used types of charts?
3. What are the two major categories of printers? What are the differences between the two?
4. How does a dot matrix printer produce an image? What effect on the quality of print does this method have? What techniques are used on dot matrix printers to improve the print quality?
5. What does the term "letter quality" mean? What types of printers print with letter quality?
6. Describe some of the print capabilities of dot matrix printers with respect to graphics and character size and style.
7. How does an ink jet printer produce images? What are some advantages of ink jet printers?
8. Explain how a laser printer works. What are some advantages of laser printers?
9. What are the three major types of high-speed printers? List the characteristics such as speed and manner of printing for each one.
10. What types of screens are used with computers? List some screen features.
11. List the steps involved in displaying an image on a CRT screen.
12. Describe some of the different types of plotters and the manner in which they produce drawings.
13. List several advantages of microfilm over printed reports.
14. Describe the two ways of creating voice output.

CONTROVERSIAL ISSUES

1. Some experts in business management have pointed out that much of the paperwork generated within a business organization is not used. Further, they have noted that managers do not have time to examine the reams of paper they receive in order to gain the information they need to make decisions. These experts have argued that very high-speed printers contribute to the paperwork explosion and, therefore, contribute to rather than help solve the problem. Others argue that in their right place, these printers are invaluable. Take a side in this dispute and prepare an argument.
2. "Automation—The Curse of Modern Society" was the title of a speech given at a meeting of union leaders. The speaker stated that the ability of the computer to develop drawings that are equal to or better than those prepared by graphic artists directly threatens the skilled worker. Others have said that having the computer perform these jobs frees people to do more creative work. What do you think?

RESEARCH PROJECTS

1. The speed, quality, and prices of printers are constantly changing as new innovations appear. Examine a current issue of a personal computer magazine and clip out four advertisements for printers. Write to the printer manufacturers and obtain detailed information about the printers. Then make a presentation to your class concerning what you found.
2. Visit an installation in your area that uses plotters. Bring back and share with your class the drawings that are produced on the plotters.

CHAPTER 7

Auxiliary Storage

CHAPTER 7

Auxiliary Storage

OBJECTIVES

- Define auxiliary storage.
- Identify the primary devices used for personal computer auxiliary storage.
- Describe the manner in which data is stored on disks.
- Describe the methods used to back up data stored on floppy and hard disks.
- Identify the types of disk storage used with large computers.
- Explain how tape storage is used with large computers.
- List and describe three other forms of auxiliary storage: optical, solid state, and mass storage.

Storage, performed by all computers, is the fourth and final operation in the information processing cycle. Upon completion of this chapter you will be able to add the knowledge you acquire about storage operations to what you have learned in previous chapters about input, processing, and output operations. In addition, you will be familiar with the various types and capabilities of auxiliary storage devices that are used with computers.

WHAT IS AUXILIARY STORAGE?

Computer storage can be classified into two types: main memory and auxiliary storage. As you have seen, main memory temporarily stores programs and data that are being processed. **Auxiliary storage**, or **secondary storage**, stores programs and data when they are not being processed, just as a filing cabinet is used in an office to store records. Records that are not being used are kept in the file cabinet until they are needed. In the same way, data and programs that are not being used on a computer are kept in auxiliary storage until they are needed. Auxiliary storage devices that are used with computers include devices such as magnetic disk and tape (Figure 7-1).

Auxiliary storage devices provide a more permanent form of storage than main memory because they are **nonvolatile**, that is, data and programs that have been placed on auxiliary storage devices are retained when the power is turned off. Main memory is volatile, which means that when power is turned off, whatever is stored in main memory is erased.

Auxiliary storage devices can be used as both input and output devices. When they are used to receive data that has been processed by the computer they are functioning as output devices. When data that they stored is transferred to the computer for processing, they are functioning as input devices.

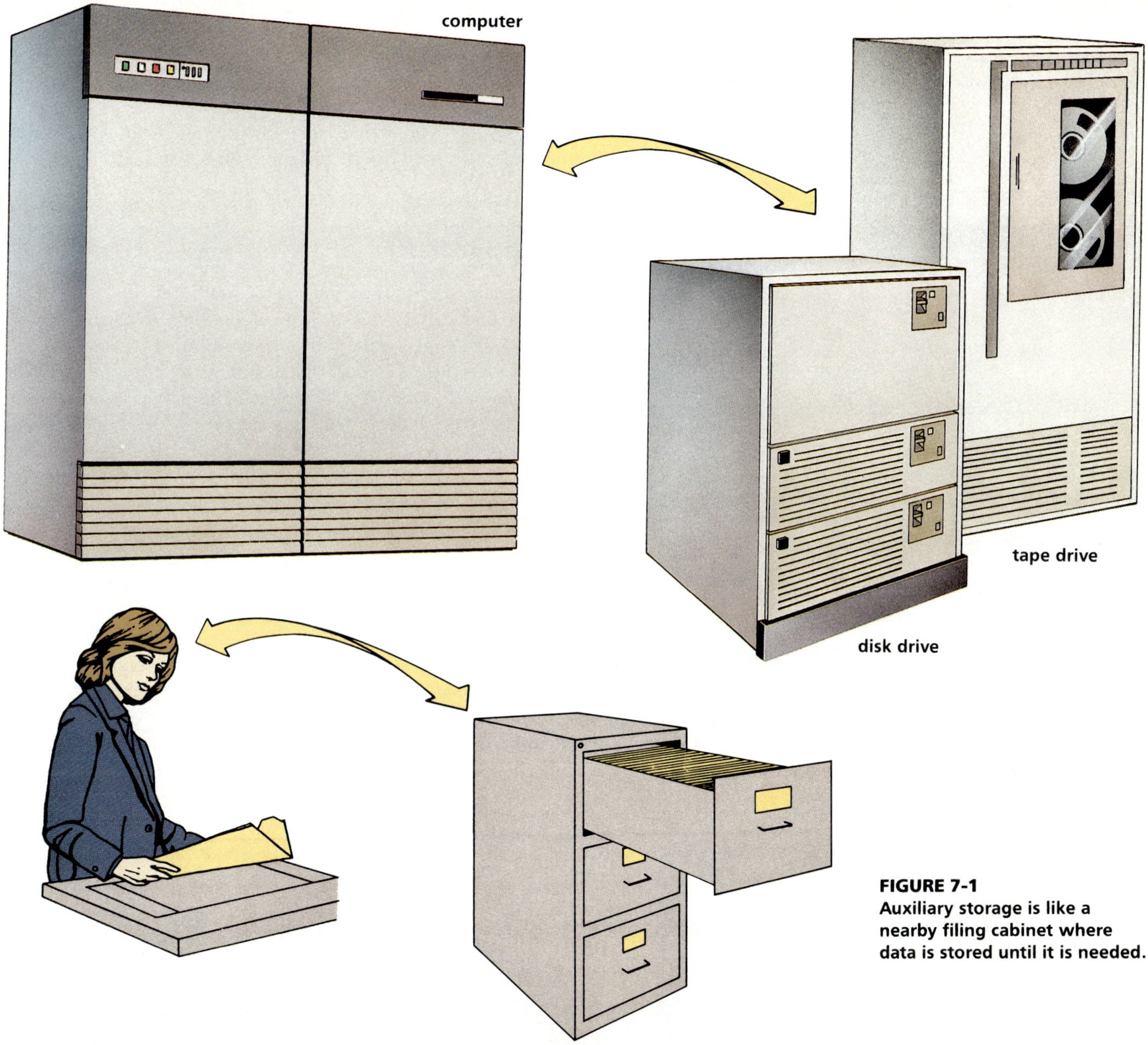

FIGURE 7-1
Auxiliary storage is like a nearby filing cabinet where data is stored until it is needed.

The auxiliary storage needs of users can vary greatly. Those who use personal computers, may find the amount of data to be stored to be relatively small. For example, the names, addresses, and telephone numbers of several hundred friends or customers of a small business might require only 20,000 bytes of auxiliary storage (200 records × 100 characters per record). Users of large computers such as banks or insurance companies, however, may need auxiliary storage devices that can store billions of characters. To meet the different needs of users, a variety of storage devices are available. In the next section we explain the devices that are designed for users with personal computers. Later in the chapter, we discuss the devices that are used with larger computer systems.

AUXILIARY STORAGE FOR PERSONAL COMPUTERS

Personal computer users have several categories of auxiliary storage from which to choose. These include floppy disks, hard disks, and removable disk cartridges.

FIGURE 7-2
In this picture, a user is inserting a diskette into the disk drive of an IBM microcomputer.

Floppy Disks

In the early 1970s IBM introduced the floppy disk and the floppy disk drive as a new type of auxiliary storage. Today, **floppy disks**, also called **diskettes**, **floppies**, or just **disks**, are used as a principal auxiliary storage medium for personal computers (Figure 7-2). This type of storage is convenient, reliable, and relatively low in cost.

Floppy disks are available in a number of different sizes. Many personal computers take disks that are 5 1/4 inches in diameter. Smaller disks, 3 1/2 inches in diameter, are also commonly used and are increasing in popularity (Figure 7-3).

A floppy disk consists of a circular piece of thin mylar plastic (the actual disk), which is coated with an oxide material similar to that used on magnetic tape. On a 5 1/4 inch disk, the circular piece of plastic is enclosed in a flexible square protective jacket. The jacket has an opening so that a portion of the disk's surface is exposed for reading and recording (Figure 7-4). On a 3 1/2 inch disk, the circular piece of plastic is enclosed in a rigid plastic cover and a piece of metal called the shutter covers the reading and recording area. When the 3 1/2 inch disk is inserted into a disk drive, the drive slides the shutter to the side to expose the disk surface (Figure 7-5).

FIGURE 7-3
The most commonly used disks for personal computers are 5 1/4 and 3 1/2 inch disks.

FIGURE 7-4
A 5 1/4 inch floppy disk, or diskette, consists of the disk itself enclosed within a protective jacket, usually made of a vinyl material. The liner of the diskette is essentially friction-free so that the disk can turn freely, but the liner does contact the disk and keep it clean. The magnetic surface of the diskette, which is exposed through the window in the jacket, allows data to be read and stored. The large hole (hub) in the diskette is used to mount the diskette in the disk drive. The small hole is used by some disk drives as an indicator for where to store data.

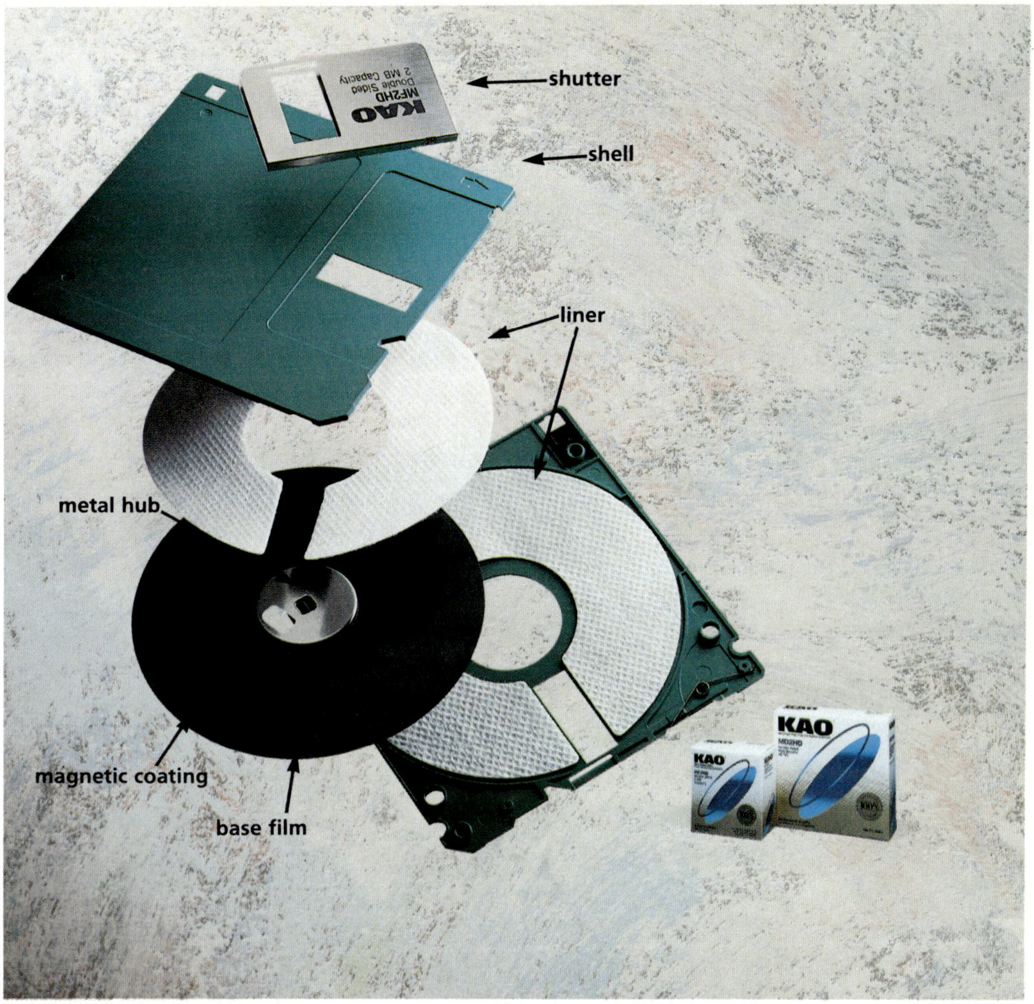

FIGURE 7-5
In a 3 1/2 inch diskette the flexible plastic disk is enclosed between two liners that clean the disk surface of any microscopic debris and help to disperse static electricity. The outside cover is made of a rigid plastic material and the recording window is covered by a metal shutter that slides to the side when the disk is inserted into the disk drive.

How Is a Floppy Disk Formatted? Before a floppy disk can be used on a microcomputer for auxiliary storage, it must be formatted. The **formatting** process includes defining the tracks and sectors on the surface of a disk (Figure 7-6). A **track** is a narrow recording band forming a full circle around the disk. Each track on the disk is divided into sectors. A **sector** is a section of a track. It is the basic storage unit of floppy disks. When data is read from a disk, a minimum of one full sector is read. When data is stored on a disk, at least one full sector is written. The number of tracks and sectors that are placed on a disk when it is formatted varies based on the capacity of the disk, the capabilities of the disk drive being used, and the specifications in the software that does the formatting. Many 5 1/4 inch disks are formatted with 40 tracks and 9 sectors on the surface of the disk. The 3 1/2 inch disks are usually formatted with 80 tracks and 9 sectors on each side. A 3 1/2 inch disk has more tracks than a 5 1/4 inch disk because even though it is smaller in size it has a larger storage capacity. When 40 tracks are recorded on a diskette, the tracks are numbered from 0 to 39. When 80 tracks are used, the tracks are numbered from 0 to 79.

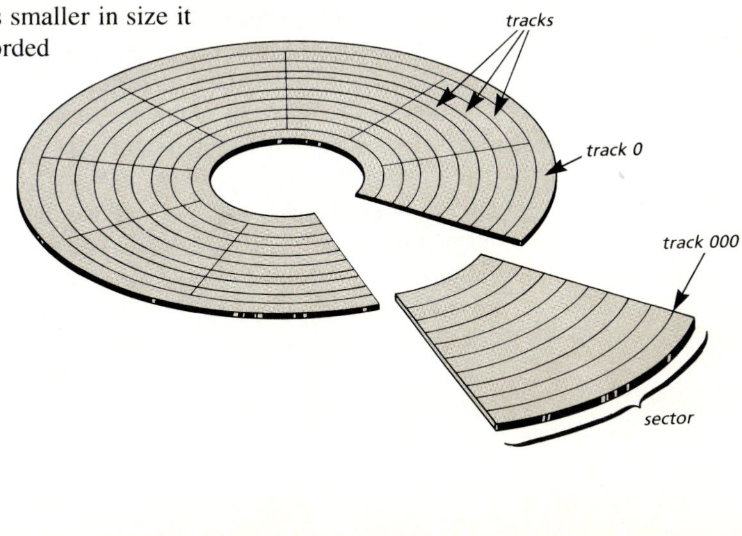

FIGURE 7-6
Each track on a diskette is a narrow, circular band. On a diskette containing 40 tracks, the outside track is called track 0 and the inside track is called track 39. The distance between track 0 and track 39 on a 5 1/4 inch diskette is less than one inch. The disk surface is divided into sectors. This example shows a diskette with nine sectors.

Hard- and Soft-Sectored Diskettes Disks and disk drives are classified as either hard-sectored or soft-sectored. A **hard-sectored disk** has a hole in front of each sector, normally near the center of the disk (Figure 7-7). These holes provide timing information to the drive. Hard-sectored disks will always contain the same number and size of sectors because the sectors are defined by the sector holes. Therefore, the exact storage capacity of a hard-sectored disk can always be determined. For example, a hard-sectored disk that contains 16 sectors with 256 bytes per sector will always be able to store a maximum of 4,096 bytes per track (16 × 256). When the disk is two-sided and contains 40 tracks per side, the total storage capacity of the disk is 327,680 bytes (4,096 × 40 × 2).

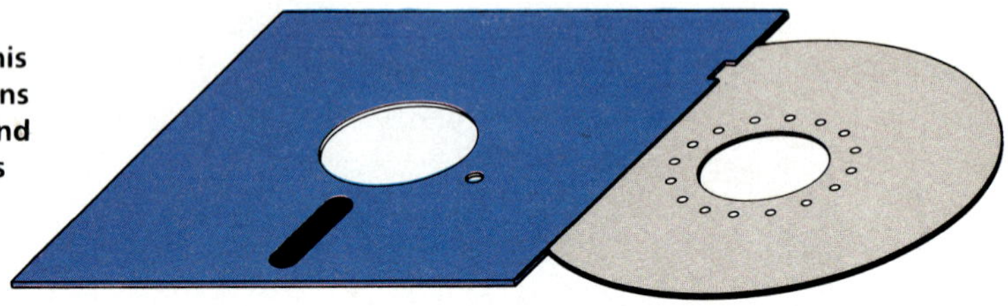

FIGURE 7-7
Within its protective jacket this hard-sectored diskette contains 16 holes, evenly spaced around a circle on the disk. The holes indicate exactly where a sector begins.

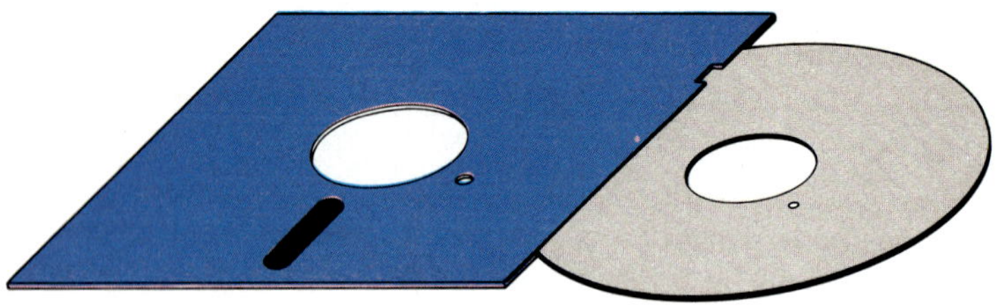

FIGURE 7-8
A soft-sectored disk has only a single index hole. The drive can use the hole to find the beginning of any track. The number of sectors on a track and the number of bytes in each sector are determined by the software that formats the disk.

A **soft-sectored disk** has a single index hole that indicates the beginning of the track (Figure 7-8). The number of sectors per track and the number of characters that can be stored in each sector are defined by the software when the disk is formatted. For example, a soft-sectored disk can be formatted with 40 tracks on each side, nine sectors per track, and 512 bytes per sector, for a total of 368,640 bytes (characters) stored on the disk.

What Is the Storage Capacity of a Floppy Disk? Knowing the storage capacity of a disk gives a user an idea of how much data or how many programs can be stored on the disk. The number of characters that can be stored on a disk depends on three basic factors: (1) the number of sides of the disk used; (2) the recording density of the bits on a track; and (3) the number of tracks on the diskette.

Some disks and drives are designed so that data can be recorded on only one side of the disk. These drives are called **single-sided drives**. Similarly, disks on which data can be recorded on one side only are called **single-sided disks**. Today, most disk drives are designed to record and read data on both sides of the disk. Drives that can read and write data on both sides of the disk are called **double-sided drives** and the disks are called **double-sided disks**. The use of double-sided drives and disks doubles the number of characters that can be stored on the disk. The term cylinder is sometimes used with double-sided disks. A **cylinder** is defined as all tracks of the same number. For example, track 0 on side 1 of the disk and track 0 on side 2 of the disk is called cylinder 0.

Another factor in determining the storage capacity of a disk is the recording density provided by the drive. The **recording density** is the number of bits that can be recorded on one inch of the innermost track on the disk. This measurement is referred to as **bits per inch (bpi)**. The higher the recording density, the higher the storage capacity of the disk.

The third factor that influences the number of characters that can be stored on a disk is the number of tracks onto which data can be recorded. This measurement is referred to as **tracks per inch (tpi)**. As we saw earlier in this chapter, the number of tracks depends on the size of the disk, the drive being used, and how the disk was formatted.

While the capacity of floppy disks can vary, a common capacity for a 5 1/4 inch disk is approximately 360K and for a 3 1/2 inch disk, 720K. On some computers floppy disks can store 2 megabytes (million characters) of data.

How Is Data Stored on a Floppy Disk? Regardless of the type of floppy disk or the formatting scheme that is used, the method of storing data on a disk is essentially the same. When a disk is inserted in a disk drive, the center hole fits over a hub mechanism that positions the disk in the unit (Figure 7-9). The circular plastic disk rotates within its cover at approximately 300 revolutions per minute. Data is stored on tracks character by character, using the same code, such as ASCII (American Standard Code for Information Interchange), that is used to store characters in main memory. Electronic impulses are placed along a track to represent the bit pattern for each character. To do this, a recording mechanism in the drive called the **read/write head** rests on the surface of the rotating disk, generating electronic impulses representing the bits to be recorded (Figure 7-10). To access different tracks on the disk, the drive moves the read/write head from track to track.

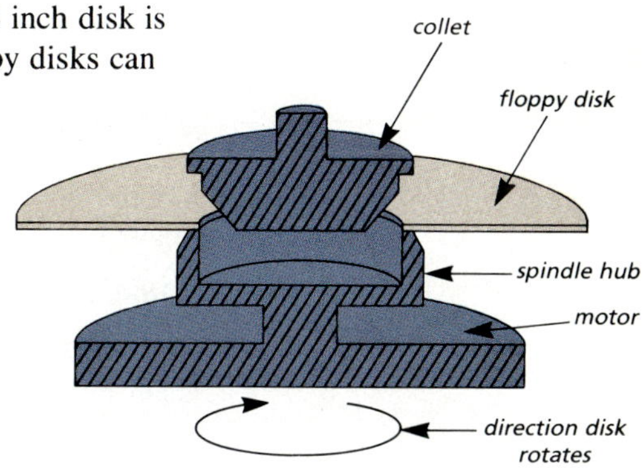

FIGURE 7-9
When a floppy disk is inserted in a drive, the center hole is positioned between the collet and the hub. After the door to the disk drive is closed and the disk is engaged, it begins rotating within the protective jacket at approximately 300 RPM.

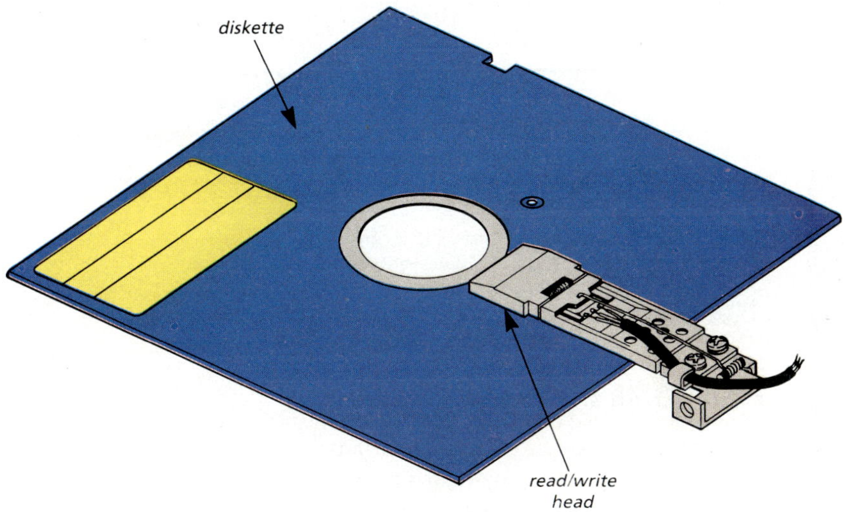

FIGURE 7-10
The read/write head moves back and forth over the opening in the protective jacket to read or write data on the disk.

What Is Access Time? Data stored in sectors on a floppy disk must be retrieved and placed in main memory to be processed. The time required to access and retrieve the data is called the **access time**.

The access time for a floppy disk drive depends on four factors:

1. **Seek time**, the time it takes to position the read/write head over the proper track.
2. **Latency**, the time it takes for the sector containing the data to rotate under the read/write head.

3. **Settling time**, the time required for the read/write head to be placed in contact with the disk.
4. **Data transfer rate**, the time required to transfer the data from the disk to main memory.

The access time for floppy disks varies from about 175 milliseconds (one millisecond equals 1/1000 of a second) to approximately 300 milliseconds. What this means to the user is that, on the average, data stored in a single sector on a diskette can be retrieved in approximately 1/5 to 1/3 of a second.

The Care of Floppy Disks With reasonable care, floppy disks provide an inexpensive and reliable form of storage. In handling floppy disks, take care to avoid exposing them to heat, magnetic fields, and contaminated environments. One advantage of the 3 1/2 inch disk is that it has a rigid plastic cover that provides more protection for the data stored on the plastic disk inside than the flexible cover on a 5 1/4 inch disk. Figure 7-11 shows ways to care for floppy disks properly.

FIGURE 7-11
Guidelines for the proper care of floppy disks.

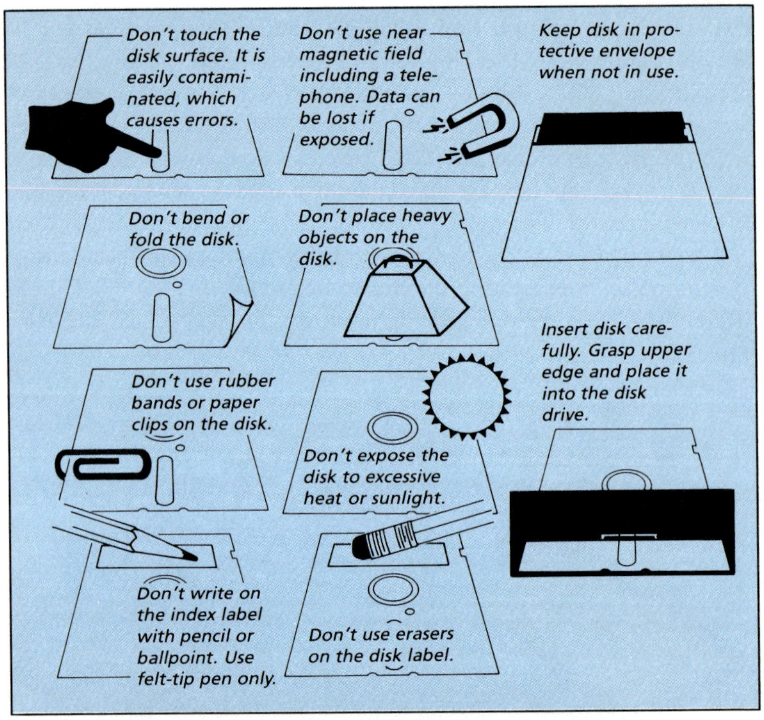

Hard Disks

Hard disks provide larger and faster auxiliary storage capabilities for personal computers. **Hard disks** consist of one or more rigid metal **platters** coated with a metal oxide material that allows data to be magnetically recorded on the surface of the platters (Figure 7-12). In this section we discuss the two types of hard disks used on personal computers, fixed disks and hard cards.

FIGURE 7-12
A hard disk consists of one or more disk platters. Each side of the platter is coated with a metal oxide substance that allows data to be magnetically stored.

FIGURE 7-13
A hard card is a hard disk on a circuit board that can be mounted in a computer's expansion slot. In the picture below, the protective cover for the disk has been removed.

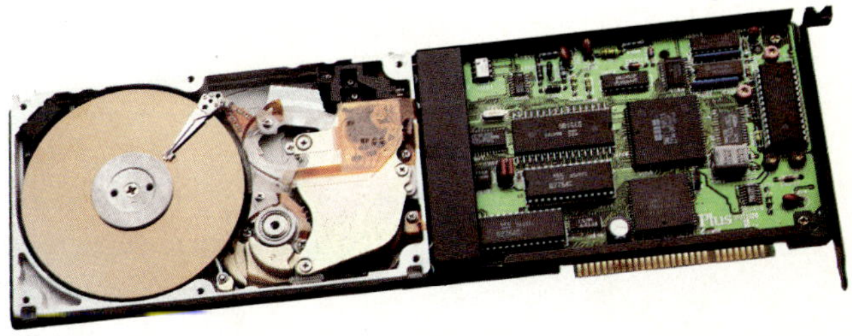

What Is a Fixed Disk? Hard disks used on personal computers are sometimes called **fixed disks** because the platters used to store the data are permanently mounted inside the computer and are not removable like floppy disks. On fixed disks, the metal disks, the read/write heads, and the mechanism for moving the heads across the surface of the disk are enclosed in a sealed case. This helps to ensure a clean environment for the disk.

The **hard card** is a circuit board that has a hard disk built onto it. Hard cards provide an easy way to expand the storage capacity of a personal computer because the board can be installed into an expansion slot of the computer (Figure 7-13).

FIGURE 7-14
This picture of a hard disk drive illustrates the access arm and the read/write heads, which are over the surface of the disks. These heads are extremely stable. They can read and write tracks very close together on the surface of the disk.
▼

How Is Data Stored on a Hard Disk? Storing data on hard disks is similar to storing data on floppy disks. Hard drives contain a spindle on which one or more disk platters are mounted. The spindle rotates the disk platters at a high rate of speed, usually 3,600 revolutions per minute. In order to read or write data on the surface of the spinning disk platter, the disk drives are designed with **access arms**, or **actuators**. The access arms or actuators contain one or more read/write heads per disk surface (Figure 7-14). These read/write heads "float" on a cushion of air and do not actually touch the surface of the disk. The distance between the head and the surface varies from approximately one-millionth of an inch to 1/2 millionth of an inch. As shown in Figure 7-15, the close tolerance leaves no room for any type of contamination. If some form of contamination is introduced or if the alignment of the read/write heads is altered by something accidentally jarring the computer, the disk head can collide with and damage the disk surface, causing a loss of data. This event is known as a **head crash**. Because of the time needed to repair the disk and to reconstruct the data that was lost, head crashes can be extremely costly for users.

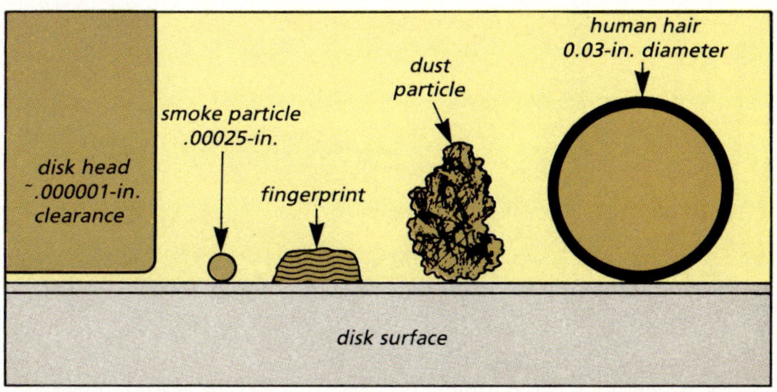

◀ **FIGURE 7-15**
The clearance between a disk head and the disk surface is about 1 millionth of an inch. With these tolerances, contamination such as a smoke particle, fingerprint, dust particle, or human hair could render the drive unusable. Sealed disk drives are designed to minimize contamination.

When reading data from the disk, the read/write head senses the magnetic spots that are recorded on the disk along the various tracks and transfers the data to main memory. When writing, the read/write head transfers data from main memory and stores it as magnetic spots on the tracks on the recording surface of one or more of the disks. As the disk rotates at a high rate of speed, the read/write heads move across its surface.

The number of platters permanently mounted on the spindle in the drive can vary. For 5 1/4 inch drives, the number varies between one and four platters. On many drives, each surface of a platter can be used to store data. Thus, if one platter is used in the drive, two surfaces are available for data. If two platters are used, four surfaces are available for data, and so on. Naturally, the more platters, the more data that can be stored on the drive.

The storage capacity of hard drives is measured in megabytes or millions of bytes (characters) of storage. Common sizes for personal computers range from 10MB to 100MB of storage and even larger sizes are available. As an idea of how much data these storage capacities represent, 10MB of storage is equivalent to approximately 5,000 double-spaced typewritten pages.

In addition to a larger storage capacity, hard disks provide faster access time than floppy disks. The typical access time of a hard disk for a personal computer is between 25 and 80 milliseconds.

The use of a hard disk drive on a personal computer provides many advantages for users. Because of its large storage capacity, a hard disk can store many software application programs and data files. When a user wants to run a particular application or access a particular data file on a hard disk, it is always available. The user does not have to find the appropriate floppy disk and insert it into the drive. In addition, the faster access time of a hard disk reduces the time needed to load programs and access data.

Disk Cartridges Another variation of disk storage available for use with personal computers is the removable **disk cartridge**. Disk cartridges, which can be inserted and removed from a computer (Figure 7-16), offer the storage and fast access features of hard disks and the portability of floppy disks. Disk cartridges are often used when data security is an issue. At the end of a work session, the disk cartridge can be removed and locked up, leaving no data on the computer.

FIGURE 7-16
This photo shows a removable hard disk cartridge, which allows a user to remove and transport the entire hard disk from computer to computer or to lock it up in a safe.

Protecting Data Stored on a Disk

Regardless of whether you are using floppy disks, hard disks, or removable disk cartridges on a personal computer, you must protect the data you store on the disk from being lost. Disk storage is reusable and data that is stored on a disk may be overwritten and replaced with new data. This is a desirable feature allowing users to remove or replace unwanted files. However, it also raises the possibility of accidentally removing or replacing a file that you really wanted to keep. To protect programs and data stored on disks, there are several things you can do.

How Is the Write-Protect Notch Used? One way to protect the data and programs stored on a floppy disk is to use the write-protect notch. On the 5 1/4 inch disks, this notch is located on the side of the disk. To prevent writing to a disk, a user covers this notch with a small piece of removable tape. Before writing data onto a disk, the disk drive checks the notch. If the notch is open the drive will proceed to write on the disk. If the notch is covered the disk drive will not write on the disk (Figure 7-17).

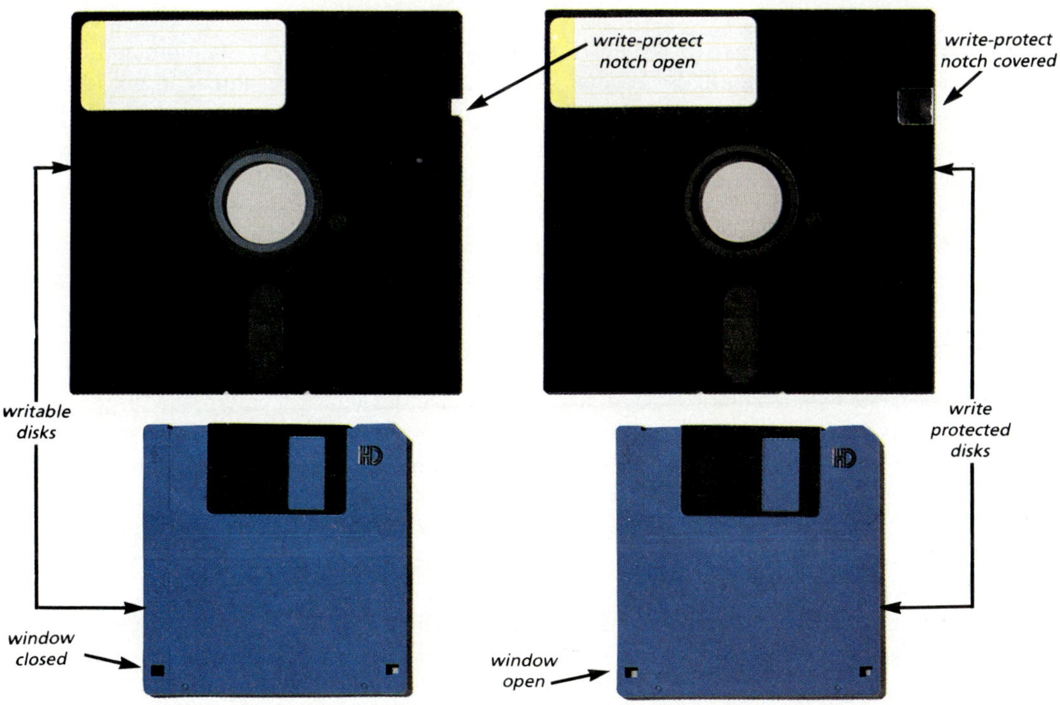

FIGURE 7-17
The write-protect notch of the 5 1/4 inch disk on the left is open and therefore data could be written to the disk. The notch of the 5 1/4 inch disk on the right, however, is covered. Data could not be written to this disk. The reverse situation is true for the 3 1/2 inch disk. Data cannot be written on the 3 1/2 inch disk on the right because the small black piece of plastic is not covering the window in the lower left corner. Plastic covers the window of the 3 1/2 inch disk on the left, so data can be written on this disk.

On 3 1/2 inch disks, the situation is reversed. The write-protect notch is a small window in the corner of the disk. A piece of plastic in the window can be moved to open and close the window. If the write-protect window is closed, the drive can write on the disk. If the window is open, the drive will not write on the disk.

Backup Storage Another way to protect programs and data stored on disks is by creating backup storage. As discussed in Chapter 3, backup storage means creating a duplicate copy of important programs and data on a separate disk. To back up floppy disks, simply copy the data on one disk to another floppy disk. When using hard disks, however, the user is faced with a more difficult problem. The amount of data that can be stored on a hard disk can fill many floppy disks. For example, to back up a hard disk containing 10 million characters, approximately thirty 5 1/4 inch diskettes that could each store 360,000 characters would be required. For this reason, cartridge tape is sometimes used to back up hard disk storage.

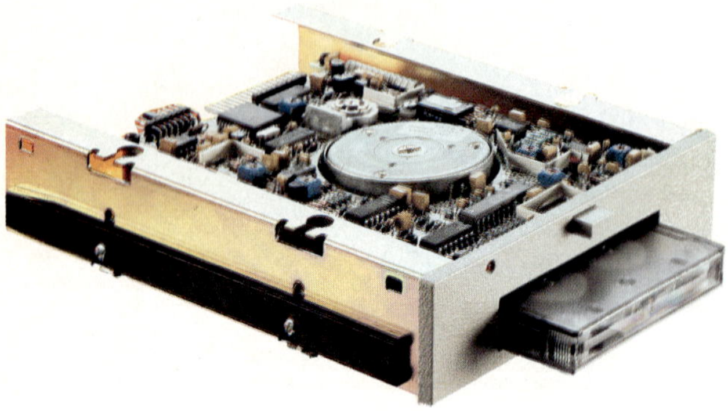

FIGURE 7-18
Cartridge tape drives are an effective way to back up and store data that would otherwise require numerous diskettes.

Cartridge Tape A device commonly used to back up hard disks on personal computers is the **cartridge tape drive** (Figure 7-18). When these devices are available on a personal computer, the data and programs that are stored on a hard disk can be copied onto the tape cartridge for backup storage.

Some cartridge tape drives can operate in a **streaming mode**, without the normal stopping and starting usually associated with tape operations. Tape streaming results in more data being recorded in less time. Using the streaming method, a cartridge tape unit can completely copy a 20 million byte hard disk in approximately four minutes.

AUXILIARY STORAGE FOR MEDIUM AND LARGE COMPUTERS

A wide variety of devices are available for use as auxiliary storage on medium and large computers. Most of these devices use storage techniques that are similar, if not identical, to the devices that we discussed for personal computers. As you would expect, however, storage devices used for medium and large computers provide greater storage capacity and faster retrieval rates than devices used with small systems. For discussion purposes, we group storage devices for medium and large computers into three categories: magnetic disk, magnetic tape, and other storage devices.

Magnetic Disk

Magnetic disk is the most common type of auxiliary storage device for medium and large computers. Disks for medium and large computers are similar to devices used on personal computers but have larger capacities, usually as a result of having more recording surfaces. Some disk devices used on large computers can store billions of characters of information. Because of their ability to retrieve data directly from a specific location on the disk, disk devices for medium and large computers are sometimes referred to as **direct-access storage devices (DASD)**.

One difference between auxiliary storage for a personal computer and for larger computers is that many more disk devices can be attached to larger computers. While most personal computers are limited to two to four disks, medium computers can support 8 to 16 disk devices and large computers can support over 100 high-speed disk devices. Figure 7-19 shows a large number of disk units attached to a single mainframe computer.

FIGURE 7-19
A mainframe computer can have dozens of fixed disk storage devices attached to it.

Disk devices for medium and large computers fall into two categories: fixed disks and removable disks.

Fixed Disks Fixed disks, the most commonly used disks for medium and large computers, can be either mounted in the same cabinet as the computer or enclosed in their own stand-alone cabinet. As with fixed disks in personal computers, fixed disks on medium and large computers contain nonremovable platters that are enclosed in airtight cases to prevent contamination (Figure 7-20).

FIGURE 7-20
A high-speed, high-capacity fixed disk drive in a stand-alone cabinet.

Removable Disks Removable disk units were introduced in the early 1960s and were the most prevalent type of disk storage for nearly 20 years. During the 1980s, however, removable disks began to be replaced by fixed disks that offered larger storage capacities and higher reliability.

Removable disk devices consist of the drive unit, which is usually in its own cabinet, and the removable recording media, called a **disk pack**. Removable disk packs consist of 5 to 11 metal platters that are used on both sides for recording data. The recording capacity of these packs varies from 10 to 300 megabytes of data. One advantage of removable disk packs is that the data on a disk drive can be quickly changed by removing one pack and replacing it with another. This can be accomplished in minutes. When removable disk packs are not mounted in a disk drive they are stored in a protective plastic case. When the packs are being used, the plastic case is usually placed on top of the drive unit. Figure 7-21 shows a large installation of removable disk devices with the empty protective disk pack cases on top of the drives.

FIGURE 7-21
A large installation of removable disk drives showing the protective disk pack cases on top of the drive units.

How Is Data Physically Organized on a Disk? Depending on the type of disk drive, data is physically organized in one of two ways on disks used with medium and large computers. One way is the sector method and the other is the cylinder method.

As with the floppy disks and hard disks used with personal computers, the **sector method** for physically organizing data on disks divides each track on the disk surface into individual storage areas called sectors (Figure 7-22). Each sector can contain a specified number of bytes. Data is referenced by indicating the surface, track, and sector where the data is stored.

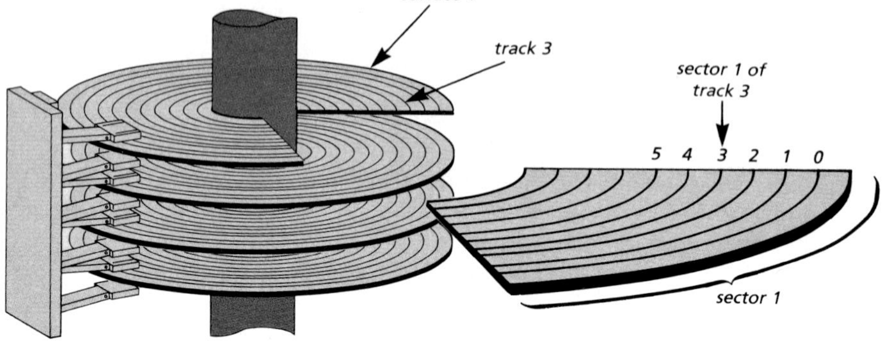

FIGURE 7-22
The sector method of disk addressing divides each track into a number of sectors. To locate data, the surface, track, and sector where the data is stored are specified.

With the **cylinder method**, all tracks of the same number on each recording surface are considered part of the same cylinder (Figure 7-23). For example, if each platter contained 200 tracks, the tenth track on all surfaces would be considered part of the tenth cylinder. All twentieth tracks would be part of the twentieth cylinder, and so on. When the computer requests data from a disk using the cylinder method, it must specify the cylinder, recording surface, and record number. Because the access arms containing the read/write heads all move together, they are always over the same track on all surfaces. Thus, using the cylinder method to record data "down" the disk surfaces reduces the movement of the read/write head during both reading and writing of data.

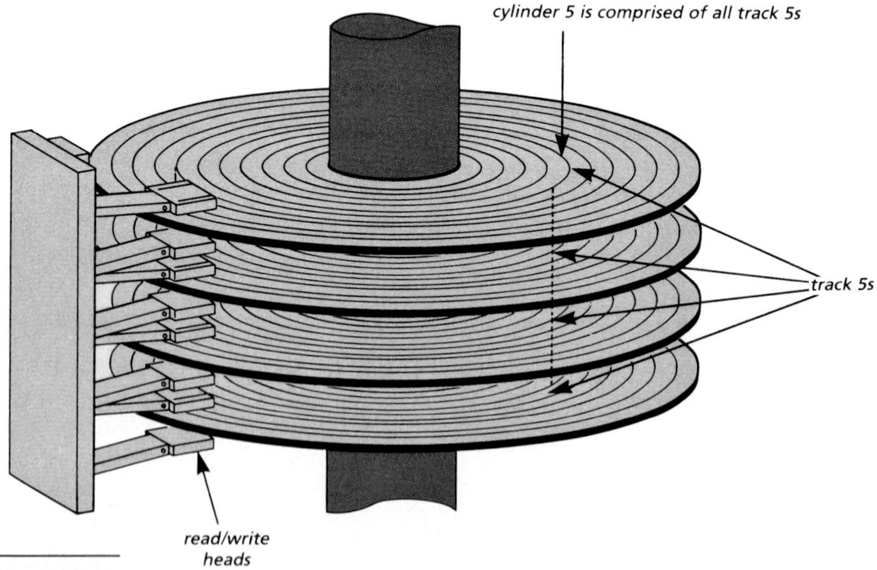

FIGURE 7-23
The cylinder method reduces the movement of the read/write head (thereby saving time) by writing information "down" the disk on the same track of successive surfaces.

Magnetic Tape

During the 1950s and early 1960s, prior to the introduction of removable disk pack drives, magnetic tape was the primary method of storing large amounts of data. Today, even though tape is no longer used by medium and large computers as the primary method of auxiliary storage, it still functions as a cost-effective way to store data that does not have to be accessed immediately. In addition, tape serves as the primary means of backup for most medium and large systems and is often used when data is transferred from one system to another.

Magnetic tape consists of a thin ribbon of plastic. The tape is coated on one side with a material that can be magnetized to record the bit patterns that represent data. The most common types of magnetic tape devices are reel-to-reel and cartridge. Reel-to-reel tape is usually 1/2 inch wide and cartridge tape is 1/4 inch wide (Figure 7-24).

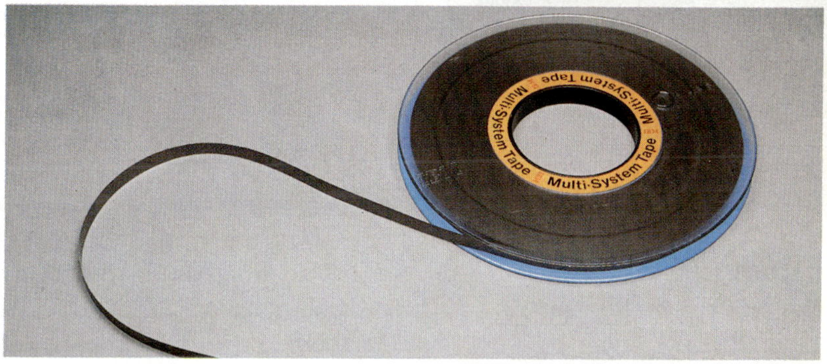

FIGURE 7-24 ▲
In the top picture a computer operator is positioning a reel of magnetic tape on a tape device. Below is a standard 10 1/2-inch reel of magnetic tape.

Reel-to-Reel Tape Devices

Reel-to-reel tape devices use two reels: a supply reel to hold the tape that will be read or written on, and the take-up reel to temporarily hold portions of the supply reel tape as it is being processed. At the completion of processing, tape on the take-up reel is wound back onto the supply reel. As the tape moves from one reel to another, it passes over a read/write head (Figure 7-25), an electromagnetic device that can read or write data on the tape.

Older style tape units (Figure 7-26) are vertical cabinets with vacuum columns that hold five or six feet of slack tape to prevent breaking during sudden start or stop operations.

Newer style tape units (Figure 7-27) allow a tape to be inserted through a slot opening similar to the way videotapes are loaded in a videocassette recorder. This front-loading tape drive takes less space and can be cabinet mounted. The drive automatically threads the end of the tape onto an internal take-up reel.

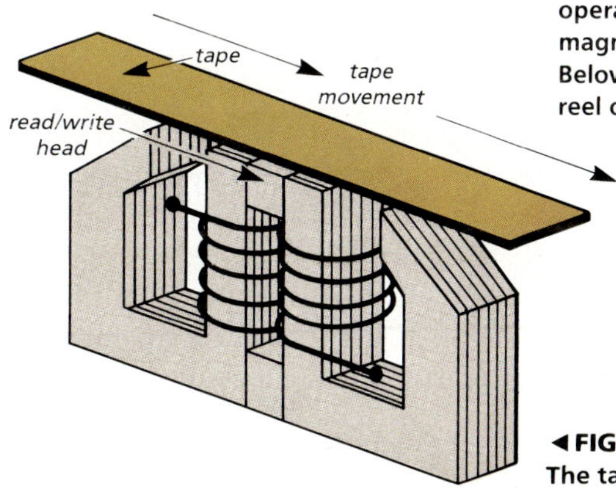

◀ FIGURE 7-25
The tape read/write head senses and records the electronic bits that represent data.

FIGURE 7-26 ▲
Older style reel-to-reel magnetic tape storage devices.

FIGURE 7-27 ▶
Newer style tape drives allow the user to slide the tape into a slot at the front of the unit. The drive automatically threads the tape.

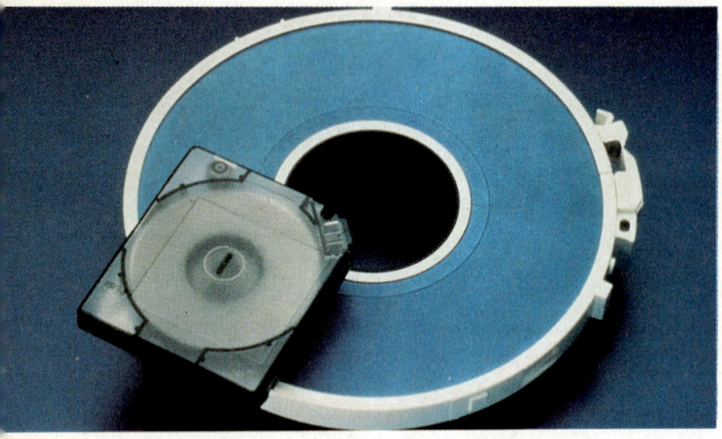

FIGURE 7-28
The four inch by five inch tape cartridge can hold 20% more data than the 10 1/2 inch reel of tape.

Reels of tape usually come in lengths of 300, 1,200, 2,400 and 3,600 feet and can store up to 100 megabytes of data.

Cartridge Tape Devices Cartridge tape devices for medium and large computers are identical to units previously discussed for personal computers. They are becoming increasingly popular because they can store more data and take less space than the traditional 10 1/2 inch diameter reels of tape (Figure 7-28).

How Is Data Stored on Magnetic Tape? Data is recorded on magnetic tape in the form of magnetic spots that can be read and transferred to main memory. The magnetic spots on the tape are organized into a series of horizontal rows called channels. The presence or absence of magnetic spots representing bits is used to represent a given character on the tape.

Several different coding structures are used with magnetic tape, including both ASCII and EBCDIC. The coding structure for EBCDIC divides half-inch tape into nine horizontal channels. A combination of bits in a vertical column that consists of the nine horizontal channels is used to represent characters and the error-checking parity bit on the tape (Figure 7-29).

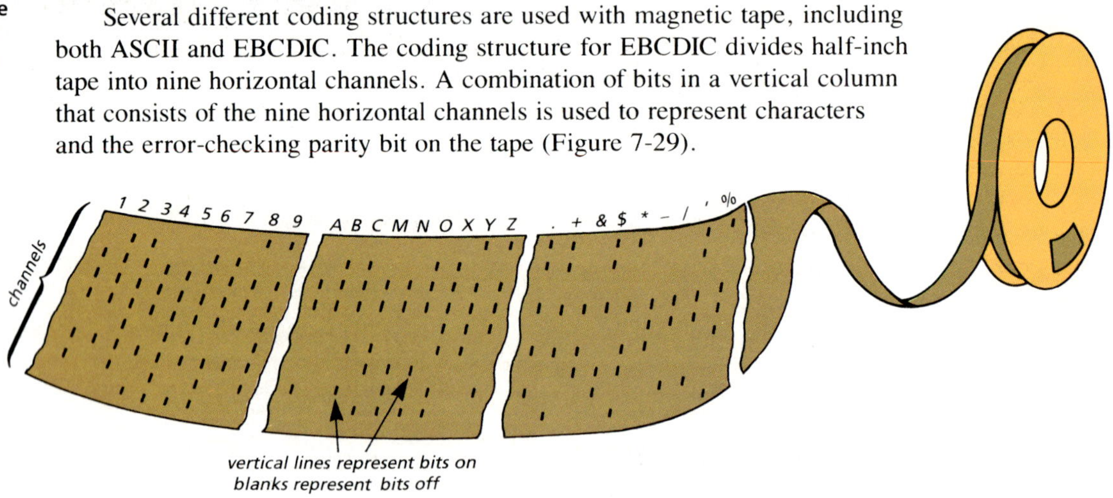

FIGURE 7-29
One of the most common coding structures found on magnetic tape is the EBCDIC code, which is stored in nine channels on the tape. Eight channels are used to store the bits representing a character. The ninth channel is a parity error-checking channel.

Tape density is the number of characters or bytes that can be stored on an inch of tape. Tape density is expressed in bytes per inch or bpi. Commonly used tape densities are 800, 1,600, 3,200 and 6,250 bpi. Some of the newer cartridge tape devices can record at densities of over 38,000 bpi. The higher the density, the more data that can be stored on a tape.

Tape is considered a **sequential storage** media because the computer must read tape records one after another until it finds the one it wants. Tapes do not have fixed data storage location addresses like disk drives that allow direct access of a record.

In order to allow some room for starting and stopping, tapes use **interblock gaps (IBG)**, also called **interrecord gaps (IRG)** (Figure 7-30). These spaces are usually about .6 inch long. To increase recording efficiency, **blocked records** are normally used. Blocking refers to placing two or more individual records, called **logical records**, into a block to form a **physical record** (Figure 7-31). A logical record refers to the amount of data that a program uses when it processes one record. A physical record refers to the amount of data that is physically transferred into memory from the tape. For example, there could be three employee payroll (logical) records contained within one block or (physical) record on a tape. Using blocking has two advantages. First, the tape is used more efficiently. More data can be stored because the gap between each logical record is eliminated. Second, because an entire physical record is read into memory each time data is read from the tape, reading data takes place faster. Two or more logical records are read each time data is transferred from the tape to main memory.

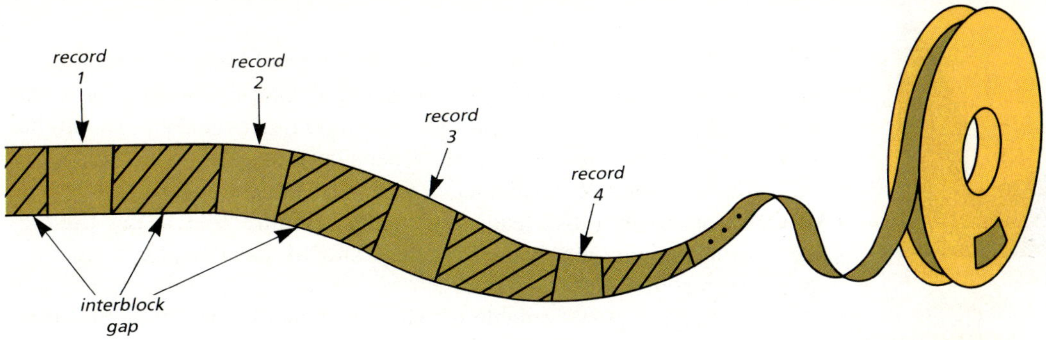

FIGURE 7-30
Records stored on tape are stored sequentially, separated by an interblock gap that allows for the starting and stopping of the tape drive. The interblock gap is typically .6 inch wide.

FIGURE 7-31
Three logical records are stored in each block or physical record in this diagram. An entire block of records is brought into main memory each time the tape file is read.

OTHER FORMS OF AUXILIARY STORAGE

While the conventional disk and tape devices described above comprise the majority of auxiliary storage devices and media, several other means for storing data are used. These include optical storage technology, solid-state devices, and mass storage devices.

Optical Storage Technology

Optical storage technology is one of the newest and most promising methods of data storage. Enormous quantities of information can be stored on **optical disks** by using a laser to burn microscopic holes on the surface of a hard plastic disk (Figure 7-32). A lower power laser reads the disk by reflecting light off the disk surface. The reflected light is converted into a series of bits that the computer can process.

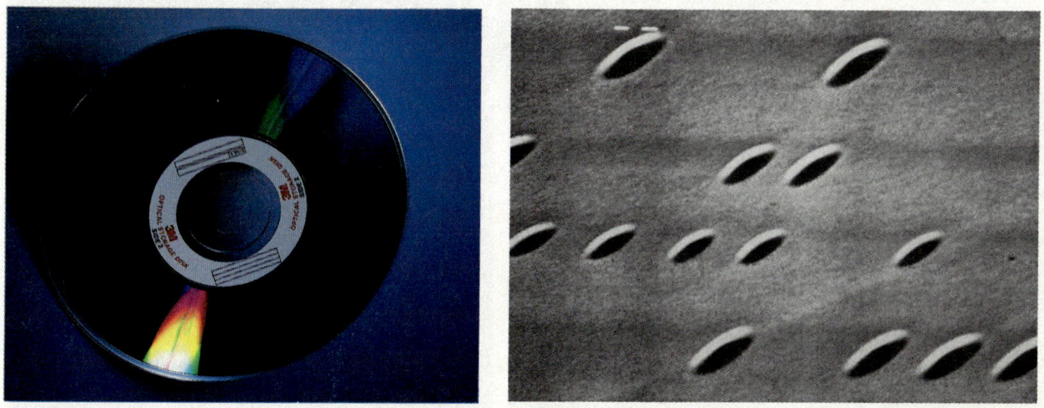

FIGURE 7-32
To record data on an optical disk (left), a laser burns microscopic holes on the surface (right).

FIGURE 7-33
An optical compact disk can store hundreds of times the data as on a comparable-size floppy disk.

A full-size 12 inch optical disk can store several billion characters of information. The smaller disks, just under five inches in diameter, can store over 800 million characters or approximately 800 times the data that can be stored on a 5 1/4 inch floppy diskette. That's enough space to store approximately 400,000 pages of typed data. The smaller optical disks are called **CDROM**, for compact disk read-only memory (Figure 7-33). They use the same laser technology that is used for the CDROM disks that have become popular for recorded music.

The disadvantage of optical disks now available is that they cannot be modified once the data is recorded. Most optical disks are prerecorded but some devices provide for one-time recording. These units are called **WORM** devices, for write once, read many. Recently announced optical disk devices will be able to erase and rerecord disks.

Even as read-only devices, optical disks have great potential. Because of their tremendous storage capacities, entire catalogs or reference materials can be stored on a single disk. Some people predict that optical disks will soon replace data now stored on film such as microfiche.

Solid-State Devices

To the computer, solid-state storage devices look and act just like disk drives, only faster. But as their name suggests, they contain no moving parts, only electronic circuits. **Solid-state storage devices** use the latest in random-access memory (RAM) technology to provide high-speed data access and retrieval. Rows of RAM chips (Figure 7-34) provide megabytes of memory that can be accessed much faster than the fastest conventional disk drives. Solid-state storage devices are significantly more expensive than conventional disk drives offering the same storage capacity.

Mass Storage Devices

Mass storage devices provide for the automated retrieval of data from a "library" of storage media such as cartridge tapes or floppy disks. Mass storage is ideal for extremely large databases that require all information to be readily accessible even though any one portion of the database may be infrequently required. Mass storage systems take less room than conventional tape storage and can retrieve and begin accessing records within seconds. Figure 7-35 shows a mass storage system that uses tape cartridges.

FIGURE 7-34
Solid-state storage devices use megabytes of RAM chips to simulate a conventional disk drive. ▼

FIGURE 7-35▶
This mass storage system can access any one of thousands of tape cartridges in an average of 11 seconds. Each cartridge is a 4 × 4 inch square and about 1 inch thick.

SUMMARY OF AUXILIARY STORAGE

Auxiliary storage is used to store programs and data that are not currently being processed by the computer. This chapter discussed the various types of auxiliary storage used with computers. The chart in Figure 7-36 provides a summary of the auxiliary storage devices. What you have learned about these devices and storage operations in general can now be added to what you have learned about the input, processing, and output operations of the information processing cycle.

FIGURE 7-36
A summary of some of the more common auxiliary storage devices.

DEVICE	DESCRIPTION
Personal Computers	
Floppy disk	Plastic storage media that is reliable and low in cost.
Hard disk	Fixed metal storage media that provides large storage capacity and fast access.
Hard card	Fixed disk that is built on a circuit board and installed in an expansion slot of a personal computer.
Disk cartridge	Combines storage and access features of hard disk and portability of floppy disks.
Tape cartridge	Used to back up hard disks on personal computers.
Medium and Large Computers	
Fixed disk	Large multiplatter fixed disk with high storage capacity and fast access.
Removable disk	Disk drives with removable disk packs.
Reel tape	Magnetic tape device using the reel-to-reel method of moving tape.
Tape cartridge	Magnetic tape device using cartridge method of holding tape.
Other Storage Devices	
Optical storage	Uses lasers to record and read data on a hard plastic disk. High quality and large storage capacity.
Solid state	Uses RAM chips to provide high-speed data access and retrieval.
Mass storage	Automated retrieval of storage media such as tape cartridges and floppy disks.

CHAPTER SUMMARY

1. **Auxiliary storage** is used to store data that is not being processed on the computer.
2. The **floppy disk** or **diskette** is used as a primary auxiliary storage medium with personal computers.
3. Most personal computers use a diskette 5 1/4 inches in diameter. Smaller diskettes (approximately 3 1/2 inches in diameter) are also available and are increasing in popularity.
4. A floppy disk consists of a plastic disk enclosed within a square protective jacket. A portion of the surface of the disk is exposed so data can be stored on it.
5. Data is stored on a disk in tracks. A **track** is a narrow recording band forming a full circle around the diskette.
6. The number of tracks most often found are 40 tracks or 80 tracks per diskette.
7. Each track on a disk is divided into **sectors**, the basic unit of disk storage. A minimum of one full sector of data is read from a diskette: a minimum of one sector is written on a diskette.
8. A **hard-sectored disk** contains holes in the diskette indicating where each sector begins.
9. A **soft-sectored disk** contains one hole indicating where the tracks begin. The number of sectors and the number of characters in each sector are determined by the software that formats the disk.

10. The factors affecting disk storage capacity are the number of sides of the disk used; the recording density of the bits; and the number of tracks on the disk.
11. **Single-sided drives** read and record data on only one side of a diskette. **Double-sided drives** read and record data on both sides of the disk.
12. The **recording density** is stated as the number of bits that can be recorded on one inch of the innermost track on a disk. The measurement is referred to as **bits per inch (bpi)**.
13. To read or write data on a disk, the disk is placed in the disk drive. Within its protective covering the disk rotates at about 300 revolutions per minute. The **read/write head** rests on the disk and senses or generates electronic impulses representing bits.
14. The time required to access and retrieve data stored on a diskette is called the **access time**.
15. Access time depends on four factors: (1) **seek time**, the time it takes to position the read/write head on the correct track; (2) **latency time**, the time it takes for the data to rotate under the read/write head; (3) **settling time**, the time required for the head to be placed in contact with the disk; and (4) **data transfer rate**, the amount of data that can be transferred from the disk to main memory.
16. Floppy disks should not be exposed to heat or magnetic fields. With proper care, floppy disks provide an inexpensive and reliable form of storage.
17. A **hard disk** consists of one or more rigid metal **platters** coated with a metal oxide material.
18. On **fixed disks**, the metal disks, read/write heads, and access arm are enclosed in a sealed case. These disks provide high storage capabilities and fast access times.
19. To read and write data on a hard disk, an **access arm** moves read/write heads in and out. The heads float very close to the surface of the disk, generating or sensing electronic impulses that represent bits.
20. The number of platters in a hard disk for a microcomputer can vary from one to four. On many disks, both sides of the platters can be used for storing data.
21. The typical access time for a microcomputer hard disk is between 25 and 85 milliseconds.
22. **Removable disk cartridges** offer the storage and access features of hard disks with the portability of floppy disks.
23. The write-protect notch on floppy disks can be used to protect the data stored on a disk from being overwritten.
24. To backup storage means to create a duplicate copy of important programs and data on a separate disk or tape.
25. The normal method for floppy disk backup is to copy the data onto another disk. For hard disk, the disk is often copied to a **cartridge tape**.
26. Disk drives used with large computers can be categorized as either fixed disks or removable disks.
27. **Fixed disks** are sealed in an enclosure and permanently mounted in the disk drive.
28. **Disk packs** contain between 5 and 11 platters that can be mounted and removed from the disk drive.
29. The **sector method** (identifying the surface, track, and sector number) or the **cylinder method** (identifying the cylinder, recording surface, and record number) can be used to physically organize and address data stored on disk.
30. The tracks that can be referenced at one position of the access arm are called a **cylinder**.
31. **Magnetic tape** is used primarily for backup purposes in large computer installations.
32. Data is recorded on **magnetic tape** as a series of magnetic spots along a horizontal channel. Each spot represents a bit in a coding scheme. Large computers commonly use the EBCDIC coding scheme on nine-track tape.
33. **Tape density** is the number of characters or bytes that can be stored on one inch of tape. Common densities are 800, 1,600, 3,200, and 6,520 bytes per inch.
34. **Sequential organization** means records are stored one after the other on the tape.
35. An **interblock gap** separates records stored on tape.
36. **Blocked records** mean two or more **logical records** are stored in a **physical record** on the tape.
37. **Optical disks** use a laser beam recording and reading method and can store enormous quantities of data.
38. RAM chips are used in **solid-state storage devices**. These devices act just like disk drives but provide faster data access and retrieval.
39. Automated retrieval of storage media is provided by **mass storage devices**.

KEY TERMS

Access arms *7.9*
Access time *7.7*
Actuators *7.9*
Auxiliary storage *7.2*
Bits per inch (bpi) *7.7*
Blocked records *7.16*
Cartridge tape drive *7.12*
CDROM *7.18*
Cylinder *7.6*
Cylinder method *7.14*
Data transfer rate *7.8*
Direct-access storage devices (DASD) *7.12*
Disk cartridge *7.10*
Diskette *7.4*
Disk pack *7.13*
Disks *7.4*
Double-sided disk *7.6*
Double-sided drive *7.6*
Fixed disk *7.9*
Floppies *7.4*
Floppy disk *7.4*
Formatting *7.5*
Hard card *7.9*
Hard disk *7.8*
Hard-sectored disk *7.6*
Head crash *7.9*
Interblock gap (IBG) *7.16*
Interrecord gap (IRG) *7.16*
Latency *7.7*
Logical records *7.16*
Magnetic tape *7.15*
Mass storage devices *7.18*
Nonvolatile *7.2*
Optical disks *7.17*
Physical record *7.16*
Platters *7.8*
Read/write head *7.7*
Recording density *7.7*
Reel-to-reel *7.15*
Secondary storage *7.2*
Sector *7.5*
Sector method *7.14*
Seek time *7.7*
Sequential storage *7.16*
Settling time *7.8*
Single-sided disk *7.6*
Single-sided drive *7.6*
Soft-sectored disk *7.6*
Solid-state storage devices *7.18*
Streaming mode *7.12*
Tape density *7.16*
Track *7.5*
Tracks per inch (TPI) *7.7*
WORM *7.18*

REVIEW QUESTIONS

1. Differentiate between the uses of main memory and auxiliary storage.
2. Draw a diagram of a diskette and label the main parts.
3. What does formatting a disk mean?
4. What are the three factors influencing the storage capacity of a disk? Briefly describe each of them.
5. Describe the care and handling of floppy disks.
6. Identify the factors that influence the access time of a disk drive.
7. Describe the characteristics of a fixed disk drive. What sizes are commonly used with personal computers?
8. What is disk backup? How are floppy disks normally backed up? How are hard disks backed up?
9. Describe the differences between fixed disks and removable disks on large computers.
10. Describe the sector method of disk organization and the cylinder method of disk organization.
11. How is data stored on magnetic tape? What are typical tape densities?
12. Describe optical storage technology. Why is it one of the most promising methods of data storage?

CONTROVERSIAL ISSUES

1. A study of personal computer owners found that less than 10 percent regularly backup the files and databases they use. The consensus of these users was that new auxiliary storage devices, particularly the hard disk drives, are so reliable and error free that backup is a waste of time and storage. Experts who reviewed this study commented that these users were inviting disaster because even a few failures are enough to justify full file and database backup. Who is right? Take a position on this issue.
2. The cost of semiconductor memory has decreased significantly in recent years. In addition, research is being done constantly to find new ways for storing data. As a result, some experts believe magnetic memory such as disk and tape will be obsolete in a few years. Others say this will never happen. What is your opinion?

RESEARCH PROJECTS

1. The storage capacities of hard disks vary considerably. Obtain the names of five different manufacturers of hard disk drives used with personal computers. Write to each of the manufacturers to obtain literature concerning their drives. Prepare a report summarizing the information you have collected.
2. The storage capacities of optical disks allow complete reference works to be stored on a single compact disk. Write a paper on possible applications of this technology.
3. Data storage requirements vary based on the type of organization. Write a paper on the storage requirements of a bank, a retailer with online cash registers, and the government agency that issues passports. Consider the amount and type of storage required and the necessity of having immediate access to the stored data.

CHAPTER 8

File Organization and Databases

CHAPTER 8

File Organization and Databases

OBJECTIVES

- Describe sequential files, indexed files, and direct (or relative) files.
- Explain the difference between sequential retrieval and random retrieval of records from a file.
- Describe the data maintenance procedures for updating files, including adding, changing, and deleting data in a file or database.
- Discuss the advantages of a database management system (DBMS).
- Describe a relational database system.
- Describe a hierarchical database system.
- Describe a network database system.
- Explain the use of a query language.
- Describe the responsibilities of a database administrator.

The data and information that a company has accumulated is usually considered a valuable asset. For data and information to provide maximum benefit to a company, they must be carefully organized, used, and managed. While you are now familiar with the auxiliary storage devices used to store data and information, it is equally important that you understand the various ways in which the data and information stored on these devices is organized, used, and managed. The purpose of this chapter is to explain (1) how files on auxiliary storage are organized, retrieved and maintained (kept current); and (2) the advantages, organization, use, and management of databases.

As you read this chapter, you will notice that several of the file and database concepts that are discussed were introduced earlier in the text. With the computer knowledge that you now have, especially about auxiliary storage devices, you are ready for a more in-depth look at these topics. The first part of this chapter concentrates on how files are organized and used. The second part of this chapter discusses the advantages, organization, and use of databases. Learning this information will help you to better understand how data and information is stored and managed on a computer.

WHAT IS A FILE?

A *file* is a collection of related records that is usually stored on an auxiliary storage device. A *record* is a collection of related fields and a *field*, also called a *data item* or *data element*, is a fact (Figure 8-1). Files contain data that pertains to one topic. For example, a business can have separate files that contain data related to personnel, inventory, customers, vendors, and so forth. Most companies have hundreds, sometimes thousands of files that store the data pertaining to their business. Files that are stored on auxiliary storage devices can be organized in several different ways and there are advantages and disadvantages to each of these types of file organization.

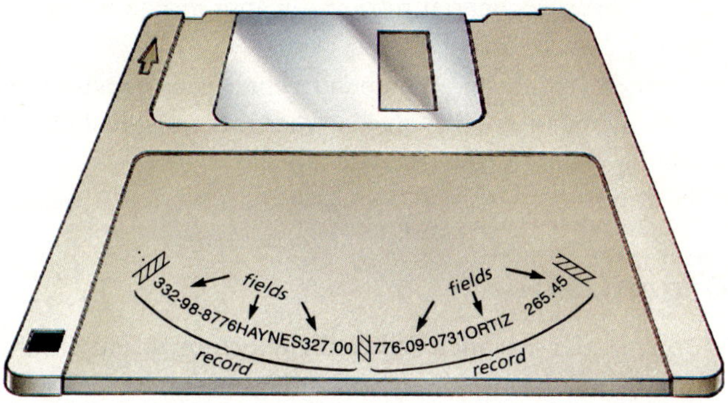

FIGURE 8-1
This payroll file stored on a diskette contains payroll records. Each payroll record contains a social security field, a name field, and a paycheck amount field.

TYPES OF FILE ORGANIZATION

Three types of file organization are used on auxiliary storage devices. These are sequential, indexed, and direct, or relative, file organization.

Sequential File Organization

Sequential file organization means that records are stored one after the other, normally in ascending or descending order, based on a value in each record called the key. The **key** is a field that contains data, such as a social security number, that is used to sequence the records in a file (Figure 8-2). Files that are stored on tape are always sequential files. Files on disk may be sequential, indexed, or direct.

FIGURE 8-2
The student records in this file are stored sequentially in ascending order using the social security number as the key field. The records in this file will be retrieved sequentially.

Records that are stored using sequential file organization are also retrieved sequentially. **Sequential retrieval**, also called **sequential access**, means that the records in a file are retrieved one record after another in the same order that the records are stored. For example, in Figure 8-2, the file contains student records stored in sequence by social security number. The data in the file is retrieved one record after another in the same sequence that it is stored in the file.

Sequential retrieval has a major disadvantage—since records must be retrieved one after another in the same sequence as they are stored, the only way to retrieve a record is to read all preceding records first. Therefore, in Figure 8-2, if the record for Joan Schwartz must be retrieved, the records for Tom Lee and for Ray Ochoa must be read before retrieving the Joan Schwartz record. Because of this, sequential retrieval is not used when fast access to a particular record is required. However, sequential retrieval is appropriate when records are processed one after another.

A common use of sequential files in a computer center is as backup files, where data from a disk is copied onto a tape or another disk so that if the original data becomes unusable, the original file can be restored from the backup file.

Indexed File Organization

A second type of file organization is called **indexed file organization**. Just as in a sequential file, records are stored in an indexed file in an ascending or descending sequence based on the value in the key field of the record.

An indexed file, however, also contains an index. An **index** consists of a list containing the values of the key field and the corresponding disk address for each record in a file (Figure 8-3). In the same way that an index for a book points to the page where a particular topic is covered, the index for a file points to the place on a disk where a particular record is located. The index is usually stored with a file when the file is created. The index is retrieved from the disk and placed in main memory when the file is to be processed.

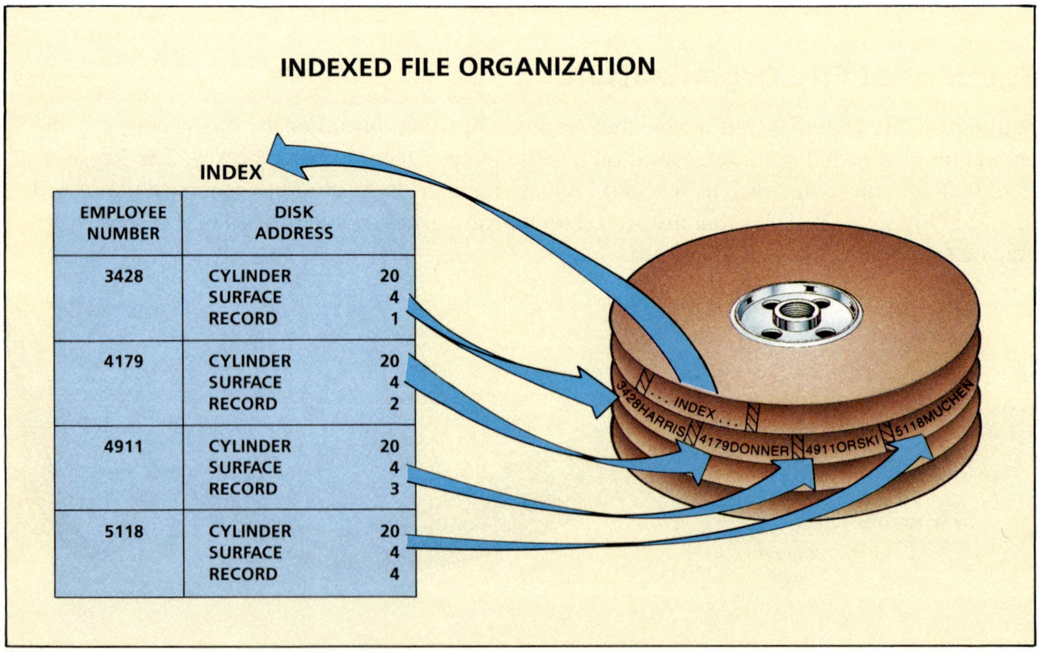

FIGURE 8-3
The index in an indexed file contains the record key value and the corresponding disk address for each record in the file. In this example, the index contains the employee number, which is the key for the employee file, and the disk address for the corresponding employee record.

Records can be accessed in an indexed file both sequentially and randomly. As previously discussed, sequential retrieval means that the records in a file are retrieved one record after another in the same order that the records are stored. **Random retrieval**, also called **random access**, means any record in a file can be directly accessed (retrieved) regardless of where it is stored in the file. For example, the 50th record in a file can be retrieved first, followed by the 3rd record, and then the 20th record. Random retrieval is used when fast access to a record is required, as in a reservation system. For random retrieval to be used, files must be stored on disk.

To randomly access a record in an indexed file, the index is searched until the key of the record to be retrieved is found. The address of the record (also stored in the index) is then used to retrieve the record directly from the file without reading any other records. For example, if an inquiry was received from the personnel office asking the name of employee number 5118, the index could be searched until key 5118 was found (Figure 8-4). The corresponding disk address (cylinder 20, surface 4, record 4) would then be used to read the record directly from the disk into main memory.

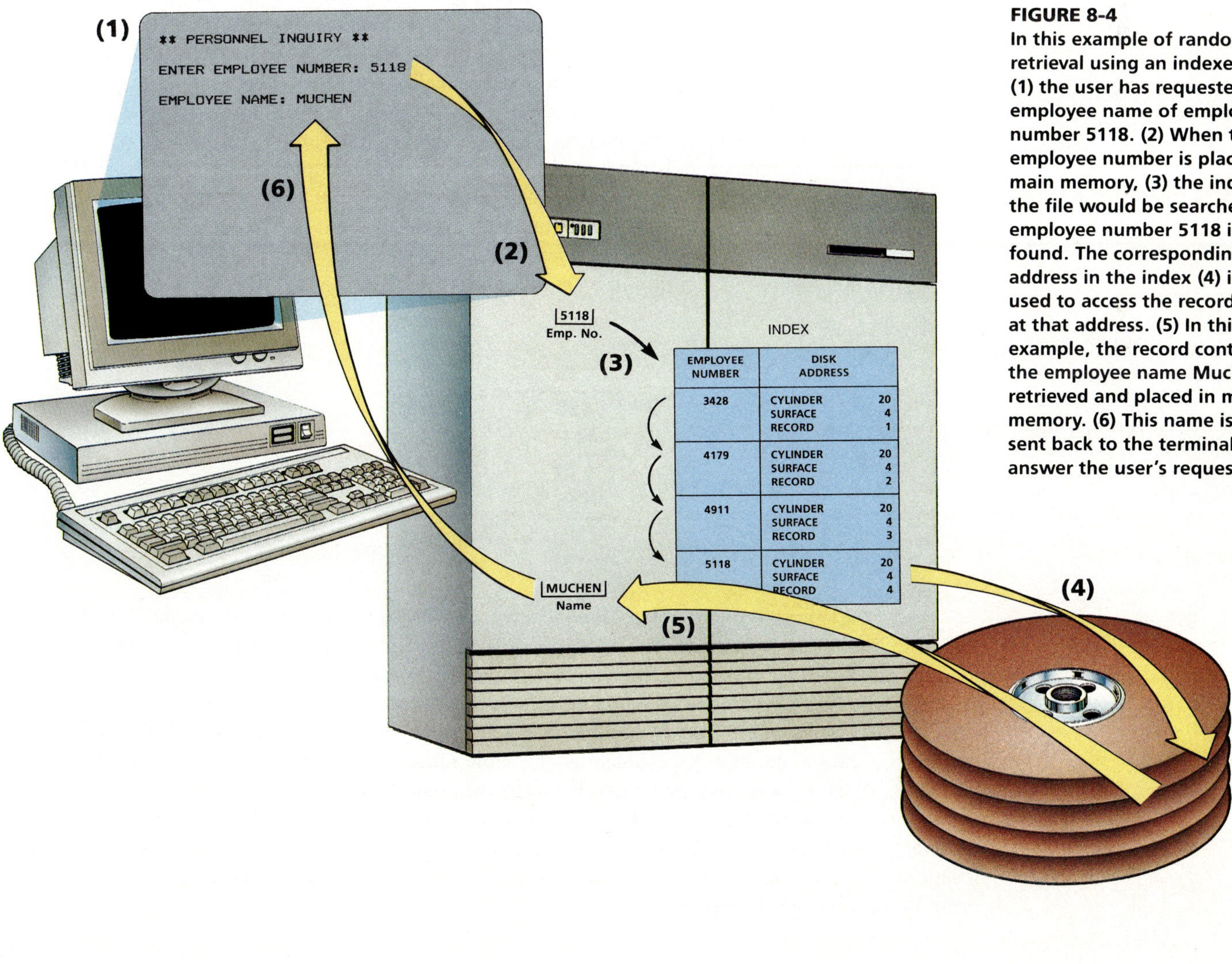

FIGURE 8-4
In this example of random retrieval using an indexed file, (1) the user has requested the employee name of employee number 5118. (2) When the employee number is placed in main memory, (3) the index for the file would be searched until employee number 5118 is found. The corresponding disk address in the index (4) is then used to access the record stored at that address. (5) In this example, the record containing the employee name Muchen is retrieved and placed in main memory. (6) This name is then sent back to the terminal to answer the user's request.

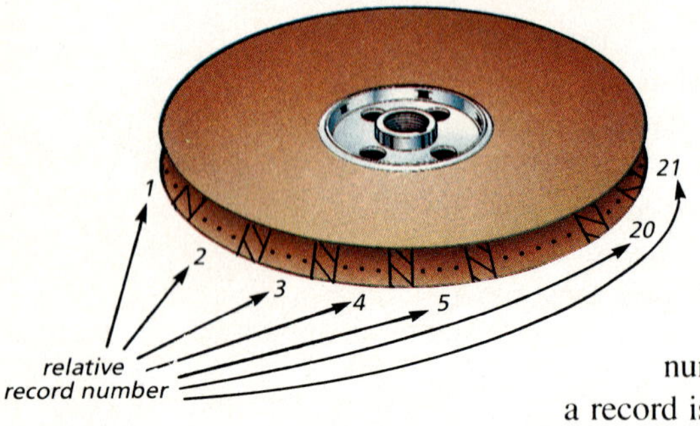

FIGURE 8-5
The relative address of a record is the same as the numeric position of the record in the file. The fifth record has a relative address of 5.

Direct or Relative File Organization

A **direct file** or **relative file** (occasionally called a random file) contains records that are stored and retrieved according to either their disk address or their position within a file. This means that the program that stores and accesses records in a direct file must specify either the exact physical address of a record in the file (for example, cylinder, surface and track number, or track and sector number), or the relative location (position) where a record is stored in the file, such as the first, tenth, or fiftieth record (Figure 8-5).

The location where a record is stored is based on a key value found in the record. For example, a program could establish a file that has nine locations where records can be stored. These locations are sometimes called **buckets**. A bucket can contain multiple records. If the key in the record is a one-digit value (1–9), then the value in the key would specify the relative location within the file where the record was stored. For example, the record with key 3 would be placed in relative location or bucket 3; the record with key 6 would be placed in relative location 6, and so on.

Usually the storage of records in a file is not so simple. For instance, what if the maximum number of records to be stored in a direct file is 100 and the key for the record is a four-digit number? In this case, the key of the record could not be used to specify the relative or actual location of the record because the four-digit key could result in up to 9,999 records. In cases such as these, an arithmetic formula must be used to calculate the relative or actual location in the file where the record is stored. The process of using a formula and performing the calculation to determine the location of a record is called **hashing**.

One hashing method is the division/remainder method. Using this method, a prime number close to but not greater than the number of records to be stored in the file is chosen. A **prime number** is a number divisible by only itself and 1. For example, suppose you have 100 records. The number 97 is the closest prime number to 100 without being greater than 100. The key of the record is then divided by 97 and the remainder from the division operation is the relative location where the record is stored. For example, if the record key is 3428, the relative location where the record will be stored in the file is location 33 (Figure 8-6).

FIGURE 8-6
When the value 3428 is divided by the prime number 97, the remainder is 33. This remainder is used as the bucket where the record with key 3428 is stored in the direct file.

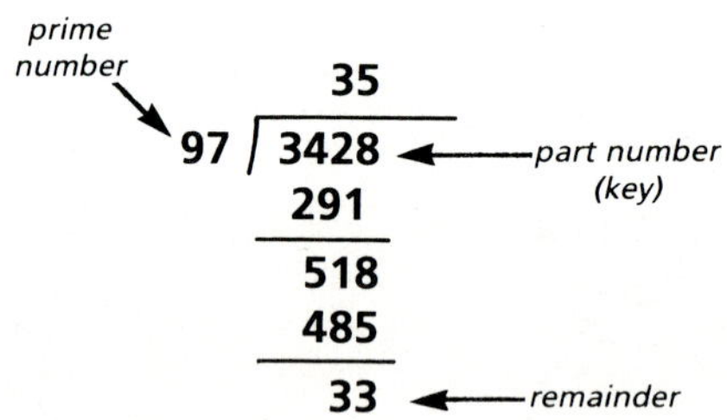

Direct files present one problem not encountered with sequential or indexed files. In all three file organization methods, the key in the record must be unique so that it can uniquely identify the record. For example, the employee number, when acting as the key in an employee file, must be unique. When a hashing technique is used to calculate a disk address, however, it is possible that two different keys could identify the same location on disk. For example, employee number 3331 generates the same relative location (33) as employee number 3428. When the locations generated from the different keys are the same they are called **synonyms**. The occurrence of this event is called a **collision**. A method that is often used to resolve collisions is to place the record that caused the collision in the next available storage location. This location may be in the same bucket (if multiple records are stored in a bucket) or in the next bucket (Figure 8-7).

Once a record is stored in its relative location within a direct file, it can be retrieved either sequentially or randomly. The method normally used with direct files is random retrieval. In order to randomly retrieve a record from a direct file three steps are performed:

1. The program must obtain the key of the record to be retrieved. The value of the key is entered into the computer by a user or as data from an input device.
2. The program determines the location of the record by performing the same hashing process as when the record was initially stored. Thus, to retrieve the record with key 3428, the key value would be divided by the prime number 97. The remainder, 33, specifies the location of the bucket where the record will be found.
3. The software then directs the computer to bucket 33 to retrieve the record.

Sequential retrieval from a direct file can be accomplished by indicating that the record from the first relative location is to be retrieved, followed by the record from the second relative location, and so on. All the records in the file are retrieved based on their relative location in the file.

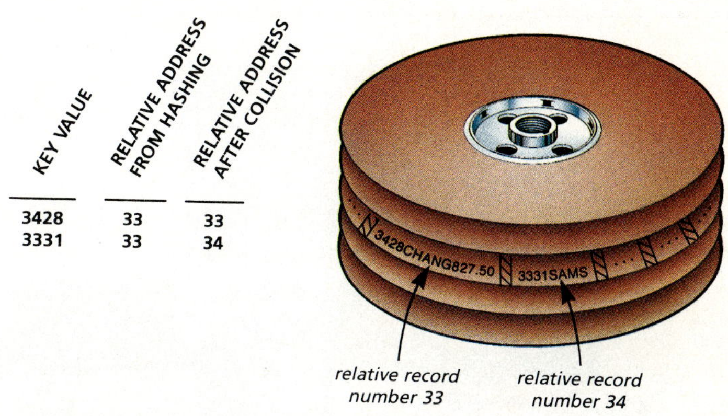

FIGURE 8-7
Sometimes the hashing computation produces synonyms, or records that have the same relative address. In this example, both records have a relative address of 33. When the computer tries to store the second record and finds that location 33 is already full, it stores the second record at the next available location. In this example, record 3331 would be stored in location 34.

FILE TYPE	TYPE OF STORAGE	ACCESS METHOD
Sequential	Tape or Disk	Sequential
Indexed	Disk	Random* or Sequential
Direct (Relative)	Disk	Random* or Sequential

* *Primarily accessed as random files*

FIGURE 8-8
The chart shows the type of storage and the access methods that can be used with each of the three file types.

Summary of File Organization Concepts

Files are organized as either sequential, indexed, or direct files. Sequential file organization can be used on tape or disk and requires that the records in the file be retrieved sequentially. Indexed files must be stored on disk and the records can be accessed either sequentially or randomly. Direct files are stored on disk and are usually accessed randomly (Figure 8-8).

HOW IS DATA IN FILES MAINTAINED?

Data stored on auxiliary storage must be kept current to produce accurate results when it is processed. To keep the data current, the records in the files must be updated. **Updating** records within a file consists of adding records to the file, changing records within the file, and deleting records from the file.

Adding Records

Records are added to a file when additional data is needed to make the file current. For example, if a customer opens a new account at a bank, a record containing the data for the new account must be added to the bank's account file. The process that would take place to *add* this record to the file is shown in Figure 8-9.

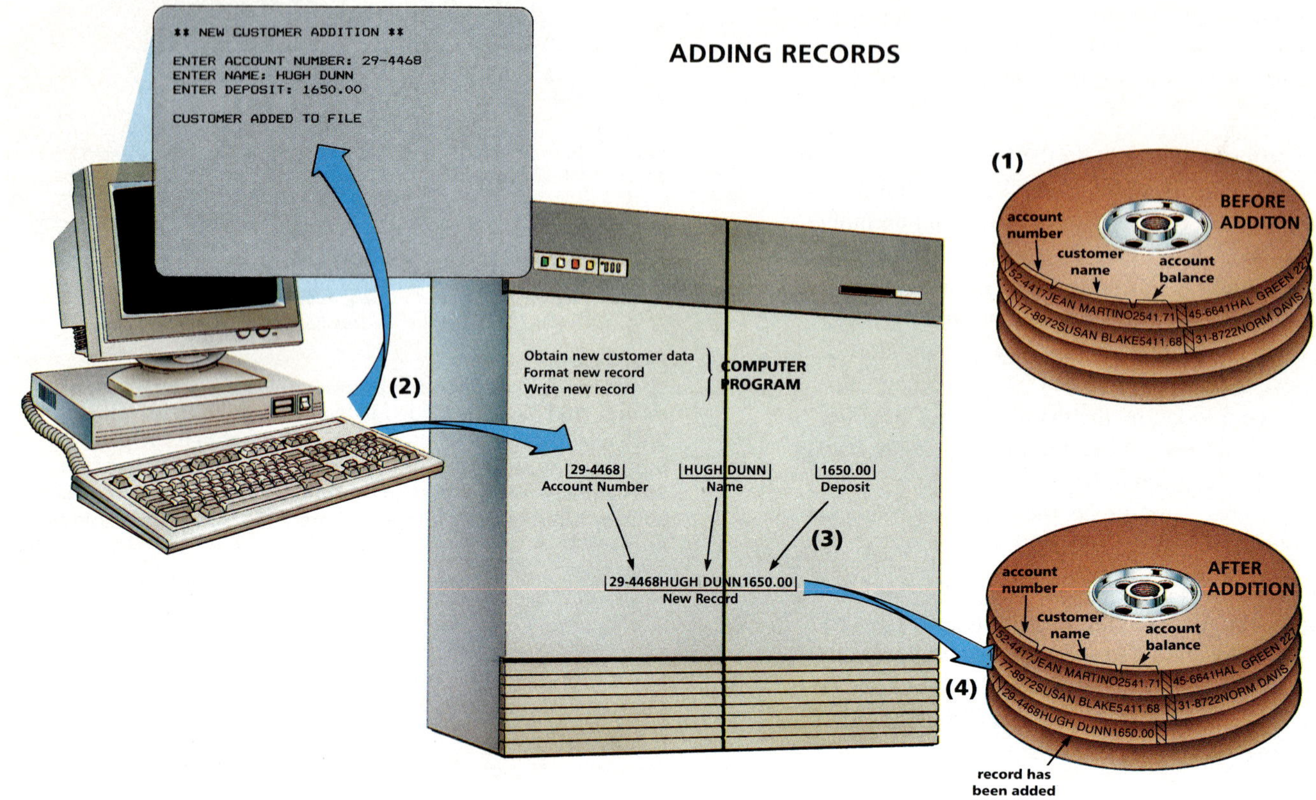

FIGURE 8-9
In this example of adding records, (1) the file first exists without the new account. (2) The teller enters the account number, customer name, and deposit. (3) This data is used to create a record that is then (4) added to the file.

1. A bank teller enters the new customer data into the computer through a terminal. The data includes the account number, the customer name, and the deposit that will become the account balance.
2. The update program moves the data entered by the user into the new record area in main memory.
3. The update program writes the new record to the file. The location on the disk where the record is written is determined by the program. In some cases, a new record will be written between other records in the file. In other cases, such as illustrated in this example, the added record is added to the end of the file.

Whenever data is stored on auxiliary storage for subsequent use, the ability to add records must be present in order to keep the data current.

Changing Records

The second task that must be accomplished when updating data is to *change* data that is currently stored in a record. Changes to data stored on auxiliary storage take place for two primary reasons: (1) to correct data that is known to be incorrect, and (2) to update data when new data becomes available.

As an example of the first type of change, assume in Figure 8-9 that instead of entering HUGH DUNN as the name for the customer, the teller enters HUGH DONE. The error is not noticed and thc customer leaves the bank. Later in the day, when the customer returns to question the transaction, the name stored in the file must be changed so that it contains the correct spelling. Therefore, the teller would enter HUGH DUNN as a change to the name field in the record. This change is made to replace data known to be incorrect with data known to be correct.

The bank account example also illustrates the second reason for change—to update data when new data becomes available. This type of change is made when a customer deposits or withdraws money. In Figure 8-10, Jean Martino has withdrawn \$500.00. The record for Jean Martino must be changed to reflect her withdrawal. The following steps occur:

1. The teller enters Jean Martino's account number 52-4417 and the amount 500.00.
2. The update program retrieves the record for account number 52-4417 and stores the record in main memory.
3. The program subtracts the withdrawal amount from the account balance in the record. This changes the account balance to reflect the correct balance in the account.
4. After the balance has been changed in memory, the record is written back onto the disk. After the change, the account balance has been updated, and the record stored on auxiliary storage contains the correct account balance.

Changing data stored on auxiliary storage to reflect the correct and current data is an important part of the updating process that is required for data.

CHANGING RECORDS

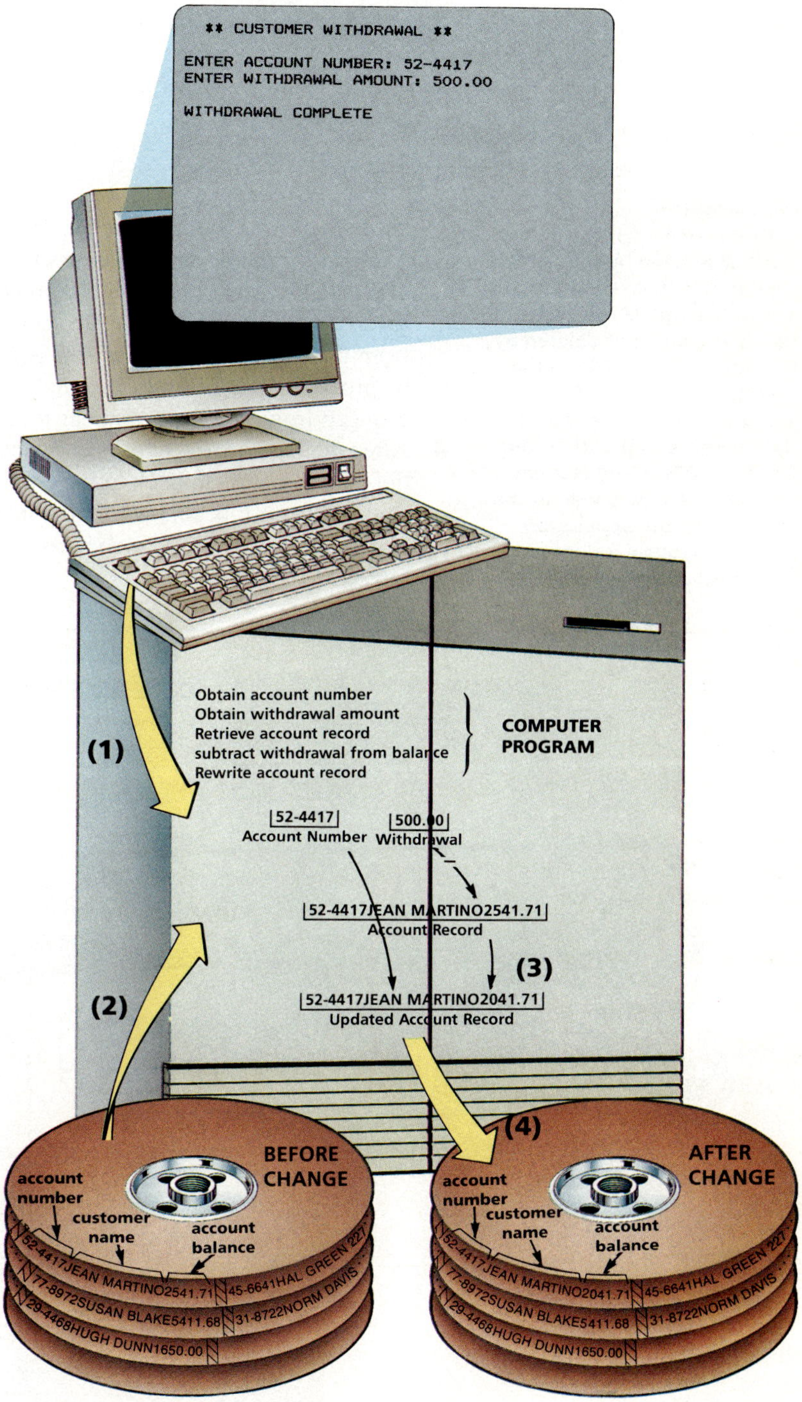

FIGURE 8-10
When Jean Martino withdraws \$500.00, the bank's records must be changed to reflect her new account balance. In this example, (1) the teller enters Jean Martino's account number and withdrawal amount, (2) the account number is used to retrieve Jean's account balance record; and (3) the account balance is reduced by the amount of the withdrawal (\$500.00). The record is then rewritten back onto the disk (4).

Deleting Records

The third major type of activity that must occur when updating data is to delete records stored in a file or database. Records are deleted when they are no longer needed as data. Figure 8-11 shows the updating procedures to *delete* a record for Hal Gruen who has closed his account. The following steps occur:

1. The teller enters Hal Gruen's account number (45-6641).
2. The update program retrieves the record from the disk using the account number as the key. The record is placed in main memory.
3. The actual processing that occurs to delete a record from a file depends on the type of file organization being used and the processing requirements of the application. Sometimes the record is removed from the file. Other times, as in this example, the record is not removed from the file. Instead, the record is *flagged*, or marked, in some manner so that it will not be processed again. In this example, the first three characters of the account number are changed from the actual number to the letters DEL (short for delete).
4. After the letters DEL have been placed in the first three characters of the account number, the record is written back to the file. The application program will not process the record again because it begins with DEL instead of a valid account number. Even though the record is still physically stored on the disk, it is effectively deleted because it will not be retrieved for processing.

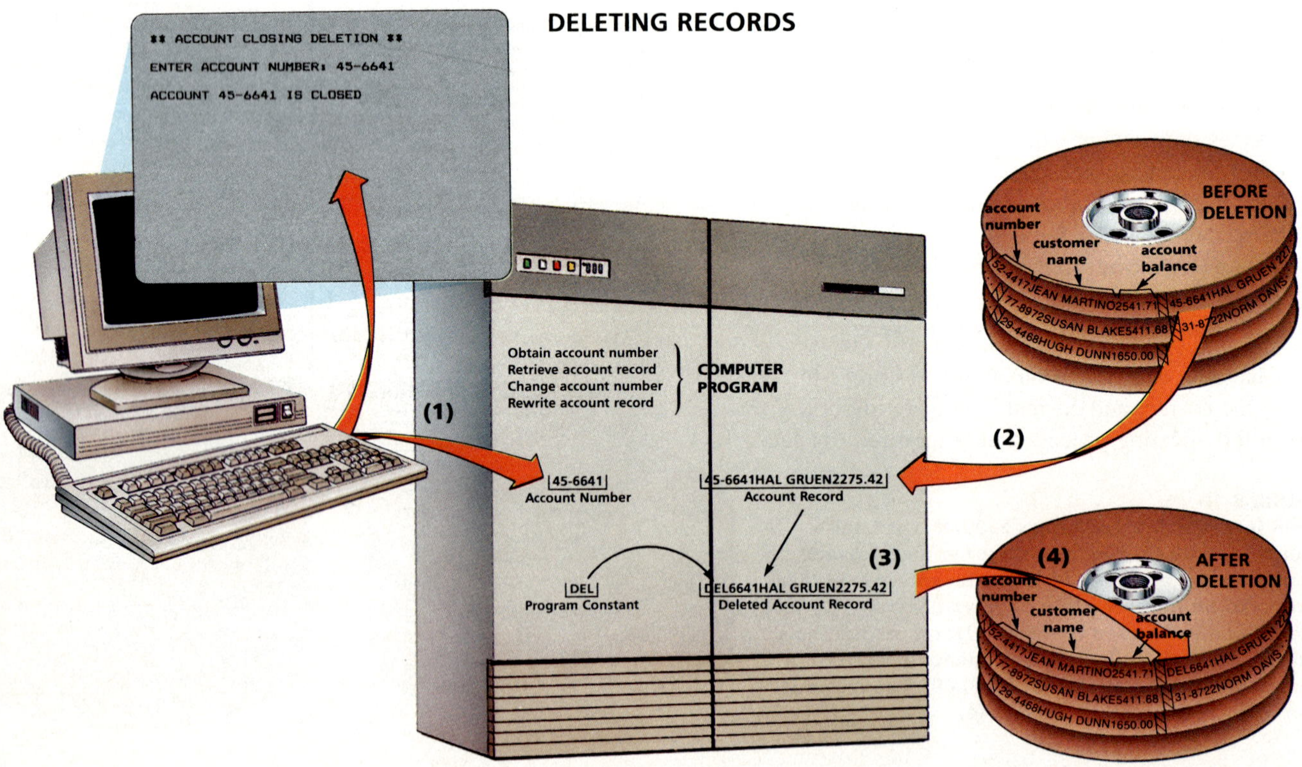

FIGURE 8-11
In this example, (1) the account number entered by the teller is used to (2) retrieve Hal Green's account record. (3) The account record is marked as deleted by placing the letters DEL In the first three positions of the account number. The record is then rewritten (4) back to the file. With DEL in the account number, the record will not be retrieved by the application program because it does not have a valid key value.

Deleting records from auxiliary storage is important because it provides a way of either removing or flagging records that are no longer needed for processing. This is necessary to keep data accurate.

Summary of How Data Is Maintained

Data maintenance is updating or adding, changing, and deleting data stored on auxiliary storage. The maintenance of data is critical if information derived from the processing of that data is to be reliable. When updating data, it does not matter if the data is stored as a single file or if it is part of a series of files organized into a database. The concept of adding, changing, and deleting data to keep it current remains the same.

DATABASES: A BETTER WAY TO MANAGE DATA AND INFORMATION

As stated at the beginning of this chapter, more and more businesspeople realize that next to the skills of their employees, data (and the information it represents) is one of a company's most valuable assets. They recognize that the information that has been accumulated on sales trends, competitors' products and services, employee skills, and production processes is a valuable resource that would be difficult if not impossible to replace.

Unfortunately, in many cases this resource is located in different files in different departments throughout the organization, often known only to the individuals who work with their specific portion of the total information. In these cases, the potential value of the information goes unrealized because it is not known to people in other departments who may need it or it cannot be accessed efficiently. In an attempt to organize their information resources and provide for timely and efficient access, many companies have implemented databases.

WHAT IS A DATABASE?

Previously in this chapter, we've discussed how data elements (characters, fields, and records) can be organized in files. In file-oriented systems, each file is independent. In a **database**, the data is organized in multiple related files. These related files are not independent of one another and it is possible for them to obtain data from one another. A **database management system (DBMS)** is the software that allows the user to create, maintain, and report the data and file relationships. Note that a **file management system**, sometimes mistakenly referred to as a database management system, is software that only allows the user to create, maintain, and access a single file at a time.

WHY USE A DATABASE?

The following example (Figure 8-12) illustrates some of the advantages of a database system as compared to a file-oriented system. Assume that a business periodically mails catalogs to its customers. If the business is using a file-oriented system, it would probably have a file used for the catalog mailing application that contains information about the catalog plus customer information, such as customer account number, name, and address. Files that are used in a file-oriented system are independent of one another. Therefore, other applications, such as the sales application, that also need to have customer information would each have files that contain the same customer information stored in the catalog mailing file. Thus in a file-oriented system, the customer data would be duplicated several times in different files. This duplication of data wastes auxiliary storage space. In addition, it makes maintaining the data difficult because when a customer record must be updated, all files containing that data must be individually updated.

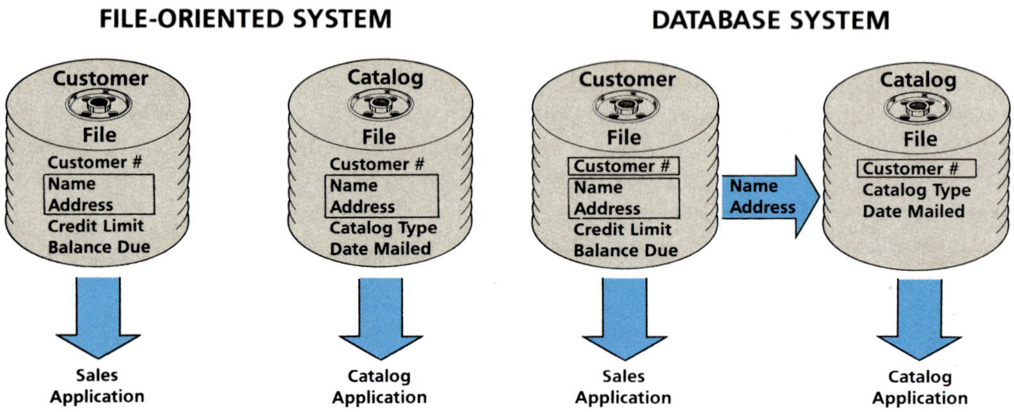

FIGURE 8-12
In a file-oriented system, each file contains the customer name and address. In the database system, only the customer file contains the name and address. Other files, such as the catalog file, use the customer number to retrieve the customer name and address when it is needed for processing.

In a database system, however, only one of the applications would have a file containing the customer name and address data. That is because in a database system, files are integrated; related files are linked together by the database software either through predefined relationships or through common data fields. In this example, the link could be the customer account number. If the sales file contained the customer account number, name, and address, the catalog mailing file would only need to contain the customer's account number plus the other catalog information. When the catalog application software is executed, the customer's name and address would be obtained from the sales file. The advantage of the database is that because the files are integrated, the customer name and address would only be stored once. This saves auxiliary storage space. It also allows data to be maintained more easily because update information only needs to be entered once.

As the previous example illustrates, a database system offers a number of advantages over a file-oriented system. These advantages and several others are summarized in the following list:

1. **Reduced data redundancy.** Redundant or duplicate data is greatly reduced in a database system. Frequently used data elements such as names, addresses, and descriptions are stored in one location. Having such items in one instead of many locations lowers the cost of maintaining the data.
2. **Improved data integrity.** Closely related to reduced data redundancy is the database advantage of improved data integrity. Because data is only stored in one place, it is more likely to be accurate. When it is updated, all applications that use the data will be using the most current version.
3. **Integrated files.** As demonstrated by the catalog mailing example (Figure 8-12), a key advantage of a database management system is its ability to "integrate" or join together data from more than one file for inquiry or reporting purposes.
4. **Improved data security.** Most database management systems allow the user to establish different levels of security over information in the database. For example, a department manager may have "read only" privileges on certain payroll data: the manager could inquire about the data but not change it. The payroll supervisor would have "full update"

privileges: the supervisor could not only inquire about the data but could also make changes. A nonmanagement employee would probably have no access privileges to the payroll data and could neither inquire about nor change the data.

Now that we've discussed some of their advantages, let's discuss the different types of databases.

TYPES OF DATABASE ORGANIZATION

There are three major types of database organization: relational, hierarchical, and network. The relational database structure is the most recent of the three methods and is considered a trend for the future. The relational database structure takes advantage of large-capacity direct-access storage devices that were not available when the hierarchical and network methods were developed.

Relational Database

In a **relational database**, data is organized in tables that in database terminology are called **relations**. The tables are further divided into rows (called **tuples**) and fields (called **attributes**). The tables can be thought of as files and the rows as records. The description or name of a particular attribute is called a **domain**. Figure 8-13 illustrates these terms with a student name and address file.

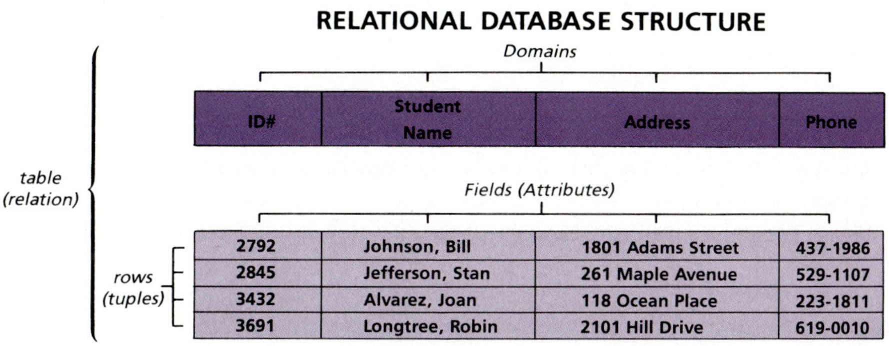

FIGURE 8-13
This example illustrates the terms used to identify the data in a relational database. A relational database is made up of multiple tables that can be thought of as files. In this example, other tables would probably exist for student grades, courses, faculty, and other logical groups of data.

As previously mentioned, a key advantage of a database is its ability to link multiple files together. A relational database accomplishes this by using a common field, sometimes called a **link**, that exists in each file. For example, in a database for a college, the link between files containing student information could be the student identification number. Hierarchical and network databases can also extract data from multiple files, but in these database structures, the data relationships that will enable the multiple file combination must be defined *when the database is created*. The advantage of a relational database is that the data relationships do not have to be predefined. The relational database only needs a common field in both data files to make a relationship between them. Because it is sometimes difficult to know ahead of time how data will be used, the flexibility provided by a relational database is an important advantage.

Another advantage of a relational database is its ability to add new fields. All that needs to be done is to define the fields in the appropriate table. With hierarchical and network database systems, the entire database has to be "redefined": existing relationships have to be reestablished to include the new fields.

Hierarchical Database

In a **hierarchical database** (Figure 8-14), data is organized in a series like a family tree or organization chart (the term hierarchy means an organized series). Like a family tree, the hierarchical database has branches made up of parent and child records. Each **parent record** can have multiple child records. However, each **child record** can only have one parent. The parent record at the top of the database is referred to as the **root** record.

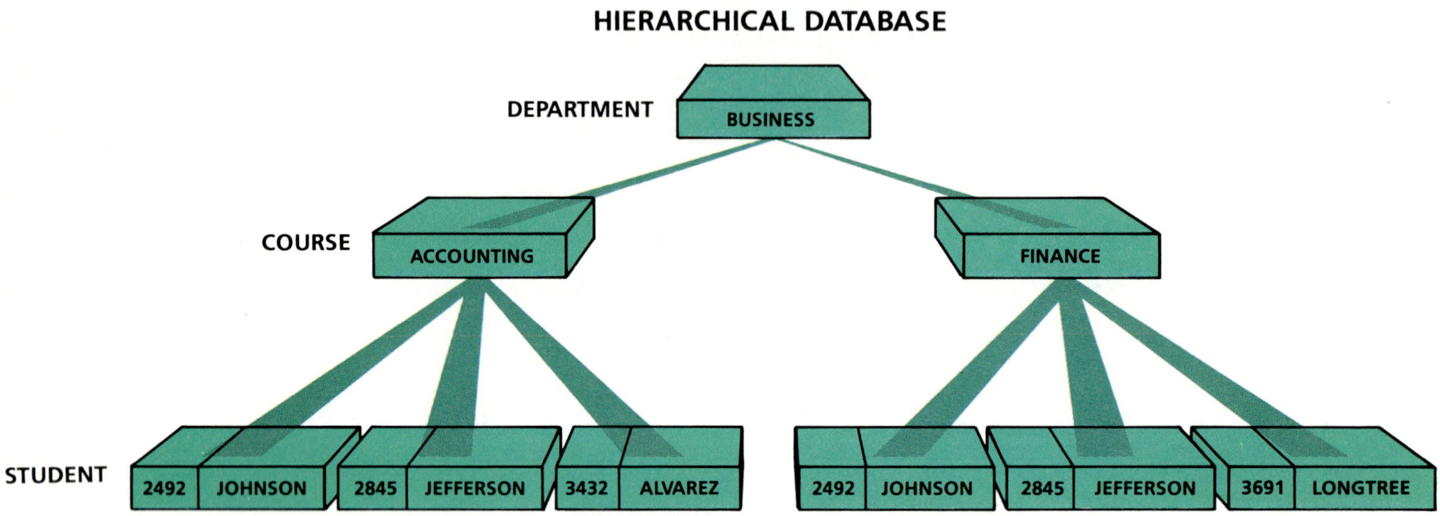

FIGURE 8-14
In this hierarchical database, Johnson, Jefferson, and Longtree are the children of Finance and Finance is their parent. Finance and Accounting are the children of Business and Business is their parent. These relationships must be established before the database can be used.

Hierarchical databases are the oldest form of database organization and reflect the fact that they were developed when the disk and memory capacity of computers was limited and most processing was done in batch mode. Data access is sequential in the sense that an inquiry begins at the root record and proceeds down the branch until the requested data is found. All parent-child relationships must be established before the user can access the database. These relationships are defined by the person who is responsible for designing the database and are established when the database is created in a separate process that is sometimes called "generating the database."

After the database is created, access must be made through the established relationships. This points out two disadvantages of hierarchical databases. First, records located in separate branches of the database cannot be accessed easily at the same time. Second, adding new fields to database records or modifying existing fields, such as adding the four-digit zip code extension, requires the redefinition of the entire database. Depending on the size of the database, this redefinition process can take a considerable amount of time. The advantage of a hierarchical database is that because the data relationships are predefined, access to and updating of data is very fast.

Network Database

A **network database** (Figure 8-15) is similar to a hierarchical database except that each child record can have more than one parent. In network database terminology, a child record is referred to as a **member** and a parent record is referred to as an **owner**. Unlike the hierarchical database, the network database is able to establish relationships between different branches of the data and thus offers increased access capability for the user. However, like the hierarchical database, these data relationships must be established prior to the use of the database and must be redefined if fields are added or modified.

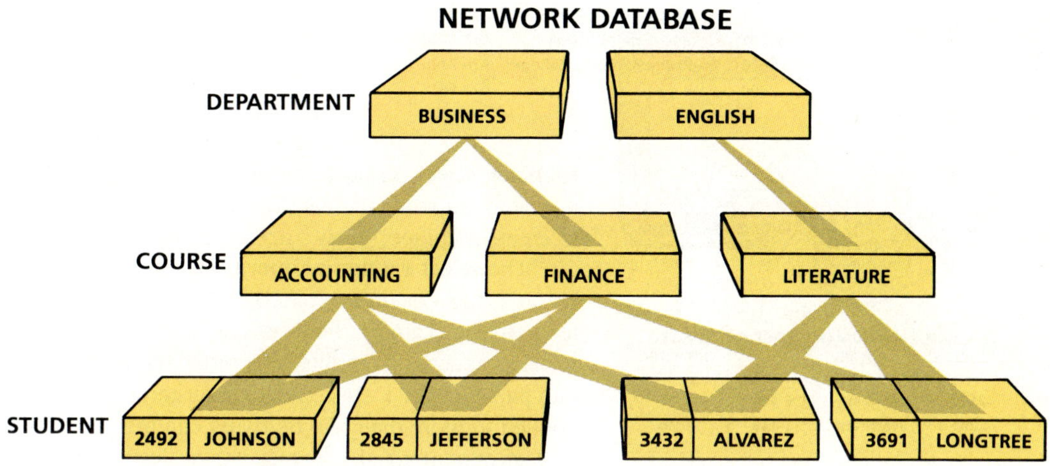

FIGURE 8-15
In a network database, lower level (member) records can be related to more than one higher level (owner) record. For example, Longtree's owners are Finance and Literature. Accounting has three members, Johnson, Jefferson, and Alvarez. As in a hierarchical database, these relationships must be established before the database can be used.

DATABASE MANAGEMENT SYSTEMS

Database management systems, the software that manage the creation, maintenance and reporting of database data, have a number of common features. These features include:

1. **Data dictionary.** The **data dictionary** defines each data field that will be contained in the database files. The dictionary is used to record the field name, size, description, type of data (e.g., text, numeric, or date), and relationship to other data elements.
2. **Utilities.** Database management system utility programs provide for a number of maintenance tasks including creating files and dictionaries, monitoring performance, copying data, and deleting unwanted records.
3. **Security.** Most database management systems allow the user to specify different levels of user access privileges. The privileges can be established for each user for each type of access (retrieve, update, and delete) to each data field. Note that without some type of access security, the data in a database is more subject to unauthorized access than in a decentralized system of individual files.
4. **Query language.** The query language is one of the most valuable features of a database management system. It allows the user to retrieve information from the database based on the criteria and in the format specified by the user.

QUERY LANGUAGES: ACCESS TO THE DATABASE

A **query language** is a simple English-like language that allows users to specify what data they want to see on a report or screen display. Although each query language has its own grammar, syntax, and vocabulary, these languages can generally be learned in a short time by persons without a programming background.

Query: Display customer name and quantity ordered for all sales orders for Part C-143

SALES ORDERS

SALES ORDER NO.	CUSTOMER NUMBER	PART #	QUANTITY ORDERED
1421	1100	M-200	100
1422	2600	C-143	15
1423	1425	A-101	65
1424	2201	C-143	1000
1425	1087	B-231	4
1426	2890	D-388	140

CUSTOMERS

CUSTOMER NUMBER	NAME	ADDRESS	PHONE
1087	Smith	1820 State	436-8800
1100	Ramirez	231 Elm	619-2200
1425	Gilder	3300 Main	232-0108
2201	Hoffman	675 Oak	457-7030
2600	Redman	1400 College	976-2400
2890	Ingles	117 Adams	629-9021

Select: Part C-143

Join: by Customer Number

Project: Customer Name

SALES ORDER	CUSTOMER NUMBER	CUSTOMER NAME	PART #	QUANTITY ORDERED
1422	2600	Redman	C-143	15
1424	2201	Hoffman	C-143	1000

Response to Query

FIGURE 8-16
This example illustrates the three relational operations (select, project, and join) that would be used to produce a response to the query.

A Query Example

Figure 8-16 shows how a user might query a relational database. This example illustrates the relational operations that may be performed when a relational database inquiry is made.

These three **relational operations** are select, project, and join. They allow the user to manipulate the data from one or more files to create a unique "view" or subset of the total data.

The **select relational operation** selects certain records (rows or tuples) based on user-supplied criteria. In the example, the user queries the database to select records from the sales order file that contain part number C-143. Selection criteria can be applied to more than one field and can include tests to determine if a field is greater than, less than, equal to, or not equal to a value specified by the user. Connectors such as AND and OR can also be used.

The **project relational operation** specifies the fields (attributes) that appear on the query output. In the example, the user wants to see the names of the customers who placed orders for part number C-143.

The **join relational operation** is used to combine two files (relations or tables). In the example, the link used to join the two files is the customer number, a field contained in each file.

After the query is executed, most query languages allow the user to give the query a unique name and save it for future use.

Structured Query Language: An Emerging Standard

One of the most widely used query languages is **Structured Query Language**, often referred to as **SQL**. Originally developed during the 1970s by IBM, SQL has been incorporated into a number of relational database software packages including ORACLE by Oracle Corporation and INGRES by Relational Technology. IBM actively supports SQL and incorporates it into their two major relational database system products, SQL/DS and DB2. SQL received increased support as the emerging relational database management system query language when, in 1985, the American National Standards Institute formed a committee to develop industry standards for SQL. The standards were issued in 1987. Today, it is difficult to pick up a computer industry publication and not read about at least one database software vendor announcing plans to incorporate SQL into its product. The standardization of SQL will further accelerate its implementation on a wide range of computer systems from micros to supercomputers. This fact, coupled with the increasing dominance of relational databases, will mean that SQL will be used by many computer users.

FIGURE 8-17
The database administrator plays a key role in the managing of a company's data. The DBA should possess good technical as well as good management skills.

DATABASE ADMINISTRATION

The centralization of an organization's data into a database requires a great deal of cooperation and coordination on the part of the database users. In file-oriented systems, if a user wanted to keep track of some data he or she would just create another file, often duplicating some data that was already being tracked by someone else. In a database system, the user must first check to see if some or all of the data is already on file and if not, how it can be added to the system. The role of coordinating the use of the database belongs to the database administrator.

The Database Administrator

The **database administrator**, or **DBA**, is the person responsible for coordinating all database activities (Figure 8-17). In small organizations, this person usually has other responsibilities such as the overall management of the computer resources. In medium and large organizations, the role of DBA is a full-time job for one or more people. The job of DBA usually includes the following responsibilities:

1. **Database design.** The DBA determines the initial design of the database and specifies where to add additional data files and records when they are needed.
2. **User coordination.** The DBA is responsible for letting users know what data is available in the database and how the users can retrieve it. The DBA also reviews user requests for additions to the database and helps establish priorities for their implementation.
3. **Backup and recovery.** The centralization of data in a database makes an organization particularly vulnerable to a computer system failure. It is often the responsibility of the DBA to minimize this risk, making sure that all data is regularly backed up and that contingency plans are prepared (and periodically tested) for a prolonged equipment or software malfunction.
4. **System security.** It is the DBA's responsibility to establish and monitor system access privileges to prevent the unauthorized use of an organization's data.
5. **Performance monitoring.** The performance of the database, usually measured in terms of response time to a user request, can be affected by a number of factors such as file sizes and the types and frequency of inquiries during the day. Most database management systems have utility programs that enable the DBA to monitor these factors and make adjustments to provide for more efficient database use.

In addition to the DBA, the user also has a role in a database management system.

The Responsibility of the User in a Database Management System

One of the user's first responsibilities is to become familiar with the data in the existing database. First-time database users are often amazed at the wealth of information available to help them perform their jobs more effectively.

Another responsibility of the user, in organizations of any size, is to play an active part in the specification of additions to the database. The maintenance of an organization's database is an ongoing task that must be constantly measured against the overall goals of the organization. Therefore users must participate in designing the database that will be used to help them achieve those goals and measure their progress.

MANAGING DATA ON A PERSONAL COMPUTER

A variety of data management systems are available for personal computers, ranging from simple file management programs to full relational database management systems. As with large system packages, many personal computer software vendors are developing or modifying existing packages to support Structured Query Language (SQL). The advantage of SQL packages for personal computers is that they can directly query mainframe databases that support SQL.

The increased computing power of the latest personal computers has also allowed database management packages originally written for mainframe computers to be modified to run on the smaller systems. ORACLE (Oracle Corporation) and INGRES (Relational Technology) are two SQL-based packages that have been adapted to personal computers.

Perhaps the best known and most widely used personal computer-based database management system is the dBASE series from Ashton-Tate Corporation. dBASE III PLUS offers a relational database manager, a programming language, and application development tools. dBASE IV includes a complete implementation of SQL.

With so many data management packages available (a recent survey included 43), it's difficult to decide which one to choose. For those with simple needs, a file management package is probably all that is necessary. For larger databases with multiple files, one of the more popular database management systems will offer increased capability and growth potential. For complex database requirements, the packages originally developed on mainframes should provide all the database resources required. If you need to select a database software package for your personal computer, you may want to refer to the section in Chapter 2 that discusses how to choose software packages for a personal computer.

SUMMARY OF DATABASES

Databases provide a better way of organizing data by relating items in multiple files. With databases, redundant data is minimized and data integrity improved. Database query languages allow data to be retrieved according to the criteria and in the format specified by the user.

Understanding the database and file concepts that have been presented in this chapter will help you to have a better understanding of how data and information are organized and managed on the auxiliary storage of a computer. Whether you are a home computer user who wants to store personal data on floppy disks or a hard drive, or a mainframe user accessing the database of the company where you are employed, a fundamental knowledge of how data is organized and managed will be useful to you.

CHAPTER SUMMARY

1. A file is a collection of related records that is usually stored on an auxiliary storage device. The three types of file organization are sequential, indexed, and direct or relative.
2. When **sequential file organization** is used, records are stored one after the other, normally in ascending or descending order by the value in the **key** field.
3. **Sequential retrieval** means that the records on a tape or disk file are retrieved (accessed) one after another in the same order that the records are stored on the tape or disk.

4. With **indexed file organization**, the records are stored on the disk in an indexed file in ascending or descending sequence based on a key field. An index is used to retrieve records.
5. An **index** consists of entries containing the key to the records and the disk addresses of the records.
6. **Random retrieval**, or access, allows the records in a disk file to be accessed in any order based on the value in a key field or on the location of a record in a file. Random retrieval is used when fast access to a record is required.
7. Random access and sequential access can be used with indexed files.
8. A **direct file** or **relative file** contains records that are stored and retrieved according to their disk address or their physical location within the file.
9. The locations on a disk where records in a direct file can be stored are called **buckets**.
10. **Hashing** means using a formula or performing a calculation to determine the location (position) where a record will be placed on a disk.
11. A **collision** occurs when the hashing operation generates the same disk location (called **synonyms**) for records with different key values.
12. Data maintenance refers to the process of **updating** files and databases by adding, changing, or deleting data from a file.
13. A **database** uses multiple related files to organize data.
14. A **database management system (DBMS)** is the software that allows the user to create, maintain, and report the data and file relationships used in a database.
15. By contrast, a **file management system** allows a user to access only one file at a time.
16. **Reduced data redundancy** (data that is duplicated in several different files), **improved data integrity** (data accuracy), **integrated files** (joining data from more than one file), and **improved data security** (ensuring that the data is accessible only to those with the proper authorization) are the major advantages of using a database.
17. A **relational database** is organized into tables called **relations**. The relations are divided into **tuples** (rows) and **attributes** (fields). Each attribute is given a unique name, called the **domain**.
18. In a relational database, a common attribute or **link** is used to connect multiple files.
19. The advantage of a relational database is that the data relationships do not need to be predefined.
20. A **hierarchical database** is organized in a top to bottom series of parent-child relationships. Each **parent record** can have multiple child records. However, each **child record** can have only one parent. The parent record at the top of the hierarchy is called the **root** record.
21. A **network database** is organized similar to a hierarchical database except each child record (called a **member**) may have more than one parent record (called an **owner**).
22. Data relationships in both the hierarchical database and the network database must be established prior to the use of the database.
23. The database management system consists of a **data dictionary** that defines each data field to be used in the database; utility programs (usually referred to as utilities) that provide a number of special functions (such as copying data, creating files, and deleting records); security levels that control access to the data; and a **query language** that allows users to specify what data they wish to view.
24. The **relational operations** of a relational database include the select relational operation, the project relational operation, and the join relational operation.
25. The **select relational operation** selects specific records based on the specifications provided by the user.
26. The **project relational operation** specifies the fields to be displayed.
27. The **join relational operation** is used to combine two files.
28. A widely used query language is **Structured Query Language (SQL)**.
29. The **database administrator (DBA)** is the person who coordinates all use of the database.
30. The database administrator is responsible for database design, user coordination, backup and recovery, database security, and database performance monitoring.
31. Users should become familiar with the data in their organization's database and should actively participate in the specification of additions to the database that will affect their jobs.

KEY TERMS

Attributes *8.13*
Backup and recovery *8.17*
Buckets *8.6*
Child record *8.14*
Collision *8.6*
Database *8.11*
Database administrator (DBA) *8.17*
Database design *8.17*
Database management system (DBMS) *8.11*
Data dictionary *8.15*
Direct file *8.6*
Domain *8.13*
File management system *8.11*
Hashing *8.6*
Hierarchical database *8.14*
Improved data integrity *8.12*
Improved data security *8.12*
Index *8.4*
Indexed file organization *8.4*
Integrated files *8.12*
Join relational operation *8.16*
Key *8.3*
Link *8.13*
Member *8.15*
Network database *8.15*
Owner *8.15*
Parent record *8.14*
Performance monitoring *8.17*
Prime number *8.6*
Project relational operation *8.16*
Query language *8.16*
Random access *8.5*
Random retrieval *8.5*
Reduced data redundancy *8.12*
Relational database *8.13*
Relational operations *8.16*
Relations *8.13*
Relative file *8.6*
Root *8.14*
Security *8.15*
Select relational operation *8.16*
Sequential access *8.4*
Sequential file organization *8.3*
Sequential retrieval *8.4*
Structured Query Language (SQL) *8.16*
Synonyms *8.6*
System security *8.17*
Tuples *8.13*
Updating *8.7*
User coordination *8.17*
Utilities *8.15*

REVIEW QUESTIONS

1. Describe sequential file organization. How are records in sequential files retrieved?
2. What is an indexed file? Describe how the index is used to retrieve records from an indexed file.
3. How is the location where a record is stored in a direct file determined?
4. What is a collision? What are synonyms?
5. List the three data maintenance procedures that are used to update files. Give an example of each.
6. Write a definition for the term database.
7. What is the difference between a database management system and a file management system?
8. What are the advantages of a database management system over a file-oriented system?
9. In a relational database, how are different files related to one another?
10. What is the difference between the structures of a hierarchical and a network database?
11. How is a data dictionary used?
12. Why is access security important in a database system?
13. How is a database query used?
14. What are the responsibilities of a database administrator?
15. What are the responsibilities of the user in a database management system?

CONTROVERSIAL ISSUES

1. Security experts have said that the risk of computer crime increases when a database is used in a company as opposed to when application-related files are used. They theorize that since all the data is accessible in one place, it would be easier to manipulate the data for illegal purposes. Database management system developers maintain that with proper security measures, databases are just as secure as files, if not more secure. What do you think?
2. Government attempts to establish a database on all citizens have been opposed by people who claim that it would be an invasion of privacy. Discuss the possible advantages and possible misuse of such a database.

RESEARCH PROJECTS

1. Find articles on relational databases in recent journals and magazines. Report on the performance characteristics of relational databases, particularly with respect to the time required to retrieve and display information from more than one file (a joint operation).
2. Prepare a report on various databases available for use on personal computers.
3. Prepare a report on a database management system that supports Structured Query Language (SQL).

Data Communications

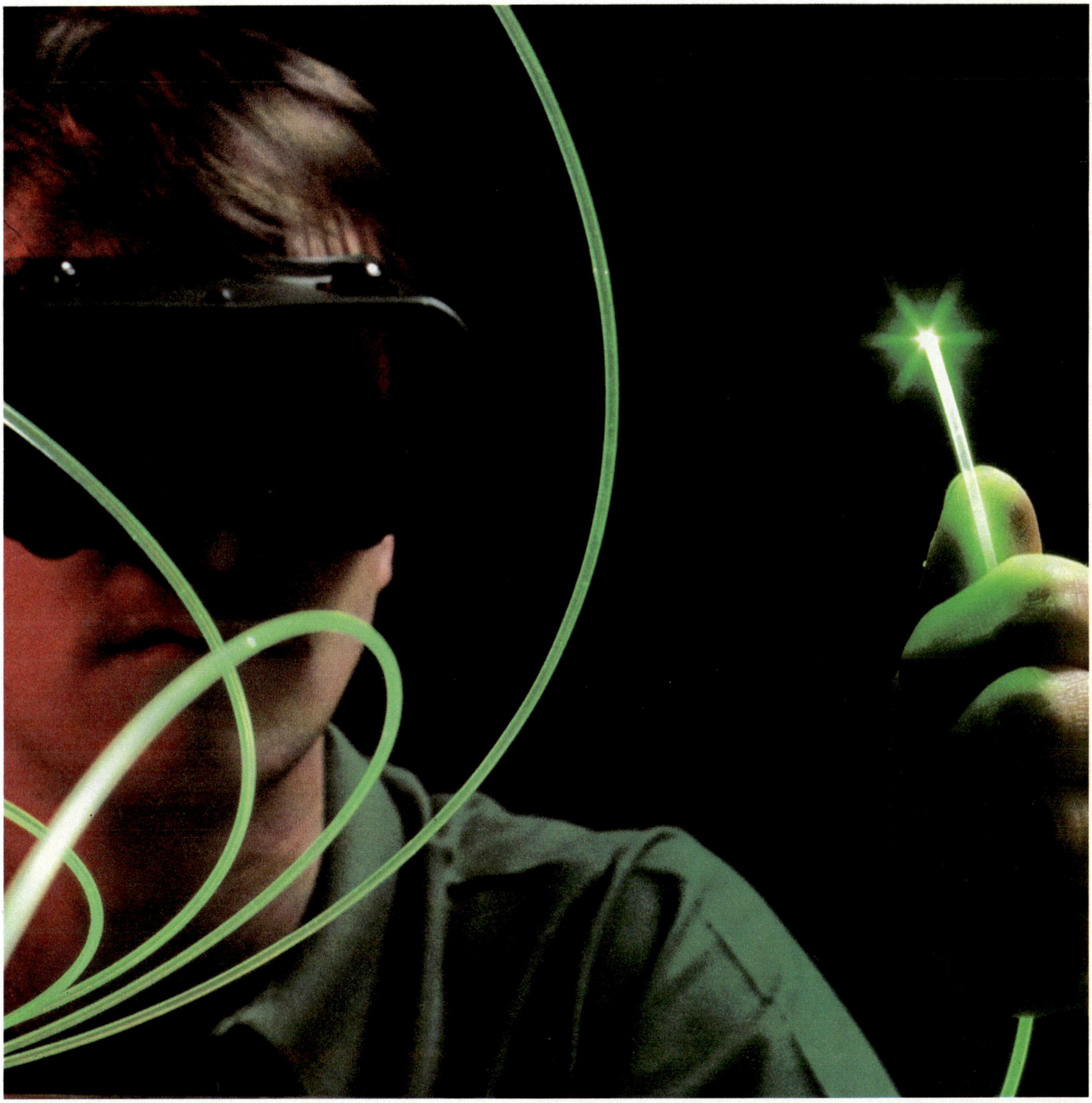

CHAPTER 9

Data Communications

OBJECTIVES

- Define data communications.
- Describe the basic components of a data communications system.
- Describe the various transmission media that are used for communication channels.
- Describe the different types of line configurations.
- Describe how data is transmitted.
- Identify and explain the communications equipment that can be used in a data communications system.
- Describe the functions that communications software can perform.
- Explain the two major categories of networks and describe the common network configurations.
- Discuss how personal computers can use data communications.

Computers are well recognized as important computing devices. They should also be recognized as important communication devices. It is now possible for a computer to communicate with other computers anywhere in the world. This capability allows users to quickly and directly access data and information that otherwise would have been unavailable or that probably would have taken considerable time to acquire. Banks, retail stores, airlines, hotels, and many others businesses use computers for communication purposes. Personal computer users communicate with other personal computer users and also access special databases available on larger machines to quickly and conveniently obtain information such as weather reports, stock market data, airline schedules, news stories, or even theater and movie reviews.

This chapter provides an overview of data communications and explains some of the terminology, equipment, procedures, and applications that relate to computers and their use as communication devices.

WHAT IS DATA COMMUNICATIONS?

Data communications is the transmission of data over a communication channel, such as a standard telephone line, between one computer (or a terminal) and another computer.

Figure 9-1 shows the basic components of a data communications system. These components include:

1. A computer or a terminal.
2. Data communication equipment that sends (and can usually receive) data.
3. The communication channel over which the data is sent.
4. Data communications equipment that receives (and can usually send) data.
5. Another computer.

As you will see, the basic model of a data communications system illustrated in Figure 9-1 can be applied to virtually all data communications systems.

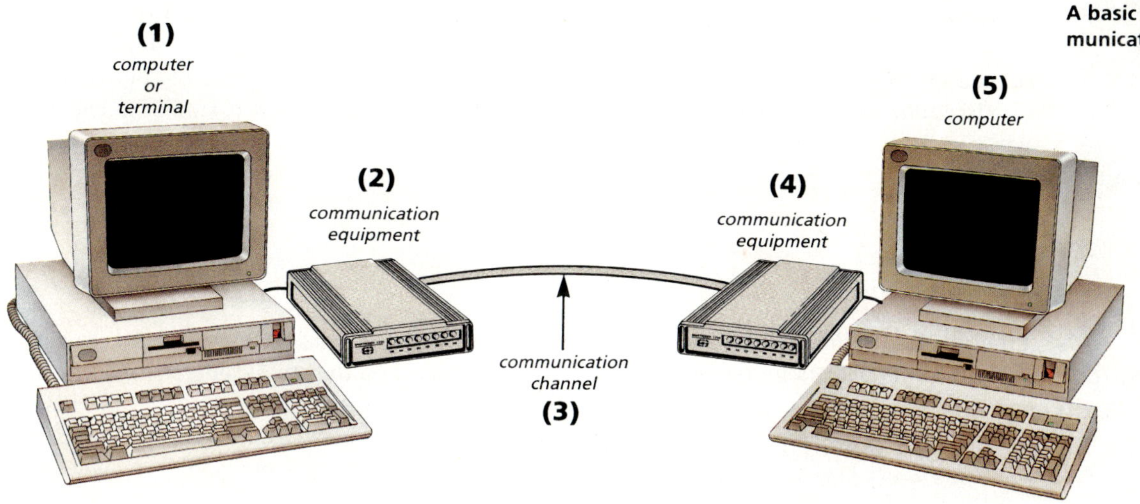

FIGURE 9-1
A basic model of a data communications system.

COMMUNICATION CHANNELS

A **communication channel** is the link or path that the data follows as it is transmitted from the sending equipment to the receiving equipment in a data communications system. These channels are made up of one or more **transmission media**, including twisted pair wire, coaxial cable, fiber optics, microwaves, and communication satellites.

Twisted Pair Wire

Twisted pair wire (Figure 9-2) consists of pairs of copper wires that are twisted together. To insulate and identify the wires, each wire is covered with a thin layer of colored plastic. Twisted pair wire is commonly used for telephone lines. It is an inexpensive transmission medium, and it can be easily strung from one location to another. The disadvantage of twisted pair wire is that it is susceptible to outside electrical interference generated by fans or air conditioners. This interference can garble the data as it is sent over the line, causing transmission errors to occur.

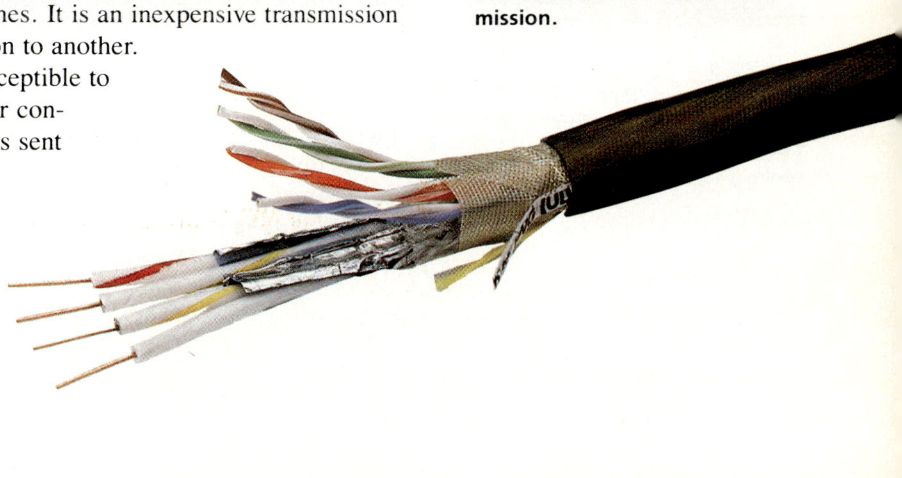

FIGURE 9-2
Twisted pair wire is most commonly used as telephone wire. It is inexpensive but susceptible to electrical interference that can cause errors in data transmission.

FIGURE 9-3
This photograph shows several types of coaxial cable that can be used to transmit data.

Coaxial Cable

A **coaxial cable** is a high-quality communication line that is used in offices, laid under the ground and under the ocean. Coaxial cable consists of a wire or central conductor surrounded by a nonconducting insulator that is in turn surrounded by a woven metal shielding layer, and finally a plastic outer coating (Figure 9-3). Because of its more heavily insulated construction, coaxial cable is not susceptible to electrical interference and can transmit data at higher data rates over longer distances than twisted pair telephone wire.

There are two types of coaxial cable, named for the transmission techniques they support: baseband and broadband. **Baseband** coaxial cable carries one signal at a time. The signal, however, can travel very fast—in the area of ten million bits per second for the first 1,000 feet. The speed drops off significantly as the length of cable increases and special equipment is needed to amplify (boost) the signal if it is transmitted more than approximately one mile.

Broadband coaxial cable can carry multiple signals at one time. It is similar to cable TV where a single cable offers a number of channels to the user. A particular advantage of broadband channels is that data, audio, and video transmission can take place over the same line.

Fiber Optics

Fiber optics (Figure 9-4) is a technology that may eventually replace conventional wire and cable in communication systems. This technology is based on the ability of smooth hair-thin strands of material to conduct light with high efficiency. The major advantages of fiber optics over wire cables include substantial weight and size savings and increased speed of transmission. A single fiber-optic cable can carry several hundred thousand voice communications simultaneously. Although fiber optics is not yet used on a large scale, it is frequently being used in new installations and promises to dramatically increase data communication capabilities.

FIGURE 9-4
The two-strand fiber-optic cable can transmit as much information as the 1500-pair copper cable.

Microwaves

Microwaves are a type of radio waves that can be used to provide high-speed transmission of both voice and data. Data is transmitted through the air from one microwave station to another in a manner similar to the way radio signals are transmitted. A disadvantage of microwaves is that they are limited to line-of-sight transmission. This means that microwaves must be transmitted in a straight line and that there can be no obstructions, such as buildings or mountains, between microwave stations. For this reason, microwave stations are characterized by antennas positioned on tops of buildings, towers, or mountains (Figure 9-5). Because of the curvature of the earth, the maximum distance between microwave stations is about thirty miles.

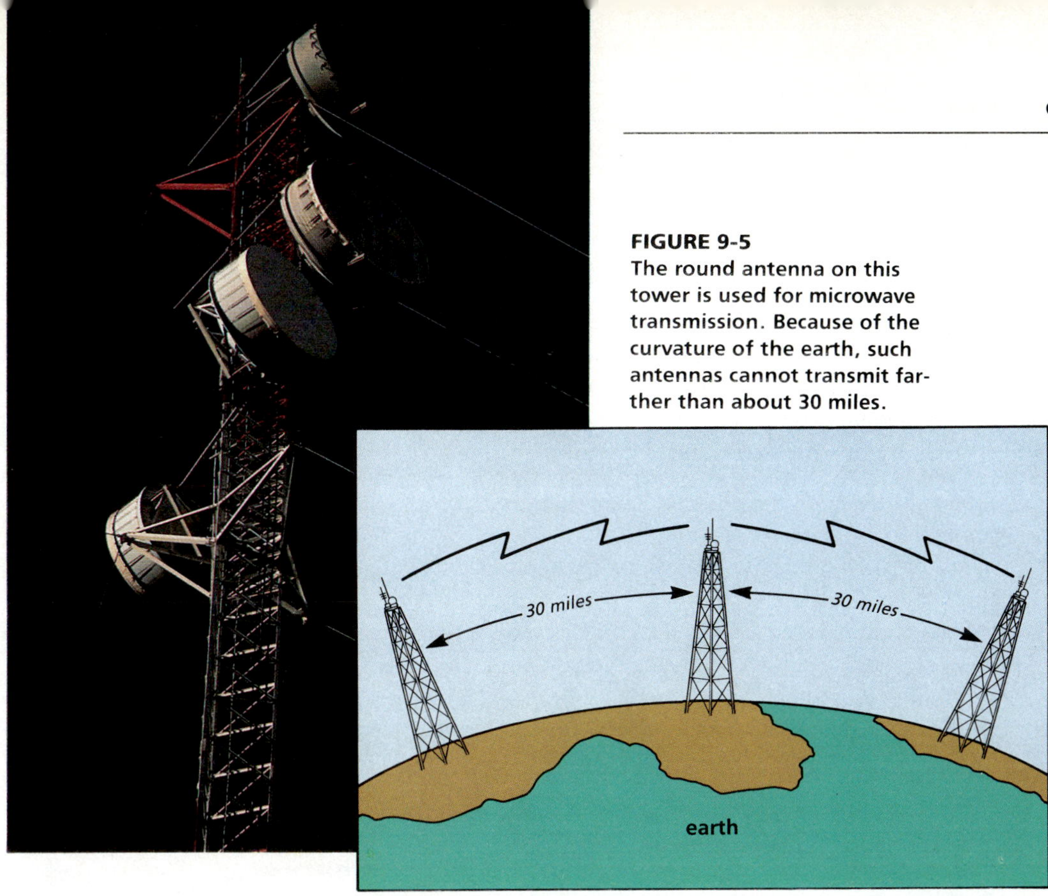

FIGURE 9-5
The round antenna on this tower is used for microwave transmission. Because of the curvature of the earth, such antennas cannot transmit farther than about 30 miles.

FIGURE 9-6
Earth stations use large dish antennas to communicate with satellites and microwave antennas. ▼

Communication Satellites

Communication satellites have the ability to receive signals from earth, amplify the signals, and retransmit the signals back to the earth. **Earth stations** (Figure 9-6) are communication facilities that use large dish-shaped antennas to transmit and receive data from satellites. The transmission to the satellite is called an **uplink** and the transmission from the satellite to a receiving earth station is called a **downlink**. Communication satellites are normally placed about 22,000 miles above the earth in a geosynchronous orbit (Figure 9-7). This means that the satellite rotates with the earth, so that the same dish antennas on earth that are used to send and receive signals can remain fixed on the satellite at all times.

◀ **FIGURE 9-7**
Communication satellites are placed in geosynchronous orbits approximately 22,000 miles above the earth. This satellite is shown emerging from the cargo bay of a space shuttle.

An Example of a Communication Channel

When data is transmitted over long distances, it is likely that a number of different types of transmission media will be used to make a complete communication channel. The diagram in Figure 9-8 illustrates some of the various transmission media that could be used to transmit data from a personal computer on the west coast of the United States to a large computer on the east coast. The steps that could occur are:

1. An entry is made on the personal computer. The data is sent over telephone lines from the computer to a microwave station.
2. The data is then transmitted between microwave stations that are usually located no more than thirty miles apart.
3. The data is transmitted from the last microwave station to an earth station.
4. The earth station transmits the data to the communications satellite.
5. The satellite relays the data to another earth station on the other side of the country.
6. The data received at the earth station is transmitted to microwave stations.
7. The data is sent by the telephone lines to the large computer.

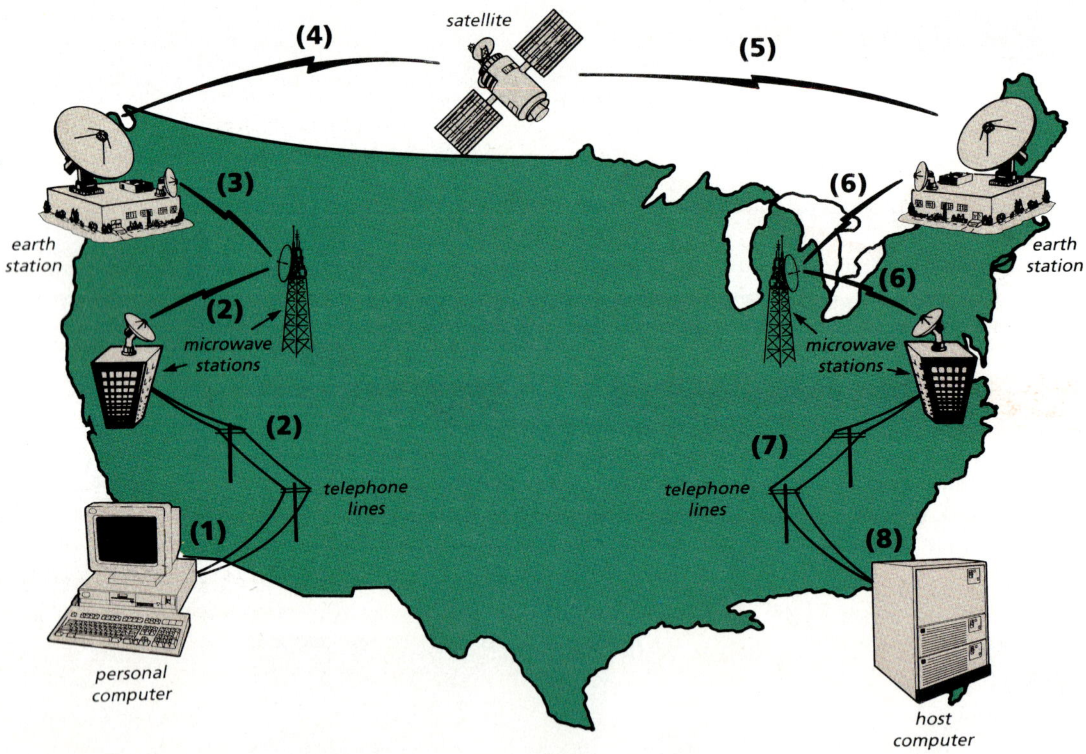

FIGURE 9-8
This diagram illustrates the use of telephone wires, microwave transmission, and a communication satellite to allow a personal computer to communicate with a large host computer.

The entire transmission process just described would take less than one second.

Not all data transmission is as complex as this example, but such sophisticated communication systems do exist to satisfy the needs of some users.

LINE CONFIGURATIONS

There are two major **line configurations** (types of line connections) that are commonly used in data communications: point-to-point lines and multidrop or multipoint lines.

Point-to-Point Lines

A **point-to-point line** is a direct line between a sending and a receiving device. It may be one of two types: a switched line or a dedicated line (Figure 9-9).

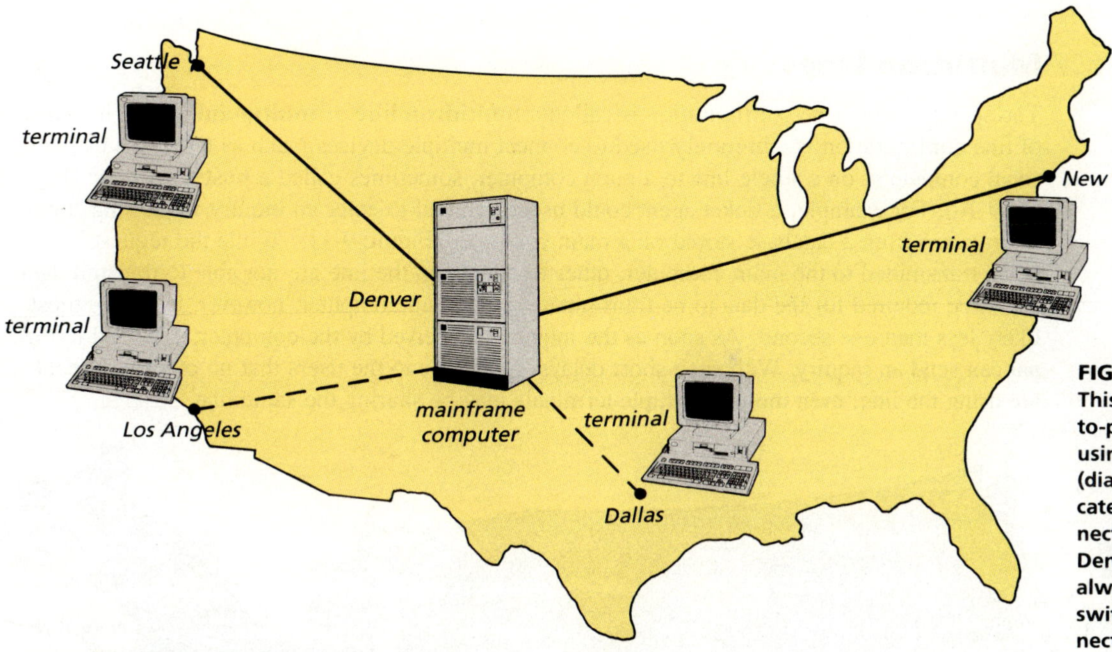

FIGURE 9-9
This diagram illustrates a point-to-point line configuration using both switched phone (dial up) lines (- - - -) and dedicated leased lines (——) connected to a main computer in Denver. The leased lines are always connected whereas the switched lines have to be connected each time they are used.

Switched Line A **switched line** uses a regular telephone line to establish a communication connection. Each time a connection is made, the line to be used for the call is selected by the telephone company switching stations (hence the name switched line). Using a switched line is the same as one person using a phone to call another person. The communication equipment at the sending end dials the phone number of the communication equipment at the other end. When the communication equipment at the receiving end answers the call, a connection is established and data can be transmitted. When the transmission of data is complete, the communication equipment at either end terminates the call by "hanging up" and the line is disconnected.

An advantage of using switched lines is that a connection can be made between any two locations that have phone service and communication equipment. For example, a personal computer could dial one computer to get information about the weather and then hang up and place a second call to another computer to get information about the stock market. A disadvantage of a switched line is that the quality of the line cannot be controlled because the line is chosen at random by the telephone company switching equipment. A switched line used for data communication is charged the same rate as a regular phone call.

Dedicated Line A **dedicated line** is a line connection that is always established (unlike the switched line where the line connection is reestablished each time it is used). The communication device at one end is always connected to the device at the other end. A user can create a dedicated line connection by running a wire or cable between two points, such as between two offices or buildings, or the dedicated line can be provided by an outside organization such as the phone company or some other communication service company. If the dedicated line is provided by an outside organization, it is sometimes called a **leased line** or a **private line**. Because a dedicated line is always established, the quality and consistency of the connection is better than on a switched line. Dedicated lines provided by outside organizations are usually charged on a flat fee basis: a fixed amount each month regardless of how much time the line is actually used to transmit data. The cost of dedicated lines varies based on the distance between the two connected points and, sometimes, the speed at which data will be transmitted.

Multidrop Lines

The second major line configuration is called a **multidrop line** or **multipoint line**. This type of line configuration is commonly used to connect multiple devices, such as terminals or personal computers, on a single line to a main computer, sometimes called a **host computer** (Figure 9-10). For example, a ticket agent could use a terminal to enter an inquiry requesting flight information from a database stored on a main computer (Figure 9-11). While the request is being transmitted to the main computer, other terminals on the line are not able to transmit data. The time required for the data to be transmitted to the main computer, however, is short—most likely less than one second. As soon as the inquiry is received by the computer, a second terminal can send an inquiry. With such short delays, it appears to the users that no other terminals are using the line, even though multiple terminals may be sharing the same line.

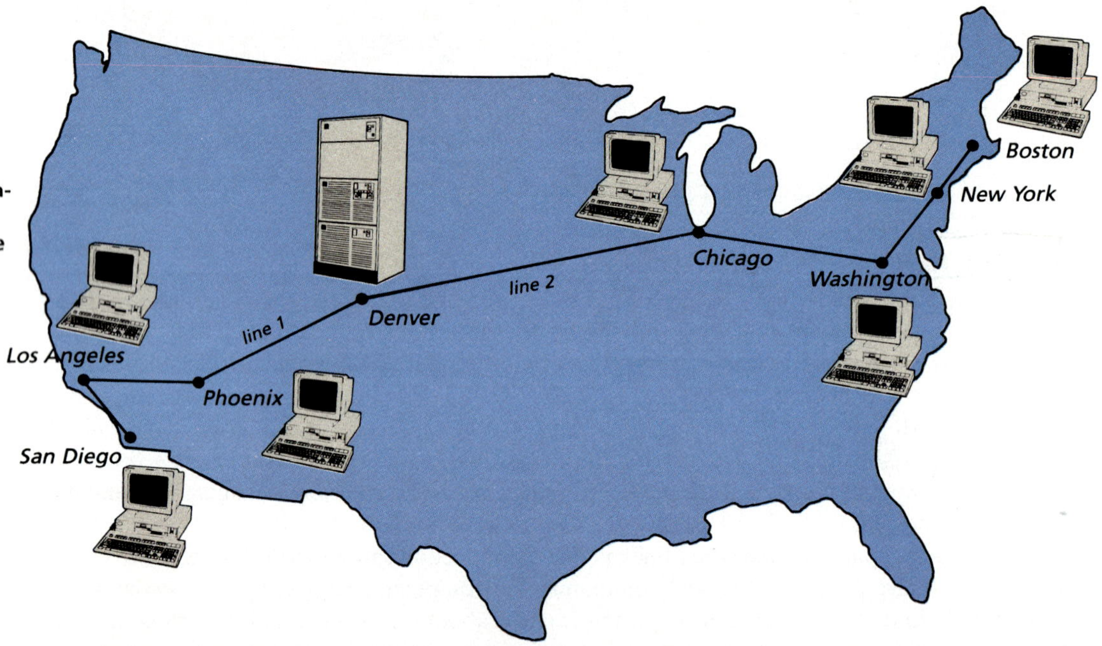

FIGURE 9-10
This diagram illustrates two multidrop lines connecting several cities with a computer in Denver. Each line is shared by terminals at several locations. Multidrop line configurations are less expensive than individual lines to each remote location.

The number of terminals to be placed on one line is a decision made by the designer of the system based on the amount of traffic that will be found on the line. For example, 100 or more terminals could be contained on a single line, provided each of them was only going to be sending short messages, such as inquiries, and each terminal was going to use the communication line only a few hours per day. But if longer messages such as reports were required and the terminals were to be used almost continuously, the number of terminals on one line would have to be smaller.

A leased line is almost always used for multidrop line configurations. The use of multidrop lines can decrease line costs considerably because one line is used by many terminals.

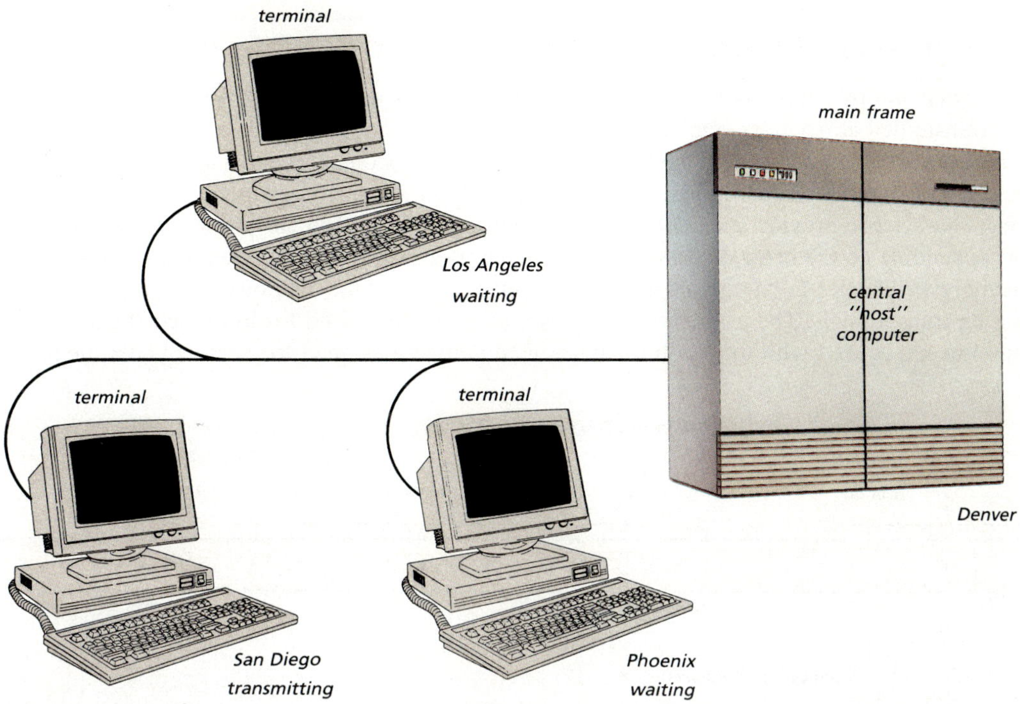

FIGURE 9-11
On a multidrop line, several terminals share the same line. Only one terminal at a time can transmit data to the host computer.

CHARACTERISTICS OF COMMUNICATION CHANNELS

The communication channels we have discussed can be categorized by a number of characteristics, including the type of signal, transmission mode, transmission direction, and transmission rate.

Types of Signals: Digital and Analog

Computer equipment is designed to process data as **digital signals**, individual electrical pulses that can represent the bits that are grouped together to form characters. However, telephone equipment was originally designed to carry only voice transmission, which is comprised of a continuous electrical wave called an **analog signal** (Figure 9-12). Therefore, in order to use voice phone lines to carry data, a special piece of equipment called a **modem** is used to convert the digital signals into analog signals. We discuss modems in more detail later in this chapter.

FIGURE 9-12
Individual electrical pulses of the digital signal are converted into analog (electrical wave) signals for transmission over voice phone lines. At the main computer receiving end, another modem converts the analog signals back into digital signals that can be processed by the computer.

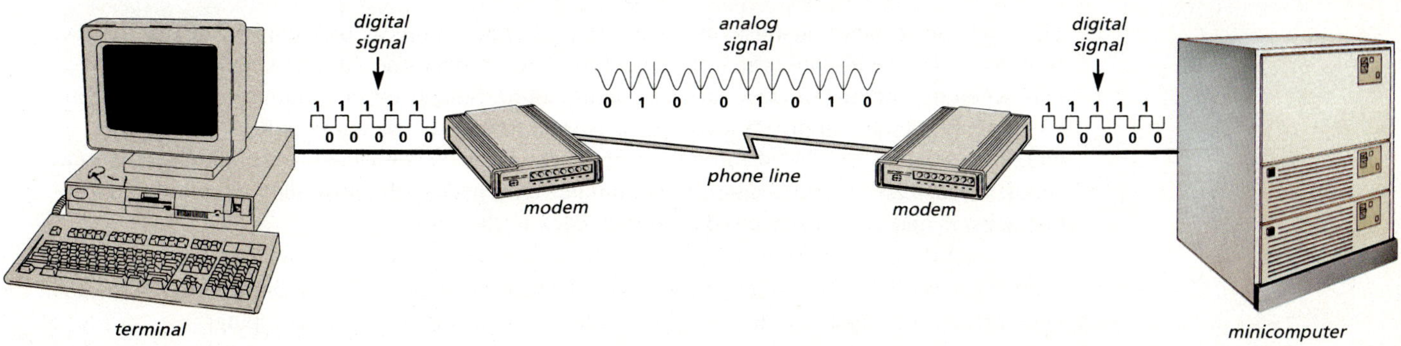

Transmission Modes: Asynchronous and Synchronous

In **asynchronous transmission mode** (Figure 9-13), individual characters (made up of bits) are transmitted at irregular intervals, for example, as they are entered by a user. To distinguish where one character stops and another starts, the asynchronous communication mode uses a start and a stop bit. An additional bit called a **parity bit** is sometimes included at the end of each character to provide a way of checking against data loss. The parity bit is turned on or off depending on the error detection method being used. As you recall from the discussion on memory in Chapter 5, parity bits are used to detect if one of the data bits has been changed during transmission. The asynchronous transmission mode is used for lower speed data transmission and is used with most communication equipment designed for personal computers.

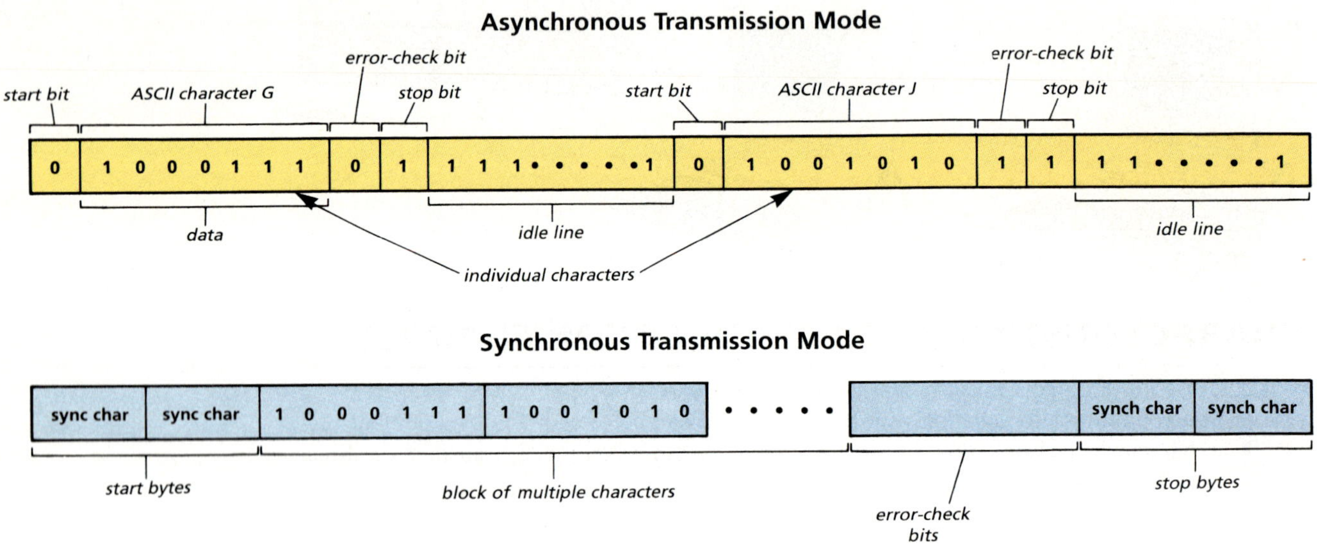

FIGURE 9-13
In asynchronous transmission mode, individual characters are transmitted. In synchronous transmission mode, multiple characters are sent in a block. Synchronous transmission is faster and more accurate.

In the **synchronous transmission mode** (also shown in Figure 9-13), large blocks of data are transmitted at regular intervals. Timing signals synchronize the communication equipment at both the sending and receiving ends and eliminate the need for start and stop bits for each character. Error-checking bits and start and end indicators called sync bytes are also transmitted. Synchronous transmission requires more sophisticated and expensive equipment but does give much higher speeds and accuracy than asynchronous transmission.

Direction of Transmission: Simplex, Half-Duplex, and Full-Duplex

The direction of data transmission is classified as either simplex, half-duplex, or full-duplex (Figure 9-14). In **simplex transmission**, data flows in only one direction. Simplex is used only when the sending device, such as a temperature sensor, never requires a response from the computer. For example, if a computer is used to control the temperature of a building, numerous sensors are placed throughout it. Each sensor is connected to the computer with a simplex transmission line because the computer only needs to receive data from the temperature sensors and does not need to send data back to the sensors.

In **half-duplex transmission**, data can flow in both directions but in only one direction at a time. An example is a citizens band radio. The user can talk or listen but not do both at the same time. Half-duplex is often used between terminals and a central computer.

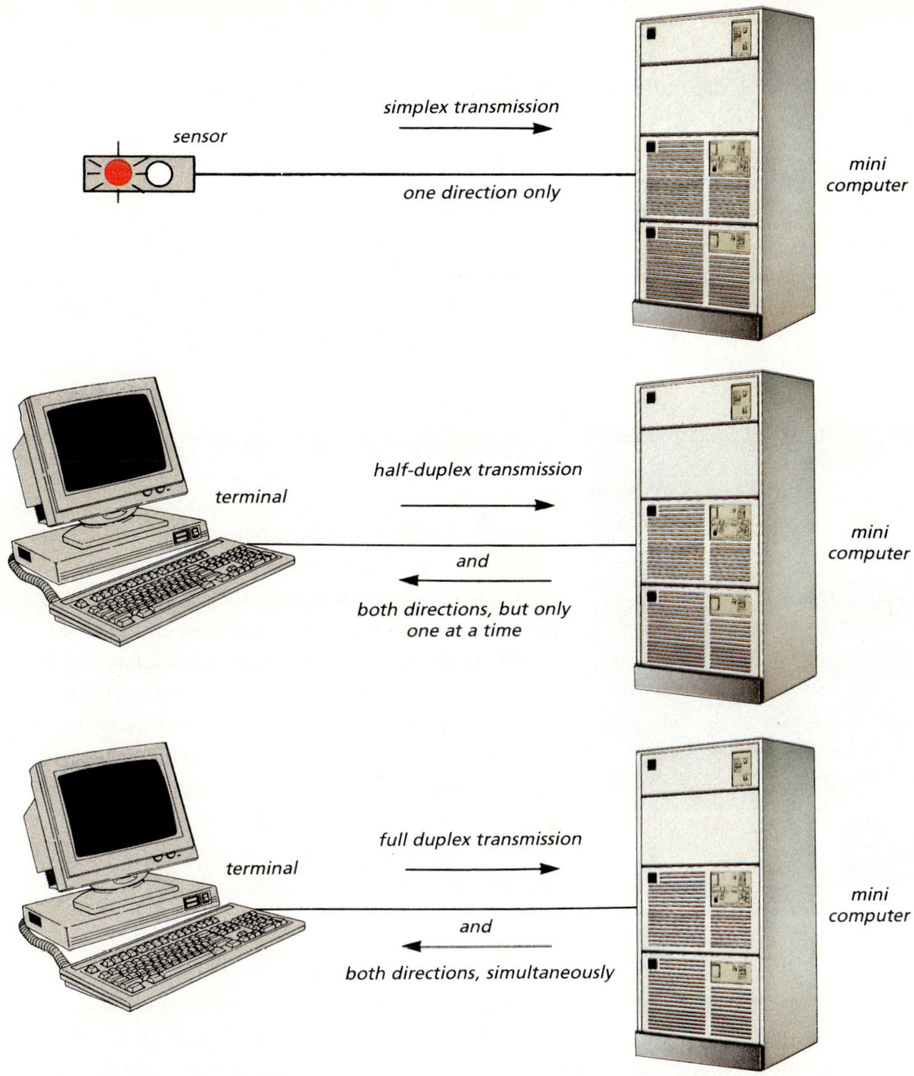

FIGURE 9-14
Simplex transmission allows data to flow in only one direction. Half-duplex allows data to flow in both directions but not at the same time. Full-duplex allows data to flow in both directions simultaneously.

In **full-duplex transmission**, data can be sent in both directions at the same time. A normal phone line is an example of full-duplex transmission. Both parties can talk at the same time. Full-duplex transmission is used for most interactive computer applications and for computer-to-computer data transmission.

Transmission Rate

The transmission rate of a communication channel is determined by its bandwidth and its speed. The **bandwidth** is the range of frequencies that a channel can carry. Since transmitted data can be assigned to different frequencies, the wider the bandwidth, the more frequencies, and the more data that can be transmitted at the same time. Figure 9-15 summarizes the bandwidths of the communication channels we have discussed.

FIGURE 9-15
Bandwidth and relative carrying capacity of communication channels. Bandwidth is measured in Hertz or cycles per second. A megahertz is one million cycles per second; a gigahertz is one billion cycles per second; and a terahertz is one trillion cycles per second.

TRANSMISSION CHANNEL	BANDWIDTH (HERTZ)	RELATIVE CARRYING CAPACITY
Twisted pair	10–100,000	1
Coaxial cable	1–1000 megahertz	1000
Microwave	1–10 gigahertz	10,000
Satellite	2–40 gigahertz	40,000
Fiber optics	100–1000 terahertz	1,000,000,000

The speed at which data is transmitted is usually expressed as bits per second or as a baud rate.

Bits per second (bps) is the number of bits that can be transmitted in one second. Using a 10-bit byte to represent a character (7 data bits, 1 start, 1 stop, and 1 parity bit), a 2,400 bps transmission would transmit 240 characters per second. At this rate, a 20-page single-spaced report would be transmitted in approximately five minutes.

The **baud rate** is the number of times per second that the signal being transmitted changes. With each change, one or more bits can be transmitted. At speeds up to 2,400 bps, usually only one bit is transmitted per signal change and thus the bits per second and the baud rate are the same. To achieve speeds in excess of 2,400 bps, more than one bit is transmitted with each signal change and thus the bps will exceed the baud rate.

FIGURE 9-16
An external modem is connected to a terminal or computer and to a phone outlet.

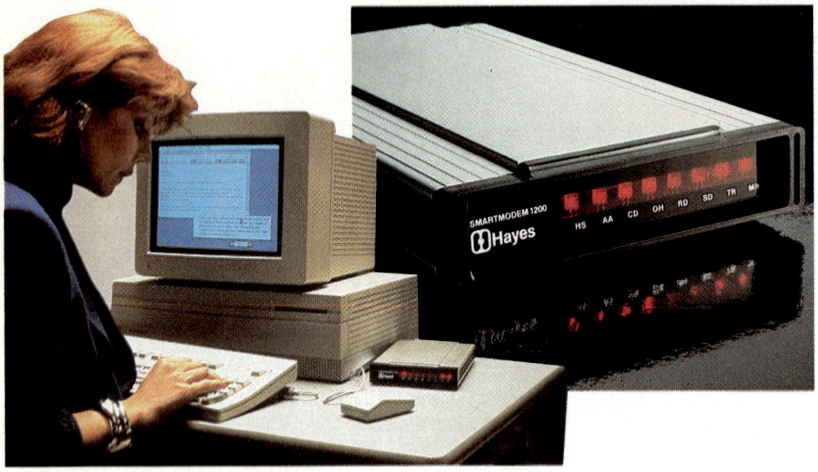

COMMUNICATION EQUIPMENT

If a terminal or a personal computer is within approximately 1,000 feet of another computer, the two devices can usually be directly connected by a cable. Over 1,000 feet, however, the electrical signal weakens to the point that some type of special communication equipment is required to increase or change the signal to transmit it farther. A variety of complex communication equipment exists to perform this task, but the equipment that a user is most likely to encounter is a modem, a multiplexor, and a front-end processor.

Modems

A **modem** converts the digital signals of a terminal or computer to analog signals that can be transmitted over phone equipment. The word modem comes from a combination of the words *mo*dulate, which means to change into a sound or analog signal, and *de*modulate, which means to convert an analog signal into a digital signal. A modem must be present at both the sending and receiving ends of a communication channel.

An **external modem** (Figure 9-16) is a separate or stand-alone device that is attached to the computer or terminal by a cable and to the phone outlet by a standard phone cord. An advantage of an external modem is that it may be moved from one terminal or computer to another.

FIGURE 9-17
An internal modem is mounted inside a personal computer.

An **internal modem** (Figure 9-17) is a circuit board that is installed inside a computer or terminal. Internal modems are generally less expensive than comparable external modems but once installed, they are not as easy to move.

An **acoustic modem**, also called an **acoustic coupler**, is designed to be used with a phone handset (Figure 9-18). The acoustic coupler converts the digital signals generated by the terminal or personal computer into a series of audible tones, which are picked up by the mouthpiece in the headset in the same manner that a telephone picks up a person's voice. The analog signals are then transmitted over the

FIGURE 9-18
The acoustic coupler in the lower left corner of this picture allows a portable computer user to communicate with another computer over telephone lines. Note that the telephone handset is placed in the molded rubber cups on the acoustic coupler.

communication channel. An acoustic coupler provides portability but is generally less reliable than an internal or external modem, because small outside sounds can be picked up by the acoustic coupler and cause transmission errors. Acoustic couplers are not common and are primarily used for special applications, such as with portable computers.

Modems can transmit data at rates from 300 to 38,400 bits per second (bps). Most personal computers would use either a 1,200 or 2,400 bps modem. Business or heavier volume users would use faster and more expensive modems.

Multiplexors

A **multiplexor** combines more than one input signal into a single stream of data that can be transmitted over a communication channel (Figure 9-19). The multiplexor at the sending end codes each character it receives with an identifier that is used by the multiplexor at the receiving end to separate the combined data stream into its original parts. A multiplexor may be connected to a separate modem or may have a modem built in. By combining the individual data streams into one, a multiplexor increases the efficiency of communications and saves the cost of individual communication channels.

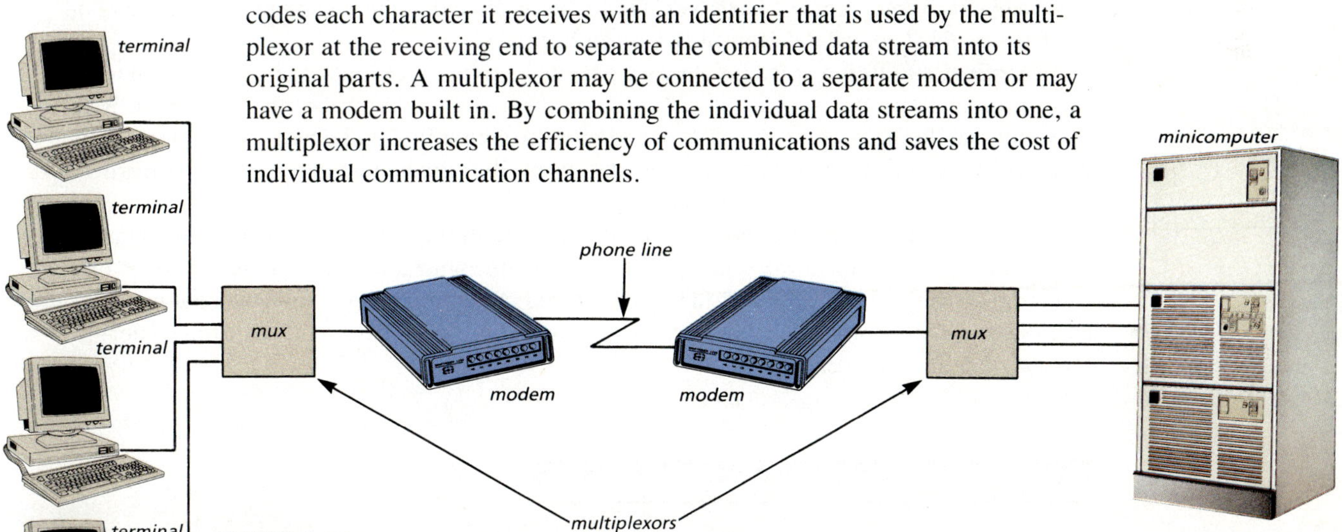

FIGURE 9-19
At the sending end, a multiplexor combines separate data transmissions into a single data stream. At the receiving end, the multiplexor separates the single stream into its original parts.

Front-End Processors

A **front-end processor** (Figure 9-20) is a computer that is dedicated to handling the data communication requirements of a larger computer. Relieved of these tasks, the activity of the large computer is dedicated to processing data, while the front-end processor communicates the data. Tasks that the front-end processor would handle include **polling** (checking the connected terminals or computers to see if they have data to send), error checking and correction, and access security to make sure that a connected device or the user of the connected device is authorized to access the computer.

FIGURE 9-20
This IBM Series 1 minicomputer is often used as a front-end processor to relieve the main computer of data communication tasks.

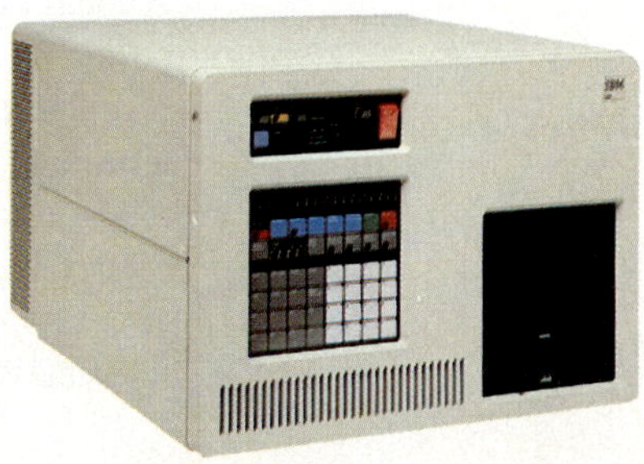

FIGURE 9-21
Communication software performs a variety of tasks that assist the user in using data communications equipment.

COMMUNICATION SOFTWARE

Sometimes communications equipment is preprogrammed to accomplish its designed communication tasks. In other cases, the user must load a program before beginning data transmission. These programs, referred to as **communications software**, can perform a number of tasks including dialing (if a switched phone line is used), terminal emulation, and data encryption (Figure 9-21).

Dialing software allows the user to store, review, select and dial phone numbers of computers that can be called. The software provides a variety of meaningful messages to assist the user in establishing a connection before transmitting data. For example, a person who uses a personal computer at home to communicate with a computer at the office could use dialing software to establish the communication connection. The software would display the office computer's phone number on the user's personal computer screen. The user would enter the appropriate command for the dialing software, working with a modem, to begin dialing the office computer and to establish a connection. During the 10 or 15 seconds that this process takes, the software would display messages to indicate specifically what was happening, such as "DIALING," "CARRIER DETECT" (which means that the office computer has "answered"), and "CONNECTED" (to indicate that the communication connection has been established and data transmission can begin).

Terminal emulation software allows a personal computer to imitate or appear to be a specific type of terminal so that the personal computer can connect to another computer. Most mini and mainframe computers are designed to work with a limited number of terminals that have specific characteristics such as speed and parity. Terminal emulation software performs the necessary speed and parity conversion.

Data encryption is used to protect confidential data during transmission. **Data encryption** is the conversion of data at the sending end into an unrecognizable string of characters or bits and the reconversion of the data at the receiving end. Without knowing how the data was encrypted, someone who intercepted the transmitted data would have a difficult time determining what the data meant.

COMMUNICATION NETWORKS

A communication **network** is a collection of terminals, computers, and other equipment that use communication channels to share data. Networks can be classified as either local area networks or wide area networks.

Local Area Networks (LANs)

A **local area network** or **LAN** is a communications network that is privately owned and that covers a limited geographic area, such as an office, a building, or a group of buildings.

The LAN consists of a communication channel that connects either a series of computer terminals together with a minicomputer or, more commonly, a group of personal computers to one another. Very sophisticated LANs may connect a variety of office devices, such as word processing equipment, computer terminals, video equipment, and personal computers.

Two common applications of local area networks are hardware resource sharing and information resource sharing. **Hardware resource sharing** allows each personal computer in the network to access and use devices that would be too expensive to provide for each user or would not be justified for each user because of only occasional use. For example, when a number of personal computers are used on the network, each may need to use a laser printer. Using a LAN, a laser printer could be purchased and made a part of the network. Whenever a user of a personal computer on the network needed the laser printer, it could be accessed over the network.

To illustrate, the drawing in Figure 9-22 depicts a simple local area network consisting of four personal computers linked together by a cable. Three of the personal computers (computer 1 in the sales and marketing department, computer 2 in the accounting department, and computer 3 in the personnel department) are available for use at all times. Computer 4 is used as a **network control unit**, sometimes called a **server**, which is dedicated to handling the communication needs of the other computers in the network. The users of this LAN have connected the laser printer to the network control unit. Using the LAN, all computers and the network control unit can use the printer.

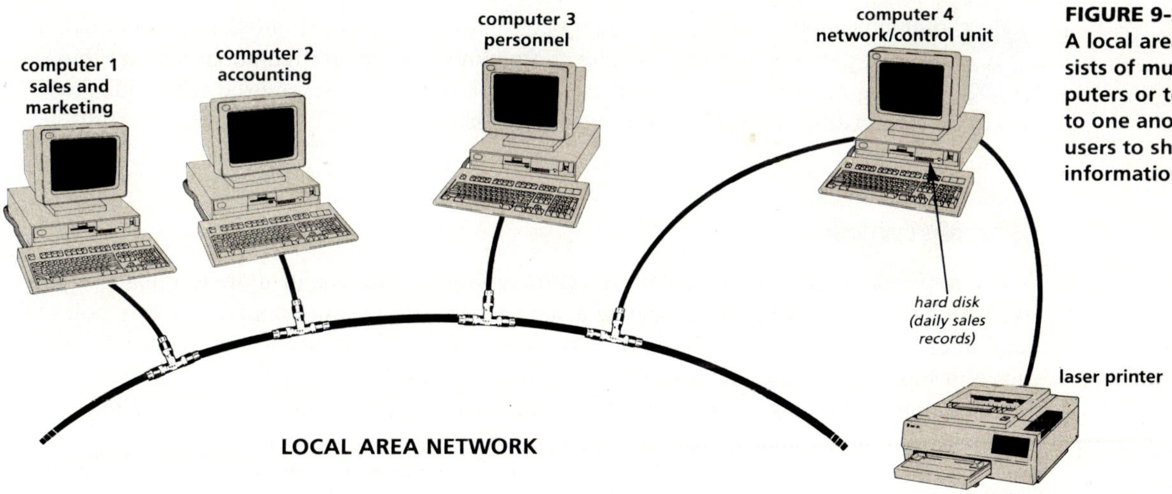

FIGURE 9-22
A local area network (LAN) consists of multiple personal computers or terminals connected to one another. The LAN allows users to share hardware and information.

Information resource sharing allows anyone using a personal computer on the local area network to access data stored on any other computer in the network. In actual practice, hardware resource sharing and information resource sharing are often combined. For example, in Figure 9-22, the daily sales records could be stored on the hard disk associated with the control unit personal computer. Anyone needing access to the sales records could use this information resource. The ability to access and store data on common auxiliary storage is an important feature of many local area networks.

Frequently used software is another type of resource that is often shared on a local area network. For example, if all users need access to word processing software, the software can be stored on the hard disk and accessed by all users as needed. This is much more convenient and faster than having the software stored on a floppy disk and available at each computer. For software written in-house, this is a common approach. Note, however, that the licensing agreement from many software companies does not permit the purchase of a single software package for use by all the computers in a network; therefore, it may be necessary to obtain a special agreement, called a **site license**, if a commercial software package is to be stored on hard disk and accessed by many users. Many software vendors now sell a network version of their packages.

Wide Area Networks (WANs)

A **wide area network** or **WAN** is one that is geographic in scope (as opposed to local) and uses phone lines, microwaves, satellites, or a combination of communication channels. Public wide area network companies include so-called "common carriers" such as the telephone companies. In recent years, telephone company deregulation has encouraged a number of companies to build their own wide area networks and others, such as MCI, to build WANs to compete with the telephone companies. Some common carriers are now offering **Integrated Services Digital Network (ISDN)** services. ISDN establishes an international standard for the digital transmission of data using different channels and communication companies.

NETWORK CONFIGURATIONS

Communication networks are usually configured or arranged in one or a combination of three patterns, sometimes called a **topology**. These configurations are star, bus, and ring networks. Although these configurations can also be used with wide area networks, we illustrate them with local area networks.

Star Network

A **star network** (Figure 9-23) contains a central computer and one or more terminals or personal computers connected to it, forming a star. A pure star network consists of only point-to-point lines between the terminals and the computer, but most star networks, such as the one shown in Figure 9-23, include both point-to-point lines and multidrop lines. A star network configuration is often used when the central computer contains all the data required to process the input from the terminals, such as an airline reservation system. For example, if inquiries are being processed in the star network, all the data to answer the inquiry would be contained in the database stored on the central computer.

A star network can be relatively efficient and close control can be kept over the data processed on the network. Its major disadvantage is that the entire network is dependent on the central computer and the associated hardware and software. If any of these elements fail, the entire network is disabled. Therefore, in most large star networks, backup systems are available in case the primary system fails.

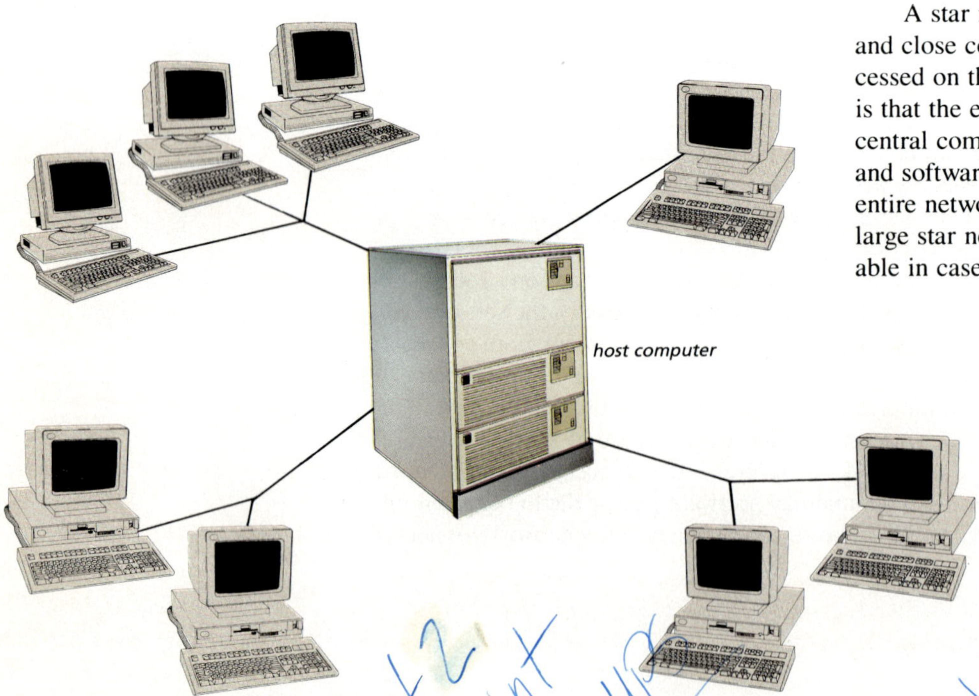

FIGURE 9-23
A star network contains a single, centralized host computer with which all the terminals or personal computers in the network communicate. Both point-to-point and multidrop lines can be used in a star network.

Bus Network

When a **bus network** is used, all devices in the network are connected to and share a single cable. Information is transmitted in either direction from any one personal computer to another. Any message can be directed to a specific device. An advantage of the bus network is that devices can be attached or detached from the network at any point without disturbing the rest of the network. In addition, if one computer on the network fails, this does not affect the other users of the network. Figure 9-22 illustrates a simple bus network.

Ring Network

A **ring network** does not utilize a centralized host computer. Rather, a series of computers communicate with one another (Figure 9-24). A ring network can be useful when all the processing is not done at a central site, but at local sites. For example, computers could be located in three departments: the accounting department, the personnel department, and the shipping and receiving department. The computers in each of these departments could perform the processing required for each of the departments. On occasion, however, the computer in the shipping and receiving department could communicate with the computer in the accounting department to update certain data stored on the accounting department computer. Ring networks have not been extensively implemented for data communications systems that are used for long-distance communication; they are used more for local communications.

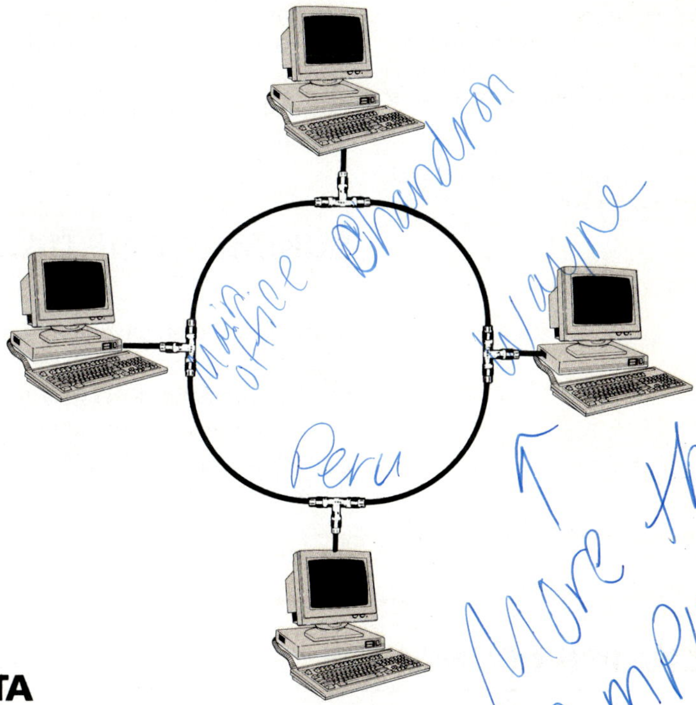

FIGURE 9-24
In a ring network, all computers are connected in a continuous loop. Data flows around the ring in only one direction.

THE PERSONAL COMPUTER AND DATA COMMUNICATIONS

The increased use of personal computers and the decreasing cost of communications equipment has resulted in a number of services that are now available to the individual personal computer user. To use these services, all that is required is a personal computer, a modem, communications software, and a phone line (Figure 9-25). These services include home banking, electronic shopping, commercial databases, and electronic bulletin boards.

Home banking, sometimes called electronic banking, allows a user to schedule payments to creditors, make transfers from one account to another, review bank statements and cleared checks, and inquire about current account balances.

Electronic shopping allows a user to select from a catalog of merchandise that the service offers for sale. The catalog is displayed on the user's screen. Theoretically, these items cost no more or cost less than comparable items found in stores because the electronic shopping seller doesn't have to operate a showroom. In addition, an electronic shopper has the added convenience of not having to go out to make the purchase.

Commercial databases offer a wealth of information in hundreds of subject areas. These services are literally electronic libraries containing information on such topics as economics, education, science, law, and a variety of business subjects. One service, NEXIS, offers access

FIGURE 9-25
This person is using a personal computer to schedule checking account payments with a home banking service. This is one of many services that are now available to individual personal computer users.

to the complete text of the *Encyclopaedia Britannica*. CompuServe offers a variety of databases that include information on world and business news, travel, and weather. Dow Jones provides business and financial information including access to the full text of the *Wall Street Journal*. To access commercial databases, users generally pay an initial subscription fee and additional charges based on the amount of use.

Electronic bulletin boards, like their physical counterparts, allow users to post messages on virtually any subject. These bulletin boards are usually maintained by computer clubs or vendors for local users although some have been established for wider use. Some bulletin boards offer members access to public domain software, programs that are available free to anyone who wants to use them. These programs can be **downloaded** or transferred to the user's own personal computer. If the user wants to contribute a program to the public domain software, it is **uploaded** or transferred to the bulletin board system.

SUMMARY OF DATA COMMUNICATIONS

Data communications will continue to have an increasing impact on the way people work and the way they use computers. Individuals and organizations are no longer limited to local data resources but instead, with communication capabilities, can obtain information from anywhere in the world at electronic speed. With data communications technology rapidly changing, today's businesses are challenged to find ways to adapt the technology to provide better products and services for their customers and make their operations more efficient. For individuals, the new technology offers increased access to worldwide information and services, and provides new opportunities for education.

CHAPTER SUMMARY

1. The transmission of data from one computer (or terminal) to another computer over communication channels is called **data communications**.
2. The basic components of a data communications system are: (1) a personal computer or terminal; (2) data communications equipment that sends (and can usually receive) data; (3) the communication channel over which data is sent; (4) data communications equipment that receives (and can usually send) data; and (5) a computer.
3. A **communication channel** is the link or path that the data follows as it is transmitted from the sending device to the receiving device in a data communications system.
4. A communication channel can consist of various **transmission media** including twisted pair wire, coaxial cable, fiber optics, microwaves, and communication satellites.
5. **Twisted pair wire** is the color-coded copper wires that are twisted together and commonly used as telephone wire.
6. **Coaxial cable** is high-quality underground or suboceanic communication lines consisting of a central conductor or wire that is surrounded by a nonconducting insulator and encased in a woven metal shield.
7. Coaxial cable can be either **baseband**, carrying one signal at a time at very high rates of speed, or **broadband**, carrying multiple signals at a time.
8. **Fiber optics** uses technology based on the ability of smooth, hair-thin strands of material that conduct light waves to rapidly and efficiently transmit data.
9. **Microwaves** are high-speed radio transmissions sent through the air between microwave stations.

10. **Communication satellites** are man-made space devices that receive, amplify, and retransmit signals from earth.
11. **Earth stations** are communication facilities that contain large dish-shaped antennas used to transmit data to and receive data from communication satellites.
12. **Line configurations** can be either point-to-point lines or multidrop lines.
13. A **point-to-point line** is a direct line between a sending and receiving device. It may be either a **switched line** (a connection established through regular telephone lines) or a **dedicated line** (a line whose connection between devices is always established).
14. A **multidrop line**, also known as a **multipoint line**, uses a single line to connect multiple devices to a main computer.
15. Computer equipment processes data as **digital signals**, which are individual electrical pulses representing the bits that are grouped together to form characters.
16. **Analog signals** are continuous electrical waves that are used to transmit data over standard telephone lines.
17. A **modem** is a special piece of equipment that converts the digital signals used by computer equipment into analog signals that are used by telephone equipment.
18. There are two modes of transmitting data: **asynchronous transmission mode**, which transmits one character at a time at irregular intervals using start and stop bits, and **synchronous transmission mode**, which transmits blocks of data at regular intervals using timing signals to synchronize the sending and receiving equipment.
19. Transmissions may be classified according to the direction in which the data can flow on a line: sending only (**simplex transmission**); sending or receiving, but in only one direction at a time (**half-duplex transmission**); and sending and receiving at the same time (**full-duplex transmission**).
20. The transmission rate of a communication channel depends on the **bandwidth** and its speed. The wider the bandwidth, the greater the number of signals that can be carried on the channel at one time, and the more data that can be transmitted.
21. **Bits per second (bps)** is the number of bits that can be transmitted in one second.
22. There are three basic types of modems: an **external modem**, which is a separate stand-alone device attached to the computer or terminal by a cable and to the phone outlet by a standard phone cable; an **internal modem**, which is a circuit board installed inside a computer or terminal; and an **acoustic modem** or **acoustic coupler**, which is a device used with a phone handset.
23. A **multiplexor** combines more than one input signal into a single stream of data that can be transmitted over a communications channel.
24. A **front-end processor** is a computer dedicated to handling the data communications requirements of a larger computer.
25. **Communication software** consists of programs that perform tasks such as dialing (software that stores, selects, and dials phone numbers); **terminal emulation** (software that allows the personal computer to imitate or appear to be a specific type of terminal so that the personal computer can connect to specific types of computers); and **data encryption** (software that can code and decode transmitted data for security purposes).
26. A **network** is a collection of terminals, computers, and other equipment that use communication channels to share data.
27. A **local area network (LAN)** is a communications network that covers a limited geographic area and is privately owned.
28. Two common uses of local area networks are **hardware resource sharing**, which allows all network users to access a single piece of equipment rather than each user having to be connected to his or her own device, and **information resource sharing**, which allows the network users to access data stored on other computers in the network.
29. A **wide area network** or **WAN** is a network that covers a large geographical area.
30. Network **topology** describes the pathways by which devices in a network are connected to each other.
31. A **star network** contains a central computer and one or more terminals or computers connected to it, forming a star.
32. In a **bus network** all devices in the network are connected to and share a single cable.
33. A **ring network** has a series of computers connected to each other in a ring.
34. For a personal computer to access other computers through data communications, it must have a modem, communications software, and a phone line.
35. Some of the data communication services available to personal computer users are home banking, electronic shopping, commercial databases, and electronic bulletin boards.

KEY TERMS

Acoustic coupler *9.12*
Acoustic modem *9.12*
Analog signal *9.9*
Asynchronous transmission mode *9.10*
Bandwidth *9.11*
Baseband *9.4*
Baud rate *9.12*
Bits per second (bps) *9.12*
Broadband *9.4*
Bus network *9.17*
Coaxial cable *9.4*
Communication channel *9.3*
Communication satellites *9.5*
Communications software *9.14*
Data communications *9.2*
Data encryption *9.14*
Dedicated line *9.7*
Digital signal *9.8*
Downlink *9.5*
Downloaded *9.18*
Earth stations *9.5*
External modems *9.12*
Fiber optics *9.4*
Front-end processors *9.13*
Full-duplex transmission *9.11*
Half-duplex transmission *9.11*
Hardware resource sharing *9.14*
Host computer *9.8*
Information resource sharing *9.15*
Integrated Services Digital Network (ISDN) *9.16*
Internal modem *9.12*
Leased line *9.7*
Line configuration *9.6*
Local area network (LAN) *9.14*
Microwaves *9.4*
Modem *9.9*
Multidrop line *9.8*
Multiplexor *9.13*
Multipoint line *9.8*
Network *9.14*
Network control unit *9.15*
Parity bit *9.10*
Point-to-point line *9.7*
Polling *9.13*
Private line *9.7*
Ring network *9.17*
Server *9.15*
Simplex transmission *9.10*
Site license *9.15*
Star network *9.16*
Switched line *9.7*
Synchronous transmission mode *9.10*
Terminal emulation *9.14*
Topology *9.16*
Transmission media *9.3*
Twisted pair wire *9.3*
Uplink *9.5*
Uploaded *9.18*
Wide area network (WAN) *9.16*

REVIEW QUESTIONS

1. Define data communications. What are the basic components of a data communications system?
2. List five kinds of transmission media used for communication channels.
3. Describe the two major types of line configurations. What are the advantages and disadvantages of each?
4. List and describe the three types of data transmission (direction) that are used.
5. Why is a modem used? Describe some of the types of modems available.
6. Describe some of the tasks that communications software can perform.
7. Compare and contrast a local area network and a wide area network.
8. Discuss the reasons for using a local area network.
9. Name three topologies or configurations that are used with networks. Draw a diagram of each.
10. Describe several data communications services that are available to personal computer users.

CONTROVERSIAL ISSUES

1. Some personal computer users have used communication equipment and software to illegally gain access to private databases. These individuals, known as "hackers," often claim that their illegal access was only a harmless prank. Do you think this type of computer usage is harmless? Explain your position.
2. The use of data communications equipment now allows some individuals to work for their company from their homes. These individuals "commute" electronically and do their work via a computer terminal or personal computer connected by a communication channel to their company's main computer. Discuss the advantages and disadvantages of such a working relationship.

CHAPTER 10

Operating Systems and System Software

CHAPTER 10

Operating Systems and System Software

OBJECTIVES

- Define the terms operating system and system software.
- Describe the various types of operating systems and explain the differences in their capabilities.
- Describe the functions of an operating system, including allocating system resources, monitoring system activities, and using utilities.
- Explain the difference between proprietary and portable operating systems.
- Name and briefly describe the major operating systems that are being used today.

When most people think of software they think of applications software such as the word processing, spreadsheet, and database software that we discuss in this text. However, for application software to run on a computer, another type of software is needed to interface between the user, the applications software, and the equipment. This software consists of programs that are referred to as the operating system. The operating system is part of what is called the system software.

WHAT IS SYSTEM SOFTWARE?

System software consists of all the programs including the operating system that are related to controlling the operations of the computer equipment. System software differs from applications software. Applications software tells the computer how to produce information, such as how to calculate the correct amount to print on a paycheck. In contrast, some of the functions that system software perform are: starting up the computer; loading, executing, and storing application programs; storing and retrieving files; and performing a variety of utility functions such as formatting disks, sorting data files, and translating program instructions into machine language. The most important part of the system software is the operating system.

WHAT IS AN OPERATING SYSTEM?

All computers utilize an operating system. An **operating system (OS)** consists of one or more programs that manage the operations of a computer. These programs function as an interface between the user, the application programs, and the computer equipment (Figure 10-1).

For a computer to operate, the essential and most frequently used instructions in the operating system must be stored in main memory. This portion of the operating system is called by many different names: the **supervisor**, **monitor**, **executive**, **master program**, **control program** and **kernel**. The remaining part of the operating system is usually stored on disk and can be loaded into main memory whenever it is needed.

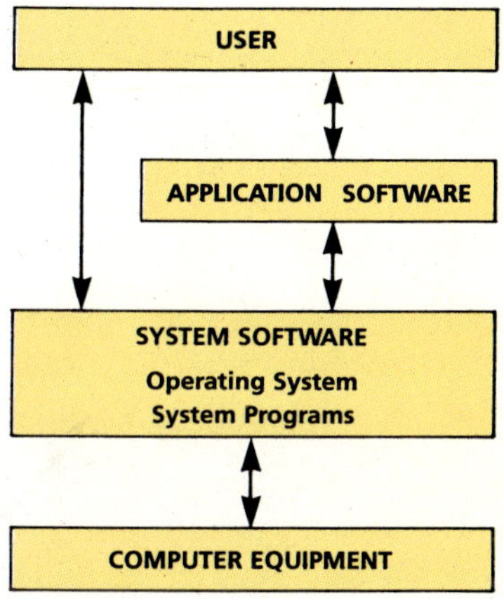

FIGURE 10-1
The operating system and other system programs act as an interface between the user, the application software, and the computer equipment.

LOADING AN OPERATING SYSTEM

The process of loading an operating system into the main memory of the computer is called **booting** the system. Figure 10-2 shows the steps that occur when an operating system is loaded on a personal computer. While this process is not identical to that used on large computers, the functions performed are similar:

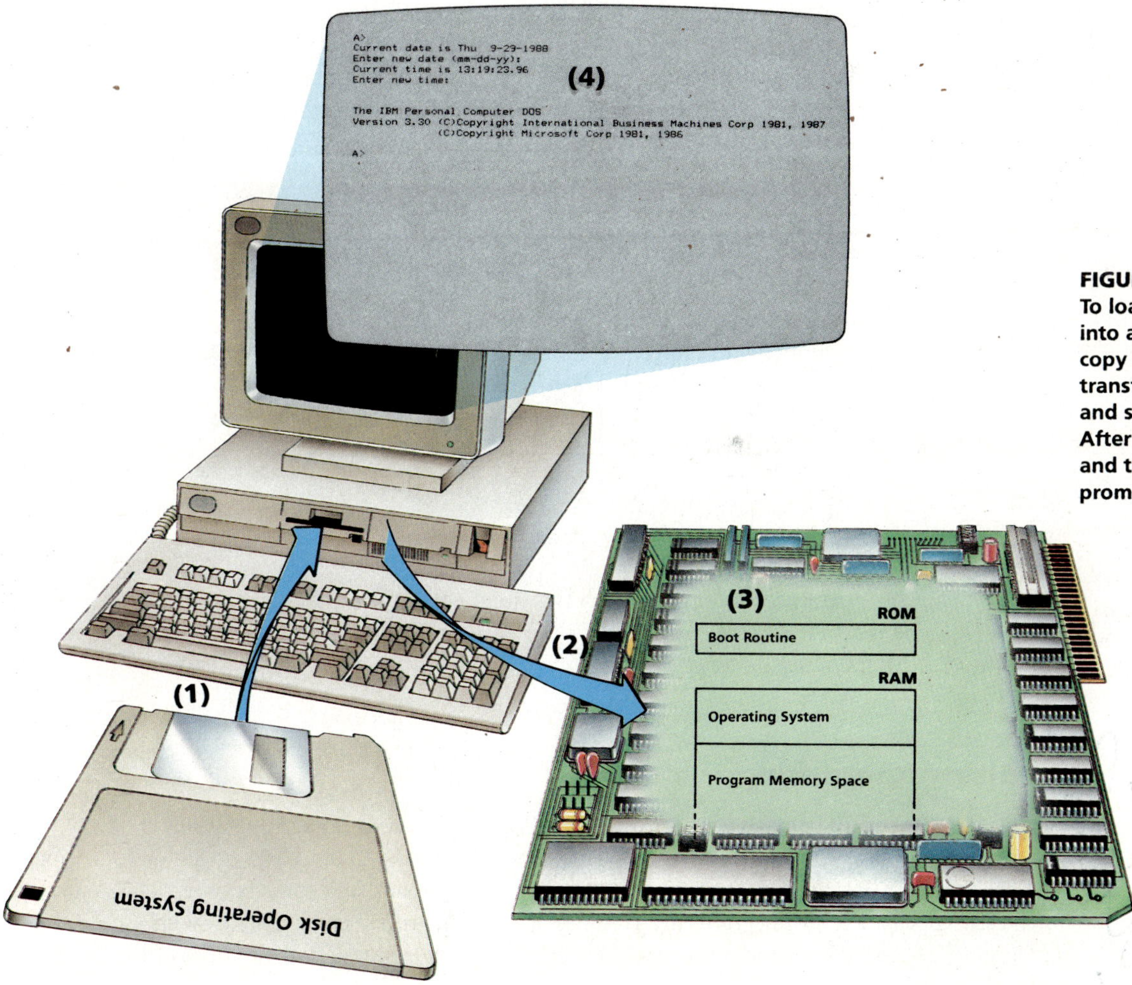

FIGURE 10-2
To load the operating system into a personal computer (1), a copy of the operating system is transferred from the disk (2) and stored in main memory (3). After the user enters the date and time (4), the system prompt (A>) is displayed.

1. A floppy disk that contains the operating system is placed in the disk drive. Note that if the operating system was stored on a hard disk, the floppy disk would not be used.
2. When the computer is turned on, the boot routine, which is stored in ROM, issues the commands to load the operating system into main memory. To do this, a copy of the operating system is transferred from the floppy disk or hard disk into main memory.
3. The boot instructions that loaded the operating system transfer control of the computer to the operating system. In many cases, the operating system requests that the user enter the correct date and time, after which the **operating system prompt** is displayed. The prompt indicates to the user that the operating system is ready to accept a command such as to run an application program.

Once the operating system is loaded into main memory, it usually remains in memory until the computer is turned off. The operating system controls the loading and manages the execution of each application program that is requested by the user. When an application program completes its task, the operating system queries the user by displaying the system prompt. The prompt indicates that the operating system is ready to receive a command specifying the next program or operation that is to be performed.

TYPES OF OPERATING SYSTEMS

The various types of operating systems include single program, multiprogramming, multiprocessing, and virtual machine operating systems. These operating systems can be classified by two criteria: (1) whether or not they allow more than one user to use the computer at the same time and (2) whether or not they allow more than one program to run at the same time (Figure 10-3).

	SINGLE PROGRAM	MULTIPROGRAMMING	MULTIPROCESSING	VIRTUAL MACHINE
NUMBER OF PROGRAMS RUNNING	One	More than one	More than one on each CPU	More than one on each operating system
NUMBER OF USERS	One	One or more than one (Multiuser)	More than one on each CPU	More than one on each operating system

FIGURE 10-3
Operating systems can be classified by whether they allow more than one user and more than one program to be operating at one time.

Single Program

Single program operating systems allow only a single user to run a single program at one time. This was the first type of operating system developed. Today, many personal computers use this type of operating system.

Multiprogramming

Multiprogramming operating systems, also called **multitasking** operating systems, allow more than one program to be run at the same time. Even though the CPU is only able to work on one program instruction at a time, its ability to switch back and forth between programs makes it appear that all programs are running at the same time. For example, with a multiprogramming operating system the computer could be performing a complex spreadsheet calculation and at the same time be downloading a file from another computer while the user is writing a memo with the word processing program.

Multiprogramming operating systems on personal computers can usually support a single user running multiple programs. Multiprogramming operating systems on some personal computers and most mini and mainframe computers can support more than one user running more than one program. This version of a multiprogramming operating system is sometimes called a **multiuser-multiprogramming** operating system. Most of these operating systems also allow more than one user to be running the same program. For example, a wholesale distributor may have dozens of terminal operators entering sales orders using the same order entry program.

Multiprocessing

Computers that have more than one CPU are called **multiprocessors**. A **multiprocessing** operating system coordinates the operations of multiprocessor computers. Because each CPU in a multiprocessor computer can be executing one program instruction, more than one instruction can be executed simultaneously. Besides providing an increase in performance, most multiprocessors offer another advantage. If one CPU fails, work can be shifted to the remaining CPUs. The ability to continue processing when a major component fails is called **fault tolerance**.

Virtual Machine

A **virtual machine (VM)** operating system, available on some large computers, allows a single computer to run two or more different operating systems. The VM operating system allocates system resources to each operating system. To users it appears that they are working on separate systems. The advantage of this approach is that an organization can concurrently (at the same time) run different operating systems that are best suited to different tasks. For example, some operating systems are best for interactive processing and others are best for batch processing. With a VM operating system both types of operating systems can be run at the same time.

FUNCTIONS OF OPERATING SYSTEMS

The operating system performs a number of functions that allow the user and the application software to interact with the computer. These functions apply to all operating systems but become more complex for operating systems that allow more than one program run at a time. The functions can be grouped into three areas: allocating system resources, monitoring system activities, and utilities (Figure 10-4).

ALLOCATING RESOURCES	MONITORING ACTIVITIES	UTILITIES
CPU management Memory management Input/output management	System performance System security	File management Sorting Editing

FIGURE 10-4
Operating system functions.

Allocating System Resources

The primary function of the operating system is to allocate the resources of the computer system. These resources include the CPU, main memory, and the input and output devices such as disk and tape drives and printers. Like a police officer directing traffic, the operating system decides what resource will currently be used and for how long.

CPU Management Because a CPU can only work on one program instruction at a time, a multiprogramming operating system must keep switching the CPU among the different instructions of the programs that are waiting to be performed. A common way of allocating CPU processing is time slicing. A **time slice** is a fixed amount of CPU processing time, usually measured in milliseconds (thousandths of a second). With this technique, each user in turn receives a time slice. Since some instructions take longer to execute than others, some users may have more instructions completed in their time slice than other users. When a user's time slice has expired, the operating system directs the CPU to work on another user's program instructions and the most recent user moves to the "end of the line" to await the next time slice (Figure 10-5). Unless the system has a heavy workload, however, users may not even be aware that their program has been temporarily set aside. Before they notice a delay, the operating system has allocated them another time slice and their processing continues.

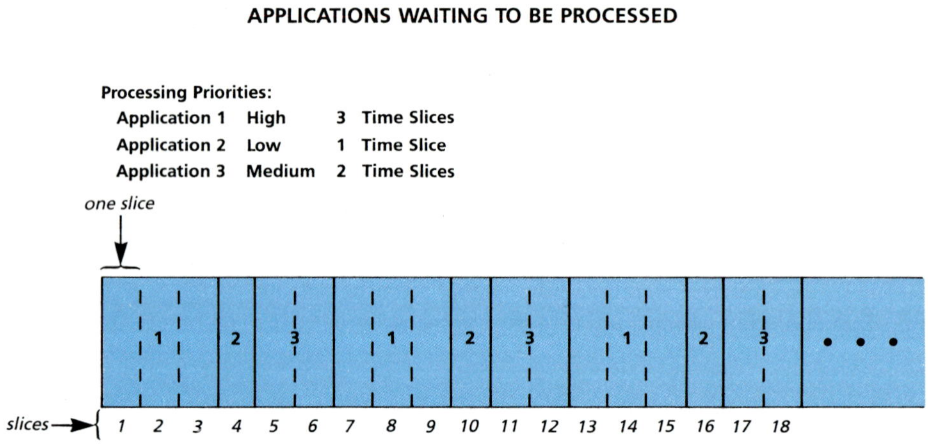

FIGURE 10-5
With the time slice method of CPU management, each application is allocated one or more fixed amounts of time called slices. Higher priority applications receive more consecutive slices than lower priority applications. When its processing time has expired, an application goes to the end of the line until all other applications have received at least one time slice.

Because some work is more important than other work, most operating systems have ways to adjust the amount of time slices a user receives, either automatically or based on user-specified criteria. One technique for modifying time slices is to have different priorities assigned to each user. The highest priority would receive several consecutive time slices for each time slice received by the lowest priority. For example, it would be logical to assign a higher priority to a program that processes orders and records sales than to an accounting program that could be run at a later time. Another way of allocating time slices is based on the type of work being performed. For example, some operating systems automatically allocate more time slices to interactive processes such as keyboard entry than they do to CPU-only processes such as calculations or batch processing.

Memory Management During processing, memory is used to store a variety of items including the operating system, application program instructions for one or more programs, data waiting to be processed, and workspace used for calculations, sorting, and other temporary tasks. Data that has just been read or is waiting to be sent to an output device is stored in reserved areas of memory called **buffers**. It is the operating system's job to keep track of all this data by allocating memory.

All operating systems allocate at least some portion of memory into fixed areas called partitions (Figure 10-6). Some operating systems allocate all memory on this basis while others use partitions only for the operating system instructions and buffers. Another way of allocating memory is called virtual memory management or virtual storage.

Virtual memory management increases the effective (or "virtual") limits of memory by expanding the amount of main memory to include disk space (Figure 10-7). Without virtual memory management, an entire program must be loaded into main memory during execution. With virtual memory management, only a portion of the program that is currently being used is required to be in main memory. Virtual memory management is used with multiprogramming operating systems to maximize the number of programs that can be using memory at the same time. The operating system performs virtual memory management by transferring data and instructions to and from memory and the disk by using one or both of the following methods: segmentation and paging.

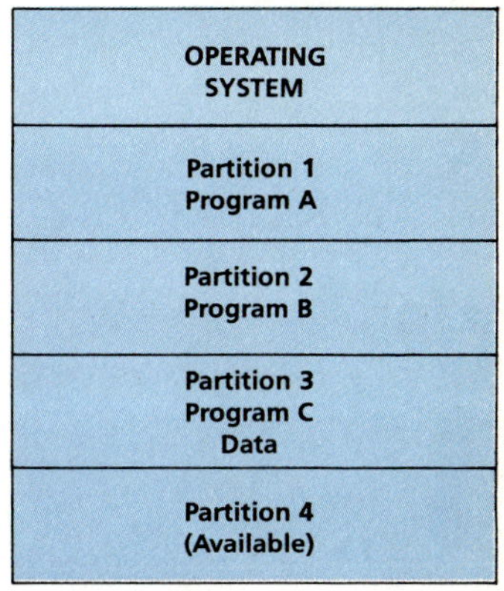

FIGURE 10-6
Some computer systems allocate memory into fixed blocks called partitions. The CPU then keeps track of programs and data by assigning them to a specific partition.

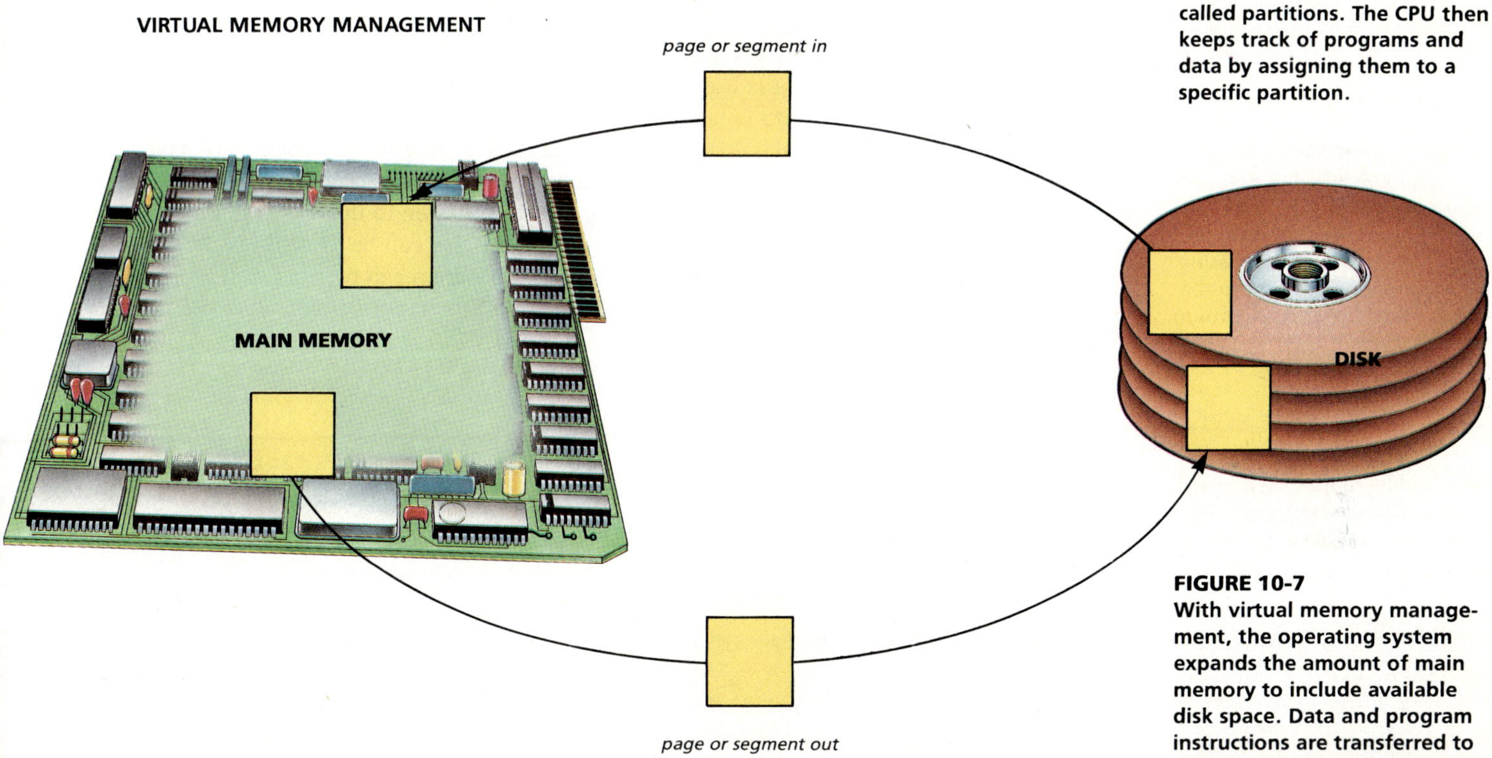

FIGURE 10-7
With virtual memory management, the operating system expands the amount of main memory to include available disk space. Data and program instructions are transferred to and from memory and disk as required. The segmentation technique transfers logical portions of programs that may be of different sizes. The paging technique transfers pages of the same size. To make room for the new page or segment, the least recently used page or segment is "swapped," or written back to the disk.

In **segmentation**, programs are divided into logical portions called **segments**. Because the segments are based on logical portions of a program, some segments are larger than others. When a particular program instruction is required, the segment containing that instruction is transferred from the disk into main memory.

In **paging**, a fixed amount of space, generally from 512 to 4K bytes, is transferred from the disk each time data is required. This fixed amount of data is called a **page** or a **frame**. Because a page is a fixed amount of space, it may not correspond to a logical division of a program.

In both segmentation and paging, a time comes when memory is full but another page or segment needs to be read into memory. When this occurs, the operating system makes room for the new data by writing back to disk one or more of the pages or segments currently in memory. This process is referred to as **swapping**. The operating system usually chooses the least recently used page or segment to transfer back to disk.

Input and Output Management At any one time, a number of different input devices can be trying to send data to the computer. At the same time, the CPU could be ready to send data to an output device such as a terminal or printer or a storage device such as a disk. It is the operating system's responsibility to manage these input and output processes.

Some devices, such as a tape drive, are usually allocated to a specific user or application program. This is because tape is a sequential storage medium and generally it would not make sense to have more than one application writing records to a single tape. Disk drives are usually allocated to all users because the programs and data files that users need are stored on these devices. The operating system keeps track of disk read and write requests, stores these requests in buffers along with the associated data for write requests, and usually processes them sequentially. A printer may be allocated to all users or restricted to a specific user. A printer would be restricted to a specific user, for example, if the printer was going to be used with preprinted forms such as payroll checks.

Because the printer is a relatively slow device compared to other computer system devices, the technique of spooling is used to increase printer efficiency and reduce the number of printers required. With **spooling** (Figure 10-8), a report is first written (saved) to the disk before being printed. Writing to the disk is much faster than writing to the printer. For example, a report that may take half an hour to print (depending on the speed of the printer) may only take one minute to write to the disk. After the report is written to the disk, the CPU is available to process other programs. The report saved on the disk can be printed at a later time or, on a multiprogramming operating system, a print program can be run (at the same time other programs are running) to process the **print spool** (the reports on the disk waiting to be printed).

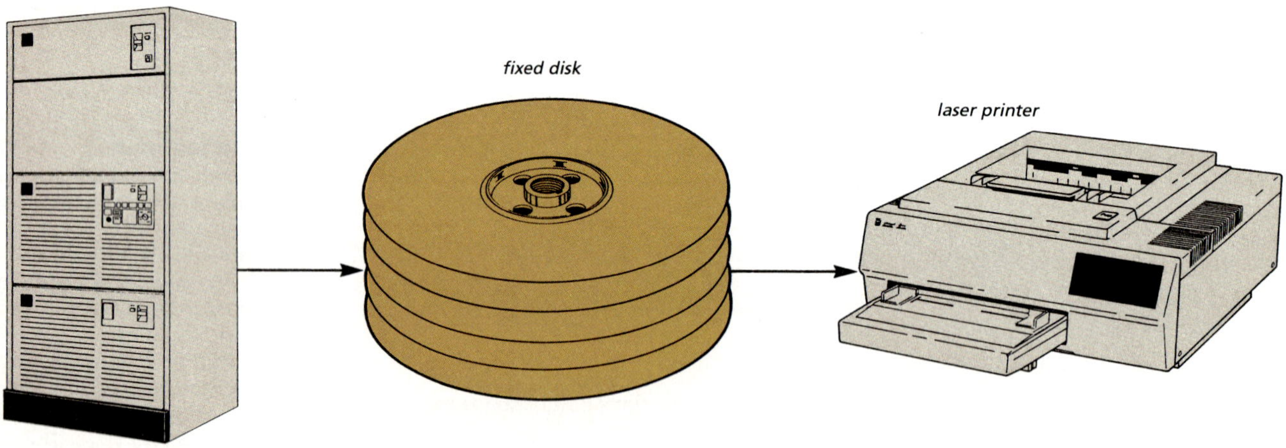

FIGURE 10-8
Spooling increases both CPU and printer efficiency by writing reports to the disk before they are printed. After the reports are written to disk, the CPU is able to begin processing other programs. Writing to the disk is much faster than writing directly to the printer.

Monitoring System Activities

Another function of the operating system is monitoring the system activity. This includes monitoring system performance and system security.

System Performance System performance can be measured in a number of ways but is usually gauged by the user in terms of response time. **Response time** is the amount of time from the moment a user enters data until the computer responds. Response time can vary based on what the user has entered. If the user is simply entering data into a file, the response time is usually within a second or two. However, if the user has just completed a request for a display of sorted data from several files, the response time could be minutes.

A more precise way of measuring performance is to run a program that is designed to record and report system activity. Among other information, these programs usually report **CPU utilization**, the amount of time that the CPU is working and not idle, waiting for data to process. Figure 10-9 shows a CPU performance measurement report.

Another measure of performance is to compare the CPU utilization with the disk input and output rate, referred to as disk I/O. We previously discussed how a virtual memory management operating system swaps pages or segments from disk to memory as they are needed. Systems with heavy workloads and insufficient memory or CPU power can get into a situation called **thrashing**, where the system is spending more time moving pages to and from the disk than processing the data. System performance reporting can indicate this problem.

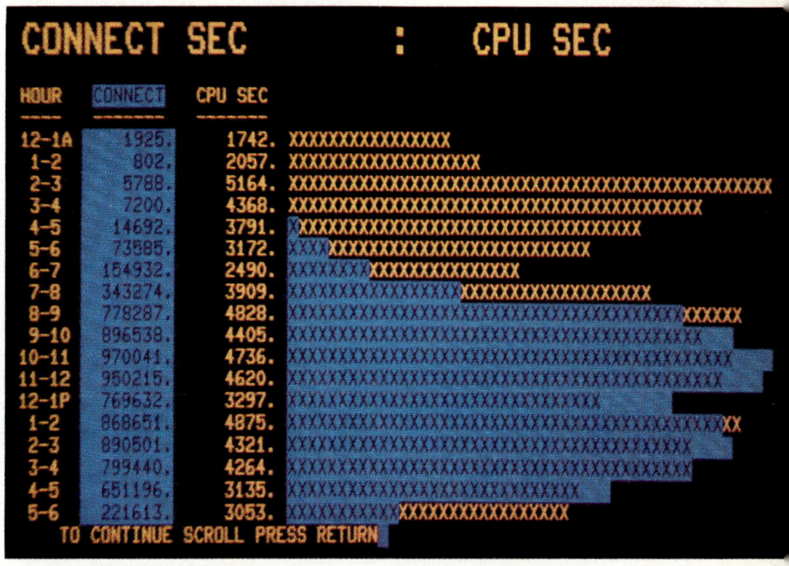

FIGURE 10-9
System performance measurement programs report the amount of time the CPU is actually working and not waiting to process data.

System Security Most multiuser operating systems provide for a logon code, a user ID, and a password that must all be entered correctly before a user is allowed to use an application program (Figure 10-10). Each is a word or series of characters. A **logon code** usually identifies the application that will be used, such as accounting, sales or manufacturing. A **user ID** identifies the user, such as Jeffrey Ryan or Mary Gonzales. The **password** is usually confidential; often it is known only to the user and the data processing manager. The logon code, user ID, and password must match entries in an authorization file. If they don't match, the user is denied access to the system. Both successful and unsuccessful logon attempts are often recorded in a file so that managers can review who is using or attempting to use the system. These logs can also be used to allocate data processing expenses based on the percentage of system use by an organization's various departments.

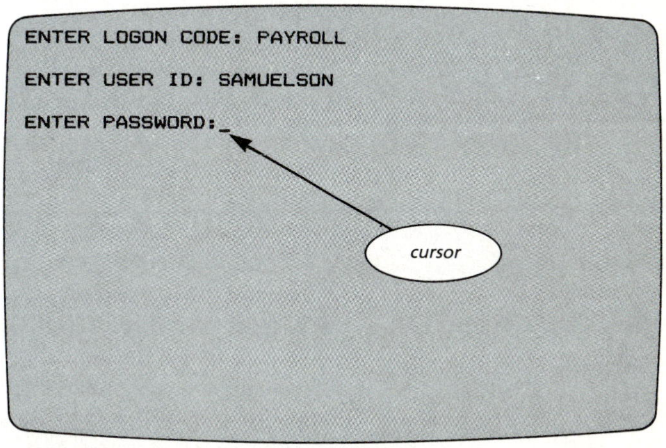

FIGURE 10-10
The logon code, user ID, and password must all be entered correctly before the user is allowed to use the computer. Because the password is confidential, it is usually not displayed on the screen when the user types it in.

Utilities

In addition to allocating system resources and monitoring system activities, most operating systems contain programs called **utilities** that can perform functions such as file management, sorting, and editing. Some of the functions that the file management utility programs can perform include formatting disks and diskettes, deleting files from a disk, copying files from one auxiliary storage device to another, and renaming stored files. Sort utilities are used to place the data stored in files into ascending or descending order based on a value stored in the key field of each record in a file. For example, a sort utility program could be used to sort the records in a personnel file in alphabetical order by the employees' last names. **Editors** allow users to make direct changes to programs and data. An editor would be used by a programmer to change a program instruction that was incorrect or had to be modified.

POPULAR OPERATING SYSTEMS

The first operating systems were developed by manufacturers for the computers in their product line. When the manufacturers came out with another computer or model, they often produced an "improved" and different operating system. Since programs are designed to be used with a particular operating system, this meant that users who wanted to switch computers, either from one vendor to another or to a different model from the same vendor, would have to convert their existing programs to run under the new operating system. Today, however, the trend is away from operating systems limited to a specific model and toward operating systems that will run on any model by a particular manufacturer. For example, part of Digital Equipment Corporation's success in recent years has been attributed to the fact that their VMS operating system is used on all their computer systems. Going even further, many computer users are supporting the move away from **proprietary operating systems** (meaning privately owned) and toward **portable operating systems** that will run on many manufacturers' computers. The advantage of portable operating systems is that the user is not tied to a particular manufacturer. Using a portable operating system, a user could change computer systems, yet retain existing software and data files, which usually represents a sizable investment in time and money. One of the most popular portable operating systems is UNIX, which we will discuss along with the popular personal computer operating system, MS-DOS, and IBM's latest personal computer operating system, O/S 2.

UNIX

The **UNIX** operating system was developed in the early 1970s by scientists at Bell Laboratories. It was specifically designed to provide a way to manage a variety of scientific and specialized computer applications. Because of federal regulations, Bell Labs (a subsidiary of AT&T) was prohibited from actively promoting UNIX in the commercial marketplace. Instead, for a low fee Bell Labs licensed UNIX to numerous colleges and universities where it obtained a wide following. With the deregulation of the telephone companies in the 1980s, AT&T was allowed to enter the computer system marketplace. With AT&T's increased promotion and the trend toward portable operating systems, UNIX has aroused tremendous interest. One of the advantages of UNIX is its extensive library of over 400 instruction modules that can be linked together to perform almost any programming task. Today, most major computer manufacturers offer a multiuser version of the UNIX operating system to run on their computers.

With all its strengths, however, UNIX has not yet obtained success in the commercial business systems marketplace. Some people attribute this to the fact that UNIX has never been considered "user friendly." For example, most of the UNIX program modules are identified by obscure names such as MAUS, SHMOP, and BRK. Other critics contend that UNIX lacks the file management capabilities to support the online interactive databases that more and more businesses are implementing. With the support of most major computer manufacturers, however, these problems are being worked on and UNIX has a good chance of becoming one of the major operating systems of the coming years.

MS-DOS

The Microsoft Disk Operating System or **MS-DOS** was released by Microsoft Corporation in 1981. MS-DOS was originally developed for IBM for their first personal computer system.

IBM calls their equivalent version of the operating system **PC-DOS**. Because so many personal computer manufacturers followed IBM's lead and chose MS-DOS for their computers, MS-DOS quickly became an industry standard. Other personal computer operating systems exist, but by far the majority of personal computer software is written for MS-DOS. This single-user operating system is so widely used that it is often referred to simply as DOS.

OS/2

In 1988, IBM released the **OS/2** operating system for its new family of PS/2 personal computers (Figure 10-11). Microsoft Corporation, which developed OS/2 for IBM, also released their equivalent version, called MS-OS/2. OS/2 is designed to take advantage of the increased computing power of the 80286 and 80386 microprocessors and will only run on systems that use these chips. OS/2 also requires a lot more computing power to operate. For example, OS/2 requires 5MB of hard disk and a minimum of 2MB of main memory just to run the operating system. Additional features offered by OS/2 include the ability to run larger and more complex programs and the ability to do multiprogramming (OS/2 can have up to 12 programs running at the same time).

There are two versions and two editions of OS/2. One of the versions includes the *Presentation Manager*, a graphic windowing environment similar to that available on the Apple Macintosh. The difference between the Standard Edition and the Extended Edition of OS/2 is that the Extended Edition includes database management and communications capabilities.

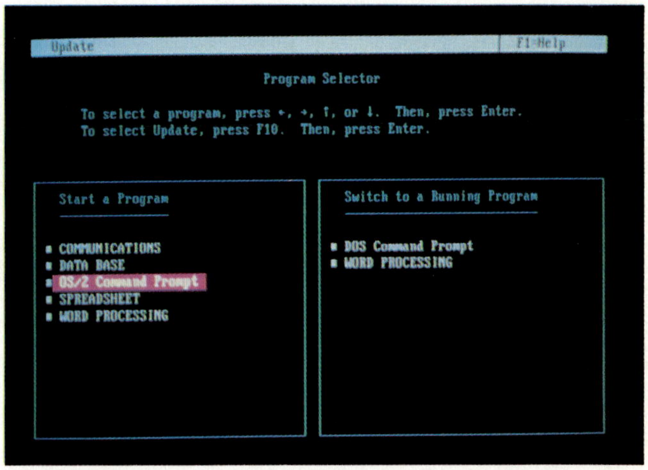

FIGURE 10-11
IBM's OS/2 operating system takes advantage of the increased processing power of the latest personal computer systems.

Other Operating Systems

A number of other popular operating systems exist in addition to the ones just discussed. The Apple Macintosh multiprogramming operating system, currently available only on Apple systems, provides a unique graphic interface that uses icons (figures) and windows (Figure 10-12) that many people find easy to learn and use. The ProDos operating system is used on many of Apple's other computer systems. The PICK operating system is another portable operating system that runs on personal, mini, and mainframe computers. The PICK operating system incorporates a relational database manager and has had much success in the business data processing marketplace. Most mainframe operating systems are unique to a particular make of computer or are designed to be compatible with one of IBM's operating systems such as DOS/VS, MVS, or VM, IBM's virtual machine operating system.

FIGURE 10-12
The Macintosh operating system offers a unique graphic interface and the ability to display information in separate "windows."

SUMMARY OF OPERATING SYSTEMS AND SYSTEM SOFTWARE

System software and the operating system are essential parts of any computer system and should be understood by users who want to obtain the maximum benefits from their computer. This is especially true for the latest personal computer operating systems that include features such as virtual memory management and multiprogramming. Understanding and being able to use these and other features will give users even more control over their computer resources.

CHAPTER SUMMARY

1. **System software** consists of all the programs including the operating system that are related to managing the operations of the computer.
2. An **operating system** consists of one or more programs that manage the operations of a computer.
3. Operating systems function as an interface between the user, the application programs, and the computer equipment.
4. The essential and most frequently used instructions in an operating system are sometimes called the **supervisor** and must be stored in the main memory of a computer for the computer to operate.
5. **Booting** the system is the process of loading the operating system into the main memory of a computer.
6. **Single program** operating systems allow a single user to run a single program at one time.
7. **Multiprogramming** operating systems, also called **multitasking** operating systems, allow more than one program to be run at the same time.
8. A multiprogramming operating system that allows multiple users is called a **multiuser–multiprogramming** operating system.
9. A **multiprocessor** computer has more than one CPU. **Multiprocessor** operating systems coordinate the operations of these computers.
10. A **virtual machine (VM)** operating system allows a single computer to run two or more different operating systems.
11. The functions of an operating system include allocating system resources, monitoring system activities, and utilities.
12. The system resources that the operating system allocates include the CPU, main memory, and the input/output devices.
13. **Time slicing** is a common way for an operating system to allocate the CPU.
14. **Virtual memory management** expands the main memory by using portions of the disk space. With virtual memory management, the operating system transfers data between main memory and the disks by **segmentation** or **paging**.
15. The operating system is responsible for managing the input and output processes of the computer.
16. **Response time** is the amount of time from the moment a user enters data until the computer responds.
17. System performance can be measured by the response time and by comparing the **CPU utilization** with the disk I/O to determine if the system is **thrashing**.
18. System security is monitored by the operating system through the use of **passwords**.
19. Most operating systems contain programs called **utilities** that can perform functions such as file management and sorting.
20. Many computer users are supporting the move away from **proprietary operating systems** and toward **portable operating systems**.
21. Some of the popular operating systems being used today include UNIX, MS-DOS, and OS/2.

KEY TERMS

Booting *10.3*
Buffers *10.7*
Control program *10.3*
CPU utilization *10.9*
Editors *10.9*
Executive *10.3*
Fault tolerance *10.5*
Frame *10.7*
Kernel *10.3*
Logon code *10.9*
Master program *10.3*
Monitor *10.3*
MS-DOS *10.11*
Multiprocessing *10.5*
Multiprocessors *10.5*
Multiprogramming *10.4*
Multitasking *10.4*
Multiuser-multiprogramming *10.5*
Operating system (OS) *10.3*
Operating system prompt *10.4*
OS/2 *10.11*
Page *10.7*
Paging *10.7*
Password *10.9*
Portable operating system *10.10*
Print spool *10.8*
Proprietary operating system *10.10*
PC-DOS *10.11*
Response time *10.8*
Segments *10.7*
Segmentation *10.7*
Single program *10.4*
Spooling *10.8*
Supervisor *10.3*
Swapping *10.8*
System software *10.2*
Time slice *10.6*
Thrashing *10.9*
UNIX *10.10*
User ID *10.9*
Utilities *10.9*
Virtual machine (VM) *10.5*
Virtual memory management *10.7*

REVIEW QUESTIONS

1. Define system software. List some of the functions of system software.
2. Describe how to boot an operating system on a personal computer.
3. List the various types of operating systems and briefly describe their capabilities.
4. The functions of an operating system can be grouped into three areas. What are they?
5. How does an operating system use time slicing?
6. What is virtual memory management?
7. Describe how system performance can be measured.
8. What are three types of authorizations that an operating system uses to provide system security?
9. List several functions that the utilities of an operating system provide.
10. Explain the difference between proprietary and portable operating systems. Name and briefly describe three popular operating systems.

CONTROVERSIAL ISSUE

1. Some users argue that portable operating systems should be avoided because they do not take full advantage of the unique capabilities of a computer. Other users feel that the advantages of using portable operating systems make them a better choice than proprietary operating systems. How do you feel? Be prepared to present your reasons in a class discussion.

RESEARCH PROJECT

1. Visit a computer store and obtain information about the operating systems that are available for personal computers. Prepare a paper on the information you obtained.

CHAPTER 11

Commercial Application Software

CHAPTER 11

Commercial Application Software

OBJECTIVES

- Define commercial application software.
- Describe the difference between general applications and functional applications.
- Describe the difference between horizontal and vertical applications.
- Discuss the factors to be considered in developing or buying application software.
- Discuss each of the five steps of acquiring commercial application software.
- Discuss the information that should be included on a request for proposal (RFP) for application software.
- Identify several sources for commercial application software.

The first computer users had few if any choices when it came to software. If users wanted the computer to perform a specific task, they usually had to develop and write their own computer programs to do the job. Today, however, users have several options when acquiring software. In addition to developing their own software, users may purchase prewritten software packages. Prewritten software is available for computers of all sizes. Most users know about the numerous application packages available for microcomputers. In addition, users should be aware that numerous packages are available for larger machines. This chapter discusses the type of prewritten application software that is available, how to determine your software requirements, and how to acquire the software you need. This information is important to know because it is very likely that some day you will either acquire application software for yourself or participate in software selection for your organization.

WHAT IS COMMERCIAL APPLICATION SOFTWARE?

Commercial application software is software that has already been written and is available for purchase. It may be designed to perform either general or specific tasks. An example of software that performs a general task is word processing. Word processing is considered a "general" task because it can be performed by individuals throughout an organization to create documents. An example of a specific task is medical insurance claim processing. Software that performs this task would only be useful to a company that processes medical insurance claims. Software designed to perform general tasks is called general application software. Software designed to perform specific tasks is called functional application software. In the following sections, we discuss both of these categories in more detail.

GENERAL APPLICATION SOFTWARE

General application software provides a way for tasks that are commonly performed in all types of businesses to be done on a computer. These applications are sometimes referred to as **productivity tools** because when they are used, they provide users with a more efficient way to do their work so that they become more productive. There are many popular types of general application software (Figure 11-1). The most common include word processing, spreadsheets, database, and graphics applications. In addition, three others that are commonly used include desktop publishing, electronic mail, and project management.

TYPE	PURPOSE	POPULAR PACKAGES
Word processing	Creates documents	WordPerfect Microsoft Word
Spreadsheet	Manipulates rows and columns of numbers	Lotus 1-2-3 Excel
Database	Stores, organizes, and retrieves data	dBASE III, RBASE
Graphics	Pictorial representation of data	Chart-Master Harvard Graphics
Electronic mail	Transmits electronic messages	Microsoft Mail In Box
Desktop Publishing	Lay out and create documents containing text and graphics	Ventura PageMaker
Project Management	Schedule and track a project's events and resources	Timeline Super Project Expert

FIGURE 11-1
A list of general application software packages. These packages can be used by most organizations and are not limited to a specific type of business.

Review of the Four User Tools

The four user tools described in Chapter 2, word processing, electronic spreadsheets, database, and graphics software, are all examples of general applications software. To review, word processors are used to create documents; spreadsheets are used to manipulate rows and columns of numbers; databases allow data to be stored, organized, and retrieved efficiently; and graphics provide a way of representing data pictorially.

Desktop Publishing

Desktop publishing (DTP) software allows users to design and produce professional-looking documents that contain both text and graphics (Figure 11-2). In business, this software is used to produce documents, such as newsletters, marketing literature, technical manuals, and annual reports, that were previously created by more traditional publishing methods. By using desktop publishing both the cost and time of producing quality documents is significantly decreased.

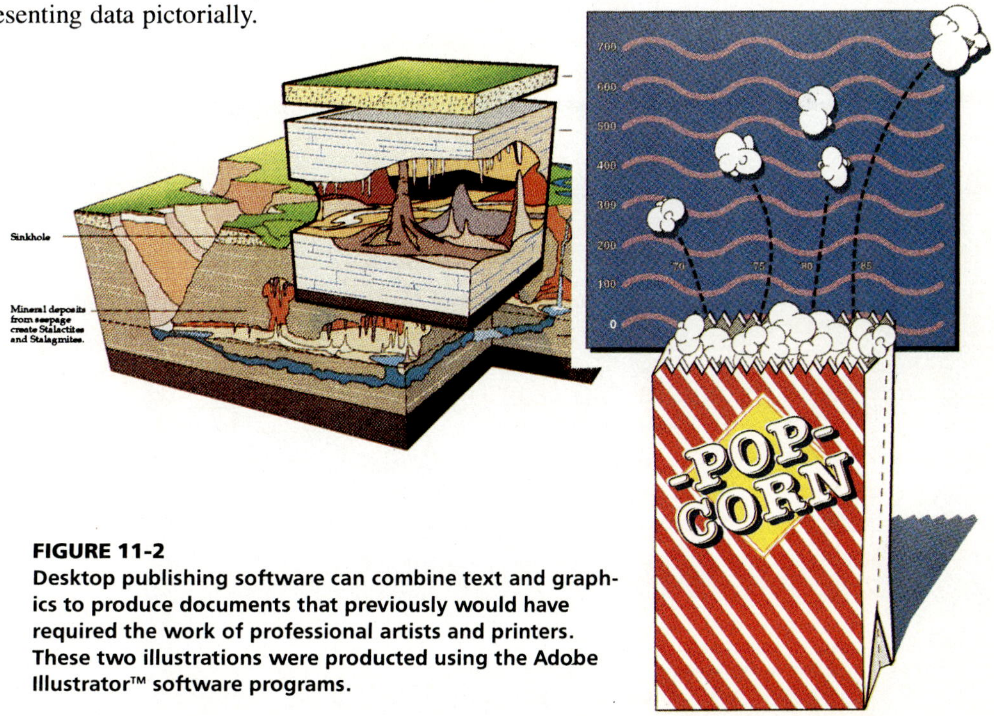

FIGURE 11-2
Desktop publishing software can combine text and graphics to produce documents that previously would have required the work of professional artists and printers. These two illustrations were producted using the Adobe Illustrator™ software programs.

An important feature of desktop publishing is page composition. This means that a user is able to design on the screen an exact image of what a printed page will look like. This capability is called **WYSIWYG**—an acronym for "What You See Is What You Get." Some of the page composition or layout features that are available include the use of columns for text, the choice of different font (type) styles, and the placement and size of art on the page.

The art used in the documents created with desktop publishing usually comes from one of three sources:

1. It can be created on the computer with software that has graphics capabilities, such as software packages that are specifically designed to create graphics, or software such as spreadsheet packages that can create pie, line, and bar charts.
2. A scanner can be used to digitize pictures, photographs, and drawings and store them as files on auxiliary storage for use with desktop publishing software.
3. Art can be selected from "clip art" collections. These are collections of art that are stored on disks and are designed to integrate with popular desktop publishing packages (Figure 11-3).

FIGURE 11-3
Clip art consists of previously created figures, shapes, and symbols that can be added to documents. Users specify the numbers of the piece they want to use.

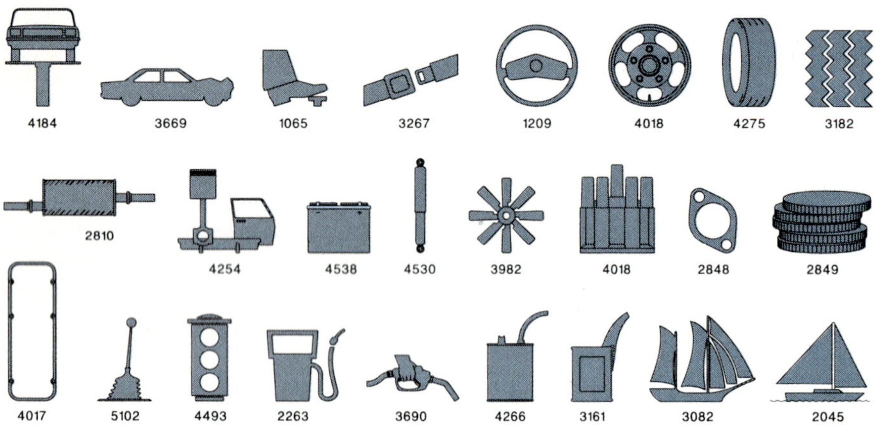

While the text for a document can be created with desktop publishing software, the word processing features of many desktop publishing packages are not as complete as those offered by word processing packages. Therefore, text is usually created with a word processor and then transferred into the desktop publishing package. As new versions of word processing and desktop publishing software are introduced, the capabilities of both applications will increase and the differences between the two applications will decrease. A number of word processing packages now offer desktop publishing features and the word processing features of desktop publishing packages continue to improve (Figure 11-4).

Desktop publishing software is usually executed on a microcomputer with graphics capabilities. Remember from the chapter on Output that graphics capability means that the computer can individually turn on or off the thousands of phosphor dots that make up the display screen. This ability is necessary in DTP to create different sizes and styles of letters and to produce other special DTP effects. Dot matrix and laser printers are used to print the letters and special graphic effects.

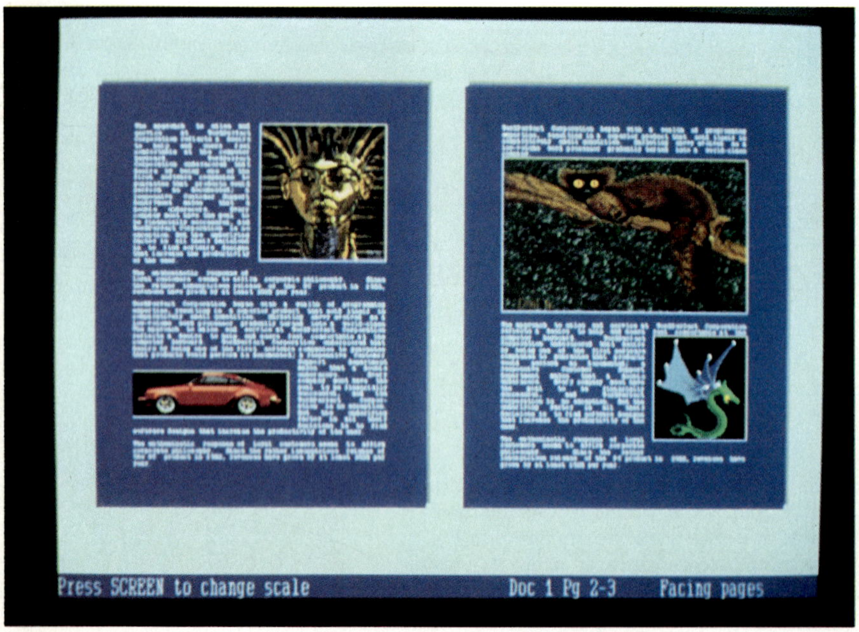

FIGURE 11-4
This document was created using WordPerfect 5.0, which allows graphics to be imported into text.

Electronic Mail

Another type of general application software is electronic mail. **Electronic mail** software provides the ability for users to communicate directly with other users by sending text messages electronically over communication channels (Figure 11-5). For example, if the sales manager, Florence Bolduc, wants to send a message congratulating Terry Willis and Sue Rodriguez for closing a recent sale, she would use the electronic mail software to (1) enter the message on her computer, (2) specify that Terry and Sue are to receive the message, and (3) enter a command to send the message. The software places the message in a file referred to as an electronic mailbox. When Terry and Sue use their computers to check for electronic mail, the message from Florence is displayed on their screens. This method of communication is much more efficient than the traditional method of creating and physically delivering a printed document. Correspondence that once took days to reach an individual can now be electronically transmitted from one user to another in seconds.

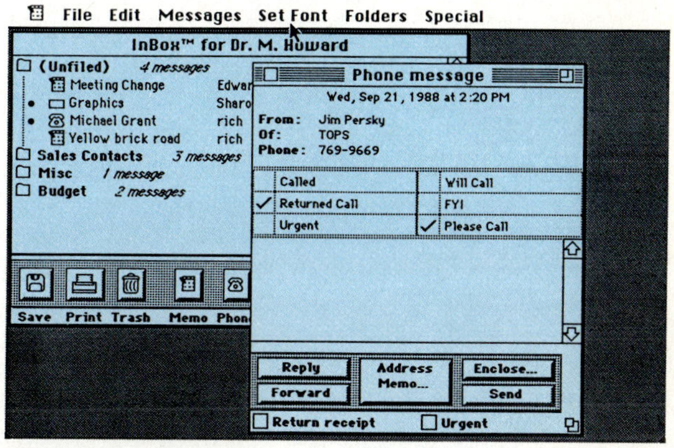

FIGURE 11-5
Electronic mail software allows a user to transmit and receive messages without paperwork. Messages can be saved for future reference or sent back to the sender with a reply.

Project Management

Project management software allows users to plan, schedule, track, and analyze the events, resources, and costs of a project (Figure 11-6). For example, a construction company might use this type of software to manage the building of an apartment complex or a campaign manager might use it to coordinate the many activities of a politician running for office. The value of project management software is that it provides a method for managers to control and manage the variables of a project to help ensure that the project will be completed on time and within budget.

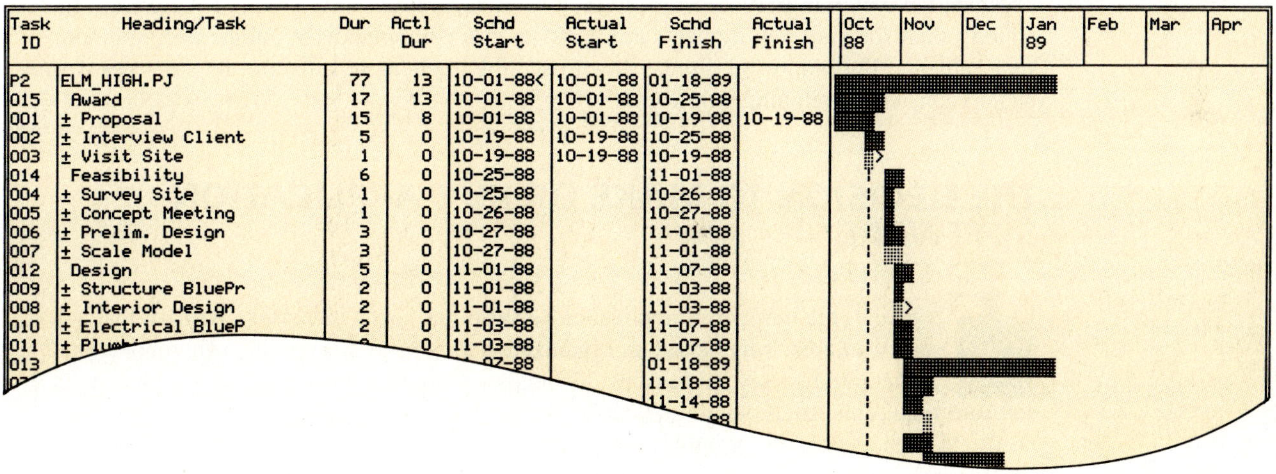

Task ID	Heading/Task	Dur	Actl Dur	Schd Start	Actual Start	Schd Finish	Actual Finish	Oct 88	Nov	Dec	Jan 89	Feb	Mar	Apr
P2	ELM_HIGH.PJ	77	13	10-01-88<	10-01-88	01-18-89								
015	Award	17	13	10-01-88	10-01-88	10-25-88								
001	± Proposal	15	8	10-01-88	10-01-88	10-19-88	10-19-88							
002	± Interview Client	5	0	10-19-88	10-19-88	10-25-88								
003	± Visit Site	1	0	10-19-88	10-19-88	10-19-88								
014	Feasibility	6	0	10-25-88		11-01-88								
004	± Survey Site	1	0	10-25-88		10-26-88								
005	± Concept Meeting	1	0	10-26-88		10-27-88								
006	± Prelim. Design	3	0	10-27-88		11-01-88								
007	± Scale Model	3	0	10-27-88		11-01-88								
012	Design	5	0	11-01-88		11-07-88								
009	± Structure BluePr	2	0	11-01-88		11-03-88								
008	± Interior Design	2	0	11-01-88		11-03-88								
010	± Electrical BlueP	2	0	11-03-88		11-07-88								
011	± Plumb[illegible]	[illegible]	0	11-03-88		11-07-88								
013	[illegible]			[illegible]-07-88		01-18-89								
[illegible]						11-18-88								
						11-14-88								
						[illegible]-88								

FUNCTIONAL APPLICATION SOFTWARE

FIGURE 11-6
This output was prepared using project management software. It shows the individual tasks that make up the project and the elapsed time that each task is scheduled to take.

Now that we've covered general applications, we'll discuss **functional application software**, software developed to perform a specific task or function.

With the increasing use of computers, a list of all functional applications might be as long as this book. It's probably safe to say that at least some part of every type of busi-

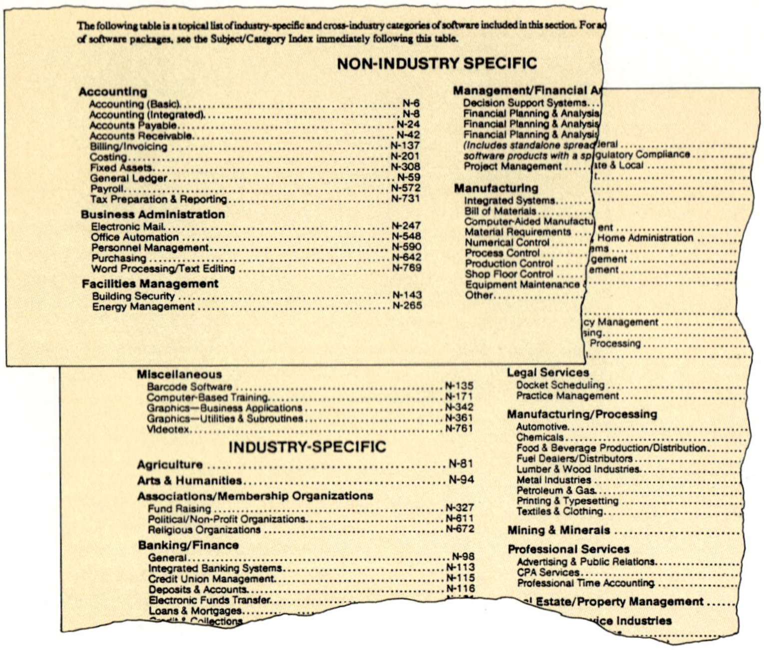
The following table is a topical list of industry-specific and cross-industry categories of software included in this section. For a
of software packages, see the Subject/Category Index immediately following this table.

NON-INDUSTRY SPECIFIC

Accounting
Accounting (Basic) N-6
Accounting (Integrated) N-8
Accounts Payable N-24
Accounts Receivable N-42
Billing/Invoicing N-137
Costing N-201
Fixed Assets N-308
General Ledger N-59
Payroll N-572
Tax Preparation & Reporting N-731

Business Administration
Electronic Mail N-247
Office Automation N-548
Personnel Management N-590
Purchasing N-642
Word Processing/Text Editing N-769

Facilities Management
Building Security N-143
Energy Management N-265

Management/Financial A
Decision Support Systems...
Financial Planning & Analysis
Financial Planning & Analysis
Financial Planning & Analysis
(Includes standalone sprea
software products with a sp
Project Management ......

Manufacturing
Integrated Systems.......
Bill of Materials..........
Computer-Aided Manufactu
Material Requirements ....
Numerical Control ....
Process Control ....
Production Control .....
Shop Floor Control .....
Equipment Maintenance
Other.............

Miscellaneous
Barcode Software N-135
Computer-Based Training N-171
Graphics—Business Applications N-342
Graphics—Utilities & Subroutines N-361
Videotex N-761

INDUSTRY-SPECIFIC

Agriculture N-81
Arts & Humanities N-94

Associations/Membership Organizations
Fund Raising N-327
Political/Non-Profit Organizations N-611
Religious Organizations N-672

Banking/Finance
General N-98
Integrated Banking Systems N-113
Credit Union Management N-115
Deposits & Accounts N-116
Electronic Funds Transfer ....
Loans & Mortgages ....

Legal Services
Docket Scheduling ....
Practice Management ....

Manufacturing/Processing
Automotive ....
Chemicals ....
Food & Beverage Production/Distribution ....
Fuel Dealers/Distributors ....
Lumber & Wood Industries ....
Metal Industries ....
Petroleum & Gas ....
Printing & Typesetting ....
Textiles & Clothing ....

Mining & Minerals ....

Professional Services
Advertising & Public Relations ....
CPA Services ....
Professional Time Accounting ....

FIGURE 11-7
This is a category listing from an application software catalog that contains information on over 20,000 individual software packages.

ness, government branch, or recreational pastime has been computerized. Figure 11-7 is a category listing from an applications software catalog. Within each category, there are numerous programs available to perform different types of tasks. This catalog contains listings for over 20,000 individual software packages. Notice that this list is divided into two parts: non–industry specific and industry specific. More commonly used terms are horizontal and vertical applications.

Horizontal application software is software that can be used by many different types of organizations. Accounting packages are a good example of horizontal applications because they apply to most organizations. If, however, an organization has a unique way of doing business, then it requires a package that has been developed specifically for that job. Software developed for a unique way of doing business, usually within a specific industry, is called **vertical application software**. Examples of specific industries that utilize vertical software include food service, construction, and real estate. Each of these industries has unique information processing requirements.

The difference between horizontal and vertical application software is important to understand. If you become involved in selecting software, one of the first things you will have to decide is how unique is the task for which you are trying to obtain software. If the task is not unique to your business, you will probably be able to use a horizontal application package. Horizontal application packages tend to be more widely available (because they can be used by a greater number of organizations) and less expensive. If your task is unique to your type of organization, you will probably have to look for a vertical software solution. Often an organization's total software requirements are made up of a combination of unique and common requirements. But before we discuss how to acquire application software, let's discuss if you should consider developing it yourself.

THE DECISION TO MAKE OR BUY APPLICATION SOFTWARE

Each year, the number of application software packages increases. With all that software available, why would an organization choose to develop its own applications? There could be several reasons. The most common reason is that the organization's software requirements are so unique that it is unable to find a package that will meet its needs. In such a case, the organization would choose to develop the software itself or have it developed specifically for them. Application software that is developed by the user or at the user's request is called **custom software**. An example of a requirement for custom software might be a government agency that is implementing a new medical assistance service. If the service has new forms and procedures and is different from previous services, it is unlikely that any appropriate software exists. Another reason to develop rather than buy software is that the new software must work with existing custom software. This is an important point to keep in mind; once an organization chooses to use custom software, it will usually choose custom software for future applications as well. This is because it is often difficult to make custom software work with purchased software. The following example illustrates this point.

Let's say a company that has previously developed a custom inventory control software system now wants to computerize their order entry function. Order entry software packages allow the user to sell merchandise from stock and therefore must work closely with the inventory files. In fact, many order entry systems are sold together with inventory control systems. If the company wants to retain its existing inventory control application, it would probably have a hard time finding a commercial order entry package that would be able to work with its custom inventory files. This is because the software and the file structures used in the commercial package will not be the same as the existing software. For this reason, the company would probably decide to develop a custom order entry application.

Both custom and commercial software have their advantages and disadvantages. The advantage of custom software is that if it is correctly done, it will match an organization's exact requirements. The disadvantages of custom software are that it is "one of a kind," difficult to change, often poorly documented, and usually more expensive than commercial software. In addition, custom software projects are often difficult to manage and complete on time.

The advantage of commercial software is that it's ready to install immediately. After sufficient training, usually provided by the vendor who developed or sold the software, people can begin using the software for productive work. The disadvantage of commercial software is that an organization will probably have to change some of its methods and procedures to adapt to the way the commercial software functions.

A good guideline for evaluating your need for custom or commercial software is to look for a package with an 80% or better "fit" with your requirements. If there is less than an 80% fit, an organization should either consider custom software or reevaluate its requirements. Figure 11-8 shows the most likely software solutions for different application requirements.

APPLICATION CHARACTERISTICS	APPLICATION EXAMPLE	MOST LIKELY SOFTWARE SOLUTION
Applicable to many different types or organizations	Accounts receivable	Horizontal application package
Specific to a particular type of business or organization	Hotel room reservations	Vertical application package
Unique to a specific organization or business	Space shuttle launch program	Custom software

FIGURE 11-8
A guide to the types of functional software applications.

HOW TO ACQUIRE COMMERCIAL APPLICATION SOFTWARE

The first companies to develop commercial application software were the computer manufacturers. Having software to solve specific problems made it easier for them to sell computers. Today, most mini and mainframe computer manufacturers still sell application software, but numerous other sources are available as well. The process of acquiring software involves five steps: (1) evaluating the application requirements, (2) identifying potential software vendors, (3) evaluating software alternatives, (4) making the purchase, and (5) installing the software.

Evaluating the Application Requirements

Evaluating the application requirements is the first and probably the most important step in acquiring commercial application software. Decisions made during this step can determine the eventual success or failure of the software package implementation. The actual evaluation process can and should vary depending on the type of application, how many people will be using it, and how critical it is to the organization. For example, an application to keep track of office supplies is not as critical to an organization as one for processing the payroll. All evaluations should include at least the following steps:

1. **Identify the key features of the application.** If the application is an important one, you should prepare a key features list with features that are considered essential to the application. For example, if an organization is a wholesale distributor that makes (or loses) sales based on whether or not it has an item in stock, it would want current inventory status to be part of any order entry program it acquires. Software that only updates the inventory once a day probably would not be acceptable. Therefore, current inventory status should be listed as a key feature.
2. **Determine your current transaction volumes and estimate their growth over the next one to three years.** Figure 11-9 shows a transaction volume summary for an organization's accounts payable application. The figure shows that projected growth over the next year is moderate but increases significantly during the second and third years. This information needs to be considered for both the application software and the equipment that the software will run on. The user would want to be assured that the software and equipment could handle the increased volume of transactions and the corresponding increase in file storage requirements.
3. **Decide if the software for the new application needs to work with any existing software or equipment.** It may be important that the new application transfer data to or receive data from an existing application. An example would be an accounts payable package that passes data to the general ledger, where all accounting transactions are summarized. In addition, if you already have a particular type of computer, you'll probably want to find software for that system first. On the other hand, if you don't have any equipment, make the decision about the software *first*. It's the software that is the most important element in any system. Choosing the software first is especially important with mini and mainframe systems. Application software for these systems is usually written for a specific manufacturer's computer.

FIGURE 11-9
A transaction volume summary should be prepared to avoid acquiring software that won't handle the projected growth.

MONTHLY VOLUME			
	CURRENT	1 YEAR	3 YEARS
# of Vendors	50	60	200
# of Invoices	100	120	400
# of Debit Memos	20	25	80
# of Checks	75	100	300

One way organizations summarize their software requirements is in a request for proposal. A **request for proposal** or **RFP** is a written list of an organization's software requirements that is given to prospective software vendors to help the vendors determine if they have a product that is a possible software solution. Just as the depth of application evaluations varies, so too do RFPs. RFPs for simple applications may be only a single page consisting of the key features and a transaction volume summary. Other RFPs for large systems may consist of over a hundred pages that identify both key and secondary desired features. An example of a page from an RFP is shown in Figure 11-10.

FIGURE 11-10
A request for proposal (RFP) documents the key features that a user wants in a software package.

REQUEST FOR PROPOSAL

ACCOUNTS PAYABLE

Features	Standard Feature	Comments
1. Interface to general ledger	✓	
2. Matching to receiving documents	✓	
3. Matching to purchasing documents	✓	
4. Automatic check printing	✓	
5. Recurring payments		PLANNING FOR NEXT RELEASE
6. Flexible payment selection	✓	
7. Checking statement reconciliation		WILL DO ON CUSTOM BASIS
8. Consolidated check preparation	✓	
9. Duplicate invoice check		NO PLANS FOR THIS FEATURE
10. Manual check processing	✓	
Reports		
1. Vendor listing	✓	BYNAME, BUYER
2. Invoice register	✓	
3. Check register	✓	
4. Cash requirements	✓	WEEKLY & MONTHLY
5. Detail aging	✓	30, 60, 90, 120 + DAYS
6. Form 1099 reports		PLANNED FOR NEXT RELEASE
7. Account distribution	✓	
8. Bank statement reconciliation		WILL DO ON CUSTOM BASIS

Identifying Potential Software Vendors

After you have an idea of the software features you want, the next step is to locate potential vendors that sell the type of software you are interested in buying. If the software will be implemented on a personal computer, a good place to start looking for software is a local computer store. Most computer stores have a wide selection of application software and can suggest several alternatives to consider. If you have prepared an RFP, even a simple one, it will help the store representative to narrow the choices. If software is required for a mini or mainframe computer, however, you won't find it at the local personal computer store. For this type of software, which can cost tens to hundreds of thousands of dollars, the best place to start is the computer manufacturer. In addition to having some software themselves, most manufacturers have a list of software companies that they work with—companies that specialize in developing software for the manufacturer's equipment. **Software houses** are businesses that specialize in developing software for sale. **System houses** not only sell software but sell the equipment as well. System houses usually take full responsibility for equipment, software, installation, and training. Sometimes they even provide equipment maintenance, although this is usually left to the equipment manufacturer. The advantage of dealing with a system house is that the user only has to deal with a single company for the entire system.

Another place to find software suppliers, especially for vertical applications, is to look in trade publications, magazines written for specific businesses or industries. Companies and individuals who have written software for these industries often advertise in the trade publications. Some industry trade groups also maintain lists of companies that provide specific software solutions.

For horizontal applications, most computer magazines publish regular reviews of individual packages and often have annual reviews of several packages of the same type. Figure 11-11 shows a software review of an accounting package.

Another way to identify software suppliers is to hire a knowledgeable consultant. Although the fees paid to a consultant will increase the overall software investment, it may be worth it, considering the real cost of making a bad decision. Many consultants specialize in assisting organizations of all sizes identify and implement software packages. A good place to start looking for a consultant would be to contact professional organizations in your industry. Your accountant may also be able to recommend a possible software solution or a consultant.

INFO WORLD THE PC NEWS WEEKLY

REPORT CARD

ACCOUNTING SOFTWARE

PEACHTREE COMPLETE II

VERSION 4.21

Criterion	(Weighting)	Score
Performance	(400)	Good
Documentation	(80)	Excellent
Ease of learning	(40)	Very Good
Ease of use	(120)	Very Good
Error handling	(80)	Very Good
Support		
Policies	(40)	Satisfactory
Technical Support	(40)	Satisfactory
Value	(200)	Excellent
Final score		**7.5**

PRODUCT SUMMARY

Company: Peachtree Software, 4355 Shackleford Road, Norcross, GA 30093; (800) 247-3224 or (404) 564-5800.
List Price: $199.
Requires: IBM PC or compatible, PS/2 or compatible; 384K of RAM; hard disk; DOS 2.0 or later.
Support: No cost-free support from vendor. Charge: $1 per minute, $20 minimum, with toll-free number; useability warranty; 30-day money-back guarantee (minus $20 charge) if purchased direct from Peachtree.
Pros: Superb value; great manuals; easy to use.
Cons: Reporting capabilities rather inflexible; broad range of modules but shallow in depth; no cost-free support.
Summary: An entry-level accounting package with functions for general ledger, accounts receivable, accounts payable, inventory, job costing, fixed assets, and payroll.

FIGURE 11-11
Many publications regularly evaluate application software. This review also included a narrative discussion of this accounting package.

Evaluating Software Alternatives

After you've identified several possible software solutions, you have to sort them out and choose one. First, match each choice against your original requirements list. Be as objective as possible—try not to be influenced by the salesperson or representative demonstrating the software or the appeal of the marketing literature. Match each package against your list or RFP and give each package a score. If some key features are more important than others, take that into consideration. Try to complete this rating either during or immediately after a demonstration of the package while the features are still fresh in your mind (Figure 11-12).

FIGURE 11-12
You should ask to see a demonstration of any program you are considering purchasing. During or after the demonstration, you should rate how well the package meets your requirements.

The next step is to talk to existing users of the software. For mini and mainframe software packages, software vendors routinely provide user references. For personal computer packages, if the computer store can't provide references, call the software manufacturer directly. User references are important because if a software package does (or doesn't) work for some organization like yours, it probably will (or won't) work for you.

Finally, try the software yourself. For a small application, this may be as simple as entering a few simple transactions using a demonstration copy of the software at the computer store. For large applications, it may require one or more days of testing at the vendor's office or on your existing computer to be sure that the software meets your needs.

If you are concerned about the ability of the software to handle a certain transaction volume efficiently, you may want to perform a benchmark test. A **benchmark test** involves measuring the time it takes to process a set number of transactions. For example, a benchmark might consist of measuring the time it takes a particular software package to produce a sales summary report using 1,000 sales transactions. Comparing the time it takes different packages to perform the same task using the same data and the same equipment is one way of measuring the packages' relative performance.

FIGURE 11-13
A software license grants the purchaser the right to use the software but does not include ownership rights.

Making the Purchase

When you purchase software you usually don't own it. What you are actually purchasing is a **software license** (Figure 11-13), the right to use the software under certain terms and conditions. One of the usual terms and conditions is that you can use the software on a single computer only. In fact, some software is licensed to a specific computer and the serial number of the system is recorded in the license agreement. Other license restrictions include prohibitions against making the software available to others (for example, renting it or leasing it) and modifying or translating the software into another language. These restrictions are designed to protect the rights of the software developer who doesn't want someone else to benefit unfairly from the developer's work. For personal computer users, software license terms and conditions usually cannot be modified. But for mini and mainframe users, terms of the license agreements can be modified and therefore should be carefully reviewed and considered a part of the overall software selection process. Modifications to the software license are generally easier to obtain before the sale is made than after.

FIGURE 11-14
Most application software comes with detailed installation instructions. Some packages include toll-free telephone numbers in case the user needs to call for assistance. The software seller will also usually offer support.

Installing the Software

After you've acquired the software, the next step is to install it. On small applications this could be a ten-minute task. On large systems, installation of a complete business system could be scheduled over a period of a year or more. Installation includes loading the software on the computer system, training the users, and testing to make sure the software is functioning correctly. Personal computer software can usually be installed by following the instructions in the user manual (Figure 11-14). Mini and mainframe computer software, however, usually requires a written installation plan tailored to the individual organization.

SUMMARY OF COMMERCIAL APPLICATIONS SOFTWARE

This chapter discussed various aspects of commercial applications software including the types of software applications that are available, how to determine your software needs, and how to acquire applications software packages. Whether you need software for personal use or are involved in selecting software for your organization, a knowledge of commercial applications software and how to acquire it is useful.

CHAPTER SUMMARY

1. **Commercial application software** is software that has already been written and is available for purchase.
2. Two categories of commercial application software are general application software and functional application software.
3. **General application software** provides a way for tasks that are commonly performed in all types of businesses to be done on a computer.
4. Software that allows a user to create professional-looking documents that include both text and graphics is called **desktop publishing** software.
5. Page composition, or the ability to design on the screen an exact image of what a printed page will look like, is an important feature of desktop publishing. This capability is called **WYSIWYG**, an acronym for "What You See Is What You Get."
6. **Electronic mail** software provides the ability for users to directly communicate with other users by sending text messages electronically over communication channels.
7. **Project management software** allows users to plan, schedule, track, and analyze the events, resources, and costs of a project.
8. **Functional application software**, developed to perform a specific task or function, can be classified as either horizontal or vertical applications.
9. Software packages that can be used by many different types of organizations, such as accounting packages, are called **horizontal applications**.
10. Software developed for a unique way of doing business, usually within a specific industry, is called **vertical application software**.
11. Application software that is developed by a user, or at the user's request, is called **custom software**.
12. The process of acquiring software involves five steps: evaluating the application requirements, identifying potential software vendors, evaluating software alternatives, making the purchase, and installing the software.
13. Evaluating the application requirements includes: identifying the key features of the application; determining your current transaction volumes and estimating their growth over the next three years; and deciding if the software for the new application needs to work with any existing software or equipment.
14. A **request for proposal** is a written list of an organization's software requirements that is given to prospective software vendors.
15. Identifying potential software vendors for personal computers can usually be done at a local computer store. For larger applications sources include computer manufacturers, **software houses**, **system houses**, trade publications, computer periodicals, and consultants.
16. To evaluate software alternatives, match the features of each possible solution against the original requirements list or RFP.
17. A **benchmark test** involves measuring the time it takes to process a set number of transactions.
18. A **software license** is the right to use software under certain terms and conditions.
19. Installation of the software includes loading the software on the computer system, training the users, and testing to make sure the software is functioning correctly.

KEY TERMS

Benchmark test *11.10*
Commercial application software *11.2*
Custom software *11.6*
Desktop publishing (DTP) *11.3*
Electronic mail *11.5*
Functional application software *11.5*
General application software *11.3*
Horizontal application software *11.6*
Productivity tools *11.3*
Project management software *11.5*
Request for proposal (RFP) *11.8*
Software houses *11.9*
Software license *11.10*
System houses *11.9*
Vertical application software *11.6*
WYSIWYG *11.4*

REVIEW QUESTIONS

1. What is commercial application software? Describe the difference between software that performs a general task and software that performs a specific task.
2. List several types of general applications software. Why are these applications called productivity tools?
3. What does the page composition feature of desktop publishing allow a user to do? What is WYSIWYG?
4. Explain the difference between horizontal and vertical applications.
5. What is custom software and why is it appropriate for some applications?
6. List the five steps in acquiring commercial applications software.
7. Describe the information that an RFP should contain and how the RFP is used.
8. List several ways to find sources for commercial applications software.
9. Describe several things that a user can do to evaluate a software package before purchasing it. What is a benchmark test?
10. What is a software license? Describe some of the terms and conditions that are included in a software license.

CONTROVERSIAL ISSUES

1. Some personal computer users who have purchased application software off the shelf in a computer store have found that learning to use the software has been difficult and time consuming. Many of these users claim that the store that sold the software should provide training on how to use it. While some computer stores do provide limited training, other stores say that training is not their responsibility and explain that they cannot afford to provide training services for customers on all the various software packages that they sell. Do you think that software stores should provide training to customers?
2. Some organizations claim that consultants have saved them considerable sums of money when acquiring application software? Others say that they would have been better off not using a consultant. What role, if any, do you feel a consultant should play in helping an organization to select application software?

RESEARCH PROJECTS

1. Compare the license agreements for three different microcomputer software packages. Prepare a report that discusses the terms and conditions of each license.
2. Visit a store that sells microcomputer software. Select three accounting packages and prepare a report that discusses the features of each package. In the conclusion of your report, state which package you would buy and give the reasons for your selection.

CHAPTER 12

The Information System Development Life Cycle

CHAPTER 12

The Information System Development Life Cycle

OBJECTIVES

- Describe the six elements of an information system: equipment, software, data, personnel, users, and procedures.
- Define the term information system and describe the different types of information systems.
- Explain the five phases of the information system development life cycle: analysis, design, development, implementation, and maintenance.
- Explain the importance of documentation and project management in the information system development life cycle.
- Describe how various analysis and design tools, such as data flow diagrams, are used.
- Explain how program development is part of the information system development life cycle.
- Explain several methods that can be used for a conversion to a new system.
- Discuss the maintenance of an information system.

Every day, factors such as competition and government regulations cause people to face new challenges in obtaining the information they need to perform their jobs. A new product, a new sales commission plan, or a change in tax rates are just three examples of events that require a change in the way an organization processes information. Sometimes these challenges can be met by existing methods but other times, meeting the challenge requires an entirely new way of processing data. In these cases, a new or modified information system is needed. As a computer user, either as an individual or within your organization, it is very likely that someday you will participate in the development or modification of such a system. This chapter discusses information systems and how they are developed. To better explain the chapter material, we illustrate each phase of the system development cycle with a case study about the wholesale auto parts division of the Sutherland Company.

WHAT IS AN INFORMATION SYSTEM?

An **information system** is a collection of elements that provide accurate, timely, and useful information. As discussed in Chapter 1, an information system is comprised of six elements: equipment, software, data, personnel, users, and procedures. Each element is important in order to obtain quality information from an information system.

The term information system is frequently used to describe the entire computer operation of an organization, as in a computer information system or the information system(s) department. The term is also used to mean an individual application or "system" that is processed on the computer. For example, an accounting system or an inventory control system can each be thought of as an information system.

Regardless of the scope implied by the use of the term information system, all information systems that are implemented on a computer are comprised of the six elements previously listed. Each element—equipment, software, data, personnel, users, and procedures—contributes to a successful information system and conversely, a weakness in any of these elements can cause an information system to fail. To help ensure success, all six elements should be considered by the people responsible for creating or changing any type of information system.

FIGURE 12-1
Operational systems process the day-to-day transactions of an organization, such as the tax forms that are shown being entered into an IRS computer.

TYPES OF INFORMATION SYSTEMS

The types of information systems that use a computer fall into four broad categories: (1) operational systems; (2) management information systems; (3) decision support systems; and (4) expert systems.

Operational Systems

An **operational system** is designed to process data generated by the day-to-day business transactions of a company. Examples of operational systems are accounting systems, billing systems, inventory control systems, and order entry systems (Figure 12-1).

Management Information Systems

When computers were first used for processing business applications, the information systems developed were primarily operational systems. Usually, the purpose was to "computerize" an existing manual system. This approach often resulted in faster processing, reduced clerical costs, and improved customer service.

Managers soon realized, however, that computer processing could be used for more than just day-to-day transaction processing. The computer's ability to perform rapid calculations and compare data could be used to produce meaningful information for management. This led to the concept of management information systems.

Although the term management information system has been defined in a number of ways, today a **management information system (MIS)** refers to a computer-based system that generates timely and accurate information for the top, middle, and lower levels of management. For example, to process a sales order, the operational system would record the sale, update the customer's accounts receivable balance, and make a deduction from the inventory. In the related management information system, reports would be produced that show slow or fast moving items, customers with past due accounts receivable balances, and inventory items that need reordering. In the management information system, the focus is on the information that management needs to do its job (Figure 12-2).

FIGURE 12-2
Management information systems focus on the summary information and exceptions that managers use to perform their jobs.

Decision Support Systems

Frequently management needs information that is not routinely provided by operational and management information systems. For example, a vice president of finance may want to know the effect on company profits if sales increase by 10% and costs increase by 5%. This type of information is not usually provided by operational or management information systems. To provide this information, decision support systems have been developed.

FIGURE 12-3
Decision support systems often use graphics to help the user evaluate decision data.

A **decision support system** is a system designed to help someone reach a decision by summarizing or comparing data from either or both internal and external sources. Internal sources include data from an organization's database such as sales, manufacturing, or financial data. Data from external sources could include information on interest rates, population trends, or new housing construction. Decision support systems often include query languages, statistical analysis capabilities, spreadsheets, and graphics to help the user evaluate the decision data (Figure 12-3). More advanced decision support systems also include capabilities that allow users to create a model of the factors affecting a decision. A simple model for determining the best product price would include factors for the expected sales volume at each price level. With a model, users can ask "what if" questions by changing one or more of the factors and seeing what the projected results would be. Many people use electronic spreadsheets for simple modeling tasks.

Expert Systems

Expert systems combine the knowledge on a given subject of one or more human experts into a computerized system that simulates the human experts' reasoning and decision making processes (Figure 12-4). Thus, the computer also becomes an "expert" on the subject. Expert systems are made up of the combined subject knowledge of the human experts, called the **knowledge base** and the **inference rules** that determine how the knowledge is used to reach decisions. Although they may appear to "think," the current expert systems actually operate within narrow preprogrammed limits and cannot make decisions based on "common sense" or on information outside of their knowledge base. Expert systems have been successfully applied to problems as diverse as diagnosing illnesses, searching for oil, and making soup. These systems are part of an exciting branch of computer science called **artificial intelligence**, the application of human intelligence to computer systems.

FIGURE 12-4
NEXpert Object is a powerful software tool that allows relatively unsophisticated users to create their own expert system.

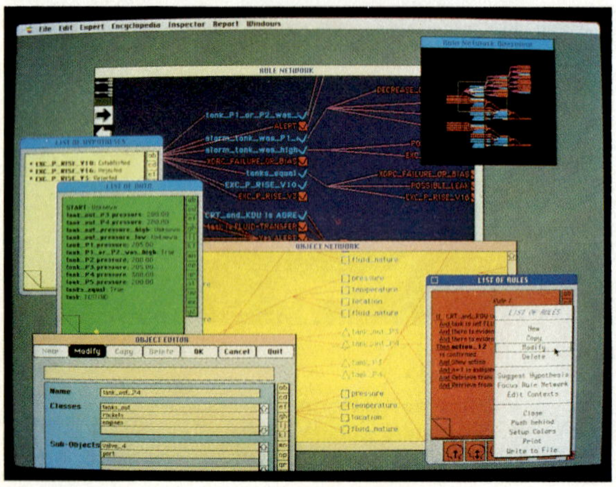

The Integration of Information Systems

With today's sophisticated software, it can be difficult to classify a system as belonging uniquely to one of the four types of information systems. For example, much of today's application software provides both operational and management information system information and some of the more advanced software even includes some decision support capabilities. Although expert systems still operate primarily as separate systems, the trend is clear: to combine all of an organization's information needs into a single integrated information system.

To develop the information systems they need, many organizations use the information system development life cycle.

WHAT IS THE INFORMATION SYSTEM DEVELOPMENT LIFE CYCLE?

The **information system development life cycle (SDLC)** is an organized approach to developing an information system.

Regardless of the type or complexity of an information system, the structured process of the information system development life cycle should be followed whenever an information system is developed. Although some experts group them differently, this chapter divides the activities of the information system development life cycle into five phases.

The Five Phases of the Information System Development Life Cycle

Each of the five phases of the information system development life cycle includes important activities that relate to the development of an information system. The five phases are (Figure 12-5):

Phase 1 Analysis
Phase 2 Design
Phase 3 Development
Phase 4 Implementation
Phase 5 Maintenance

Before explaining each of the phases, we will discuss project management and documentation because these two activities are ongoing processes that are performed throughout the cycle. In addition, we will identify the information system specialists and users who participate in the various phases of the SDLC.

FIGURE 12-5
The five phases of the information system development life cycle.

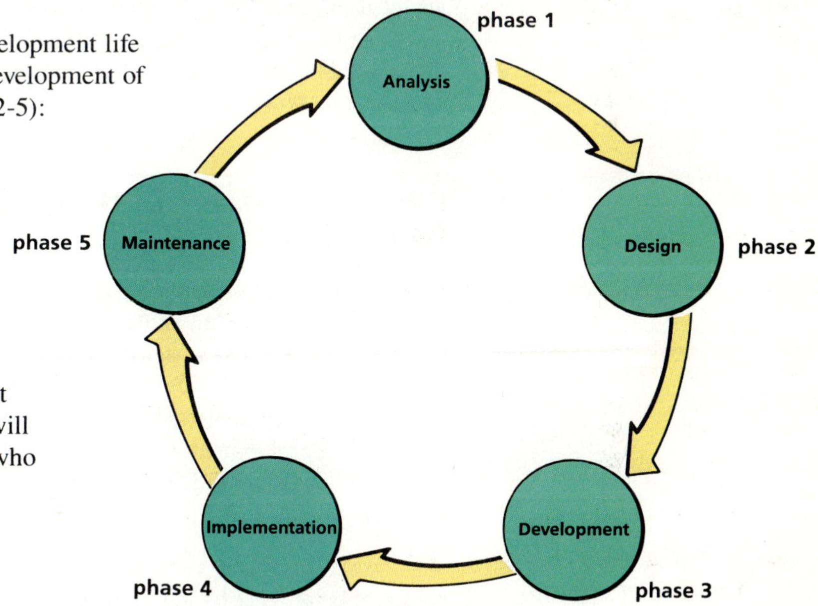

Project Management

Project management involves planning, scheduling, reporting, and controlling the individual activities that make up the information system development life cycle. These activities are usually recorded in a **project plan** on a week-by-week basis that includes an estimate of the time to complete the activity and the start and finish dates. As you might expect, the start of many activities depends on the successful completion of other activities. For example, implementation (Phase 4) activities can't begin until you have completed at least some, if not all, of the development activities (Phase 3). An effective way of showing the relationship of project activities is with a Gantt chart (Figure 12-6).

FIGURE 12-6
A Gantt chart is often used in project management to show the time relationships of the project activities.

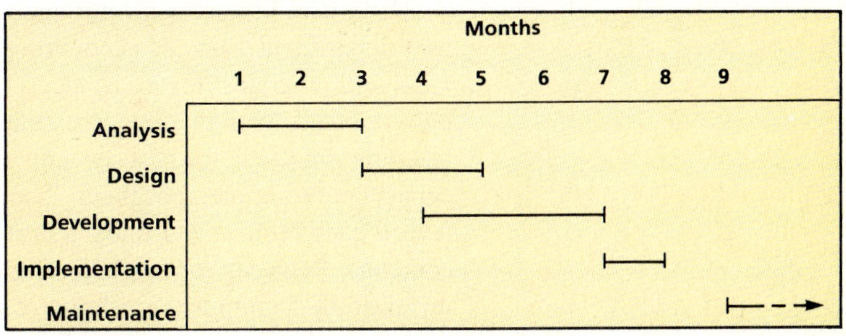

The importance of maintaining a realistic schedule for project management cannot be overstated. Without a realistic schedule, the success of a development project is in jeopardy from the start. If project members don't believe the schedule is realistic, they may not participate to the full extent of their abilities. Project management is a place for realistic and not wishful thinking.

Project management is a task that should be done *throughout* the development process. In most projects, activities need frequent rescheduling. Some activities will take less time than originally planned and others will take longer. To measure the impact of the actual results and revised estimates, they should be recorded regularly and a revised project plan issued. A number of project management software packages are available to assist in this task.

Documentation

Documentation refers to written materials that are produced as part of the information system development life cycle, such as a report describing the overall purpose of the system or layout sheets that are used to design reports and screens. Documentation should be identified and agreed on prior to beginning the project. Well-written, thorough documentation makes it easier for users and others to understand why particular decisions are made. Too often, documentation is put off until the completion of a project and is never adequately finished. Documentation should be an ongoing part of the entire development process and should not be thought of as a separate phase.

Who Participates in the Information System Development Life Cycle?

Every person who will be affected by the new system should have the opportunity to participate in its development. The participants fall into two categories: users and information system personnel such as systems analysts and computer programmers. As discussed in Chapter 1, the systems analyst works closely with both the users and the programmers. The systems analyst's job is challenging, requiring good communication, analytical, and diplomatic skills to keep the development process on track and on schedule. Good communication skills are especially important during analysis, the first phase of the information system development life cycle.

PHASE 1—ANALYSIS

Analysis is the separation of a system into its parts to determine how the system works. In addition, the analysis phase of a development project also includes the identification of a proposed solution to the problems identified in the current system.

A system project can originate in several ways, but a common way is for the manager of a user department, such as accounting or personnel, to contact the information systems department with a request for assistance. The initial request may be oral, but it is eventually written on a standard form that becomes the first item of documentation (Figure 12-7). In most organizations, requests for new system projects exceed the capacity of the information systems department to implement them. Therefore, the manager of the systems department must review each request and make a preliminary determination as to the potential benefit for the company. Requests for large development projects, such as an entirely new system, are often reviewed by committees made up of both user and information systems personnel and representatives of top management. When the managers of both the user and information systems departments determine that a request warrants further review, one or more systems analysts will be assigned to begin a preliminary investigation, the first step in the analysis phase.

The Preliminary Investigation

The purpose of the **preliminary investigation** is to determine if a request justifies further detailed investigation and analysis. The most important aspect of the preliminary investigation is **problem definition**, the identification of the true nature of the problem. Often the stated problem and the real problem are not the same. For example, the investigation of a request for a new accounts receivable report may reveal that the real problem is that customer payments are not being recorded in a timely manner. The existing accounts receivable reports may be fine if the payments are recorded when received instead of once a week. The purpose of the preliminary investigation is to determine the real source of the problem.

The preliminary investigation begins with an interview of the manager who submitted the request. Depending on the scope of the request, other users may be interviewed as well.

The duration of the preliminary investigation is usually quite short when compared to the remainder of the project. At the conclusion of the investigation, the analyst presents the findings to both user and information system management and recommends the next course of action. Sometimes the results of a preliminary investigation indicate an obvious solution that can be implemented at minimal cost. Other times, however, the only thing the preliminary investigation does is confirm that there is a problem that needs further study. In these cases, detailed system analysis is recommended.

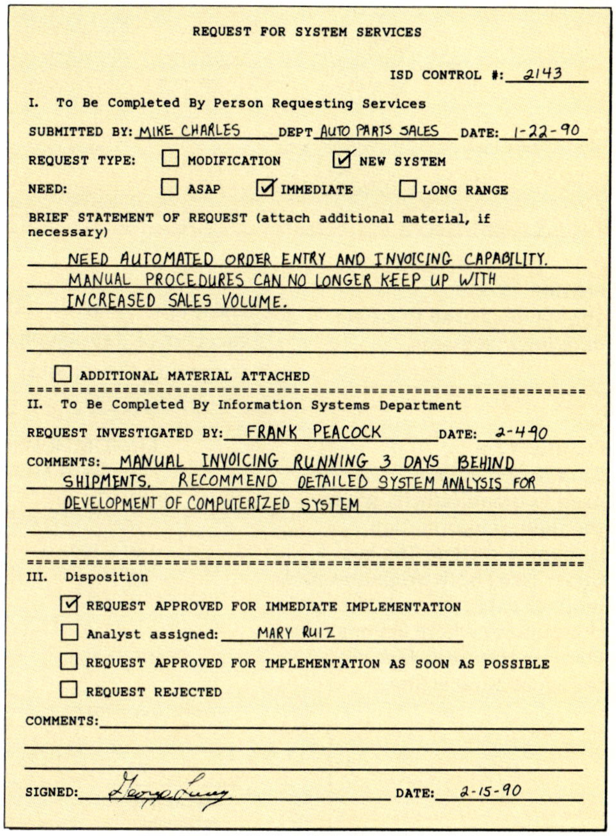
REQUEST FOR SYSTEM SERVICES

ISD CONTROL #: 2143

I. To Be Completed By Person Requesting Services

SUBMITTED BY: MIKE CHARLES DEPT AUTO PARTS SALES DATE: 1-22-90

REQUEST TYPE: ☐ MODIFICATION ☑ NEW SYSTEM

NEED: ☐ ASAP ☑ IMMEDIATE ☐ LONG RANGE

BRIEF STATEMENT OF REQUEST (attach additional material, if necessary)

NEED AUTOMATED ORDER ENTRY AND INVOICING CAPABILITY. MANUAL PROCEDURES CAN NO LONGER KEEP UP WITH INCREASED SALES VOLUME.

☐ ADDITIONAL MATERIAL ATTACHED

II. To Be Completed By Information Systems Department

REQUEST INVESTIGATED BY: FRANK PEACOCK DATE: 2-4-90

COMMENTS: MANUAL INVOICING RUNNING 3 DAYS BEHIND SHIPMENTS. RECOMMEND DETAILED SYSTEM ANALYSIS FOR DEVELOPMENT OF COMPUTERIZED SYSTEM

III. Disposition

☑ REQUEST APPROVED FOR IMMEDIATE IMPLEMENTATION

☐ Analyst assigned: MARY RUIZ

☐ REQUEST APPROVED FOR IMPLEMENTATION AS SOON AS POSSIBLE

☐ REQUEST REJECTED

COMMENTS:

SIGNED: George Lung DATE: 2-15-90

FIGURE 12-7
The system development project usually starts with a request from a user. The request should be documented on a form such as the one shown here to provide a record of the action taken.

Detailed System Analysis

Detailed system analysis involves both a thorough study of the current system and at least one proposed solution to any problems found.

The study of the current system is important for two reasons. First, it helps increase the analyst's understanding of the activities that the new system will perform. Second, and perhaps most important, studying the current system builds a relationship with the user. The analyst will have much more credibility with users if the analyst understands how the users currently do their job. This may seem an obvious point, but surprisingly, many systems are created or modified without studying the current system or without adequately involving the users.

The basic fact-gathering techniques used during the detailed system analysis are: (1) interviews; (2) questionnaires; (3) reviewing current system documentation; (4) observing current procedures. During this phase of the system study, the analyst must develop a critical, questioning approach to each procedure within the current system to determine what is actually taking place. Often it is found that operations are being performed not because they are efficient or effective, but because "they have always been done this way."

Information gathered during this phase includes: (1) the output of the current system; (2) the procedures used to produce the output; (3) the input to the current system.

An increasingly popular method for documenting this information is called structured analysis. **Structured analysis** is the use of analysis and design tools such as data flow diagrams, data dictionaries, structured English, and decision tables and trees to document the specifications of an information system.

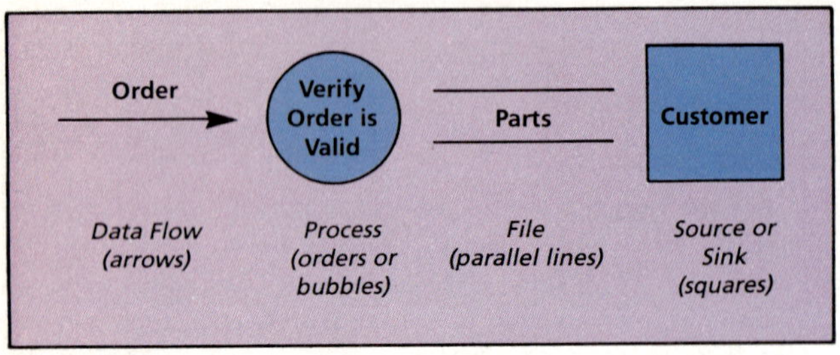

FIGURE 12-8
The symbols used to create data flow diagrams.

Data Flow Diagrams One of the difficulties with the analysis of any system is documenting the results in a way that others can understand. Structured analysis addresses this problem by using graphics to represent the flow of data between processes and files. These graphics are represented by data flow diagrams.

Data flow diagrams (DFD) graphically show the flow of data through a system. The key elements of a DFD (Figure 12-8) are arrows or vectors called data flows, representing data; circles (also called "bubbles") representing processes, such as verifying an order or creating an invoice; parallel lines representing data files; and squares, called sources or sinks, that represent either or both an originator or a receiver of data, such as a customer. Because they are visual, DFDs are particularly useful for reviewing the existing or proposed system with the user. (See Figure 12-9).

FIGURE 12-9
Data flow diagrams (DFD) are used to graphically illustrate the flow of information through a system. The customer (box) both originates and receives data (arrows). The circles indicate where actions take place on the data. Files are shown as parallel lines.

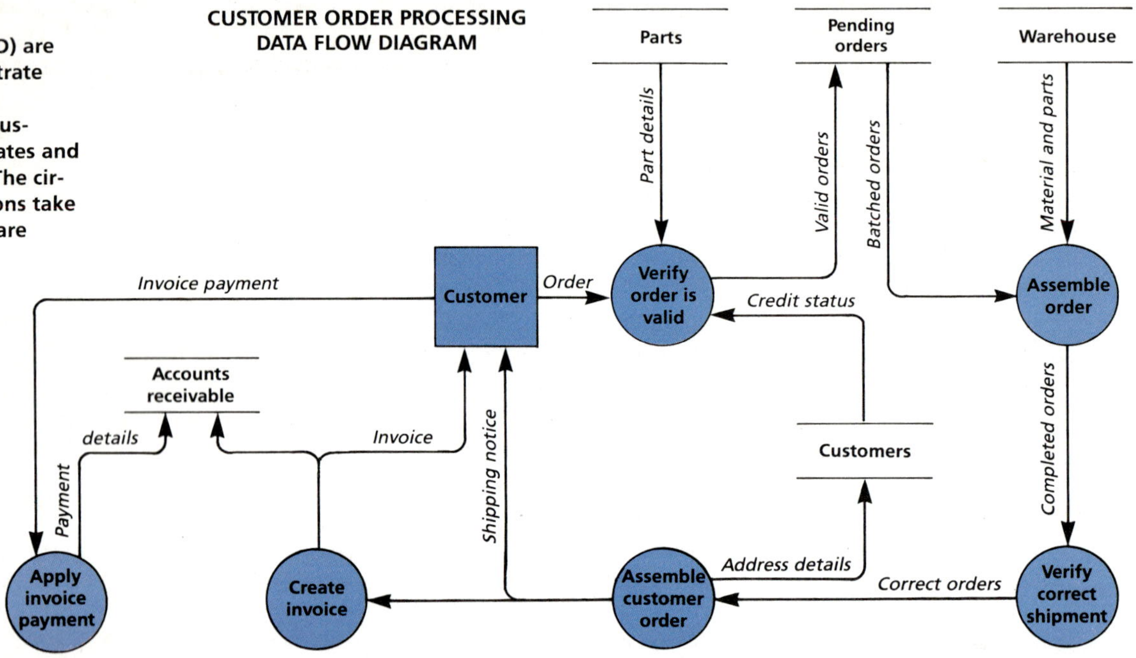

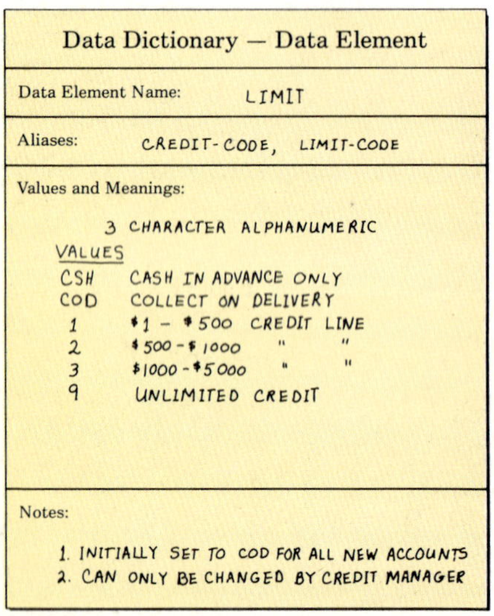

Data Dictionary — Data Element

Data Element Name: LIMIT

Aliases: CREDIT-CODE, LIMIT-CODE

Values and Meanings:

3 CHARACTER ALPHANUMERIC

VALUES

CSH CASH IN ADVANCE ONLY
COD COLLECT ON DELIVERY
1 $1 - $500 CREDIT LINE
2 $500 - $1000 " "
3 $1000 - $5000 " "
9 UNLIMITED CREDIT

Notes:

1. INITIALLY SET TO COD FOR ALL NEW ACCOUNTS
2. CAN ONLY BE CHANGED BY CREDIT MANAGER

Data Dictionaries The **data dictionary** describes the elements that make up the data flow. Elements can be thought of as equivalent to fields in a record. The data dictionary (Figure 12-10) includes information about the attributes of an element, such as length; where the element is used (what files and data flows include the element); and any values or ranges the element might have, such as a value of 2 for a credit limit code to indicate a purchase limit of $1,000.00. The data dictionary is created in the analysis phase and is used in all subsequent phases.

FIGURE 12-10
The data dictionary is used to document the elements that are included in the data flows. This illustration shows the information on length, type of data, and possible values that is recorded for each data element in the dictionary.

Structured English **Process specifications** document what action is taken on the data flows. Referring to the DFD in Figure 12-9, process specifications will describe what goes on in each of the circles. One way of writing process specifications is to use **structured English**, a style of writing and presentation that highlights the alternatives and actions that are part of the process. Figure 12-11 shows an example of a structured English process specification describing a policy for order processing.

```
If the order amount exceeds $1,000,
   If customer has any unpaid invoices over 90 days old,
      Do not issue order confirmation,
      Write message on order reject report.
   Otherwise (account is in good standing),
      Issue order confirmation.
Otherwise (order is $1,000 or less),
   If customer has any unpaid invoices over 90 days old,
      Issue order confirmation,
      Write message on credit follow-up report.
   Otherwise (account is in good standing),
      Issue order confirmation.
```

FIGURE 12-11▲
Structured English is an organized way of describing what actions are taken on data. This structured English example describes an order processing policy.

Decision Tables and Decision Trees Another way of documenting the system during the analysis phase is with a decision table or decision tree. A **decision table** or **decision tree** identifies the actions that should be taken under different conditions. Figures 12-12 and 12-13 show a decision table and decision tree for the order processing policy described with structured English in Figure 12-11. Decision tables and trees are an excellent way of showing the desired action when the action depends on multiple conditions.

	Rules			
	1	2	3	4
Conditions				
1. Order > $1,000	Y	Y	N	N
2. Unpaid invoices over 90 days old	Y	N	Y	N
Actions				
1. Issue confirmation	N	Y	Y	Y
2. Reject order	Y	N	N	N
3. Credit follow-up	N	N	Y	N

◄FIGURE 12-12
Decision tables help a user quickly determine the course of action based on two or more conditions. This decision table is based on the order processing policy described in Figure 12-11. For example, if an order is $1,000 or less and the customer has an unpaid invoice over 90 days old, the policy is to issue an order confirmation but to perform a credit follow-up on the past due invoice.

Making the Decision on How To Proceed

Just as at the completion of the preliminary investigation, at the completion of the analysis phase, the user, systems analyst, and management face another decision on how to proceed. At this point the analyst should have completed a study of the current system and, using the same tools and methods, developed one or more proposed solutions to the current system's identified problems. Sometimes the systems analyst is asked to prepare a feasibility study and a cost/benefit analysis. These two reports are often used together. The **feasibility study** discusses whether the proposed solution is practical and capable of being accomplished. The **cost/benefit analysis** identifies the estimated costs of the proposed solution and the benefits (including potential cost savings) that are expected. If there are strong indications at the beginning of the project that some type of new system will be developed, the feasibility study and cost/benefit analysis are sometimes performed as part of the preliminary investigation.

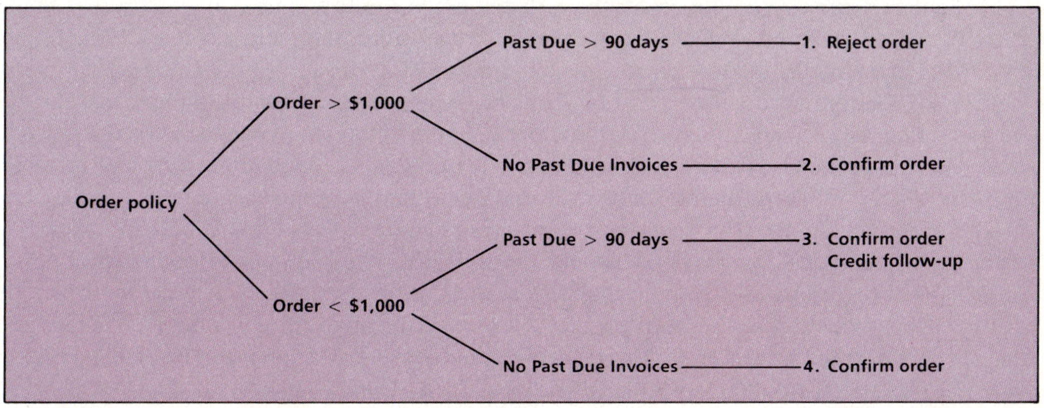

◄FIGURE 12-13
Like a decision table, a decision tree illustrates the action to be taken based on the given conditions, but presents it graphically. This decision tree is based on the order processing policy described in Figure 12-11.

The results of the analyst's work are presented in a written report (Figure 12-14) to both user and information systems management who consider the alternatives and the resources, such as time, people, and money, of the organization. The end of the analysis phase is usually where organizations decide either to acquire commercial software from an outside source, contract outside the organization for system development, or develop the system internally. If a decision is made to proceed, the project enters the design phase.

DATE: April 1
TO: Management Review Committee
FROM: George Lacey, Corporate Systems Manager
SUBJECT: Detailed Investigation and Analysis of Order Entry System

Introduction

A detailed system investigation and analysis of the order entry system was conducted as a result of approval given by the Management Review Committee on March 1. The findings of the investigation are presented below.

Objectives of Detailed Investigation and Analysis

The study was conducted to investigate two major complaints of the wholesale auto parts order entry system. Complaints have been received that orders were not being shipped promptly, and customers were not notified of out-of-stock conditions for many days after sending in orders. In addition, billing invoices are running several days behind shipments. The objective of this study was to determine where the problems existed and to develop alternative solutions.

Findings of the Detailed Investigation and Analysis

The following problems appear to exist within the order entry system:

2. Place the order entry and invoicing systems on the computer. Computer terminals would be installed in the sales department for order entry clerks. As orders are received, they would be entered into the computer. Orders could be immediately edited for proper customer and part numbers and a check could be made to determine if stock is available. Billing invoices could be mailed the same day as shipments. Estimated costs: (1) Systems analysis and design-$26,000; (2) Programming and implementation-$40,000; (3) Training, new forms, and maintenance-$7,000; (4) Equipment (four terminals)-$6,000.

Recommended Action

The systems department recommends the design of a computerized order entry and invoicing system utilizing alternative 2, which is believed to offer the most effective solution.

George Lacey

FIGURE 12-14
Written reports summarizing the analyst's work are an important part of the development project. This report was prepared at the end of the analysis phase and recommends the development of a computerized order entry and invoicing system.

PHASE 1—ANALYSIS AT SUTHERLAND

The Sutherland Company is a large corporation with separate divisions that sell tools, electric motors, and auto parts, respectively. Although the tool and electric motor divisions have been computerized for some time, the low sales volume of the auto parts division, started just two years ago, enabled it to rely on manual procedures. In the last six months, however, auto parts sales doubled and the manual order entry and invoicing systems were unable to keep up with the increased workload.

Because he believed the increased sales volume would continue, Mike Charles, the auto parts sales manager, turned in a request for system services to the information systems department that provided computer services for all three Sutherland divisions. Frank Peacock, a systems analyst, was assigned to investigate the request.

As part of the preliminary investigation, Frank interviewed Mike to try to determine the problem. During his interview with Mike and a subsequent tour of the auto parts sales department, Frank discovered that invoices were not being sent to customers until three days after their parts orders had shipped. In addition, Frank found that customers were complaining about shipments being late and about not being notified when parts they ordered were not available. As a result of his preliminary investigation, Frank recommended a detailed system analysis. George Lacey, the corporate systems manager, agreed with Frank's recommendation and assigned systems analyst Mary Ruiz.

Mary reviewed Frank's notes and began to perform a detailed analysis of the auto parts order entry and invoicing systems. As part of her study, Mary interviewed several people in the auto parts division and prepared several documents including a data flow diagram (Figure 12-9), a data dictionary definition for the different credit limits assigned to customers (Figure 12-10), and a structured English statement of the order processing policy (Figure 12-11).

After studying the manual procedures for a week, Mary discussed her findings with her supervisor, George Lacey. Based on Mary's work, George wrote a report to the management review committee recommending that the order entry and invoicing systems be computerized. The report contained two alternative solutions, one utilizing a separate minicomputer system and the other, considered the most effective solution, utilizing terminals connected to the company's central computer. The management review committee meets every month to review requests for additional computer equipment and software. The committee is made up of top management representatives from each division, the finance department, and the information systems department. Based on George's report, the management review committee authorized the corporate systems department to design a computerized order entry and invoicing system.

PHASE 2—DESIGN

The proposed solution developed as part of the analysis phase usually consists of what is called a **logical design**, which means that the design was deliberately developed without regard to a specific computer or programming language and no attempt was made to identify which procedures should be automated and which procedures should be manual. This approach avoids early assumptions that may limit the possible solutions. During the **design** phase the logical design will be transformed into a **physical design** that will identify the procedures to be automated, choose the programming language, and specify the equipment needed for the system.

Structured Design Methods

The system design usually follows one of two methods, top-down design or bottom-up design.

Top-Down Design **Top-down design**, also called **structured design**, focuses on the major functions of the system, such as recording a sale or generating an invoice, and keeps breaking those functions down into smaller and smaller activities, sometimes called modules, that can eventually be programmed. Top-down design is an increasingly popular method because it focuses on the "big picture" and helps users and systems analysts reach an early agreement on what the major functions of the new system are.

Bottom-Up Design **Bottom-up design** focuses on the data, particularly the output of the system. The approach used is to determine what output is needed and move "up" to the processes needed to produce the output.

In practice, most system analysts use a combination of the two methods. Some information requirements like payroll checks, for example, have data elements that lend themselves to bottom-up design. Other requirements, such as management-oriented exception reports, are better suited to a top-down design.

Regardless of the structured design method used, the system analyst will eventually need to complete the design activities.

Design Activities

Design activities include a number of individual tasks that a system analyst performs to design an information system. These include designs for the output, input, database, processes, system controls, and testing.

Output Design The design of the output is critical to the successful implementation of the system because it is the output that provides the information to the users and that is the basis for the justification of most computerized systems. For example, most users don't know (or necessarily care) how the data will be processed, but they usually do have clear ideas on how they want the information output to look. Often requests for new or modified systems begin with a user-prepared draft of a report that the current system doesn't produce. During **output design**, the system analyst and the user document specific screen and report layouts that will be used for output to display or report information from the new system. The example in Figure 12-15 illustrates a report layout sheet.

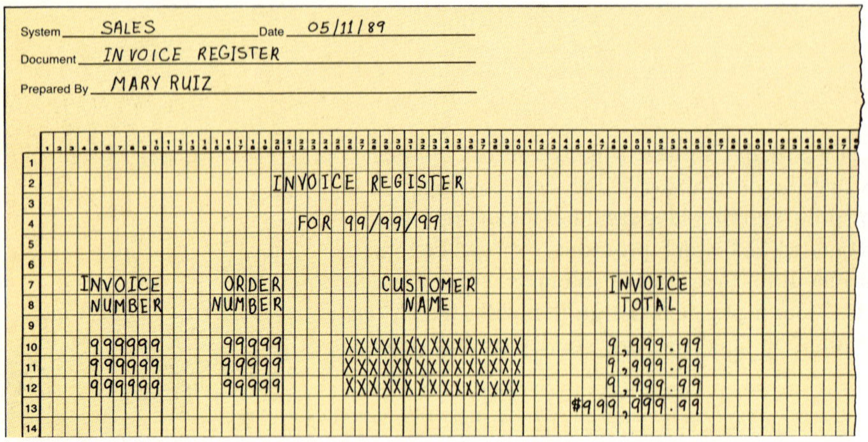

FIGURE 12-15
The report layout form is used to design printed output. Column titles, data width, and report totals are shown on the layout form.

Input Design During **input design** the analyst and user identify what information needs to be entered into the system to produce the desired output and where and how the data will be entered. With interactive systems, the systems analyst and user must determine the sequence of inputs and computer responses, called a **dialogue**, that the user will encounter when entering data. Figure 12-16 shows a display screen layout sheet commonly used to document the format of a screen display.

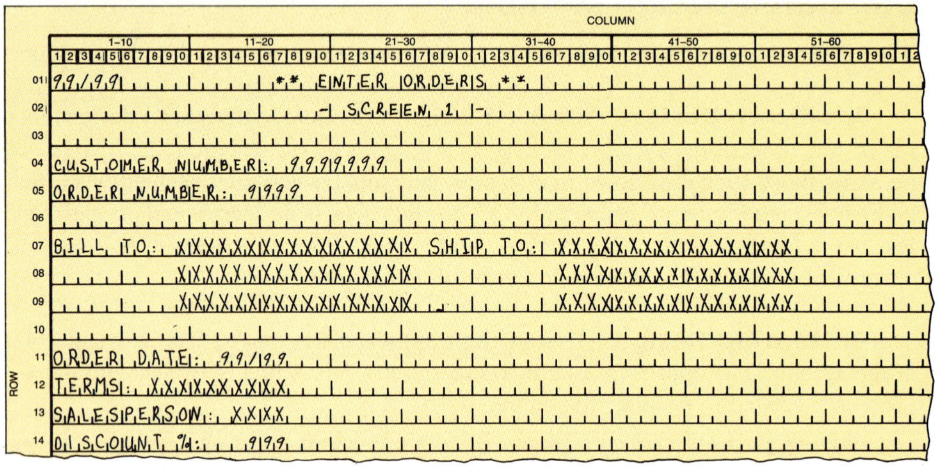

FIGURE 12-16
The display screen layout sheet is similar to the report layout form. Each row and column correspond to a row and column on the screen.

Database Design During **database design** the systems analyst uses the data dictionary information developed during the analysis phase and merges it into new or existing system files. During this phase of the design, the analyst works closely with the database administrator to identify existing database elements that can be used to satisfy design requirements.

Efficient file design can be a challenging task, especially with relational database systems that stress minimum data redundancy (duplicate data). The volume of database activity must also be considered at this point. For example, large files that will be frequently accessed may need a separate index file (discussed in Chapter 8) to allow inquiries to be processed in an amount of time acceptable to the user.

Process Design During **process design** the system analyst specifies exactly what actions will be taken on the input data to create output information. Decisions on the timing of actions are added to the logical processes identified in the analysis phase. For example, the analysis phase might have found that an exception report should be produced if inventory balances fall below a certain level. During the process design phase, the frequency of the report would be determined.

One way to document the relationship of different processes is with a **system flowchart** (Figure 12-17). The system flowchart shows the major processes (each of which may require one or more programs), reports (including their distribution), data files, and the types of input devices such as terminals or tape drives, that will provide data to the system. The special symbols used in a system flowchart are shown in Figure 12-18.

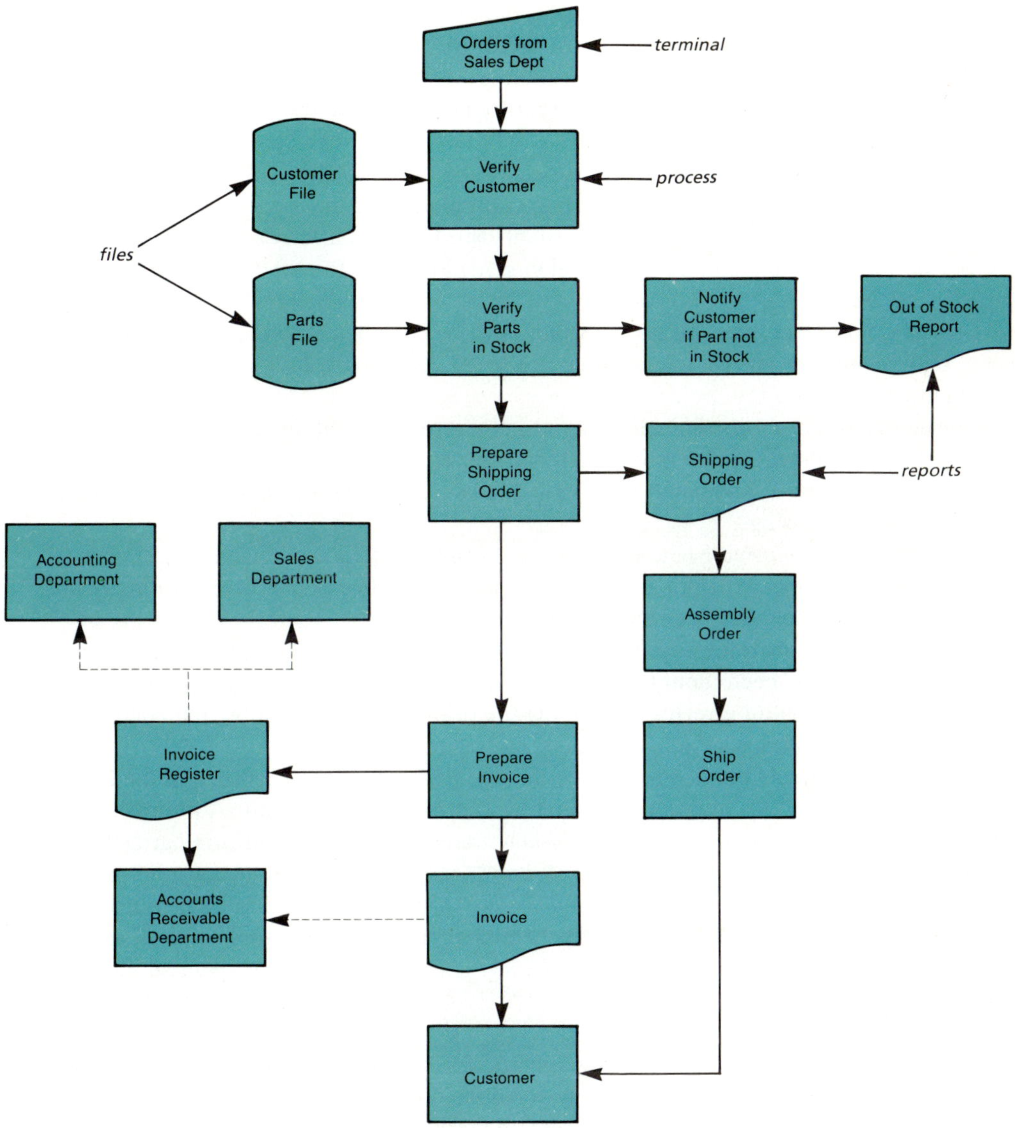

FIGURE 12-17
The system flowchart documents the equipment used to enter data, such as the terminals for the salespeople and the order department, the processes that will take place, such as "Verify Customer," the files that will be used, such as the Parts and Customer files, and the reports that will be produced, such as the shipping order. Dotted lines indicate additional copies of reports, such as the copy of the invoice that is sent to the accounts receivable department.

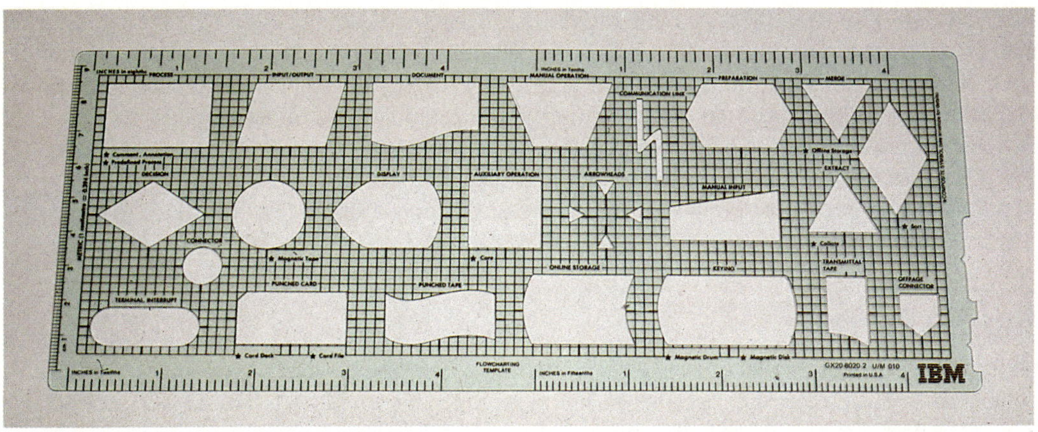

FIGURE 12-18
Symbols used for preparing a system flowchart.

During process design the system analyst, the user, and other members of the development project sometimes meet to conduct a **structured walkthrough**, a step-by-step review of the process design. The purpose of these sessions is to identify any design logic errors and to continue the communication between the systems analyst and the user.

System Controls An important aspect of the design phase is the establishment of a comprehensive set of system controls. **System controls** ensure that only valid data is accepted and processed. Adequate controls must be established for two basic reasons: (1) to ensure the accuracy of the processing and the information generated from the system; (2) to prevent computer-related fraud.

There are four basic types of controls that must be considered by the systems analyst. These controls are: (1) source document controls; (2) input controls; (3) processing controls; (4) accounting controls.

Source document controls include serial numbering of input documents such as invoices and paychecks, document registers in which each input document is recorded and time-stamped as it is received, and batch totaling and balancing to predetermined totals to assure the accuracy of processing.

Input controls are established to assure the complete and accurate conversion of data from the source documents or other sources to a machine-processable form. Editing data as it enters the system is the most important form of input controls.

Processing controls refer to procedures that are established to determine the accuracy of information after it has been input to the system. For example, the accuracy of the total accounts receivable could be verified by taking the prior day's total, adding the current day's sales invoices, and subtracting the current day's payments.

Accounting controls provide assurance that the dollar amounts recorded in the accounting records are correct. An important accounting control is an audit trail. An **audit trail** is one or more reports that provide a history of how transactions have been summarized before they are recorded in the general ledger. For example, an audit trail for sales would include a daily sales register that shows each individual sale transaction, a monthly sales journal that shows the total sales for each day, and the general ledger that has an entry for total sales for the month. With an audit trail, a user can trace any summary entry in the general ledger back to the individual transactions that make it up.

Testing Design During the design phase, test specifications are developed. The exact tests to be performed should be specified by someone other than the user or the systems analyst, although both should be consulted. Users and systems analysts have a tendency to test only what has been designed. An impartial third party, who has not been actively involved in the design, is more likely to design a test for, and therefore discover, a procedure or type of data that may have been overlooked in the design. Sometimes organizations avoid test design and test their systems with actual transactions. While such "live" testing is valuable, it might not test all conditions that the system is designed to process. This is especially true of error or exception conditions that do not occur regularly. For example, payroll systems are usually designed to reject input for hours worked over some limit, say 60 hours in a week. If only actual data are used to test the system, this limit may not be tested. Thus it is important to design testing specifications that will test each system control that is part of the system.

Design Review

At the end of the design phase, management performs a **design review** and evaluates the work completed so far to determine whether or not to proceed (Figure 12-19). This is a critical point in any development project and all parties must take equal responsibility for the decision.

Usually the design review will result only in requests for clarification of a few items. But sometimes an entire project may be terminated. Although canceling or restarting a project from the beginning is a difficult decision, in the long run it is less costly than implementing the wrong or an inadequate solution. If the decision is made to proceed, the project enters the development phase. Before discussing the development phase, we describe prototyping, a development method that can be used in several phases of a system development project.

FIGURE 12-19
The design review is a critical point in the development process. Representatives from the user and information systems departments and top management meet to determine if the system should be developed as designed or if additional design work is necessary.

Prototyping

Prototyping is building a working model of the new system. The advantage of prototyping is that it lets the user actually experience the system before it is completed. Some organizations use prototyping during the analysis phase, others use it during the design phase. Still other companies use prototyping to go directly from preliminary investigation to an implemented system. These companies just keep refining the prototype until the user says that it is acceptable. The disadvantage of such an accelerated approach is that key features of a new system, especially exception conditions, may be overlooked. Another disadvantage is that documentation, an important part of any system development effort, is usually not as well or as thoroughly prepared. When used as a tool to show the user how the system will operate, however, prototyping can be an important system development tool.

PHASE 2—DESIGN AT SUTHERLAND

Upon approval by the management review committee, Mary Ruiz began designing the order entry and invoicing system. After studying existing manually prepared documents and talking to users, Mary designed printed reports and screen displays. According to Mike Charles, one of the most important reports is the daily invoice register. Using a report layout form (Figure 12-15), Mary showed Mike what the report would look like after it was programmed. Using a similar form for screen displays (Figure 12-16), Mary also showed Mike what the order clerks would see when they enter auto parts orders. To graphically show how the overall system would work, Mary prepared a system flowchart (Figure 12-17). The system flowchart showed that auto parts orders would be entered on terminals in the sales department and would use data in the Parts and Customer files to verify that the orders were valid. Shipping orders and invoices were two of the reports produced. An important part of Mary's design time involved specifying the system controls used during processing. These controls included verifying the customer number before processing the order and checking to see if the ordered part is in stock. If the ordered part is not in stock, the customer is notified immediately.

After completing her design work, Mary met with representatives from the user and information systems departments and top management to review her design. After Mary explained the design, the committee agreed to develop the system.

PHASE 3—DEVELOPMENT

Once the system design phase has been completed, the project enters the system development phase. There are two parts to **development**: program development and equipment acquisition.

Program Development

The process of developing the software, or programs, required for a system is called **program development** and includes the following steps: (1) reviewing the program specifications; (2) designing the program; (3) coding the program; (4) testing the program; and (5) finalizing the program documentation. The primary responsibility for completing these tasks is assumed by computer programmers who work closely with the system analyst who designed the system. Chapter 13 explains program development in depth. The important concepts to understand now are that this process is a part of the development phase of the information system life cycle and that its purpose is to develop the software required by the system.

Equipment Acquisition

During the development phase, final decisions will be made on what additional equipment, if any, will be required for the new system. A preliminary review of the equipment requirements would have been done during the analysis phase and included in the written report prepared by the systems analyst. Making the equipment acquisition prior to the development phase would be premature because any equipment selected should be based on the requirements of the approved design from Phase 2. Equipment selection is affected by factors such as the number of users who will require terminals and the disk storage that will be required for new files and data elements. In some cases, even a new or upgraded CPU is required.

PHASE 3—DEVELOPMENT AT SUTHERLAND

During the development phase, Mary worked closely with the two programmers who were assigned to the project. She regularly met with the programmers to answer questions about the design and to check on the progress of their work. Prior to starting the programming, Mary arranged for the programmers to meet with the auto parts sales employees so that the programmers would have a better understanding of the purpose of the new system.

When the programming was close to completion, Mary arranged for the terminals to be installed in the sales department.

PHASE 4—IMPLEMENTATION

Implementation is the phase of the system development process when people actually begin using the new system. This is a critical phase of the project that usually requires careful timing and the coordination of all project participants. Important parts of this phase that will contribute to the success of the new system are training and education, conversion, and postimplementation evaluation.

Training and Education

Someone once said, "If you think education is expensive, you should consider the cost without it." The point is that untrained users can prevent the estimated benefits of a new system from ever being obtained or worse, contribute to less efficiency and more costs than when the old system was operational. Training consists of showing people exactly how they will use the new system (Figure 12-20). This may include classroom-style lectures but should definitely include hands-on sessions with the equipment they will be using, such as terminals, and realistic sample data. Education consists of learning new principles or theories that help people to understand and use the system. For example, before implementing a modern manufacturing system, many companies now require their manufacturing personnel to attend classes on material requirements planning (MRP), shop floor control, and other essential manufacturing topics.

FIGURE 12-20
All users should be trained on the system before they have to use it to process actual transactions. Training could include both classroom and hands-on sessions.

Conversion

Conversion refers to the process of changing from the old system to the new system. A number of different methods of conversion may be used including direct, parallel, phased, and pilot.

With **direct conversion**, the user stops using the old system one day and begins using the new system the next. The advantage of this approach is that it is fast and efficient. The disadvantage is that it is risky and can seriously disrupt operations if the new system does not work correctly the first time.

Parallel conversion consists of continuing to process data on the old system while some or all of the data is also processed on the new system. Results from both systems are compared, and if they agree, all data is switched to the new system (Figure 12-21).

Phased conversion is used with larger systems that can be broken down into individual modules that can be implemented separately at different times. An example would be a complete business system that could have the accounts receivable, inventory, and accounts payable modules implemented separately in phases. Phased conversions can be direct, parallel, or a combination of both.

Pilot conversion means that the new system will be used first by only a portion of the organization, often at a separate location such as a plant or office.

FIGURE 12-21
During parallel conversion, the user compares results from both the old and the new system to determine if the new system is operating properly.

Postimplementation Evaluation

After a system is implemented, it is important to conduct a **postimplementation evaluation** to determine if the system is performing as designed, if operating costs are as anticipated, and if any modifications are necessary to make the system operate more effectively.

PHASE 4—IMPLEMENTATION AT SUTHERLAND

Before they began using the new system to enter real transactions, the users participated in several training sessions about the equipment and the software. Because this was the first application in the auto parts division to be computerized, Mary began the training sessions with an overview of how the central computer system processes data. She conducted a basic data entry class to teach the employees how to use the terminals (Figure 12-20).

Before the system could be used, the Parts and Customer files had to be created from existing manual records. Temporary employees trained in data entry skills were hired for this task. Their work was carefully reviewed each day by Mike Charles and other permanent department employees.

Although he knew it would mean extra work, Mike decided that a parallel conversion would be the safest way to implement the new system. Using this method, Mike could verify the results of the new system with those of the existing manual system. Actual use of the system began on the first business day of the month so that transaction totals could be balanced to accounting reports.

Because they were thoroughly trained, the order clerks felt comfortable when they began entering real orders. A few minor problems were encountered, such as orders for special parts that were not on the Parts file. These errors became less frequent and at the end of the month, after comparing manual and computerized report totals, Mike decided to discontinue the use of the manual system.

During the postimplementation review, Mike and Mary discovered that nine out of ten customer orders were now shipped the same day as the order was received. Before the new system was implemented, less than half the orders were shipped within two days of receipt. Invoices, which once lagged three days behind shipments, were now mailed on the same day. Perhaps the most positive benefit of the new system was that customer complaints about order processing were practically eliminated.

PHASE 5—MAINTENANCE

Maintenance is the process of supporting the system after it is implemented. Maintenance consists of three activities: performance monitoring, change management, and error correction.

Performance Monitoring

Performance monitoring is the ongoing process of comparing response times, file sizes, and other system performance measures against the estimates that were prepared during the analysis, design, and implementation phases. Variances from these estimates may indicate that the system requires additional equipment resources, such as more memory or faster disk drives.

Change Management

Change is an inevitable part of any system and should be provided for with methods and procedures that are made known to all users of the system. Sometimes changes are required because existing requirements were overlooked. Other times, new information requirements caused by external sources such as government regulations will force change. A key part of change management is documentation. The same documentation standards that were followed during the analysis and design phases should also be used to record changes. In fact, in many organizations, the same document that is used to request new systems (Figure 12-7) is used to request changes to an existing system (Figure 12-22). Thus the information system development cycle continues as Phase 1 (analysis) begins on the change request.

Error Correction

Error correction deals with problems that are caused by programming and design errors that are discovered after the system is implemented. Often these errors are minor problems, such as the zip code not appearing on a name and address report, that can be quickly fixed by a programmer. Other times, however, the error requires some level of investigation by the systems analyst before a correction can be determined.

PHASE 5—MAINTENANCE AT SUTHERLAND

During the months following the system implementation, a number of minor programming errors were discovered. Most of these errors were quickly corrected by the programming staff but in one case involving special credit terms for a large customer, Mary Ruiz had to become involved and had to prepare specifications for the necessary program changes.

Approximately one year after Mike Charles submitted his original request for a computerized order entry and invoicing system, he submitted another request (Figure 12-22) for a change to the system to provide for a new county sales tax. This type of request does not require a preliminary investigation and will be assigned to Mary Ruiz as soon as she is available. Mike submitted his request five months before the tax was scheduled to go into effect, which should allow ample time for the necessary program changes to be implemented.

REQUEST FOR SYSTEM SERVICES

ISD CONTROL #: 4703

I. To Be Completed By Person Requesting Services

SUBMITTED BY: MIKE CHARLES DEPT AUTO PARTS SALES DATE: 2-1-91

REQUEST TYPE: ☑ MODIFICATION ☐ NEW SYSTEM

NEED: ☑ ASAP ☐ IMMEDIATE ☐ LONG RANGE

BRIEF STATEMENT OF REQUEST (attach additional material, if necessary)

SALES INVOICE PROGRAM NEEDS TO PROVIDE FOR 1% COUNTY TAX THAT WILL GO INTO EFFECT JULY 1, 1991.

☑ ADDITIONAL MATERIAL ATTACHED COUNTY TAX RATE SCHEDULE

II. To Be Completed By Information Systems Department

REQUEST INVESTIGATED BY: ______ DATE: ______

COMMENTS: ______

III. Disposition

☐ REQUEST APPROVED FOR IMMEDIATE IMPLEMENTATION

☐ Analyst assigned: ______

☐ REQUEST APPROVED FOR IMPLEMENTATION AS SOON AS POSSIBLE

☐ REQUEST REJECTED

COMMENTS: ______

SIGNED: ______ DATE: ______

FIGURE 12-22
The same form that was used to request a new system (see Figure 12-7) is also used to request a modification to an existing system.

SUMMARY OF THE INFORMATION SYSTEM DEVELOPMENT LIFE CYCLE

Although the information system development process may appear to be a straightforward series of steps, in practice it is a challenging activity that calls for the skills and cooperation of all involved. New development tools have made the process more efficient but the success of any project always depends on the commitment of the project participants. The understanding you have gained from this chapter will help you participate in information system development projects and give you an appreciation for the importance of each phase.

CHAPTER SUMMARY

1. An **information system** is a collection of six elements, equipment, software, data, personnel, users, and procedures, that provide accurate, timely and useful information.
2. There are four types of information systems: (1) **operational systems**; (2) **management information systems**; (3) **decision support systems**; and (4) **expert systems**.
3. The trend is to combine all of an organization's information needs into a single integrated information system.
4. The **information system development life cycle** is an organized approach to developing an information system and consists of five phases: analysis, design, development, implementation, and maintenance.
5. Planning, scheduling, reporting, and controlling the individual activities that make up the information system development life cycle is called **project management**. These activities are usually recorded in a **project plan**.
6. **Documentation** refers to written materials that are produced throughout the information system development life cycle.
7. All users and information system personnel who will be affected by the new system should have the opportunity to participate in its development.
8. The systems analyst's job is a challenging one requiring good communication, analytical, and diplomatic skills to keep the development process on track and on schedule.
9. The **analysis** phase is the separation of a system into its parts in order to determine how the system works. This phase consists of the preliminary investigation, detailed system analysis, and making the decision to proceed.
10. The purpose of the **preliminary investigation** is to determine if a request warrants further detailed investigation. The most important aspect of this investigation is **problem definition**.
11. **Detailed system analysis** involves both a thorough study of the current system and as least one proposed solution to any problems found.
12. **Data flow diagrams** are a **structured analysis** tool that graphically show the flow of data through a system.
13. Other tools that are used in the analysis phase include **data dictionaries**, **process specifications**, **structured English**, **decision tables**, and **decision trees**.
14. A **feasibility study** and **cost/benefit analysis** are often prepared to show whether the proposed solution is practical and to show the estimated costs and benefits that are expected.
15. During the **design** phase the **logical design** that was created in the analysis phase is transformed into a **physical design**.
16. There are two major structured design methods: **top-down design** (or **structured design**) and **bottom-up design**.
17. **Output design**, **input design**, and **database design** all occur during the design phase.
18. When designing interactive systems, the systems analyst and user determine the sequence of inputs and computer responses, called a **dialogue**.
19. During the **process design** the systems analyst specifies exactly what actions will be taken on the input data to create output information.
20. One method of documenting the relationship of different processes is with a **system flowchart**.
21. A **structured walkthrough**, or a step-by-step review, is sometimes performed on the process design.
22. **System controls** ensure that only valid data is accepted and processed. Types of system controls include **source document controls**, **input controls**, **processing controls**, and **accounting controls**, including an **audit trail**.
23. At the end of the design phase, a **design review** is performed to evaluate the work completed so far.
24. **Prototyping** is building a working model of the new system.
25. The **development** phase consists of program development and equipment acquisition.
26. **Program development** includes: (1) reviewing the program specifications; (2) designing the program; (3) coding the program; (4) testing the program; and (5) finalizing the program documentation.
27. The **implementation** phase is when people actually begin using the new system. This phase includes training and education, conversion, and the **postimplementation evaluation**.
28. The process of changing from the old system to the new system is called a **conversion**. The conversion methods that may be used are **direct**, **parallel**, **phased**, and **pilot**.
29. The **maintenance** phase is the process of supporting the information system after it is implemented. It consists of three activities: **performance monitoring**, change management, and error correction.

KEY TERMS

Accounting controls *12.14*
Analysis *12.6*
Artificial intelligence *12.4*
Audit trail *12.14*
Bottom-up design *12.11*
Conversion *12.17*
Cost/benefit analysis *12.9*
Database design *12.12*
Data dictionary *12.8*
Data flow diagram (DFD) *12.8*
Decision support systems *12.4*
Decision table *12.9*
Decision tree *12.9*
Design *12.11*
Design review *12.14*
Detailed system analysis *12.7*
Development *12.16*
Dialogue *12.12*
Direct conversion *12.17*
Documentation *12.6*
Expert systems *12.4*
Feasibility study *12.9*
Implementation *12.16*
Inference rules *12.4*
Information system *12.2*
Information system development life cycle (SDLC) *12.5*
Input controls *12.14*
Input design *12.12*
Knowledge base *12.4*
Logical design *12.11*
Maintenance *12.18*
Management information system (MIS) *12.3*
Operational system *12.3*
Output design *12.11*
Parallel conversion *12.17*
Performance monitoring *12.18*
Phased conversion *12.17*
Physical design *12.11*
Pilot conversion *12.17*
Postimplementation evaluation *12.17*
Preliminary investigation *12.7*
Problem definition *12.7*
Process design *12.12*
Processing controls *12.14*
Process specifications *12.9*
Program development *12.16*
Project management *12.5*
Project plan *12.5*
Prototyping *12.15*
Source document controls *12.14*
Structured analysis *12.8*
Structured design *12.11*
Structured English *12.9*
Structured walkthrough *12.14*
System controls *12.14*
System flowchart *12.12*
Top-down design *12.11*

REVIEW QUESTIONS

1. List the six elements of an information system.
2. What are the four types of information systems? What is meant by integrated information systems?
3. List the five phases of the information system development life cycle.
4. Describe project management and when it should be performed.
5. What is the preliminary investigation? What is the most important aspect of the preliminary investigation?
6. Briefly describe detailed system analysis. What are the fact-finding techniques used during detailed system analysis?
7. What are the symbols used in data flow diagrams? Why are data flow diagram useful?
8. Explain the difference between the logical and physical design of an information system.
9. What are the two methods of structured design? Briefly describe each method.
10. List and describe four basic types of system controls.
11. What is prototyping?
12. What are the steps in program development?
13. Write a description of the four types of conversion methods.
14. Describe the three major activities of system maintenance.

CONTROVERSIAL ISSUES

1. Large systems may take several years to design and implement. Some experts argue that undertaking such a task is ridiculous because the needs of the users and the technology will change so much during the time it takes to implement the system that it will be obsolete before it is implemented. Others point out that there are really no alternatives. What do you think?
2. "The difficulty in developing and implementing an information processing system is the user," proclaimed a systems analyst. "Users never know what they want. When they are shown what the system will do, they give their approval, but when the system is implemented they are never happy. They always want changes. It's impossible to satisfy them." How do you feel about these comments? Are the systems analyst's comments about users correct?

RESEARCH PROJECTS

1. Today there are many software packages available for personal computers to help systems analysts with the tasks they perform during the information system development life cycle. Write a report on one of these packages and be prepared to discuss it in class.
2. Prepare a data flow diagram of how you registered for class. Document your work by obtaining copies of any forms that were used during the registration process.

CHAPTER 13

Program Development

CHAPTER 13

Program Development

OBJECTIVES

- Define the term computer program.
- Describe the five steps in program development: review of program specifications, program design, program coding, program testing, and finalizing program documentation.
- Explain the concepts of structured program design including modules, control structures, and single entry/single exit.
- Explain and illustrate the sequence, selection, and iteration control structures used in structured programming.
- Define the term programming language and discuss the various categories of programming languages.
- Briefly discuss the programming languages that are commonly used today, including BASIC, COBOL, C, FORTRAN, Pascal, Ada, and RPG.
- Explain and discuss application generators.
- Explain the factors that should be considered when choosing a programming language.

As we discussed in Chapter 12, the information system development life cycle covers the entire process of taking a plan for processing information through various phases until it becomes a functioning information system. During the development phase of this cycle, computer programs are written. The purpose of these programs is to process data and produce output as specified in the information system design. This chapter focuses on the steps taken to write a program and the available tools that make the program development process more efficient. In addition, this chapter discusses the different languages used to write programs.

Although you may never write a program yourself, it is likely that you will someday request information that will require a program to be written or modified. Therefore it is important for you to understand the process that takes place when a computer program is developed.

WHAT IS A COMPUTER PROGRAM?

A **computer program** is a detailed set of instructions that directs a computer to perform the tasks necessary to process data into information. These instructions, usually written by a computer programmer, can be coded (written) in a variety of programming languages that will be discussed later in this chapter. To create programs that are correct (produce accurate information) and maintainable (easy to modify), programmers follow a process called program development.

WHAT IS PROGRAM DEVELOPMENT?

In the early days of computing, programming was considered an "art" and the programming process was left to the "interpretation" of the programmer. While there is still room for creativity, **program development**, the process of producing one or more programs to perform one or more specific tasks on a computer, has evolved into a series of five steps that most experts agree should take place when any program is developed. These five steps (Figure 13-1) are:

1. Review of program specifications. The programmer reviews the specifications created by the system analyst during the system design phase.
2. Program design. The programmer determines the specific actions the program will take to accomplish the desired tasks.
3. Coding. The programmer writes the actual program instructions.
4. Testing. The written programs are tested to make sure they perform as intended.
5. Finalizing documentation. The documentation produced during the program development process is brought together and organized.

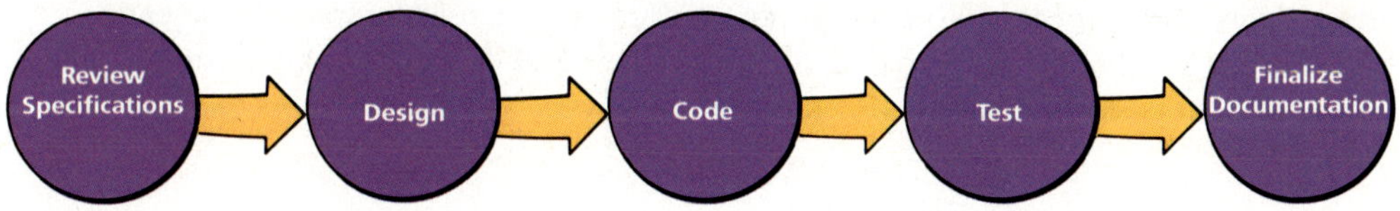

FIGURE 13-1
The five steps of program development.

STEP 1—REVIEW OF PROGRAM SPECIFICATIONS

The first step in the program development cycle is a review of the program specifications. **Program specifications** can consists of data flow diagrams, system flowcharts, process specifications that indicate the action to be taken on the data, a data dictionary identifying the data elements that will be used, screen formats, and report layouts. These documents help the programmer understand the work that needs to be done by the program. Because it is important that the programmer understands the purpose of the program from the user's point of view, one or more meetings are usually held between the programmer, the user, and the systems analyst who designed the system.

If the programmer believes some aspect of the design should be changed, such as a screen layout, it is discussed with the analyst and the user. If the change is agreed on, the design specification is changed. However, the programmer should not change the specified system without the agreement of the analyst and user. If a change is authorized, it should be recorded in the system design. The analyst and user, through the system design, have specified *what* is to be done. It is the programmer's job to determine *how* to do it.

Large programming jobs are usually assigned to more than one programmer. In these situations, a good system design is essential so that each programmer can be given a logical portion of the system to be programmed.

STEP 2—PROGRAM DESIGN

After the program specifications have been carefully reviewed, program design begins. During **program design** a logical solution to the programming task is developed and documented. The logical solution or **logic** for a program is a step-by-step solution to a programming problem. Determining the logic for a computer program can be an extremely complex task. To aid in program design and development, a method called structured program design is commonly used.

Structured Program Design

Structured program design is a methodology that emphasizes three main program design concepts: modules, control structures, and single entry/single exit. Use of these concepts helps to create programs that are easy to write, read, understand, check for errors, and modify.

Modules With structured design, programming problems are "decomposed" (separated) into smaller parts called modules. Each **module**, sometimes referred to as a **subroutine** in programming, performs a given task within the program. The major benefit of this technique is that it simplifies program development because each module of a program can be developed individually. When the modules are combined, they form a complete program that accomplishes the desired result.

Structure charts, also called **hierarchy charts**, are often used to decompose and represent the modules of a program. When the program decomposition is completed, the entire structure of a program is illustrated by the hierarchy chart and the relationship of the modules within the program is shown (Figure 13-2).

FIGURE 13-2
A structure chart graphically illustrates the relationship of individual program modules.

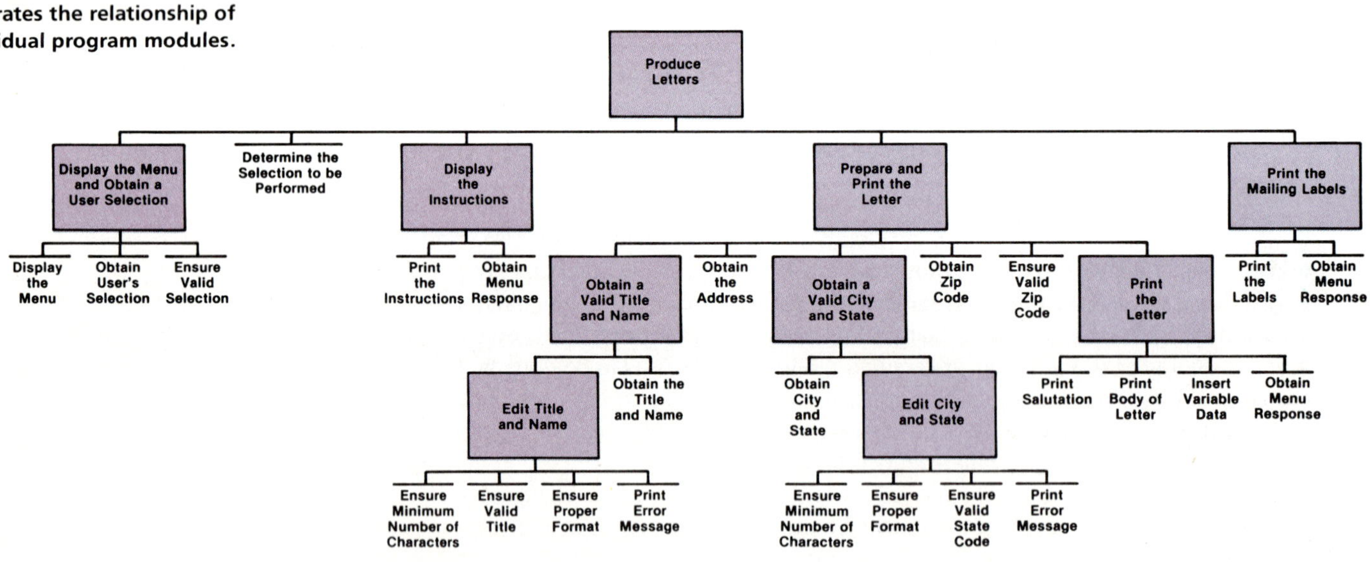

Control Structures In structured program design three basic **control structures** are used to form the logic of a program. All logic problems can be solved by a combination of these structures. The three basic control structures are: sequence, selection, and iteration.

In the **sequence structure**, one process occurs immediately after another. In Figure 13-3, each rectangular box represents a particular process that is to take place. For example, a process could be a computer instruction to move data from one location in main memory to another location. Each process takes place in the exact sequence specified, one process followed by the next.

The second control structure, called the **selection** or **if-then-else structure**, gives programmers a way to represent conditional program logic (Figure 13-4). Conditional program logic can be expressed in the following way: *If* the condition is true, *then* perform the true condition processing, *else* perform the false condition processing. When the if-then-else control structure is used, the "if" portion of the structure tests a given condition. The true portion of the statement is executed if the condition tested is true and the false portion of the statement is executed if the condition is false. For example, in a payroll program the number of hours worked might be tested to determine if an employee worked overtime. If the person did work overtime, the true portion of the statement would be executed and overtime would be calculated. If the employee did not work overtime, then the false portion of the statement would be executed and overtime would not be calculated. The selection or if-then-else structure is used by programmers to represent conditional logic problems.

The third control structure, called **iteration** or **looping**, means that one or more processes continue to occur so long as a given condition remains true. There are two forms of this control structure: the **do-while structure** and the **do-until structure** (Figure 13-5). In the do-while structure a condition is tested. If the condition is true, the process is performed. The program then "loops" back and tests the condition again. If the condition is still true, the process is performed again. This looping continues until the condition being tested is false. At that time, the program exits the loop and performs some other processing. An example of this type of testing would be a check to see if all records have been processed. The do-until control structure is similar to the do-while except that the conditional test is at the end instead of the beginning of the loop. Processing continues "until" the condition is met.

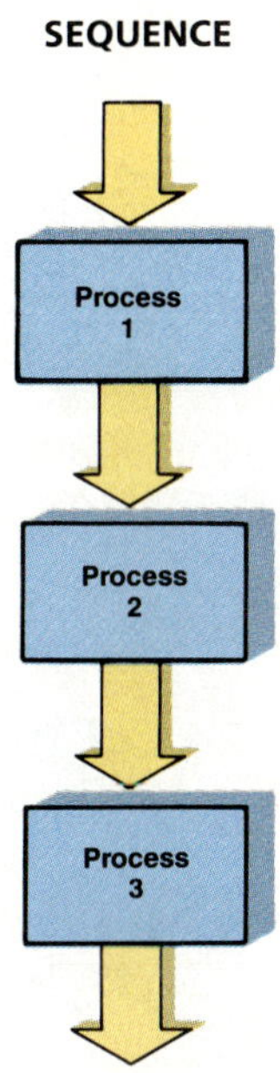

FIGURE 13-3 ▶
Each box in the sequence control structure represents a process that will take place immediately after the preceding process.

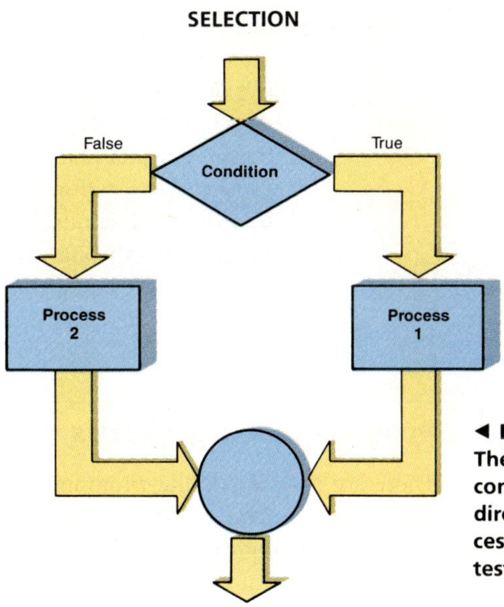

◀ FIGURE 13-4
The selection or if-then-else control structure is used to direct the program to one process or another based on the test of a condition.

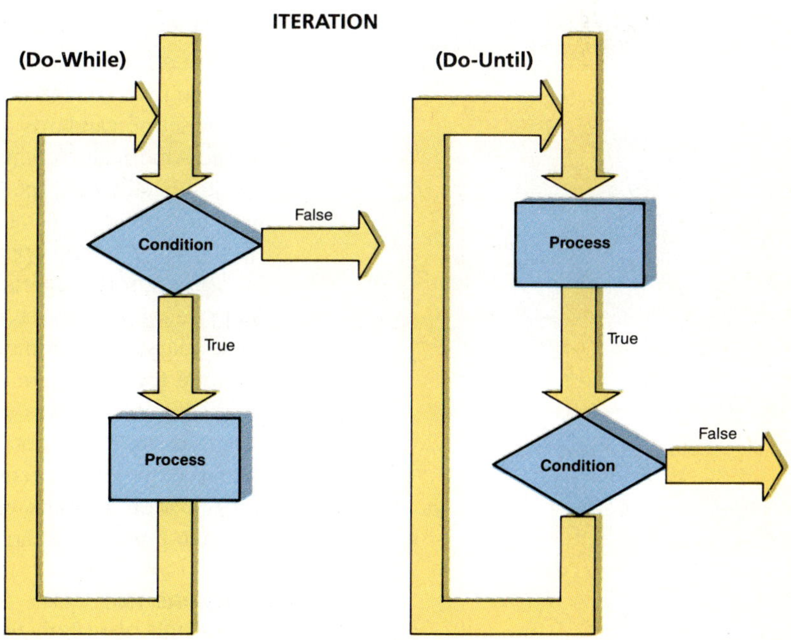

FIGURE 13-5 ▶
The iteration control structure has two forms, do-while and do-until. In the do-while structure, the condition is tested before the process. In the do-until structure, the condition is tested after the process.

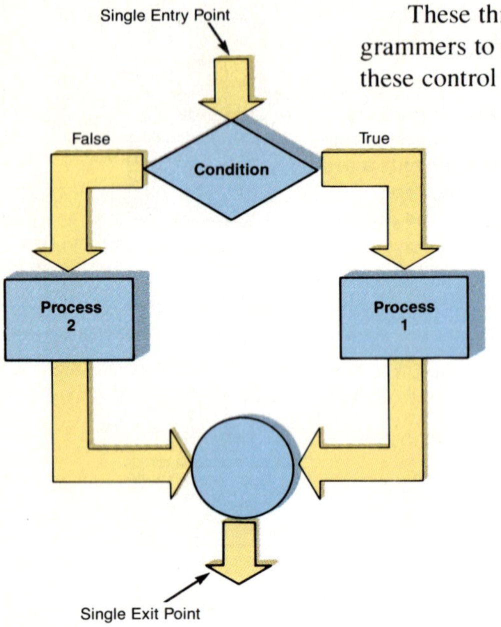

FIGURE 13-6 ▲
Structured programming concepts require that all control structures have a single entry point and a single exit point. This contributes to programming logic that is easier to understand.

These three control structures, sequence, selection, and iteration, are combined by programmers to create program logic solutions. A structured program design rule that applies to these control structures and how they are combined is the single entry/single exit rule.

Single Entry/Single Exit An important concept in structured programming is **single entry/single exit**, meaning that there is only one entry point and one exit point for each of the three control structures. An **entry point** is the point where a control structure is entered. An **exit point** is the point where the control structure is exited. For example, in Figure 13-6, when the if-then-else structure is used, the control structure is entered at the point where the condition is tested. When the condition is tested, one set of instructions will be executed if the condition is true and another set will be executed if the condition is false. Regardless of the result of the test, however, the structure is exited at the single exit point.

This feature substantially improves the understanding of a program because, when reading the program, the programmer can be assured that whatever happens within the if-then-else structure, the control structure will always be exited at a common point. Prior to the use of structured programming, many programmers would transfer control to other parts of a program without following the single entry/single exit rule. This practice led to poorly designed programs that were extremely difficult to read, check for errors, and modify.

Program Design Tools

There are several popular program design tools through which structured program design concepts can be applied. These design tools are used by computer programmers to develop and document the logical solutions to the problems they are programming. Three of these design tools are program flowcharts, pseudocode, and Warnier-Orr.

Program Flowcharts Program flowcharts were one of the first program design tools. Figure 13-7 shows a flowchart drawn in the late 1940s by Dr. John von Neumann, a computer scientist and one of the first computer programmers. In a **program flowchart** all the logical steps of a program are represented by a combination of symbols and text.

A set of standards for program flowcharts was published in the early 1960s by the American National Standards Institute (ANSI). These standards, which are still used today, specify symbols, such as rectangles and diamonds, that are used to represent the various operations that can be performed on a computer (Figure 13-8 on the opposite page).

Program flowcharts were used as the primary means of program design for many years prior to the introduction of structured program design. During these years, programmers designed programs by focusing on the detailed steps required for a program and creating logical solutions for each new combination of conditions as it was encountered. Developing programs in this manner led to programs that were poorly designed. Today, programmers are taught to apply the structured design concepts when preparing program flowcharts (Figure 13-9). When the basic control structures are utilized, program flowcharts are a valuable program design tool.

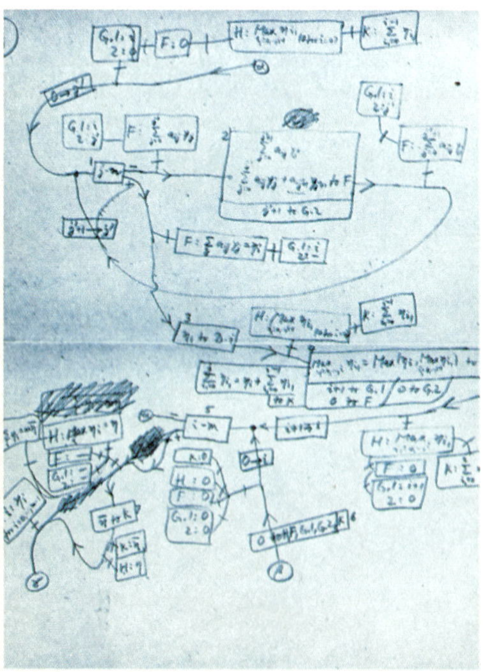

◄ FIGURE 13-7
An example of an early flowchart developed by computer scientist Dr. John von Neumann in the 1940s to solve a problem involving game theory.

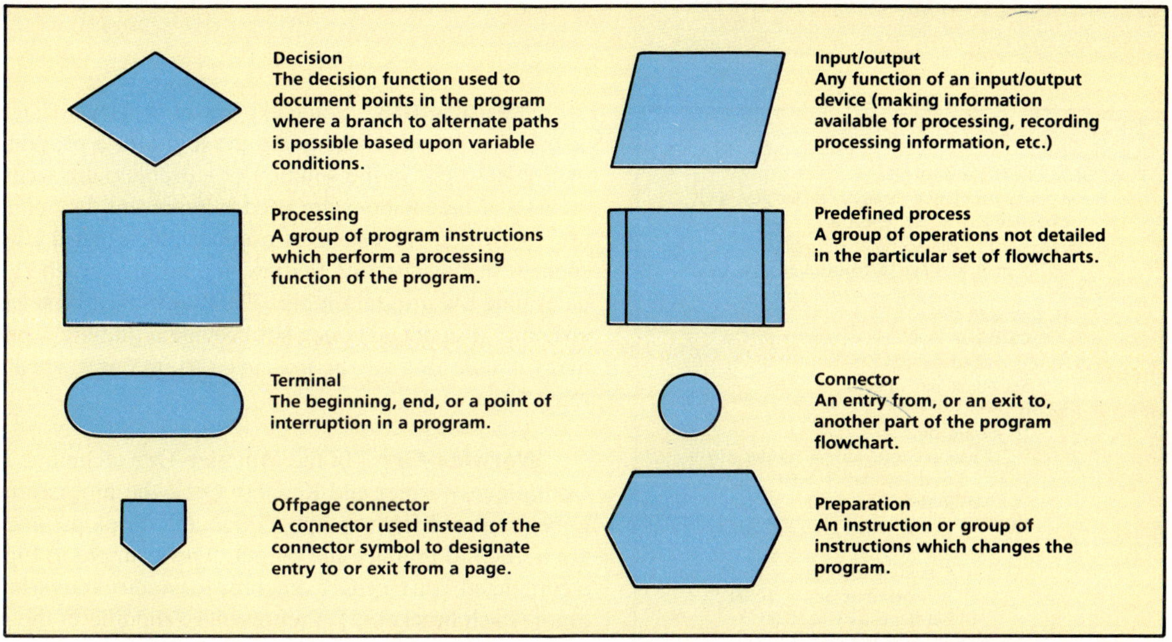

FIGURE 13-8
The standard symbols used to prepare program flowcharts.

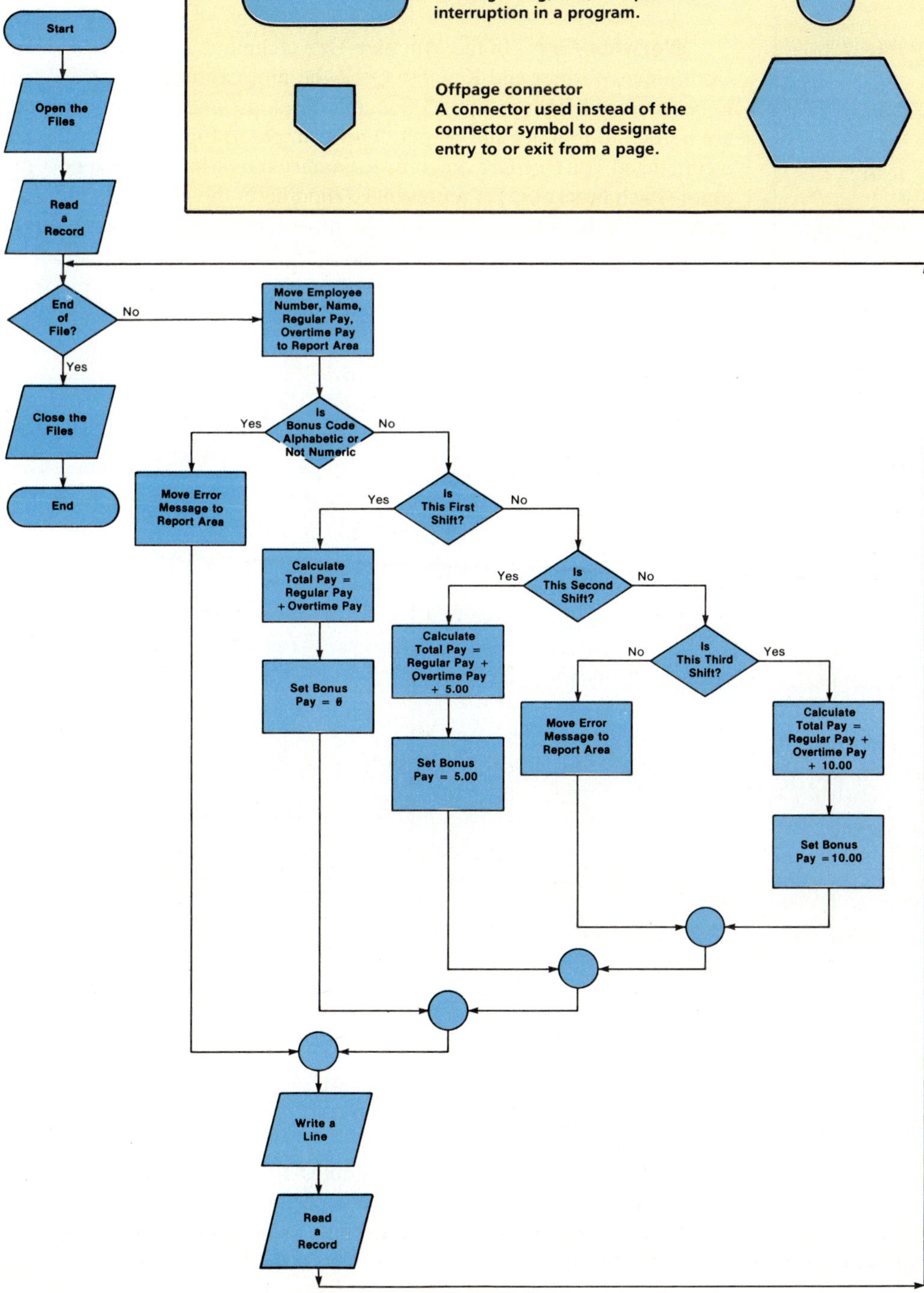

FIGURE 13-9
This flowchart illustrates the use of standard flowcharting symbols and the three control structures used in structured programming. It displays the logic required to solve a payroll calculation task.

```
Open the files
Read a record
PERFORM UNTIL end of file
    Move employee number, name, regular pay, and
        overtime pay to the report area
    IF bonus code is alphabetic or not numeric
        Move error message to report area
    ELSE
        IF first shift
            Calculate total pay = regular pay +
                overtime pay
            Set bonus pay to zero
        ELSE
            IF second shift
                Calculate total pay = regular pay +
                    overtime pay + 5.00
                Set bonus pay to 5.00
            ELSE
                IF third shift
                    Calculate total pay = regular pay +
                        overtime pay + 10.00
                    Set bonus pay to 10.00
                ELSE
                    Move error message to report area
                ENDIF
            ENDIF
        ENDIF
    ENDIF
    Write a line
    Read a record
ENDPERFORM
Close the files
End the program
```

FIGURE 13-10
This pseudocode is another way of documenting the logic shown in the flowchart in Figure 13-9.

Pseudocode Some experts in program design advocate the use of pseudocode when designing the logic for a program. In **pseudocode** the logical steps in the solution of a problem are written as English statements and indentations are used to represent the control structures (Figure 13-10). An advantage of pseudocode is that it eliminates the time spent with flowcharting to draw and arrange symbols while attempting to determine the program logic. The major disadvantage is that unlike flowcharting, pseudocode does not provide a graphic representation, which many people find useful and easier to interpret when examining programming logic.

Warnier-Orr In the **Warnier-Orr** technique (named after Jean-Dominique Warnier and Kenneth Orr), the programmer analyzes output to be produced from an application and develops processing modules that are needed to produce the output. The example in Figure 13-11 illustrates a completed Warnier-Orr diagram for a checkbook-balancing report program. Each bracket ({) represents a module in the program. The statements within the brackets identify the processing that is to occur within the modules.

Regardless of the design tool used, it is important that the program design is efficient and correct. To help ensure this, many organizations use structured walkthroughs.

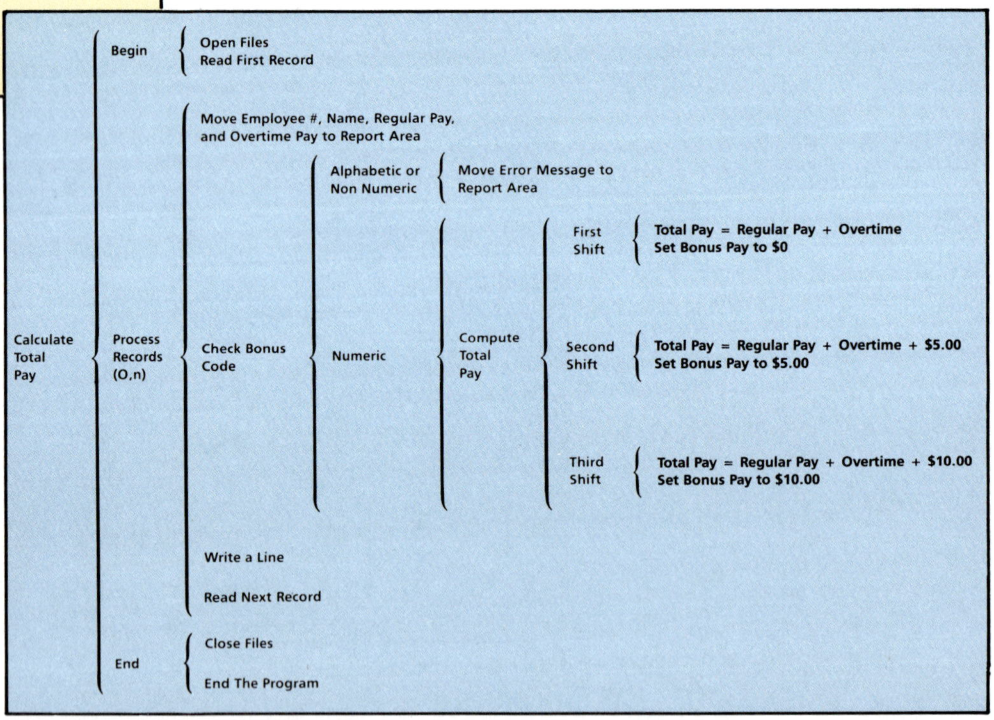

FIGURE 13-11
This Warnier-Orr diagram illustrates the logic for the payroll calculation problem also used for Figures 13-9 and 13-10.

Structured Walkthroughs

After a program has been designed, the programmer schedules a structured walkthrough of the program. The programmer, other programmers in the department, and the systems analyst attend. During the walkthrough, the programmer who designs the program explains the program logic. The purpose of the design walkthrough is to review the logic of the program for errors, and if possible, improve program design. It is much better to find errors and make needed changes to the program during the design step than to make them later in the program development process.

Once the program design is complete, the coding of the program begins.

STEP 3—PROGRAM CODING

Coding the program refers to the process of writing the program instructions that will process the data and produce the output specified in the program design. As previously mentioned, programs are written in different languages that each have particular rules on how to instruct the computer to perform specific tasks, such as read a record or multiply two numbers. The differences in these languages will be discussed later in this chapter.

If a thorough program design has been produced, the coding process is greatly simplified and can sometimes be a one-for-one translation of a design step into a program step. Today, program code, or instructions, are usually entered directly into the computer via a terminal and stored on a disk drive. Using this approach, the programmer can partially enter a program at one time and finish entering it at a later time. Program instructions are added, deleted, and changed until the programmer believes the program design has been fully translated into program instructions and the program is ready for testing.

STEP 4—PROGRAM TESTING

Before a program is used to process "real" data and produce information that people rely on, it should be thoroughly tested to make sure it is functioning correctly. Several different types of tests can be performed.

Desk checking is the process of reading the program and mentally reviewing its logic. This is a simple process that can be performed by the programmer who wrote the program or by another programmer. This process can be compared with proofreading a letter before you put it in the mail. The disadvantage of this method is that it is difficult to detect other than obvious errors.

Another type of testing identifies program **syntax errors**, violations of the grammar rules of the language in which the program was written. An example of a syntax error would be the program command READ being misspelled REED. Syntax errors missed by the programmer are discovered by the computer when it decodes the program instructions.

Logic testing is what most programmers think of when the term testing is used. During **logic testing**, the sequence of program instructions is tested to make sure they provide the correct result. Logic errors may be the result of a programming oversight, such as using the wrong data to perform a calculation, or a design error, such as forgetting to specify that some customers do not have to pay sales tax when they purchase merchandise.

Logic testing is performed with **test data**, data that simulates the type of input that the program will process when it is implemented. In order to obtain an independent and unbiased test of the program, test data and the review of test results should be the responsibility of someone other than the programmer who wrote the program. The test data should be developed by referring to the system design but should also try to "break" the program by including data outside the range of data that will be input during normal operations. For example, even though a payroll program should never have more than 60 hours per week input, the program should be designed, coded, and tested to properly process transactions in excess of 60 hours by displaying an error message or in some other way indicating that an invalid number

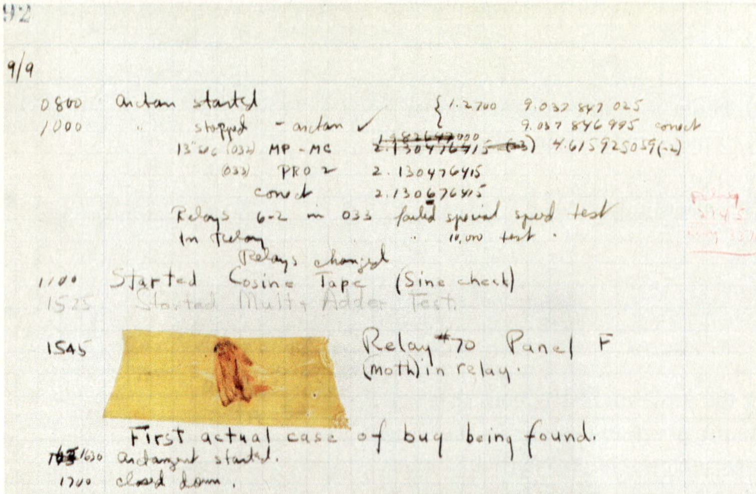

FIGURE 13-12
In 1945, the cause of the temporary failure of the world's first electromechanical computer, the Mark I, was traced to a dead moth caught in the electrical components. The term "bug," meaning a computer error, has been part of computer jargon ever since.

of hours has been entered. Other similar tests should include alphabetic data when only numeric data is expected, and negative numbers when only positive numbers are normally input.

One of the more colorful terms of the computer industry is **debugging**, which refers to the process of locating and correcting program errors or **bugs** found during testing. The term was coined when the failure of one of the first computers was traced to a moth that had become lodged in the electronic components (Figure 13-12).

STEP 5—FINALIZING PROGRAM DOCUMENTATION

Documentation is an essential but sometimes neglected part of the programming process. As reflected in the title of this section, documentation should be an ongoing part of developing a program and should only be finalized, meaning organized and brought together, after the program is successfully tested and ready for implementation. The difficulty in sometimes obtaining adequate documentation is that many programmers can and do develop programs without it; when the program is completed, they have little incentive to go back and complete the documentation "after the fact." In addition to helping programmers develop programs, documentation is valuable because it helps the next programmer who, six months or one year later, is asked to make a change to the program. Proper documentation can substantially reduce the amount of time the new programmer will have to spend learning enough about the program to know how best to make the change.

Documentation developed during the programming process should include a narrative description of the program, program flowcharts, pseudocode, program listings, and test results. Comments in the program itself are also an important part of program documentation (Figure 13-13).

FIGURE 13-13
Most programming languages allow explanatory comments to be placed directly in the program. This is an effective way of documenting the program.

```
100 REM TELLIST              SEPTEMBER 22              SHELLY/CASHMAN
110                                                               REM
120 REM THIS PROGRAM DISPLAYS THE NAME, TELEPHONE AREA CODE
130 REM AND PHONE NUMBER OF INDIVIDUALS.
140                                                               REM
150 REM VARIABLE NAMES:
160 REM    A.....AREA CODE
170 REM    T$....TELEPHONE NUMBER
180 REM    N$....NAME
190                                                               REM
200 REM ***** DATA TO BE PROCESSED *****
210                                                               REM
220 DATA 714, "749-2138", "SAM HORN"
230 DATA 213, "663-1271", "SUE NUNN"
240 DATA 212, "999-1193", "BOB PELE"
250 DATA 312, "979-4418", "ANN SITZ"
260 DATA 999, "999-9999", "END OF FILE"
270                                                               REM
280 REM ***** PROCESSING *****
290                                                               REM
300 READ A, T$, N$
310                                                               REM
320 WHILE N$<> "END OF FILE"
330   PRINT N$, A, T$
340   READ A, T$, N$
350 WEND
360                                                               REM
370 PRINT " "
380 PRINT "END OF TELEPHONE LISTING"
390 END
```

comments

PROGRAM MAINTENANCE

Program maintenance includes all changes to a program once it is implemented and processing real transactions. Sometimes maintenance is required to correct errors that were not found during the testing step. Other times, maintenance is required to make changes that are the result of the user's new information requirements. It may surprise you to learn that the majority of all business programming today consists of maintaining existing programs, not writing new programs.

Because so much time is spent on maintenance programming, it should be subject to the same policies and procedures, such as design, testing, and documentation, that are required for new programs. Unfortunately, this is not always the case. Because maintenance tasks are usually shorter than new programming efforts, they often aren't held to the same standards. The result is that over time, programs can become unrecognizable when compared with their original documentation. Maintaining high standards for program maintenance can not only lower overall programming costs, but also lengthen the useful life of a program.

SUMMARY OF PROGRAM DEVELOPMENT

The key to developing quality programs for an information system is to follow the steps of the program development process. Program specifications must be carefully reviewed and understood. Structured concepts should be used to design programs that are modular, use the three control structures, and follow the single entry/single exit rule. The program should be carefully coded and tested. Documentation should be finalized. If each of these steps is followed, quality programs will be developed that are correct and that can be easily read, understood, and maintained.

WHAT IS A PROGRAMMING LANGUAGE?

As mentioned at the beginning of this chapter, computer programs can be written in a variety of programming languages. People communicate with one another through language, established patterns of words and sounds. A similar definition can also be applied to a **programming language**, which is a set of written words and symbols that allow the programmer or user to communicate with the computer. Just like English, Spanish, Chinese, or other spoken languages, programming languages have rules, called syntax, that govern their use.

CATEGORIES OF PROGRAMMING LANGUAGES

There are hundreds of programming languages, each with its own syntax. Some languages were developed for specific computers and others, because of their success, have been standardized and adapted to a wide range of computers. Programming languages can be classified into one of four categories: machine language, assembly language, high-level languages, and fourth-generation languages.

Machine Language

A **machine language** is the fundamental language of the computer's processor. Programs written in all other categories of languages are eventually converted into machine language before they are executed. Individual machine language instructions exist for each of the commands in the computer's instruction set, the operations such as add, move, or read that are specific to each computer. Because the instruction set is unique for a particular processor, machine languages are different for computers that have different processors. The advantage of writing a program in machine language is that the programmer can control the computer directly and accomplish exactly what needs to be done. Therefore, well-written machine language programs are very efficient. The disadvantages of machine language programs are that they take a long time to write and they are difficult to review if the programmer is trying to find an error. In addition, because they are written using the instruction set of a particular processor, the programs will only run on computers with the same type of processor. Because they are written for specific processors, machine languages are also called **low-level languages**. Figure 13-14a shows an example of machine language instructions.

FIGURE 13-14
This chart shows program instructions for: (a) machine language (printed in a hexadecimal form); (b) assembly language; and (c) a high-level language called C. The machine language and assembly language instructions shown in this example correspond to the high-level instructions and were generated when the high-level language statements were translated into machine language.

(a) Machine Language	(b) Assembly Language	(c) High-level Language
9b df 46 0c 9b d9 c0 9b db 7e f2 9b d9 46 04 9b d8 c9 9b d9 5e fc	fild WORD PTR [bp+12];qty fld ST(0) fstp TBYTE PTR [bp-14] fld DWORD PTR [bp+4];price fmul ST(0),ST(1) fstp DWORD PTR [bp-4];gross	gross = qty * price;
9b d9 c0 9b dc 16 ac 00 9b dd d8 9b dd 7e f0 90 9b 8a 66 f1 9e 9b dd c0 76 19	fld ST(0) fcom QWORD PTR $T20002 fstp ST(0) fstsw WORD PTR [bp-16] fwait mov ah,BYTE PTR [bp-15] sahf ffreeST(0) jbe $I193	if (qty > ceiling)
9b d9 46 fc 9b d9 46 fc 9b dc 0e b4 00 9b de e9 9b d9 5e 08 90 9b	fld DWORD PTR [bp-4];gross fld DWORD PTR [bp-4];gross fmul QWORD PTR $T20003 fsub fstp DWORD PTR [bp+8];net fwait	net = gross - (gross * discount_rate);
eb 0d 90	jmp SHORT $I194 nop $I193:	else
8b 46 fc 8b 56 fe 89 46 08 89 56 0a	mov ax,WORD PTR [bp-4];gross mov dx,WORD PTR [bp-2] mov WORD PTR [bp+8],ax ;net mov WORD PTR [bp+10],dx $I194:	net = gross;

Assembly Language

To make it easier for programmers to remember the specific machine instruction codes, assembly languages were developed. An **assembly language** is similar to a machine language, but uses abbreviations called **mnemonics** or **symbolic operation code** to represent the machine operation code. Another difference is that assembly languages usually allow **symbolic addressing**, which means that a specific computer memory location can be referenced by a name or symbol, such as TOTAL, instead of by its actual address as it would have to be referenced in machine language. Assembly language programs can also include **macroinstructions** that generate more than one machine language instruction. Assembly language programs are converted into machine language instructions by a special program called an **assembler**. Even though assembly languages are easier to use than machine languages, they are still considered a low-level language because they are so closely related to the specific design of the computer. Figure 13-14b shows an example of assembly language instructions.

High-Level Languages

The evolution of computer languages continued with the development of high-level languages in the late 1950s and 1960s. **High-level languages** more closely resemble what most people would think of as a language in that they contain nouns, verbs, and mathematical, relational, and logical operators that can be grouped together to form what appear to be sentences (Figure 13-14c). These sentences are called **program statements**. Because of these characteristics, high-level languages can be "read" by programmers and are thus easier to learn and use than machine or assembly languages. Another important advantage over low-level languages is that high-level languages are usually machine independent, which means they can run on different types of computers.

As mentioned previously, all languages must be translated into machine language before they can instruct the computer to perform processing. High-level languages are translated in one of two ways: with a compiler or an interpreter.

A **compiler** converts an entire program into machine language that is usually stored on a disk for later execution. The program to be converted is called the **source program** and the machine language produced is called the **object program** or **object code**. Compilers check the program syntax, perform limited logic checking, and make sure that data that is going to be used in comparisons or calculations, such as a discount rate, is properly defined somewhere in the program. An important feature of compilers is that they produce an error listing of all program statements that do not meet the program language rules. This listing helps the programmer make the necessary changes to correct the program. Figure 13-15 illustrates the process of compiling a program.

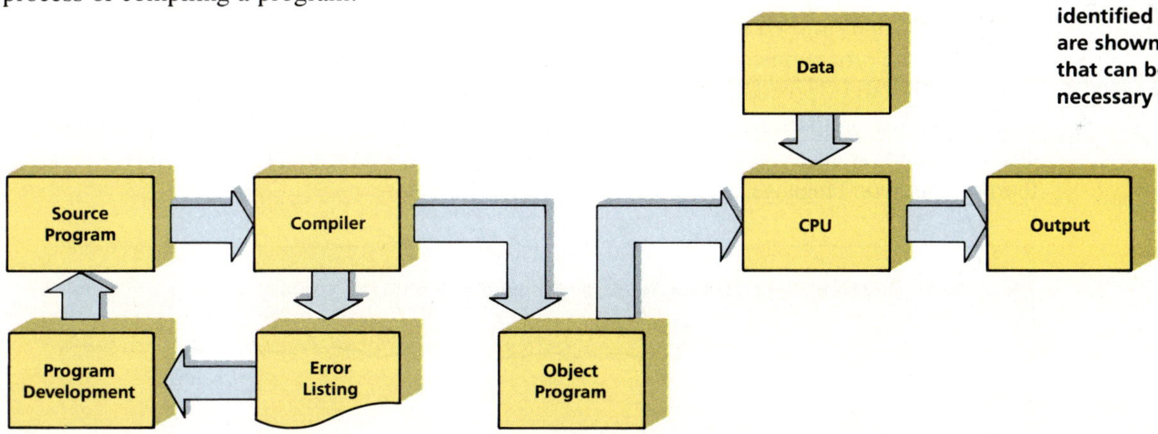

FIGURE 13-15
When a compiler is used, a source language program is compiled into a machine language object program. Usually, both the source and object programs are stored on disk. When the user wants to run the program, the object program is loaded into the main memory of the CPU and the program instructions begin executing. Errors in the source program identified during compilation are shown on an error listing that can be used to make the necessary corrections.

Because machine language is unique to each processor, different computers require different compilers for the same language. For example, a mainframe, minicomputer, and personal computer would each have different compilers that would translate the same source language program into the specific machine language for each computer.

While a compiler translates an entire program, an **interpreter** translates one program statement at a time and then executes the resulting machine language before translating the next program statement. When using an interpreter, each time the program is run, the source program is interpreted into machine language and executed. No object program is produced. Figure 13-16 illustrates this process.

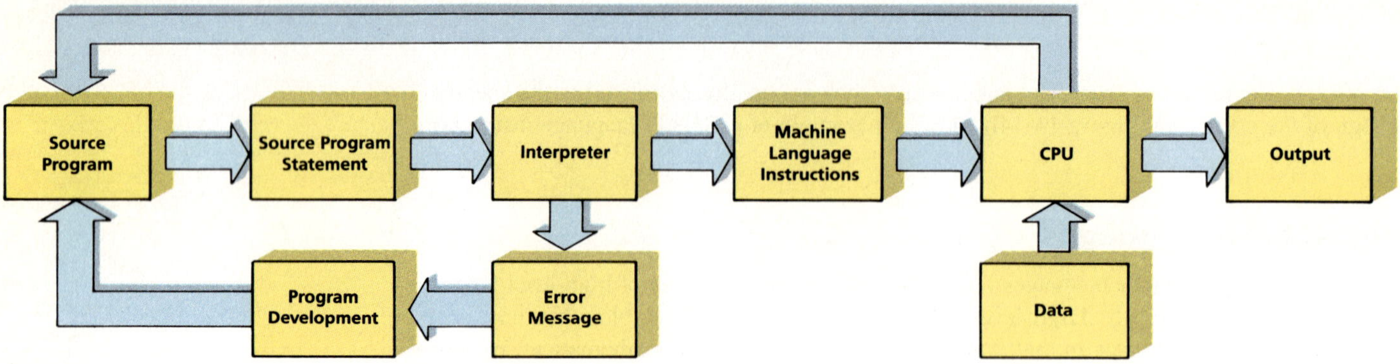

FIGURE 13-16
When an interpreter is used, one source language statement at a time is interpreted into machine language instructions that are executed immediately. Error messages indicating an invalid source language statement are produced as each source program statement is interpreted.

Interpreters are often used with personal computers that do not have the memory or computing power required by compilers. The advantage of interpreters is that the compiling process is not necessary before program changes can be tested. The disadvantage of interpreters is that interpreted programs do not run as fast as compiled programs because the translation to machine language occurs each time the program is run. Compilers for most high-level languages are now available for the newer and more powerful personal computers.

Fourth-Generation Languages

The evolution of computer languages is sometimes described in terms of "generations" with machine, assembly, and high-level languages considered the first, second, and third generations, respectively. Each generation offered significant improvements in ease of use and programming flexibility over the previous generation. Although a clear definition doesn't yet exist, **fourth-generation languages (4GLs)**, sometimes called **very high-level languages**, continue the programming language evolution by being even easier to use than high-level languages for both the programmer and the nonprogramming user.

A common term used to describe fourth-generation languages is **nonprocedural**, which means that the programmer does not specify the procedures to be used to accomplish a task as is done with lower "procedural" language generations. Instead of telling the computer *how* to do the task, the programmer tells the computer *what* is to be done, usually by describing the desired output. A database query language (Figure 13-17) is an example of a nonprocedural fourth-generation language.

FIGURE 13-17
This database query is considered an example of a fourth-generation language because it tells the computer what the user wants, not how to perform the processing.

```
LIST CUSTOMERS CUSTOMER.NAME WITH BALANCE.DUE > '1000'
```

The advantage of fourth-generation languages is that they are "results" oriented ("what" is to be done, not "how") and they can be used by nonprogramming personnel such as users. The disadvantage of fourth-generation languages is that they do not provide as many processing options to the programmer nor are they as efficient as other language generations. Most experts, however, believe that their ease of use far outweighs these disadvantages and predict that fourth-generation languages will continue to be more widely used.

An extension of fourth-generation languages, sometimes called the fifth generation, is a natural language. A **natural language** is a type of query language that allows the user to enter a question as if the user were speaking to another person. For example, a fourth-generation query might be stated as LIST SALESPERSON TOTAL-SALES BY REGION. A natural language version of that same query might be TELL ME THE NAME OF EACH SALESPERSON AND THE TOTAL SALES FOR EACH REGION. The natural language allows the user more flexibility in the structure of the query and can even ask the user a question if it does not understand what is meant by the initial query statement.

PROGRAMMING LANGUAGES USED TODAY

Although there are hundreds of programming languages, only a few are used extensively enough to be recognized as industry standards. Most of these are high-level programming languages that can be used on a variety of computers. This section discusses the popular programming languages that are commonly used, their origins, and their primary purpose.

To help you understand the differences, we show program code for each of the most popular languages. The code is from programs that solve the same problem, the computation of the net sale price using a discount if the gross sale is over $100.00.

BASIC

BASIC, which stands for **B**eginner's **A**ll-purpose **S**ymbolic **I**nstruction **C**ode, was developed by John Kemeny and Thomas Kurtz in 1964 at Dartmouth College (Figure 13-18). Originally designed to be a simple, interactive programming language for college students to learn and use, BASIC has become one of the most commonly used programming languages on microcomputers and minicomputers.

```
5010 REM *****************P R O C E S S    A N D    D I S P L A Y********
5040 GROSS = QTY * SLSPR
5050 IF QTY > CEILING THEN NET = GROSS - (GROSS * DISC) ELSE NET = GROSS
5070 PRINT "THE NET SALES IS $";
5080 PRINT USING "$$#,###.##"; NET
5090 RETURN
```

FIGURE 13-18
An excerpt from a BASIC program.

COBOL

COBOL (**CO**mmon **B**usiness **O**riented **L**anguage) was introduced in 1960. Backed by the Department of Defense, COBOL was developed by a committee of representatives from both government and industry. Rear Admiral Grace M. Hopper was a key person on the committee and is recognized as one of the prime developers of the COBOL language. COBOL is one of the most widely used programming languages for business applications (Figure 13-19). Using an English-like format, COBOL instructions are arranged in "sentences" and grouped into "paragraphs." The English format makes COBOL easy to write and read, but also makes it a wordy language that produces lengthy program code. COBOL is very good for processing large files and performing relatively simple business computations. Other languages are stronger at performing complex mathematical formulas and functions.

```
016200 C010-PROCESS-AND-DISPLAY.
016400*****************************************************************
016600* FUNCTION:                              CALCULATE NET SALES AMOUNT     *
016700*                                        AND DISPLAY RESULTS            *
016800* ENTRY/EXIT:                            B000-LOOP-CONTROL              *
016900* CALLS:                                 NONE                           *
017100*****************************************************************
017300     COMPUTE GROSS-SALES-WRK = QUANTITY-SOLD-WRK * SALES-PRICE-WRK.
017500     IF QUANTITY-SOLD-WRK IS GREATER THAN CEILING
017600         COMPUTE NET-SALES-WRK = GROSS-SALES-WRK -
017700              (GROSS-SALES-WRK * DISCOUNT-RATE)
017800     ELSE
017900         MOVE GROSS-SALES-WRK TO NET-SALES-WRK.
018100     MOVE NET-SALES-WRK TO NET-SALES-OUTPUT.
018300      DISPLAY CLEAR-SCREEN.
018500     WRITE PRINT-LINE FROM DETAIL-LINE
018600          AFTER ADVANCING 2.
```

FIGURE 13-19
An excerpt from a COBOL program.

C

The **C** programming language was developed at Bell Laboratories in 1972 by Dennis Ritchie (Figure 13-20). Originally designed as a programming language for writing systems software, it is now considered a general-purpose programming language. C is a powerful programming language that requires professional programming skills to be used effectively. The use of C to develop various types of software on microcomputers and minicomputers is increasing.

FIGURE 13-20
An excerpt from a C program.

```
float gross;
gross = qty * price;
if (qty > ceiling)
    net = gross - (gross * discount_rate);
else
    net = gross;
return(net);
```

FORTRAN

FORTRAN (**FOR**mula **TRAN**slator), developed by IBM and released in 1957, was designed as a programming language to be used by scientists, engineers, and mathematicians (Figure 13-21). The language is noted for its ability to easily express and efficiently calculate mathematical equations.

FIGURE 13-21
An excerpt from a FORTRAN program.

```
67.000          SUBROUTINE CALC(QTY,SALES,DISC,MAX,GROSS,NET)
68.000          REAL SALES, DISC, MAX, GROSS, NET
69.000          INTEGER QTY
70.000          GROSS = QTY * SALES
71.000          IF(QTY .GT. MAX) THEN
72.000    1        NET = GROSS - (GROSS * DISC)
73.000    1     ELSE
74.000    1        NET = GROSS
75.000    1     ENDIF
76.000          PRINT *, "    "
77.000          RETURN
```

Pascal

The **Pascal** language was developed by Niklaus Wirth, a computer scientist at the Institut fur Informatik in Zurich, Switzerland, in 1968. The name Pascal is not an abbreviation or acronym, but rather the name of a mathematician, Blaise Pascal (1623–1662), who developed one of the earliest calculating machines. Pascal, available for use on both personal and large computers, was one of the first programming languages that provided statements to encourage the use of structured program design (Figure 13-22).

FIGURE 13-22
An excerpt from a Pascal program.

```
BEGIN                                    (* Begin procedure *)
    GROSS := SALES * QTY;
    IF QTY > CEILING
        THEN NET := GROSS - (GROSS * DISCOUNT_RATE)
        ELSE NET := GROSS;
    WRITELN('THE NET SALES IS $',NET:6:2);
END;                                     (* End of procedure *)
```

Ada

The programming language **Ada** is named for Augusta Ada Byron, Countess of Lovelace, a mathematician in the 1800s, who is thought to have written the first program. Introduced in 1980, the development of Ada was supported by the Department of Defense. Ada was designed to facilitate the writing and maintenance of large programs that would be used over a long period of time. The language encourages coding of readable programs that are also portable, allowing them to be transferred from computer to computer (Figure 13-23).

```
GROSS_SALES_PRICE := FLOAT(QUANTITY * SALES_PRICE);
if GROSS_SALES_PRICE > 100.0 then
    GROSS_SALES_PRICE := GROSS_SALES_PRICE - (GROSS_SALES_PRICE * 0.05);
end if;
```

FIGURE 13-23
An excerpt from an Ada program.

RPG

RPG, which stands for **R**eport **P**rogram **G**enerator, was developed by IBM and introduced in 1964. As the name indicates, this language was primarily designed to allow reports to be generated quickly and easily. Instead of writing a set of instructions as in other languages, in RPG special forms are filled out that describe the desired report (Figure 13-24). With a minimum of training, a user can be taught to fill out the forms, enter the information into the computer, and produce the desired reports without having to design and develop a computer program.

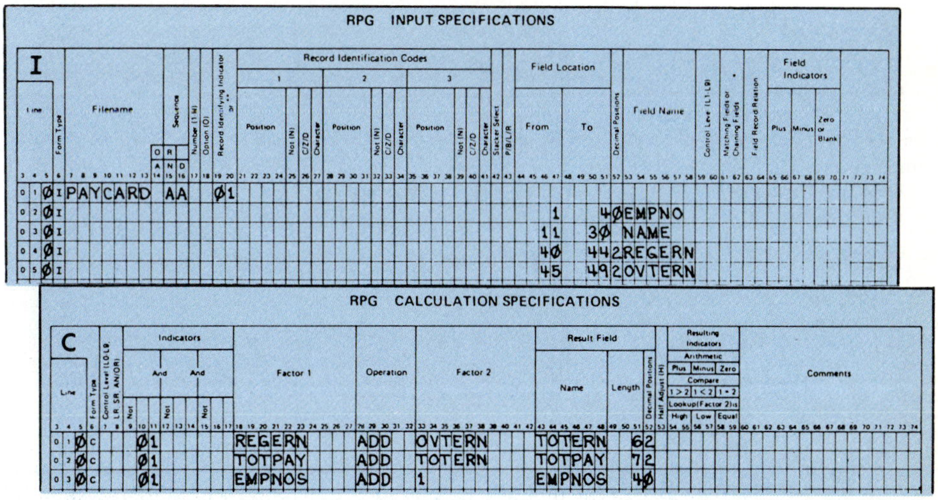

FIGURE 13-24
Special forms help the RPG programmer to quickly specify the input, calculation, and output requirements of a program. The input and calculation forms are shown in this illustration.

Other Popular Programming Languages

In addition to the commonly used programming languages just discussed, there are several other popular languages. Figure 13-25 lists some of these languages and their primary uses.

Language	Description
ALGOL	ALGOrithmetic Language. Structured programming language used for scientific and mathematical applications.
APL	A Programming Language. A powerful, easy to learn language that is good for processing data stored in a table (matrix) format.
FORTH	Similar to C. Creates fast and efficient program code. Originally developed to control astronomical telescopes.
LISP	LISt Processing. Popular artificial intelligence language.
LOGO	Primarily known as an educational tool to teach problem-solving skills.
MODULA-2	Similar to Pascal. Used primarily for developing systems software.
PILOT	Programmed Inquiry Learning Or Teaching. Used by educators to write computer-aided instruction programs.
PL/1	Programming Language/One. Business and scientific language that combines many of the features of FORTRAN and COBOL.
PROLOG	PROgramming in LOGic. Used for artificial intelligence.

FIGURE 13-25
Other popular computer languages.

APPLICATION GENERATORS

Application generators, also called **program generators**, are programs that produce source language programs, such as BASIC or COBOL, based on input, output, and processing specifications entered by the user. Application generators can greatly reduce the amount of time required to develop a program. They are based on the fact that most programs are comprised of standard processing modules, such as routines to read, write, or compare records, that can be combined together to create unique programs. These standard processing modules are stored in a library and are selected and grouped together based on user specifications. Application generators often use menu and screen generators to assist in developing an application.

A **menu generator** lets the user specify a menu (list) of processing options that can be selected. The resulting menu is automatically formatted with heading, footing, and prompt line text (Figure 13-26).

FIGURE 13-26
The screen on the left is part of a menu generator from Oracle Corporation that can be used to quickly create professional-looking menus, as shown in the screen on the right.

A **screen generator**, sometimes called a **screen painter**, allows the user to design an input or output screen by entering the names and descriptions of the input and output data directly on the screen. The advantage is that the user enters the data exactly as it will appear after the program is created. As each data name, such as Order No., is entered, the screen generator asks the user to specify the length and type of data that will be entered and what processing, if any, should take place before or after the data is entered. The order entry screen shown in Figure 13-27 was created in just one hour using SQL*FORMS, a screen generator product from ORACLE Corporation.

FIGURE 13-27
This order entry screen and the program to process the data were created in just one hour using a screen generator from Oracle Corporation. Using the traditional programming technique of writing individual program instructions would have taken considerably longer.

HOW TO CHOOSE A PROGRAMMING LANGUAGE

Although each programming language has its own unique characteristics, selecting a language for a programming task can be a difficult decision. Following are some of the factors that should be considered in making a choice:

- The programming standards of the organization. Many organizations have programming standards that specify that a particular language is used for all applications.
- The need to interface with other programs. If a program is going to work with other existing or future programs, ideally it should be programmed in the same language as the other programs.
- The suitability of a language to the application to be programmed. As we discussed, most languages are best suited to a particular type of application. For example, FORTRAN works well with applications requiring many calculations.
- The expertise of the available programmers. Unless another language is far superior, the language used by the existing programmers probably should be chosen.
- The availability of the language. Not all languages are available on all machines.
- The need for the application to be portable. If the application will have to run on different machines, a common language should be chosen so the program only has to be written once.
- The anticipated maintenance requirements. If the user anticipates that the application will have to be modified frequently, a language that can be maintained easily and that supports structured programming concepts should be considered.

SUMMARY OF PROGRAMMING LANGUAGES

Although procedural languages such as COBOL and BASIC will continue to be used for many years, there is a clear trend toward the creation of programs using nonprocedural tools, such as fourth-generation and natural languages, that allow users to specify what they want accomplished. Your knowledge of programming languages will help you to better understand the process that takes place when the computer converts data into information and to obtain better results if you directly participate in the programming process.

CHAPTER SUMMARY

1. A **computer program** is a detailed set of instructions that directs a computer to perform the tasks necessary to process data into information.
2. **Program development** is a series of five steps that take place when a computer program is developed.
3. The five steps in program development are: (1) review of the program specifications; (2) program design; (3) program coding; (4) program testing; and (5) finalizing the documentation.
4. **Program specifications** can include many documents such as data flow diagrams, system flowcharts, process specifications, a data dictionary, screen formats, and report layouts.
5. During **program design** a logical solution or **logic** for a program is developed and documented.
6. **Structured program design** is methodology that emphasizes three main program design concepts: modules, control structures, and single entry/single exit.
7. **Modules** or **subroutines**, which perform a given task within a program, can be developed individually and then combined to form a complete program.
8. **Structure charts** or **hierarchy charts** are used to decompose the modules of a program.
9. The three **control structures** are: **sequence** where one process occurs immediately after another; **selection** or **if-then-else**, which is used for conditional program logic; and **iteration** which is used for **looping**.
10. The two forms of iteration are the **do-while structure** and the **do-until structure**.
11. **Single entry/single exit** means that there is only one **entry point** and one **exit point** from each of the control structures.
12. Three commonly used program design tools are **program flowcharts**, **pseudocode**, and **Warnier-Orr**.
13. Structured walkthroughs are used to review the design and logic of a program.
14. **Coding** is the process of writing the program instructions.
15. Before a program is used to process "real" data it should be thoroughly tested to make sure it is functioning correctly. A simple type of testing is **desk checking**.
16. Programs can be tested for **syntax errors** (grammar). **Logic testing** checks for incorrect results using **test data**.
17. **Debugging** refers to the process of locating and correcting program errors or **bugs** found during testing.
18. **Program maintenance** includes all changes to a program once it is implemented and processing real transactions.
19. A **programming language** is a set of written words and symbols that allow a programmer or user to communicate with the computer.
20. Programming languages fit into one of four categories: machine language; assembly language; high-level languages; and fourth-generation languages.
21. Before they can be executed, all programs are converted into **machine language**, the fundamental language of computers, also called **low-level language**.
22. **Assembly language** is a low-level language that is closely related to machine language. It uses **mnemonics** or **symbolic operation code**.
23. Assembly languages use **symbolic addressing** and include **macroinstructions**. Assembly language programs are converted into machine language instructions by an **assembler**.
24. **High-level languages** are easier to learn and use than low-level languages. They use sentences called **program statements**.
25. **Compilers** and **interpreters** are used to translate high-level **source programs** into machine language **object code** or **object programs**.
26. **Fourth-generation languages**, also called **very high-level languages**, are **nonprocedural**, which means that the user tells the computer "what" is to be done, not "how" to do it.
27. A **natural language** allows the user to enter a question as if the user were speaking to another person.
28. Commonly used programming languages include **BASIC**, **COBOL**, **C**, **FORTRAN**, **Pascal**, **Ada**, and **RPG**.
29. **BASIC** is one of the most commonly used programming languages on microcomputers and minicomputers.
30. **COBOL** is the most widely used programming language for business applications.
31. **C** is an increasingly popular programming language that requires professional programming skills to be used effectively.
32. **FORTRAN** is noted for its ability to easily express and efficiently calculate mathematical equations.

33. **Pascal** contains programming statements that encourage the use of structured program design.
34. **Ada**, developed and supported by the Department of Defense, was designed to facilitate the writing and maintenance of large programs that would be used over a long period of time.
35. **RPG** was primarily designed to generate reports quickly and easily.
36. **Application generators** or **program generators** produce source language programs based on input, output, and processing specifications entered by the user.
37. A **menu generator** lets the user specify a menu of options.
38. A **screen generator** or **screen printer** allows the user to design an input or output screen.
39. Some of the factors that should be considered when choosing a programming language are: the programming standards of the organization; the need to interface with other programs; the suitability of a language to the application to be programmed; the expertise of the available programmers; the availability of the language; the need for the application to be portable; and the anticipated maintenance requirements.

KEY TERMS

Ada *13.17*
Application generators *13.18*
Assembler *13.12*
Assembly language *13.12*
BASIC *13.15*
Bugs *13.10*
C *13.16*
COBOL *13.15*
Coding *13.9*
Compiler *13.13*
Computer program *13.2*
Control structures *13.4*
Debugging *13.10*
Desk checking *13.9*
Do-until structure *13.5*
Do-while structure *13.5*
Entry point *13.6*
Exit point *13.6*
FORTRAN *13.16*
Fourth-generation language (4GL) *13.14*
Hierarchy charts *13.4*
High-level languages *13.13*
If-then-else structure *13.5*
Interpreter *13.13*
Iteration *13.5*
Logic *13.4*
Logic testing *13.9*
Looping *13.5*
Low-level language *13.12*
Machine language *13.12*
Macroinstruction *13.12*
Menu generator *13.18*
Mnemonics *13.12*
Module *13.4*
Natural language *13.14*
Nonprocedural *13.14*
Object code *13.13*
Object program *13.13*
Pascal *13.16*
Program design *13.4*
Program development *13.3*
Program flowchart *13.6*
Program generators *13.18*
Program maintenance *13.11*
Programming language *13.11*
Program specifications *13.3*
Program statements *13.13*
Pseudocode *13.8*
RPG (Report Program Generator) *13.17*
Screen generator *13.18*
Screen painter *13.18*
Selection structure *13.5*
Sequence structure *13.4*
Single entry/single exit *13.6*
Source program *13.13*
Structure charts *13.4*
Structured program design *13.4*
Subroutine *13.4*
Symbolic addressing *13.12*
Symbolic operation code *13.12*
Syntax errors *13.9*
Test data *13.9*
Very high-level languages *13.14*
Warnier-Orr *13.8*

REVIEW QUESTIONS

1. What is a computer program?
2. List the five steps in program development and give a brief description of each step.
3. What is the purpose of reviewing the program specifications? List at least four types of documents that may be included in the program specifications.
4. Draw the three control structures used in structured program design.

5. Briefly describe three types of program design tools that are used by programmers.
6. What is the difference between a syntax error and a logic error?
7. Describe the four categories of programming languages.
8. Explain how a compiler and an interpreter work. What is a source program? What is an object program?
9. Why are high-level languages referred to as machine-independent languages?
10. List five commonly used programming languages and explain their primary uses.
11. How do application generators reduce the amount of time required to program?
12. List seven factors that should be considered when choosing a programming language.

CONTROVERSIAL ISSUE

1. Computer literacy is defined in different ways. Some people believe that to be computer literate a person should learn a programming language and have experience programming a computer. Other people believe that programming knowledge is inappropriate for the general user and should be reserved for those who plan to become computer professionals. What do you think?

RESEARCH PROJECT

1. Review the employment advertisements in your local newspaper for computer programming positions. Prepare a report discussing which programming languages are in demand.

CHAPTER 14

Career Opportunities in the Age of Information Processing

CHAPTER 14

Career Opportunities in the Age of Information Processing

OBJECTIVES

- Discuss the three areas that provide the majority of computer related jobs.
- Describe the career positions available in an information systems department.
- Describe information processing career opportunities in sales, service and repair, consulting, and education and training.
- Discuss the compensation and growth trends for information processing careers.
- Discuss the three fields in the information processing industry.
- Discuss career development, including professional organizations, certification, and professional growth and continuing education.

In discussing career opportunities and computers, it's difficult to decide what to exclude. As society becomes more information oriented, computers are becoming an integral part of most jobs. For this reason, the knowledge you have gained from this text will apply in some way to any career you choose. Some of you, however, may want to consider a career in the information processing industry itself. The purpose of this chapter is to show you the opportunities that exist in the industry, present computer industry career trends, and discuss how to prepare for a career in information systems. Even if you don't choose a computer industry career, it is important to have an understanding of them, as it is likely that any job you choose will at some time provide contact with one or more computer industry representatives.

THE INFORMATION PROCESSING INDUSTRY

The information processing industry is one of the largest industries in the world with annual sales of well over $100 billion. Job opportunities in the industry come primarily from three areas: the companies that provide the computer equipment; the companies that develop computer software; and the companies that hire information processing professionals to work with these products. As in any major industry, there is also a large group of service companies that support each of these three areas. An example would be a company that sells computer supplies such as printer paper and disks.

The Computer Equipment Industry

The computer equipment or hardware industry includes all manufacturers and distributors of computers and computer-related equipment such as disk and tape drives, terminals, printers, and communication equipment (Figure 14-1). The five largest mini and mainframe computer manufacturers in the United States, IBM, Digital Equipment Corporation, UNISYS, Hewlett-Packard, and NCR, are huge organizations with tens of thousands of employees worldwide. Major microcomputer manufacturers include IBM, Apple, Compaq, and Tandy. The largest company, IBM, has had annual sales of over $54 billion. In addition to the major companies, the computer equipment industry is also known for the many new "start-up" companies that appear each year. These new companies take advantage of rapid changes in equipment technology, such as laser printers, video disks, and fiber optics, to create new products and new job opportunities. Besides the companies that make end user equipment, thousands of companies make components that most users never see. These companies manufacture chips (processor, memory, etc.), power supplies, wiring, and the hundreds of other parts that go into computer equipment.

FIGURE 14-1
This photo shows newly manufactured computer keyboards being tested before shipping.

The Computer Software Industry

The computer software industry includes all developers and distributors of application and system software. In the early days, computer software was almost exclusively produced by the computer manufacturers. However, during the 1960s, numerous companies began producing software to compete with that offered by manufacturers. Today, thousands of companies provide a wide range of software from operating systems to complete business systems. The personal computer boom in the early 1980s provided numerous opportunities in the software industry. Thousands of individuals went into business for themselves by creating useful programs for the new microcomputers. Many of these people started by working out of their homes, developing their first software products on their own time while holding other jobs.

Today, software alone is a huge industry whose leaders include companies such as MSA, ASK, Microsoft, Lotus, and Ashton-Tate, with annual sales in the hundreds of millions of dollars. Most of these companies specialize in one particular type of software product such as business application software or productivity tools like word processing or spreadsheets.

FIGURE 14-2
Computer professionals must be able to understand the end user's point of view and often meet with the user to review information processing requirements.

Information Processing Professionals

Information processing professionals are the people that put the equipment and software to work to produce information for the end user (Figure 14-2). This includes people such as programmers and systems analysts who are hired by companies to work in an information systems department. These and other positions available in the information processing industry will be discussed in the next section.

WHAT ARE THE CAREER OPPORTUNITIES IN INFORMATION PROCESSING?

The use of computers in so many aspects of life has created thousands of new jobs. Some of these occupations, such as personal computer software sales representative, didn't even exist ten years ago. The following section describes some of the career opportunities that currently exist.

Working in an Information Systems Department

In Chapter 1 we discussed the various types of career positions that exist within an information systems department. These positions include: data entry personnel, computer operators, computer programmers, systems analysts, database administrator, manager of information systems, and vice president of information systems.

The people in these positions work together as a team to meet the information demands of their organizations. Throughout this book, the responsibilities associated with many of these positions were discussed, including the role of the systems analysts in the information system development life cycle (Chapter 12) and the steps programmers perform in program development (Chapter 13). Another way to visualize the positions and their relationships is to look at an organization chart such as the one shown in Figure 14-3. In addition to management, the jobs in an information systems department can be classified into five categories:

1. Operations
2. Data administration
3. Systems analysis and design
4. Programming
5. Information center

Operations personnel are responsible for carrying out tasks such as operating the computer equipment that is located in the computer center. The primary responsibility of data administration is the maintenance and control of an organization's database. In systems analysis and design the various information systems needed by an organization are created and maintained. Programming develops the programs needed for the information systems, and the information center provides teaching and consulting services within an organization to help users meet their departmental and individual information processing needs. As you can see, an information systems department provides career opportunities for people with a variety of skills and talents.

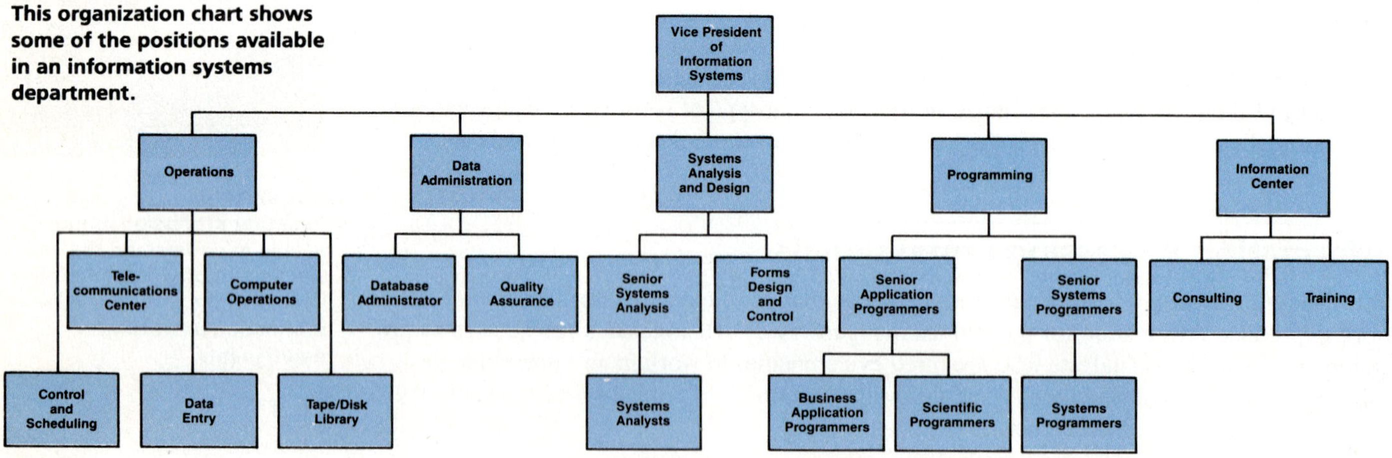

FIGURE 14-3
This organization chart shows some of the positions available in an information systems department.

Sales

Sales representatives must have a general knowledge of computers and a specific understanding of the product they are selling. Strong interpersonal or "people" skills are important, including the ability to listen and the ability to communicate effectively both verbally and in writing. Sales representatives are usually paid based on the amount of product they sell, and top sales representatives are often the most highly compensated employees in a computer company.

FIGURE 14-4
Computer retailers, such as Computerland, need salespeople who understand personal computers and have good "people" skills.

Some sales representatives work directly for equipment and software manufacturers and others work for resellers. Most personal computer products are sold through dealers such as Computerland or Businessland (Figure 14-4). Some dealers, such as Egghead Discount Software, specialize in selling the most popular software products.

Service and Repair

Being a **service and repair technician** is a challenging job for persons who like to troubleshoot and solve problems and who have a strong background in electronics (Figure 14-5). In the early days of computers, repairs were often made at the site of the computer equipment. Today, however, malfunctioning components, such as circuit boards, are usually replaced and taken back to the service technician's office or sent to a special facility for repair. Many equipment manufacturers are now including special diagnostic software with their computer equipment that helps the service technician identify the problem. Using a modem, some advanced computer systems can automatically telephone a computer at the service technician's office and leave a message that a malfunction has been detected.

FIGURE 14-5
Computer service and repair is one of the fastest growing computer-related professions. A knowledge of electronics is essential for this occupation.

Consulting

After building experience in one or more areas, some individuals become **consultants**, people who draw upon their experience to give advice to others. Consultants must not only have strong technical skills in their area of expertise, but must also have the people skills to convince their clients to follow their advice. Qualified consultants are in high demand for such tasks as computer system selection, system design, and communication network design and installation.

Education and Training

The increased sophistication and complexity of today's computer products has opened wide opportunities in computer education and training (Figure 14-6). Qualified instructors are needed in schools, colleges, and universities and in private industry as well. In fact, the high demand for teachers has created a shortage at the university level, where many instructors have been lured into private industry because of higher pay. This shortage probably will not be filled in the near future; the supply of Ph.D.s, usually required at the university level, is not keeping up with the demand.

FIGURE 14-6
There is a high demand in schools and industry for qualified instructors who can teach information processing subjects.

COMPENSATION AND GROWTH TRENDS FOR INFORMATION PROCESSING CAREERS

Compensation is a function of experience and demand for a particular skill. Demand is influenced by geographic location, with metropolitan areas usually having higher pay than rural areas where, presumably, the cost of living is lower. Figure 14-7 shows the result of a salary survey of over 70,000 computer professionals across the United States and Canada. These amounts represent an average increase of approximately 7% over the prior year. As shown in Figure 14-8, some industries pay higher than others for the same job position. According to the survey, the communications, utility, and aerospace industries paid the highest salaries. These industries have many challenging applications and are willing to pay the highest rate to obtain the best qualified employees. According to the U.S. Bureau of Labor Statistics, the fastest growing computer career positions between 1982 and 1995 will be systems analyst, applications programmer, machine operator, and computer repair technician (Figure 14-9).

FIGURE 14-7
This table shows salary levels for various computer industry positions based on the number of years of experience. (Source: Source Edp, The Going Rate: 1988 Salaries.)

PROGRAMMING:	YRS. EXP.	20%	MEDIAN	80%
Commercial	<2	19.9	24.3	28.7
	2–3	23.5	28.0	32.5
	4–6	25.8	30.4	35.0
	>6	30.6	36.0	42.5
Engineering/Scientific	<2	23.4	30.0	34.2
	2–3	24.5	30.6	35.5
	4–6	29.6	34.8	40.7
	<6	32.8	40.0	48.4
Microcomputer	<2	18.0	22.0	27.1
	2–3	20.0	25.0	29.8
	4–6	26.1	33.0	38.9
	>6	34.8	43.0	51.6
Minicomputer	<2	19.3	23.2	28.8
	2–3	22.4	27.0	32.9
	4–6	25.4	31.0	37.2
	>6	30.3	37.0	45.9
Software Engineer	<2	23.2	28.6	31.7
	2–3	24.9	29.0	33.6
	4–6	29.1	35.0	40.6
	>6	33.6	41.5	50.2
Systems Software	<2	23.7	27.6	31.5
	2–3	23.5	28.0	31.9
	4–6	26.9	32.0	37.8
	>6	36.1	42.0	50.0
MANAGEMENT:				
Data Center Operations		33.2	40.0	52.0
Programming Development		39.8	48.0	58.1
Software Development		44.0	53.0	64.1
Systems Development		44.8	54.0	65.3
Technical Services		42.5	50.0	61.5
MIS Director		49.2	60.0	76.8
BUSINESS SYSTEMS:				
Consultant	<4	25.4	31.0	37.2
	4–6	30.1	35.0	41.3
	>6	38.7	45.0	53.6
Project Leader	<4	25.8	31.5	37.8
	4–6	30.1	35.0	41.3
	>6	36.1	42.0	50.0

BUSINESS SYSTEMS (Cont.):	YRS. EXP.	20%	MEDIAN	80%
System Analyst	<4	24.0	29.3	35.2
	4–6	28.4	33.0	38.9
	>6	32.7	38.0	45.2
SPECIALISTS:				
Communications Analyst	<4	27.6	32.5	37.4
	4–6	27.3	35.0	44.5
	>6	32.0	41.0	48.8
Database/Management Analyst	<4	20.7	28.0	33.6
	4–6	28.5	33.5	40.5
	>6	34.9	41.5	49.4
Information Center Analyst	<4	20.0	26.0	29.1
	4–6	23.4	30.0	36.0
	>6	30.2	38.2	45.8
Office Automation Analyst	<4	20.0	26.0	29.1
	4–6	25.7	33.0	39.6
	>6	30.5	38.6	46.3
SALES:				
Hardware		30.4	44.0	63.4
Software		26.7	43.8	62.6
Services		28.9	43.1	62.9
Technical Support	<2	18.6	23.2	27.1
	2–3	23.9	29.5	35.1
	4–6	26.6	32.4	39.9
	>6	36.0	45.0	54.0
Management		45.5	61.5	85.5
OTHER:				
Computer Operator	<2	15.2	19.5	21.6
	2–3	16.0	20.0	22.8
	4–6	23.3	28.8	34.3
	>6	26.3	33.7	41.5
Edp Auditor	<4	30.8	35.0	42.0
	4–6	32.5	38.2	48.9
	>6	34.0	40.0	48.4
Technical Writer or Editor	<4	17.2	21.0	24.8
	4–6	27.3	32.5	40.0
	>6	31.2	39.5	47.8

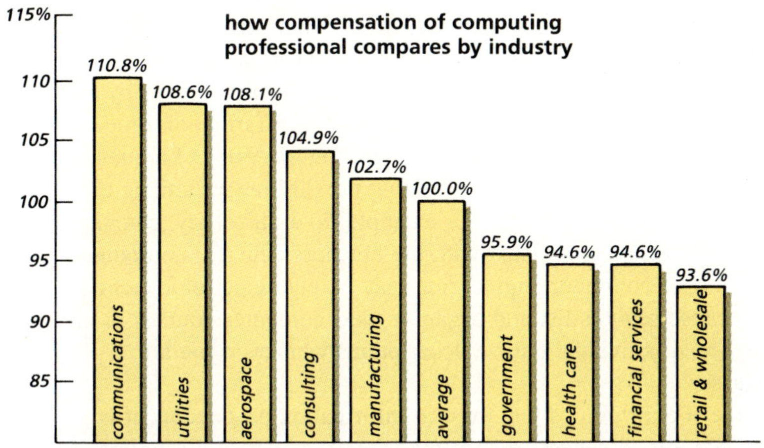

FIGURE 14-8
This chart shows that some industries pay more for the same job position.

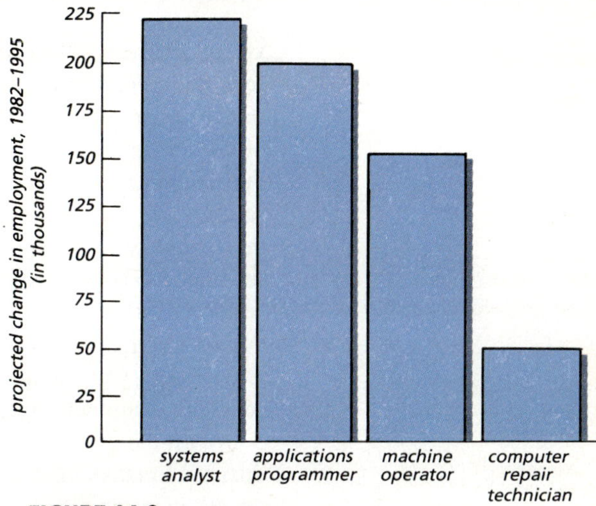

FIGURE 14-9
This chart shows computer careers with the highest projected growth, as compiled by the U.S. Bureau of Labor Statistics.

PREPARING FOR A CAREER IN INFORMATION PROCESSING

To prepare for a career in the information processing industry, individuals must decide what computer field they are interested in and obtain education in the chosen field. This section discusses the three major computer fields and some of the opportunities for obtaining education in those fields.

FIGURE 14-10
There are three broad fields of study in the information processing industry. Each field has specialized study requirements.

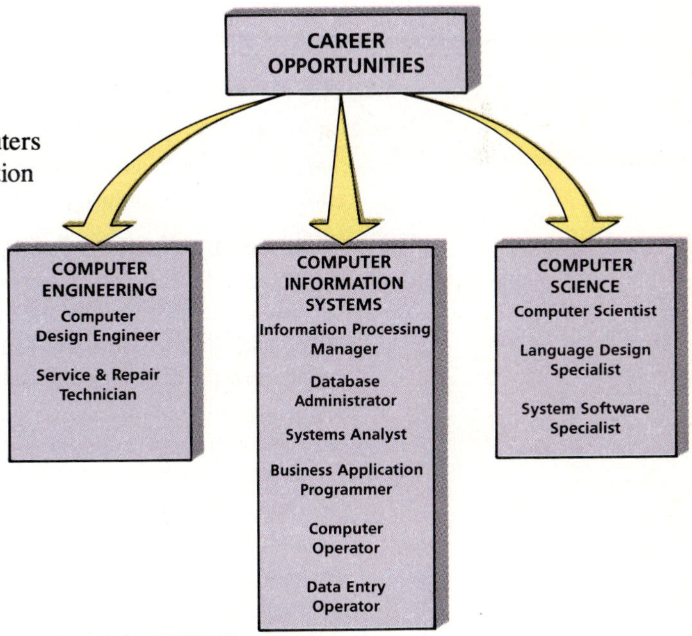

What Are the Fields in the Information Processing Industry?

While this book has primarily focused on the use of computers in business, there are actually three broad fields in the information processing industry (Figure 14-10): computer information systems; computer science; and computer engineering. **Computer information systems (CIS)** refers to the use of computers in areas relating to business. The field of **computer science** includes the technical aspects of computers such as hardware operation and systems software. **Computer engineering** deals with the design and manufacturing of electronic computer components and computer hardware. Each field provides unique career opportunities and has specialized study requirements. Several avenues of study are available to persons interested in obtaining formal education in information processing.

Obtaining Education for Information Processing Careers

The expanded use of computers in today's world has increased the demand for properly trained computer professionals. Educational institutions have responded to this demand by providing a variety of options for students to study information systems. Trade schools, technical schools, community colleges, colleges and universities offer formal education and certification or degree programs in computer-related fields. If you are evaluating a program offered by one of these institutions, it is important that you remember the three areas of information processing: computer information systems, computer science, and computer engineering. Frequently schools will have separate programs for each area. Understanding the differences among the three fields will help you to find the courses you want. For example, in a university, courses relating to computer information systems may be listed with the business courses, computer science courses may be with math, and computer engineering may be with electronic technology or electrical engineering. Because schools list and organize their computer courses in different ways, you should carefully read individual course descriptions whenever you are selecting computer education classes.

With the wide variety of career opportunities that exist in information processing, it is difficult to make anything other than broad general statements when it comes to discussing degree requirements for employment in the industry. As in most other industries, the more advanced degree an individual has in a chosen field, the better that individual's chances are for success. While not having a degree may limit a person's opportunities for securing a top position, it will not prevent entry nor preclude success in information processing.

CAREER DEVELOPMENT IN THE INFORMATION PROCESSING INDUSTRY

There are several ways for persons employed in the information processing industry to develop their skills and increase their recognition among their peers. These include professional organizations, certification, and professional growth and continuing education activities.

Professional Organizations

A number of computer-related organizations have been formed by people who have common interests and a desire to share their knowledge. Some of the organizations that have been influential in the industry include:

- **Association for Computing Machinery (ACM)**. An association composed of persons interested in computer science and computer science education. The association has many special interest groups such as computer graphics, database, and business.
- **Association of Information Systems Professionals**. This association was originally aimed at word processing professionals, but now includes a much broader interest area, including office automation.
- **Association of Systems Management (ASM)**. A group composed of individuals interested in the improvement of the systems analysis and design field.
- **Data Processing Management Association (DPMA)**. A professional association of programmers, systems analysts, and information processing managers.
- **Institute of Electrical and Electronic Engineers (IEEE)** and **IEEE Computer Society**. Organizations primarily composed of computer scientists and engineers.

Each of the above organizations has chapters throughout the United States (several throughout the world), offers monthly meetings, and sponsors periodic workshops, seminars, and conventions. Some organizations have student chapters or offer reduced membership fees for students. Attending professional meetings provide an excellent opportunity for students to learn about the information processing industry and to meet and talk with professionals in the field. In addition to these and other professional organizations, user groups exist for most makes of computers. Most metropolitan areas have one or more local computer societies that meet monthly to discuss topics of common interest about personal computers. For anyone employed or just interested in the computer industry, these groups can be an effective and rewarding way to learn and continue career development.

Certification

Many professions offer certification programs as a way of encouraging and recognizing the efforts of their members to attain a level of knowledge about their profession. The best known certification program in the information processing industry is the **Certificate in Data Processing (CDP)**, originated by DPMA but now administered by the **Institute for the Certification of Computer Professionals (ICCP)**. The CDP (Figure 14-11) is awarded to persons who pass an examination that has five parts: (1) computer equipment; (2) computer programming and software; (3) principles of management; (4) accounting and quantitative methods; and (5) systems analysis and design. To be eligible to take the examination, a person must have a minimum of five years of experience in the information processing industry. People who pass the examination are authorized to place the initials CDP after their name.

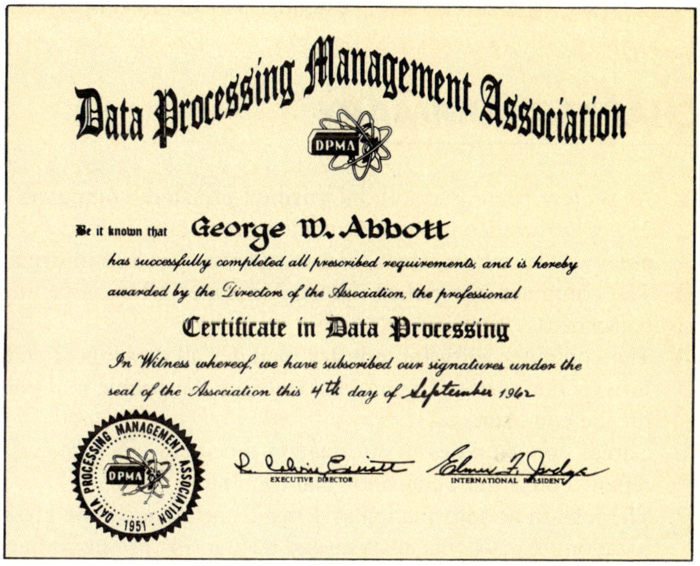

Data Processing Management Association

DPMA

Be it known that George W. Abbott has successfully completed all prescribed requirements and is hereby awarded by the Directors of the Association, the professional

Certificate in Data Processing

In Witness whereof, we have subscribed our signatures under the seal of the Association this 4th day of September 1962

DATA PROCESSING MANAGEMENT ASSOCIATION DPMA 1951

EXECUTIVE DIRECTOR

INTERNATIONAL PRESIDENT

FIGURE 14-11
The Certificate in Data Processing (CDP) recognizes a high level of knowledge that the recipient has demonstrated by passing a five-part examination. This is a copy of the first CDP ever awarded.

Professional Growth and Continuing Education

Because of rapid changes in technology, staying aware of new products and services in the information processing industry can be a challenging task. One way of keeping up is by participating in professional growth and continuing education activities. This broad category includes events such as conferences, workshops, conventions, and trade shows that provide both general and specific information on equipment, software, services, and issues affecting the industry, such as computer security. Workshops and seminars usually last a day or two while conferences, conventions, and trade shows often last a week. Some of the larger trade shows, such as **COMDEX (COMputer Dealer EXposition)**, bring together over a thousand vendors to display their latest products and services (Figure 14-12).

FIGURE 14-12
COMDEX is one of the largest computer product trade shows in the world. Thousands of vendors come together to demonstrate their new equipment, software, and services to prospective customers.

SUMMARY OF COMPUTER CAREER OPPORTUNITIES

With the increased use of computers, the prospects for computer-related career opportunities are excellent. Not only are the numbers of traditional information processing jobs, such as programmer and systems analyst, expected to increase, but the application of the computer to existing occupations will create additional job opportunities. Regardless of an individual's career choice, a basic understanding of computers should be an essential part of any employee's job skills.

CHAPTER SUMMARY

1. As society becomes more information oriented, computers are becoming an integral part of most jobs.
2. Job opportunities in the information processing industry come from three areas: computer equipment companies, computer software companies, and companies that hire information processing professionals.
3. The computer equipment industry includes all manufacturers and distributors of computers and computer-related equipment.
4. The computer software industry includes all developers and distributors of application and system software.
5. Information processing professionals are the people that put the equipment and software to work to produce information for the end user.
6. Career opportunities in information processing include: working in an information systems department; sales; service and repair; consulting; education and training.
7. The jobs in an information systems department can be classified into five categories: (1) operations; (2) data administration; (3) systems analysis and design; (4) programming; and (5) information center.
8. **Sales representatives** are often the most highly compensated employees in a computer company.
9. Being a **service and repair technician** is a challenging job for persons who like to solve problems and who have a strong background in electronics.
10. **Consultants**, people who draw upon their experience to give advice to others, are in high demand for such tasks as computer system selection, system design, and communication network design and installation.
11. According to the U.S. Bureau of Labor and Statistics, the fastest growing computer career positions between 1982 and 1995 will be systems analyst, applications programmer, machine operator, and computer repair technician.
12. The three fields in information processing are computer information systems; computer science; and computer engineering.
13. **Computer information systems** refers to the use of computers in areas relating to business.
14. **Computer science** includes the technical aspects of computers such as hardware operation and systems software.
15. **Computer engineering** deals with the design and manufacturing of electronic computer components and computer hardware.
16. Trade schools, technical schools, community colleges, colleges, and universities offer formal education and certification or degree programs in computer related fields.
17. Computer professionals may continue to develop their skills and increase their recognition among their peers through professional organizations, certification, and professional growth and continuing education activities.
18. Professional organizations, such as the **Data Processing Management Association (DPMA)**, have been formed by people who have common interests and a desire to share their knowledge.
19. The **Certificate in Data Processing (CDP)** is the best known certification program in the information processing industry.
20. Computer professionals stay current by participating in professional growth and continuing education activities such as conferences, workshops, conventions, and trade shows.

KEY TERMS

Association for Computing Machinery (ACM) *14.8*
Association of Information Systems Professionals *14.8*
Association of Systems Management (ASM) *14.8*
Certificate in Data Processing (CDP) *14.9*
COMDEX *14.9*
Computer engineering *14.7*
Computer information systems (CIS) *14.7*
Computer science *14.7*
Consultants *14.5*
Data Processing Management Association (DPMA) *14.8*
Institute for the Certification of Computer Professionals (ICCP) *14.9*
Institute of Electrical and Electronic Engineers (IEEE) *14.8*
Sales representatives *14.5*
Service and repair technician *14.5*

REVIEW QUESTIONS

1. Briefly discuss the computer hardware and software industries.
2. The positions in an information systems department can be classified into what five categories?
3. List and discuss four information career opportunities other than working in an information systems department.
4. What are the four fastest growing computer career positions?
5. Describe the three fields in information processing.
6. List five computer-related professional organizations.
7. What are the five parts of the CDP exam?

CONTROVERSIAL ISSUE

1. Some people believe that computer professions such as programming should be subject to mandatory certification or licensing, like certified public accountants. Others believe that because the industry is changing so rapidly, certification programs should be encouraged but remain voluntary. Discuss the advantages and disadvantages of mandatory programs.

RESEARCH PROJECT

1. Contact one of the professional computer organizations listed in the chapter. Either attend a local meeting or write for membership information and prepare a report for your class.

CHAPTER 15

Trends and Issues in the Information Age

CHAPTER 15

Trends and Issues in the Information Age

OBJECTIVES

- Discuss the electronic devices and applications that are part of the automated office.
- Describe the technologies that are developing for the automated factory, including CAD, CAE, CAM, and CIM.
- Discuss the use of personal computers in the home.
- Explain guidelines for purchasing personal computers.
- Discuss social issues related to computers, such as computer crime and privacy.

After reading the preceding chapters, you know what a computer is, what a computer does, how it does it, and why a computer is so powerful. You have learned about computer equipment and software, and how the system development process is used to combine these elements with data, personnel, users, and procedures to create a working information system. The purpose of this chapter is to talk about current and future trends, including changes taking place in information systems in the workplace. We also discuss the use of personal computers in the home and some of the social issues related to computers, such as security and computer crime, privacy, ethics, and health.

INFORMATION SYSTEMS IN BUSINESS

The largest single user of computers is business. Millions of systems ranging from mainframes to microcomputers are installed and used for applications such as inventory control, billing, and accounting. This section discusses how these traditional applications will be affected by changes in technology and methods. It also discusses two other areas of business applications, the automated office and the automated factory. Although the term automated can be applied to any process or machine that can operate without human intervention, the term is commonly used to describe computer-controlled functions.

How Will Existing Information Systems Change?

Existing business information systems will continue to undergo profound changes as new technology, software, and methods are applied to the huge installed base of traditional business system users. Important overall trends include more online, interactive systems and less batch processing. In addition, the increased use of relational database systems means that users have a wider variety of data and information available for decision making, and more flexibility, presenting information on reports and displays (Figure 15-1).

FIGURE 15-1
Trends that will affect information systems of tomorrow.

EQUIPMENT

- Increased use of personal computers networked to other personal computers and to central mini or mainframe computers.
- Increased storage capacity of disks using improved and new technologies such as laser disks.
- Terminals that can display 132 or more characters per line, as well as graphics and images.
- Faster, better quality printers.
- Reduced instruction set computers (RISC) and parallel processing that will greatly increase the number of instructions that can be processed at one time.

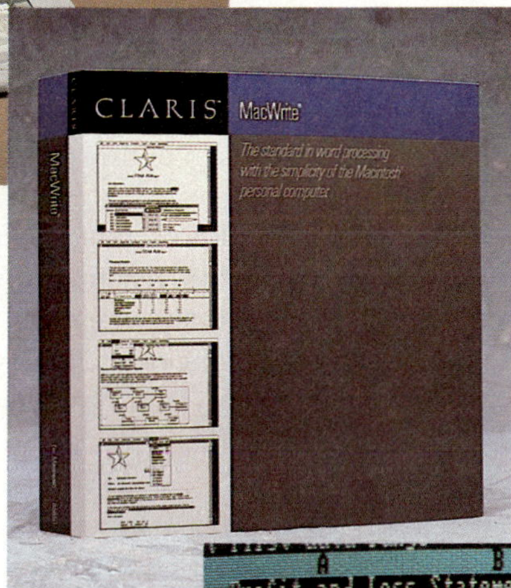

SOFTWARE

- Fourth-generation and natural languages that will enable the user to communicate with the computer in a more conversational manner.
- Computer-aided software engineering (CASE) that will shorten the system development time frame.
- Increased use of decision support and artificial intelligence systems to help users make decisions.
- Increased implementation of graphic interfaces using icons and symbols to represent information and processes.

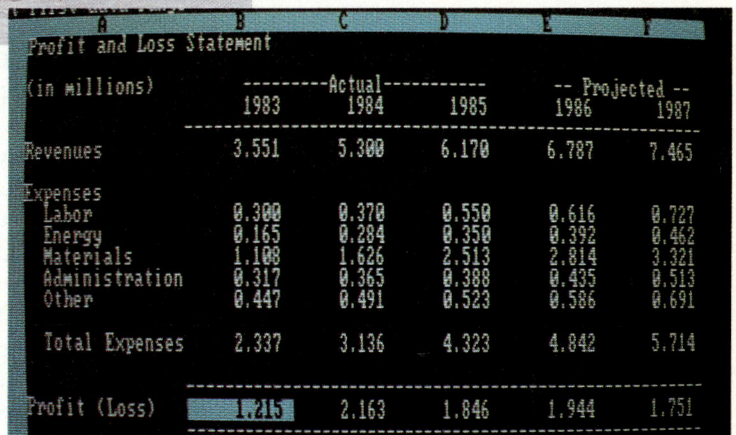

Profit and Loss Statement

(in millions)	Actual 1983	Actual 1984	Actual 1985	Projected 1986	Projected 1987
Revenues	3.551	5.300	6.170	6.787	7.465
Expenses					
Labor	0.300	0.370	0.550	0.616	0.727
Energy	0.165	0.284	0.350	0.392	0.462
Materials	1.108	1.626	2.513	2.814	3.321
Administration	0.317	0.365	0.388	0.435	0.513
Other	0.447	0.491	0.523	0.586	0.691
Total Expenses	2.337	3.136	4.323	4.842	5.714
Profit (Loss)	1.215	2.163	1.846	1.944	1.751

DATA

- Automatic input of data at the source where it is created.
- Storage and use of non-text data such as voice and image.

INFORMATION SYSTEMS PERSONNEL

- Increased interface with users.
- Emphasis will shift from how to capture and process data to how to use the available data more effectively.

USERS

- Most people will be computer literate, with a basic understanding of how computers work and how they can use them in their jobs.

The Automated Office

The **automated office**, sometimes referred to as the **electronic office**, is the term that describes the use of electronic devices such as computers, facsimile machines, and computerized telephone systems to make office work more productive. As was the case with traditional business applications such as accounting, automated office applications such as word processing, electronic mail, voice mail, desktop publishing, facsimile, image processing, and teleconferencing started out as separate, stand-alone applications. In recent years, however, the trend has been to integrate these applications into a network of devices and services that can share information. A brief review of each of these capabilities follows.

Word Processing Word processing is the ability to electronically create, store, revise, and print written documents. For many organizations, word processing was the first office application to be automated and among all organizations, word processing still ranks as the most widely used office automation technology. Today, most word processing systems are integrated with other applications. This allows the word processing applications to extract data such as names and addresses or financial data from other application files.

Electronic Mail Electronic mail is the ability to use computers to transmit messages to and receive messages from other computer users. The other users may be on the same computer network or on a separate computer system reached through the use of a modem or some other communications device. Electronic mail eliminates the need to hand deliver messages or use a delivery service, such as the post office or Federal Express. Electronic mail usage will grow as previously separate personal computers are attached to local area networks.

Voice Mail **Voice mail** can be considered verbal electronic mail. Made possible by the latest computerized telephone systems, voice mail reduces the problem of "telephone tag," where two people trying to reach each other wind up leaving a series of messages to "please call back." With voice mail, the caller can leave a message, similar to leaving a message on an answering machine. The difference is that with a voice mail system, the caller's message is digitized (converted into binary ones and zeros) so that it can be stored on a disk like other computer data. This allows the party who was called to hear the message later (by reconverting it to an audio form) and also, if desired, add a reply or additional comments and forward the message to someone else who has access to the system.

Desktop Publishing Desktop publishing involves the use of computers to produce printed documents that can combine different sizes and styles of text and graphics. Desktop publishing allows the user to control the process of creating high quality newsletters, brochures, and other documents that previously would have to have been developed by professional artists. The availability of desktop publishing systems for different computers and levels of user sophistication will increase their use in small as well as large organizations.

Facsimile **Facsimile** or **Fax** machines are used to transmit a reproduced image of a document over standard phone lines (Figure 15-2). The document can be printed, hand written, or a photograph. Fax machines optically scan the document and convert the image into digitized data that can be transmitted, using a modem, over the phone. A compatible Fax machine at the receiving end converts the digitized data back into its original image. Besides the separate Fax machines, plug-in circuit boards are also available for personal computers. Using a modem, these boards can directly transmit computer-prepared documents or documents that have been digitized with the use of a scanner. Fax machines are having an increasing impact on the way businesses transmit documents. Many documents that were previously sent through the mail are now sent by Fax. With the speed and convenience of a phone call, a document sent by Fax can be transmitted anywhere in the world.

FIGURE 15-2
This facsimile (Fax) machine can send and receive copies of documents to and from any location where there is phone service and a compatible Fax machine.

Image Processing Image processing is the ability to store and retrieve a reproduced image of a document. Image processing is often used when an original document, such as an insurance claim, must be seen to verify data. Image processing and traditional applications will continue to be combined in many areas. For example, in 1988 American Express began sending cardholders copies of the individual charge slips that were related to the charges on their statement. These charge slips were recorded by an image processing system and then merged with the customer statement program.

Teleconferencing Teleconferencing once meant three or more people sharing a phone conversation. Today, however, **teleconferencing** usually means **video conferencing**, the use of computers and television cameras to transmit video images and the sound of the conference participants to other participants with similar equipment at a remote location (Figure 15-3). Special software and equipment is used to digitize the video image so that it can be transmitted along with the audio over standard communication channels. Although the video image is not as clear for moving objects as is commercial television, it does contribute to the conference discussion and is adequate for nonmoving objects such as charts and graphs.

FIGURE 15-3
Video conferencing is used to transmit and receive video and audio signals over standard communication channels.

Summary of the Automated Office The trend toward integrated automated office capabilities will continue. Incompatible devices will be standardized or will be provided with software that will enable them to communicate and transfer data with other devices. The increased productivity provided by automated office devices will encourage more and more organizations to adopt them to help control costs and remain competitive.

The Automated Factory

As in the automated office, the goal of the **automated factory** is to increase productivity through the use of automated, and often computer-controlled, equipment. Technologies used in the automated factory include computer-aided design, computer-aided engineering, computer-aided manufacturing, and computer-integrated manufacturing.

FIGURE 15-4
Computer-aided design (CAD) is an efficient way to develop plans for new products.

Computer-Aided Design (CAD) **Computer-aided design (CAD)** uses a computer and special graphics software to aid in product design (Figure 15-4). The CAD software eliminates the laborious drafting that used to be required and allows the designer to dynamically change the size of some or all of the product and view the design from different angles. The ability to store the design electronically offers several advantages over traditional manual methods. For one thing, the designs can be changed more easily than before. For another, the design database can be reviewed more easily by other design engineers. This increases the likelihood that an existing part will be used in a product rather than a new part designed. For example, if a support bracket was required for a new product, the design engineer could review the design database to see if any existing products used a support bracket that would be appropriate for the new product. This not only decreases the overall design time but increases the reliability of the new product by using proven parts.

Computer-Aided Engineering (CAE) **Computer-aided engineering (CAE)** is the use of computers to test product designs. Using CAE, engineers can test the design of an airplane or a bridge before they are built (Figure 15-5). Sophisticated programs are available to simulate the effects of wind, temperature, weight, and stress on product shapes and materials. Before the use of CAE, prototypes of products had to be built and subjected to testing that often destroyed the prototype.

Computer-Aided Manufacturing (CAM) **Computer-aided manufacturing (CAM)** is the use of computers to control production equipment. CAM production equipment includes software-controlled drilling, lathe, and milling machines as well as robots (Figure 15-6). The use of robots has aroused much interest, partially because of preconceived ideas of robots as intelligent, humanlike machines. In practice, most industrial robots rarely look like a human and can only perform preprogrammed tasks. Robots are often used for repetitive tasks in hazardous or disagreeable environments, such as welding or painting areas.

FIGURE 15-5 Computer-aided engineering (CAE) allows the user to test product designs before they are built and without damaging the product.

FIGURE 15-6 Computer-aided manufacturing (CAM) is used to control production equipment such as these welding robots on an automobile assembly line.

Computer-Integrated Manufacturing (CIM) **Computer-integrated manufacturing (CIM)** is the total integration of the manufacturing process using computers (Figure 15-7). Using CIM concepts, individual production processes are linked so that the production flow is balanced and optimized, and products flow smoothly through the factory. In a CIM factory, automated design processes are linked to automated machining processes that are linked to automated assembly processes that are linked to automated testing and packaging. Under ideal CIM conditions, a product will move through the entire production process under computer control. Because of its complexity, many companies may never fully implement CIM. But CIM's related concepts of minimum inventory and efficient demand-driven production are valid and will be incorporated into many manufacturers' business plans.

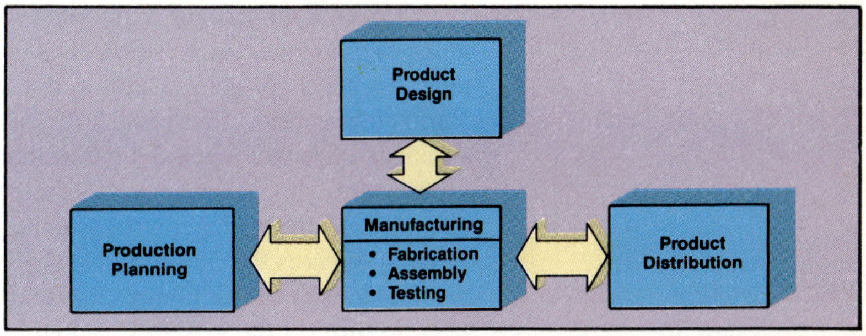

FIGURE 15-7
The concept of computer-integrated manufacturing (CIM) is to use computers to integrate all phases of the manufacturing process from planning and design to manufacturing and distribution.

BRINGING THE INFORMATION AGE HOME

Since personal computers became available in the mid-1970s, millions of personal computers have been purchased for home use. It is expected that the use of personal computers in the home will continue to increase. Just as the use of computers in the workplace will change how we work, the use of computers in our homes will change various aspects of our personal lives. The next two sections discuss how personal computers are used in the home, including some possible new applications, and things you should consider when purchasing a personal computer system.

The Use of Personal Computers in the Home

Personal computers can be used in many different ways in the home. Five general areas of use include: (1) personal services; (2) control of home systems; (3) telecommuting; (4) education; and (5) entertainment.

Personal Services In many ways running a home is similar to running a small business. The productivity tools that are used in the office, such as word processing, spreadsheet, and database, can also be used in the home to aid with creating documents, financial planning and analysis, and filing and organizing data. Personal computer software is also available to assist with home accounting applications such as balancing checkbooks, making household budgets, and preparing tax returns. In addition, using a personal computer to transmit and receive data over telephone lines allows home users to access a wealth of information and services. For example, teleshopping and electronic banking are two services that are becoming more popular, and information such as stock prices and airline schedules is available to home users who subscribe to database services such as CompuServe and The Source. The personal services provided by home computer use allows people to perform personal and business-related tasks quickly and conveniently in the comfort of their own homes. Without a personal computer, completing similar activities would take considerably more time because it would frequently require travel to other locations to conduct business and acquire information.

Control of Home Systems Another use of computers in the home is to control home systems such as security, environment control, lighting, and landscape sprinkler systems. Personal computers used in this manner are usually linked to special devices such as alarms for security; thermostats for environmental control; and timing devices for lighting and sprinkler systems. When the personal computer system has communication capabilities, a homeowner who is away can use a telephone or another computer to call home and change the operation of one of the control systems. For example, suppose a homeowner is on vacation in Texas and learns that heavy rains have been falling at home in Pennsylvania. It is possible for the homeowner to call home and use the keys of a touch-tone telephone to instruct the computer to turn off the garden sprinkler system. Near Orlando, Florida, an example of the ways that computers may be used in homes of the future is demonstrated in a showcase model called the Xanadu House. In this home computers are used in many ways including controlling home systems.

Telecommuting **Telecommuting** refers to the ability of individuals to work at home and communicate with their offices by using personal computers and communication lines. With a personal computer, an employee can access the main computer at the office. Electronic mail can be read and answered. Databases can be accessed and completed projects can be transmitted. It has been predicted that by the end of the 1990s 10 percent of the workforce will be telecommuters. Most of these people will probably arrange their business schedules so that they can telecommute two or three days a week. Telecommuting provides flexibility, allowing companies and employees to work out arrangements that can increase productivity and at the same time meet the needs of individual employees. Some of the advantages possible with telecommuting include reducing the time needed to commute to the office each week; eliminating the need to travel during poor weather conditions; providing a convenient and comfortable work environment for disabled employees or workers recovering from injuries or illnesses; and allowing employees to combine work with personal responsibilities such as child care.

Education The use of personal computers for education, called **computer-aided instruction (CAI)**, is another rapidly growing area. While CAI is frequently used to describe software that is developed and used in schools, much of the same software is available for home users. CAI software can be classified into three main types: drill and practice; tutorials; and simulations.

Drill and practice software uses a "flashcard" approach to teaching by allowing users to practice skills in subjects such as math and language. A problem or word is displayed on the computer screen and the user enters the answer. The computer accepts the answer and responds by telling the student whether or not the answer was correct. Sometimes the user gets second and third chances to select the correct answer before the computer software will display the correct answer. With **tutorial software**, the computer software displays text and graphics and sometimes uses sound to teach a user concepts about subjects such as chemistry, music theory, or computer literacy. Following the instruction, tutorial software may quiz the user with true/false or multiple choice questions to help ensure that the concepts being taught are understood. The increased use of optical disk storage that provides high quality graphics and direct access capability promises to greatly enhance this type of CAI.

The third type of CAI, **simulation software**, is designed to teach a user by creating a model. For example, many simulation packages are available to teach business concepts. One program designed for children simulates running a lemonade stand and another program for adults simulates the stock market. In the lemonade simulation, the user makes decisions about "How many quarts of lemonade to make" and "What price to charge customers for a glass of lemonade." The computer software accepts the user's decisions, performs computations using the software model, and then responds to the user with the amount of profit or loss for the day. Good CAI software is designed to be user friendly and motivate the user to succeed (Figure 15-8).

FIGURE 15-8
Computer-aided instruction (CAI) software provides a structured yet motivating way to learn. This software package helps the user to develop deductive reasoning, reference, and research skills while learning geography, history, economics, government, and culture.

In addition to CAI software, some trade schools, colleges and universities are now allowing students with personal computers to take electronic correspondence courses from their homes. Lessons and assignments for classes are transmitted between the student and the school over communication lines.

Education in the home through CAI or electronic correspondence courses allow home users to learn at their own pace, in the convenience of their home, and at a time that fits into their personal schedule. Well-written educational software can be so entertaining that it is sometimes difficult to distinguish between it and entertainment software.

Entertainment Entertainment software, or game playing, on home computers has always had a large following among the younger members of the family. However, many adults are surprised to find that entertainment software can also provide them with hours of enjoyment. Popular types of entertainment software include arcade games, board games, simulations, and interactive graphics programs. Most people are familiar with the arcade-type games (similar to video games such as Pac-Man) that are available for computers. A popular board game is computer chess. Simulations include games such as baseball and football and a variety of flight simulators that allow users to pretend they are controlling and navigating different types of aircraft (Figure 15-9). Also available are a wide variety of interactive graphic adventure games that range from rescuing a princess from a castle's dungeon to solving a murder mystery. Many of these games can be played either individually or in small groups. The software usually allows players to adjust the level of play to their skill level, that is, beginner through advanced. With entertainment software, the computer becomes a fun, skillful, and challenging game partner.

FIGURE 15-9
Flight simulators can be part fun and part educational. Some simulators offer realistic instrument consoles and flight patterns that help teach the user about flying.

A different type of entertainment available to users who have personal computers with communication capabilities is the access and use of electronic **bulletin board systems**, called **BBSs**, that allow users to communicate with one another and share information (Figure 15-10). While some bulletin boards provide specific services such as buying and selling used computer equipment, many bulletin boards function as electronic clubs for special interest groups and are used to share information about hobbies as diverse as stamp collecting, music, genealogy, and astronomy. Some BBSs are strictly social; users meet new friends and conduct conversations by entering messages through their keyboards.

FIGURE 15-10
This is a list of just some of the bulletin boards available in the San Diego, California area. Bulletin board systems are an excellent source for answers to questions about personal computer equipment and software.

300/1200 BPS

A&B Express	447-1009	* Z
Adventure Board	224-2636	
The After World	679-7159	
Back County PCBBS	789-6377	
The BBS	447-8143	
The C-64 Exchange	292-9351	
The Candy Shoppe	474-5966	
Clue Line	566-2562	
CMS—Bell Junior High	267-2807	
CMS—Kearny Mesa	565-1321	
CMS—Patrick Henry	287-2644	
CMUG	433-3162	
The Commodore Shop	423-7910	*
Cougar Country	480-3056	Z
Cuyamaca College	465-3792	
Digex—SDCS DIGSIG	454-8078	
Disk-Connection	562-1989	
Educational Technologies	265-3428	
Eight-Bit Tandy	571-6366	
Empty V	425-5808	Z
The Evergreen Forest	426-2057	*
F&L BBS	670-7462	
The Fifth Dimension	670-3969	* Z
Frog's Bible Board	275-0506	
The Fun House	282-9124	
Guardian's Cavern	563-9004	
Heath SIG MS/PC-DOS Support	461-2417	
His Majesty's Secret Service	480-8403	Z
JSR Service Net	258-9078	
Kit's Hideout	741-0692	
The Knight's Realm	746-2029	
The Lemonade Stand	941-6158	
The Looney Bin	390-9470	
Maui's CoCo Hotspot	486-4249	
Micro-80 of Oceanside	439-9169	
Money Works	579-1403	
The Monsoon	259-1507	
My Board	743-7194	
My House	447-1422	
Ocean Beach BBS	224-4878	
Outer Limits	941-2424	
Paulette's Playhouse	743-3138	
The Post Office	479-8558	
P.O.C.	437-1911	
Private Resort	484-6437	
Ramona Country BBS	789-6235	
Real-Net BBS	464-4540	
Sanyo Users Group BBS	454-8876	
SCCG-TIBBS	278-8155	
ST—SDACE	284-3821	
ST SIG Atari ST & Others	726-4419	
SunSplash	297-3230	
The 64 & More Store	258-0951	
Smart Users Group	480-9686	
also	726-4419	
Software, Etc.	291-5790	Z
Special Integrated Designs	464-0048	
The Surf Shack	967-6017	
The Torture Chamber	452-2893	
Zeke	755-5675	

300/1200/2400 BPS

Adventures In Palancia	222-1785	
The Amiga Exchange	223-2734	Z
Apokolips	488-4714	
Bear Country	541-7048	
Brian Smith's BBS	582-0875	
Camelot 3000	462-0542	
Classified Connection	566-1745	
CMS—El Cajon	444-5442	
COM2: Remote BBS	471-8730	
Computer Boulevard	589-0565	
ComputorEdge On-Line	573-1675	
Computer Outlet	282-6815	Z
Computer Outlet, North County	740-0113	* Z
The Computer Room	287-6006	
CORE BBS	295-2912	
Cornucopia	283-0498	
Coronado Wildcat!	435-8070	
Dollars and Bytes	483-5477	Z
The Dream Clinic	670-9522	
The Enchanted World	692-9518	
Enigma—The Next Generation	453-1819	
The Fish Express	792-1653	
Faultline BBS	481-7340	
FSMAO-2	725-6322	
The Flare Path	561-2999	
The Fun House	282-9124	
The Information Center	696-2568	
Imperial Beach BBS	575-1562	
The Key Of David	479-2104	
Kingdom Age BBS	586-7973	
The Knowledge Works BBS	528-1058	*
Lakeside PC Board	390-7328	
MacBonsall	726-1591	
The MacConnection	259-8735	
Mainstreet Data	439-6624	
Mac INFONET	944-3646	
Milliway's	268-9614	
Morning Star	575-3310	
Mouse Trap BBS	462-3975	*
Multitech PC	578-9221	
Nassau Xpress	433-9777	
NEXUS Z-Node #63	486-0735	
North San Diego Apple Club	571-9010	
Nova	489-6975	
PD-SIG	749-2741	
also	749-2589	
also	566-6329	
also	466-3118	
also	727-0202	
P-Net (pnet01)	444-7006	
P-Net (pnet03)	569-9195	
P-Net (pnet08)	450-0052	
Prides Crossing	464-6271	
ProLine [avalon]	271-0131	
ProLine [beagle]	452-5565	
ProLine [mercury]	697-0261	
The Rasta Connection	282-1211	
The RPC Library	283-6365	
Sabaline	692-1961	
San Diego Computer Society	549-3788	
San Diego Live	584-1715	$
also	584-4172	$
Scanline	298-2023	
Seastalker BBS	581-9379	
Sharky's MAChine	747-8719	
SomeWares Between Heaven & Hell	436-9861	
ST MIDI Connection	452-7535	
Star Base 23	560-2996	
Surfer's Paradise	724-9520	*
Sysport MIDI BBS	698-7155	
TeleMac	576-1820	$
Turnkey Technology	563-6688	
Z Node #9	270-3148	

300/1200/2400/9600 HST STANDARD

Another System	792-0634	
Bootcamp I	941-0996	
Bytes 'R Us	428-9773	
Casino West	470-0771	
Dead Zone	755-3350	
DOOGER'S PLACE	588-8931	
Dworkin's Castle	438-5256	
MediaLine BBS	454-1629	
The Final Experience	670-4445	
Sawyer College of Business BBS	286-8614	Z
Mushin BBS	535-9580	
Night Owl, Ham Radio	279-3921	
Nuggo's Place	222-3097	
ProLine [simasd]	239-1397	
ProLine [sol]	670-5379	*
PD-SIG	749-6222	
also	749-3432	
SCANIS	565-0785	
Serenity	259-7757	
South Bay BBS	421-3189	
Starhelm Graystaff	479-3006	

300/1200/2400/9600 BPS Trailblazer

People-Net (pnet12)	259-3704	*

300/1200/2400/9600 BPS Racial Vadic

PD-SIG	749-6384	*

LEGEND
* New or updated information.
Z After hours or weekends.
$ Requires a one-time donation for access.

ComputorEdge acknowledges this is not a complete listing of all BBSs in San Diego area. We reserve the right to reject or cancel any submission for publication.

62 October 14, 1988 COMPUTOREDGE

In addition to sharing hobby information with other computer users on a BBS, some personal computer users use their home computer as a tool for personal hobbies. Computers are used by hobbyists to design quilt and stained glass patterns, run model trains, organize stamp, doll, and photography collections, and write, transpose, play, and print musical scores.

Summary of the Use of Personal Computers in the Home As you can see, personal computers are used in homes in a variety of ways. Whether or not you now use a personal computer in your home, it is very probable that you will at some time in the near future. In fact, it is very possible that within the next decade you will have multiple computers in your home. Because computers can be used in so many different ways and also because computer technology is changing so rapidly, it is important that you carefully choose any computer system that you may purchase. Some general guidelines for purchasing personal computers are discussed in the next section.

Guidelines for Buying a Personal Computer

When purchasing a personal computer, make every effort to select a computer system that matches your individual needs as closely as possible. Six general steps recommended for purchasing a personal computer system include:

Step 1. Become computer literate. This is truly the first step and an important step in making a wise purchase. You might be surprised that many people go straight out and buy computer equipment without understanding the capability of a personal computer or the tasks it can and cannot perform. Many times these people buy a computer like the one their neighbor or friend purchased, and expect it to meet their needs. Sometimes it does, but frequently they are disappointed. Hopefully this will not happen to you. You already have an advantage because by reading this book, you now know a great deal about computers and have developed a foundation of knowledge on which you can base your software and equipment decisions. In short, you already are computer literate. Because computer technology is changing rapidly, to stay computer literate you will need to stay current with the changes in the field. You can do this by reading periodicals or attending seminars on "state of the art" computer technology.

Step 2. Define and prioritize the type of tasks you want to perform on your computer. This step will help you to see more clearly exactly what you want to do with your computer and will help you to select software and equipment that will match these needs. Define your needs in writing. Create a numbered list with the most important application at the top and the least important application at the bottom. General applications like word processing, spreadsheets, database, and communications are easy to include on the list. You may, however, have a special application in mind, such as controlling a household security system. Being computer literate will help you to know if a special application is feasible. It will also help you to discuss any special needs you may have with computer professionals who can help you. Once your list is completed you can begin to evaluate the available software.

Step 3. Select the software packages that best meet your needs. Periodicals, computer stores, and user groups are all good resources when it comes to evaluating the available software. For more on evaluating software, review the section in Chapter 2, "Guidelines for Purchasing Microcomputer Applications Software."

In addition to purchasing commercial software, another possibility is to consider selecting shareware and public domain software. **Shareware** is software that users may try out on their own systems before paying a fee. If a user decides to keep and use the software a registration fee is sent to the software publisher (Figure 15-11). **Public domain software** is free software that is not copyrighted and can therefore be distributed among users. While the quality of shareware and public domain software varies greatly, some of the software is quite good. This type of software can be obtained from BBSs and also from public domain software libraries.

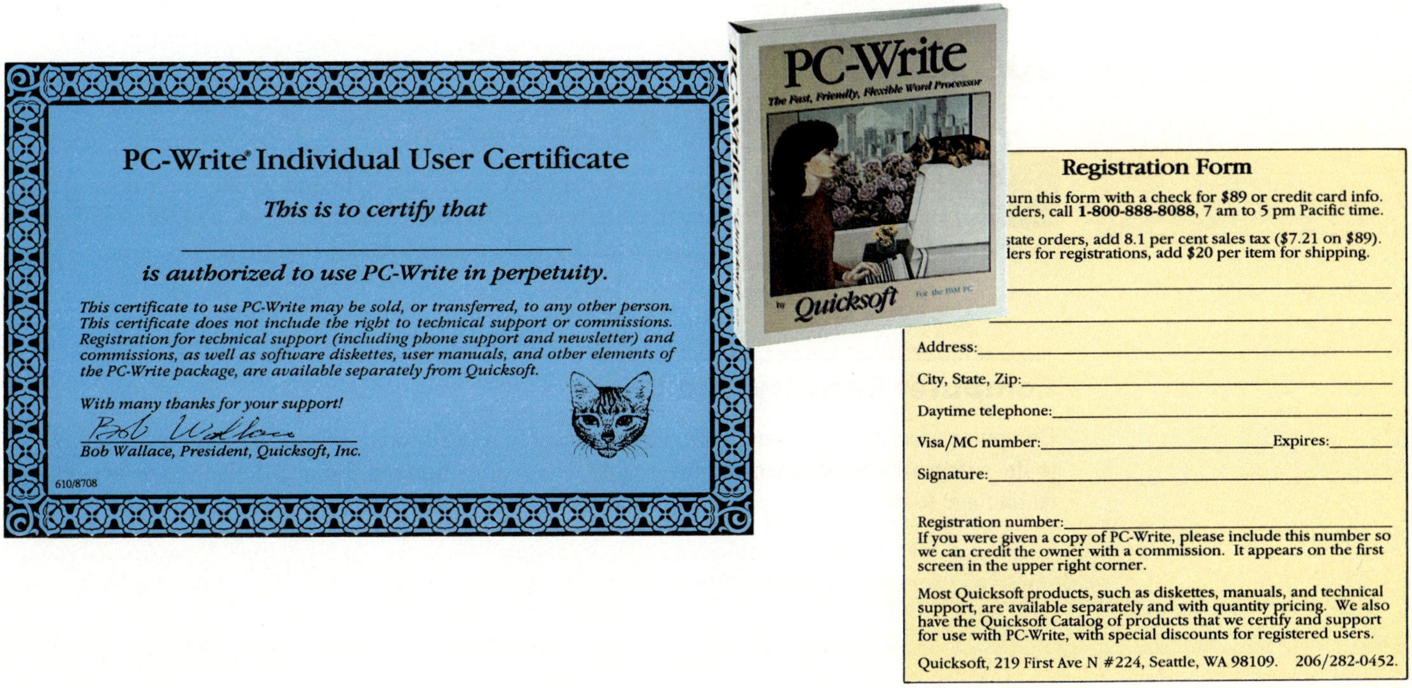

FIGURE 15-11
After trying the PC-Write software, users fill out a registration form and mail it with a fee to Quicksoft, the publisher of PC-Write. A user certificate is then sent to the user.

Step 4. Select equipment that will run the software you have selected. The capabilities of the different types of personal computers vary greatly. For example, some personal computers can perform extensive graphics while others cannot. Selecting the software that meets your needs before selecting your equipment guides you in selecting appropriate equipment. Some software only runs on certain types of personal computers. Also, knowing the software you want to run prevents overbuying (purchasing a machine that is more powerful than you need) or underbuying (purchasing a machine that is not powerful enough). Other things to consider when evaluating equipment include: processing speed of the microprocessor, memory size, system expandability, compatibility of the system with other personal computers, monochrome or color display, amount and type of auxiliary storage, printer type and speed, and communications capabilities.

Step 5. Select the suppliers for the software and equipment. Options include used equipment and software, mail order, and computer stores. Price, warranties, training, service, and repair are all things to consider when selecting a supplier. Obtaining the best overall value may not mean paying the lowest price. A store that is willing to provide you with assistance in assembling your system or providing some training may be well worth a slightly higher price.

Step 6. Purchase the software and equipment. If you have followed these guidelines you will probably feel both excited and confident with the decisions you have made. Your efforts to define your computing needs and to select software, equipment, and a supplier that will meet those needs should have helped you to select a personal computer system that is appropriate for you and with which you will be satisfied.

Summary of Bringing the Information Age Home

Personal computers are used in homes to aid in a variety of tasks such as personal services, control of home systems, telecommuting, education, and entertainment. When purchasing a personal computer system for the home, users should first become computer literate and evaluate their computer processing needs, and then purchase software and equipment that meets those needs. The trend is clear. Personal computers will continue to bring the information age into our homes.

The changes that accompany the information age raise several issues that are related to society as a whole. Some of these issues will be discussed in the following section.

SOCIAL ISSUES

Significant inventions such as the automobile and television have always challenged existing values and caused society to think about the right and wrong ways to use the new invention. So too has the computer. This section discusses some of the social issues related to computers, including security and computer crime and privacy.

Computer Security and Crime

Computer security and computer crime are closely related topics. **Computer security** refers to the safeguards established to prevent and detect unauthorized use and deliberate or accidental damage to computer systems and data. **Computer crime** is the use of a computer to commit an illegal act. This section discusses the types of crimes that can be committed and the security measures that can be taken to prevent and detect them.

Software Theft Software theft, often called **software piracy**, became a major problem with the increased use of personal computers. Some people have a hard time understanding why they should pay hundreds, perhaps thousands of dollars for what appears to be an inexpensive diskette or tape, and instead of paying for an authorized copy of the software they make an illegal copy. This leads software manufacturers to install elaborate copy protection schemes designed to prevent anyone from copying the software. However, the copy protection also prevents authorized users who have paid the license fee from making backup copies of the software for security purposes. Today, software piracy is still an issue. It is estimated that for every authorized copy of a commercial program, there is at least one illegal copy. Although many companies have abandoned copy protection, they still take illegal copying seriously and vigorously prosecute offenders when caught. For large users, the financial incentives for stealing software have been lowered by site licensing and multiple copy discounts. Site licensing allows organizations to pay a single fee for multiple copies of a program used at a single location. Multiple copy discounts reduce the fee of each additional copy of a program license.

Unauthorized Access and Use **Unauthorized access** can be defined as computer trespassing, in other words, being logged on a system without permission. Many so-called computer hackers boast of the number of systems that they have been able to access by using a modem. These hackers usually don't do any damage and merely "wander around" the accessed system before logging off.

Unauthorized use is the use of a computer system or computer data for unapproved and possibly illegal activities. Unauthorized use may range from an employee using the company computer for keeping his child's soccer league scores to someone gaining access to a bank funds system and creating an unauthorized transfer. Unauthorized use could also include the theft of computerized information such as customer lists or product plans.

The key to preventing both unauthorized access and unauthorized use is an appropriate level of authorization. Authorization techniques range from simple passwords to advanced biometric devices that can identify individuals by their fingerprint, voice, or eye pattern. The level of authorization should match the degree of risk and should be regularly reviewed to determine if the level is still appropriate.

Malicious Damage Malicious or deliberate damage to the data in a computer system is often difficult to detect because the damaged data may not be used or carefully reviewed on a regular basis. A disgruntled employee or an outsider may gain access to the system and delete or alter individual records or an entire file. One of the most potentially dangerous types of malicious damage is done by a **virus**, a computer program designed to copy itself into other software and spread through multiple computer systems. Figure 15-12 on the following page shows how a virus can spread from one system to another. Although they have been known for a long time, it is only in recent years that viruses have become a serious problem. Besides developing specific programs called "vaccines" to locate and remove viruses, organizations are becoming more aggressive in prosecuting persons suspected of planting viruses. In what was described as the first computer virus trial, in 1988 a former programmer was convicted in Texas of planting a program in his employer's computer system that deleted 168,000 sales commission records.

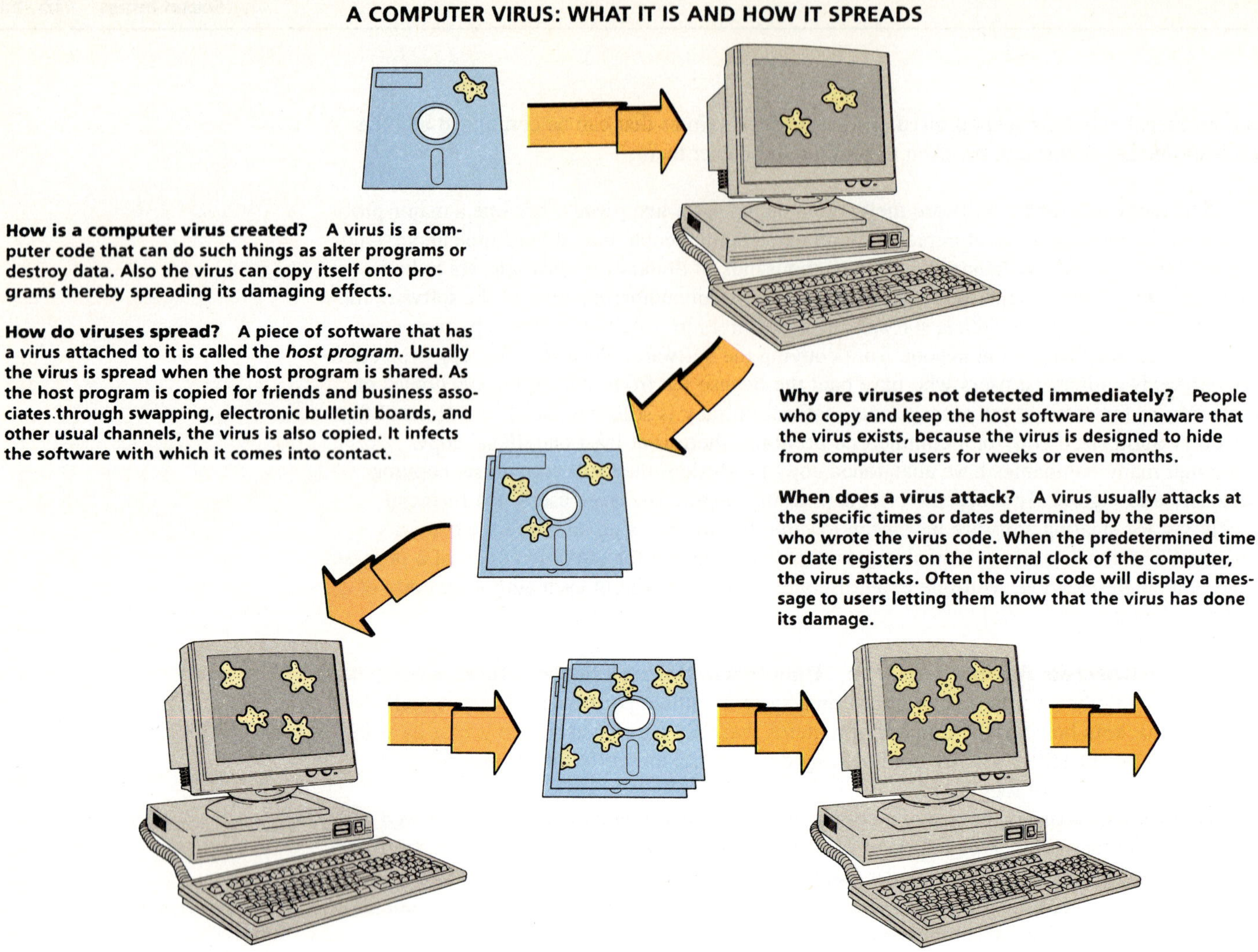

FIGURE 15-12
This illustration shows how a virus program can be transmitted from one computer system to another.

Single acts of malicious damage, especially when performed by employees with authorized access to the computer system, are very difficult to prevent. The best protection against this type of act remains adequate backup files that enable damaged data to be restored.

Privacy

In the past, one way to maintain privacy was to keep information in separate locations—individual stores had their own credit files, government agencies had separate records, doctors had separate files, and so on. However, it is now technically and economically feasible to store large amounts of related data about individuals in one database. Some people believe that the easier access to the data increases the possibility for misuse. Others worry that the increased storage capacity of computers may encourage the storage of unnecessary personal data.

The concern about information privacy has led to federal and state laws regarding the storage and disclosure of personal data. Common points in these laws include: (1) Information collected and stored about individuals should be limited to what is necessary to carry out the function of the business or governmental agency collecting the data. (2) Once collected, provisions should be made to restrict access to the data to those employees within the organization who need access to it to perform their job duties. (3) Personal information should be released outside the organization collecting the data only when the person has agreed to its disclosure. (4) When information is collected about an individual, the individual should know that data is being collected and have the opportunity to determine the accuracy of the data.

SUMMARY OF TRENDS AND ISSUES IN THE INFORMATION AGE

Based on current and planned developments, the impact of computers and the information age will be even greater in the future than it has been to date. However, as a society and as individuals, we have an obligation to use the computer responsibly and not abuse the power it provides. This presents constant challenges that sometimes weigh the rights of the individual against increased efficiency and productivity. The computer must be thought of as a tool whose effectiveness is determined by the skill and experience of the user. As a computer literate member of society, you will be better able to participate in decisions on how to best use computerized information systems.

CHAPTER SUMMARY

1. Existing business information systems will continue to undergo profound changes as new technology, software, and methods become available.
2. Trends will include more online, interactive systems; less batch processing; and increased use of relational database systems.
3. The **automated office**, sometimes referred to as the **electronic office**, is the term that describes the use of electronic devices such as computers, facsimile machines, and computerized telephone systems to make office work more productive.
4. Word processing is the ability to electronically create, store, revise, and print written documents.
5. Electronic mail is the ability to transmit messages to and receive messages from other computer users.
6. **Voice mail** can be considered verbal electronic mail.
7. Desktop publishing involves the use of computers to produce printed documents that can combine different sizes and styles of text and graphics.
8. **Facsimile** or **Fax** machines are used to transmit a reproduced image of a document over standard phone lines.
9. Image processing is the ability to store and retrieve a reproduced image of a document.
10. **Teleconferencing** usually means **video conferencing**, the use of computers and television cameras to transmit video images and the sound of the conference participants to other participants with similar equipment at a remote location.
11. The goal of the **automated factory** is to increase productivity through the use of automated, and often computer-controlled, equipment.
12. **Computer-aided design (CAD)** uses a computer and special graphics software to aid in product design.
13. **Computer-aided engineering (CAE)** is the use of computers to test product designs.
14. **Computer-aided manufacturing (CAM)** is the use of computers to control production equipment.
15. **Computer-integrated manufacturing (CIM)** is the total integration of the manufacturing process using computers.
16. Personal computers are used in the home in many different ways, including: (1) personal services; (2) control of home systems; (3) telecommuting; (4) education; and (5) entertainment.
17. The personal services provided by home computer use allow people to perform personal and business-related tasks quickly and conveniently in the comfort of their own homes.
18. Another use of computers in the home is to control home systems such as security, environment control, lighting, and landscape sprinkler systems.
19. **Telecommuting** refers to the ability of individuals to work at home and communicate with their offices by using personal computers and communication lines.
20. The use of personal computers for education, called **computer-aided instruction (CAI)**, is a rapidly growing area.
21. CAI software can be classified into three main types: **drill and practice software**; **tutorial software**; and **simulation software**.
22. Popular types of entertainment software include arcade games, board games, simulations, and interactive graphics programs.

23. Electronic **bulletin board systems**, called **BBSs**, allow users to communicate with one another and share information.
24. The guidelines for purchasing a personal computer recommend that you: (1) become computer literate; (2) define and prioritize the type of tasks you want to perform on your computer; (3) select the software packages that best meet your needs; (4) select equipment that will run the software you have selected; (5) select the suppliers for the software and equipment; (6) purchase the software and equipment.
25. **Shareware** is software that users may try out on their own systems before paying a fee.
26. **Public domain software** is not copyrighted and can therefore be distributed among users.
27. **Computer security** refers to the safeguards established to prevent and detect unauthorized use and deliberate or accidental damage to computer systems and data.
28. **Computer crime** is the use of a computer to commit an illegal act.
29. Today, **software piracy** is still an issue and it is estimated that for every authorized copy of a commercial program, there is at least one illegal copy.
30. **Unauthorized access** can be defined as computer trespassing, in other words, being logged on a system without permission.
31. **Unauthorized use** is the use of a computer system or computer data for unapproved and possibly illegal activities.
32. The key to preventing both unauthorized access and unauthorized use is an appropriate level of authorization.
33. One of the most potentially dangerous types of malicious damage is done by a **virus**, a computer program designed to copy itself into other software and spread through multiple computer systems.
34. The concern about information privacy has led to federal and state laws regarding the storage and disclosure of personal data.

KEY TERMS

Automated factory *15.6*
Automated office *15.4*
Bulletin board systems (BBSs) *15.10*
Computer-aided design (CAD) *15.6*
Computer-aided engineering (CAE) *15.6*
Computer-aided instruction (CAI) *15.8*
Computer-aided manufacturing (CAM) *15.6*
Computer crime *15.13*
Computer-integrated manufacturing (CIM) *15.7*
Computer security *15.13*
Drill and practice software *15.8*
Electronic office *15.4*
Facsimile (Fax) *15.4*
Public domain software *15.11*
Shareware *15.11*
Simulation software *15.9*
Software piracy *15.13*
Telecommuting *15.8*
Teleconferencing *15.5*
Tutorial software *15.8*
Unauthorized access *15.13*
Unauthorized use *15.13*
Video conferencing *15.5*
Virus *15.13*
Voice mail *15.4*

REVIEW QUESTIONS

1. List three electronic devices that are used in an automated office. What is voice mail? How is a Fax machine used?
2. What is the goal of the automated factory? Briefly explain the four technologies that are used.
3. What are some of the personal services available to home computer users?
4. Describe the three general categories of educational software.
5. List the six guidelines for buying a personal computer. Why is it recommended that you select your software before your equipment?
6. What is software piracy?
7. What is unauthorized access and unauthorized use? How can they be prevented?
8. Explain why computer viruses are malicious. What is a "vaccine" program?
9. Discuss the four common points covered in the state and federal information privacy laws.

Introduction to DOS

Introduction to DOS

OBJECTIVES

You will have mastered the basics of using DOS when you can:

- "Boot" your microcomputer
- Enter the time and date, if required
- Establish the system default disk drive
- List a disk directory
- Cancel commands
- Format diskettes, using /S and /V
- Use file specifications to address files on various disks
- Copy files on the same disk and from one disk to another
- Rename and erase files
- Organize and manage file subdirectories on a hard disk
- Start application programs

INTRODUCTION

An **operating system** is one or more programs that control and manage the operation of the computer. These programs provide an interface among the user, the computer equipment, and the application programs. For instance, to use a computer to print a memo, you'd first use the operating system to start the computer. Next, you would enter a keyboard command that the operating system processes to activate the word processing program. When the word processing program instructs the computer to print the memo, the operating system finds the proper file on the disk, retrieves the data from the disk, and routes the output to the printer. The operating system is not part of the application program itself, but it provides essential services that the application program uses to perform its functions.

Operating Systems for IBM PCs

Microsoft Corporation joined forces with IBM to develop the program known as **DOS**, an acronym for **Disk Operating System**, used since 1981 in IBM PC and IBM-compatible computers. **PC-DOS** is the name for versions of DOS distributed by IBM for its Personal Computer and Personal System/2 lines. All IBM-compatible computers use versions of this operating system distributed by Microsoft as **MS-DOS**. This book uses the term DOS to refer to any of the various editions of PC- or MS-DOS and covers information applicable to all versions of DOS, unless otherwise noted.

DOS Versions

The numbers following the abbreviation DOS indicate the specific version and release of the product (Figure 1). The **version** number is the whole number and signifies a major improvement of the product. The **release** number is the decimal number and identifies minor corrections or changes to a version of the product. For example, DOS 1.1 corrected some minor problems with DOS 1.0.

Software developers try to maintain **upward compatibility**, that is, that all the features of an earlier version remain supported by a later one. However, "downward" compatibility is not common. Programs or equipment that require the features of DOS 3.3, for example, will not function with DOS 3.2 or earlier versions.

DOS VERSION RELEASE	MAJOR FEATURE SUPPORTED	YEAR
3.3	Introduction of PS/2	1987
3.2	Token-Ring Networks, 3.5" Diskette	
3.1	Addition of Networking, 1.2 mb 5.25 Diskette	
3.0	Introduction of PC/AT	1985
2.1	Enhancements to 2.0	
2.0	Introduction of PC/XT	1983
1.1	Enhancements to 1.0	
1.0	Introduction of IBM/PC	1981

FIGURE 1

USING THE DISK OPERATING SYSTEM (DOS)

Starting the Computer

DOS programs are normally stored on a diskette or on a hard disk. To begin using the operating system, it must be read into main memory, a process known as **booting**. If you are using a system with two diskette drives, insert the diskette containing DOS into drive A of the computer and turn on the computer (Figure 2). If you are using a system with a hard disk, DOS is already available on the hard disk. Turn on the computer (Figure 3) and be certain you do not insert a diskette before the system has completed its startup process. If the computer is already on and your DOS diskette is in drive A (or DOS is on the hard disk and drive A is empty), you can restart the system by pressing the CTRL, ALT, and DEL keys simultaneously (Figure 4).

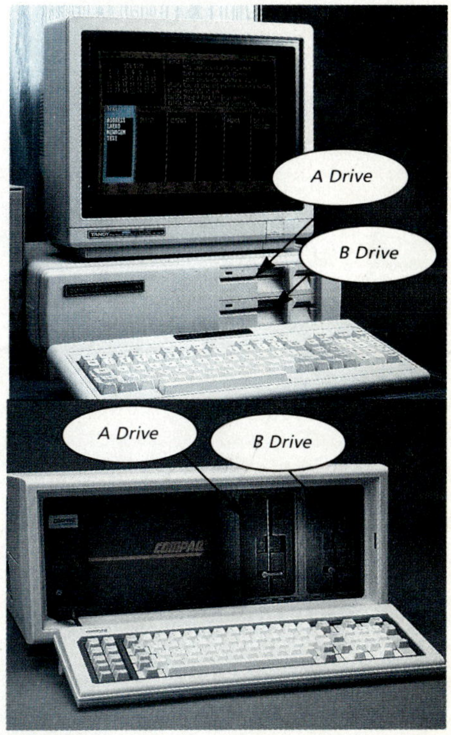

FIGURE 2

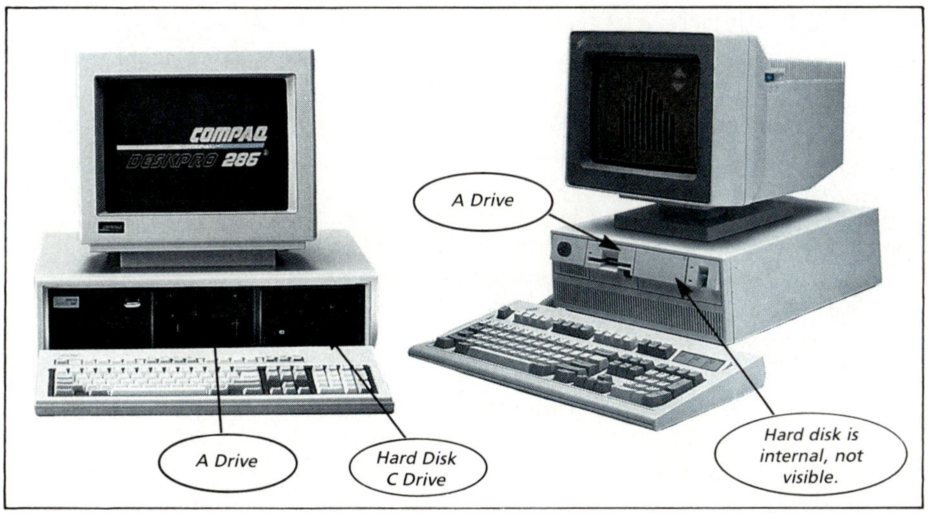

FIGURE 3

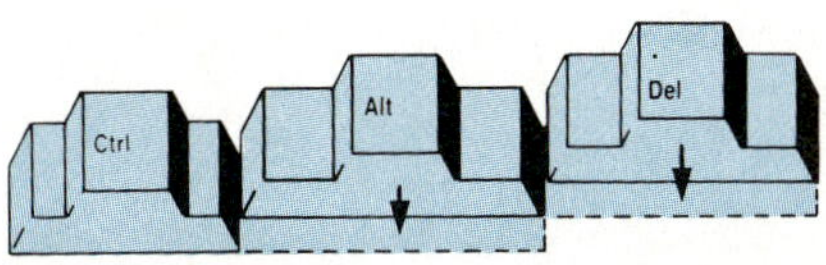

FIGURE 4

The Cold Start. Starting the computer by turning on the power switch is known as a **cold start** or **cold boot**. The computer will first run some tests to diagnose its own circuitry (known on some computers as a **power-on self-test**, or **POST** process). After running this test, the computer will begin to read the DOS diskette.

The Warm Start or Reset. Restarting the operating system by pressing the CTRL, ALT, and DEL keys simutaneously is called a **warm start**, or **warm boot**, because the computer has already been turned on. This procedure does not repeat the POST process, but it does erase all programs and data from main memory and reloads DOS. Do not worry about losing data from diskettes during this process, however, because data properly stored on diskettes will remain there.

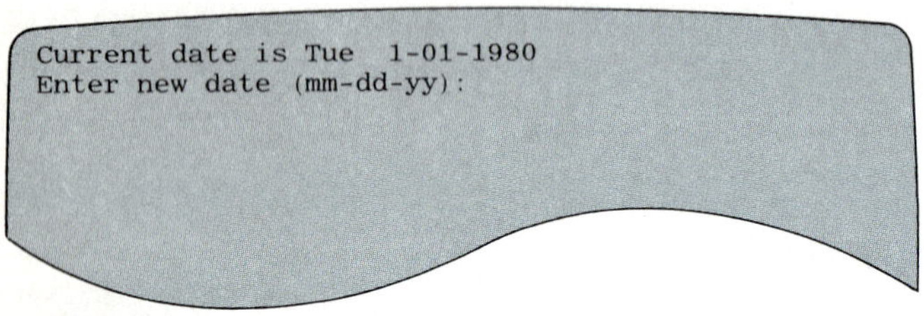

FIGURE 5

Loading DOS. While the system is being booted, the status light on the disk drive flashes on and off, and the disk drive whirls for a few seconds. During this time, the program from the operating system is being loaded into main memory. When DOS has been loaded into main memory, an image similar to Figure 5 appears on the screen. When DOS has been loaded into main memory, the system will perform various activities depending upon how the startup procedure has been tailored for the specific computer.

Setting the Date and Time

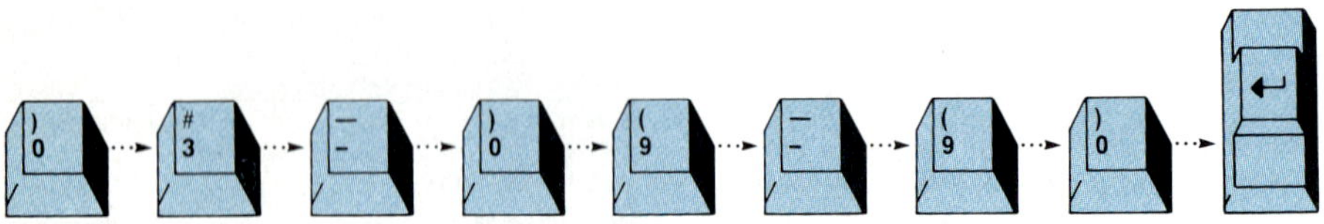

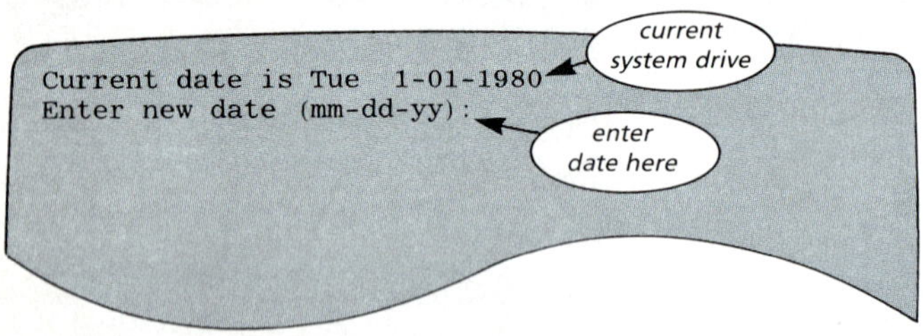

FIGURE 6

Although not required, it is a good practice to enter the date and time so that files you create are accurately documented. Enter the current date when the computer screen displays the message shown in Figure 6. To enter the date, always enter the month, day, and year separated by hyphens (-), slashes (/), or, in DOS 3.30 and later versions, periods (.). For example, assume that today is March 9, 1990. Type 03-09-90. Then press the Enter key (Figure 7).

If the date displayed is already correct—which it may be if your computer has an internal clock—you do not need to enter the date. Instead, press the Enter key when the message "Enter new date:" appears on the screen.

You enter the time in the format hh:mm:ss.xx, where hh stands for hours, mm stands for minutes, ss stands for seconds, and xx stands for hundredths of a second. As with the date, you are not required to enter the time, although it is a good practice to do so. For practice, type the time as 11:50 and press the Enter key (Figure 8). (If you do not include seconds and hundredths of seconds, the operating system assumes a value of zero for them.)

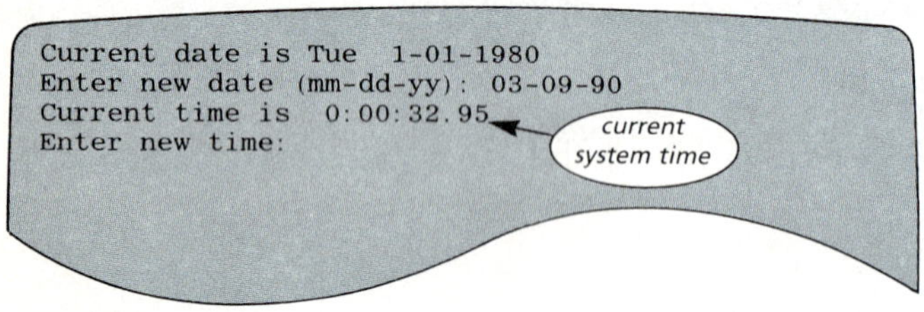

FIGURE 7

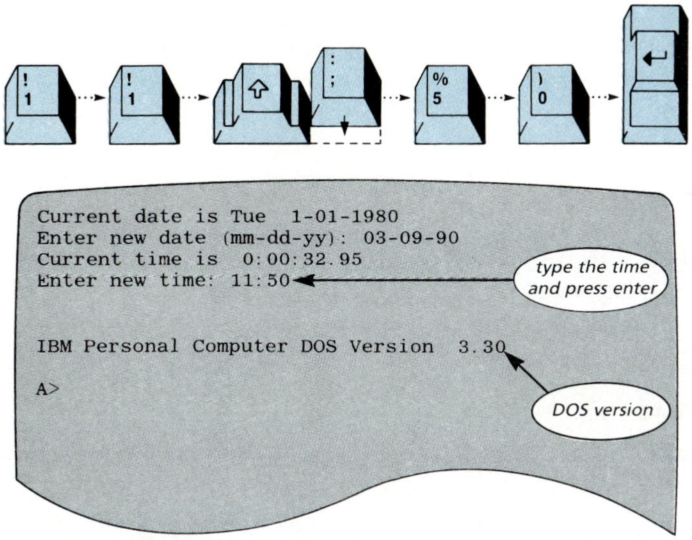

FIGURE 8

The DOS Prompt

After the messages are displayed, the **system prompt**, also called the **DOS prompt**, indicates that the operating system is ready to receive your commands (Figures 9 and 10). The letter displayed within the prompt > indicates which drive has been assigned as the default disk drive. The **default drive** is the disk drive in which the operating system assumes the disk or diskette containing the operating system and other programs is located. Another term used for the default drive is **current drive**, because it is the drive that is assumed to be in current use.

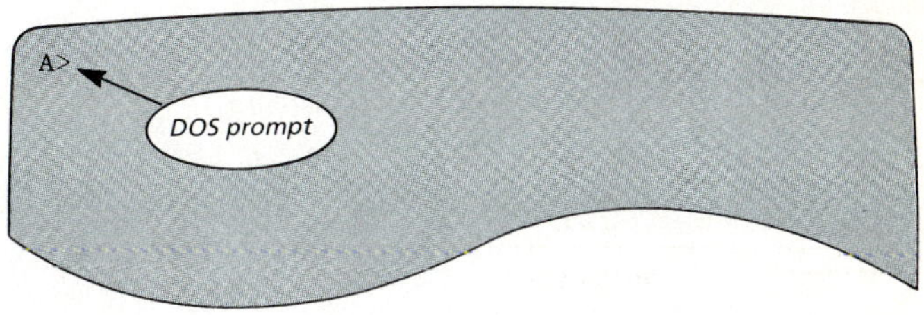

FIGURE 9

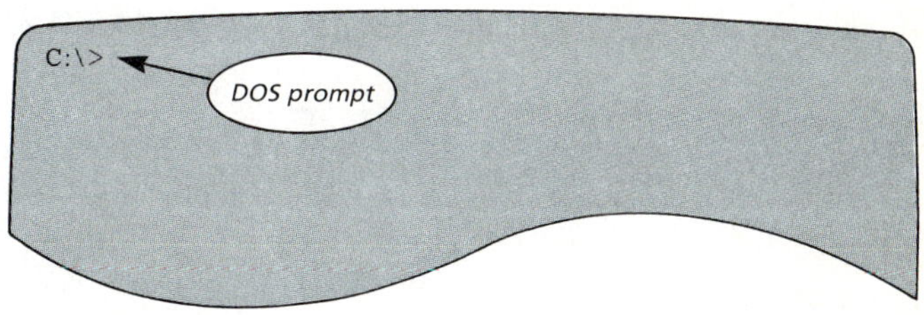

FIGURE 10

The Default Drive

The default drive assignment will vary depending upon the specific hardware you are using. A two-diskette system typically assigns drive A as the default drive (Figure 9). If your computer has a hard disk, the default drive will initially be drive C, and the prompt will appear as it is shown in Figure 10.

At times you will need to change the default drive assignment. Before you do so, be certain that the new drive is ready. A hard disk is always installed, but in a two-diskette system the disk drive must have a diskette inserted before it can be assigned as the default drive. If the drive does not have a diskette in it, the computer will give you an error message.

To change the drive assignment, type the letter of the new drive to be used, followed by a colon, and then press the Enter key. For example, to change the default to drive B, type the letter B, followed by a colon (:), and then press the Enter key (Figure 11, step 1). The prompt will display drive B as the default drive. Now, change the default drive back to drive A by typing A:↵ (Figure 11, step 2).

FIGURE 11

Step 1: Change the default drive from A to B. **Step 2: Change the default drive from B to A.**

In most of the examples in this text, the default drive will be drive A. You will be told when the procedures for a hard disk are different than those for a diskette system. Figure 12 shows how to change the default drive for a hard disk system from drive C to drive A (step 1) and back to drive C (step 2).

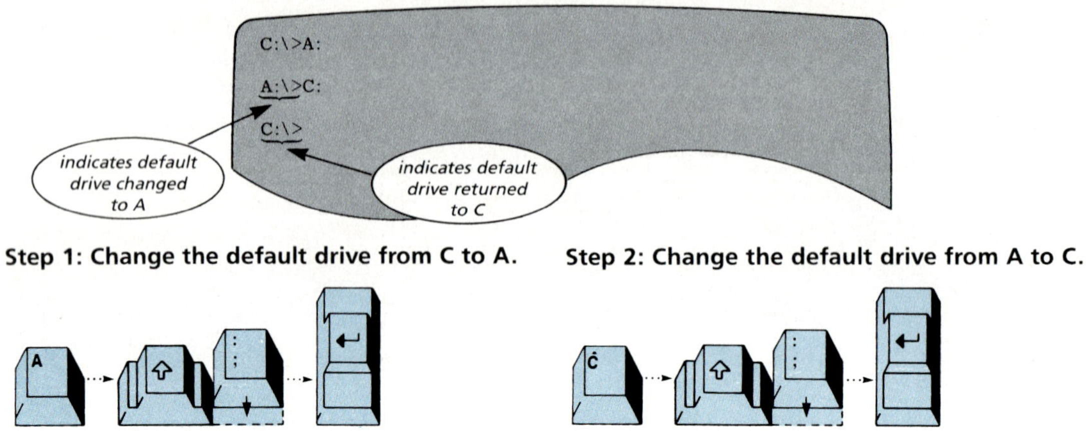

FIGURE 12

ENTERING DISK OPERATING SYSTEM (DOS) COMMANDS

Now that you have booted the DOS system, you are able to enter commands to instruct the computer. DOS includes a variety of commands to assist you in using the computer. Some of the commands might be called "status" or "informative" commands because they instruct DOS to give you information about the system's operation. The directory command, DIR, is one such informative command. It lists the names of files stored on a disk. Other commands support DOS functions, helping you use the computer. FORMAT, for instance, prepares a new disk for use in storing files.

The DOS commands you have entered so far have been typed in capital letters. You can type capital letters either by pressing the Caps Lock key or by holding down one of the two shift keys. However, you do not have to enter all DOS commands in capital letters. Commands, drive specifiers, and other entries to the operating system can be entered in any combination of uppercase and lowercase letters.

Internal and External Commands

An **internal command** is part of the operating system program. Once you have loaded DOS into main memory, an internal command is always started there. You can enter an internal command at any time. It does not matter whether the DOS system diskette is in the default drive. DIR, COPY, CLS, ERASE, RENAME, and DEL are examples of internal commands.

External commands, on the other hand, are stored on the DOS system disk as program files. They must be read from the disk into main memory before they can be executed. This means that the DOS system disk must be in the default drive or the specified drive so that the program can be found on the disk and loaded into main memory for execution. FORMAT and CHKDSK are examples of external commands. Another easy way to identify external commands is to look for the extensions .BAT, .COM, or .EXE following the filename, such as FORMAT.EXE.

DIRECTORY COMMAND (DIR)

One of the functions of the operating system is to store files containing both programs and data on diskettes. To facilitate that storage, the operating system maintains a directory of all the files stored on a diskette. To display the directory of the diskette you have placed in drive A of your computer, use the **DIR command**. At the A> prompt, type DIR and press the Enter key (Figure 13).

The directory of the diskette in the default drive will then be displayed as in Figure 14. Because the default drive is drive A (as specified by the system's A> prompt), the directory of the diskette in drive A is displayed. If you are using a hard disk and your default disk is drive C, the DIR command will display the directory of your hard disk.

The directory itself consists of the names of the files on the diskette, the number of bytes required to store the file on the diskette, the date of the last change of the file, and for some files, the time of the last change of the file. The message at the end of the directory listing indicates the number of files on the diskette (in Figure 14 there are 15 files on the diskette) and the remaining space available on the diskette (181248 unused bytes remain on the diskette in Figure 14). At the end of the directory display, the system prompt reappears on the screen, indicating that the system is ready for your next command.

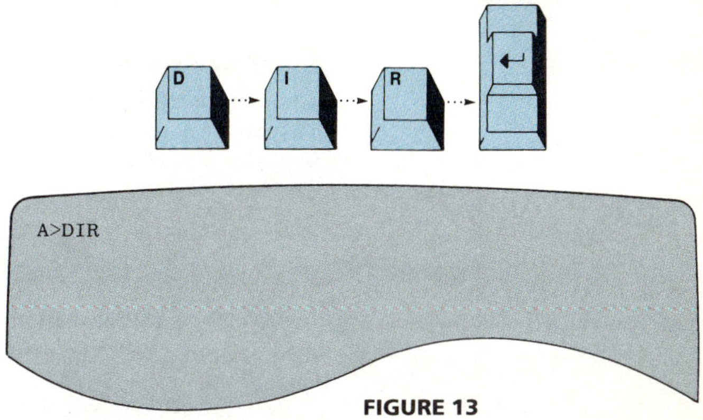

FIGURE 13

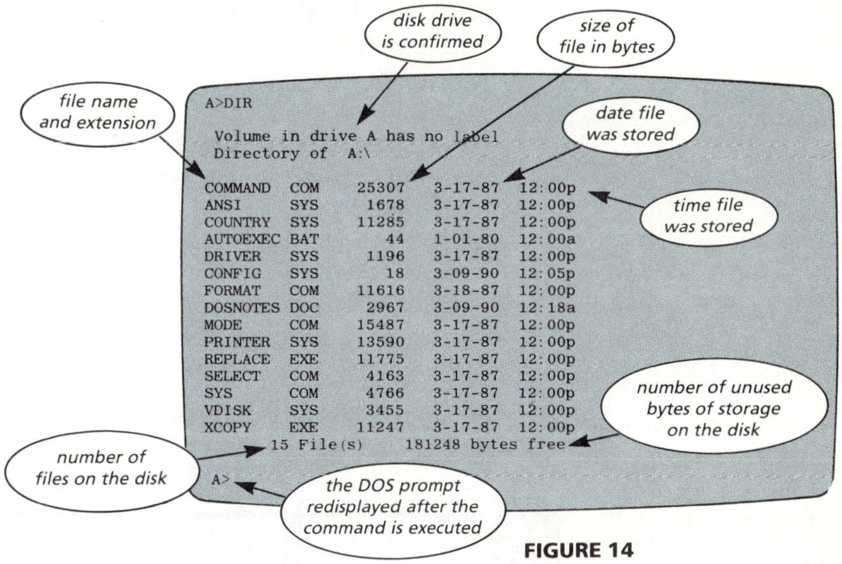

FIGURE 14

Displaying Directories of Other Disks

The directories of files on diskettes in other disk drives of the computer can be displayed as well. For practice, remove your system diskette from drive A and move it to drive B. To display the directory, type the command DIR B: and press the Enter key, as in Figure 15. You have directed the operating system to display the directory of the diskette located in drive B. The entry B: specifies that drive B is to be used.

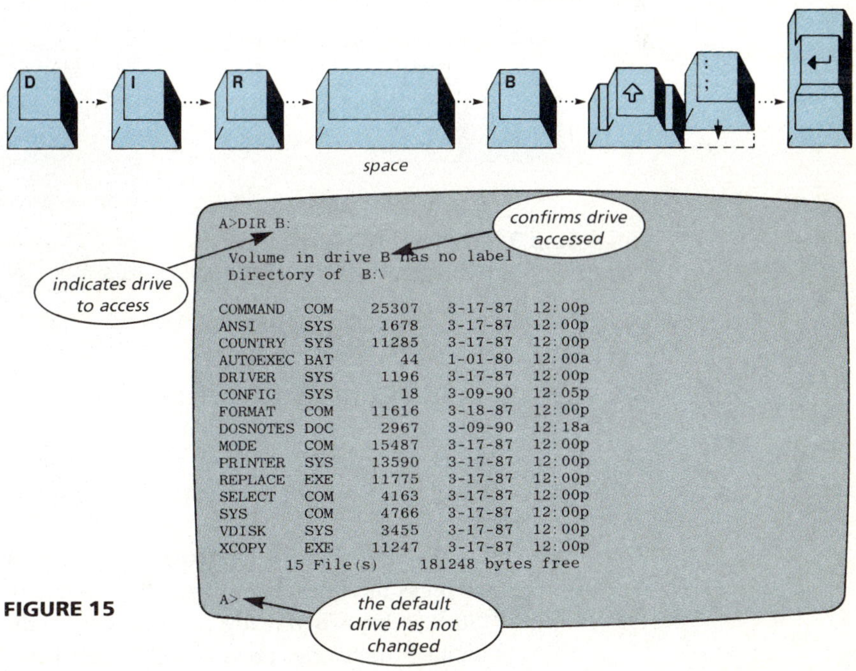

FIGURE 15

If your computer has a hard disk and you have been using drive C as the default drive, you can insert a diskette into drive A and then list the directory of that diskette drive by typing DIR A: and pressing the Enter key (Figure 16).

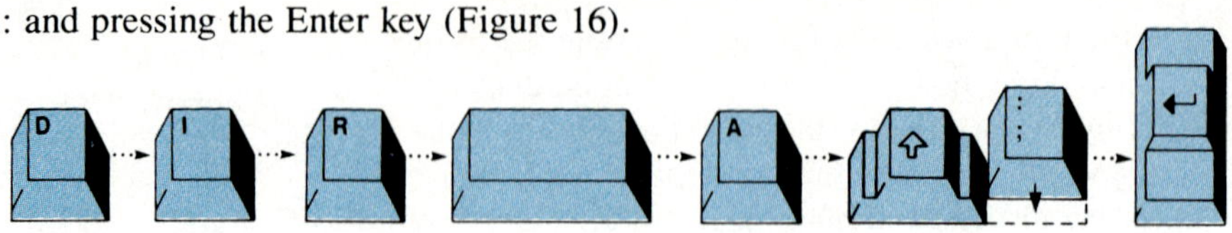

FIGURE 16

Note the use of the **colon, :**, with the disk drive letter. Whenever you refer to a specific disk drive, type the letter designating the drive followed by the colon, such as A:, B:, or C:.

Pausing Directory Listings

The directory of your diskette will often contain more files than can be displayed on the screen at one time. DOS has two methods of handling this situation: the pause screen option and the DIR command options.

Pause Screen (Control S). To use a **pause screen** function, first make certain that your DOS diskette is in drive A. Type DIR and press the Enter key (Figure 17, step 1). When approximately one screenful of information is displayed, press Control-S. The directory display immediately halts (Figure 17, step 2). You can then examine the screen for any information you require. To continue the display, press any character key on the keyboard. The directory display will continue to scroll as if it had never halted. This pause screen operation can be used with many DOS commands.

Step 1: Display a directory of the default drive.

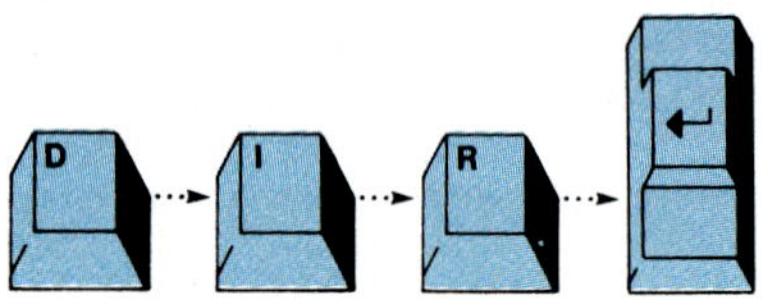

Step 2: Halt the directory listing.

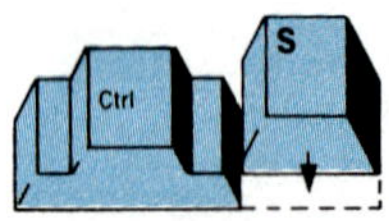

Step 3: Continue the display by pressing any character key.

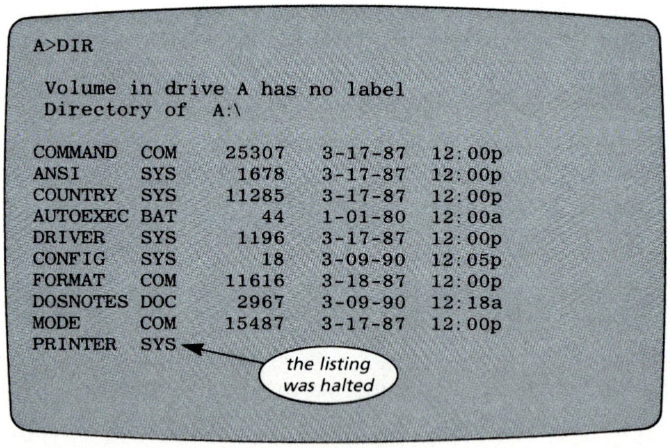

FIGURE 17

DIR Command Options. It is not always easy to pause the directory listing where you want it. Therefore, you might want to use two other options with the DIR command. One option, /P, causes the screen to pause. The second option, /W, displays more data on the screen by increasing the **width** of the display area.

/P—the Pause Option. To demonstrate the pause option, type DIR followed by /P and press the Enter key (Figure 18). When the screen is full, the listing stops and the message "Strike a key when ready . . ." appears at the bottom of the screen. When you are ready to continue the listing, press any character key.

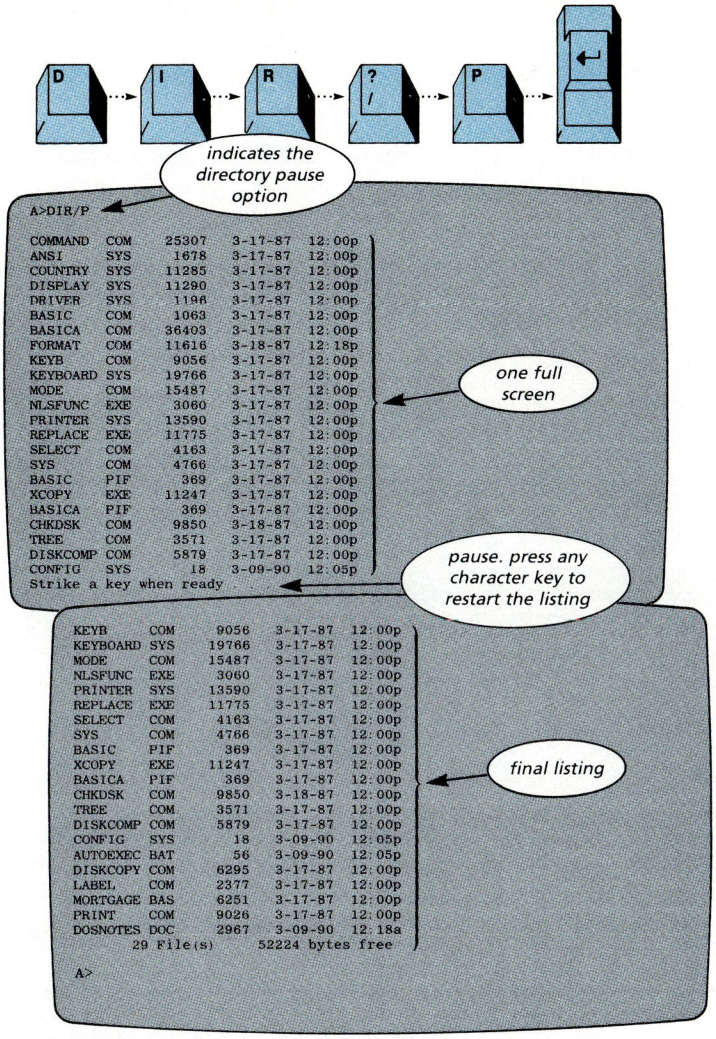

FIGURE 18

/W—the Wide Display Option. The second option for displaying a long list of files is the **/W option**, which displays the information in a wide format. To use the /W option, type DIR /W, then press the Enter key (Figure 19). Note that only the file and directory names are listed, not the size, time, or date of the files.

Canceling a Command (Break)

In some cases, you only need to see a portion of the directory and so you might want to cancel the DIR command after you have seen that portion. To cancel a command you use the Break key. Locate this key on your keyboard; on many keyboards it is on the side of a key, often on the Scroll Lock key or the Pause key. When you press Ctrl-Break the characters ^C appear on the screen and the system prompt reappears. You will often hear this keystroke combination referred to as **Control-Break** or the **Break key**. The characters **^C** indicate that you canceled the command by using the Break key. In general, you can cancel any DOS command that has been initiated by pressing Control-Break. An alternate method of canceling DOS commands is pressing Control-C (Figure 20).

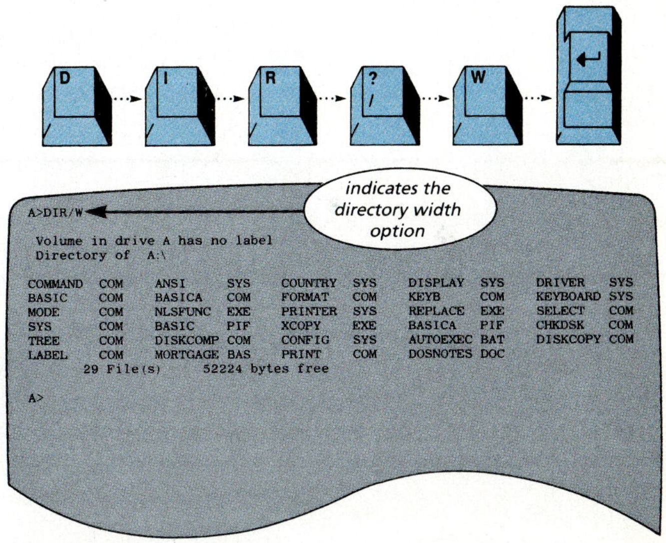

FIGURE 19

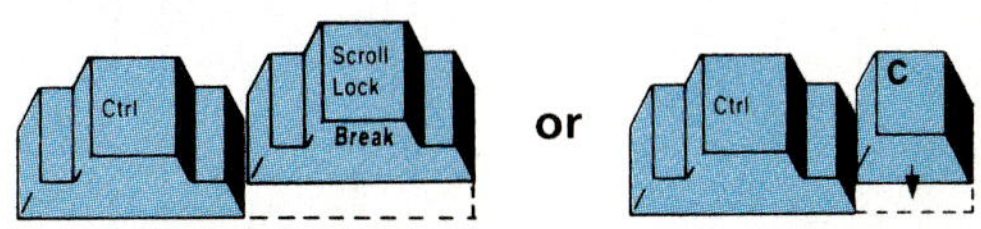

FIGURE 20

FORMATTING A DISKETTE

You cannot use a brand new diskette to store files. The diskette must first be formatted using the DOS FORMAT program. The **formatting** process establishes sectors on the diskette and performs other functions that allow the diskette to store files. Be careful when selecting disks to be used with the FORMAT command. Formatting a diskette destroys all files previously stored on the diskette. Therefore, you must be extremely careful to place the correct diskette in the drive and to make the correct drive letter designation. With a hard disk, extra precaution is necessary to avoid losing files by formatting the hard disk accidentally. DOS versions 3.0 and later provide some protection against accidental formatting of a hard disk, but your own precautions are still the best insurance.

The FORMAT Command

To initiate the FORMAT program, select a new diskette, or one that may be erased. (Use the DIR command to check the contents of your diskette if you are not certain it may be erased.) Because FORMAT is an external DOS command, the FORMAT.COM program file must be on the system disk in the computer when you use this command.

To format a diskette on a two-diskette system, place the DOS diskette in drive A. Type the command FORMAT B: and press the Enter key (Figure 21).

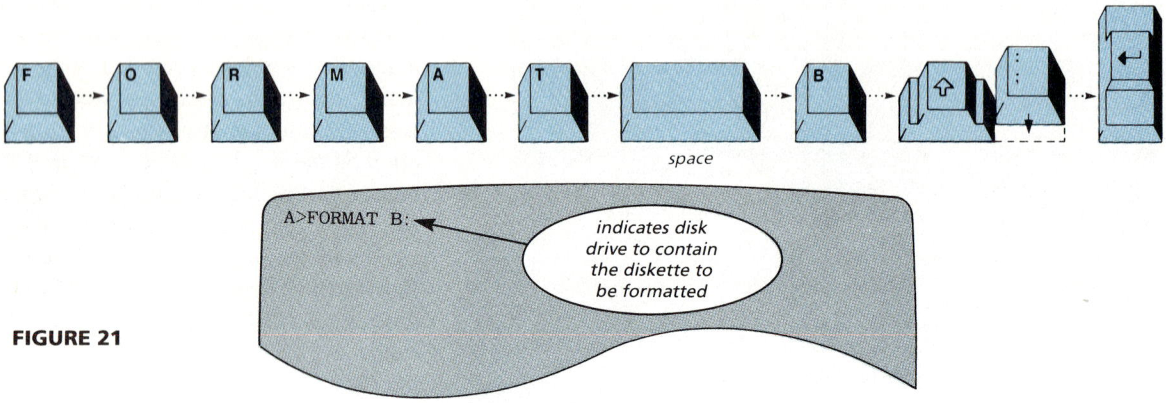

FIGURE 21

When you press the Enter key, the FORMAT program is loaded into main memory and is executed. A message appears on the screen instructing you to "Insert new diskette for drive B: and strike ENTER when ready" (Figure 22). If the disk you want to format is already in drive B, simply press the Enter key.

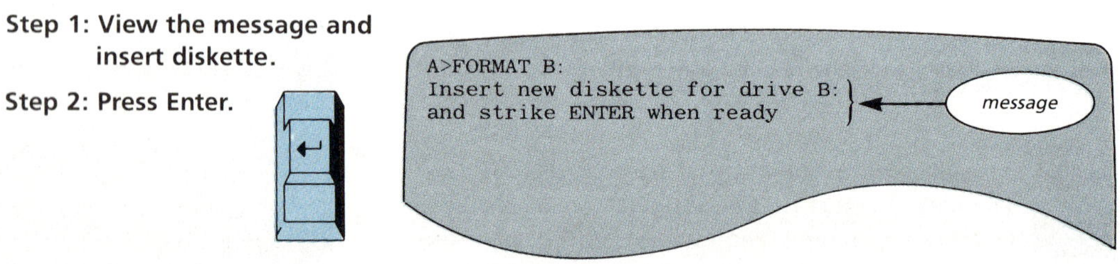

FIGURE 22

The FORMAT procedure on a hard-disk system is essentially the same as for a two-diskette system, except that the FORMAT program is stored on drive C, the hard disk. Be careful NOT to format drive C accidentally. To format a diskette in drive A at the C> prompt, type FORMAT A: and press the Enter key (Figure 23). The program will instruct you when to place the diskette to be formatted into drive A (Figure 24).

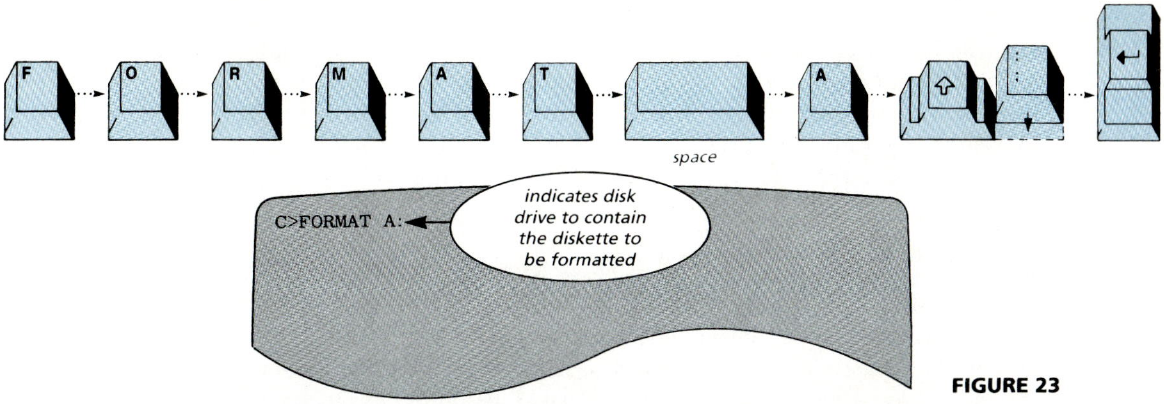

FIGURE 23

To complete the format process, place the diskette to be formatted into the appropriate drive (drive B for a two-diskette system; drive A for a computer with a hard-disk) and press the Enter key. While formatting occurs, a message appears indicating that the process is underway. Figure 25 shows the message from a two diskette system and Figure 26 illustrates the message on a computer with a hard-disk. Messages may differ slightly depending upon the version of DOS you are using. When the formatting process is complete, the messages shown in Figure 27 or 28 appear.

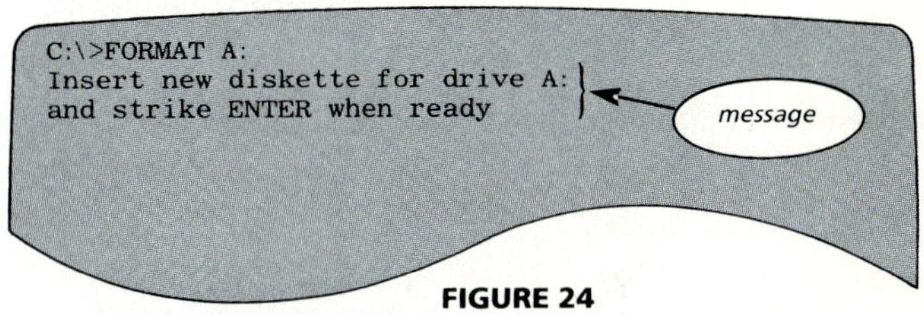

FIGURE 24

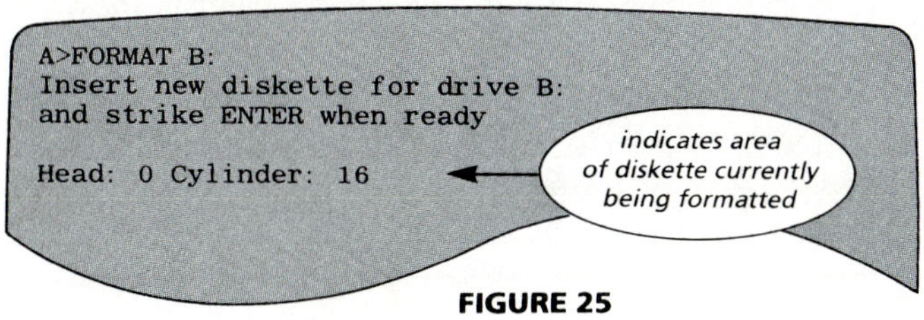

FIGURE 25

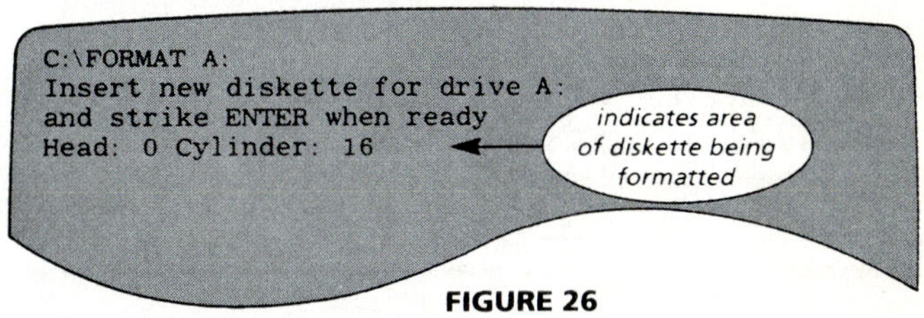

FIGURE 26

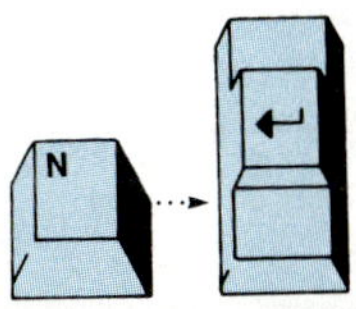

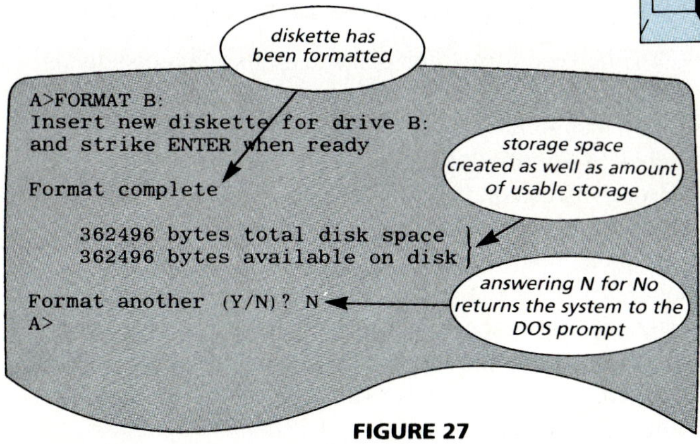

FIGURE 27

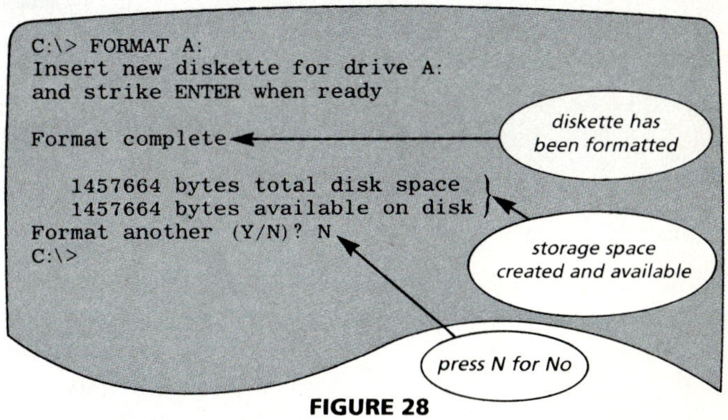

FIGURE 28

The FORMAT program specifies that the diskette is formatted for a total number of bytes and that all of these bytes are available for storage. Finally, the FORMAT program asks if there are other diskettes to be formatted. If there are, press the letter Y and then the Enter key to continue the formatting process. If there are no more diskettes to be formatted, press the letter N and then the Enter key to end the FORMAT program.

Formatting a System Disk (/S Option)

The FORMAT command shown in Figures 26 and 27 will format a diskette so that it can be used for both data files and program files. However, the diskette cannot be used to boot the system because it does not contain the special system programs that are required for booting. To format a diskette so that it contains these special programs, thus creating what is called a **system disk**, you must use the **/S option**.

Use the same diskette you used in the last exercise. If you are using a two-diskette system, use the following commands. If you are using a hard-disk system, use drive C as the default drive and place the diskette to be formatted in drive A. Be very certain NOT to format drive C accidentally.

To create a system disk on a two-diskette system, type FORMAT B:/S and press the Enter key (Figure 29). On a hard-disk system, type FORMAT A:/S. You will be prompted to insert a new diskette in drive B (or A); if the diskette you formatted earlier is still in the disk drive, simply press the Enter key. After the diskette is formatted, the "System transferred" message appears. In general, if you are formatting a diskette to be used only for storing data files, do not place system programs on the diskette so that more space is available for the data files.

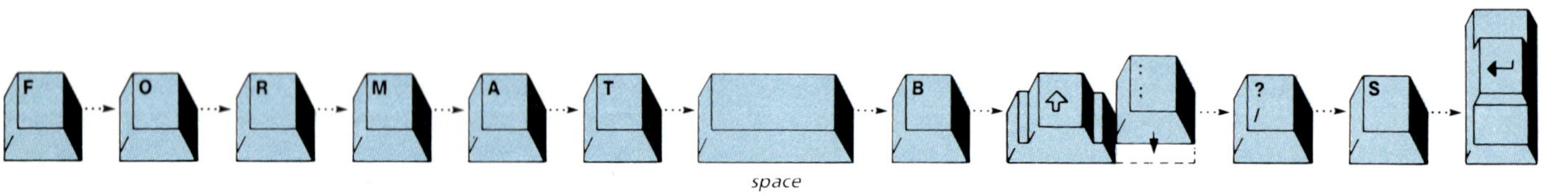

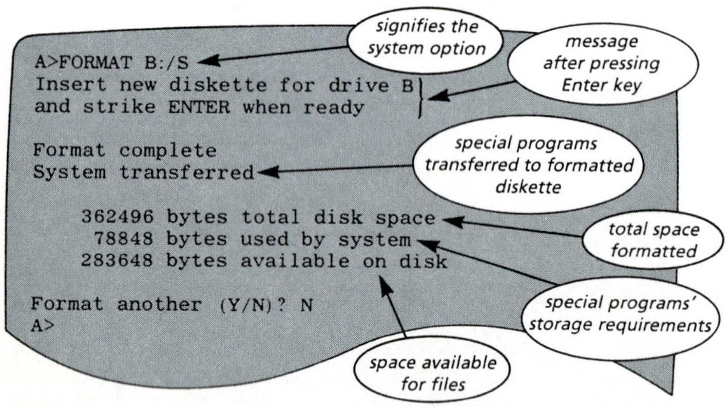

FIGURE 29

Assigning a Volume Label (/V Option)

Whether you format the diskette as a system disk using the /S option or only for data and program files, it is a good idea to identify each diskette by assigning a volume label. A **volume label** is an entry that appears before the listing of files on the diskette to help you verify which diskette is being accessed. You use the /V command to assign a volume label.

To assign a volume label, you would type FORMAT B:/V and press the Enter key (Figure 30). You will again be instructed to insert a diskette into drive B. Insert a new diskette, or press the Enter key if the diskette from the previous exercise is still in drive B. When the format process is complete, you will receive the message "Volume label (11 characters, ENTER for none)?" as a prompt to enter your label. You may use 11 characters—letters, numbers, or spaces—but not punctuation or special characters. After you enter a label and press the Enter key, a message appears asking if you want to format another diskette. You would press N and the Enter key to return to the DOS prompt.

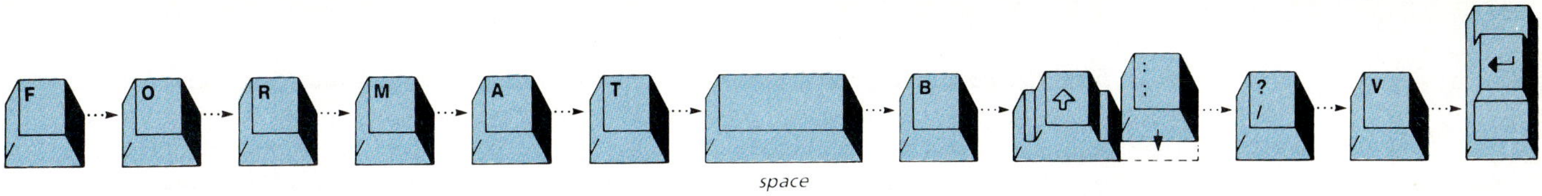

FIGURE 30

CLS COMMAND

Quite often, as you issue several commands or perform lengthy processes, the display screen will become crowded and difficult to read and interpret (Figure 31). To clear the screen and place the system prompt on the first line of the screen, you can use the CLS (Clear Screen) command. Type the letters CLS, then press the Enter key to execute the Clear Screen command.

MANAGING DATA AND PROGRAM FILES ON DISKS

A **data file** is a collection of data created by application or system programs and used by the programs. The data can be the figures used for a spreadsheet showing sales revenues, names and addresses in a database file, or a word processing document announcing the arrival of a new employee. A **program file** contains machine-readable instructions that the computer follows to perform its tasks. The program might be an operating system program or one of the application programs such as word processing that uses data files. Both data files and program files require your attention to be stored on a disk correctly.

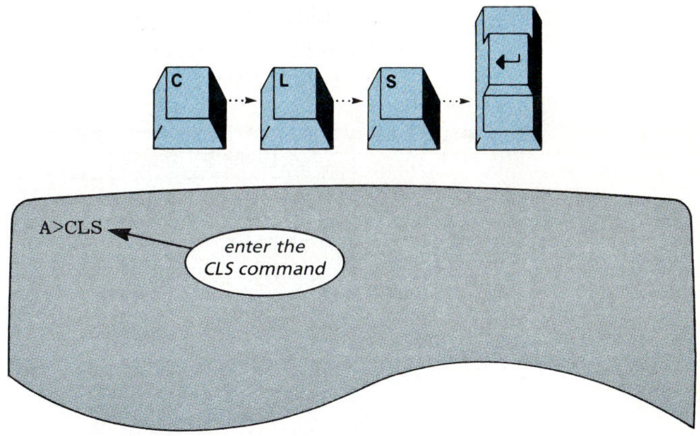

FIGURE 31

Assigning File Specifications

DOS identifies the files on a disk by a combination of several specifications (Figure 32). A **file specification** lets DOS know exactly where to search for a file and gives its exact name. There are four parts to a DOS file specification: (1) the drive specifier, which you already know as drive A: or B: or C:, if there is a hard disk; (2) a directory specification (explained later); (3) the filename; (4) the filename extension.

FIGURE 32

LEGEND	DEFINITION
d:	The disk drive letter specifies the drive containing the file you are requesting. For example, A: specifies disk drive A. If you omit the drive letter, DOS assumes the file is located on the default drive. A disk drive letter is always followed by a colon (:).
\path	A path is an optional reference to a subdirectory of files on the specified disk. It is preceded, and sometimes followed, by a backslash (\).
filename	The filename consists of from one to eight characters.
.ext	A filename may contain an optional extension of a period followed by from one to three characters. The extension is used to add further identity to files.

Filenames. Regardless of the type of data in the file, you must assign a filename to every data file, as well as to every program file. A **filename** consists of one to eight characters and is used by DOS to identify a specific file. You may use any combination of characters except: period (.), quotation mark ("), slash (/), backslash (\), brackets ([ ]), colon (:), less than (<), greater than (>), plus (+), equals (=), semicolon (;), and comma (,).

In general, your filename should reflect the data stored in it. For example, if your file contains employee records, it is more meaningful to use the filename EMPLOYEE than to use the filename FILE1, even though DOS will accept either filename.

Filename Extensions. A filename can be made more specific by an optional extension. A **filename extension** consists of a period followed by one to three characters. The same characters that are permitted for a filename are permitted for a filename extension. The filename extension can identify a file more specifically or describe its purpose (Figure 33). For example, if you wish to create a copy of the EMPLOYEE file, you could use the filename extension .CPY to identify the file as a copied file. The entire file specification for the file would be EMPLOYEE.CPY.

FIGURE 33

.COM Files		.EXE Files		.BAT Files	
COMMAND	COM	APPEND	EXE	AUTOEXEC	BAT
ASSIGN	COM	ATTRIB	EXE	WP	BAT
BACKUP	COM	FASTOPEN	EXE	INSTALL	BAT
BASIC	COM	FIND	EXE		
BASICA	COM	JOIN	EXE		
CHKDSK	COM	NLSFUNC	EXE		
COMP	COM	REPLACE	EXE		
DEBUG	COM				
DISKCOMP	COM				
DISKCOPY	COM				
FORMAT	COM				
LABEL	COM				

Certain programs associated with the Disk Operating System use special filename extensions. All files with the filename extensions .COM or .EXE are executable programs. Files with the extension .BAT are **DOS batch files** and contain a series of DOS commands to be executed in sequence. Any DOS command with one of these filename extensions is an external command. You can execute any external command simply by typing the filename (the extension is not required) and pressing the Enter key.

COPY COMMAND

Once you have formatted a diskette and are ready to use it to store data or program files, you will need a method of placing these files on the diskette. Use the **COPY command** to copy one file or a series of files to the same or a different diskette. As a DOS internal command, COPY may be used at any time, with or without the system disk.

Using the COPY Command

The COPY command is often used to make working copies of program and data diskettes. Copying original files from one diskette creates a second diskette that can be used for everyday work to protect the original disk from damage. A similar use for COPY is to make a **backup copy** of a diskette to guard against accidental loss of data. One frequently used technique is to make a backup copy of a file whenever you work on revisions to an existing file. In fact, some application programs will make a backup file automatically, using the filename extension .BAK or .BAC to indicate that it is a backup file.

Copying Files from One Diskette to Another

In the following examples of the COPY command, you will copy files from drive A to drive B. Check to see that you have the Data Diskette provided to instructors in drive A and your formatted diskette in drive B. If you are using a hard disk system, use drive C as the default drive, copying the files to drive A.

For practice, copy the file DOSNOTES.DOC from drive A to drive B. Your instructor will make the DOSNOTES.DOC file available to you or will give you the name of another file to copy. Type COPY DOSNOTES.DOC B: and press the Enter key. Note that after the word COPY you leave one or more spaces, then state the file specification of the file to be copied. In DOS terminology, this file is called the **source file**. In Figure 34, the filename DOSNOTES.DOC is specified as the source file. Since no drive specification is included, the operating system assumes the file is located on the default drive, drive A.

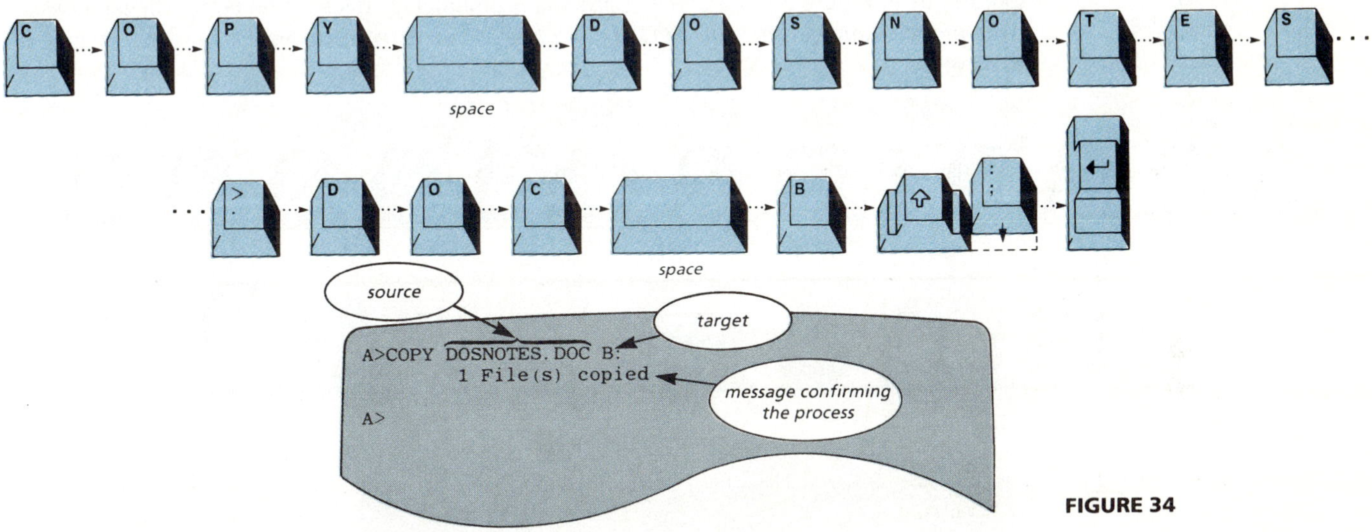

FIGURE 34

Following the source file is one or more blank spaces. Then, the **file specification**, which can include the drive specification, and the name of the **target file**, that is, the filename and filename extension of the source file after it is copied, is specified. In Figure 34, the drive specification B: states that the file is to be copied to a diskette in drive B. Because no filename is specified for the target file on drive B, DOS defaults to the same name as the source file, and so the name of the file on drive B will be DOSNOTES.DOC. The message "1 File(s) copied" signals that the command is completed.

When you copy a file from a diskette in one drive to a diskette in another drive, you can assign a new name to the target file. To copy the file DOSNOTES.DOC from the diskette in drive A to the diskette in drive B, giving the new file the name NOTECOPY on drive B, type COPY DOSNOTES.DOC B:NOTECOPY and press the Enter key (Figure 35). Again, the message "1 File(s) copied" appears when the task is completed, as in Figure 34.

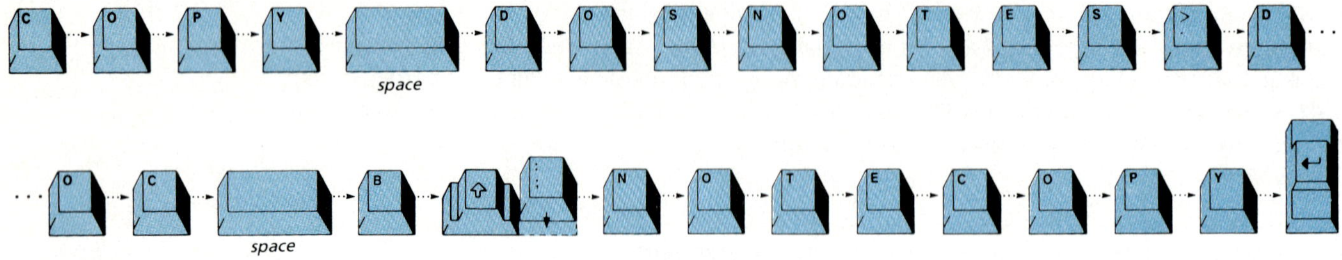

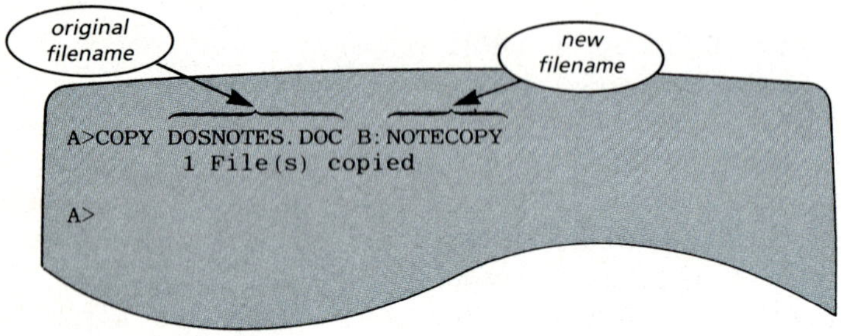

FIGURE 35

Copying to the Default Disk

It is also possible to copy a file from the second drive to the default drive. In the next exercise, you will copy a file from the diskette in drive B to the diskette in drive A, the default drive. You will not change the filename. To accomplish this procedure, type COPY B:NOTECOPY A: and press the Enter key. This command copies the file named NOTECOPY from the diskette in drive B to the diskette in drive A. When the message "1 File(s) copied" appears, as in Figure 36, the copying process is completed. Because no target filename was given in the command, the file NOTECOPY will be on drive A under the same name as it is on drive B.

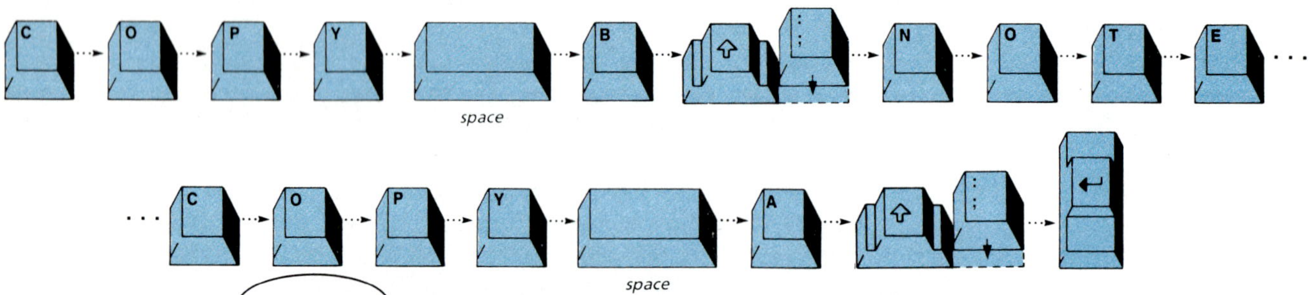

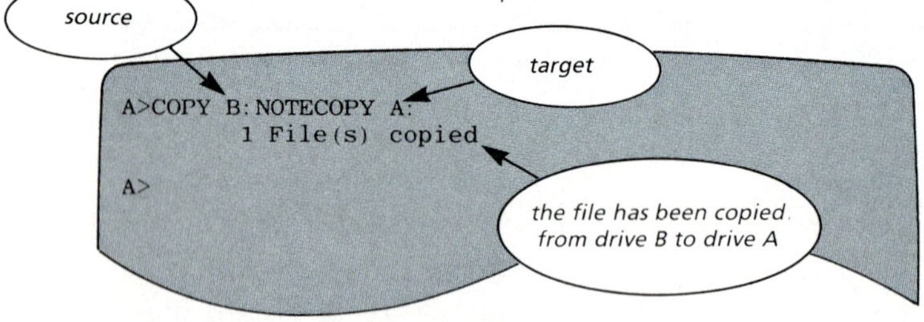

FIGURE 36

Copying a File to the Same Diskette

It is possible to copy a file to the same diskette, but you must use a different filename. For practice, copy the file named DOSNOTES.DOC stored on drive A onto the same diskette. Give the filename DOSNOTES.BAK to the target file. Type the command COPY DOSNOTES.DOC DOSNOTES.BAK and press the Enter key.

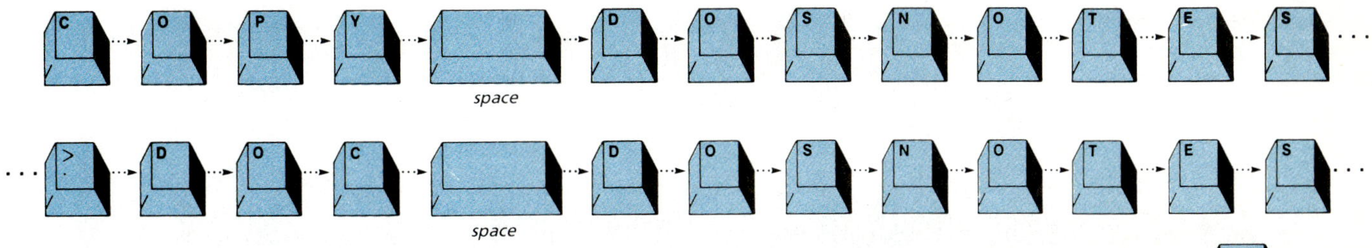

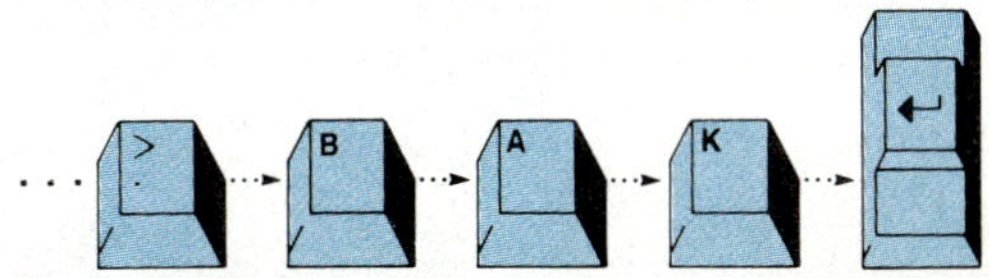

When your COPY command is executed, the file DOSNOTES.DOC in drive A is copied to the same diskette on drive A as DOSNOTES.BAK (Figure 37). The file extension .BAK is used to distinguish the files. If you had used the same filename to designate both the target and source files on the same diskette, an error message would be displayed, stating that a file cannot be copied onto itself. You would then have to reenter the COPY command using a different name for the target file.

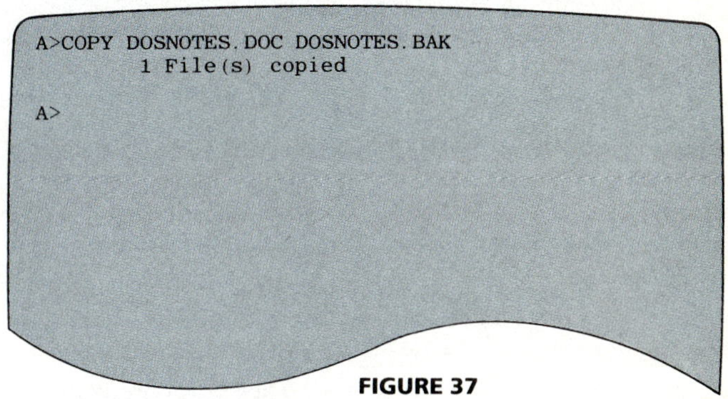

FIGURE 37

Global Filename Characters (''Wildcards'')

You can copy more than one file at a time using a single COPY command. To copy more than one file, you use **global characters**, or **wildcards**. These are special characters indicating that any character may occupy that specific location in the filename. The two global characters are the ***** (asterisk) and the **?** (question mark).

To use wildcards, you need to know the files stored on the diskette. Figure 38 shows the directory of the diskette in drive A. (Your directory may look different.) Notice that the files DOSNOTES.BAK and NOTECOPY appear, a result of the COPY commands you used earlier. Notice also that several files have the same filename extensions. It is not uncommon, on any disk with many files, to find several files with similarities in filenames or extensions. These similarities can be exploited by using wildcard characters.

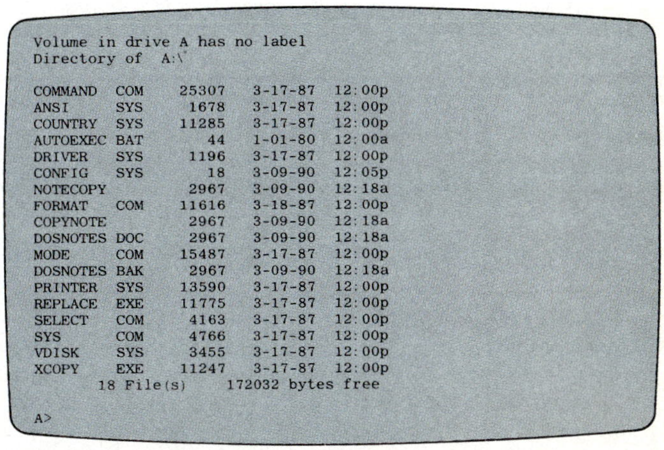

FIGURE 38

The * Character. You can use the global character ***** (asterisk) to indicate a portion of the filename or extension. When the * global character appears, any character can occupy that position and all the remaining positions in the filename or the filename extension.

For example, let us use the wildcard asterisk (*) to copy files with the filename extension .COM from the diskette in drive A to the diskette in drive B. Type COPY *.COM B: and press the Enter key. In Figure 39, the source files are specified by the entry *.COM. The asterisk (*) in the filename portion of the specification means that any filename can be used. The file extension .COM states that the file specification must include the file extension .COM. In Figure 38, five filenames satisfy this criterion: COMMAND.COM, FORMAT-.COM, MODE.COM, SELECT.COM, and SYS.COM.

FIGURE 39

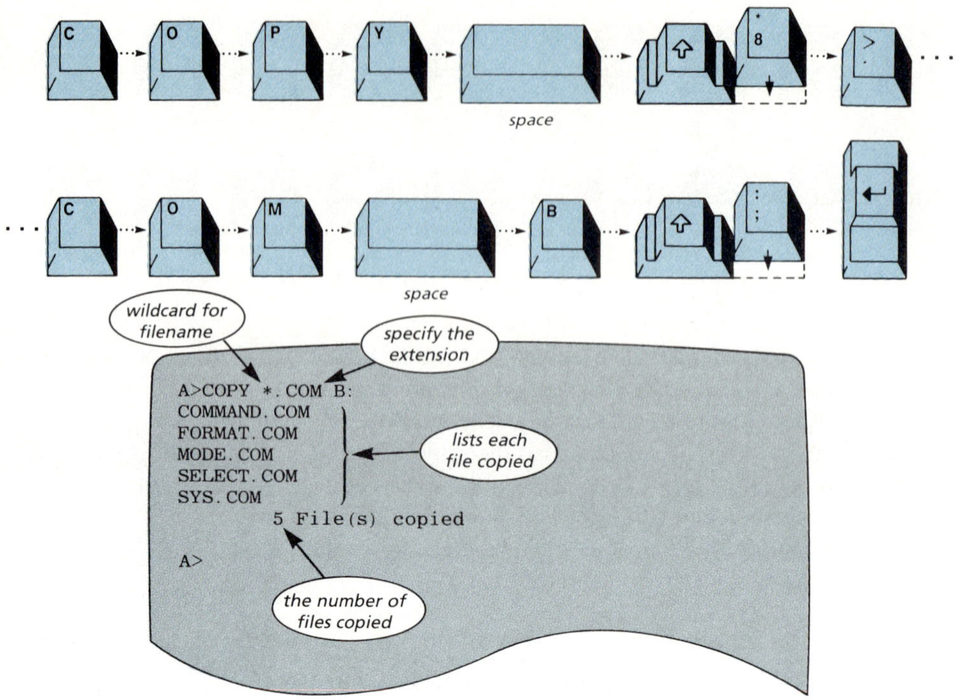

These files are copied to the diskette in disk drive B. The filenames for the copied files on the diskette in drive B remain the same as the source filenames on the diskette in drive A because you specified no new names in the copy command. When you copy files with a COPY command using the * global character, all files copied are listed by the COPY command. Figure 39 lists the five copied files.

You can also specify the global character * as the filename extension to copy a specific filename with any extension. For example, the diskette contains two files with the name DOSNOTES, DOSNOTES.BAK and DOSNOTES.DOC. Type the command COPY DOSNOTES.* B: as in Figure 40 and press the Enter key to copy both the files with the filename DOSNOTES to drive B.

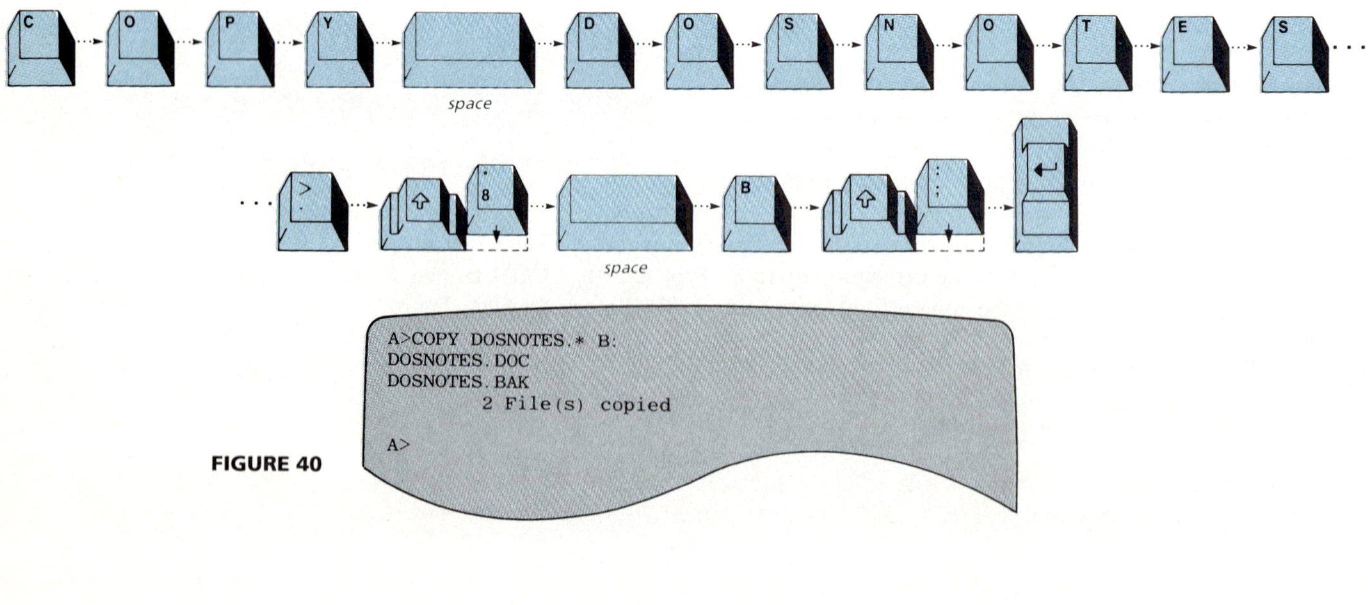

FIGURE 40

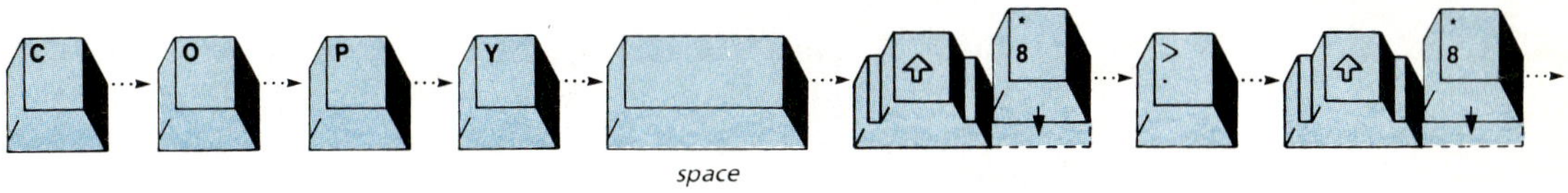

Copying All Files from One Diskette to Another. You can also use the COPY command to copy all of the files on one diskette to another diskette by using the * global character. This technique is useful in making backup or working copies of entire diskettes. You use the * wildcard in both the filename and extension positions to signify "all filenames.all extensions" in the command. Practice by typing COPY *.* B: and pressing the Enter key to copy all files on drive A to drive B (Figure 41).

The ? Character. The ? (question mark) global character can also be used to represent any character occupying the position in which the wildcard character appears. However, the ? represents only a single character replacement, whereas the * can represent one or more characters. You can use a single ? or several in a command to identify files. Practice this option by typing COPY DOSNOTES.BA? B: and pressing the Enter key to copy DOSNOTES.BAK to drive B (Figure 42).

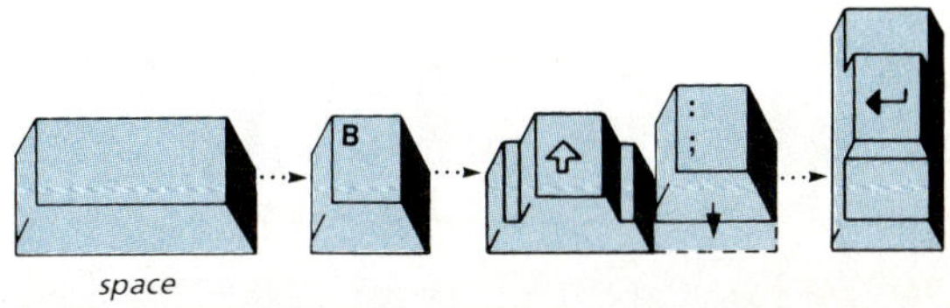


```
A>COPY *.* B:
COMMAND.COM
ANSI.SYS
COUNTRY.SYS
AUTOEXEC.BAT
DRIVER.SYS
CONFIG.SYS
NOTECOPY
FORMAT.COM
COPYNOTE
DOSNOTES.DOC
MODE.COM
DOSNOTES.BAK
PRINTER.SYS
REPLACE.EXE
SELECT.COM
SYS.COM
VDISK.SYS
XCOPY.EXE
        18 File(s) copied

A>
```

FIGURE 41

Using Wildcards with DOS Commands

You have learned to use the wildcard characters with the COPY command. Many DOS commands support the use of global replacement characters. For example, you can use the wildcards with the DIR command to look for files of a common type. To look at all DOS batch files on a diskette, you would type the command DIR *.BAT and press the Enter key to display all files with the filename extension .BAT.

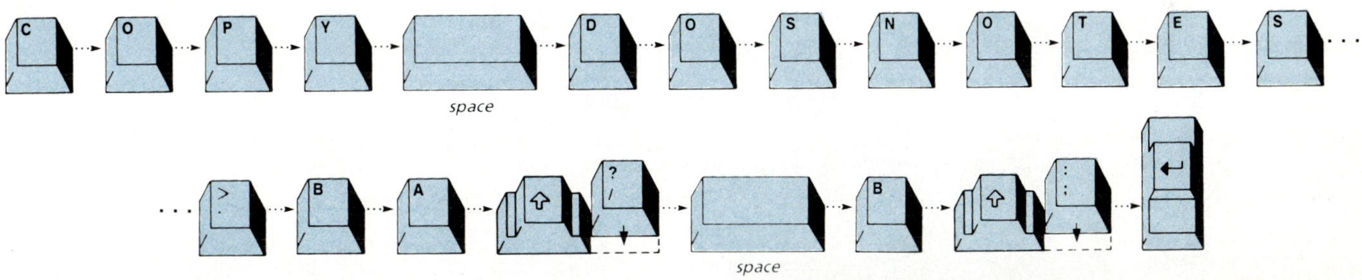


```
A>COPY DOSNOTES.BA? B:
DOSNOTES.BAK
        1 File(s) copied

A>
```

the ? is replaced by the letter K

FIGURE 42

RENAME COMMAND

Use the **RENAME command** when you want to rename a file on a diskette. If you assign a filename already used by a file currently on the diskette, DOS creates the new file on the diskette and destroys the previously existing file with that name. You will not receive any warning that this has happened. Thus, you should periodically check the filenames on a diskette to avoid accidental replacement of files. If you discover a filename you might reuse, you can use the RENAME command to change the name of the file.

In the example in Figure 43, the file with the filename NOTECOPY on drive A is to be renamed DOSFILE. Type the command RENAME NOTECOPY DOSFILE immediately after the system prompt and press the Enter key. When you press the Enter key, the filename on the diskette in drive A is changed from NOTECOPY to DOSFILE.

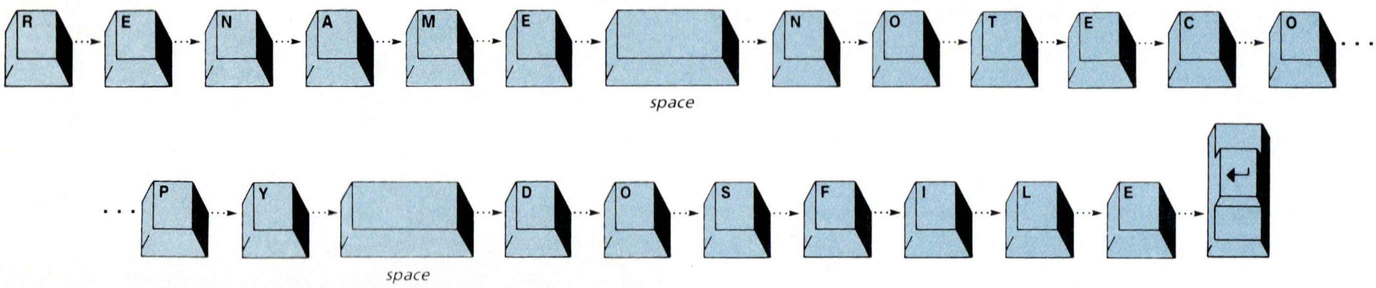

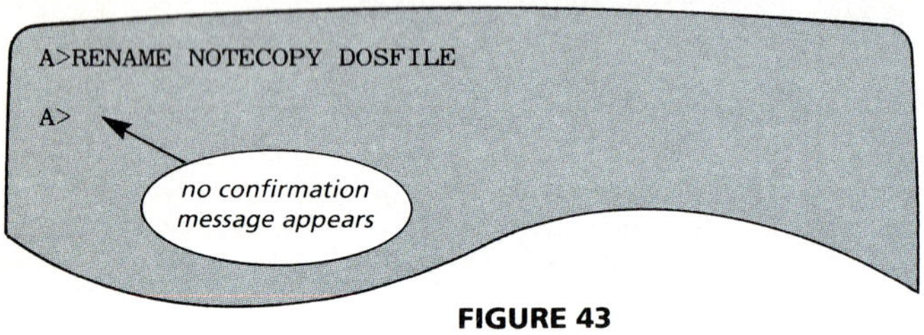

FIGURE 43

You can use the global characters * and ? with the RENAME command. In Figure 44, all files with the file extension .BAK are renamed with a file extension .BAC. Type the wildcard character * with the command RENAME *.BAK *.BAC and press the Enter key. All characters represented by the * will remain the same in the new filename. Thus, in Figure 44, all the filenames in the renamed files will remain the same, but the file extensions will change from .BAK to .BAC. RENAME does not confirm the operation on the screen, so you should use the DIR command before and after you use the RENAME command to assure the command was executed (Figure 45).

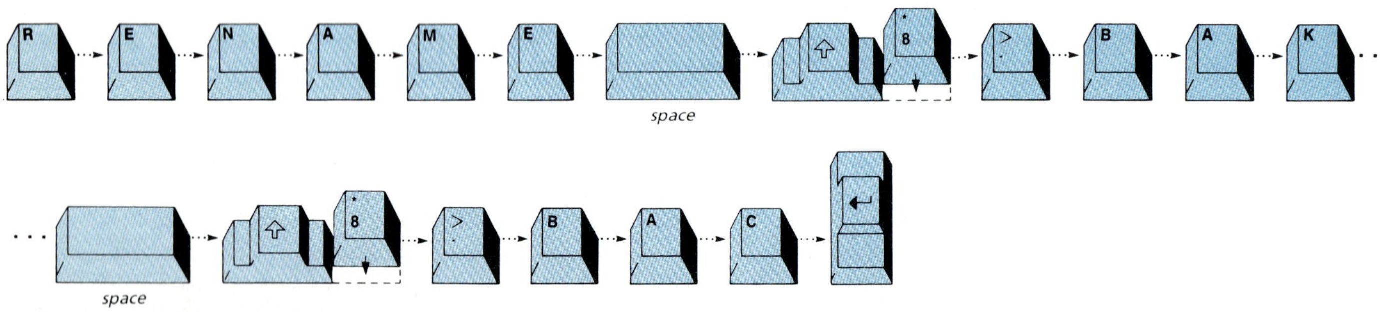

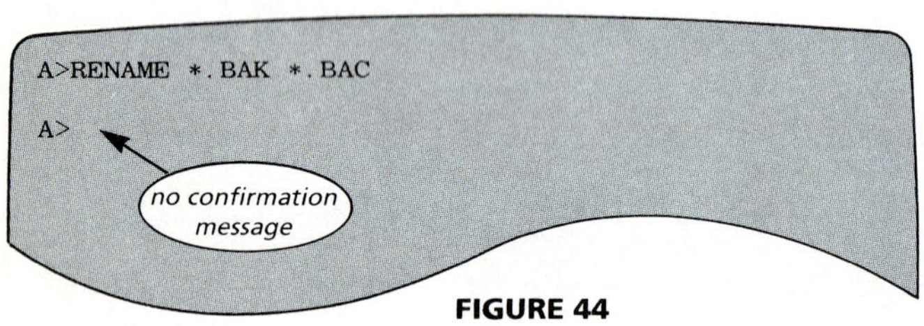

FIGURE 44

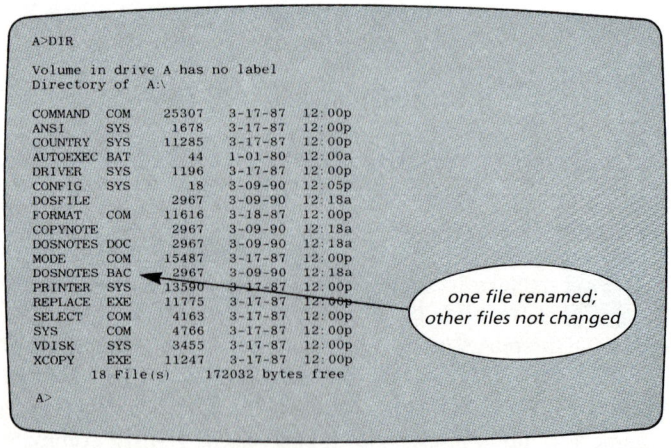

FIGURE 45

ERASE AND DEL COMMANDS

As a part of diskette file management, you should periodically remove unneeded files from your diskette. The **ERASE command** will erase, or remove, a file from a diskette. An alternative command that functions like the erase command is the **DEL** (delete) command. Take care when using the ERASE or DEL commands, because once a file has been erased from the directory, it cannot be easily recovered. Such inadvertent erasing of a file is another reason for keeping backup files.

Removing Files

We will begin by removing a single file, DOSFILE, from drive A. Type ERASE DOSFILE and press the Enter key, as shown in Figure 46. (You could use the DEL command instead, typing DEL DOSFILE and pressing the Enter key.) Use the DIR command to assure that the file has been removed from the diskette.

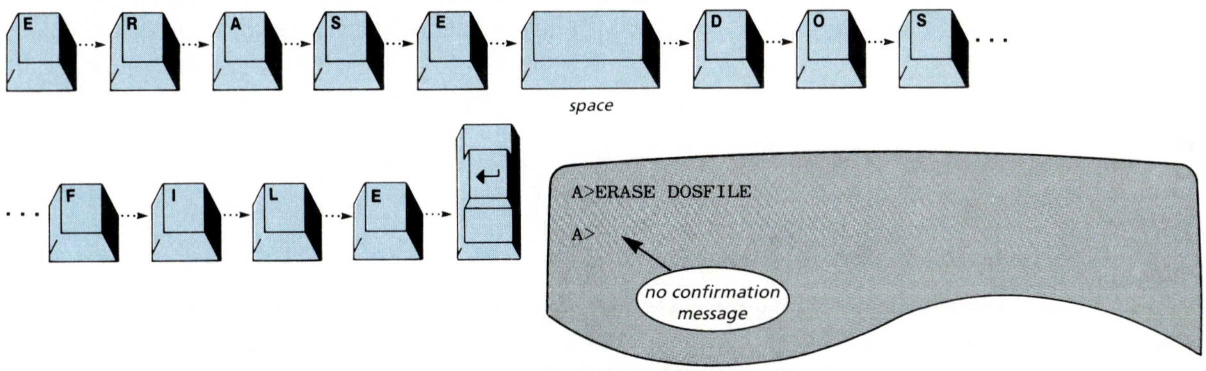

FIGURE 46

USING DIRECTORIES AND SUBDIRECTORIES

Directory Entries and Subdirectories

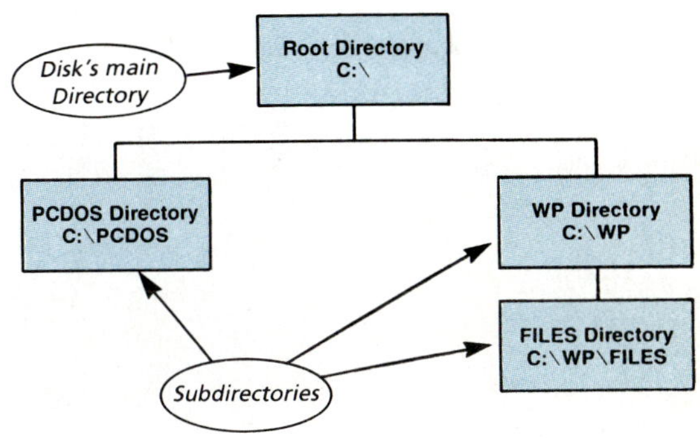

FIGURE 47

When you need to view the files on any disk, the computer does not actually read the entire disk looking for the file. Instead, a **file directory** or listing of each of the filenames on the disk is searched. This directory, created when the diskette is formatted, is called the **root directory**. Entries for subdirectories are made in the root directory. The root directory is the highest level directory of a disk (Figure 47).

You can make three types of entries into a disk directory: (1) the filename and extension, (2) the volume label, (3) a subdirectory entry. We have previously discussed (1) and (2).

You can create a **subdirectory** to group all files of a similar type together (Figure 47). For example, you can create a subdirectory containing all the files related to DOS.

There are at least two good reasons to use subdirectories. First, the operating system provides a limited number of entries in the file directory. A diskette has room for only 112 entries; a hard disk allows up to 512 entries. This capacity may be sufficient on a diskette, but a hard disk with many millions of bytes of storage may have more files than the directory permits.

It is also easier to find files that are organized by related groups than to search randomly through all the files on a disk.

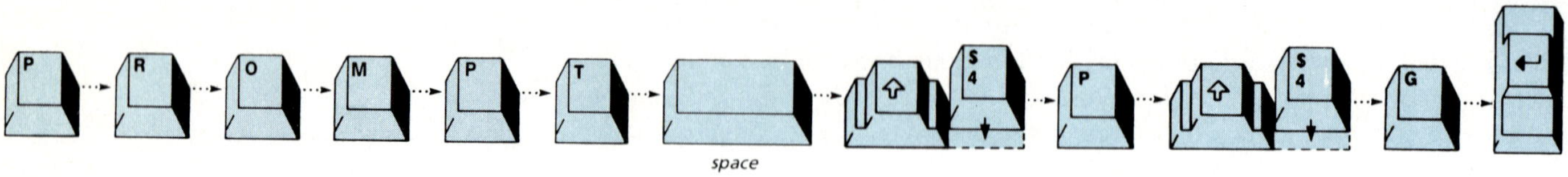

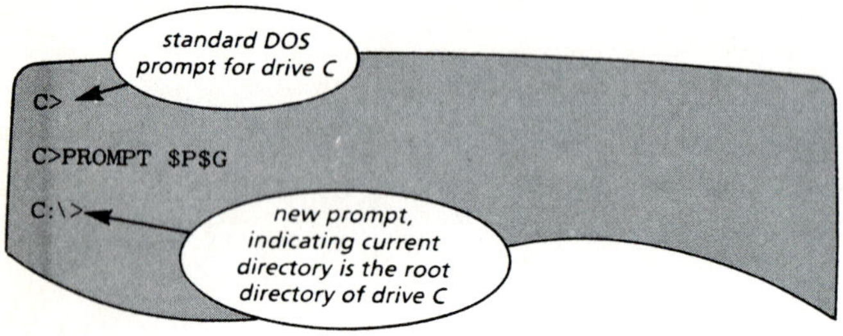

FIGURE 48

The PROMPT Command

The standard DOS prompt, A>, B>, or C>, does not tell you what subdirectories you are using. DOS provides a way for you to monitor which directory is in use through the **PROMPT command**. To have DOS include the subdirectory information as a part of the DOS prompt, type PROMPT PG and press the Enter key (Figure 48). Whenever you change disk drive addresses, you will see the subdirectory information as a part of the prompt.

Making Subdirectories

To create a subdirectory, use the **MKDIR command**, usually abbreviated as **MD**. If you have a hard disk, and *if your instructor approves*, create a subdirectory on drive C. Otherwise, practice the command on a diskette in drive A. To create a subdirectory called "PCDOS" on your diskette or disk drive, type MD A:\PCDOS and press the Enter key (Figure 49).

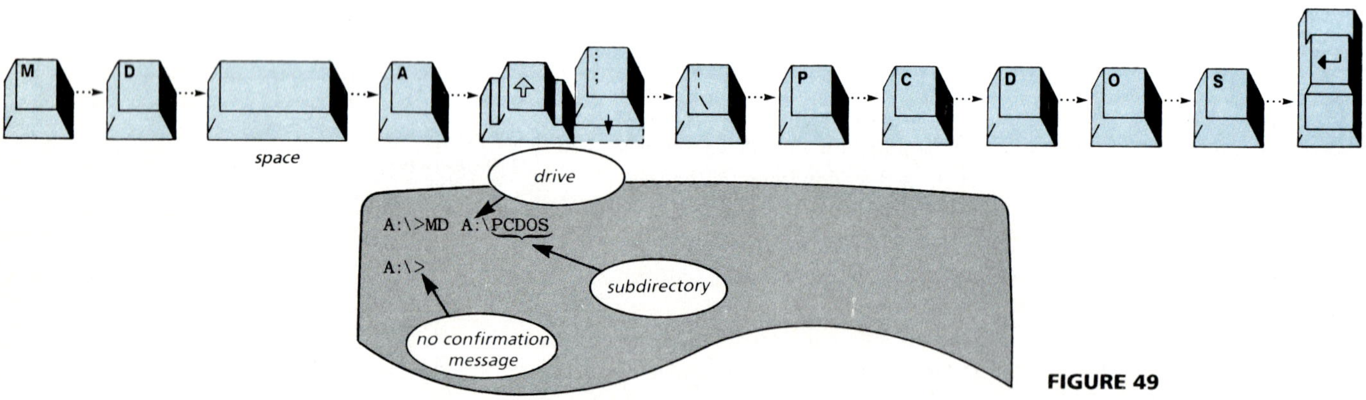

FIGURE 49

There are specific steps to the MD command. (1) Start a subdirectory entry with the drive designation. If the directory is to be on drive C, enter C: immediately after the MD command. Use the command MD A:\PCDOS to use drive A on a diskette. You can omit the drive specification if you are creating the directory on the default drive.

(2) Begin a subdirectory entry with the **backslash** character, \. The root directory for your hard disk is designated by a backslash alone. For example, C:\ designates the root

directory of drive C. The subdirectory made for the DOS files is C:\PCDOS. Notice that because you have issued the PROMPT command, the DOS prompt now includes the root or subdirectory name, C:\> or C:\PCDOS>.

(3) The subdirectory name, like any filename, can contain one to eight characters, followed optionally by a period and one to three characters in an extension. (Generally, subdirectory names do not include extensions.)

(4) You can assign a subdirectory entry to an existing subdirectory. For instance, you can create a subdirectory for a word processing program and a subordinate subdirectory for the data files created by the program. To create the word processing subdirectories shown in Figures 50 and 51, make the word processing subdirectory by typing MD A:\WP and press the Enter key. To make the subordinate subdirectory, type MD A:\WP\FILES and press the Enter key. The program subdirectory is A:\WP, and the word processing files can be stored in a second subdirectory, A:\WP\FILES. These two operations result in a series of related directories. Refer back to Figure 47 to see the relationships among the directories and subdirectories we have created.

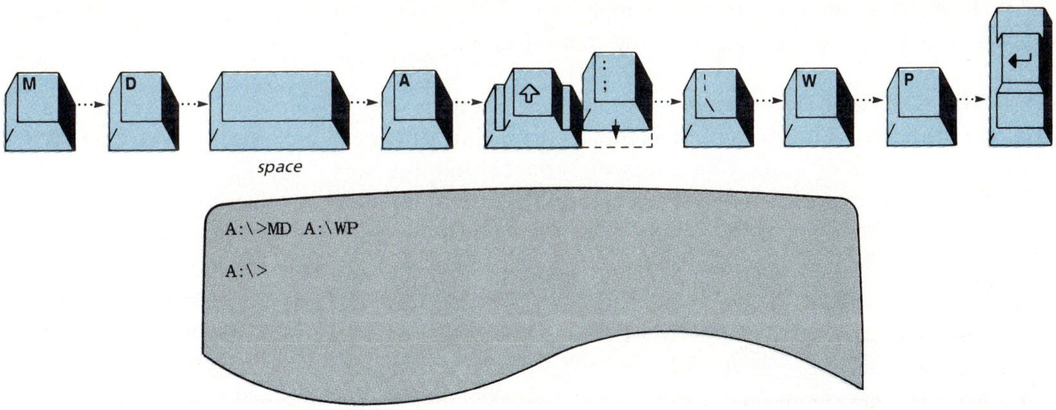

FIGURE 50

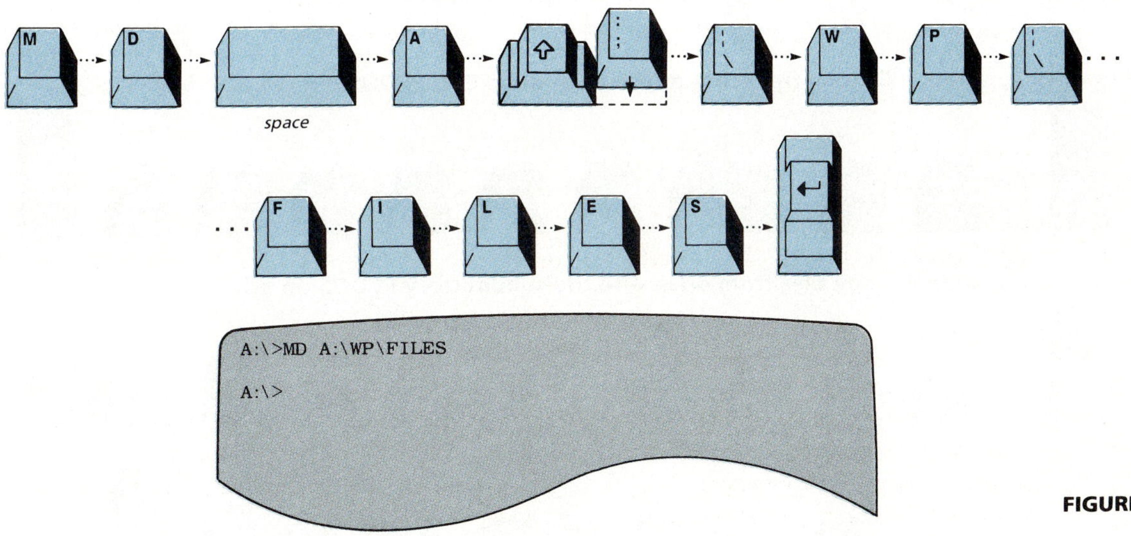

FIGURE 51

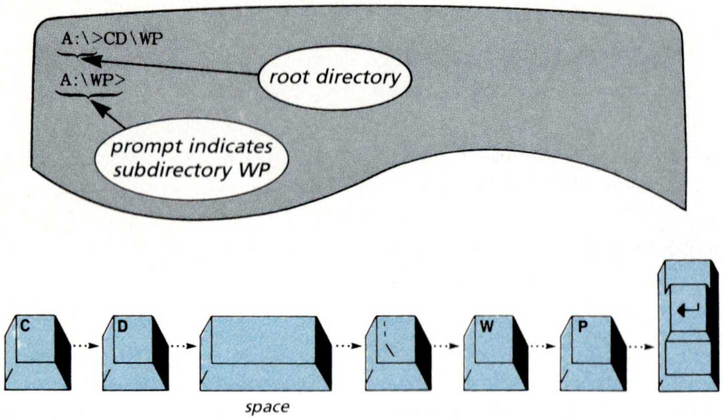

FIGURE 52

Changing Directories

Use the **CHDIR command** to move from one directory to another. Enter the letters CD immediately following the DOS prompt. Then type the backslash character and the subdirectory name and press the Enter key. To change from the root directory to the WP directory, for instance, type the entry CD \WP and press the Enter key. The result shown in Figure 52 should appear on your screen. To move to a lower subdirectory, such as the FILES subdirectory, type CD \WP\FILES and press the Enter key.

If you are moving to a directory that is subordinate to the current subdirectory, you can simply type CD and the subdirectory name. For instance, if your current directory is WP, you can move to the FILES subdirectory by entering CD FILES. Note that the entry omits both the reference to WP (the current directory) and the backslash character.

To return to the root directory simply type CD\ and press the Enter key. The backslash character entered by itself signifies the root directory.

The Current Directory. Just as there is a default or current disk drive, there is a current directory. The **current directory** is the one in which you are currently working. When you first access a disk, the root directory is the current directory. You can, however, direct DOS to a subdirectory, which then becomes the current directory for that disk. If you temporarily set another drive as the default drive, the named directory remains the current directory for the first disk.

FIGURE 53

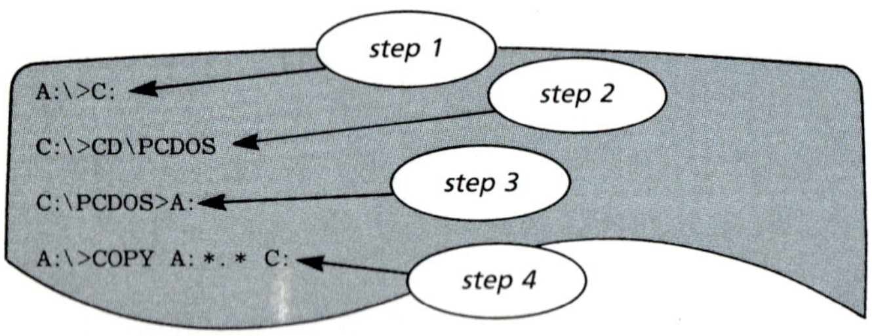

For practice, set your default drive to drive C by entering C: (Figure 53, step 1). Then set PCDOS as the current subdirectory for drive C by entering CD \PCDOS (step 2). Switch to drive A as the default drive (step 3) and copy files from drive A to drive C: type the copy command COPY A:*.* C: (step 4). Files are copied from the A drive to the PCDOS subdirectory on drive C even though the subdirectory is not specified in the copy command.

Step 1: Change default to drive C.

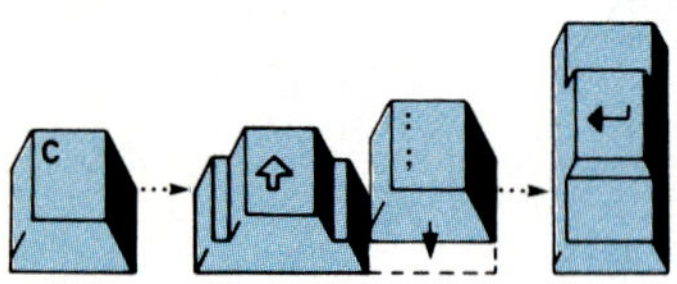

Step 2: Change from root directory of drive C to PCDOS directory.

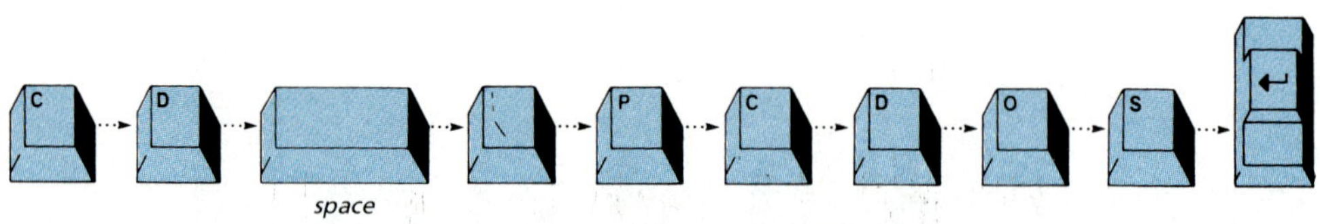

Step 3: Return to A drive.

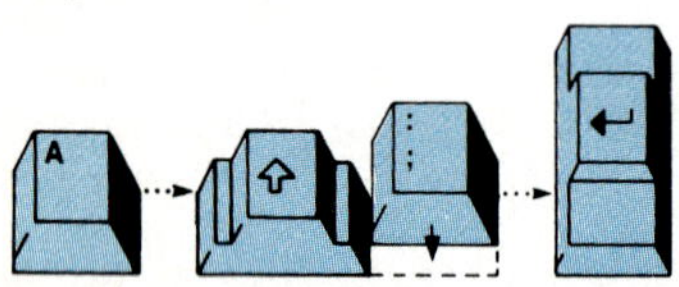

Step 4: Copy files from drive A to the subdirectory PCDOS on drive C.

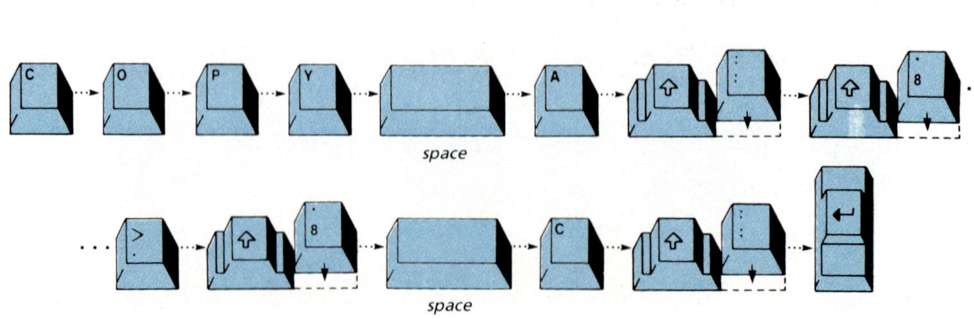

Specifying a Path to Subdirectories and Files

You will find it very convenient to group files in subdirectories. To use the technique you must learn to specify the path to a file. The **path** includes three components: (1) the drive, (2) the name of the subdirectories, (3) the name of the file. The path specifies the route DOS is to take from the root directory through subdirectories leading to a file. Specify the path whenever you wish to access a file for DIR, COPY, or similar commands. Unless you specify a path, DOS may not find the file you desire because it would search only the current directory of the default drive.

Specifying Paths in Commands. One way to specify the path is to include it in the command you are using. For example, you can make a backup copy on a diskette of a file named DOSNOTES.DOC stored in the FILES subdirectory under the WP subdirectory, by typing the command COPY C:\WP\FILES\DOSNOTES.DOC A:. The COPY command includes the source drive (C:), both directories specified together (\WP\FILES), and the filename preceded by a backslash (\DOSNOTES.DOC). On drive A, the file is stored simply as DOSNOTES.DOC under the root directory, because no subdirectory has been made or referenced on that disk.

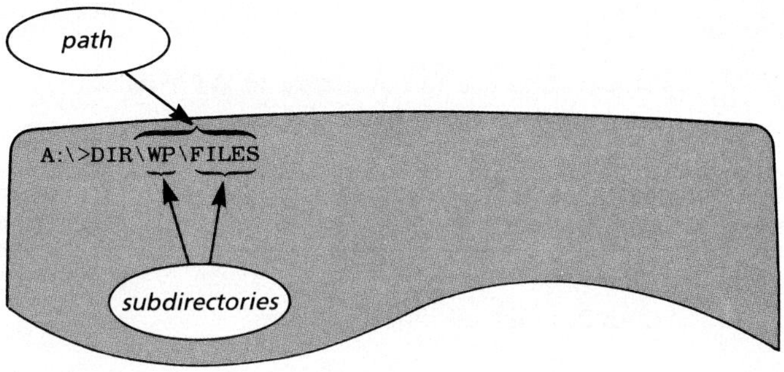

FIGURE 54

You can use this style with other DOS commands and when specifying files in many programs. For example, to display the file contents of the FILES subdirectory, enter DIR \WP\FILES and press the Enter key (Figure 54). Enter DIR \WP to list the program files for the word processing software stored under the WP subdirectory.

Managing Files Within Subdirectories

To copy files or data to subdirectories, you can use the COPY command or any file storage techniques offered by your application program. Some programs may not recognize the subdirectory structure on your diskette, so you may need to set the current directory before you use the program. The RENAME, DIR, ERASE, and other DOS commands work in subdirectories in nearly the same way as they do in the main directory.

Removing Subdirectories

When you no longer need a subdirectory, you can remove it. Use the **RMDIR command**, abbreviated to **RD**, to remove a specified directory from a disk.

Erasing Subdirectory Files. To remove a subdirectory, you must first remove all files stored within it. You can do so by using the global character * with the ERASE command. You can issue this command from the subdirectory to be removed or from another directory if you give the full path specification. If you issue the command from another directory, make certain to use the correct subdirectory and path information or you might inadvertently erase files from another part of the disk.

For practice, delete the FILES subdirectory (Figure 55, step 1). First, enter the FILES subdirectory by typing the command CD\WP\FILES and pressing the Enter key. Next, empty the subdirectory of files by typing ERASE *.* and pressing the Enter key (step 2). You will receive the message "Are you sure (Y/N)?", to which you must press Y and then the Enter key (step 3).

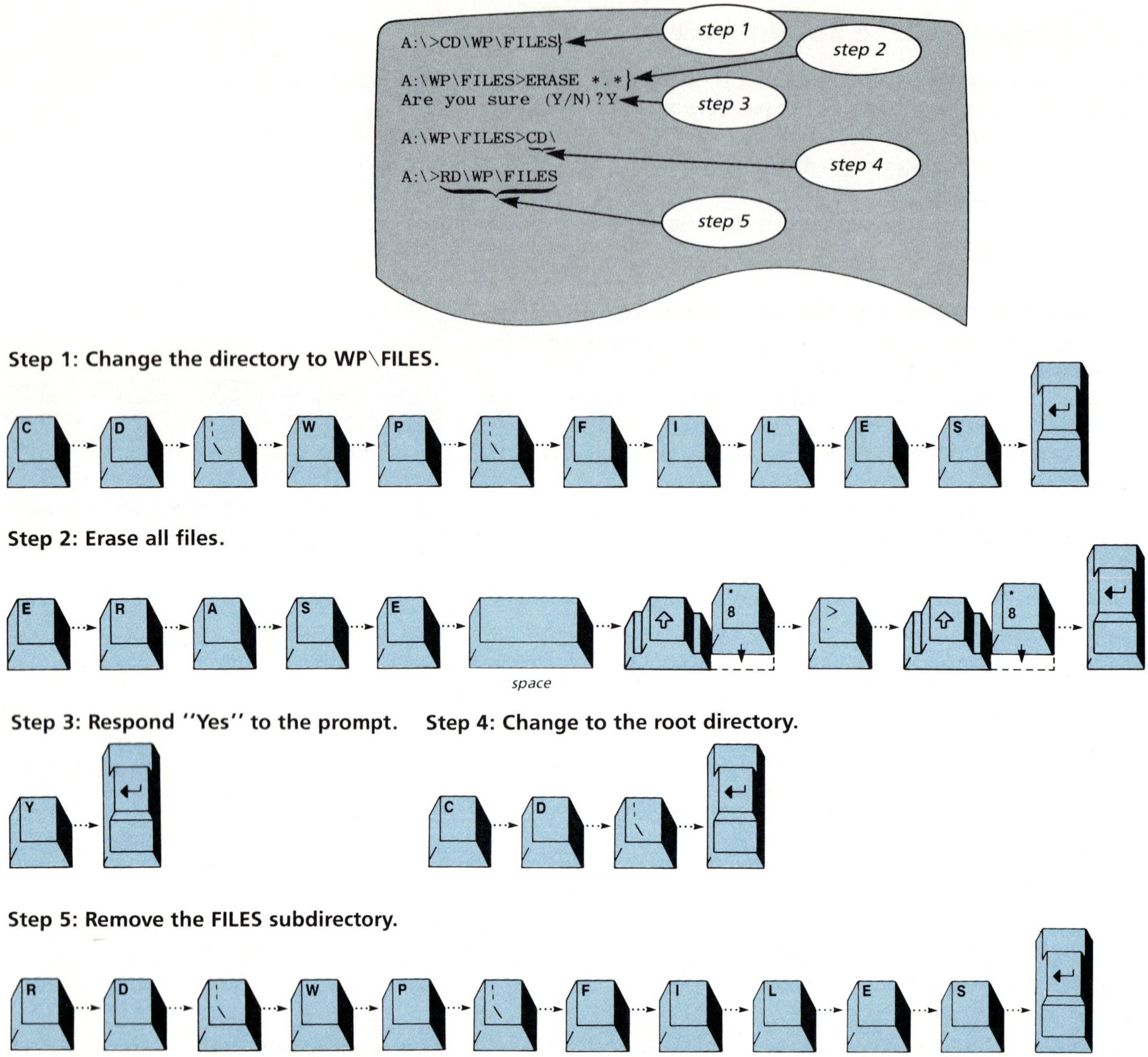

FIGURE 55

Removing a Subdirectory. After you have emptied the subdirectory files, you can remove the subdirectory. Enter the root directory by typing the command CD\ and pressing the Enter key (step 4). To remove the FILES subdirectory, enter RD \WP\FILES and press the Enter key (step 5). Note that you must specify the full path, even though the WP directory is to remain. You must specify the full path so that DOS follows the path from the root directory, where the WP directory entry is stored, through the WP directory to find and remove the FILES entry.

LOADING A PROGRAM

A **program** is a series of instructions that specifies the steps your computer must perform to accomplish a specific purpose. To execute a program, you must first load the program into main memory from diskette or disk storage. The program must be stored either on a diskette, which you have inserted into one of the disk drives, or on the internal hard disk. If you are using a two-diskette system, place the diskette containing the program to be executed in the default drive, usually drive A. Then type the program name (or name abbreviation) and press the Enter key. (Notice that loading and executing an application program is essentially the same as issuing an external DOS command.)

SUMMARY

1. An **operating system** is one or more programs that control and manage the operation of a computer.
2. The operating system for an IBM Personal Computer is **PC-DOS**. Other compatible computers use a similar program called **MS-DOS**.
3. The **version** number of a program is the whole number and signifies a major improvement of the product. The **release** number is the decimal number and identifies minor corrections or changes to a version of the product.
4. "**Booting**" the computer refers to loading the operating system from a disk into main memory.
5. The computer can be "booted" by turning it on with the operating system located on a disk in the computer. This is called a "cold start."
6. To reload the operating system when the computer is already switched on, hold down the **Control** and **Alternate** keys and press the **Delete** key. This process is called a "warm start" or "reset."
7. The operating system will **prompt** you for its commands. DOS has two general types of commands: (1) **internal commands** that are executed from the program stored in the main memory; (2) **external commands** that are programs loaded from a disk as the command is executed.
8. After the operating system has been loaded into main memory, you may be prompted to enter the date or time. Some systems have an internal clock that provides this information for you.
9. The **DOS prompt** includes the letter address of the **default disk drive**, the disk that is currently in use for data or program access.
10. The default drive of a two-diskette computer is usually drive A. A computer with a hard disk drive will generally use drive C as its default drive.
11. You can change the default drive by entering a valid drive letter, followed by a colon, and pressing the Enter key.
12. To examine files on a disk, issue the **DIR** (directory) command. Use the **/P** option to pause a long directory listing when the screen is full. Use the **/W** option to list files across the width of the screen.
13. Give the **pause-screen** command by holding down the Control key and pressing the S key.
14. Many commands can be canceled by holding down the **Control** key and pressing the **Break** key or by pressing Control-C.
15. Use the **FORMAT** command to prepare diskettes for storing data or program files. Several options are available for various types of diskettes. Use **/S** to format the diskette as a **system disk**. The **/V** option prompts a **volume label**.
16. Filenames must be created by following specific rules. A **filename** may consist of up to eight letters, numbers, or certain symbols. The filename **extension** is an optional one- to three-character addition, separated from the filename by a period.
17. Files with the extensions **.BAT**, **.COM**, or **.EXE** are external, executable command files.
18. Use the COPY command to transfer a file to another diskette or to create a backup file on the same diskette.
19. **Wildcards**, the ***** and **?** characters, can be used in conjunction with many DOS commands to replace specific characters.
20. A file to be copied is the **source** file. The resulting copy is called the **target** file.
21. You can change a file's name by specifying the target file used during the COPY command or by using the **RENAME** command.
22. To remove a file from a disk, execute the **ERASE** or the **DELETE** command.
23. Disks can be better organized through the use of **subdirectories**. A disk's primary directory is the **root** directory, signified by a **backslash** following the drive letter, such as C:\.
24. Use the **MKDIR** or the **MD** command to create a subdirectory. The entry includes the drive, backslash, and directory name, such as C:\WP.
25. To switch from one directory to another, use the **CHDIR** or **CD** command, for example, CD\WP.
26. A directory can be removed by first erasing all the files in the directory, then using the REMOVE DIRECTORY command, **RD**.
27. To **load a program** for execution, type the name of the program file at the DOS prompt.

STUDENT ASSIGNMENTS

True/False Questions

Instructions: Which of the following statements are true and which are false?

1. PC-DOS and MS-DOS are essentially the same operation system.
2. When DOS is updated for a new version, programs operating in prior versions may not work under the newer edition.
3. The programs comprising an operating system such as PC-DOS can be stored on a diskette.
4. "Booting" the computer refers to the procedure of starting the operating system.
5. DOS commands are divided into two types: internal and external commands.
6. As a part of the system startup procedures, you are requested to enter the computer's serial number.
7. After the operating system has been loaded, you can type the command DIR and press the Enter key to display a directory of the diskette in the default drive.
8. The computer may have a built-in clock that the operating system automatically accesses to input the date and time.
9. The symbol A>, which appears on the computer screen, is called the DOS prompt.
10. A defective disk drive is one that improperly stores data.
11. To change the disk drive assignment to drive C, type C:↵.
12. All DOS commands must be entered in uppercase characters.
13. You can list the directory of the default disk drive by typing DIR and pressing the Enter key.
14. The option /P used with the DIR command will cause the listing to pause when the screen is full.
15. Holding down the Control key and then pressing the Break key will cancel a command function.
16. To format a diskette, put the diskette to be formatted in disk drive A and enter the command FORMAT B:.
17. The command Copy A: can be used to copy all files from one disk drive to another.
18. The ERASE command can be used to remove a file from the file directory.
19. To include the operating system on a formatted disk, use the command FORMAT B:/S.
20. When you use the FORMAT option /V, the system will prompt you to enter a volume label.
21. To cancel a command, hold down the ALT key and press the END key.
22. A DOS filename may contain from 1 to 11 characters plus an optional extension of 1 to 3 characters.
23. The disk containing the file to be copied is known as the source disk.
24. Global replacement characters include *, ?, and \.
25. Hard disk drives are generally addressed as drive C.
26. Subdirectories on disks are used to group filename entries for convenient storage and retrieval.
27. A disk's main file directory is called the root directory.
28. The current directory is the one in which you are currently working.
29. To move from one current directory to another, use the MD command.
30. A file address contains the disk drive letter, the subdirectory path, and the filename.
31. A program cannot be loaded from a disk unless the program disk is in the current drive.

Multiple-Choice Questions

1. "Booting" the computer refers to
   a. loading the operating system
   b. placing covers over the disk drives
   c. using application programs to access disk drives
   d. the system interface
2. "DOS" stands for
   a. Digital Organizing Software
   b. Data Output Stream
   c. Disk Operating System
   d. Dielectric Orthanographic Startup
3. PC-DOS is used on IBM Personal Computers and Personal System/2 systems. IBM-compatible computers generally use
   a. PC-OMD
   b. MS-DOS
   c. XD-DOS
   d. CP/DUZ
4. A term describing your ability to use newer editions of software while retaining features and data used in earlier ones is
   a. software generation
   b. compatibility curve
   c. upward compatibility
   d. version control
5. When you start up the computer, you load the operating system
   a. from a diskette in drive A
   b. from the computer's internal memory
   c. from the fixed disk if the computer is so equipped
   d. both a and c
6. The term for restarting the operating system in a computer already powered on is
   a. warm start
   b. cold start
   c. warm boot
   d. both a and c
7. The symbol A>
   a. is called a DOS prompt
   b. indicates the name of a program
   c. indicates the default disk drive
   d. both a and c
8. Listing the files on a disk is accomplished by
   a. typing DIR and pressing the Enter key
   b. typing LIST and pressing the Enter key
   c. typing CHKDSK and pressing the Enter key
   d. typing RUN FILES and pressing the Enter key

9. To pause a listing on the screen, press
   a. Control and Break
   b. Alternate, Control, and Delete
   c. Control and S
   d. either b or c
10. To cancel a command, press
    a. Control and Break
    b. Alternate, Control, and Delete
    c. Control and S
    d. either c or d
11. The ________ command establishes sectors on a diskette and performs other functions that allow the diskette to store files.
    a. CHKDSK
    b. DIR
    c. REUSE
    d. FORMAT
12. A valid DOS filename specification consists of
    a. 10 alphanumeric characters
    b. a 9-character filename
    c. an 11-character name, separated by a period at any position within the name
    d. an 8-character filename plus an optional extension of a period followed by 3 characters
13. A common use of the COPY command is to make working copies of program and data disks, producing
    a. file disks
    b. backup copies
    c. extension disks
    d. authorized disks
14. To copy the file PROGRAM.EXE from drive A to drive B, type the command
    a. COPY PROGRAM.EXE TO DRIVE B
    b. COPY A:PROGRAM.EXE TO B:PROGRAM.EXE
    c. COPY A:PROGRAM.EXE B:
    d. either b or c
15. To copy all files on drive A to drive C, type the command
    a. COPY DRIVE A TO DRIVE C
    b. COPY ALL FILES TO C
    c. COPY A:*.* C:*.*
    d. COPY A: C:
16. To change the name of a file from FILEX.DOC to FILEA.DOC, enter
    a. ALTER FILEX.DOC TO FILEA.DOC
    b. CHANGE FILEX.DOC TO FILEA.DOC
    c. ASSIGN FILEX.DOC AS FILEA.DOC
    d. RENAME FILEX.DOC FILEA.DOC
17. To remove a file from a disk, type
    a. REMOVE FILE
    b. DELETE FILEX.DOC
    c. ERASE FILEX.DOC
    d. either b or c
18. Filenames are grouped on disks into
    a. index lists
    b. directories and subdirectories
    c. subject and filename entries
    d. internally labeled entries

19. The MKDIR, or MD, command will
    a. manage directory files
    b. make a directory on a disk
    c. create a file copy
    d. either a or b
20. To shift from the root directory to a directory of files under a word processing directory, type the command
    a. CH /FILES
    b. GOTO WP FILES
    c. CD \WP\FILES
    d. C:\WP\FILES*.*

Projects

1. Start your computer without a DOS disk in drive A. What is the display on the screen? Why did this display appear? Insert a DOS disk in drive A and restart the computer by pressing the Ctrl Alt Del keys simultaneously.
2. Start your computer with the DOS disk in the default disk drive. If permitted in your computer lab, prepare a new diskette as a system disk using the proper FORMAT command options for the task at hand and for the specific diskette your computer uses.
3. Prepare a diskette to be a file disk using the FORMAT command. Give the diskette a volume label using your own name. Determine the proper type of diskette to use on the computer and, after formatting, determine the amount of free space remaining on the diskette.
4. If permitted in your computer lab, create a working copy of your application program diskettes.
    a. First, format a new diskette. Will there be enough room on the diskette to contain both the operating system and the program? How can you know?
    b. Using one command, copy all files from the master copy of the disk to your newly prepared diskette.
5. Create a subdirectory named SUB1 on your diskette.
6. Make subdirectory SUB1 the current directory. Copy all .DOC files into SUB1 and display the directory.
7. Erase the files in SUB1. Change to the root directory and remove subdirectory SUB1.

DOS Index

* (asterisk) character, **DOS 17**
? (question mark) character, **DOS 19**
: (colon), **DOS 8**

Asterisk (*) character, **DOS 17**

Backslash, DOS 22
Booting, **DOS 3**
Break key (^C), **DOS 9**

^C (break key), **DOS 9**
CHDIR (change directory) command, **DOS 24**
CLS (clear screen) command, **DOS 13**
Cold boot, **DOS 4**
Colon (:), **DOS 8**
Commands (See DOS commands)
Control-Break, **DOS 9**
COPY command, **DOS 14** (See also Copying)
Copying
  all files from one diskette to another, DOS 19
  to default disk, DOS 16
  global characters and, DOS 17–19
  from one diskette to another, DOS 15
  to same diskette, DOS 16–17
Current directory, **DOS 24**
Current drive (See Default drive)

Data file, **DOS 13**
Date, setting, DOS 4
Default drive, **DOS 5**
  changing, DOS 5–6
  copying to, DOS 16
DEL (delete) command, **DOS 21**
DIR (directory) command, **DOS 7**
Directories
  changing, DOS 24
  current, DOS 24
  file, DOS 7–9, DOS 21
  in other disk drives, DOS 7
  pausing display of, DOS 8
  root, DOS 21
  using, DOS 21–24
  wide display of, DOS 9
Diskette, formatting, DOS 9–12
Disk Operating System (See DOS)
DOS, **DOS 2**
  batch files (.BAT), **DOS 14**
  file specification, DOS 13–14
  loading, DOS 4
  prompt in, DOS 5
  using, DOS 3–6
  versions of, DOS 3
DOS commands
  canceling, DOS 9
  CHDIR, DOS 24
  CLS, DOS 13
  COPY, DOS 14–19
  DEL, DOS 21
  DIR, DOS 7–9
  entering, DOS 6
  ERASE, DOS 21
  external, DOS 6
  FORMAT, DOS 10–12
  internal, DOS 6
  paths in, DOS 25
  RENAME, DOS 19–20
  RMDIR, DOS 25
  using wildcards with, DOS 19

ERASE command, **DOS 21**
External command, **DOS 6**

File(s)
  data, DOS 13
  naming, DOS 14
  path to, DOS 25
  program, DOS 13
  source, DOS 15
  in subdirectories, DOS 25
  target, DOS 15
File directory, DOS 7–9, **DOS 21**
Filename, **DOS 14**
  renaming, DOS 19–20
Filename extension, **DOS 14**
File specification, **DOS 13, DOS 15**
FORMAT command, DOS 10–12
Formatting, **DOS 9**
  system disk, DOS 12
  volume label, DOS 12

Global characters, **DOS 17**

Hard disk
  booting, DOS 3
  directories, DOS 7, 8
  formatting, DOS 10
  prompt, DOS 5

IBM PCs, operating systems for, DOS 2–3
Internal command, **DOS 6**

MKDIR command, (MD), **DOS 22**
MS-DOS, **DOS 2** (See also DOS)

Operating system, **DOS 2** (See also DOS)

/P (pause) option, **DOS 8**
Path, **DOS 25**
Pause (/P) option, **DOS 8**
PC-DOS, **DOS 2** (See also DOS)
Power-on self-test (POST) process, **DOS 4**
Program, **DOS 26**
Program file, **DOS 13**
PROMPT command, **DOS 22**

Question mark (?) character, **DOS 19**

Release number, **DOS 3**
RENAME command, **DOS 19**
RMDIR (remove directory) command, **DOS 25**
Root directory, **DOS 21**

/S (system) option, **DOS 12**
Software compatibility, DOS 3
Source file, **DOS 15**
Subdirectories, DOS 22
  file management in, DOS 25
  path to, DOS 25
  removing, DOS 25–26
  using, DOS 25–26
System disk (/S), **DOS 12**
System prompt, **DOS 5**

Target file, **DOS 15**
Time, setting, DOS 4

Upward compatibility, **DOS 3**
User interface, DOS 2

/V (volume label) option, **DOS 12**
Version number, **DOS 3**
Volume label (/V), **DOS 12**

/W (wide) option, **DOS 9**
Warm boot, **DOS 4**
Wide display (/W) option, **DOS 9**
Wildcards, **DOS 17**

Photo Credits: **Opening Page and Figure 2a**, Radio Shack, a division of Tandy Corp.; **Figures 2b and 3a**, Compaq Computer Corp.; **Figure 3b**, International Business Machines Corp.

Programming in QuickBASIC

PROJECT 1
An Introduction to Programming in QuickBASIC
THE PROGRAMMING PROCESS
SAMPLE PROGRAM 1 — PATIENT LISTING
THE DATA STATEMENT
THE CLS, PRINT, AND END STATEMENTS
VARIABLES
THE READ STATEMENT
THE DO WHILE AND LOOP STATEMENTS
TRY IT YOURSELF EXERCISES
THE QB OPERATING ENVIRONMENT
EXECUTING PROGRAMS AND HARD-COPY OUTPUT
SAVING, LOADING, AND ERASING PROGRAMS
THE QB ADVISOR ON-LINE HELP SYSTEM
TRY IT YOURSELF EXERCISES
STUDENT ASSIGNMENTS

PROJECT 2
Basic Arithmetic Operations and Accumulating Totals
THE LET STATEMENT
SAMPLE PROGRAM 2 — AUTO EXPENSE REPORT
REPORT EDITING
PRINTING A REPORT ON THE PRINTER
TRY IT YOURSELF EXERCISES
STUDENT ASSIGNMENTS

PROJECT 3
Decisions
THE IF STATEMENT
CODING IF-THEN-ELSE STRUCTURES
SAMPLE PROGRAM 3 — VIDEO RENTAL REPORT
LOGICAL OPERATORS
THE SELECT CASE STATEMENT
TRY IT YOURSELF EXERCISES
STUDENT ASSIGNMENTS

PROJECT 4
Interactive Programming, For Loops, and An Introduction to the Top-Down Approach
THE INPUT STATEMENT
THE BEEP AND LOCATE STATEMENTS
EDITING DATA ENTERED THROUGH THE KEYBOARD
SAMPLE PROGRAM 4 — ITEM COST REPORT
THE FOR AND NEXT STATEMENTS
AN INTRODUCTION TO THE TOP-DOWN APPROACH
THE GOSUB AND RETURN STATEMENTS
TRY IT YOURSELF EXERCISES
STUDENT ASSIGNMENTS

PROJECT 5
Sequential File Processing
FILE ORGANIZATION
CREATING A SEQUENTIAL DATA FILE
SAMPLE PROGRAM 5A — CREATING A SEQUENTIAL DATA FILE
READING DATA FROM A SEQUENTIAL DATA FILE
SAMPLE PROGRAM 5B — PROCESSING A SEQUENTIAL DATA FILE
TRY IT YOURSELF EXERCISES
STUDENT ASSIGNMENTS

PROJECT 6
Arrays and Functions
ARRAYS
THE DIM STATEMENT
SAMPLE PROGRAM 6 — CUSTOMER ACCOUNT TABLE LOOKUP
FUNCTIONS
TRY IT YOURSELF EXERCISES
STUDENT ASSIGNMENTS

APPENDIX
QuickBASIC Debugging Techniques
EXAMINING VALUES THROUGH THE IMMEDIATE WINDOW
EXECUTING ONE STATEMENT AT A TIME
BREAKPOINTS
TRACING
SET NEXT STATEMENT
RECORDING
WATCH VARIABLES AND WATCHPOINTS

PROJECT 1

An Introduction to Programming in QuickBASIC

In Project 1 we provide an introduction to the principles of program design and computer programming using the QuickBASIC programming language. QuickBASIC was developed for the personal computer (PC) by Microsoft Corporation, one of the largest microcomputer software companies in the world. Today, QuickBASIC is one of the most widely used programming languages on PCs.

Our approach in illustrating QuickBASIC is to present a series of applications that can be processed using a PC. We carefully explain the input data, the output to be produced, and the processing. Through the use of a flowchart, we illustrate the program design and logic. The flowchart is followed by an explanation of the QuickBASIC statements required to implement the logic. We then present the complete QuickBASIC program. The program solution, when entered into the PC and executed, will produce the output from the specified input.

THE PROGRAMMING PROCESS

Computer programs can vary significantly in size and complexity. A simple program may contain only a few statements. A complex program can contain hundreds and even thousands of statements. Regardless of the size of the program, it is extremely important that the task of computer programming be approached in a professional manner, as computer programming is one of the most precise of all activities.

Learning computer programming should not be approached as a trial-and-error-type of activity. By carefully reviewing the sample problems, the program design, and the QuickBASIC code we present within these projects, you should be able to write well-designed programs that produce correct output when executed on a PC.

Computer programming is not *naturally* an error-prone activity. Errors enter into the design and coding of the computer program only through carelessness or lack of understanding of the programming process. With careful study and attention to detail, you can avoid errors. Just as it is the job of the accountant, the mathematician, the engineer, and the scientist to produce correct results, so too it is the job of the computer programmer to produce a program that is reliable, easy to read, and produces accurate results.

The actual programming process involves the activities described in Figure 1-1. When you use this careful approach to program design and coding, you can develop programs that are easy to read, efficient, reliable, and execute properly.

STEP	DESCRIPTION
1	Define the problem to be solved precisely in terms of input, processing, and output.
2	Design a detailed logic plan using flowcharts or some other logic tool.
3	Desk check the logic plan as if you are the computer.
4	Code the program.
5	Desk check the code as if you are the computer.
6	Enter the program into the computer.
7	Test the program until it is error free.
8	Run the program using the input data to generate the output results.

FIGURE 1-1 The program development cycle

SAMPLE PROGRAM 1 — PATIENT LISTING

In this first sample program we generate a patient listing on the screen. The input data consists of the series of patient records shown in Figure 1-2. Each record contains a patient name, a doctor name, and a room number.

PATIENT NAME	DOCTOR NAME	ROOM NUMBER
Tim Krel	Nance	112
Mary Lepo	Gold	102
Tom Pep	King	245
Joe Ruiz	Ward	213
EOF	End	0

FIGURE 1-2 The patient records

The data taken as a group is called a **file**. The data about a single individual is called a **record**. Each unit of data within the record is called a **field**, or **data item**. Thus, the input data consists of a file of patient records. Each record contains a patient name field, a doctor name field, and a room number field.

In the list of records in Figure 1-2, the last record contains the patient name `EOF`, the doctor name `End`, and the room number `0`. This record is called a trailer record, or sentinel record. A **trailer record** is added to the end of the file to indicate when all the valid records have been processed.

The output for this sample program is a listing on the PC screen of each record in the patient file. The output listing is shown in Figure 1-3.

```
            Patient Listing

Room             Patient          Doctor

 112             Tim Krel         Nance
 102             Mary Lepo        Gold
 245             Tom Pep          King
 213             Joe Ruiz         Ward

End of Patient List
```

FIGURE 1-3 The required output for Sample Program 1

The patient list includes the room number, the patient name, and the doctor name for each record. Notice that the sequence of the fields displayed on the screen is different from the sequence of the fields in the input record. Column headings identify each field. After all records have been processed, the message `End of Patient List` displays.

Program Flowchart

The flowchart, QuickBASIC program, and output for Sample Program 1 are shown in Figure 1-4. The flowchart illustrates a simple looping structure. After the headings are displayed, a record is read. This read statement, prior to the loop, is called a **primary read**, or **lead read**.

A. PROGRAM FLOWCHART

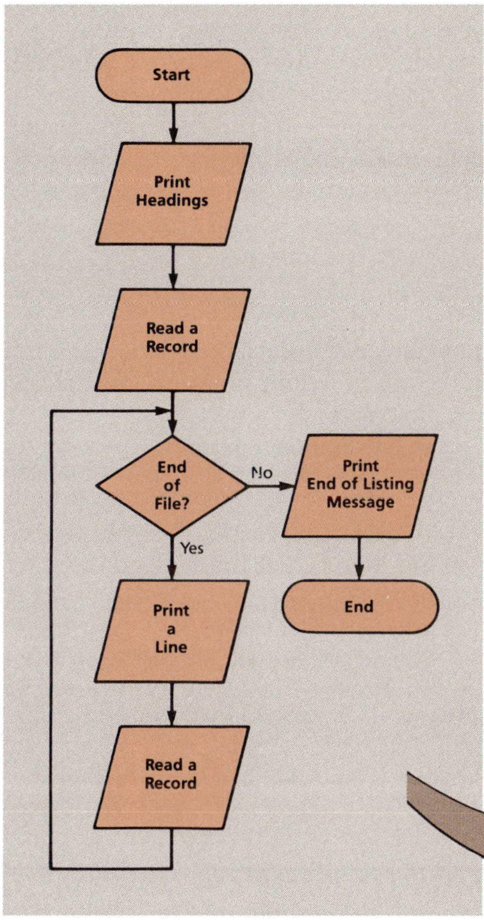

B. PROGRAM LISTING

```
' ******************************************************************
' *  Sample Program 1                            September 15, 1994  *
' *  Patient Listing                                                 *
' *  J. S. Quasney                                                   *
' *                                                                  *
' *  This program displays the room number, patient name             *
' *  and doctor name of hospital patients.                           *
' *                                                                  *
' *  Variables:  Patient.Name$ -- Name of patient                    *
' *              Doctor.Name$  -- Name of doctor                     *
' *              Room.Number   -- Room number                        *
' ******************************************************************
' ********************* Initialization *********************
CLS  ' Clear Screen
PRINT TAB(11); "Patient Listing"
PRINT
PRINT "Room", "Patient", "Doctor"
PRINT
' ********************** Process File **********************
READ Patient.Name$, Doctor.Name$, Room.Number
DO WHILE Patient.Name$ <> "EOF"
   PRINT Room.Number, Patient.Name$, Doctor.Name$
   READ Patient.Name$, Doctor.Name$, Room.Number
LOOP
' ************************ Wrap-Up *************************
PRINT
PRINT "End of Patient List"
' ********************** Data Follows **********************
DATA Tim Krel, Nance, 112
DATA Mary Lepo, Gold, 102
DATA Tom Pep, King, 245
DATA Joe Ruiz, Ward, 213
DATA EOF, End, 0
END
```

C. OUTPUT RESULTS

```
          Patient Listing

Room          Patient       Doctor

 112          Tim Krel      Nance
 102          Mary Lepo     Gold
 245          Tom Pep       King
 213          Joe Ruiz      Ward

End of Patient List
```

FIGURE 1-4 The program flowchart (A), program listing (B), and output results (C) for Sample Program 1

Following the lead read in the program flowchart in Figure 1-4, a test is performed to determine if the record just read was the trailer record containing the patient name EOF. If so, there are no more records to process. If not, then more records remain to be processed. This decision determines if the loop should be entered. If the end-of-file has not been reached, the loop is entered. Within the loop the previously read record is displayed on the screen and another record is read. Control then returns to the decision symbol at the top of the loop. As long as the trailer record has not been read, the looping continues.

When the trailer record is read, the looping process stops and an end-of-job message displays followed by termination of the program. This basic logic is appropriate for all applications which involve reading records and displaying the fields from the record read on an output device.

The QuickBASIC Program

Programs should be well documented, easy to read, easy to understand, and easy to modify and maintain. For these reasons, programming standards have been developed to guide the beginning programmer in the task of writing programs. We illustrate and explain these standards in all sample programs we present in these programming projects.

A program written using QuickBASIC consists of a series of statements which serve one of three functions:

1. Document the program
2. Cause processing to occur
3. Define data

A quality program is well documented. This means the program contains information which helps a reader understand the program. Documentation within the program should include the following:

- A prologue, including the program name, program title, an author identification, the date the program was written, a brief description of the program, and a description of the variable names used in the program. The first 12 lines of Sample Program 1 (Figure 1-5) contain the prologue.
- Remark lines should come before any major module in a program. In Sample Program 1, lines 14, 21, 28, and 32 are remark lines that precede major modules.

```
1   ' *****************************************************************
2   ' *  Sample Program 1                           September 15, 1994 *
3   ' *  Patient Listing                                               *
4   ' *  J. S. Quasney                                                 *
5   ' *                                                                *
6   ' *  This program displays the room number, patient name,         *
7   ' *  and doctor name of hospital patients.                         *
8   ' *                                                                *
9   ' *  Variables:  Patient.Name$ -- Name of patient                  *
10  ' *              Doctor.Name$  -- Name of doctor                   *
11  ' *              Room.Number   -- Room number                      *
12  ' *****************************************************************
```

FIGURE 1-5
The prologue for Sample Program 1

Documentation within a QuickBASIC program is accomplished through the use of the REM statement. The general form of the REM statement is shown in Figure 1-6.

```
REM comment
   or
' comment
```

FIGURE 1-6
The general form of the REM statement

The remark statement begins with REM or an apostrophe (') followed by any characters, numbers, or words required to document the program. Notice that in these programming projects, we use the apostrophe (') rather than the keyword REM to initiate a remark line. Asterisks (*) are used in the remark lines to highlight the documentation.

Blank lines, such as lines 13, 20, 27, and 31 of Sample Program 1 (Figure 1-4), are used to end any major module. For example, the Initialization module (Figure 1-7) begins with a remark line and ends with a blank line. The proper use of remark lines, blank lines, and indentations can substantially improve the readability of a program. We suggest that you follow the format illustrated in Sample Program 1 when coding all QuickBASIC programs.

The apostrophe (') can also be used to include in-line remarks as shown following the `CLS` statement in line 15 of Figure 1-7. All characters that follows the apostrophe in an in-line remark are considered to be part of the documentation.

Remember that remark lines and blank lines can be added before or after any line in a program. In addition, they are strictly for human comprehension and have no effect on the outcome of the program.

```
14  ' *********************** Initialization ***********************
15  CLS   ' Clear Screen
16  PRINT TAB(11); "Patient Listing"
17  PRINT
18  PRINT "Room", "Patient", "Doctor"
19  PRINT
20
```

FIGURE 1-7
The Initialization module of Sample Program 1

THE DATA STATEMENT

Sample Program 1 employs `DATA` statements to define the data. The `DATA` statements for Sample Program 1 are shown in Figure 1-8.

```
32  ' *********************** Data Follows ***********************
33  DATA Tim Krel, Nance, 112
34  DATA Mary Lepo, Gold, 102
35  DATA Tom Pep, King, 245
36  DATA Joe Ruiz, Ward, 213
37  DATA EOF, End, 0
```


FIGURE 1-8
The data to be processed by Sample Program 1

In Figure 1-8, line 33 defines the first patient record. Line 34 defines the second patient record, and so on. `DATA` statements begin with the keyword `DATA` followed by a space and the data. The `DATA` statement in line 33 contains the patient name (Tim Krel), the doctor name (Nance), and the room number (112). As shown in Figure 1-8, each of the data items must be separated by a comma.

The last `DATA` statement is the trailer record, when a trailer record is used in this manner, you must include an entry for each field. In line 37, the phrase `EOF` is included for the patient name, the word `End` is included in place of the doctor name, and the numeric value `0` is included for the room number. These values, of course, will not be included in the listing generated by the program.

The general form of the `DATA` statement is shown in Figure 1-9.

> `DATA` data item, data item, ..., data item
>
> where each data item is a numeric or string value

FIGURE 1-9
The general form of the DATA statement

THE CLS, PRINT, AND END STATEMENTS

Up to this point, we have talked about REM and DATA statements. Both of these statements are classified as nonexecutable. Neither type of statement has anything to do with the logic shown in the flowchart in Figure 1-4. For example, the DATA statements can be moved from the bottom of the program to the top of the program with no effect on the logic of the program.

In this section we discuss the CLS, PRINT, and END statements.

The CLS Statement

The first executable statement in Sample Program 1 is the CLS statement in line 15 (Figure 1-10). The function of this statement is to clear the output screen and move the cursor to the upper left corner. The **output screen** is the one that shows the results due to the execution of a program.

```
14  ' *********************** Initialization ************************
15  CLS  ' Clear Screen
16  PRINT TAB(11); "Patient Listing"
17  PRINT
18  PRINT "Room", "Patient", "Doctor"
19  PRINT
20
```

FIGURE 1-10
The Initialization module of Sample Program 1

The PRINT Statement

The PRINT statement is used to write information on the output screen. It is commonly used to display headings and the values of variables and control spacing in a report. As shown in Figure 1-11, the PRINT statement consists of the keyword PRINT. It may also have an optional list of print items separated by commas and semicolons.

FIGURE 1-11
The general form of the PRINT statement

PRINT list

where **list** is the items to display separated by semicolons or commas

The list in a PRINT statement includes print items. The **print items** can be any of the following:

- Variables, such as Doctor.Name$, Patient.Name$, and Room.Number
- Constants, such as numeric and string values—string values must be enclosed in quotation marks (")
- Function references, such as the TAB function—the TAB function allows you to move the cursor to the right to a specified column position

Lines 16 through 19 of Sample Program 1 (Figure 1-10) display the report title and column headings. Line 16 displays the report title on line 1. The first print item in line 16 is the TAB function. It causes the cursor to move to column 11. The semicolon following the TAB function instructs the PC to display the next print item (Patient Listing) at the current cursor location (column 11). Hence, the report title Patient Listing displays beginning in column 11 on line 1. After line 16 is executed, the cursor moves down one line on the output screen to line 2.

The PRINT statement in line 17 contains no print items. A PRINT statement with no print items causes the PC to skip a line. Thus, line 2 on the output screen is left blank.

Line 18 displays the three column headings. Each column heading is surrounded by the required quotation marks. Notice that the column headings also are separated by commas. When the print items are separated by commas, the fields are displayed in predefined columns called print zones. There are five print zones per line. Each **print zone** has 14 positions for a total of 70 positions per line as shown in Figure 1-12.

FIGURE 1-12
There are five print zones of 14 positions each for a total of 70 positions

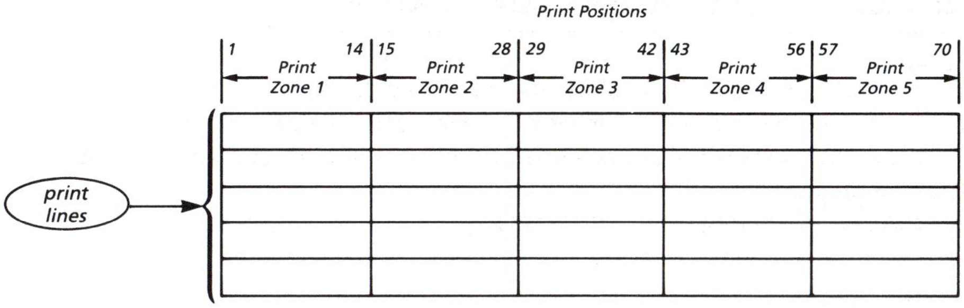

When line 18 in Sample Program 1 executes, `Room` displays beginning in column 1, `Patient` displays beginning in column 15, and `Doctor` displays beginning in column 29. Like line 17, line 19 causes the PC to skip a line on the output screen.

The END Statement

The last line in Sample Program 1 is the `END` statement. When executed, the `END` statement instructs the PC to stop executing the program. Although the `END` statement is not required, it is recommended that you always include one.

VARIABLES

In programming, a **variable** is a location in main memory whose value can change as the program executes. There are two major categories of variables—numeric and string. A **numeric variable** can only be assigned a numeric value. A **string variable** may be assigned a string of characters such as a word, name, phrase, or sentence.

A **variable name** is used to define and reference a variable in main memory. Variable names must conform to certain rules. In QuickBASIC, a variable name begins with a letter and may be followed by up to 39 letters, digits, and decimal points. You may not use a QuickBASIC keyword, such as `CLS` or `PRINT`, as a variable name. For a complete list of the QuickBASIC keywords, refer to the last page of the reference card at the back of this book.

String variable names always end with a dollar sign ($). Numeric variable names never end with a dollar sign. For example, in Sample Program 1, Room.Number is a numeric variable and Patient.Name$ and Doctor.Name$ are string variables.

With respect to the variable names used in Sample Program 1, notice how we use the decimal point (.) to better describe what the variables will hold during the execution of the program.

THE READ STATEMENT

To assign the data in the `DATA` statements to variables, we use the `READ` statement. As shown in Figure 1-13, the `READ` statement consists of the keyword `READ` followed by one or more variable names separated from each other by commas. The variable names must be specified in the `READ` statement in the order in which the data is recorded in the `DATA` statements.

FIGURE 1-13
The general form of the READ statement

`READ` variable$_1$, variable$_2$, ..., variable$_n$

where each variable is a numeric variable or string variable

When line 22 (Figure 1-14) is executed, the first data item is assigned to the first variable in the READ statement. Thus, Tim Krel is assigned to Patient.Name$. The second data item (Nance) is assigned to Doctor.Name$ and the third data item (112) is assigned to Room.Number.

Refer to Sample Program 1 in Figure 1-4 and notice that the READ statement in line 22 has the same number of variables as the DATA statements have data items. In other words, each time a READ statement is executed, one DATA statement is used. Although we recommend this style, it is not required. For example, the following shows that it is valid to write the READ statement in line 22 as three READ statements:

```
READ Patient.Name$
READ Doctor.Name$
READ Room.Number
DATA Tim Krel, Nance, 112
```

We could have also placed one data item per DATA statement as follows:

```
READ Patient.Name$, Doctor.Name$, Room.Number
DATA Tim Krel
DATA Nance
DATA 112
```

THE DO WHILE AND LOOP STATEMENTS

Following the first READ statement in line 22, lines 23 through 26 establish a **Do loop** (Figure 1-14). The DO WHILE statement in line 23 and the LOOP statement in line 26 cause the range of statements between them to be executed repeatedly as long as Patient.Name$ does not equal the string value EOF. The expression Patient.Name$ <> "EOF" following DO WHILE in line 23 is called a **condition**. A condition can be true or false. In the case of the DO WHILE, the statements within the loop are executed while the condition is true.

```
21 ' *********************** Process File ************************
22 READ Patient.Name$, Doctor.Name$, Room.Number
23 DO WHILE Patient.Name$ <> "EOF"
24    PRINT Room.Number, Patient.Name$, Doctor.Name$
25    READ Patient.Name$, Doctor.Name$, Room.Number
26 LOOP
27
28 ' ************************ Wrap-Up ***************************
29 PRINT
30 PRINT "End of Patient List"
31
```

FIGURE 1-14
The Process File and Wrap-Up modules of Sample Program 1

When Patient.Name$ does equal EOF, the condition in line 23 is false. Therefore, the PC skips the statements within the loop and continues execution at the first executable statement following the corresponding LOOP statement. The first executable statement following the LOOP statement is the PRINT statement in line 29.

One execution of a Do loop is called a **pass**. The statements within the loop, lines 24 and 25, are indented by three spaces for the purpose of readability. Collectively, lines 24 and 25 are called the **range** of statements in the Do loop.

Following execution of the lead read in line 22, Patient.Name$ is equal to Tim Krel. Hence, control passes into the Do loop and the first patient record is displayed due to the PRINT statement in line 24. Next, the READ statement in line 25 assigns the variables Patient.Name$, Doctor.Name$, and Room.Number the data items found in the second DATA statement. The LOOP statement in line 26 automatically returns control to the DO WHILE statement in line 23. This process continues while Patient.Name$ does not equal EOF.

The general forms of the DO WHILE and LOOP statements are shown in Figure 1-15.

```
DO WHILE condition
    [range of statements]
LOOP
```

FIGURE 1-15
The general forms of the DO WHILE and LOOP statements

Testing for the End-of-File

Lines 33 through 36 in Sample Program 1 (Figure 1-4) contain data for only four patients. The fifth patient in line 37 is the **trailer record**. It represents the end-of-file and is used to determine when all the valid data has been processed. To incorporate an end-of-file test, a variable must be selected and a trailer record added to the data. We selected the patient name as the test for end-of-file and the data value `EOF`. Since it guards against reading past end-of-file, the trailer record is also called the **sentinel record**. The value `EOF` is called the **sentinel value**. The value `EOF` is clearly distinguishable from all the rest of the data assigned to Patient.Name$. This sentinel value is the same as the string constant found in the condition in line 23.

After the `READ` statement in line 25 assigns Patient.Name$ the value `EOF`, the `LOOP` statement returns control to the `DO WHILE` statement. Since Patient.Name$ is equal to the value `EOF`, the `DO WHILE` statement causes the PC to pass control to line 29 which follows the corresponding `LOOP` statement. Line 29 skips a line and line 30 displays an end-of-job message. Lines 29 and 30 are referred to as an **end-of-file routine**.

Three other worthy points to consider about establishing a test for end-of-file in a Do loop are:

1. It is important that the trailer record contain enough values for all the variables in the `READ` statement. In Sample Program 1, if we only added the sentinel value `EOF` to line 37, there would not be enough data to fulfill the requirements of the three variables in the `READ` statement. We arbitrarily assigned `End` and `0` to the second and third variables in the `READ` statement.
2. The Do loop requires the use of two `READ` statements. The first `READ` statement (line 22) reads the first patient record before the PC enters the Do loop. The second `READ` statement, found at the bottom of the Do loop (line 25), causes the PC to read the next data record. This `READ` statement reads the remaining data records, one at a time, until there are no more data records left. If the first record contains the patient name `EOF`, the `DO WHILE` statement will immediately transfer control to the statement below the corresponding `LOOP` statement.
3. Sample Program 1 can process any number of patients by placing each in a `DATA` statement prior to the trailer record.

Conditions

In Figure 1-14, line 23 contains the `DO WHILE` statement

```
Patient.Name$ <> "EOF"
```

The condition is made up of two expressions and a **relational operator**. The condition specifies a relationship between expressions that is either true or false. If the condition is true, execution continues with the line following the `DO WHILE` statement. If the condition is false, then control is transferred to the line following the corresponding `LOOP` statement.

The PC makes a comparison between the two operators based on the relational operator. Figure 1-16 lists the six valid relational operators.

RELATION	MATH SYMBOL	QuickBASIC SYMBOL	EXAMPLE
Equal To	$=$	=	Educ$ = "12"
Less Than	$<$	<	Total < 25
Greater Than	$>$	>	Disc > .15
Less Than Or Equal To	$\leq$	<= or =<	Deduc <= 10
Greater Than Or Equal To	$\geq$	>= or =>	Code$ >= "A"
Not Equal To	$\neq$	<> or ><	State$ <> "TX"

FIGURE 1-16
Relational operators used in conditions

There are several important points to watch for in the application of conditions. For example, it is invalid to compare a numeric variable to a string value as in the following:

```
DO WHILE Cents > "10"
```

this condition Cents > "10" is valid

Furthermore, the condition should ensure termination of the loop. For example, look at the following logical error:

```
DO WHILE 10 > 1

     [range of statements]

LOOP
```

this condition 10 > 1 is always true

If such an error is not detected, a never-ending loop develops. There is no way to stop the endless program execution except by manual intervention, such as pressing **Ctrl + Break** on your PC keyboard. (The plus sign between two keys means hold down the first key and press the second key, and then release both keys.)

The complete QuickBASIC program and the output results are again illustrated in Figures 1-17 and 1-18.

FIGURE 1-17
Sample Program 1

```
' ******************************************************************
' *  Sample Program 1                           September 15, 1994  *
' *  Patient Listing                                                *
' *  J. S. Quasney                                                  *
' *                                                                 *
' *  This program displays the room number, patient name           *
' *  and doctor name of hospital patients.                          *
' *                                                                 *
' *  Variables:  Patient.Name$ -- Name of patient                   *
' *              Doctor.Name$  -- Name of doctor                    *
' *              Room.Number   -- Room number                       *
' ******************************************************************

' ********************** Initialization ***********************
CLS   ' Clear Screen
PRINT TAB(11); "Patient Listing"
PRINT
PRINT "Room", "Patient", "Doctor"
PRINT

' ********************** Process File ***********************
READ Patient.Name$, Doctor.Name$, Room.Number
DO WHILE Patient.Name$ <> "EOF"
   PRINT Room.Number, Patient.Name$, Doctor.Name$
   READ Patient.Name$, Doctor.Name$, Room.Number
LOOP

' ************************* Wrap-Up *************************
PRINT
PRINT "End of Patient List"

' ********************** Data Follows ***********************
DATA Tim Krel, Nance, 112
DATA Mary Lepo, Gold, 102
DATA Tom Pep, King, 245
DATA Joe Ruiz, Ward, 213
DATA EOF, End, 0
END
```

prologue (lines 1–12)

clear screen and display headings (lines 15–19)

process patient file (lines 22–26)

end-of-file routine (lines 29–30)

patient file (lines 33–37)

FIGURE 1-18
The output results due to the execution of Sample Program 1

```
          Patient Listing

Room          Patient          Doctor

 112          Tim Krel         Nance
 102          Mary Lepo        Gold
 245          Tom Pep          King
 213          Joe Ruiz         Ward

End of Patient List
```

TRY IT YOURSELF EXERCISES

1. Which of the following are valid numeric variables in QuickBASIC?
   a. X$
   b. Account
   c. 8T
   d. Inventory.No
2. Write a CLS statement and a series of PRINT statements that display the value LINE 1 beginning in column 1 of line 1, LINE 3 in column 1 of line 3, and LINE 5 in column 1 of line 5.
3. Write a PRINT statement that displays the string values Name, Account, Balance, Date in print zones 1 through 4 of the current line.
4. Use the TAB function in a PRINT statement to display the string value The answer is beginning in column 42 of the current line.
5. Given the following DATA statement:

   DATA 16723, 12, 56

   Use the variables Inventory.Number, On.Order, and On.Hand to write a READ statement that assigns Inventory.Number the value 16723, On.Order the value 12, and On.Hand the value 56.
6. State the purpose of the LOOP statement.
7. List and describe the six relational operators.
8. Which of the following are invalid DO WHILE statements? Why?
   a. DO WHILE X = 10
   b. DOWHILE Acct$ <> "End"
   c. DO WHILE 5 < Tax
   d. DO WHILE On.Hand LT 25
   e. DO WHILE Volts Equals 37
9. Determine whether the conditions below are true or false, given the following: Hours = 6, Tonnage = 12.5, and Bonus = 1.75
   a. Hours >= 10
   b. Tonnage >= 12
   c. Bonus <> 2
   d. Hours <> 6
   e. Tonnage < 12.5
   f. Bonus = 1.75

10. Write the QuickBASIC code for the Process File and Wrap-Up modules that correspond to the following program flowchart. Use the variable names specified in the Read and Print symbols. Do not include any `DATA` statements. Start each module with a remark line and end each module with a blank line. For the end-of-file test, assume the trailer record includes the following data items: `EOF, 0, 0`.

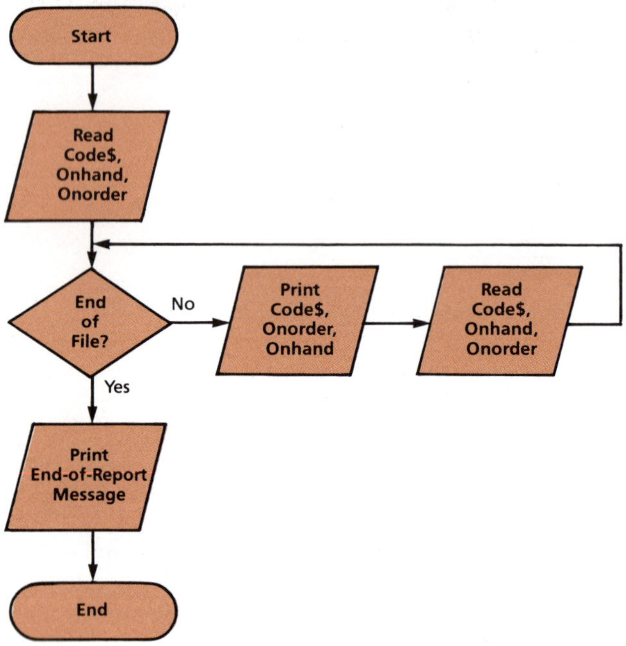

THE QB OPERATING ENVIRONMENT

To enter a program such as Sample Program 1 into the PC and execute it, you must familiarize yourself with the QB operating environment.

Starting a Session

Boot the PC using the steps outlined by your instructor, or those found in the PC's Operations manual. Once the PC is operational, do the following:

1. Place the QuickBASIC program disk in the default drive and your data disk in the other drive.
2. At the DOS prompt, enter `QBI` if you are using the textbook version of QuickBASIC or `QB` if you are using the commercial version of QuickBASIC.

Several seconds will elapse while the QuickBASIC program is loaded from the disk into main memory. The red light on the disk drive turns on during this loading process. After the QuickBASIC program is loaded into main storage, it is automatically executed.

The first screen displayed by QuickBASIC includes a Welcome message in the middle of the screen. In the Welcome message, QuickBASIC directs you to press the **Esc key** to begin entering a program or press the **Enter key** to obtain help from the QB Advisor. The **QB Advisor** is an on-line help system that answers your questions about QuickBASIC as fast as you can click the mouse or press the **F1 key**. The QB Advisor is discussed in more detail later in this section.

The QB Screen

There are four parts to the QB screen—the view window, menu bar, immediate window, and the status line. These are shown in Figure 1-19.

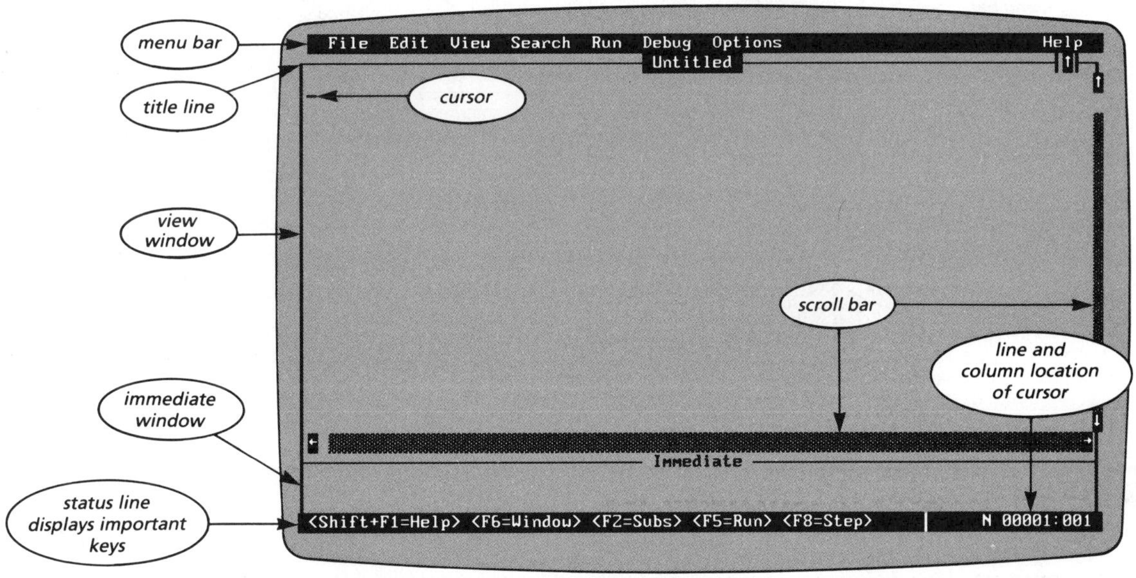

FIGURE 1-19 The QB (QuickBASIC) screen

View Window The **view window** is the largest part of the screen and the one that contains the cursor (Figure 1-19). In the view window you can enter, modify, and display programs. When the QuickBASIC program first executes, the view window is active. That is, if you start typing characters, they will appear on the first line of the view window. At the top of the view window is the title line. The **title line** displays the name of the current program. The program title is highlighted when the view window is active. The program is called "Untitled" until it is given a name. Program names will be discussed shortly.

Along the bottom and the right side of the view window are the **scroll bars**. If you have a mouse, you can move the pointer along the scroll bars and move the window in any direction to see code that does not appear in the view window.

Menu Bar The **menu bar**, the line at the very top of the QB screen (Figure 1-19), displays a list of menu names. Each menu name has a corresponding menu of commands. These commands are useful when entering and modifying programs.

To activate the menu bar, press the **Alt key**. Next, type the first letter of the name of the menu you want to open. You can also select a menu by using the **Right Arrow key** or the **Left Arrow key** to highlight the menu name. With the menu name highlighted, press the **Enter key**. QuickBASIC immediately displays a *pull-down menu* that lists a series of commands. Figure 1-20 shows the **File menu**, which is superimposed over the display of Sample Program 1. To deactivate the menu bar or any menu and activate the view window, press the **Esc key**.

FIGURE 1-20
The File menu

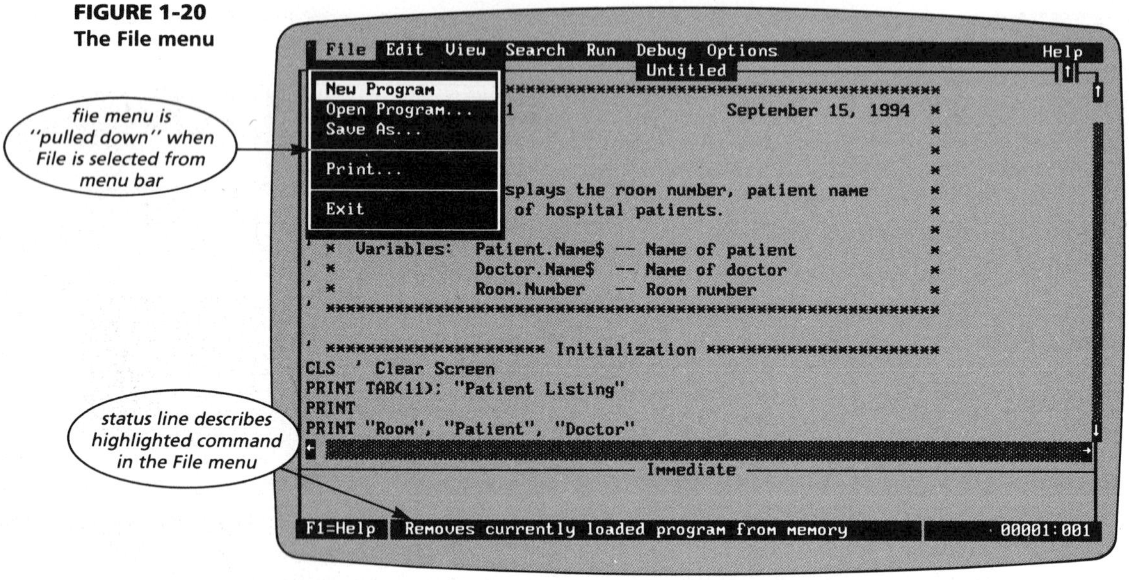

If your PC has a mouse, move the mouse pointer to the desired menu name and click the mouse button. The **mouse pointer** is a character-size, rectangular box on the screen. The **mouse button** is the left button on the mouse. To deactivate the menu bar and reactivate the view window, move the mouse pointer to any part of the view window and click the mouse button.

Immediate Window The narrow window below the view window is called the **immediate window**. The immediate window is used to execute statements as soon as they are entered. Statements entered in the immediate window are not part of the current program.

At any time, you can activate the immediate window by pressing the function key **F6**. This moves the cursor from the view window to the immediate window. QuickBASIC highlights the word Immediate. The function key **F6** is like a **toggle switch**. Press it once, and the cursor moves from the view window to the immediate window. Press it again, and the cursor moves back to the view window. You may use the immediate window as a calculator and debugging tool. For more information on the use of the immediate window, refer to the section titled Debugging Techniques in the Appendix.

If you have a mouse, move the pointer to the inactive window and click the mouse button.

Status Line The line at the very bottom of the QB screen (Figure 1-19) is the **status line**. This line contains a list of the most often used function keys and the line and column location of the cursor on the screen. Keyboard indicators, such as C for Caps Lock and N for Num Lock, display immediately to the left of the cursor line and column location counter when these keys are engaged.

If the menu bar is active and one of the menus is selected, then the status line displays the function of the highlighted command in the menu (Figure 1-20).

Dialog Boxes

QuickBASIC uses **dialog boxes** to display messages and request information from you. For example, if you use a keyword for a variable name, such as PRINT LET instead of PRINT BET, QuickBASIC displays a dialog box when you move the cursor off the line containing the invalid variable name LET. You move the cursor off the line by pressing the **Enter key** or the **Up Arrow key** or **Down Arrow key**.

The dialog box shown in Figure 1-21 displays if you attempt to end the QuickBASIC session and return control to DOS without saving the latest changes made to the current program. Dialog boxes list acceptable user responses in buttons and text boxes. **Buttons** are labeled to indicate what they represent. **Text boxes** are used to enter information such as a file name.

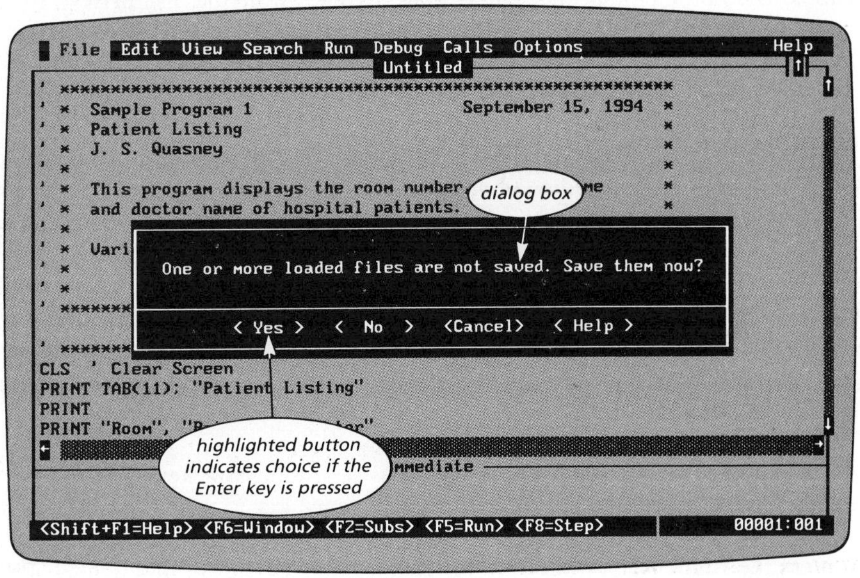

FIGURE 1-21
QuickBASIC displays a dialog box in the middle of the view window when it requires a response from the user before it can continue

In response to the message in the dialog box in Figure 1-21, you can use the **Tab key** or mouse pointer to select one of four buttons—Yes, No, Cancel, or Help. When you press the **Enter key**, the highlighted button, the one with the cursor, is selected. If your PC has a mouse, move the mouse pointer to the desired button or text box and click the mouse button.

Cursor Movement Keys

Several keys on the keyboard are used to move the cursor on the screen. These keys are called the **cursor movement keys**. The arrow keys are used to move the cursor in the windows, menu bar, or menu, one position at a time. Other keys such as the **Home key** and **End key** are used to move the cursor more than one position at a time. The cursor movement keys are summarized on the last page of the reference card at the back of this book.

Function Keys

IBM-type keyboards include a set of ten or twelve **function keys**, which are located to the far left side of the keyboard or along the top of the typewriter keys. The function keys are labeled **F1** through **F10** or **F12**. Pressing these keys instructs QuickBASIC to carry out various tasks. For example, if you press function key **F1** with the cursor in a keyword, QuickBASIC displays a help screen. If you press **Shift + F5**, QuickBASIC executes the current program in the view window. For a complete list of the function keys, refer to the last page of the reference card at the back of this book.

Terminating a QuickBASIC Session

To terminate your QuickBASIC session, press the **Alt key** to activate the menu bar. With the cursor on the word **File**, type the letter **F** or press the **Enter key** to display the **File menu** (Figure 1-20). Next, type the letter **X** for **Exit** or use the arrow keys to move the cursor to the word `Exit` and press the **Enter key**. Thus, the sequence of keystrokes **Alt**, **F**, **X** instructs the PC to return control to DOS. To quit QuickBASIC using a mouse, click on **File** in the menu bar and click on **Exit** in the **File menu**. The term *click on* means move the mouse pointer to the specified word and click the mouse button.

If you did not save the latest version of the current program, then the dialog box shown earlier in Figure 1-21 appears. QuickBASIC requests that you select one of the buttons before continuing. An alternative to selecting a button is to press the **Esc key**, which cancels the command and returns control to the view window.

When the DOS prompt appears, remove your diskettes from the disk drives. Turn the PC's power switch to Off. Turn the monitor power switch to Off. Finally, if you are using a printer, turn the power switch to Off.

Editing QuickBASIC Programs

QuickBASIC programs are entered one line at a time into the view window. The **Enter key** signals QuickBASIC that a line is complete. During the process of entering a program, you will quickly learn that it is easy to make keyboard errors and grammatical errors because of your inexperience with the QuickBASIC language and your unfamiliarity with the keyboard. Logical errors can also occur in a program if you have not considered all the details associated with the problem.

You can eliminate some of the errors if you carefully review your design and program before you enter it into the view window. Any remaining errors are resolved by editing the program. **Editing** is the process of entering and altering a program.

This section describes the most common types of editing. You will find the editing features of QuickBASIC to be both powerful and easy to use.

Deleting Previously Typed Characters Use the arrow keys or mouse to position the cursor. Press the **Delete key** to delete the character under the cursor and the **Backspace key** to delete the character to the left of the cursor. To delete a series of adjacent characters in a line, position the cursor on the leftmost character to be deleted. Hold down one of the **Shift keys** and press the **Right Arrow key** until the characters to delete are highlighted. Press the **Delete key**.

If you have a mouse, select the adjacent characters to delete by moving the pointer from the first character to the last while holding down the mouse button.

Changing or Replacing Previously Typed Lines Move the cursor to the character position where you want to make a change. Begin typing the new characters. QuickBASIC is by default in the insert mode. In the **insert mode**, the cursor is a blinking underline, and the character under the cursor and those to the right are *pushed* to the right as you enter new characters in the line. In the **overtype mode**, the cursor is a blinking box, and the character under the cursor is replaced by the one you type. Use the **Insert key** to toggle between the insert and overtype modes. As you enter new characters in this mode, they replace the old characters.

Adding New Lines Press the **Enter key** to add a new or blank line. To add a new line above the current line, move the cursor to the first character and press the **Enter key**. To add a new line below the current line, move the cursor immediately to the right of the last character and press the **Enter key**.

You should only press the **Enter key** with the cursor at the beginning or end of a line. If you press the **Enter key** in the middle of a line, it is split. To join the split lines, press the **Backspace key** with the cursor on the first character of the second line.

Deleting A Series of Lines Position the cursor at the beginning or end of the series of lines to delete. Hold down one of the **Shift keys** and press the **Up Arrow key** or **Down Arrow key** to highlight the series of lines. Press the **Delete key**.

If you have a mouse, highlight the lines to be deleted by holding down the mouse button and moving the pointer from the first character to the last in the series of lines. With the lines highlighted, press the **Delete key**.

Moving Text Moving text from one location to another in a program is called **cut and paste**. To cut and paste text, follow these steps:

1. Use the arrow keys or mouse to move to the beginning of the text you want.
2. Hold down one of the **Shift keys** and use the arrow keys to select the text. If you are using a mouse, click the mouse button and move the pointer to select the text.
3. Hold down one of the **Shift keys** and press the **Delete key** to *cut* the text. The deleted text is placed in the clipboard. The **clipboard** is a temporary storage area that contains the last text deleted through the use of the **Shift key** and **Delete key**.
4. Move the cursor to the new location using the arrow keys or the mouse. Hold down one of the **Shift keys** and press the **Insert key** to *paste* the text.

Copying Lines Copying text from one location to another in a program is called **pasting**. To paste text, follow these steps:

1. Use the arrow keys or mouse to move the cursor to the beginning of the text you want to paste.
2. Hold down one of the **Shift keys** and use the arrow keys to select the text. If you are using a mouse, hold down the mouse button and move the pointer to select the text.
3. Hold down the **Ctrl key** and press the **Insert key** to copy the text into the clipboard.
4. Move the cursor to the new location using the arrow keys or the mouse. Hold down one of the **Shift keys** and press the **Insert key** to *paste* the text.

You will find a summary of the editing keys on the last page of the reference card at the back of this book.

EXECUTING PROGRAMS AND HARD-COPY OUTPUT

The menu bar at the top of the screen contains eight menu names (Figure 1-19). Each menu name has a menu of commands. As we indicated earlier, to activate the menu bar, press the **Alt key**. Next, open a menu in one of two ways: (1) type the first letter in the menu name; or (2) use the **Left Arrow key** or **Right Arrow key** to move the cursor to the menu name and press the **Enter key**.

If you have a mouse, you can activate the menu bar and select the menu name by moving the pointer to the desired menu name and clicking the mouse button.

The two most important menu names are Run and File. The **Run menu** is primarily used to execute the current program. The **File menu** contains several important commands. One in particular, the **Print** command, is used to print all or part of the current program.

Executing the Current Program

You execute (run) the current program by selecting the **Start** command in the **Run menu** (Figure 1-22 on the next page). The **Start** command can be selected in any one of the following three ways:

1. Press the **Alt key**, **R** for **Run**, and **S** for **Start**.
2. Press **Shift + F5**.
3. If you have a mouse, click on **Run** in the menu bar and click on **Start** in the Run menu.

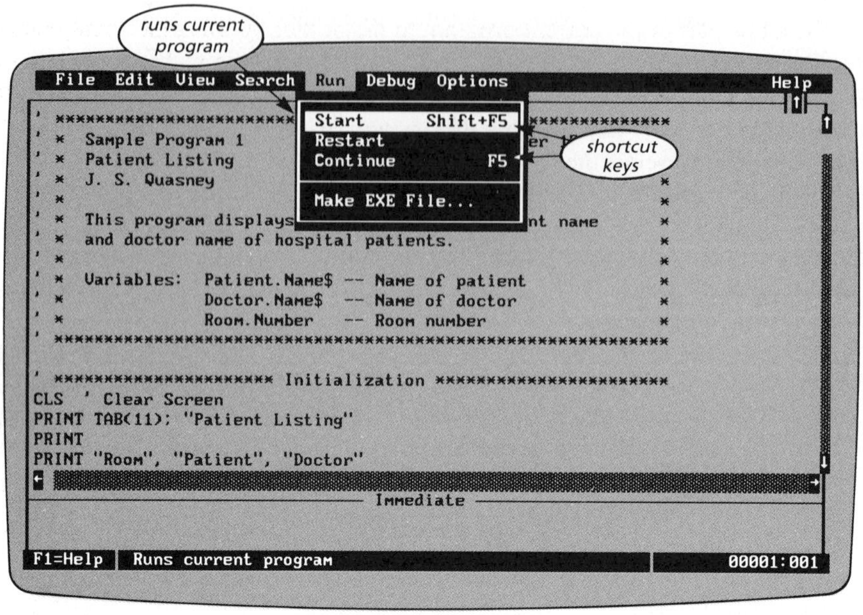

FIGURE 1-22
The Run menu

When the program first executes, QuickBASIC replaces the QB screen with the output screen. As we indicated earlier, the output screen shows the results due to the execution of the current program. Figure 1-23 shows the output screen for Sample Program 1. After you read the output results, you can redisplay the QB screen by pressing any key on the keyboard. This is indicated at the bottom of the output screen. To redisplay the output results, press the function key **F4**.

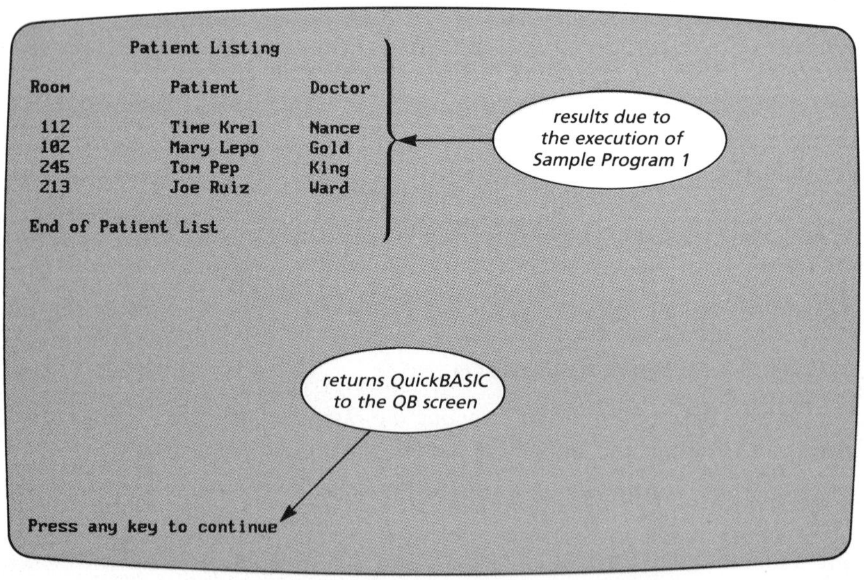

FIGURE 1-23
The output screen

Listing Program Lines to the Printer

Most programmers use a keyboard for input and a monitor (screen) for output. In many instances, it is desirable to list the program and the results on a printer. A listing of this type is called **hard-copy output**.

You can list all or part of the current program to the printer by using the **Print** command in the **File menu**. With the printer in the Ready mode, press the **Alt key** to activate the menu bar and type the letter **F** to pull down the **File menu** (Figure 1-24). Next, type the letter **P** for **Print** to print the current program. The three periods following the **Print** command mean a dialog box will appear requesting additional information. When the Print dialog box appears (Figure 1-25), make sure the bullet is next to the selection Current Module (Entire Program or Document if you are using the textbook version). Finally, press the **Enter key**.

If you have a mouse, click on **File**, click on **Print**, and click on **OK** when the Print dialog box appears.

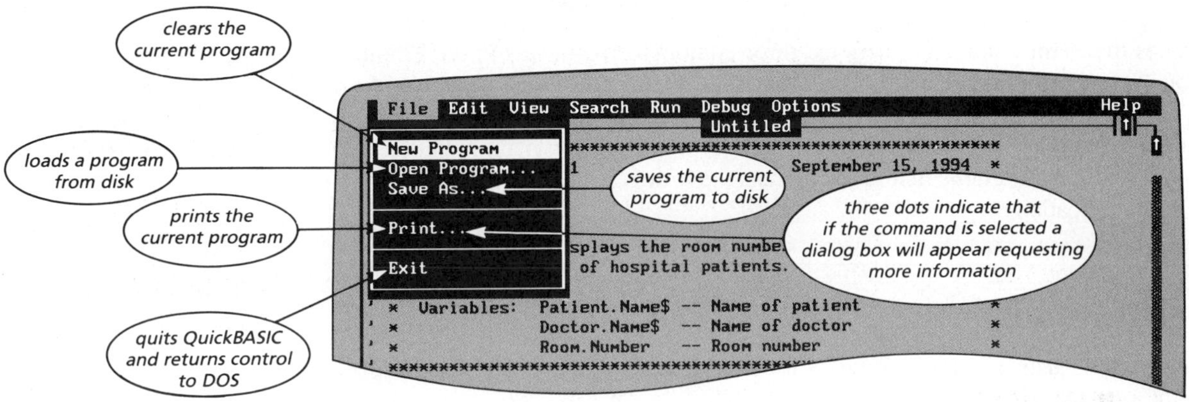

FIGURE 1-24 The File menu

Listing a Portion of the Program to the Printer

To print a portion of the current program, use the **Shift key** and arrow keys (or the mouse) to highlight the lines in the program you want to print. Next, follow the steps outlined in the previous paragraphs for printing the program. When the Print dialog box appears on the screen, the bullet should be in front of Selected Text (Figure 1-25). QuickBASIC automatically assigns the bullet to Selected Text when a series of lines is selected prior to issuing the **Print** command.

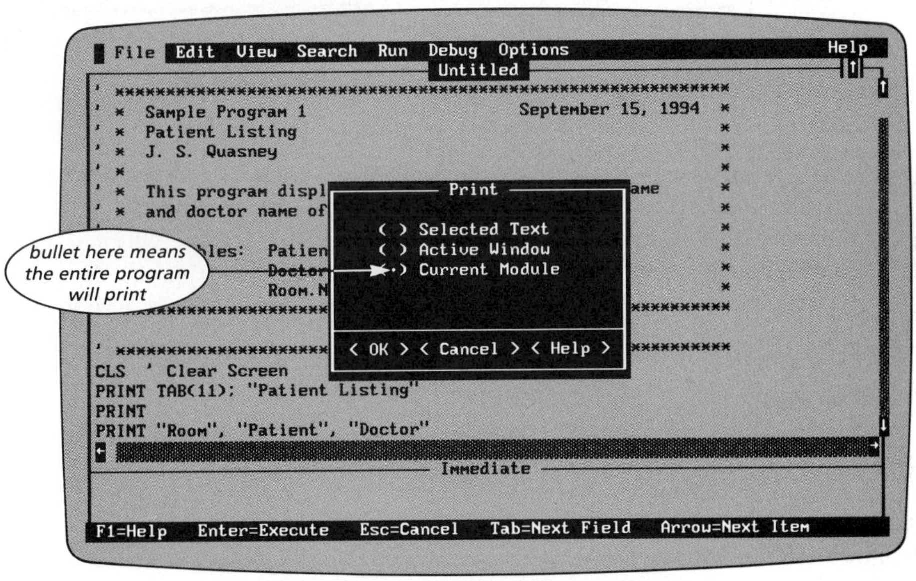

FIGURE 1-25 The dialog box for the Print command

Printing the Results on the Output Screen

To print a copy of the output screen, press **Print Screen** (**Shift + Prt Sc** on older PCs) while the output screen displays on the monitor. Later we discuss the `LPRINT` statement as an alternative means to generating hard-copy output.

SAVING, LOADING, AND ERASING PROGRAMS

Besides the **Print** command, there are three additional commands in the **File** menu (Figure 1-24) that are essential for your first session with QuickBASIC—**Save As**, **Open**, and **New**. The **Save As** command allows you to store the current program to disk. Later, you use the **Open** command to load the program from disk into main storage to make it the current one. The **New** command erases the current program from main memory. It clears the view window and indicates the beginning of a new program. Before we discuss these three commands further, it is important that you understand the concept of a file specification.

File Specifications

A **file specification**, also called a **filespec**, is used to identify programs and data files placed in auxiliary storage. A filespec is made up of a device name, file name, and extension.

filespec

device name:file name.extension

The **device name** refers to the disk drive. If no device is specified, then the filespec refers to the default drive of the PC. If a device name is included in the filespec, then it must be followed by a colon.

File names can be from 1 to 8 characters in length. Valid characters are uppercase or lowercase A–Z, 0–9, and certain special characters ($ & # @ ! % " ( ) - { } _ / \). If an extension is used, then the file name must be followed by a period.

An **extension** that is up to three characters in length may be used to classify a file. Valid characters are the same as for a file name. With QuickBASIC, the default extension is `bas`. That is, when you use a command that requires a filespec, QuickBASIC will automatically append an extension of `bas` if one is not included.

Examples of valid filespecs include `b:payroll`, `b:lab2-1`, `PAYROLL.BAS`, `Accounts`, and `S123`. The first two examples reference files on drive B. The latter three examples reference files on the default drive.

Saving the Current Program to Disk

When you enter a program through the keyboard, it is stored in main storage (RAM), and it displays in the view window. When you quit QuickBASIC or turn the computer off, the current program disappears from the screen and, more importantly, from main memory. To save a program to disk for later use, use the **Save As** command in the **File menu**.

To select the **Save As** command, press the **Alt key** to activate the menu bar. Type the letter **F** to pull down the **File menu** (Figure 1-24). Type **A** for **Save As**. Here again, the three periods following the **Save As** command mean QuickBASIC requires additional information. In this case it needs to know the filespec.

When the **Save As** dialog box appears (Figure 1-25), enter the file name and press the **Enter key**. In Figure 1-26, we entered the file name `prg-1`. QuickBASIC stores the current program using the filespec `a:prg-1.bas`. Notice in Figure 1-26 that the default drive (A:\) is specified below the file name box.

The **dirs/drives box** in the Save As dialog box includes a list of the disk drives and any subdirectories that are part of the current default drive. You may use the **Tab key** or mouse to activate this box and select a different default drive.

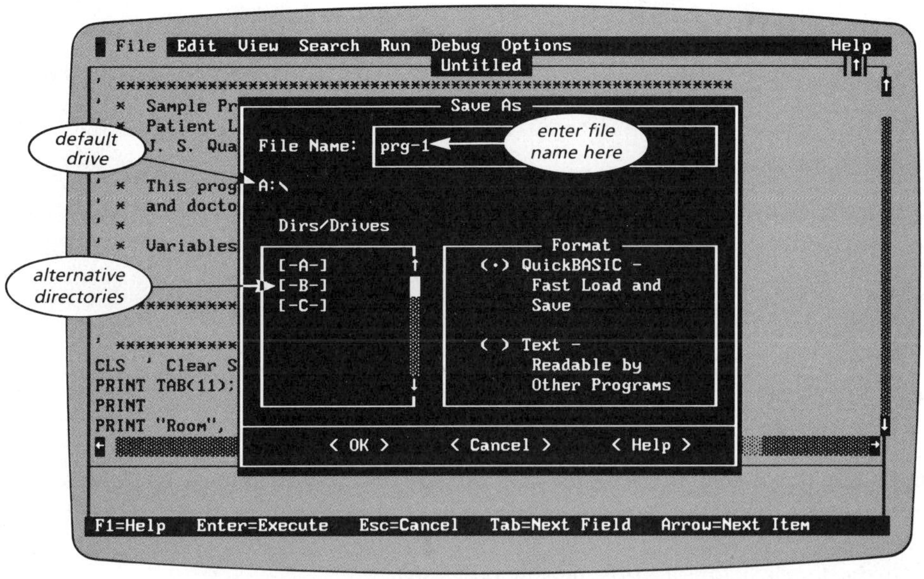

FIGURE 1-26 The dialog box for the Save As command

If you loaded the current program from disk or saved the program earlier, the file name will be in the file name box when you issue the **Save As** command. To save the program under the old file name, press the **Enter key**. To change the file name, just begin typing. What you type replaces the old name. In this case, the old file remains in its present form, and a new file is created on disk.

To save the current program using a mouse, click on **File** and click on **Save As**. Enter the name in the file name box and click on the **OK** button.

Loading a Program from Disk

To load a program stored on disk into main storage, use the **Open** command in the **File menu** (Figure 1-24). This command causes the dialog box shown on the next page in Figure 1-27 to display. In the middle of the dialog box, QuickBASIC displays the files box. The **files box** lists the file names on the default drive that have an extension of `bas`. The current default drive displays just above the files box. To display any other directory on your PC, enter the disk drive (or path) in the file name box or select one from the dirs/drive box and press the **Enter key**.

In the file name box, enter the name of the program you want to load from auxiliary storage into main storage. In Figure 1-27 we entered the file name `prg-1`. Enter the file name by typing it on the keyboard or use the **Tab key** and arrow keys to select the file name from the file names box. Each time you press an arrow key, the name of the program under the cursor displays in the file names box. To complete the command, press the **Enter key**.

If you did not save the current program before attempting to load a new one, QuickBASIC will give you the opportunity to save it before it loads the new program into main storage.

To load a program from disk using the mouse, click on **File** and click on **Open**. Double-click on the name of the program in the files box.

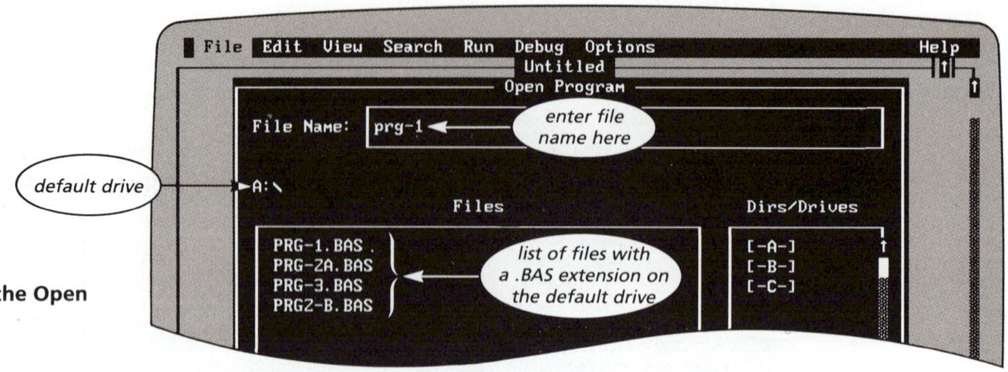

FIGURE 1-27
The dialog box for the Open Program command

Starting a New Program

The **New** command in the **File menu** (Figure 1-24) instructs QuickBASIC to erase the current program from main storage. This also clears the view window. Use this command when you are finished with the current program and wish to start a new one from scratch. Notice that it is not necessary to clear the current program if you are loading a program from disk. The **Open** command clears main storage before it loads the new program.

THE QB ADVISOR ON-LINE HELP SYSTEM

The QB Advisor is a fully integrated, on-line help system with instant access to any QuickBASIC question. You can request immediate help when you first enter QuickBASIC by pressing the **Enter key** rather than the **Esc key**. Thereafter, at any time while you are using QuickBASIC, you can interact with the QB Advisor and display help screens on any QuickBASIC topic using the keys described on the last page of the reference card at the back of this book. For example, if you press **Shift + F1**, the initial help screen shown in Figure 1-28 displays. To return to the view window, press the **Esc key**. If you press **F1**, QuickBASIC displays help for the topic in which the cursor is positioned. The QB Advisor is literally a complete reference manual at your fingertips. The best way to familiarize yourself with the QB Advisor is to use it.

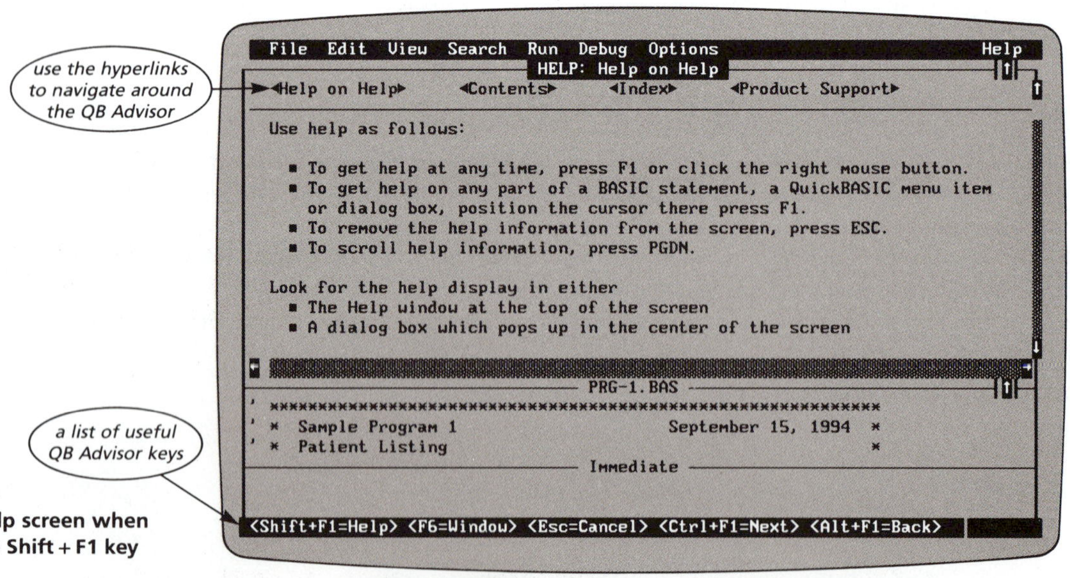

FIGURE 1-28
The initial help screen when you press the Shift + F1 key

TRY IT YOURSELF EXERCISES

1. Identify the 8 major components of the QB screen shown below.

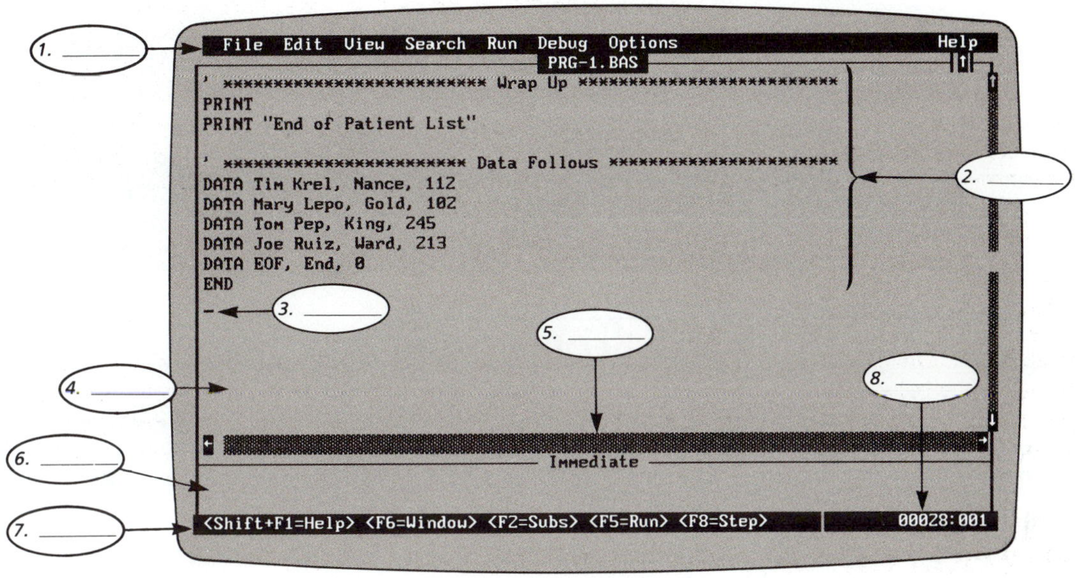

2. List the function of the following keys when a dialog box is active.
   a. Esc b. Tab c. Enter

3. List the function of the following keys when the view window is active.
   a. Alt b. Shift + Delete c. Enter
   d. Home e. End f. Ctrl + Home
   g. Ctrl + Q, X h. Shift + F5 i. F4
   j. F6 k. Backspace l. Delete
   m. Insert n. Shift + Insert o. Page Up

STUDENT ASSIGNMENTS

STUDENT ASSIGNMENT 1: Personnel Report

Instructions: Design and code a program using QuickBASIC to produce the personnel listing as shown on the next page under OUTPUT. The listing includes the employee name, department number, and pay rate for each employee shown under INPUT. Submit a program flowchart, listing of the program, and a listing of the output results. To obtain a hard copy of the output results, use the Print Screen key.

INPUT: Use the following sample data:

NAME	DEPT. NO.	PAY RATE
Sue Long	10	4.25
Chin Song	12	5.15
Mary Lopez	14	4.75
Jan Honig	14	3.85
EOF	99	9.99

Student Assignment 1 (continued)

OUTPUT: The following results are displayed:

```
              Personnel Report

Dept.            Name              Pay Rate

 10              Sue Long           4.25
 12              Chin Song          5.15
 14              Mary Lopez         4.75
 14              Jan Honig          3.85

End of Personnel Report
```

STUDENT ASSIGNMENT 2: Club Membership Report

Instructions: Design and code a program using QuickBASIC to produce the club membership listing shown under OUTPUT. The listing includes a name, birth date, and age for each member shown under INPUT. Submit a program flowchart, listing of the program, and a listing of the output results. To obtain a hard copy of the output results, use the Print Screen key.

INPUT: Use the following sample data:

BIRTH DATE	AGE	NAME
December 7	41	John Sutherlin
March 16	38	Jim Wachtel
June 9	27	Mary Hathaway
August 6	25	Loise Scott
EOF	99	End

OUTPUT: The following results are displayed:

```
         Membership Listing

Name:            John Sutherlin
Birth Date:      December 7
Age:              41

Name:            Jim Wachtel
Birth Date:      March 16
Age:              38

Name:            Mary Hathaway
Birth Date:      June 9
Age:              27

Name:            Louise Scott
Birth Date:      August 6
Age:              25

End of Membership Listing
```

PROJECT 2

Basic Arithmetic Operations and Accumulating Totals

Many applications require that arithmetic operations be performed on the input data to produce the required output. QuickBASIC includes the following basic arithmetic operators: addition (+), subtraction (–), multiplication (∗), division (/), and raising a value to a power (^). These operators are similar to those used in ordinary mathematics. The operators and an example of their use in a LET statement are illustrated in Figure 2-1.

MATHEMATICAL OPERATION	BASIC ARITHMETIC OPERATOR	EXAMPLE
Addition	+	LET Total = Sub1 + Sub2
Subtraction	–	LET Profit = Price - 5.95
Multiplication	*	LET Gross = Hours * Rate
Division	/	LET Amount = Cost / 5
Raising to a Power	^	LET Discount = Rate ^ 2

FIGURE 2-1 QuickBASIC arithmetic operators

THE LET STATEMENT

The LET statement is used to assign a variable a value. As shown in Figure 2-2, the first entry in a LET statement is the keyword LET. The keyword LET is followed by a variable name, an equal sign, and an expression.

```
LET numeric variable = numeric expression
   or
LET string variable = string expression
```

FIGURE 2-2 The general form of the LET statement

Expressions

An **expression** can be numeric or string. A **numeric expression** consists of one or more numeric constants, numeric variables, and numeric function references, all of which are separated from each other by parentheses and arithmetic operators. A **string expression** consists of one or more string constants, string variables, and string functions separated by the concatenation operator (+), which combines two strings into one. A numeric expression can only be assigned to a numeric variable. A string expression can only be assigned to a string variable.

Figure 2-3 illustrates numeric expressions in LET statements. Figure 2-4 illustrates string expressions in LET statements.

VALUE OF	LET STATEMENT	RESULTS IN
A = 15 B = 10	LET F = A + B - 10	F = 15
J = 32 H = 16	LET L = J * 2 - H	L = 48
P = 14 Y = 7	LET Q = P / Y	Q = 2
W = 4 S = 6	LET T = 6 * (S - W)	T = 12

FIGURE 2-3 **Numeric expressions in LET statements**

VALUE OF	LET STATEMENT	RESULTS IN
X$ = ABC	LET W$ = "DEF" + X$	W$ = DEFABC
F$ = WATER G$ = WINE	LET A$ = F$ + " INTO " + G$	A$ = WATER INTO WINE
S$ = "TOP"	LET S$ = S$ + "IT"	S$ = TOPIT

FIGURE 2-4 **String expressions in LET statements**

From the examples in Figures 2-3 and 2-4 you can see that when performing arithmetic operations, the calculations are specified to the right of the equal sign. The variable assigned the result of the expression is placed to the left side of the equal sign.

Order of Operations

When multiple arithmetic operations are included in a LET statement, the **order of operations** follows the normal algebraic rules. That is, the operations are completed in the following order:

- First, exponentiation is performed from left to right.
- Next, multiplication and division are performed from left to right.
- Finally, addition and subtraction are performed from left to right.

For example, the expression 27 / 3 ^ 2 + 4 * 3 is evaluated as follows:

```
27 / 3 ^ 2 + 4 * 3 = 27 / 9 + 4 * 3
                   = 3      + 4 * 3
                   = 3      + 12
                   = 15
```

If you had trouble following the logic behind this evaluation, use the following technique. Whenever a numeric expression is to be evaluated, *scan* from left to right three different times. On the first scan, every time you encounter an ^ operator, you perform exponentiation. In this example, 3 is raised to the power of 2, yielding 9.

On the second scan, moving from left to right again, every time you encounter the operators * and /, perform multiplication and division. Hence, 27 is divided by 9, yielding 3, and 4 and 3 are multiplied, yielding 12.

On the third scan, moving again from left to right, every time you detect the operators + and –, perform addition and subtraction. In this example, 3 and 12 are added to form 15. Thus, the following `LET` statement

```
LET Amount = 27 / 3 ^ 2 + 4 * 3
```

assigns 15 to the variable Amount.

The expression below yields the value of –19.37, as follows:

$$
\begin{aligned}
4 - 3 * 4 / 10 \wedge 2 + 5 / 4 * 3 - 3 \wedge 3 &= 4 - 3 * 4 / 100 + 5 / 4 * 3 - 27 \\
&= 4 - 0.12 + 3.75 - 27 \\
&= -19.37
\end{aligned}
$$

Hence, the following `LET` statement

```
LET Total = 4 - 3 * 4 / 10 ^ 2 + 5 / 4 * 3 - 3 ^ 3
```

assigns –19.37 to the variable Total.

The Use of Parentheses in an Expression

Parentheses may be used to change the order of operations. In QuickBASIC, parentheses are normally used to avoid ambiguity and to group terms in a numeric expression; they do not imply multiplication. When parentheses are inserted into an expression, the part of the expression within the parentheses is evaluated first, and then the remaining expression is evaluated according to the order of operations.

If the first example contained parentheses, as does (27 / 3) ^ 2 + 4 * 3, then it would be evaluated in the following manner:

$$
\begin{aligned}
(27 / 3) \wedge 2 + 4 * 3 &= 9 \wedge 2 + 4 * 3 \\
&= 81 + 4 * 3 \\
&= 81 + 12 \\
&= 93
\end{aligned}
$$

Use parentheses freely when you are in doubt as to the formation and evaluation of a numeric expression. For example, if you want to have the PC divide `9 * Tax` by `3 ^ Payment`, the expression may correctly be written as `9 * Tax / 3 ^ Payment`, but you may also write it as `(9 * Tax) / (3 ^ Payment)` and feel more certain of the result.

For more complex expressions, QuickBASIC allows parentheses to be contained within other parentheses. When this occurs, the parentheses are said to be **nested**. In this case, QuickBASIC evaluates the innermost parenthetical expression first and then goes on to the outermost parenthetical expression. Thus, (27 / 3) ^ 2 + (5 * (7 + 3)) is broken down in the following manner:

$$
\begin{aligned}
(27 / 3) \wedge 2 + (5 * (7 + 3)) &= 9 \wedge 2 + (5 * (7 + 3)) \\
&= 81 + (5 * 10) \\
&= 81 + 50 \\
&= 131
\end{aligned}
$$

SAMPLE PROGRAM 2 — AUTO EXPENSE REPORT

The following sample program generates an auto expense report. The program performs calculations and accumulates totals using `LET` statements. Input consists of auto expense records that contain an employee name, the license number of the employee's car, the beginning mileage for the employee's car, and the ending mileage for the car.

The auto expense file that will be processed by the sample program is shown in Figure 2-5.

NAME	LICENSE	BEGINNING MILEAGE	ENDING MILEAGE
T. Rowe	HRT-111	19,100	19,224
R. Lopez	GLD-913	21,221	21,332
C. Deck	LIV-193	10,001	10,206
B. Alek	ZRT-904	15,957	16,419
EOF	End	0	0

FIGURE 2-5 The employee auto expense file for Sample Program 2

The output generated by Sample Program 2 is a report displayed on the screen. The report contains the employee name, the automobile license number, the total mileage, and the expense. The total mileage is calculated by subtracting the beginning mileage from the ending mileage. The expense is calculated by multiplying the mileage by twenty-five cents.

The report contains both report headings and column headings. After all records have been processed, the total number of employees and total auto expenses are displayed. In addition, the average expense per employee is calculated by dividing the total auto expense by the total number of employees. The average expense per employee is then displayed followed by an end-of-report message. The format of the output is shown in Figure 2-6.

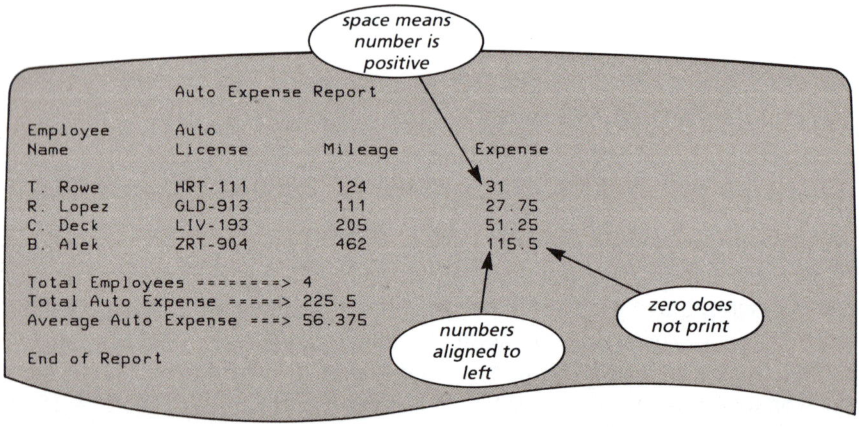

FIGURE 2-6
The report for Sample Program 2

When using the `PRINT` statement, nonsignificant zeros to the right of a decimal point are not printed. For example, Alek's expense displays as 115.5 rather than 115.50. In addition, when printing decimal numbers, the numbers are left aligned under the column heading rather than right aligned. The single space displayed to the left of each number means that the number is positive. These factors are illustrated in the output in Figure 2-6. Later in this section, we discuss the `PRINT USING` statement, which allows you to adjust the values displayed to include nonsignificant zeros and right-align numeric values under the column headings.

Accumulators

Most programs require **accumulators**, which are used to develop totals. Accumulators are initialized to a value of zero in the Initialization module, then incremented within the loop in the Process File module, and finally manipulated or displayed in the Wrap-Up module. Although QuickBASIC automatically initializes numeric variables to zero, good programming practice demands that this be done in the program. There are two types of accumulators: counters and running totals.

A **counter** is an accumulator that is used to count the number of times some action or event is performed. For example, appropriately placed within a loop, the statement

```
LET Total.Employees = Total.Employees + 1
```

causes the counter Total.Employees to increment by 1 each time a record is read. Associated with a counter is a statement placed in the Initialization module which initializes the counter to some value. In most cases the counter is initialized to zero.

A **running total** is an accumulator that is used to sum the different values that a variable is assigned during the execution of a program. For example, appropriately placed within a loop, the statement

```
LET Total.Expense = Total.Expense + Auto.Expense
```

causes Total.Expense to increase by the value of Auto.Expense. Total.Expense is called a running total. If a program is processing an employee file and the variable Auto.Expense is assigned the employee's auto expense each time a record is read, then variable Total.Expense represents the running total of the auto expense of all the employees in the file. As with a counter, a running total must be initialized to some predetermined value, such as zero, in the Initialization module.

Program Flowchart

The flowchart for the sample program, which produces an auto expense report and accumulates and prints final totals, is illustrated in Figure 2-7.

Prior to the loop in the flowchart, the accumulators are initialized, the headings are displayed, and the first employee record is read. Within the loop, the employee counter is incremented, the beginning mileage is subtracted from the ending mileage, giving the mileage driven by the employee. The auto expense is then calculated by multiplying the mileage driven times the auto cost per mile (.25). The auto expense is then added to the total auto expense accumulator. Next, a line of information is displayed. At the bottom of the loop another record is read. Control then returns to the top of the loop to determine if the trailer record was read. This looping process continues until there are no more auto expense records.

When the trailer record is read, the total number of employees and total auto expenses are displayed. Next, the total auto expense is divided by the total number of employees to give the average auto expense. Finally, the average and an end-of-report message are displayed.

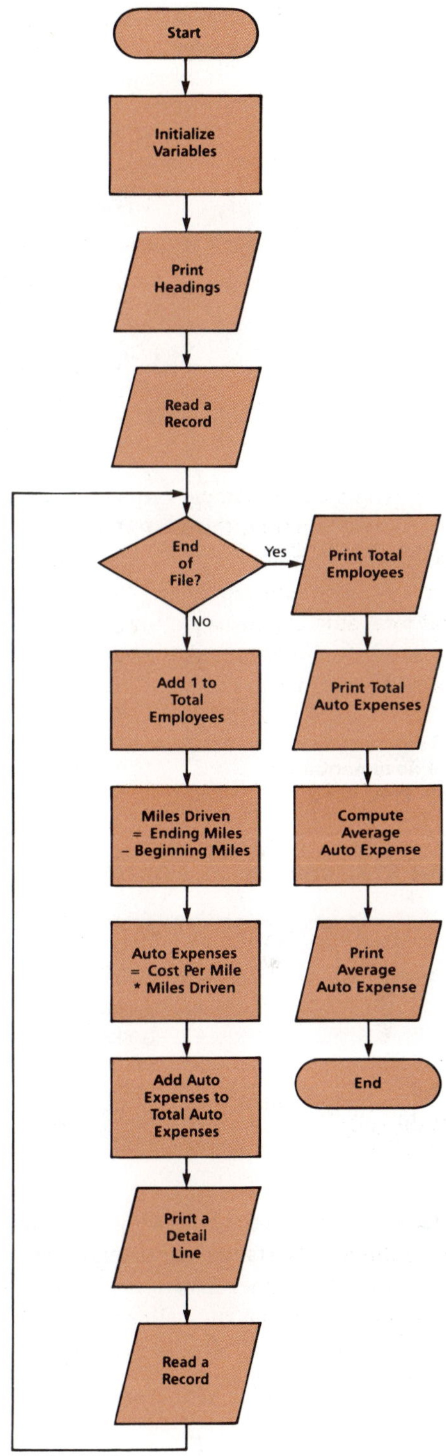

FIGURE 2-7 The flowchart for Sample Program 2

The QuickBASIC Program

The first section of the QuickBASIC program includes the initial documentation. As shown in Figure 2-8, the documentation is similar to Sample Program 1.

```
' ********************************************************************
' *  Sample Program 2                               September 15, 1994  *
' *  Auto Expense Report                                               *
' *  J. S. Quasney                                                     *
' *                                                                    *
' *  This program displays an auto expense report.  Mileage           *
' *  expense is calculated on the basis of 25 cents per mile.         *
' *  As part of the Wrap-Up module, the total number of               *
' *  employees, total auto expense, and the average expense           *
' *  per employee are displayed.                                      *
' *                                                                    *
' *  Variables:  Emp.Name$        -- Name of employee                 *
' *              License$         -- Auto license number              *
' *              Begin.Mileage    -- Beginning mileage                *
' *              End.Mileage      -- Ending mileage                   *
' *              Miles.Driven     -- Miles driven                     *
' *              Cost.Per.Mile    -- Auto cost per mile               *
' *              Auto.Expense     -- Auto expense                     *
' *              Total.Employees  -- Number of employees              *
' *              Total.Expense    -- Total auto expense               *
' *              Average.Expense  -- Average auto expense             *
' ********************************************************************

```

FIGURE 2-8
The initial documentation for Sample Program 2

The DATA Statements The DATA statements in Figure 2-9 correspond to the employee auto expense file described in Figure 2-5.

```
' ************************ Data Follows ***********************
DATA T. Rowe, HRT-111, 19100, 19224
DATA R. Lopez, GLD-913, 21221, 21332
DATA C. Deck, LIV-193, 10001, 10206
DATA B. Alek, ZRT-904, 15957, 16419
DATA EOF, End, 0, 0
END
```

FIGURE 2-9
The DATA statements for Sample Program 2

Initialization Module Following the initial program documentation shown in Figure 2-8, the Initialization module initializes the accumulators to zero and displays the report title and column headings. The Initialization module is shown in Figure 2-10.

```
' ********************** Initialization ***********************
CLS  ' Clear Screen
LET Total.Employees = 0
LET Total.Expense = 0
LET Cost.Per.Mile = .25
PRINT TAB(15); "Auto Expense Report"
PRINT
PRINT "Employee", "Auto"
PRINT "Name", "License", "Mileage", "Expense"
PRINT

```

FIGURE 2-10
The Initialization module for Sample Program 2

Lines 26 and 27 initialize the employee counter (Total.Employees) and total expense running total (Total.Expense) to zero. When these two LET statements are executed, the zeros on the right side of the equal sign are assigned to the variables Total.Employee and Total.Expense. Counters and running totals should always be set to zero at the beginning of a program.

When the LET statement in line 28 is executed, the constant 0.25 on the right side of the equal sign is assigned to Cost.Per.Mile. This variable can then be used later to compute the auto expense. The purpose of assigning 0.25 to a variable is to facilitate future changes to the program. For example, if the auto cost per mile were changed from 0.25 to 0.28, the constant value in line 28 could be changed to 0.28.

Lines 29 through 33 display the report title and column headings. The PRINT statement in line 29 displays the report title beginning in column 15. Line 30 skips a line in the report. Lines 31 and 32 display the column headings. Finally, line 33 skips a line in the report to leave space between the column headings and the first record displayed.

The Process File Module The statements that make up the Process File module for Sample Program 2 are illustrated in Figure 2-11.

```
35  ' ************************ Process File ************************
36  READ Emp.Name$, License$, Begin.Mileage, End.Mileage
37  DO WHILE Emp.Name$ <> "EOF"
38     LET Total.Employees = Total.Employees + 1
39     LET Miles.Driven = End.Mileage - Begin.Mileage
40     LET Auto.Expense = Cost.Per.Mile * Miles.Driven
41     LET Total.Expense = Total.Expense + Auto.Expense
42     PRINT Emp.Name$, License$, Miles.Driven, Auto.Expense
43     READ Emp.Name$, License$, Begin.Mileage, End.Mileage
44  LOOP
45
```

FIGURE 2-11
The Process File module for Sample Program 2

The READ statement in line 36 assigns the data in the first DATA statement (line 56 in Figure 2-9) to Emp.Name$, License$, Begin.Mileage, and End.Mileage. Next, the DO WHILE statement in line 37 tests to see if Emp.Name$ is not equal to EOF. Since Emp.Name$ does not equal EOF, control enters the loop.

The LET statement in line 38 increments the employee counter (Total.Employees). Each time this statement is executed, Total.Employees is incremented by 1. Since Total.Employees was initially set to zero (line 26 in Figure 2-10), it is equal to 1 after line 38 is executed the first time. After the statement is executed a second time, the value of Total.Employees is equal to 2. This counting continues each time through the loop. When the end-of-file is detected, the value of Total.Employees is equal to the number of records processed.

The LET statement in line 39 calculates the mileage the automobile was driven (Miles.Driven) by the employee being processed by subtracting the beginning mileage (Begin.Mileage) from the ending mileage (End.Mileage). Line 40 computes the auto expense (Auto.Expense) by multiplying the miles the automobile was driven (Miles.Driven) by the cost per mile (Cost.Per.Mile). The value 0.25 was assigned to Cost.Per.Mile in line 28 of the Initialization module (Figure 2-10).

The LET statement in line 41 adds the auto expense (Auto.Expense) to the accumulator Total.Expense. Here again, the variable Total.Expense was initialized to zero. When line 41 is executed the first time, the auto expense is added to the value zero. Hence, Auto.Expense is equal to the T. Rowe's auto expense after the first pass on the loop. When line 41 is executed the second time, the auto expense for R. Lopez is added to the auto expense for T. Rowe. Thus, the effect of this LET statement is to accumulate the auto expenses for all the employees.

The PRINT statement in line 42 displays the employee name, license number, miles driven, and the auto expense. Next, the READ statement in line 43 assigns the data for the second employee to Emp.Name$, License$, Begin.Mileage, and End.Mileage. The LOOP statement in line 44 transfers control back up to the DO WHILE statement in line 37. Notice that statements 38 through 43 are indented three spaces to illuminate the statements within the Do loop. The looping process continues until the trailer record is read, at which time control is transferred to the Wrap-Up module (line 47).

End-of-File Processing After all the records are processed, control transfers to the `PRINT` statement in line 47 (Figure 2-12), which causes the PC to skip a line in the report. The next `PRINT` statement displays the total number of employees (Total.Employees). Notice the manner in which the `PRINT` statement is written to display both a constant and a variable. The phrase `Total Employees ========>` is enclosed within quotation marks ("). The right quotation is followed by a semicolon (;). A semicolon causes the PC to display the value of Total.Employees immediately after the phrase rather than in the next print zone. Recall that if the numeric value is positive, a blank space appears before the numeric value.

After line 49 displays the total expenses, line 50 computes the average expense which is displayed by line 51. Line 52 skips a line and line 53 displays an end-of-report message. Finally, line 61 (Figure 2-9) terminates execution of the program.

```
46  ' ************************** Wrap-Up **************************
47  PRINT
48  PRINT "Total Employees ========>"; Total.Employees
49  PRINT "Total Auto Expense =====>"; Total.Expense
50  LET Average.Expense = Total.Expense / Total.Employees
51  PRINT "Average Auto Expense ===>"; Average.Expense
52  PRINT
53  PRINT "End of Report"
54
```

FIGURE 2-12
The Wrap-Up module for Sample Program 2

The Complete QuickBASIC Program The complete Sample Program 2 is illustrated in Figure 2-13. The report generated by Sample Program 2 is shown in Figure 2-14.

```
1   ' ***************************************************************
2   ' *  Sample Program 2                        September 15, 1994  *
3   ' *  Auto Expense Report                                         *
4   ' *  J. S. Quasney                                               *
5   ' *                                                              *
6   ' *  This program displays an auto expense report.  Mileage      *
7   ' *  expense is calculated on the basis of 25 cents per mile.    *
8   ' *  As part of the Wrap-Up module, the total number of          *
9   ' *  employees, total auto expense, and the average expense      *
10  ' *  per employee are displayed.                                 *
11  ' *                                                              *
12  ' *  Variables:  Emp.Name$         -- Name of employee           *
13  ' *              License$          -- Auto license number        *
14  ' *              Begin.Mileage     -- Beginning mileage          *
15  ' *              End.Mileage       -- Ending mileage             *
16  ' *              Miles.Driven      -- Miles driven               *
17  ' *              Cost.Per.Mile     -- Auto cost per mile         *
18  ' *              Auto.Expense      -- Auto expense               *
19  ' *              Total.Employees   -- Number of employees        *
20  ' *              Total.Expense     -- Total auto expense         *
21  ' *              Average.Expense   -- Average auto expense       *
22  ' ***************************************************************
23
24  ' ********************** Initialization ***********************
25  CLS  ' Clear Screen
26  LET Total.Employees = 0
27  LET Total.Expense = 0
28  LET Cost.Per.Mile = .25
29  PRINT TAB(15); "Auto Expense Report"
30  PRINT
31  PRINT "Employee", "Auto"
32  PRINT "Name", "License", "Mileage", "Expense"
33  PRINT
34
```

FIGURE 2-13
Sample Program 2

FIGURE 2-13 (continued)

```
' ************************ Process File ************************
READ Emp.Name$, License$, Begin.Mileage, End.Mileage
DO WHILE Emp.Name$ <> "EOF"
   LET Total.Employees = Total.Employees + 1
   LET Miles.Driven = End.Mileage - Begin.Mileage
   LET Auto.Expense = Cost.Per.Mile * Miles.Driven
   LET Total.Expense = Total.Expense + Auto.Expense
   PRINT Emp.Name$, License$, Miles.Driven, Auto.Expense
   READ Emp.Name$, License$, Begin.Mileage, End.Mileage
LOOP

' ************************** Wrap-Up **************************
PRINT
PRINT "Total Employees ========>"; Total.Employees
PRINT "Total Auto Expense =====>"; Total.Expense
LET Average.Expense = Total.Expense / Total.Employees
PRINT "Average Auto Expense ===>"; Average.Expense
PRINT
PRINT "End of Report"

' ************************ Data Follows ************************
DATA T. Rowe, HRT-111, 19100, 19224
DATA R. Lopez, GLD-913, 21221, 21332
DATA C. Deck, LIV-193, 10001, 10206
DATA B. Alek, ZRT-904, 15957, 16419
DATA EOF, End, 0, 0
END
```

```
                    Auto Expense Report

Employee            Auto
Name                License             Mileage             Expense

T. Rowe             HRT-111              124                 31
R. Lopez            GLD-913              111                 27.75
C. Deck             LIV-193              205                 51.25
B. Alek             ZRT-904              462                 115.5

Total Employees ========> 4
Total Auto Expense =====> 225.5
Average Auto Expense ===> 56.375

End of Report
```

FIGURE 2-14
The output results due to the execution of Sample Program 2

REPORT EDITING

Although the output in Figure 2-14 is readable, it does not conform to the format used by business and industry. For example, a column of numeric values usually has the decimal points aligned and is right-justified under the column heading. Numeric values that represent dollars and cents should include two digits to the right of the decimal point. Placing information in a format such as this is called **report editing**.

QuickBASIC provides for report editing through the use of the `PRINT USING` statement. This statement allows you to do the following:

- Specify the exact image of a line of output.
- Force decimal-point alignment when displaying numeric tables in columnar format.
- Control the number of digits displayed for a numeric result.

- Specify that commas be inserted into a number. (Starting from the units position of a number and progressing toward the left, digits are separated into groups of 3 by a comma.)
- Specify that the sign status of the number be displayed along with the number (+ or blank if positive, – if negative).
- Assign a fixed or floating dollar sign ($) to the number displayed.
- Force a numeric result to be displayed in exponential form.
- **Left-** or **right-justify** string values in a formatted field (that is, align the leftmost or rightmost characters, respectively).
- Specify that only the first character of a string be displayed.
- Round a value automatically to a specified number of decimal digits.

The general form of the `PRINT USING` statement is shown in Figure 2-15.

`PRINT USING` "format field"; list

or

`PRINT USING` string variable; list

where **format field** or **string variable** indicates the format and **list** is a variable or a group of variables separted by semicolons.

FIGURE 2-15
The general form of the PRINT USING statement

Report editing with the `PRINT USING` statement is accomplished using special characters to format the values to be displayed. When grouped together, these special characters form a **format field**. A format field is incorporated in a program as a string constant in the `PRINT USING` statement or as a string constant assigned to a string variable.

To illustrate the use of the `PRINT USING` statement, we will modify Sample Program 2. The new, formatted report is illustrated in Figure 2-16.

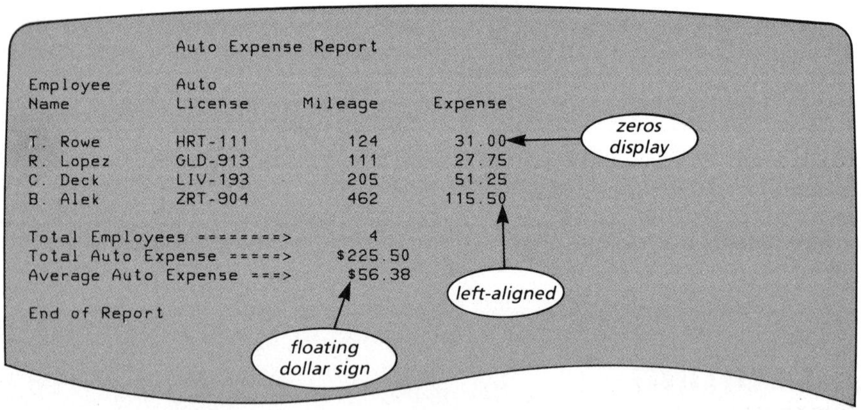

FIGURE 2-16
The formatted auto expense report

Compare the report in Figure 2-16 to the one in Figure 2-14. Notice that the mileage in the third column in Figure 2-16 is right-justified under the column heading. Also, the dollar and cents values in the expense field are right-justified under the column heading, and the decimal points are aligned. In addition, the total auto expense and the average expense per employee values are displayed with the dollar sign immediately adjacent to the leftmost digit in the number. This is known as a **floating dollar sign**.

To control the format of the displayed values, the `PRINT USING` statement is used in conjunction with a string expression that specifies exactly the image to which the output must conform. The string expression is placed immediately after the words `PRINT USING` in the form of a string constant or string variable. If the format is described by a string variable, then the string variable must be assigned the format by a `LET` statement before the `PRINT USING` statement is executed in the program. In either case, the items to display follow the string constant or string variable in the `PRINT USING` statement separated by semicolons or commas. The two methods for specifying the format for the `PRINT USING` statement are shown in Figure 2-17.

```
Method 1:

' Format Specified as a String in the PRINT USING Statement
PRINT USING "Item ### costs $$,###.##"; Item; Cost

Method 2:

' Format Specified Earlier and Assigned to a String Variable
D1$ = "Item ### cost $$,###.##"
        .
        .
        .
PRINT USING D1$; Item; Cost
```

FIGURE 2-17
The two methods for defining the format for a PRINT USING statement

In Method 1 of Figure 2-17, the string following the keywords PRINT USING instructs the PC to display the values of Item and Cost using the format found in the accompanying string constant. In Method 2, the string constant has been replaced by the string variable D1$ which was assigned the desired format in a previous statement. If Item is equal to 314 and Cost is equal to 2145.50, then the results displayed from the execution of either PRINT USING statement in Method 1 or Method 2 are as follows:

```
Item 314 costs $2,145.50
```

In Method 2 of Figure 2-17, notice that the keyword LET is not part of the LET statement. QuickBASIC considers any statement with an equal sign to be a LET statement. Hence, the keyword LET is optional. When defining format fields, we will not use the keyword LET.

Figure 2-18 illustrates how a LET statement and a PRINT USING statement are used to display the detail line in the report in Figure 2-16.

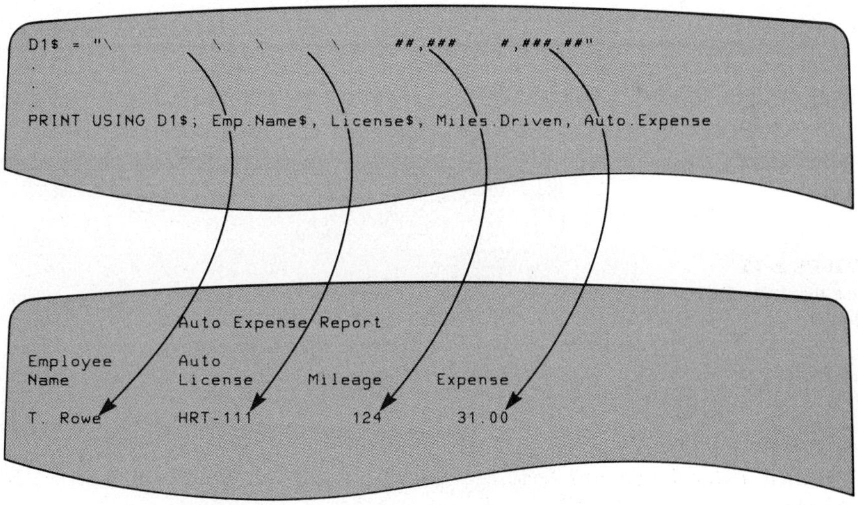

FIGURE 2-18
Using LET and PRINT USING statements to format the output

The backward slash (\) is used to create a format for string fields. The first backward slash indicates the first character position in the string field, and the second backward slash indicates the last character position in the field. Therefore, in the format field for Emp.Name$, eleven characters positions are defined—the two backward slashes and the nine spaces between them.

License$ is also a string variable. It is defined as eight characters in length by the two backward slashes and the six spaces between them. Numeric fields are defined through the use of the number sign (#). Each occurrence of a number sign corresponds to a numeric digit position. Punctuation, such as the comma and decimal point, is placed in the format field where it is to occur in the actual output. The format field for Miles.Driven includes a comma in case the value exceeds 999. Since Miles.Driven in the first line of the report is less than 1,000, the comma does not display. Similarly, a decimal point is placed in the format where it is supposed to print. For Auto.Expense, the format field `###.##` specifies three digits to the left of the decimal point and two digits to the right of the decimal point. Thus, the value displays in dollars and cents form.

Notice in Figure 2-18, following the keyword `PRINT USING`, D1$ identifies the format. This variable name is then followed by a semicolon, and the names of the fields to display are separated by semicolons. The table in Figure 2-19 illustrates additional examples of format fields.

EXAMPLE	DATA	FORMAT FIELD	RESULTS IN
1	125.62	###.##	125.62
2	005.76	###.##	bb5.76
3	.65	###.##	bb0.65
4	1208.78	#,###.##	1,208.78
5	986.05	#,###.##	bb986.05
6	34.87	$$#,###.##	bbbb$34.87
7	3579.75	$$#,###.##	b$3,579.75
8	561.93	$##,###.##	$bbb561.93
9	SALLY	\ \	SALLY
10	EDWARD	\\	ED

FIGURE 2-19 **Examples of format fields (b represents a blank character)**

You can include constants in a format field. The `LET` statement in Figure 2-20 illustrates this point.

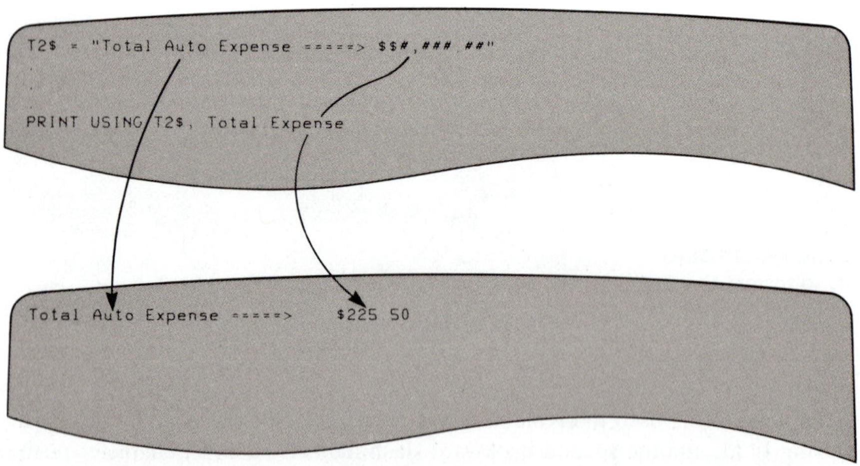

FIGURE 2-20
An example of including a constant in a format field

In Figure 2-20, the constant `Total Auto Expense =====>` is part of the string expression that includes the format field. When the variable T2$ is referenced by the `PRINT USING` statement, the constant is displayed exactly as it appears in the string expression. There are additional format symbols available with QuickBASIC. Those we present here, however, are the most widely used.

The coding in Figure 2-21 illustrates the complete program which produces the auto expense report shown on the next page in Figure 2-22. Particular attention should be paid to lines 30 through 39. These lines, when grouped together, show exactly what the report will look like when the program executes. Notice that this group of lines includes `PRINT` statements that display the report title and column headings and `LET` statements that define format fields. The column headings are within one string constant, rather than separated by commas, to better control the spacing. The format fields for the detail line (D1$) are immediately below the column headings in line 35.

We did not use the keyword `LET` in lines 35 through 39 so that all the string constants would begin in the same column in the program.

```
1  ' ************************************************************
2  ' *  Sample Program 2 Modified              September 15, 1994  *
3  ' *  Auto Expense Report                                        *
4  ' *  J. S. Quasney                                              *
5  ' *                                                             *
6  ' *  This program displays an auto expense report.  Mileage     *
7  ' *  expense is calculated on the basis of 25 cents per mile.   *
8  ' *  As part of the Wrap-Up module, the total number of         *
9  ' *  employees, total auto expense, and the average expense     *
10 ' *  per employee are displayed.                                *
11 ' *                                                             *
12 ' *  Variables:  Emp.Name$        -- Name of employee           *
13 ' *              License$         -- Auto license number        *
14 ' *              Begin.Mileage    -- Beginning mileage          *
15 ' *              End.Mileage      -- Ending mileage             *
16 ' *              Miles.Driven     -- Miles driven               *
17 ' *              Cost.Per.Mile    -- Auto cost per mile         *
18 ' *              Auto.Expense     -- Auto expense               *
19 ' *              Total.Employees  -- Number of employees        *
20 ' *              Total.Expense    -- Total auto expense         *
21 ' *              Average.Expense  -- Average auto expense       *
22 ' *              D1$, T1$, T2$, T3$, T4$  --  Print images      *
23 ' ************************************************************
24
25 ' ********************** Initialization **********************
26 CLS   ' Clear Screen
27 LET Total.Employees = 0
28 LET Total.Expense = 0
29 LET Cost.Per.Mile = .25
30 PRINT "                    Auto Expense Report"
31 PRINT
32 PRINT "Employee            Auto"
33 PRINT "Name                License      Mileage      Expense"
34 PRINT
35 D1$ = "\          \  \         \     ##,###      #,###.##"
36 T1$ = "Total Employees =========>         ###"
37 T2$ = "Total Auto Expense =====> $$#,###.##"
38 T3$ = "Average Auto Expense ===>  $$,###.##"
39 T4$ = "End of Report"
40
41 ' *********************** Process File ***********************
42 READ Emp.Name$, License$, Begin.Mileage, End.Mileage
43 DO WHILE Emp.Name$ <> "EOF"
44    LET Total.Employees = Total.Employees + 1
45    LET Miles.Driven = End.Mileage - Begin.Mileage
46    LET Auto.Expense = Cost.Per.Mile * Miles.Driven
47    LET Total.Expense = Total.Expense + Auto.Expense
48    PRINT USING D1$; Emp.Name$; License$; Miles.Driven; Auto.Expense
49    READ Emp.Name$, License$, Begin.Mileage, End.Mileage
50 LOOP
51
```

image of report

FIGURE 2-21
Sample Program 2 modified to include report editing

(continued)

FIGURE 2-21 (continued)

```
' ************************** Wrap Up **************************
PRINT
PRINT USING T1$; Total.Employees
PRINT USING T2$; Total.Expense
LET Average.Expense = Total.Expense / Total.Employees
PRINT USING T3$; Average.Expense
PRINT
PRINT T4$

' ************************ Data Follows ***********************
DATA T. Rowe, HRT-111, 19100, 19224
DATA R. Lopez, GLD-913, 21221, 21332
DATA C. Deck, LIV-193, 10001, 10206
DATA B. Alek, ZRT-904, 15957, 16419
DATA EOF, End, 0, 0
END
```

```
                   Auto Expense Report

Employee           Auto
Name               License      Mileage        Expense

T. Rowe            HRT-111          124          31.00
R. Lopez           GLD-913          111          27.75
C. Deck            LIV-193          205          51.25
B. Alek            ZRT-904          462         115.50

Total Employees ========>             4
Total Auto Expense =====>       $225.50
Average Auto Expense ===>        $56.38

End of Report
```

FIGURE 2-22
The formatted auto expense report due to the execution of the modified Sample Program 2

PRINTING A REPORT ON THE PRINTER

While the PRINT and PRINT USING statements display results on the screen, the LPRINT and LPRINT USING statements print results on the printer. Everything that has been presented with respect to the PRINT and PRINT USING statements in this section applies to the LPRINT and LPRINT USING statements. Obviously, to use these statements, you must have a printer attached to your PC and it must be in the Ready mode.

Figure 2-23 illustrates the results of the modified Sample Program 2 printed on a printer. To obtain the hard-copy results as shown in Figure 2-23, change all the PRINT and PRINT USING statements in Sample Program 2 (Figure 2-21) to LPRINT and LPRINT USING statements.

```
                   Auto Expense Report

Employee           Auto
Name               License      Mileage        Expense

T. Rowe            HRT-111          124          31.00
R. Lopez           GLD-913          111          27.75
C. Deck            LIV-193          205          51.25
B. Alek            ZRT-904          462         115.50

Total Employees ========>             4
Total Auto Expense =====>       $225.50
Average Auto Expense ===>        $56.38
```

FIGURE 2-23
A printed version of the auto expense report

TRY IT YOURSELF EXERCISES

1. Which arithmetic operation is performed first in the following numeric expressions?

   a. `5 * (Amt + 8)`
   b. `Cost - Sale + Discount`
   c. `8 / 3 * 5`
   d. `(X * (2 + Y)) ^ 2 + Z ^ (2 ^ 2)`
   e. `X + Y / Z`

2. Evaluate each of the following:

   a. `2 * 10 * 6 / 12 - 7 ^ 2 / 7`
   b. `(6 - 8) + 5 ^ 3`
   c. `12 / 6 / 2 + 7 * 3 + 5`

3. Calculate the numeric value for each of the following valid numeric expressions if Amt = 3, Sale = 4, Cost = 5, Discount = 3, S1 = 4, S2 = 1 and S3 = 2.

   a. `(Amt + Sale / 2) + 6.2`
   b. `3 * (Amt ^ Sale) / Cost`
   c. `(Amt / (Cost + 1) * 4 - 5) / 2`
   d. `S2 + 2 * S3 * Discount / 3 - 7 / (S1 - S2 / S3) - Discount ^ S1`

4. Determine the output results for each of the following programs.

   a.
```
' Exercise 4.a
X = 2.5
Y = 4 * X / 2 * X + 10
PRINT Y
Y = 4 * X / (2 * X + 10)
PRINT Y
X = -X
PRINT X
X = -X
PRINT X
END
```
   b.
```
' Exercise 4.b
C = 4
D = 1
S = C + D
PRINT S
T = D - C
PRINT T
C = S + T - C
PRINT C
D = 2 * (S + T + C) / 4
PRINT D
END
```

5. Calculate the numeric value for each of the following numeric expressions if X = 2, Y = 3, and Z = 6.

   a. `X + Y ^ 2`
   b. `Z / Y / X`
   c. `12 / (3 + Z) - X`
   d. `X ^ Y ^ Z`
   e. `X * Y + 2.5 * X + Z`
   f. `(X ^ (2 + Y)) ^ 2 + Z ^ (2 ^ 2)`

6. Insert parentheses so that each of the following results in the value indicated on the right-hand side of the arrow.

   a. `10 / 3 + 2 + 12 ----> 14`
   b. `3 ^ 2 - 1 ----> 3`
   c. `6 / 2 + 1 + 3 * 4 ----> 4`

7. For each of the following format fields and corresponding data, indicate what the PC displays. Use the letter b to indicate the space character. Notice that if a format field does not include enough positions to the left of the decimal point, the PC displays the result preceded by a percent (%) sign. If the format field does not include enough positions to the right of the decimal point, the PC rounds the result to fit the format field.

Format Field	*Data*	*Result*
a. ####	15	
b. #,###	345	
c. $$,###.##	1395.54	
d. ###.##	12.5675	
e. ##,###.###	19412.5	
f. ##.##	576.3	
g. ###.#####	32.2	
h. #.##	.234	

STUDENT ASSIGNMENTS

STUDENT ASSIGNMENT 1: Payroll Report

Instructions: Design and code a QuickBASIC program to generate the formatted payroll report shown under OUTPUT. The weekly pay is calculated by multiplying the hourly pay by the number of hours. All hours are paid at straight time. As part of the Wrap-Up module, display the total number of employees and the total weekly pay of all employees. Submit a program flowchart, listing of the program, and a listing of the output results.

INPUT: Use the following sample data:

EMPLOYEE NAME	HOURLY PAY RATE	HOURS WORKED
Joe Lomax	7.70	40
Ed Mann	6.05	38.5
Louis Orr	8.10	45
Ted Simms	9.50	39.5
Joan Zang	12.00	92
EOF	0	0

OUTPUT: The following results are displayed:

```
                Payroll Report

Employee        Hourly        Hours        Weekly
Name            Rate          Worked       Pay

Joe Lomax         7.70          40.0       308.00
Ed Mann           6.05          38.5       232.93
Louis Orr         8.10          45.0       364.50
Ted Simms         9.50          39.5       375.25
Joan Zang        12.00          92.0     1,104.00

Total Employees ========>          5
Total Weekly Pay =======>  $2,384.68

End of Report
```

STUDENT ASSIGNMENT 2: Test Score Report

Instructions: Design and code a QuickBASIC program that prints the student test report shown under OUTPUT. In each detail line, include the student's name, test scores, and average test score. The average test score is calculated by adding the score for test 1 and the score for test 2 and dividing by 2. After all records for all students have been processed, print the total number of students and the class average for all tests. To obtain a class average, add all test scores and divide by twice the number of students. Use the `LPRINT` and `LPRINT USING` statements to generate the report on the printer.

INPUT: Use the following sample data:

STUDENT NAME	TEST 1 SCORE	TEST 2 SCORE
Julie Banks	70	78
John Davis	92	93
Joe Gomez	88	84
Sally Katz	78	83
EOF	0	0

OUTPUT: The following results are printed:

```
                Test Score Report

Student
Name            Test 1      Test 2     Average

Julie Banks         70          78        74.0
John Davis          92          93        92.5
Joe Gomez           88          84        86.0
Sally Katz          78          83        80.5

Total Students ==========>      4
Class Average  ==========>  83.25

End of Report
```

PROJECT 3

Decisions

QuickBASIC includes the `IF` and `SELECT CASE` statements to instruct the PC to select one action or another on the basis of a comparison of numbers or strings. You use the `IF` statement to implement the **If-Then-Else structure** shown in Figure 3-1. When the structure in a flowchart has more than two alternative paths, you use the `SELECT CASE` statement. This type of structure is called a **case structure** and is shown in Figure 3-2.

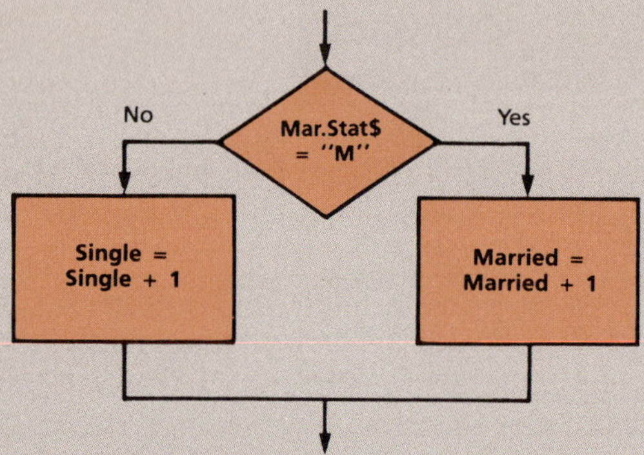


```
IF Mar.Stat$ = "M" THEN
   Married = Married + 1
ELSE
   Single = Single + 1
END IF
```

FIGURE 3-1 For the If-Then-Else structure, use the IF statement

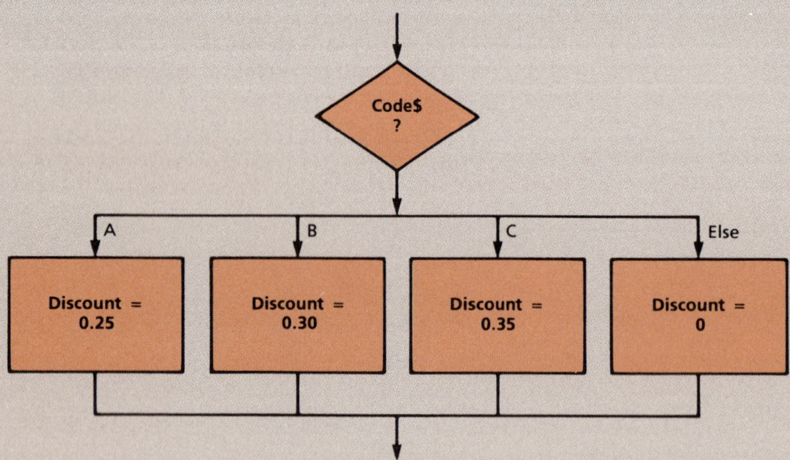


```
SELECT CASE Code$
   CASE "A"
      Discount = .25
   CASE "B"
      Discount = .30
   CASE "C"
      Discount = .35
   CASE ELSE
      Discount = 0
END SELECT
```

FIGURE 3-2 For a Case structure, use the SELECT CASE statement

THE IF STATEMENT

The `IF` statement is commonly regarded as the most powerful statement in QuickBASIC. The major function of this statement is to choose between two alternative paths. The `IF` statement has two general forms as shown in Figure 3-3.

Single-Line IF

```
IF condition THEN true task ELSE false task
```

Block IF

```
IF condition THEN
   true task
ELSE
   false task
END IF
```

FIGURE 3-3 The general form of the IF statement

In Figure 3-3, **condition** is a comparison between two expressions that is either true or false. **True task** and **false task** are statements or series of statements. If the condition is true, the PC executes the true task, also called the THEN clause, or **true case**. If the condition is false and an ELSE clause is included, the PC executes the false task, also called the ELSE clause, or **false case**. After either task is executed, control passes to the statement following the single-line IF statement or to the statement following the END IF for a block IF.

Figure 3-4 illustrates several examples of IF statements with conditions made up of numeric and string expressions. For numeric conditions, the PC evaluates not only the magnitude of each resultant expression but also its sign. For string expressions, the PC evaluates the two strings from left to right, one character at a time. With the block IF statement, the true and false tasks are indented by three spaces to improve the readability of the code.

Examples 1 through 3 in Figure 3-4 include conditions made up of numeric expressions. Examples 4 and 5 show IF statements with conditions made up of string expressions.

EXAMPLE	STATEMENT	VALUE OF VARIABLES	RESULT
1	`IF Amt = 0 THEN Dis = 4`	Amt = 0	The variable Dis is assigned the value 4, and control passes to the line following the IF statement.

2	`IF A < B THEN`
	`   PRINT X`
	`   T = T + 10`
	`ELSE`
	`   PRINT Y`
	`   Tax = Tax + 5`
	`END IF`
		A = 3
		B = 5
			The value of X is displayed; T is incremented by 10, and control passes to the line following the END IF.

3	`IF F < X - Y - 6 THEN`
	`   PRINT S`
	`END IF`
		F = 23
		X = 7
		Y = −8
			Control passes to the line following the END IF.

4	`IF C$ < D$ + E$ THEN`
	`   READ A, B, C`
	`   PRINT Y`
	`END IF`
		C$ = "JIM"
		D$ = "JA"
		E$ = "MES"
			Control passes to the line following the END IF.

5	`IF X$ = "YES" THEN`
	`   PRINT A$`
	`END IF`
		X$ = "yes"	Control passes to the line following the END IF. "YES" and "yes" are not the same string.

FIGURE 3-4 Examples of IF statements

Six types of relations can be used in a condition within an `IF` statement. These relations include determining if:

1. One value is equal to another (=)
2. One value is less than another (<)
3. One value is greater than another (>)
4. One value is less than or equal to another (< =)
5. One value is greater than or equal to another (> =)
6. One value is not equal to another (< >)

Recall that these are the same six relational operators we discussed earlier with the `DO WHILE` statement in Project 1 on page QB 9 in Figure 1-16.

CODING IF-THEN-ELSE STRUCTURES

This section describes various forms of the If-Then-Else structure and the use of `IF` statements to implement them in QuickBASIC.

Simple If-Then-Else Structures

Consider the If-Then-Else structure in Figure 3-5 and the corresponding methods of implementing the logic in QuickBASIC. Assume that the variable Age represents a person's age. If Age is greater than or equal to 18, the person is an adult. If Age is less than 18, the person is a minor. Adult and Minor are counters that are incremented as specified in the flowchart.

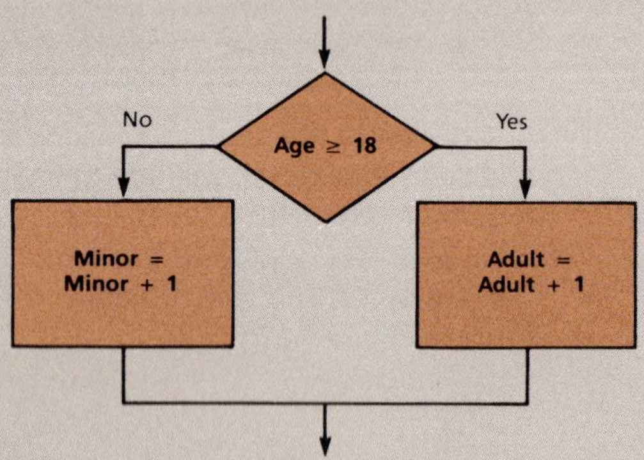

Method 1: Using a single `IF` statement.

```
IF Age >= 18 THEN
   Adult = Adult + 1
ELSE
   Minor = Minor + 1
END IF
```

Method 2: Using two `IF` statements.

```
IF Age >= 18 THEN Adult = Adult + 1
IF Age < 18 THEN Minor = Minor + 1
```

FIGURE 3-5 **Coding an If-Then-Else structure with alternative processing for the true and false cases**

In the first method shown in Figure 3-5, an `IF` statement resolves the logic indicated in the partial flowchart. The first line compares Age to 18. If Age is greater than or equal to 18, then Adult is incremented by 1. If Age is less than 18, the false task is carried out and Minor is incremented by 1. Regardless of the counter incremented, control passes to the statement following the `END IF`.

In Method 2, two single-line `IF` statements are used. Age is compared to the value 18 twice. In the first `IF` statement, the counter Adult is incremented by 1 if Age is greater than or equal to 18. In the second `IF` statement, the counter Minor is incremented by 1 if Age is less than 18.

Although both methods are valid and both satisfy the If-Then-Else structure, the first method is more efficient, as it involves fewer lines of code and less execution time. Therefore, the first method is recommended over the second.

Notice that the first method in Figure 3-5 could have been written as a single-line IF statement without the END IF. However, for readability purposes we recommend that you use the block IF statement as shown in Method 1.

As shown in Figures 3-6, 3-7, and 3-8, the If-Then-Else structure can take on a variety of appearances. In Figure 3-6, there is a task only if the condition is true.

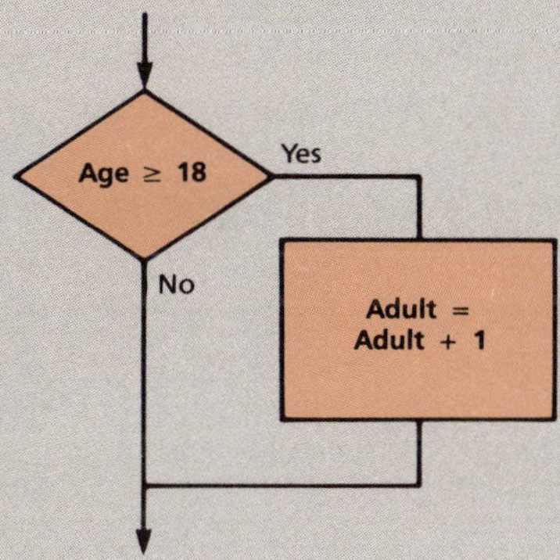

Method 1: Using an IF statement with no ELSE clause.

```
IF Age >= 18 THEN
   Adult = Adult + 1
END IF
```

Method 2: Reversing the relation.

```
IF Age < 18 THEN
ELSE
   Adult = Adult + 1
END IF
```

FIGURE 3-6
Coding an If-Then-Else structure with alternative processing for the true case

In Figure 3-6, the first method is preferred over the second since it is more straightforward and less confusing. In Method 2 of Figure 3-6, we reversed the relation. Although this method satisfies the If-Then-Else structure, it is also more difficult to understand. The second method shows that it is valid to have a null THEN clause.

The If-Then-Else structure in Figure 3-7 illustrates the incrementation of the counter Minor when the condition is false.

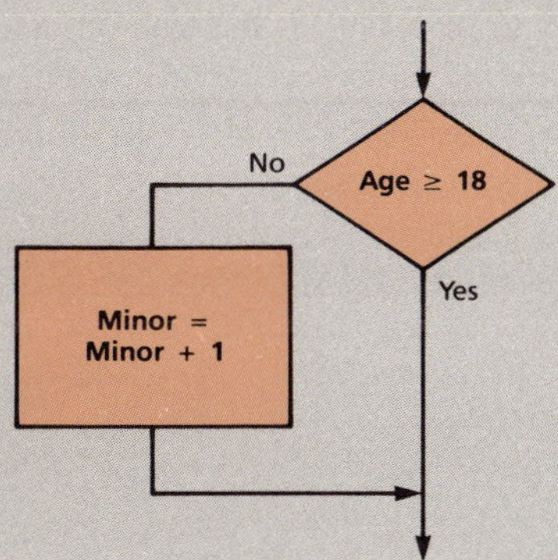

Method 1: Reversing the relation in the decision symbol and using an IF statement.

```
IF Age < 18 THEN
   Minor = Minor + 1
END IF
```

Method 2: Using an IF statement with a null THEN clause.

```
IF Age >= 18 THEN
ELSE
   Minor = Minor + 1
END IF
```

FIGURE 3-7
Coding an If-Then-Else structure with alternative processing for the false case

In Method 1, the relation in the condition that is found in the partial flowchart has been reversed. The condition Age >= 18 has been modified to read Age < 18 in the QuickBASIC code. Reversing the relation is usually preferred when additional tasks must be done as a result of the condition being false. In Method 2, the relation is the same as in the decision symbol. When the condition Age >= 18 is true, the null THEN clause simply passes control to the statement following the END IF. Either method is acceptable. Some programmers prefer always to include both a THEN and an ELSE clause, even when one of them is null. On the other hand, some prefer to reverse the relation rather than include a null clause.

On the next page in Figure 3-8, each task in the If-Then-Else structure is made up of multiple statements. We have included a suggested method of implementation.

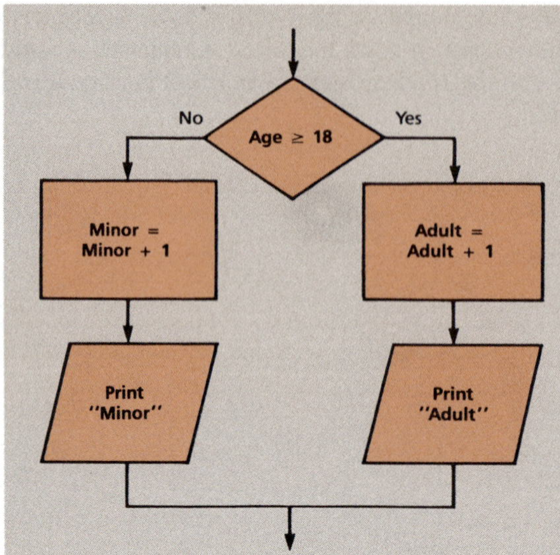


```
IF Age >= 18 THEN
   Adult = Adult + 1
   PRINT "Adult"
ELSE
   Minor = Minor + 1
   PRINT "Minor"
END IF
```

FIGURE 3-8
Coding an If-Then-Else structure with several statements for both the true and false cases

In the code in Figure 3-8, if the condition `Age >= 18` is true, the two statements in the `THEN` clause are executed. If the condition is false, the two statements in the `ELSE` clause are executed.

Although there are alternative methods for implementing the If-Then-Else structure, the method we have presented is more straightforward and involves fewer lines of code.

Nested If-Then-Else Structures

A nested If-Then-Else structure is one in which the action to be taken for the true or false case includes yet another If-Then-Else structure. The second If-Then-Else structure is considered to be nested, or layered, within the first.

Study the partial program that corresponds to the nested If-Then-Else structure in Figure 3-9.

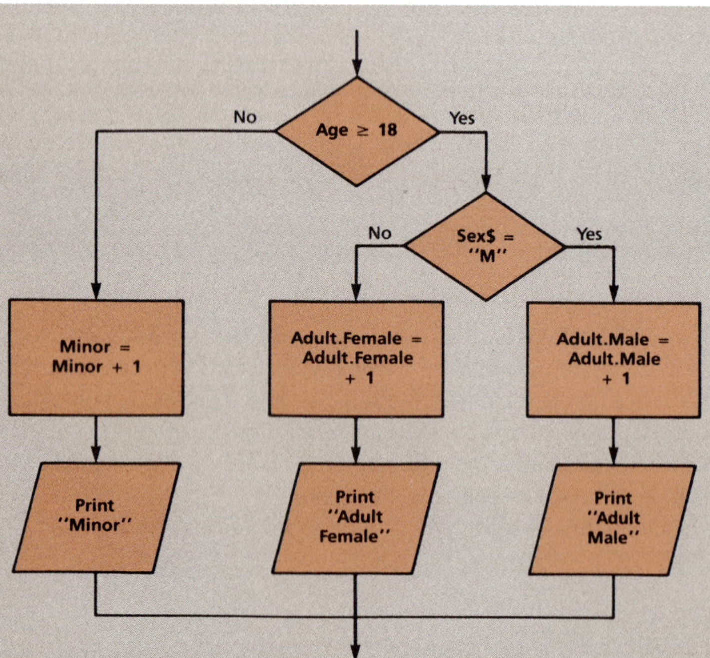


```
IF Age >= 18 THEN
   IF Sex$ = "M" THEN
      Adult.Male = Adult.Male + 1
      PRINT "Adult male"
   ELSE
      Adult.Female = Adult.Female + 1
      PRINT "Adult Female"
   END IF
ELSE
   Minor = Minor + 1
   PRINT "Minor"
END IF
```

FIGURE 3-9 Coding a nested If-Then-Else structure

In the partial program in Figure 3-9, if the condition `Age >= 18` is true, control passes to the `THEN` clause beginning with line 2. If the condition is false, the `ELSE` clause beginning in line 10 is executed. If control does pass to line 2, then a second `IF` tests to determine if Sex$ equals the value M. If the condition in line 2 is true, lines 3 and 4 are executed. If the condition is false, then the PC executes lines 6 and 7.

QuickBASIC requires that you end each block `IF` statement with an `END IF`. Hence, the block `IF` in line 1 has a corresponding `END IF` in line 12, and the block `IF` in line 2 has a corresponding `END IF` in line 8.

Notice in Figure 3-9 that only one of the three alternative tasks is executed for each record processed. Regardless of the path taken, control eventually passes to the statement immediately following the last `END IF` in line 12.

SAMPLE PROGRAM 3 — VIDEO RENTAL REPORT

To illustrate a program that uses an `IF` statement, consider the following video rental problem. In this application, if the video tape is rented for three days or less, the charge is $2.49 per day. There is a one dollar per day discount for each of the first three days for customers who are at least 65 years old. If the video tape is rented for more than three days, the charge is $3.49 per day for each day over three days.

The video records consist of the customer's name, age, video title, and the number of days rented as shown in Figure 3-10.

CUSTOMER NAME	AGE	VIDEO TITLE	DAYS RENTED
Helen Moore	47	Lost in Space	1
Hank Fisher	67	Together Again	3
Joe Frank	34	Three Lives	7
Al Jones	64	The Last Day	5
Shirley Star	65	Monday Morning	4
EOF	0	End	0

FIGURE 3-10 The video rental file for Sample Program 3

The output is a printed video rental summary report that lists the customer name, customer age, title of the video tape rented, the number of days the tape was rented, and the charge for the rental. After all records have been processed, the number of senior citizen customers, the number of tapes rented, and the total charges are printed. The format of the output is illustrated in Figure 3-11.

```
                              Video Rental Report

Customer                      Video                Days
Name               Age        Title                Rented     Charge

Helen Moore         47        Lost in Space           1         2.49
Hank Fisher         67        Together Again          3         4.47
Joe Frank           34        Three Lives             7        17.43
Al Jones            64        The Last Day            5        12.45
Shirley Star        65        Monday Morning          4         5.96

Senior Citizens ==========>     2
Videos Rented ============>     5
Total Charges ============>   $42.80

End of Report
```

FIGURE 3-11 The report for Sample Program 3

Program Flowchart

The flowchart in Figure 3-12 illustrates the logic required to produce the video rental report.

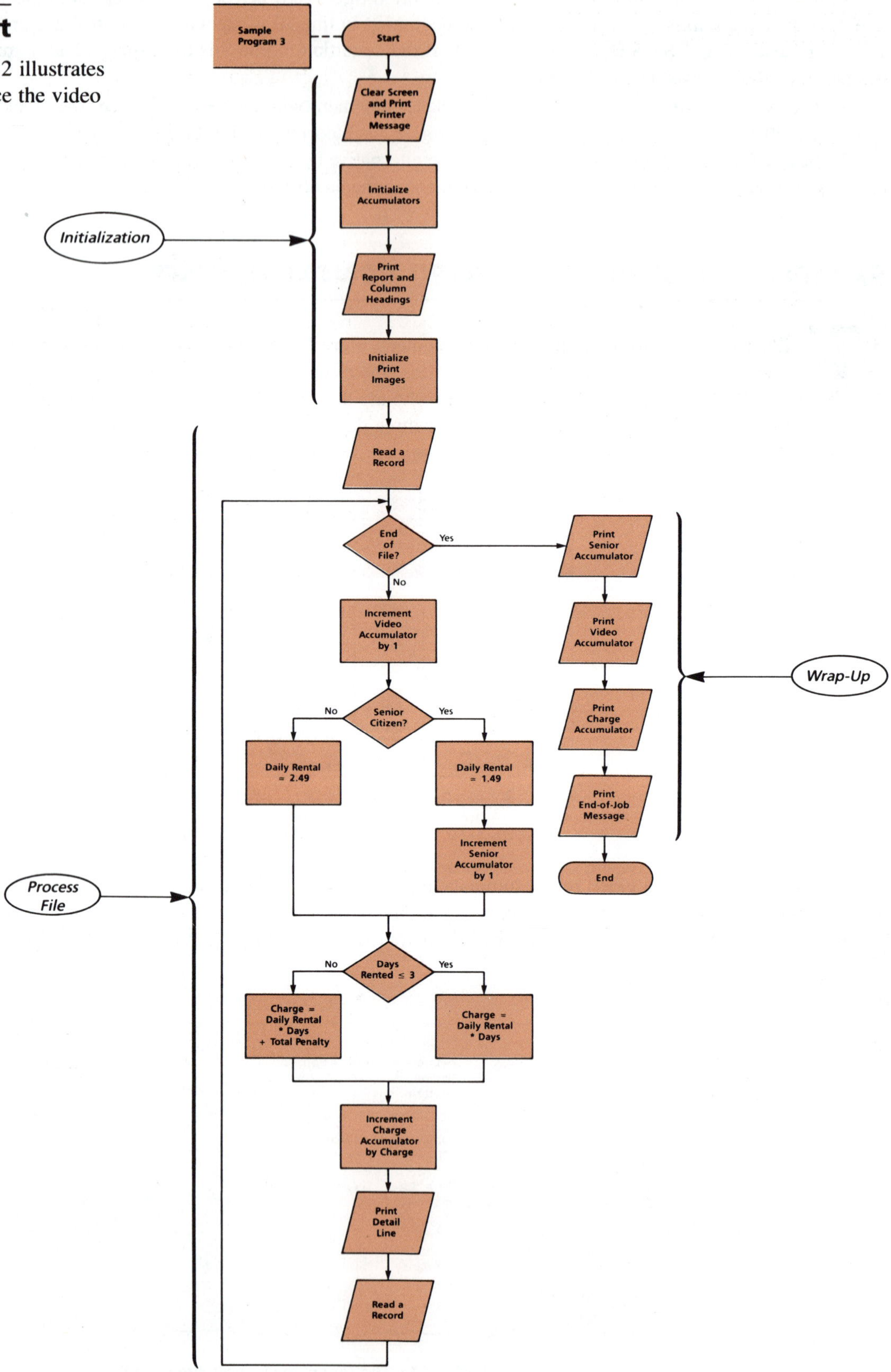

FIGURE 3-12
The flowchart for Sample Program 3

The QuickBASIC Program

The program in Figure 3-13 corresponds to the program flowchart in Figure 3-12.

FIGURE 3-13
Sample Program 3

```
'*******************************************************************
' *  Sample Program 3                         September 15, 1994    *
' *  Video Rental Report                                            *
' *  J. S. Quasney                                                  *
' *                                                                 *
' *  This program prints a video rental report.  The charge         *
' *  is based on the number of days the video is rented and         *
' *  the age of the customer.                                       *
' *       As part of the Wrap-Up module, the total number           *
' *  of videos, senior customers, and charges are printed.          *
' *                                                                 *
' *  Variables:  Cus.Name$        -- Name of customer               *
' *              Cus.Age          -- Customer age                   *
' *              Video.Title$     -- Title of video                 *
' *              Days.Rented      -- Days rented                    *
' *              Daily.Rental     -- Cost per day                   *
' *              Charge           -- Cost of renting video          *
' *              Penalty          -- Cost per day after 3 days      *
' *              Total.Videos     -- Number of videos rented        *
' *              Total.Seniors    -- Number of senior rentals       *
' *              Total.Charges    -- Total charges                  *
' *              DL1$, TL1$, TL2$, TL3$, TL4$ -- Print images       *
'*******************************************************************

' ********************** Initialization **********************
CLS  ' Clear Screen
PRINT "****** Video Rental Report Printing on Printer ******"
LET Total.Videos = 0
LET Total.Seniors = 0
LET Total.Charges = 0
LET Penalty = 3.49
LPRINT "                          Video Rental Report"
LPRINT
LPRINT "Customer                  Video                  Days"
LPRINT "Name               Age    Title                  Rented    Charge"
LPRINT
DL1$ = "\                \  ###   \                \      ###     ###.##"
TL1$ = "Senior Citizens ==========>       ###"
TL2$ = "Videos Rented ============>       ###"
TL3$ = "Total Charges ============> $$,###.##"
TL4$ = "End of Report"

```

(continued)

FIGURE 3-13 (continued)

```
43  ' ************************ Process File ************************
44  READ Cus.Name$, Cus.Age, Video.Title$, Days.Rented
45  DO WHILE Cus.Name$ <> "EOF"
46     LET Total.Videos = Total.Videos + 1
47     IF Cus.Age >= 65 THEN
48        LET Daily.Rental = 1.49
49        LET Total.Seniors = Total.Seniors + 1
50     ELSE
51        LET Daily.Rental = 2.49
52     END IF
53     IF Day.Rented <= 3 THEN
54        LET Charge = Daily.Rental * Days.Rented
55     ELSE
56        LET Charge = (Daily.Rental * Days.Rented) + Penalty * (Days.Rented - 3)
57     END IF
58     LET Total.Charges = Total.Charges + Charge
59     LPRINT USING DL1$; Cus.Name$; Cus.Age; Video.Title$; Days.Rented; Charge
60     READ Cus.Name$, Cus.Age, Video.Title$, Days.Rented
61  LOOP
62
63  ' ************************** Wrap-Up *************************
64  LPRINT
65  LPRINT USING TL1$; Total.Seniors
66  LPRINT USING TL2$; Total.Videos
67  LPRINT USING TL3$; Total.Charges
68  LPRINT
69  LPRINT TL4$
70
71  ' ************************ Data Follows **********************
72  DATA Helen Moore, 47, Lost in Space, 1
73  DATA Hank Fisher, 67, Together Again, 3
74  DATA Joe Frank, 34, Three Lives, 7
75  DATA Al Jones, 64, The Last Day, 5
76  DATA Shirley Star, 65, Monday Morning, 4
77  DATA EOF, 0, End, 0
78  END
```

Discussion of Sample Program 3

When Sample Program 3 is executed, the report shown in Figure 3-14 prints on the printer. Sample Program 3 includes a few significant points that did not appear in previous programs. They are as follows:

- When executed, line 26 clears the screen and line 27 displays a friendly message informing the user that the report is being printed on the printer.
- `LPRINT` and `LPRINT USING` statements are used throughout the program to print the report on the printer rather than display the report on the monitor.
- There are two `IF` statements that select alternative paths on the basis of the data in the video record being processed. The block `IF` in lines 47 through 52 determines whether the customer is a senior citizen. If the customer is a senior citizen, the daily rental (Daily.Rental) is set to $1.49 and the senior citizen counter is incremented. If the customer is not a senior citizen, then the daily rental is set to $2.49.

  The second block `IF` statement (lines 53 through 57) determines how much to charge the customer being processed. If the video is rented for three days or less, the charge is determined from the following `LET` statement:

  ```
  LET Charge = Daily.Rental * Days.Rented
  ```

  If the video is rented for more than three days, the charge is determined from the following `IF` statement:

  ```
  LET Charge = (Daily.Rental * Days.Rented) + Penalty * (Days.Rented - 3)
  ```

```
                        Video Rental Report

Customer                     Video                 Days
Name                  Age    Title                 Rented    Charge

Helen Moore            47    Lost in Space            1        2.49
Hank Fisher            67    Together Again           3        4.47
Joe Frank              34    Three Lives              7       17.43
Al Jones               64    The Last Day             5       12.45
Shirley Star           65    Monday Morning           4        5.96

Senior Citizens ==========>        2
Videos Rented ============>        5
Total Charges ============>   $42.80

End of Report
```

FIGURE 3-14
The report printed when Sample Program 3 is executed

LOGICAL OPERATORS

In many instances, a decision to execute a true task or false task is based upon two or more conditions. In previous examples that involved two or more conditions, we tested each condition in a separate `IF` statement. In this section, we discuss combining conditions within one `IF` statement by means of the logical operators `AND` and `OR`. When two or more conditions are combined by these logical operators, the expression is called a **compound condition**. The logical operator `NOT` allows you to write a compound condition in which the truth value of the simple condition following `NOT` is **complemented**, or reversed.

The NOT Logical Operator

A simple condition that is preceded by the logical operator `NOT` forms a compound condition that is false when the simple condition is true. If the simple condition is false, then the compound condition is true. Consider the two `IF` statements in Figure 3-15. Both print the value of Discount if Margin is less than or equal to Cost.

Method 1: Using the `NOT` logical operator.

```
IF NOT Margin > Cost THEN
   PRINT Discount
END IF
```

Method 2: Reversing the relational operator.

```
IF Margin <= Cost THEN
   PRINT Discount
END IF
```

FIGURE 3-15
Use of the NOT logical operator

In Method 1 of Figure 3-15, if Margin is greater than Cost (the simple condition is true), then the compound condition `NOT Margin > Cost` is false. If Margin is less than or equal to Cost (the simple condition is false), then the `NOT` makes the compound condition true. In Method 2, the relational operator is reversed and, therefore, the `NOT` is eliminated. Both methods are equivalent.

Because the logical operator `NOT` can increase the complexity of the decision statement significantly, use it sparingly. As shown in Figure 3-15, you can always reverse the relational operator in a condition to eliminate the logical operator `NOT`.

The AND Logical Operator

The AND operator requires that both conditions be true for the compound condition to be true. Consider the two IF statements in Figure 3-16. Both methods read a value for Selling.Price if Margin is greater than 10 and Cost is less than 8.

Method 1: Using the AND logical operator.

```
IF Margin > 10 AND Cost < 8 THEN
   READ Selling.Price
END IF
```

Method 2: Using nested IF statements.

```
IF Margin > 10 THEN
   IF Cost < 8 THEN
      READ Selling.Price
   END IF
END IF
```

FIGURE 3-16 Use of the AND operator

In Method 1 of Figure 3-16, if Margin is greater than 10 and Cost is less than 8, the READ statement assigns a value to Selling.Price before control passes to the line following the END IF. If either one of the conditions is false, then the compound condition is false, and control passes to the line following the END IF without a value being read for Selling.Price. Although both methods are equivalent, Method 1 is more efficient, more compact, and more straightforward than Method 2.

Like a single condition, a compound condition can be only true or false. To determine the truth value of the compound condition, the PC must evaluate and assign a truth value to each individual condition. Then the truth value is determined for the compound condition.

For example, if A equals 4 and C$ equals "X", the PC evaluates the following compound condition in the manner shown:

```
IF A = 3 AND C$ = "X" THEN LET F = F + 1
```

1. false (A = 3)
2. true (C$ = "X")
3. false

The PC first determines the truth value for each condition, then concludes that the compound condition is false because of the AND operator.

The OR Logical Operator

The OR operator requires that only one of the two conditions be true for the compound condition to be true. If both conditions are true, the compound condition is also true. Likewise, if both conditions are false, the compound condition is false. The use of the OR operator is illustrated in Figure 3-17.

Method 1: Using the `OR` logical operator.

```
IF Code$ = "A" OR Marital.Status$ = "M" THEN
   LET Cnt = Cnt + 1
END IF
```

Method 2: Using two `IF` statements.

```
IF Code$ = "A" THEN
   LET Cnt = Cnt + 1
END IF
IF Marital.Status$ = "M" THEN
   LET Cnt = Cnt + 1
END IF
```

FIGURE 3-17 Use of the OR operator

In Method 1 of Figure 3-17, if either Code$ equals the value A or Marital.Status$ equals the value M, the `THEN` clause is executed and Cnt is incremented by 1. If both conditions are true, the `THEN` clause is also executed. If both conditions are false, the `THEN` clause is bypassed, and control passes to the line following the `END IF`. Method 2 employs two `IF` statements to resolve the same If-Then-Else structure. Again, both methods are equivalent, but, Method 1 is easier to read and understand than Method 2.

As with the logical operator `AND`, the truth values of the individual conditions in the `IF` statement are first determined, then the truth values for the conditions containing the logical operator `OR` are evaluated. For example, if F equals 4 and H equals 5, the following condition is true:

```
IF F = 3 OR H = 5 THEN PRINT "Yes"
   1. false   2. true
        3. true
```

Combining Logical Operators

Logical operators can be combined in a decision statement to form a compound condition. The formation of compound statements that involve more than one type of logical operator can create problems unless you fully understand the order in which the PC evaluates the entire condition. Unless parentheses dictate otherwise, reading from left to right, conditions containing arithmetic operators are evaluated first; then those containing relational operators; then those containing `NOT` operators; then those containing `AND` operators; then those containing `OR` operators. Refer to the last page of the Reference Card at the back of this book for a summary listing of the order of both arithmetic and logical operators.

For the following compound condition assume, that D = 3, P = 5, R = 3, T = 5, S = 6, and Y = 3:

```
IF S > Y  OR  T = D  AND  P < 5  OR  NOT Y = R THEN READ L
  1. true    2. false     3. false       4. true
                6. false                 5. false
          7. true
                      8. true
```

The Use of Parentheses in Compound Conditions

Parentheses may be used to change the order of precedence. When there are parentheses in a compound condition, the PC evaluates that part of the compound condition within the parentheses first, then continues to evaluate the remaining compound condition according to the order of logical operations. For example, suppose variable J has a value of 2, and E has a value of 6. Consider the following compound condition:

```
IF J = 7  AND E > 5  OR  J <> 0 THEN LET Cnt = Cnt + 1
   1. false   2. true    3. true
        4. false
                 5. true
```

Following the order of logical operations, the compound condition yields a truth value of true. If parentheses surround the last two conditions, then the `OR` operator is evaluated before the `AND` condition, and the compound condition yields a truth value of false, as shown:

```
IF J = 7  AND (E > 5  OR  J <> 0) THEN LET Cnt = Cnt + 1
   4. false     1. true    2. true
                     3. true
              5. false
```

Parentheses may be used freely when the evaluation of a compound condition is in doubt. For example, if you wish to evaluate the compound condition

```
IF C > D AND S = 4 OR X < Y AND T = 5 THEN READ F
```

you may incorporate it into a decision statement as it stands. You may also write in the following way:

```
IF (C > D AND S = 4) OR (X < Y AND T = 5) THEN READ F
```

and feel more certain of the outcome of the decision statement.

THE SELECT CASE STATEMENT

The `SELECT CASE` statement is used to implement the case structure. Figure 3-18 illustrates the implementation of a case structure, which determines a letter grade (Letter.Grade$) from a grade point average (GPA) using the following grading scale:

GRADE POINT AVERAGE	LETTER GRADE
GPA ≥ 90	A
80 ≤ GPA < 90	B
70 ≤ GPA < 80	C
60 ≤ GPA < 70	D
0 ≤ GPA < 60	F
GPA < 0	Error

For example, if your GPA is 79.6, your letter grade is a C.

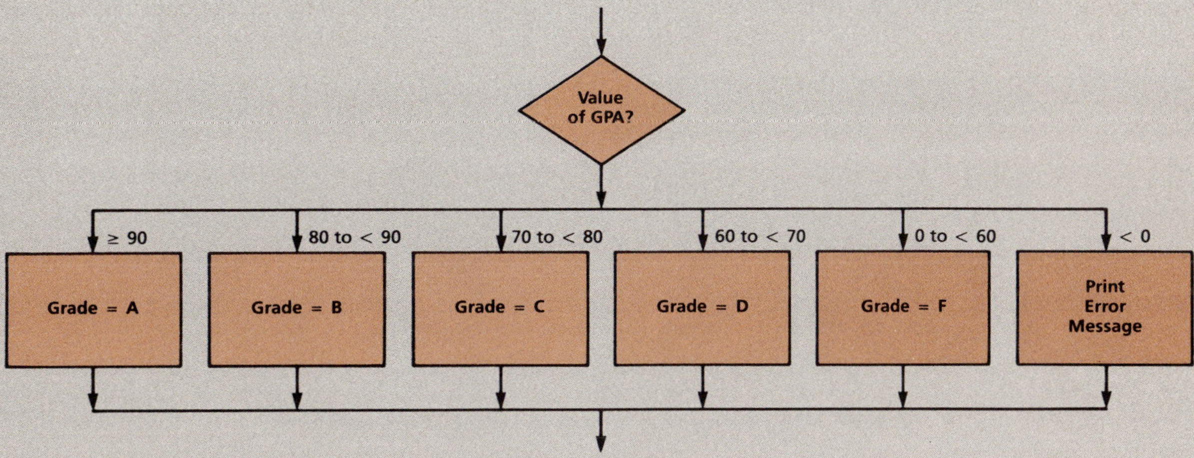


```
SELECT CASE GPA
  CASE IS >= 90
     Letter.Grade$ = "A"
  CASE IS >= 80
     Letter.Grade$ = "B"
  CASE IS >= 70
     Letter.Grade$ = "C"
  CASE IS >= 60
     Letter.Grade$ = "D"
  CASE IS >= 0, IS < 60
     Letter.Grade$ = "F"
  CASE ELSE
     PRINT "*** Error *** Negative GPA"
END SELECT
```

FIGURE 3-18 **Implementation of a case structure**

The SELECT CASE statement in Figure 3-18 is used to implement the grading scale. When the PC executes the SELECT CASE statement, it compares the variable GPA, which follows the keywords SELECT CASE, to the expressions following the keyword CASE in each CASE clause, also called a **case**. The PC begins the comparison with the first case and continues through the remaining ones until it finds a match. When a match is found, the range of statements immediately following the keyword CASE is executed. Following execution of the case, control immediately transfers to the statement following the END SELECT. The PC does not search for additional matches in the remaining cases.

For example, if GPA is equal to 79.6, then the PC finds a match in the third case. Therefore, it assigns Letter.Grade$ the value C and passes control to the statement following the END SELECT. If GPA equals a negative value, then no match is found, and the PRINT statement following the CASE ELSE is executed.

The CASE ELSE just prior to the END SELECT in Figure 3-18 instructs the PC to use this case if there is no match with any of the previous CASE clauses.

In a SELECT CASE, you place the variable, or expression, also called the **test-expression**, to test after the keywords SELECT CASE. Next, you assign the group of values, also called the **match-expression**, that make each alternative case true after the keyword CASE. Each case contains the range of statements to execute, and you may have as many cases as required. After the last case, end the SELECT CASE with an END SELECT.

The general form of the SELECT CASE statement is shown in Figure 3-19.

```
SELECT CASE test-expression
  CASE match-expression
     [range of statements]
  CASE match-expression
     [range of statements]
  .
  .
  .
  CASE ELSE
     [range of statements]
END SELECT
```

where **test-expression** is a numeric or string expression and **match-expression** indicates the values for which the case is selected.

FIGURE 3-19 The general form of the SELECT CASE statement

Valid Match-Expressions

There are several ways to construct valid match-expressions following the keyword CASE. Consider the match-expressions in Figure 3-20.

EXAMPLE	MATCH-EXPRESSION
1	CASE "F" TO "H", "S", Code$
2	CASE IS = Salary, IS = Max.Salary - 5000
3	CASE IS < 12, 20 TO 30, 48.6, IS > 100

FIGURE 3-20 Valid match-expressions in a SELECT CASE statement

In Example 1 in Figure 3-20, the match-expression is a list made up of the letters F to H, the letter S, and the value of the variable Code$. In Example 2, the match-expression includes Salary and the expression Max.Salary – 5000. If a relational operator is used, then the keyword IS is required. The second value in the list of Example 2 shows that expressions with arithmetic operators are allowed. The third example includes a list that requires the use of the keywords IS and TO. Use the keyword IS before any relational operator, such as = or >. Use the keyword TO to define a range of values.

TRY IT YOURSELF EXERCISES

1. Determine the value of Amt that will cause the condition in the following IF statements to be true:
   a.
   ```
   IF Amt > 8 OR Amt = 3 THEN
      Z = Z / 10
   END IF
   ```
   b.
   ```
   IF Amt + 10 >= 7 AND NOT Amt < 0 THEN
      PRINT "The answer is"; A
   END IF
   ```

2. Construct partial programs for each of these structures.

a.

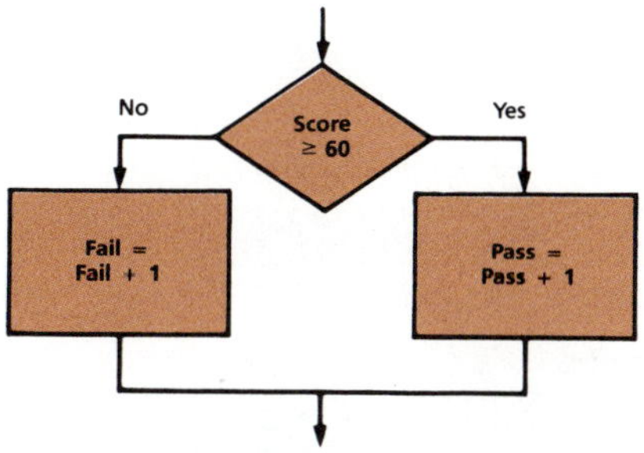

b.

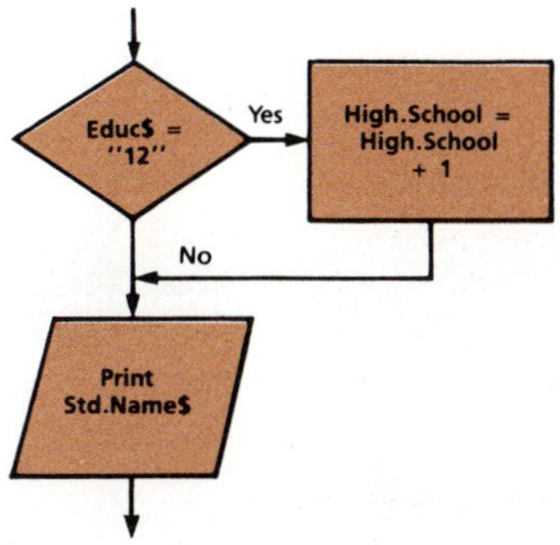

3. Construct partial programs for each of these logic structures.

a.

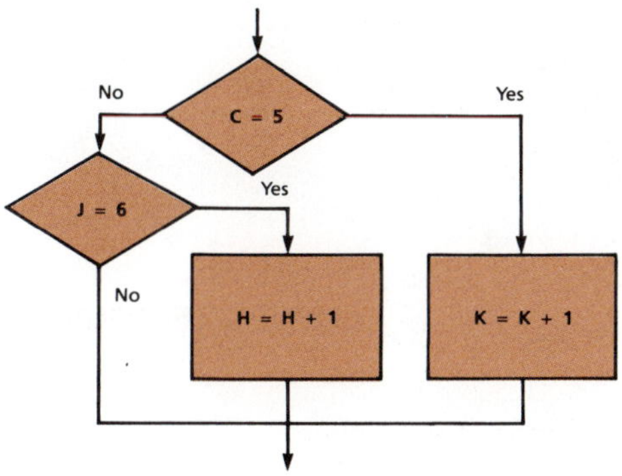

b.

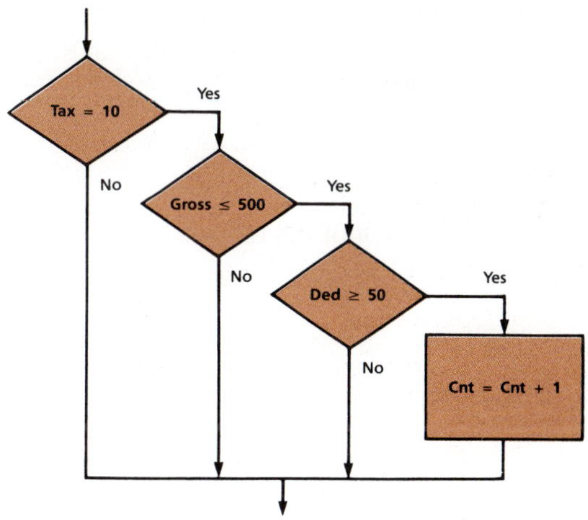

4. What is displayed if the following program is executed?

```
' Exercise 4
READ I
DO WHILE I <> -99
   SELECT CASE I
      CASE 1, 4, 7
         PRINT I, "Case 1"
      CASE IS < 8
         PRINT I, "Case 2"
      CASE 14 TO 21
         PRINT I, "Case 3"
      CASE ELSE
         PRINT I, "Case 4"
   END SELECT
   READ I
LOOP
DATA 1, 4, 7, 2, 21, 20, -99
END
```

5. Given the following:

   Emp.Num = 500
   Salary = $700
   Job.Code$ = "1"
   Tax = $60
   Insurance.Ded = $40

   Determine the truth value of the following compound conditions:

   a. `Emp.Num < 400 OR Job.Code$ = "1"`
   b. `Salary = 700 AND Tax = 50`
   c. `Salary - Tax = 640 AND Job.Code$ = "1"`
   d. `Tax + Insurance.Ded = Salary - 500 OR Job.Code$ = "0"`
   e. `NOT Job.Code$ < "0"`
   f. `NOT (Job.Code$ = "1" OR Tax = 60)`
   g. `Salary < 300 AND Insurance.Ded < 50 OR Job.Code$ = "1"`
   h. `Salary < 300 AND (Insurance.Ded < 50 OR Job.Code$ = "1")`
   i. `NOT (NOT Job.Code$ = "1")`

6. Given the following:

   T = 0, V = 4, B = 7, Y = 8, and X = 3

   Determine the action taken for each of the following:

   a.
   ```
   IF T > 0 THEN
      READ A
   END IF
   ```
   b.
   ```
   IF B = 4 OR T > 7 THEN
      IF X > 1 THEN
         READ A
      END IF
   END IF
   ```
   c.
   ```
   IF X = 3 OR T > 2 THEN
      IF Y > 7 THEN
         READ A
      END IF
   END IF
   ```
   d.
   ```
   IF X + 2 < 5 THEN
      IF B < V + X THEN
         READ A
      END IF
   END IF
   ```

7. Write a program that determines the number of negative values (Negative), number of zero values (Zero) and number of positive values (Positive) in the following data set: 4, 2, 3, –9, 0, 0, –4, –6, –8, 3, 2, 0, 0, 8, –3, 4. Use the –999999 to test for the end-of-file.
8. The values of three variables Num1, Num2, and Num3 are positive and not equal to each other. Using `IF` statements, determine which has the smallest value and assign this value to Little.
9. The IOU National Bank computes its monthly service charge on checking accounts by adding $0.50 to a value computed from the following:
   $0.21 per check for the first ten checks
   $0.19 per check for the next ten checks
   $0.17 per check for the next ten checks
   $0.15 per check for the remaining checks

   Write a sequence of statements that includes a `SELECT CASE` statement and a `PRINT` statement to display the account number (Account), the number of checks cashed (Checks), and the computed monthly charge (Charge). Assume the account number and the number of checks cashed are in `DATA` statements.

STUDENT ASSIGNMENTS

STUDENT ASSIGNMENT 1: Student Registration Report

Instructions: Design and code a QuickBASIC program to process the data shown under INPUT. Generate the student registration report shown under OUTPUT. A student with less than 12 hours is defined as part-time. The registration fee is determined from the following:

Credits Hours	Fee
Less than 12	$400.00
12 or more	$400.00 plus $30.00 per credit hour in excess of 11 hours

As part of the end-of-job routine, print the total number of part-time students, full-time students, students, and fees.

INPUT: Use the following sample data:

STUDENT NAME	CREDIT HOURS
Joe Franks	14
Ed Crane	9
Susan Lewis	18
Fred Smith	12
Jack North	10
Nikole Hiegh	17
EOF	0

OUTPUT: The following results are printed:

```
                 Student Registration

Student         Credit
Name            Hours         Fee      Status

Joe Franks         14      490.00      Full-Time
Ed Crane            9      400.00      Part-Time
Susan Lewis        18      610.00      Full-Time
Fred Smith         12      430.00      Full-Time
Jack North         10      400.00      Part-Time
Nikole Hiegh       17      580.00      Full-Time

Total Part-Time ====>           2
Total Full-Time ====>           4
Total Students =====>           6
Total Fees =========>   $2,910.00

End of Report
```

STUDENT ASSIGNMENT 2: Employee Salary Increase Report

Instructions: Design and code a QuickBASIC program to process the data shown under INPUT. Use `IF` statements with compound conditions to display on the screen the employee salary increase report shown under OUTPUT.

Determine the employee salary increase from the following:

1. All employees get a 4% salary increase
2. Employees with more than three annual merits and 10 or more years of service get an additional 2.5% salary increase
3. Employees with four or more annual merits and less than 10 years of service get an additional 1.5% salary increase

INPUT: Use the following sample data. Make sure you enclose the employee names within quotation marks, since each name includes a comma.

EMPLOYEE NAME	ANNUAL MERITS	SERVICE	CURRENT SALARY
Babjack, Bill	9	3	$19,500
Knopf, Louis	0	19	29,200
Taylor, Jane	8	12	26,000
Droopey, Joe	8	4	28,000
Lane, Lyn	2	9	19,800
Lis, Frank	6	1	21,000
Lopez, Hector	10	1	15,000
Braion, Jim	8	19	26,500
EOF	0	0	0

OUTPUT: The following results are displayed:

```
                 Employee Salary Increase Report

Employee         Annual     Current                      New
Name             Merits     Salary         Raise         Salary

Babjack, Bill       9      19,500.00     1,116.38     20,616.38
Knopf, Louis        0      29,200.00     1,168.00     30,368.00
Taylor, Jane        8      26,000.00     1,742.00     27,742.00
Droopey, Joe        8      28,000.00     1,596.00     29,596.00
Lane, Lyn           2      19,800.00       801.90     20,601.90
Lis, Frank          6      21,000.00     1,186.50     22,186.50
Lopez, Hector      10      15,000.00       862.50     15,862.50
Braion, Jim         8      26,500.00     1,775.50     28,275.50
                          ==========     ========    ==========
                          185,000.00    10,248.78    195,248.78

Total Employees ============>         8
Average Employee Raise =====>  $1,281.10

End of Report
```

STUDENT ASSIGNMENT 3: Computer Usage Report

Instructions: Design and code a QuickBASIC program to process the data shown under INPUT and prints the report shown under OUTPUT. Use the SELECT CASE statement to determine the computer charges. At the end-of-job, print the total customers, total hours in decimal, and the total charges. The monthly charges can be determined from the following:

1. $165.00 for one hour or less usage
2. $240.00 for usage greater than one hour and less than or equal to two hours
3. $300.00 for usage greater than two hours and less than or equal to three hours
4. $330.00 for usage greater than three hours and less than or equal to four hours
5. $375.00 for usage greater than four hours and less than or equal to five hours
6. $1.25 per minute if the usage is greater than five hours

INPUT: Use the following sample data:

CUSTOMER NAME	HOURS	MINUTES
Acme Inc.	2	0
Hitek	2	50
Floline	5	10
Niki's Food	1	14
Amanda Inc.	6	22
EOF	0	0

OUTPUT: The following results are printed:

```
                Computer Usage Report

Customer
Name           Hours      Minutes      Charges

Acme Inc.          2            0       240.00
Hitek              2           50       300.00
Floline            5           10       387.50
Niki's Food        1           14       240.00
Amanda Inc.        6           22       477.50

Total Customers =======>        5
Total Hours ===========>        17.60
Total Charges =========> $1,645.00

End of Report
```

PROJECT 4

Interactive Programming, For Loops, and an Introduction to the Top-Down Approach

One of the major tasks of any program is to integrate the data that is to be processed into the program. In the first three projects, the READ and DATA statements were used to integrate the data into the program. This project introduces you to another method of data integration through the use of the INPUT statement. The INPUT statement is different than the READ and DATA statements, because with the INPUT statement the data is entered *during* execution rather than as *part of the program*.

A second topic covered in this project is alternative methods for implementing loops in QuickBASIC. Through the first three projects, we have consistently created loops using the DO WHILE and LOOP statements. In this project we discuss the creation of loops using the DO and LOOP UNTIL statements and the FOR and NEXT statements. The DO and LOOP UNTIL statements allow you to create loops that test for termination at the bottom of the loop rather than at the top of the loop. The FOR and NEXT statements allow you to more efficiently establish counter-controlled loops. A **counter-controlled loop** is one that exits the loop when a counter has reached a specified number.

Finally, this project presents the top-down approach to solving problems. The top-down approach is a useful methodology for solving large and complex problems. This approach breaks the problem into smaller parts and allows you to solve each part independent of the others.

THE INPUT STATEMENT

The INPUT statement causes a program to temporarily halt execution and accept data through the keyboard as shown in Figure 4-1. After the user enters the required data (1.25 in Figure 4-1) through the keyboard, the program continues to execute.

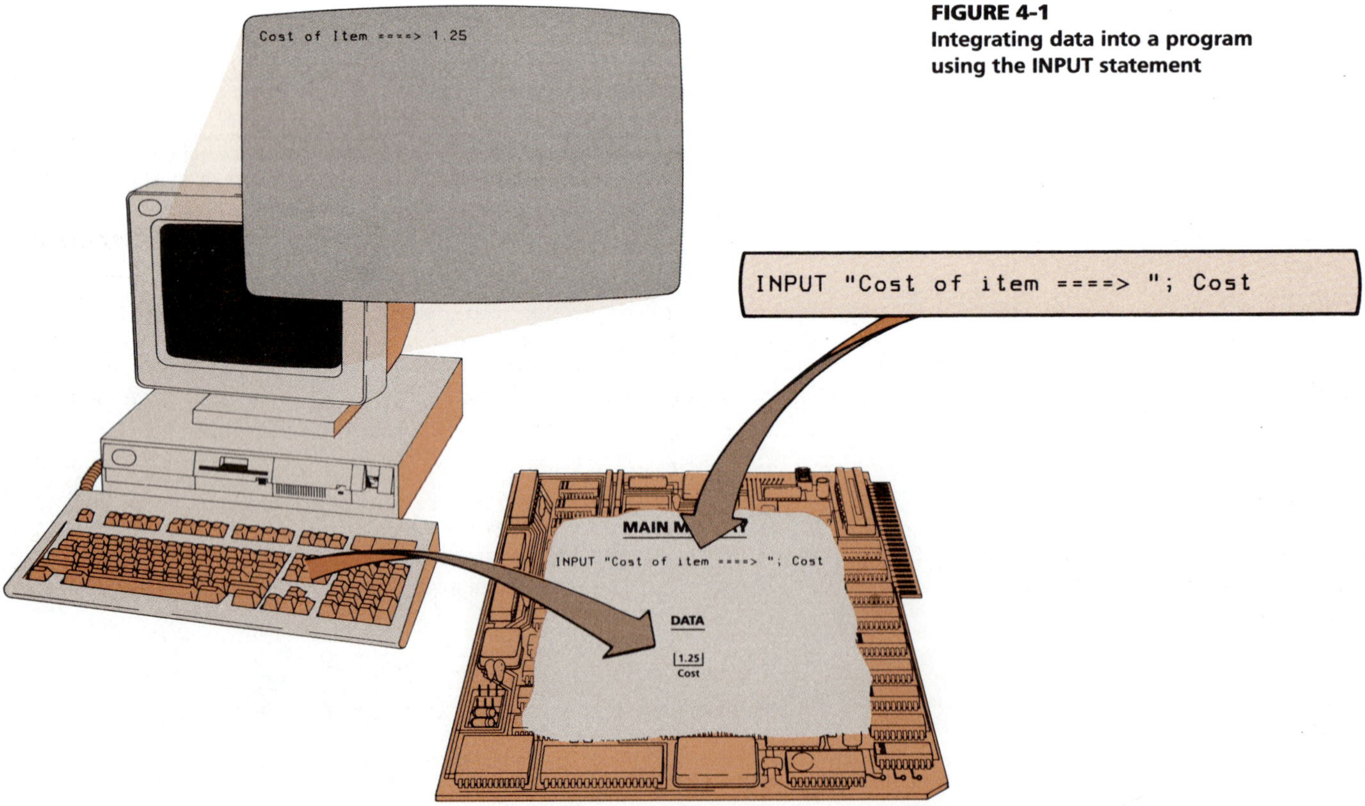

FIGURE 4-1
Integrating data into a program using the INPUT statement

The `INPUT` statement has two general forms, shown in Figure 4-2. With the first general form, the keyword `INPUT` is immediately followed by one or more variables separated by commas. When executed, this first form displays a question mark on the screen to indicate that it is waiting for the user to enter data.

The second general form of the `INPUT` statement shows that the programmer may enter a **prompt message** to inform the user of the required data. In this second and most often used form, the keyword `INPUT` is followed by the prompt message in quotation marks, a comma or semicolon after the prompt message, and a list of variables separated by commas. A semicolon after a prompt message tells the PC to display a question mark immediately after the prompt message. A comma instructs the PC not to display the question mark. Although this statement may include more than one variable, most programmers place one variable per `INPUT` statement.

No Prompt Message

`INPUT` variable, ..., variable

Prompt Message

`INPUT` "prompt message", variable, ..., variable

FIGURE 4-2 The general form of the INPUT statement

Figure 4-3 illustrates several examples of `INPUT` statements.

EXAMPLE	INPUT STATEMENT	DATA ENTERED THROUGH KEYBOARD
1	`INPUT Amount, Cost`	`125.56, 75`
2	`INPUT Cus.Name$, Age, Deduction`	`Joe Dac, 57, 25`
3	`INPUT "Discount =====>", Disc`	`.25`
4	`INPUT "What is your name"; User.Name$`	`Marci Jean`
5	`PRINT "Do you want to continue?"` `INPUT "Enter Y for Yes, else N", Control$`	`Y`

FIGURE 4-3 Examples of the INPUT statement

Examples 1 and 2 in Figure 4-3 show that it is not necessary to include a prompt message. When either `INPUT` statement is executed, a question mark displays on the screen. Examples 3 through 5 include prompt messages. In Example 3, the prompt message

```
Discount =====>
```

displays on the screen at the location of the cursor. Following the display of the prompt, the PC halts execution until the user enters the data (.25) and presses the Enter key.

In Example 4 of Figure 4-3, the following prompt displays:

```
What is your name?
```

Because we ended the prompt message with a semicolon, the PC displays the question mark after the prompt. Example 5 shows how you can utilize the `PRINT` statement along with the `INPUT` statement to display prompt messages made up of more than one line.

THE BEEP AND LOCATE STATEMENTS

Two QuickBASIC statements that are often used in tandem with the `INPUT` statement are the `BEEP` and `LOCATE` statements.

The BEEP Statement

When executed, the `BEEP` statement causes the PC's speaker to beep for a fraction of a second. Several `BEEP` statements in a row cause the PC to beep for a longer duration. The following line causes the PC to beep for approximately a second:

```
BEEP : BEEP : BEEP : BEEP
```

Notice the colons between the `BEEP` statements. In QuickBASIC, the colon allows you to place more than one statement per line. The `BEEP` statement is often used to alert the user that there is a problem with the program or data.

The LOCATE Statement

QuickBASIC defines the output screen as having 25 rows and 80 columns. The `LOCATE` statement can be used to position the cursor precisely on any one of the two thousand display positions on the screen. For example, the following line causes the PC to move the cursor to row 4, column 15:

```
LOCATE 4, 15
```

It makes no difference whether the cursor is above or below row 4 or to the right or left of column 15. The general form of the `LOCATE` statement is shown in Figure 4-4.

FIGURE 4-4
The general form of the LOCATE statement

`LOCATE` row, column

When executed, the partial program in Figure 4-5 displays the prompt message in the `INPUT` statement in row 6, column 12.

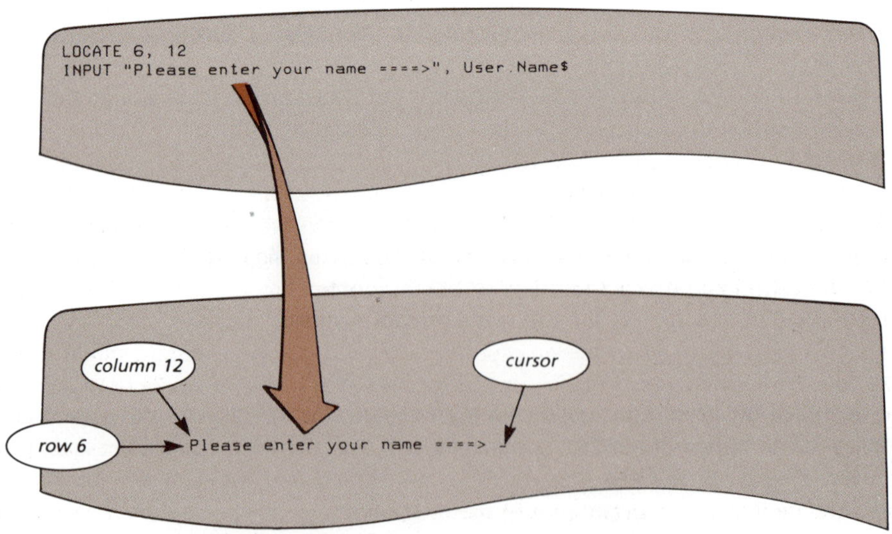

FIGURE 4-5
Use of the LOCATE statement to position the cursor

EDITING DATA ENTERED THROUGH THE KEYBOARD

In most interactive applications it is required that you check the incoming data to be sure that it is reasonable. A **reasonableness check** ensures that the data is legitimate, that is, the data is within a range of acceptable values. If the data is not validated before being used, then the PC can very well generate incorrect information.

The partial program in Figure 4-6 requests that the user enter a value for the variable Item.Cost. Assume that the program specifications state that the value of Cost must be greater than zero and less than 1,000.00.

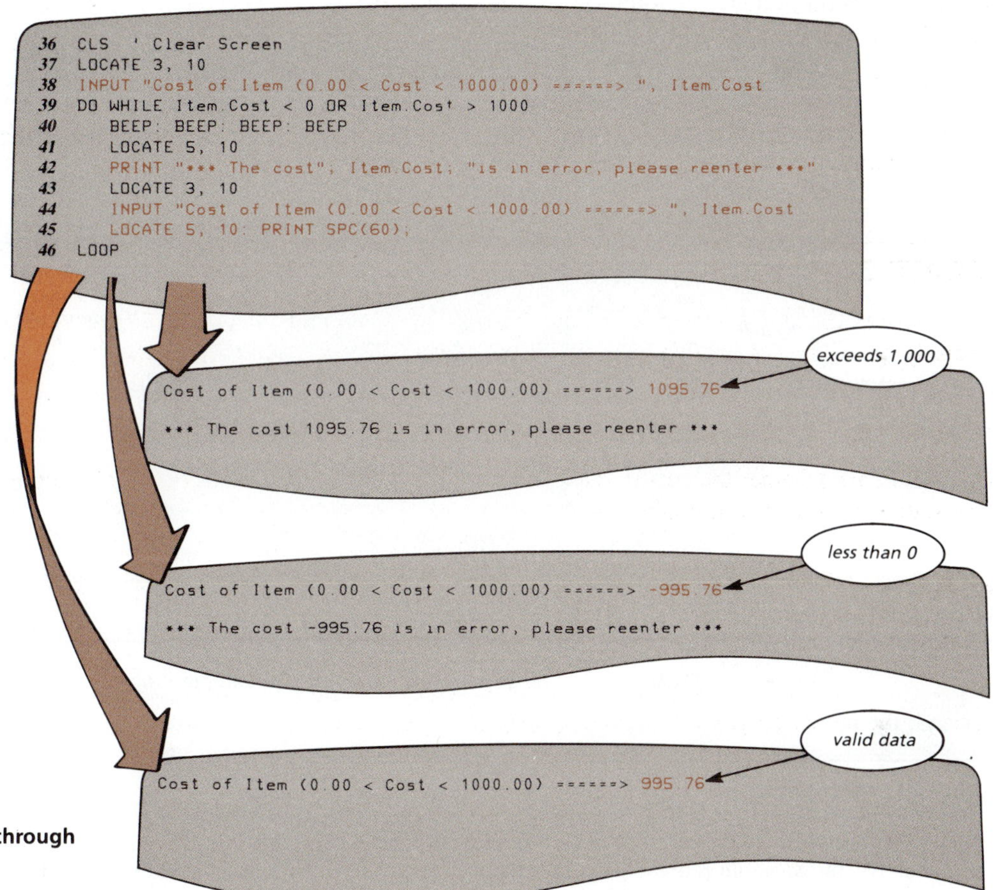

FIGURE 4-6
Editing data entered through the keyboard

When the PC executes the partial program in Figure 4-6, the `CLS` statement in line 36 clears the output screen. Line 37 moves the cursor to column 10 in row 3. The `INPUT` statement in line 38 displays the prompt message and halts execution of the program. After the user enters the value `1095.76` and presses the Enter key, the `DO WHILE` statement in line 39 tests the value of Item.Cost. Since it is greater than 1,000.00, control enters the loop. Line 40 causes the PC speaker to beep for a second. Due to lines 41 and 42, the PC displays an error message beginning at column 10 in row 5.

Lines 43 and 44 again cause the prompt message to display beginning at column 10 in row 3. After the user enters `-995.76`, the error message in row 5 is erased by the `SPC` function in the `PRINT` statement in line 45. The `SPC` function displays as many spaces as indicated in the parentheses. Thus, `SPC(60)` displays 60 spaces and in doing so erases the error message in row 5. Since `-995.76` is still outside the limits, the PC reexecutes the loop and displays the error message due to line 42. Finally, when the user enters `995.76`, the PC exits the loop and continues execution at the line following the `LOOP` statement.

Data validation is an important part of the programming process. It should be apparent that the information produced by a computer is only as accurate as the data it processes. The term **GIGO** (Garbage In—Garbage Out, pronounced GEE-GOH) is used to describe the generation of inaccurate information from the input of invalid data. Data validation should be incorporated into all programs, especially when the `INPUT` statement is used.

SAMPLE PROGRAM 4 — ITEM COST REPORT

The sample program in this project illustrates the preparation of an item cost table that contains the cost of one to ten items. The program begins by asking the user to enter the cost of an item. The cost must be greater than zero and less than 1,000.00. After validating the entry, the sample program displays the cost table. Once the table displays, the user is asked if another table should be prepared. The user must enter a Y for yes or an N for no.

If the user enters the letter Y, the loop is executed again and the user is asked to enter the cost of the next item. If the user enters the letter N, the program displays an end-of-job message followed by termination of execution. Figure 4-7 shows the desired output results for Sample Program 4.

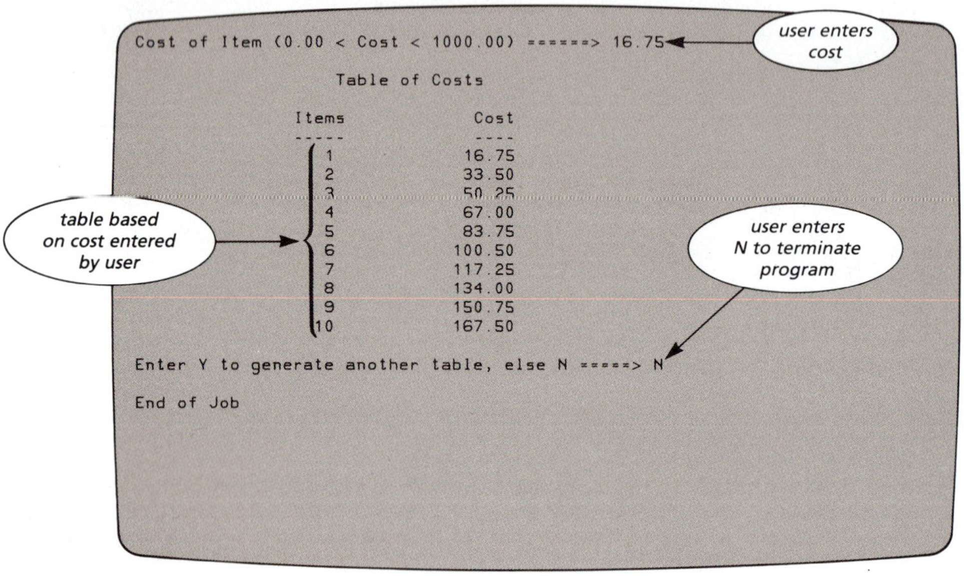

FIGURE 4-7 The desired output results for Sample Program 4

Program Flowchart

The flowchart for Sample Program 4 which produces the item cost table for one to ten items is illustrated in Figure 4-8. At the top of the flowchart, the variable representing the maximum number of items is initialized to 10 and the table format is assigned to string variables.

Control then enters the loop. Notice that this is the first time in this book that a decision symbol is not at the top of the loop. In this flowchart, the decision to terminate the loop is at the bottom. Loops that have the decision to terminate at the top are called **Do-While loops**. Loops that have the decision to terminate at the bottom are called **Do-Until loops**.

Within the major loop, the output screen is cleared and the user is requested to enter the cost of an item. Next, the cost is validated, the table headings are displayed, and a counter is initialized to one. The table is then generated by a looping process that continues while the counter is less than or equal to 10. After the table displays, the user is asked if another is desired. The decision symbol at the bottom of the Do-Until loop determines whether to continue or terminate processing on the basis of the value (Y or N) entered by the user.

Before we can code the logic shown in Figure 4-8 we need to discuss the FOR and NEXT statements.

FIGURE 4-8
The flowchart for Sample Program 4

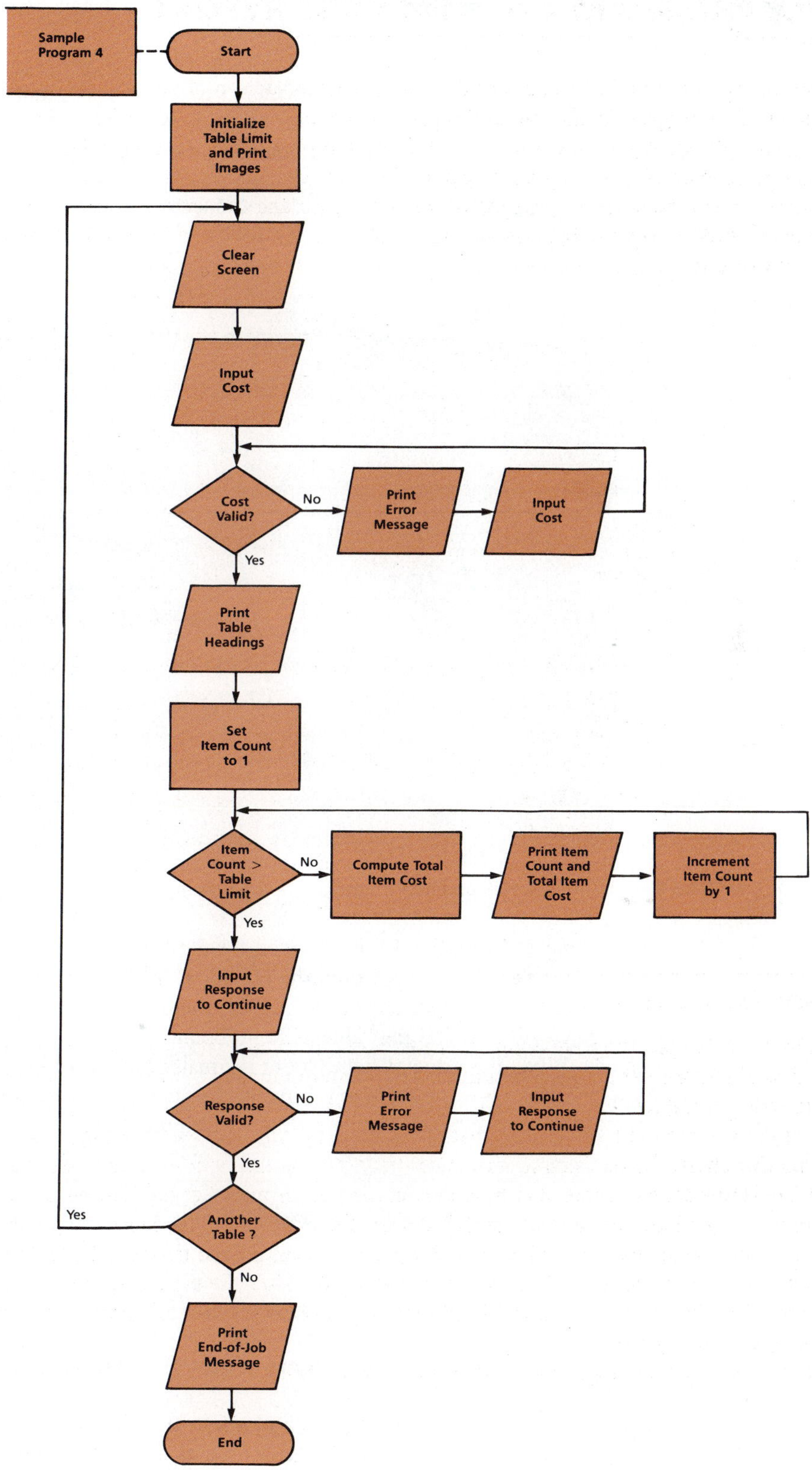

THE FOR AND NEXT STATEMENTS

The FOR and NEXT statements make it possible to execute a section of a program repeatedly, with automatic changes in the value of a variable between repetitions. Whenever you have to develop a counter-controlled loop (a loop that is to be executed a specific number of times based on a counter), the FOR and NEXT statements can be used to develop it. We call such a loop a **For loop**.

Figure 4-9 illustrates how the FOR and NEXT statements can be used to implement the loop that generates the cost table described in the flowchart for Sample Program 4.

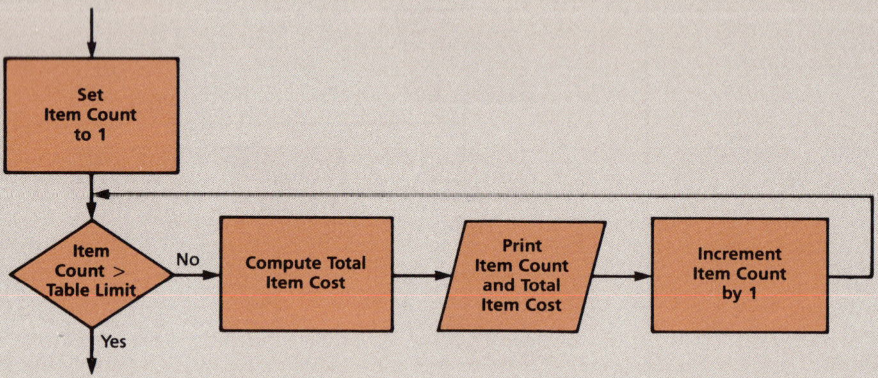


```
52   FOR Item.Count = 1 TO Max.Items STEP 1
53      LET Total.Item.Cost = Item.Count * Item.Cost
54      LOCATE , 25: PRINT USING D1$; Item.Count; Total.Item.Cost
55   NEXT Item.Count
```

FIGURE 4-9 Using the FOR and NEXT statements to implement the loop that generates the cost table

When the FOR statement in line 52 of Figure 4-9 is executed for the first time, the For loop becomes active and the variable Item.Count is set equal to one. The statements within the For loop, in this case lines 53 and 54, are executed. The NEXT statement in line 55 returns control to the FOR statement in line 52, where the value of Item.Count is incremented by the amount (1), which follows the keyword STEP. If the value of Item.Count is less than or equal to Max.Items (table limit), execution of the For loop continues. When the value of Item.Count is greater than Max.Items, control transfers to the line following NEXT Item.Count. As with other loops, notice that we indent the statements within the loop by three spaces.

The general forms of the FOR and NEXT statements are shown in Figure 4-10.

```
FOR loop-variable = initial TO limit STEP increment
    [range of statements]
NEXT loop-variable
```

FIGURE 4-10 The general forms of the FOR and NEXT statements

In Figure 4-10, the FOR statement indicates the beginning of a For loop and the NEXT statement indicates the end. The range of statements within the For loop is executed repeatedly as long as *loop-variable* is not greater than *limit*. *Loop-variable* is initially assigned the value of *initial*. Each time the range of statements is executed, *loop-variable* is increased by the value of *increment*. When *loop-variable* is greater than *limit*, control passes to the line following the corresponding NEXT statement.

If *increment* is negative, the test to terminate the For loop is reversed. The value of *loop-variable* is decremented each time through the For loop, and the For loop is executed while *loop-variable* is greater than or equal to *limit*. If the keyword STEP is not included in a FOR statement, then the increment value is automatically set to one.

Figure 4-11 illustrates several valid `FOR` statements.

EXAMPLE	FOR STATEMENT
1	FOR Count = 1 TO 100 STEP 1
2	FOR X = 5 TO Y STEP 3
3	FOR Amount = 1.25 TO 7.35 STEP .05
4	FOR Tax = A TO B STEP C
5	FOR S = 0 TO -35 STEP -3
6	FOR X = 1 TO 10

FIGURE 4-11 Examples of valid FOR statements

In Example 1 of Figure 4-11, the For loop is executed 100 times. Example 2 points out that the initial and increment values can be values other than one. Example 3 initializes Amount to 1.25 for the first pass. Thereafter, the value .05 is added to Amount each time the range of statements is executed. Hence, Amount takes on the values 1.25, 1.30, 1.35, 1.40, and so on, until Amount exceeds 7.35.

Example 4 shows that the initial, limit, and increment values can be variables. Example 5 includes a negative increment (–3). Thus, the test is reversed and S must be less than –35 before the For loop terminates. Finally, Example 6 illustrates a `FOR` statement without the keyword `STEP`. In this case, the increment value is automatically set to one.

The QuickBASIC Program

The program in Figure 4-12 corresponds to the program flowchart in Figure 4-8.

FIGURE 4-12
Sample Program 4

```
' ****************************************************************
' *  Sample Program 4                          September 15, 1994  *
' *  Item Cost Report                                              *
' *  J. S. Quasney                                                 *
' *                                                                *
' *  This program displays a table of costs of 1 to 10 items.      *
' *  The user enters the cost per item and the program             *
' *  displays the table of costs.                                  *
' *       The cost per item entered by the user is validated       *
' *  (greater than zero and less than 1000.00).  After the         *
' *  table is displayed the user is asked if another table         *
' *  should be generated.                                          *
' *       This activity continues until the user indicates         *
' *  that no more tables are to be generated.                      *
' *                                                                *
' *  Variables:   Item.Cost        -- Cost of item                 *
' *               Item.Count       -- Item count                   *
' *               Max.Items        -- Maximum number of items      *
' *                                   in table                     *
' *               Total.Item.Cost  -- Cost of items                *
' *               Control$         -- Response to continue         *
' *               H1$, H2$, H3$, D1$, T1$ -- Print images          *
' ****************************************************************

```

(continued)

FIGURE 4-12 (continued)

```
' *********************** Initialization ***********************
LET Max.Items = 10
LET H1$ = "    Table of Costs"
LET H2$ = "Items            Cost"
LET H3$ = "-----            ----"
LET D1$ = "  ##         ##,###.##"
LET T1$ = "End of Job"

' ******************** Generate Cost Table *********************
DO
   ' ************ Accept and Validate Cost of Item ************
   CLS  ' Clear Screen
   LOCATE 3, 10
   INPUT "Cost of Item (0.00 < Cost < 1000.00) ======> ", Item.Cost
   DO WHILE Item.Cost < 0 OR Item.Cost > 1000
      BEEP: BEEP: BEEP: BEEP
      LOCATE 5, 10
      PRINT "*** The cost"; Item.Cost; "is in error, please reenter ***"
      LOCATE 3, 10
      INPUT "Cost of Item (0.00 < Cost < 1000.00) ======> ", Item.Cost
      LOCATE 5, 10: PRINT SPC(60);
   LOOP

   ' **************** Generate Table of Costs *****************
   LOCATE 5, 25: PRINT H1$
   LOCATE 7, 25: PRINT H2$
   LOCATE 8, 25: PRINT H3$
   FOR Item.Count = 1 TO Max.Items STEP 1
      LET Total.Item.Cost = Item.Count * Item.Cost
      LOCATE , 25: PRINT USING D1$; Item.Count; Total.Item.Cost
   NEXT Item.Count

   ' ******** Accept and Validate Response to Continue ********
   LOCATE 20, 10
   INPUT "Enter Y to generate another table, else N =====> ", Control$
   DO WHILE Control$ <> "N" AND Control$ <> "Y"
      BEEP: BEEP: BEEP: BEEP
      LOCATE 22, 10
      PRINT "*** Response in error, please reenter ***"
      LOCATE 20, 10
      INPUT "Enter Y to generate another table, else N =====> ", Control$
      LOCATE 22, 10: PRINT SPC(50);
   LOOP

LOOP UNTIL Control$ = "N"

' ************************** Wrap-Up **************************
LOCATE 22, 10
PRINT T1$
END
```

Discussion of Sample Program 4

When Sample Program 4 is executed, the variables in lines 26 through 31 are initialized. Line 26 initializes Max.Items (table limit) to 10. Lines 27 through 31 define the table format. The variables are used later in the `PRINT` statements in lines 49 through 51, 54, and 73.

The `DO` statement in line 34 indicates the beginning of a Do-Until loop. With a Do-Until loop, the condition that determines whether the loop should continue is in the `LOOP` statement (line 69). As shown in Figure 4-13, there are two basic types of loops. The Do-While loop has the decision symbol at the top of the loop. The Do-Until loop has the decision symbol at the bottom of the loop. If the decision is at the top (Figure 4-13A), use the `DO WHILE` and `LOOP` statements. If the decision is at the bottom (Figure 4-13B), use the `DO` and `LOOP UNTIL` statements.

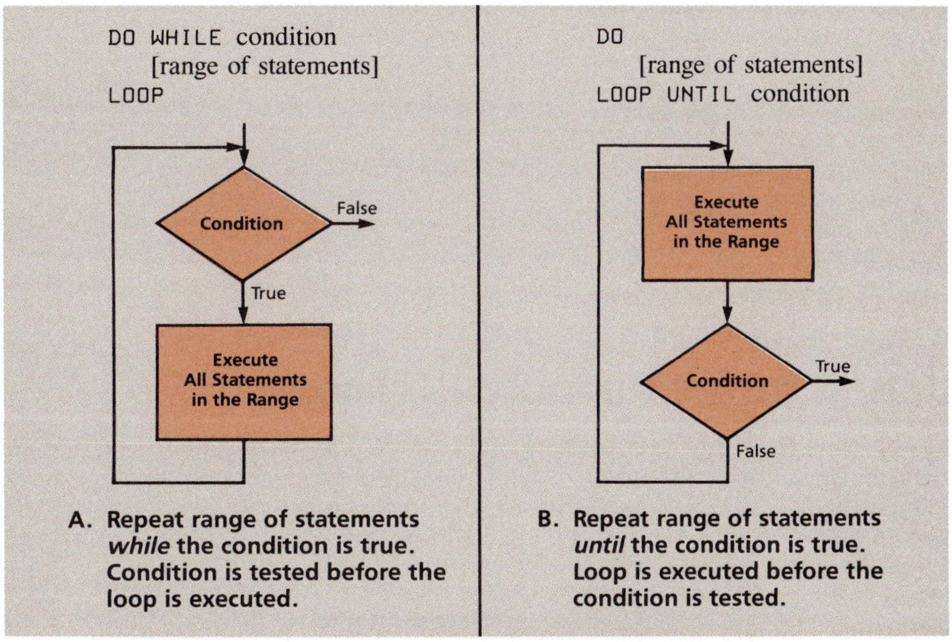

FIGURE 4-13 **The two basic types of loops and the statements in QuickBASIC which should be used to implement them**

Upon entering the Do-Until loop, the screen is cleared by line 36. Lines 37 through 46 accept and validate the cost of the item entered by the user. Lines 49 through 51 display the table title and column headings. Lines 52 through 55 compute and display the rows of the table. Notice in line 54 that the `LOCATE` statement does not include a row number. When the `LOCATE` statement is written in this fashion, it references the current row, which is one greater than the one referenced by the previously executed `PRINT` or `PRINT USING` statement. Hence, each time line 54 is executed in the For loop, the `PRINT USING` statement begins printing in column 25 of the next row. Notice in lines 49 through 51 and 54 that it is common practice to incorporate both the `LOCATE` and `PRINT` statements on the same line. Of course, it is important that you separate the two statements with the colon.

After the table is displayed on the screen, lines 58 through 67 accept and validate a response from the user that indicates whether the Do-Until loop should continue. In this case, only two values, `Y` and `N`, are acceptable (line 60). If the user enters a `Y`, line 69 causes the PC to continue execution at the top of the loop (line 34). If the user enters the value `N`, the condition in line 69 is false. Thus, control passes to line 72 and an end-of-job message is displayed followed by termination of execution of the program.

Figure 4-14 shows the display of Sample Program 4 when the value 579.46 is entered as the cost of an item.

```
Cost of Item (0.00 < Cost < 1000.00) ======> 579.46

                    Table of Costs

                Items              Cost
                -----              ----
                  1               579.46
                  2             1,158.92
                  3             1,738.38
                  4             2,317.84
                  5             2,897.30
                  6             3,476.76
                  7             4,056.22
                  8             4,635.68
                  9             5,215.14
                 10             5,794.60

Enter Y to generate another table, else N =====> N

End of Job
```

FIGURE 4-14
The results displayed due to the execution of Sample Program 4 and a cost per item of $579.46

AN INTRODUCTION TO THE TOP-DOWN APPROACH

Top-down programming is a divide and conquer strategy used by programmers to solve large problems. The first step in top-down programming is to divide the task into smaller, more manageable subtasks through the use of a top-down chart. Figure 4-15 illustrates a top-down chart for the problem solved by Sample Program 4.

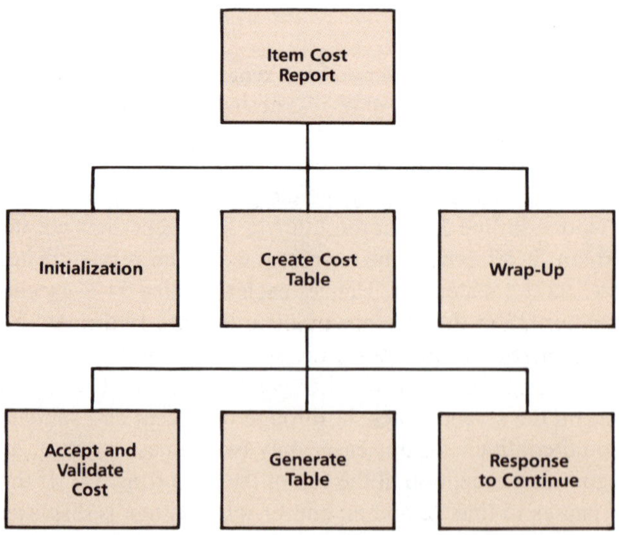

FIGURE 4-15
A top-down chart for the problem solved by Sample Program 4

A top-down chart differs from a program flowchart in that it does not show decision-making logic or flow of control. A program flowchart shows *how* to solve the problem. A top-down chart shows *what* has to be done.

A top-down chart is very similar to a company's organization chart where each lower level subtask carries out a function for its superior task. In Figure 4-15, the top box (Item Cost Report) represents the complete task. The next level of boxes (Initialization, Create Cost Table, and Wrap-Up) shows the subtasks that are required to solve the task of the top box. The lowest level of boxes (Accept and Validate Cost Item, Generate Table, and Response to Continue) indicates the subtasks required to create a table. Usually, a task is divided into lower level subtasks whenever it appears to be too complicated or lengthy to stand by itself.

Implementing the Top-Down Approach

Once the larger, more complex problem has been decomposed into smaller pieces, a solution to each subtask can be designed and coded. We call the group of statements that are associated with a single programming task a **subroutine**, or **module**.

The subroutines that formulate a program solution begin with a name, followed immediately by a colon (:), and end with a `RETURN` statement. Subroutines are *called* by their superior modules using the `GOSUB` statement. When a subroutine has completed its task, control returns to the superior module via a `RETURN` statement. The rules regarding a subroutine name are the same as for a variable name.

THE GOSUB AND RETURN STATEMENTS

The `GOSUB` statement is used to call a subroutine. As shown in Figure 4-16, the keyword `GOSUB` is immediately followed by the subroutine name to which control is transferred. Once control transfers, the instructions in the subroutine are executed.

FIGURE 4-16
The general form of the GOSUB statement

```
GOSUB subroutine-name
```

The `RETURN` statement (Figure 4-17) at the bottom of the subroutine returns control to the statement following the corresponding `GOSUB` in the superior module.

FIGURE 4-17
The general form of the RETURN statement

```
RETURN
```

Consider the partial program on the next page in Figure 4-18 and the following important points regarding the implementation of the top-down approach:

- The `END` statement is the last statement in the Main module. Control returns to DOS through this statement.
- Indent by three spaces the statements within modules.
- So that lower level modules can easily be located, they should be placed below their superior module and in the order in which they are called.

FIGURE 4-18
Implementing the top-down chart in Figure 4-15

```
' *********** Main Module **********
GOSUB Initialization
GOSUB Create.Table
GOSUB Wrap.Up
END

' ********* Initialization *********
Initialization:
      .
      .
      .
RETURN

' ******* Create Cost Table *******
Create.Table:
   GOSUB Accept.Cost.Item
   GOSUB Generate.Table
   GOSUB Accept.Response.To.Continue
RETURN

' **** Accept and Validate Cost ****
Accept.Cost.Item:
      .
      .
      .
RETURN

' ********* Generate Table *********
Generate.Table:
      .
      .
      .
RETURN

' ****** Response to Continue ******
Accept.Response.To.Continue:
      .
      .
      .
RETURN

' ************ Wrap-Up ************
Wrap.Up:
      .
      .
      .
RETURN
' ********* End of Program *********
```

place END statement here at end of main module

each subroutine begins with a name and ends with a RETURN

colon required after subroutine name

indicates physical end of program

A modified version of Sample Program 4 which utilizes the top-down approach is shown in Figure 4-19. The coding corresponds to the top-down chart in Figure 4-15.

FIGURE 4-19
A top-down version of Sample Program 4

```
' ************************************************************
' *  Sample Program 4 Modified              September 15, 1994  *
' *  Item Cost Report                                           *
' *  J. S. Quasney                                              *
' *                                                             *
' *  This program displays a table of costs of 1 to 10 items.  *
' *  The user enters the cost per item and the program         *
' *  displays the table of costs.                              *
' *       The cost per item entered by the user is validated    *
' *  (greater than zero and less than 1000.00).  After the     *
' *  table is displayed the user is asked if another table     *
' *  should be generated.                                      *
' *       This activity continues until the user indicates      *
' *  that no more tables are to be generated.                  *
' *                                                             *
' *  Variables:  Item.Cost        -- Cost of item               *
' *              Item.Count       -- Item count                 *
' *              Max.Items        -- Maximum number of items    *
' *                                  in table                   *
' *              Total.Item.Cost  -- Cost of items              *
' *              Control$         -- Response to continue       *
' *              H1$, H2$, H3$, D1$, T1$ -- Print images        *
' ************************************************************

' ************************************************************
' *                        Main Module                          *
' ************************************************************
GOSUB Initialization
GOSUB Create.Table
GOSUB Wrap.Up
END

' ************************************************************
' *                       Initialization                        *
' ************************************************************
Initialization:
   LET Max.Items = 10
   LET H1$ = "     Table of Costs"
   LET H2$ = "Items                Cost"
   LET H3$ = "-----                ----"
   LET D1$ = "  ##             ##,###.##"
   LET T1$ = "End of Job"
RETURN

' ************************************************************
' *                     Create Cost Table                       *
' ************************************************************
Create.Table:
   DO
      GOSUB Accept.Cost.Item
      GOSUB Generate.Table
      GOSUB Accept.Response.To.Continue
   LOOP UNTIL Control$ = "N"
RETURN
```

(continued)

FIGURE 4-19 (continued)

```
' ****************************************************************
' *               Accept and Validate Cost of Item               *
' ****************************************************************
Accept.Cost.Item:
   CLS  ' Clear Screen
   LOCATE 3, 10
   INPUT "Cost of Item (0.00 < Cost < 1000.00) ======> ", Item.Cost
   DO WHILE Item.Cost < 0 OR Item.Cost > 1000
      BEEP: BEEP: BEEP: BEEP
      LOCATE 5, 10
      PRINT "*** The cost"; Item.Cost; "is in error, please reenter ***"
      LOCATE 3, 10
      INPUT "Cost of Item (0.00 < Cost < 1000.00) ======> ", Item.Cost
      LOCATE 5, 10: PRINT SPC(60);
   LOOP
RETURN

' ****************************************************************
' *                  Generate Table of Costs                     *
' ****************************************************************
Generate.Table:
   LOCATE 5, 25: PRINT H1$
   LOCATE 7, 25: PRINT H2$
   LOCATE 8, 25: PRINT H3$
   FOR Item.Count = 1 TO Max.Items STEP 1
      LET Total.Item.Cost = Item.Count * Item.Cost
      LOCATE , 25: PRINT USING D1$; Item.Count; Total.Item.Cost
   NEXT Item.Count
RETURN

' ****************************************************************
' *           Accept and Validate Response to Continue           *
' ****************************************************************
Accept.Response.To.Continue:
   LOCATE 20, 10
   INPUT "Enter Y to generate another table, else N =====> ", Control$
   DO WHILE Control$ <> "N" AND Control$ <> "Y"
      BEEP: BEEP: BEEP: BEEP
      LOCATE 22, 10
      PRINT "*** Response in error, please reenter ***"
      LOCATE 20, 10
      INPUT "Enter Y to generate another table, else N =====> ", Control$
      LOCATE 22, 10: PRINT SPC(50);
   LOOP
RETURN

' ****************************************************************
' *                           Wrap-Up                            *
' ****************************************************************
Wrap.Up:
   LOCATE 22, 10
   PRINT T1$
RETURN
' ********************* End of Program *********************
```

Discussion of Sample Program 4 Modified

When the modified version of Sample Program 4 in Figure 4-19 executes, line 28 in the Main module transfers control to the Initialization module which begins at line 36. After lines 37 through 42 are executed, the RETURN statement in line 43 transfers control back to line 29 in the Main module. Next, line 29 transfers control to the Create.Table module (lines 48 through 54). In this module, the Do-Until loop includes three GOSUB statements. Each time through this loop, a cost table such as the one in Figure 4-20 is generated.

When the user enters the letter N in response to the INPUT statement in line 97, control passes back to line 53. Since the condition in line 53 is true, control passes to the RETURN statement in line 54. Line 54 returns control to line 30. Next, line 30 transfers control to the Wrap.Up module which begins at line 105. After the end-of-job message is displayed, control returns to line 31 in the Main module and the program terminates execution.

```
Cost of Item (0.00 < Cost < 1000.00) ======> 67.50

             Table of Costs

          Items           Cost
          -----           ----
            1             67.50
            2            135.00
            3            202.50
            4            270.00
            5            337.50
            6            405.00
            7            472.50
            8            540.00
            9            607.50
           10            675.00

Enter Y to generate another table, else N =====> N

End of Job
```

FIGURE 4-20 The results displayed due to the execution of the modified Sample Program 4 and a cost per item of $67.50

TRY IT YOURSELF EXERCISES

1. What is displayed if each of the following programs are executed?
   a. X is assigned the value 2, and Y is assigned the value 4.

```
' Exercise 1.a
INPUT "Enter values for X and Y ===> ", X, Y
Sum = X + Y
Diff = Y - X
Prod = X * Y
Quot = X / Y
PRINT Sum, Diff
PRINT Prod, Quot
END
```

b.

```
' Exercise 1.b
Total = 0
GOSUB Increment.Total
PRINT Total
GOSUB Increment.Total
PRINT Total
GOSUB Increment.Total
PRINT Total
Total = Total - 6
PRINT Total
END
' Increment Total
Increment.Total:
   Total = Total + 2
RETURN
```

c. Selling.Price and Discount.Rate are assigned $30.00 and 25%, respectively.

```
' Exercise 1.c
' ***********************************
' *           Main Module           *
' ***********************************
GOSUB Accept.Data
GOSUB Compute.Discount
GOSUB Display.Discount
END

' ***********************************
' *      Accept Operator Data       *
' ***********************************
Accept.Data:
   CLS  ' Clear Screen
   INPUT "Selling Price ===>", Selling.Price
   INPUT "Discount Rate in % ===>", Discount.Rate
RETURN

' ***********************************
' *        Compute Discount         *
' ***********************************
Compute.Discount:
   Discount.Rate = Discount.Rate / 100
   Discount = Discount.Rate * Selling.Price
RETURN

' ***********************************
' *         Display Amount          *
' ***********************************
Display.Discount:
   PRINT "Discount ======>"; Discount
RETURN

' *********** End of Program ********
```

2. Is the following partial program invalid? If it is invalid, indicate why.

```
' Exercise 2
' Main Module
    .
    .
    .
GOSUB Calculate
' Calculate Square
Calculate:
    X = X * X
RETURN
END
```

3. Write a sequence of `LOCATE` and `PRINT` statements that will display the word `Retail` beginning in column 12 of row 15.
4. Write a series of statements that will display the number 22 in column 22 of row 22.
5. Consider the two following types of loops:
   a. `DO WHILE . . . LOOP`
   b. `DO . . . LOOP UNTIL`

   Answer the following questions for each type of loop:

   (1) Does the loop terminate when the condition is true or false?
   (2) What is the minimum number of times the range of statements in the loop is executed?
   (3) Is the test to terminate the loop made before or after the range of statements is executed?

6. At what column and row is the cursor after the following two statements are executed?

```
LOCATE 15, 34
LOCATE 17
```

7. Identify the syntax and logic error(s), if any, in each of the following:
   a. `FOR X = 1 TO 6 STEP -1`
   b. `FOR Amt = 1 TO Sq`
   c. `FOR T$ = 0 TO 7`
   d. `FOR Value = 10 TO 1`
   e. `FOR H = A TO B STEP -B`

8. How many times does the `PRINT` statement execute when the following program is executed?

```
' Exercise 8
FOR J = 1 TO 30
   FOR N = 1 TO 20
      FOR I = 1 TO 3
         PRINT J, N, I
      NEXT I
   NEXT N
NEXT J
END
```

9. Explain the purpose of the following statement. What are the colons used for?

```
BEEP : BEEP : BEEP : BEEP
```

STUDENT ASSIGNMENTS

STUDENT ASSIGNMENT 1: Weekly Pay Rate Table

Instructions: Design and code a top-down QuickBASIC program, such as the one in Figure 4-19, to generate the weekly pay rate table shown under OUTPUT. Request that the user enter through the keyboard an hourly rate between $3.35 and $30.00, inclusive. Validate the entry. Use a For loop to generate a table of 10 hourly rates in increments of $0.50 and the corresponding weekly rates. A weekly rate is equal to 40 times the hourly rate. After the table displays, request the user to enter the letter Y to generate another table or the letter N to terminate the program. Use the following top-down chart as a guide to solving this problem:

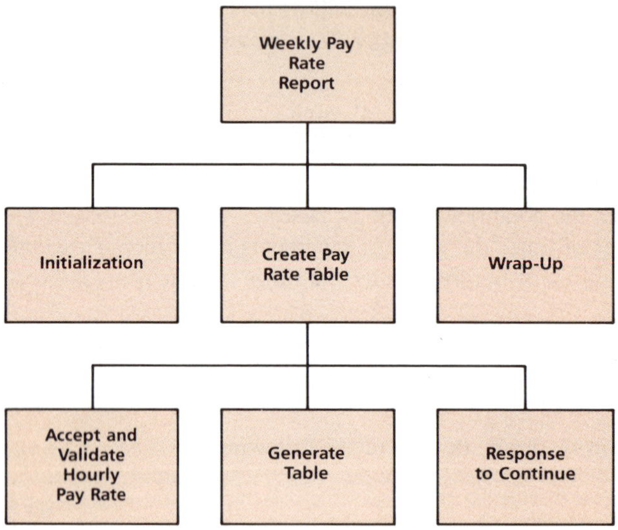

INPUT: Use the following sample data:

Table 1 – Hourly rate $6.75
Table 2 – Hourly rate $22.50

OUTPUT: The following results are displayed for the first table:

```
Initial Pay Rate (3.35 <= Cost <= 30.00) ======> 6.75

            Table of Hourly and Weekly Rates

              Hourly                      Weekly
              Rate                        Rate
              ------                      ------
                6.75                      270.00
                7.25                      290.00
                7.75                      310.00
                8.25                      330.00
                8.75                      350.00
                9.25                      370.00
                9.75                      390.00
               10.25                      410.00
               10.75                      430.00
               11.25                      450.00

Enter Y to generate another table, else N =====> Y
```

STUDENT ASSIGNMENT 2: Metric Conversion Table

Instructions: Design and code a top-down QuickBASIC program, such as the one in Figure 4-19, to generate a metric conversion table as shown on the next page in the printout. Request that the user enter through the keyboard an initial metric value, a limit metric value, and an increment metric value. Validate each entry. The initial metric value must be between 1 and 1,500, inclusive. The limit metric value must be greater than the initial metric value and less than 2,000. The increment metric value must be greater than zero and less than or equal to 100.

Use a For loop to generate a table of the metric values between the initial metric value and limit metric value. For each metric value, print the equivalent yards, feet, and inches. There are 39.37 inches in a meter, 12 inches in a foot, and 3 feet in a yard. After the table prints, request the user to enter the letter Y to generate another table or the letter N to terminate the program. Use the following top-down chart as a guide to solving this problem:

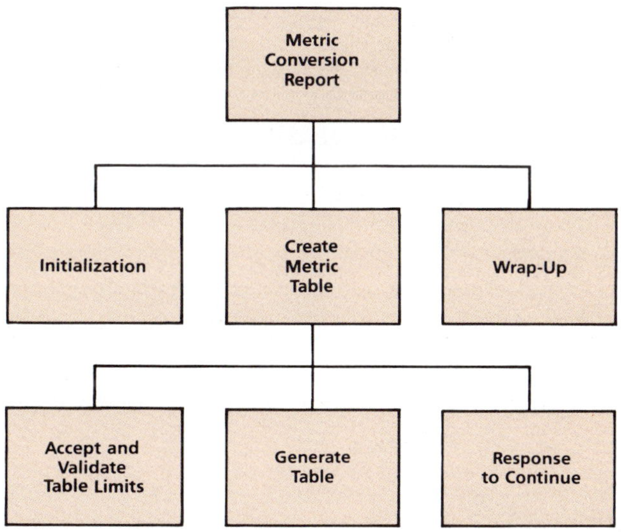

Before you print each table, use the following statement to move the paper in the printer to the top of the next page:

```
LPRINT CHR$(12);
```

This `LPRINT` statement prints the value of the function `CHR$(12)`, which is the form feed character.

INPUT: Use the following sample data:

Table 1 – Initial meters 100, Limit meters 200, Increment meters 10
Table 2 – Initial meters 140, Limit meters 160, Increment meters 2

OUTPUT: The following results display on the screen for the Table 1 data:

```
Initial Meter Value (1 <= Initial Meter <= 1500) ==> 100

Limit Meter Value (Initial Meter < Limit Meter < 2,000) ======> 200

Increment Meter Value (0 < Increment Meter <= 100) ======> 10

********* Report Being Printed On Printer *********

Enter Y to generate another table, else N =====> Y
```

Student Assignment 2 (continued)

The following results are printed on the printer for the Table 1 data:

```
            Metric Conversion Table

    Meters          Yards       Feet      Inches
    ------          -----       ----      ------
    100.00         109.36     328.08    3,937.00
    110.00         120.30     360.89    4,330.70
    120.00         131.23     393.70    4,724.40
    130.00         142.17     426.51    5,118.10
    140.00         153.11     459.32    5,511.80
    150.00         164.04     492.13    5,905.50
    160.00         174.98     524.93    6,299.20
    170.00         185.91     557.74    6,692.90
    180.00         196.85     590.55    7,086.60
    190.00         207.79     623.36    7,480.30
    200.00         218.72     656.17    7,874.00

    End of Table
```

PROJECT 5

Sequential File Processing

In the first four projects we emphasized the importance of integrating data into the program. You learned that data may be entered into a program through the use of the INPUT statement or the READ and DATA statements. This project presents a third method for entering data—the use of data files. With data files, the data is stored in auxiliary storage rather than in the program itself. This technique is used primarily for dealing with large amounts of data.

QuickBASIC includes a set of file-handling statements that allow a user to do the following:

- Open a file
- Read data from a file
- Write data to a file
- Test for the end-of-file
- Close a file

FILE ORGANIZATION

QuickBASIC provides for two types of file organization: sequential and random. A file that is organized sequentially is called a **sequential file** and is limited to sequential processing. This means that the records can be processed only in the order in which they are placed in the file. Conceptually, a sequential file is identical to the use of DATA statements within a QuickBASIC program.

The second type of file organization, **random files**, allows you to process the records in the file in any order. If the fifth record is required and it is stored in a random file, then the program may access it without reading the first four records. Random files are not discussed in this project.

CREATING A SEQUENTIAL DATA FILE

This section presents the OPEN, WRITE #n, and CLOSE statements. These statements are used to create a sequential data file. The OPEN statement is used to activate the file. The WRITE #n statement is used to write a record to the file. And the CLOSE statement is used to deactivate the file.

Opening Sequential Files

Before any file can be read from or written to, it must be opened by the OPEN statement. The OPEN statement identifies by name the file to be processed. It indicates whether the file is to be read from or written to. It also assigns the file a filenumber that can be used by statements that need to reference the file in question.

The general form of the OPEN statement is shown in Figure 5-1.

OPEN filespec FOR mode AS #filenumber

where **filespec** is the name of the file;
mode is one of the following:
APPEND opens file so that records can be added to the end of the file;
INPUT opens file to read beginning with the first record;
OUTPUT opens file to write records; and
filenumber is a numeric expression whose value is between 1 and 255.

FIGURE 5-1
The general form of the OPEN statement

As described in Figure 5-1, a sequential data file may be opened for input, output, or append. If a file is opened for input, the program can only read records from it. If a file is opened for output, the program can only write records to it. The Append mode allows you to write records to the end of a file that already has records in it. Figure 5-2 illustrates several `OPEN` statements.

EXAMPLE	STATEMENT
1	`OPEN "B:PAYROLL.DAT" FOR OUTPUT AS #4`
2	`OPEN "ACCOUNT.DAT" FOR APPEND AS #2`
3	`OPEN Filename$ FOR OUTPUT AS #1`
4	`OPEN "PART.DAT" FOR INPUT AS #1`

FIGURE 5-2
Examples of OPEN statements

The `OPEN` statement in Example 1 in Figure 5-2 opens PAYROLL.DAT on the B drive for output as filenumber 4. Since it is opened for output, you can only write records to PAYROLL.DAT. If you attempt to read a record, the PC will display a diagnostic message.

Example 2 opens the data file ACCOUNT.DAT for append as filenumber 2. Records can only be written to a data file opened for append. If ACCOUNT.DAT exists, records are written in sequence after the last record. If ACCOUNT.DAT does not exist, the PC creates it and the data file is treated as if it were open for output.

Example 3 in Figure 5-2 shows that in an `OPEN` statement you can use a string variable as the data file name. The assumption is that you will assign a file name to the string variable before the `OPEN` statement is executed.

Example 4 opens the data file PART.DAT on the default drive for input as filenumber 1. A file opened for input means we plan to read data from it. Later in this project we will show how data can be read from a data file.

Closing Sequential Files

When a program is finished reading or writing to a file, it must close the file with the `CLOSE` statement. The `CLOSE` statement terminates the association between the file and the filenumber assigned in the `OPEN` statement. If a file is being written to, the `CLOSE` statement ensures that the last record is written to the data file.

The general form of the `CLOSE` statement is shown in Figure 5-3.

`CLOSE`

or

`CLOSE` #filenumber$_1$, ..., #filenumber$_n$

FIGURE 5-3
The general form of the CLOSE statement

The `CLOSE` statement terminates access to a data file. For example, `CLOSE #1` causes the data file assigned to filenumber 1 to be closed. Any other files previously opened by the program remain open. Following the close of a specified file, the filenumber may be assigned again to the same file or to a different file by an `OPEN` statement. The keyword `CLOSE` without any filenumber, closes all opened data files.

Note that when executed, the `END` statement closes all opened files before terminating execution of the program.

Writing Data to a Sequential File

To write data to a sequential file, we use the `WRITE #n` statement. The `WRITE #n` statement writes data in a format required by the `INPUT #n` statement. The format requirement is similar to that of the `READ` and `DATA` statements—all data items are separated by commas. The `WRITE #n` statement even goes one step further by surrounding all string data items written to the file with quotation marks.

The general form of the `WRITE #n` statement is shown in Figure 5-4.

FIGURE 5-4
The general form of the WRITE #n statement

```
WRITE #filenumber, variable1, variable2, ..., variablen
```

Consider the `WRITE #n` statement in Figure 5-5. Assume that Part.No$ = 129, Description$ = Hex Bolt, On.Hand = 200, and Wholesale = 1.26. The `WRITE #n` statement transmits the record shown to the sequential file assigned to filenumber 1. The `WRITE #n` statement causes a comma to be placed between the data items in the record. Quotation marks are placed around the values of the string variables Part.No$ and Description$, and a carriage return character ↵ is appended to the last data item written to form the record.

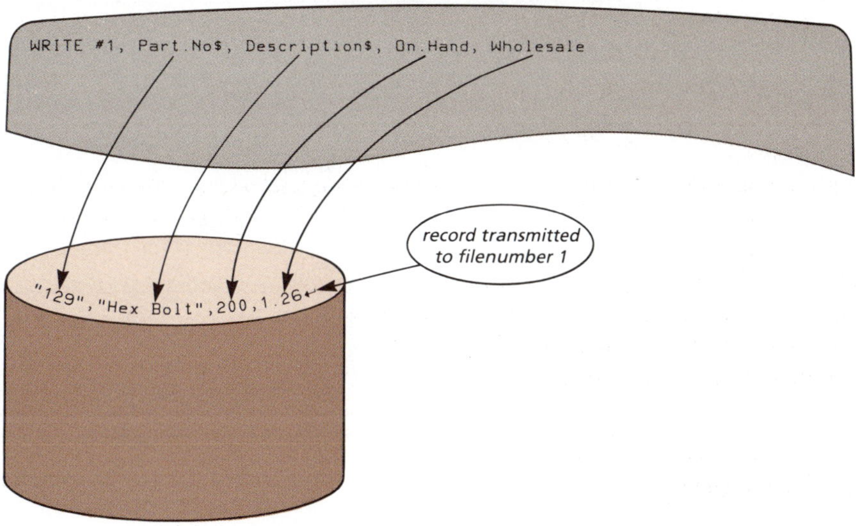

FIGURE 5-5
Writing data to a data file

SAMPLE PROGRAM 5A — CREATING A SEQUENTIAL DATA FILE

In this sample program, we create a sequential data file (PART.DAT) on the B drive from the part data shown in Figure 5-6. The data must be written in a format that is consistent with the `INPUT #n` statement. We use a series of `LOCATE`, `PRINT`, and `INPUT` statements to display the screen on the screen layout form shown on the next page in Figure 5-7. As part of the Wrap-Up module, the number of records written to PART.DAT is displayed.

PART NUMBER	DESCRIPTION	ON HAND	WHOLESALE PRICE
323	Canon PC-25	12	$799.92
432	Timex Watch	53	27.95
567	12 Inch Monitor	34	50.30
578	Epson Printer	23	179.95
745	6 Inch Frying Pan	17	9.71
812	Mr. Coffee	39	21.90
923	4-Piece Toaster	7	17.57

FIGURE 5-6 **The data to be written to the sequential file PART.DAT**

Notice that we are not validating the data entered through the keyboard in this sample program so that we can present a clear-cut example of how to create a sequential file. In a production environment, reasonableness checks are always considered for the part number, description, on hand, and wholesale price. Data should always be validated before it is written to a file.

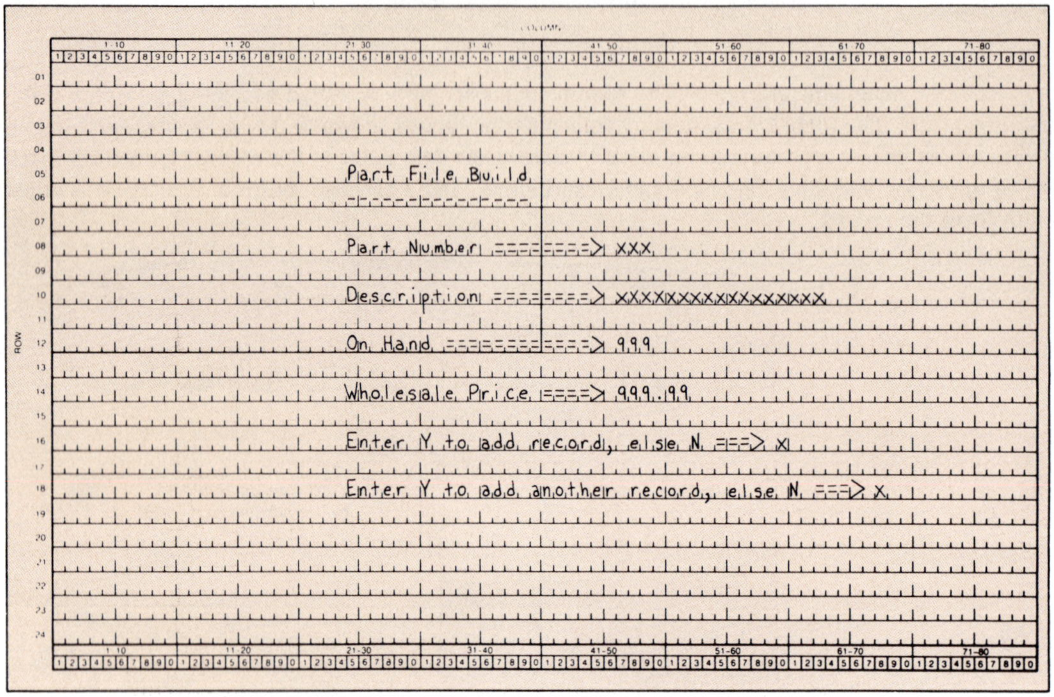

FIGURE 5-7 A screen layout form for Sample Program 5A

A top-down chart, a program flowchart for each module, a program solution, and a discussion of the program solution follow.

Top-Down Chart and Program Flowcharts

Figure 5-8 illustrates the top-down chart and corresponding program flowcharts for each module in Sample Program 5A. In the Initialization module, the record counter is initialized to zero and the data file PART.DAT is opened. The Do-Until loop in the Build File module executes until the user indicates that there are no more records to enter. Within the Do-Until loop, a part record is accepted through the keyboard. After each record is entered, the user must enter the letter Y to add the record. This entry gives the user the opportunity to cancel the record while it is displayed on the screen, but before it is added to PART.DAT. After all the records are entered, the Wrap-Up module displays the number of records written to PART.DAT.

In the program flowcharts, notice that the `OPEN`, `WRITE #n`, and `CLOSE` statements are represented by the Input/Output symbol (parallelogram).

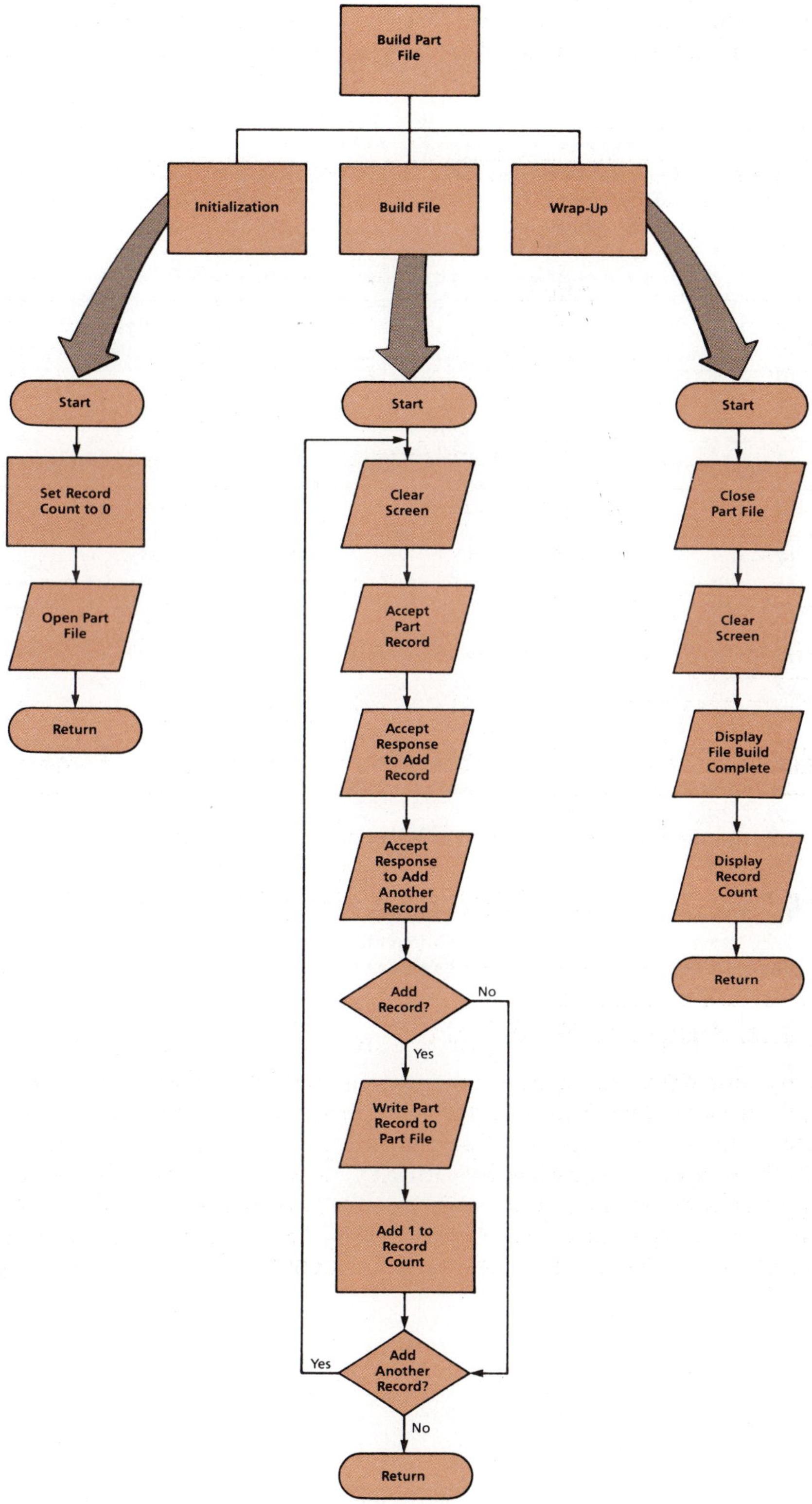

FIGURE 5-8 A top-down chart and corresponding program flowc
for Sample Program 5A

The QuickBASIC Program

The program in Figure 5-9 corresponds to the top-down chart and program flowcharts in Figure 5-8.

FIGURE 5-9
Sample Program 5A

```
' ****************************************************************
' *  Sample Program 5A                          September 15, 1994  *
' *  Build Part File                                                *
' *  J. S. Quasney                                                  *
' *                                                                 *
' *  This program builds the data file PART.DAT.                    *
' *  The user enters each part record through the keyboard.         *
' *  After the record is entered, it is written to PART.DAT.        *
' *       The number of records written to PART.DAT is              *
' *  displayed as part of the Wrap-Up module.                       *
' *                                                                 *
' *  Variables:  Part.No$         -- Part number                    *
' *              Description$     -- Part description               *
' *              On.Hand          -- Number on hand                 *
' *              Wholesale        -- Wholesale price of part        *
' *              Record.Count     -- Count of records added to      *
' *                                    PART.DAT                     *
' *              Add.Rec$         -- Indicates if record is to      *
' *                                    be written to PART.DAT       *
' *              Control$         -- Controls Do-Until loop         *
' ****************************************************************

' ****************************************************************
' *                           Main Module                           *
' ****************************************************************
GOSUB Initialization
GOSUB Build.File
GOSUB Wrap.Up
END

' ****************************************************************
' *                          Initialization                         *
' ****************************************************************
Initialization:
   Record.Count = 0
   OPEN "B:PART.DAT" FOR OUTPUT AS #1
RETURN

```

FIGURE 5-9
(continued)

```
39  ' ***************************************************************
40  ' *                          Build File                         *
41  ' ***************************************************************
42  Build.File:
43     DO
44        CLS  ' Clear Screen
45        LOCATE 5, 25: PRINT "Part File Build"
46        LOCATE 6, 25: PRINT "---------------"
47        LOCATE 8, 25: INPUT "Part Number =======> ", Part.No$
48        LOCATE 10, 25: INPUT "Description =======> ", Description$
49        LOCATE 12, 25: INPUT "On Hand ===========> ", On.Hand
50        LOCATE 14, 25: INPUT "Wholesale Price ===> ", Wholesale
51        LOCATE 16, 25: INPUT "Enter Y to add record, else N ===> ", Add.Rec$
52        LOCATE 18, 25
53        INPUT "Enter Y to add another record, else N ===> ", Control$
54        IF Add.Rec$ = "Y" OR Add.Rec$ = "y" THEN
55           WRITE #1, Part.No$, Description$, On.Hand, Wholesale
56           Record.Count = Record.Count + 1
57        END IF
58     LOOP UNTIL Control$ = "N" OR Control$ = "n"
59  RETURN
60
61  ' ***************************************************************
62  ' *                           Wrap-Up                           *
63  ' ***************************************************************
64  Wrap.Up:
65     CLOSE #1
66     CLS  ' Clear Screen
67     LOCATE 10, 15: PRINT "Creation of PART.DAT is Complete"
68     LOCATE 14, 15
69     PRINT "Total Number of Records in PART.DAT ===>"; Record.Count
70  RETURN
71
72  ' ********************** End of Program **********************
```

Discussion of the Program Solution

When Sample Program 5A is executed, line 36 of the Initialization module opens PART.DAT for output on the B drive as filenumber 1. In the Build File module, lines 45 through 53 of the Do-Until loop accepts data values through the keyboard. The display due to the execution of these lines for the first record entered by the operator is shown on the next page in Figure 5-10. Notice the two messages at the bottom of the screen. The first message (displayed due to line 51) gives the operator the opportunity to reject the transaction by assigning Add.Rec$ a value other than Y (or y). The second message (displayed due to line 53) requests that the operator enter a Y (or y) to add another record to the part file.

Owing to line 54, the part record is added by the `WRITE #n` statement if Add.Rec$ is equal to Y (or y). Line 58 controls the Do-Until loop. If Control$ equals N (or n), then the loop terminates, and control returns to line 28 of the Main module. If Control$ is equal to any other value, then the loop continues.

```
Part File Build
---------------

Part Number ========> 323

Description ========> Canon PC-25

On Hand ============> 12

Wholesale Price ====> 799.92

Enter Y to add record, else N ===> y

Enter Y to add another record, else N ===> y
```

FIGURE 5-10
The display after the first part record is entered due to the execution of Sample Program 5A

The `WRITE #n` statement in line 55 writes the record to the sequential file PART.DAT in a format that is consistent with the `INPUT #n` statement. Figure 5-11 shows the format of the data written to PART.DAT by Sample Program 5A.

```
"323","Canon PC-25",12,799.92
"432","Timex Watch",53,27.95
"567","12 Inch Monitor",34,50.3
"578","Epson Printer",23,179.95
"745","6 Inch Frying Pan",17,9.71
"812","Mr. Coffee",39,21.9
"923","4-Piece Toaster",7,17.57
```

FIGURE 5-11
A listing of PART.DAT created by Sample Program 5A

In the Wrap-Up module, line 65 closes PART.DAT. This ensures that the last record entered by the operator is physically written to the data file on auxiliary storage. Figure 5-12 shows the display due to lines 66 through 69 of the Wrap-Up module.

```
Creation of PART.DAT is Complete

Total Number of Records in PART.DAT ===> 7
```

FIGURE 5-12
The display due to the execution of the Wrap-Up module in Sample Program 5A

READING DATA FROM A SEQUENTIAL DATA FILE

The INPUT #n statement is used to read data from a data file that has been created by using the WRITE #n statement. The EOF function is used to determine when all the records have been processed. The following sections describe how the INPUT #n statement and EOF function work.

The INPUT #n Statement

The INPUT #n statement is similar to the READ statement except that it reads data from a data file instead of from DATA statements. In the following partial program,

```
OPEN "PART.DAT" FOR INPUT AS #1
  .
  .
  .
INPUT #1, Part.No$, Description$, On.Hand, Wholesale
```

the PC reads four data items from the sequential file PART.DAT.

The general form of the INPUT #n statement is shown in Figure 5-13.

```
INPUT #filenumber, variable1, variable2, ..., variablen
```

FIGURE 5-13 The general form of the INPUT #n statement

The EOF Function

When a sequential data file that was opened for output is closed, the PC automatically adds an end-of-file mark after the last record written to the file. Later, when the same sequential file is opened for input, you can use the EOF(n) function to test for the end-of-file mark. The n indicates the filenumber assigned to the file in the OPEN statement.

If the EOF function senses the end-of-file mark, it returns a value of –1 (true). Otherwise, it returns a value of 0 (false). Hence, the EOF function can be used in a DO WHILE statement to control the loop. For example, consider the partial program in Figure 5-14. In the DO WHILE statement, the EOF(1) function is used to control the Do loop. Each time the DO WHILE statement is executed, the PC checks to see whether the data pointer is pointing to the end-of-file mark in PART.DAT.

```
OPEN "PART.DAT" FOR INPUT AS #1
  .
  .
  .
DO WHILE NOT EOF(1)
   INPUT #1, Part.No$, Description$, On.Hand, Wholesale
   LET Record.Count = Record.Count + 1
   LET Total.On.Hand = Total.On.Hand + On.Hand
   LET Part.Cost = On.Hand * Wholesale
   LET Total.Part.Cost = Total.Part.Cost + Part.Cost
   LPRINT USING DL1$; Part.No$; Description$; On.Hand; Wholesale; Part.Cost
LOOP
```

FIGURE 5-14 Using the EOF function to test for end-of-file

When using the EOF function, it is important to organize your program so that the test for the end-of-file precedes the execution of the INPUT #n statement. In Figure 5-14, notice that only one INPUT #n statement is employed, and that this statement is placed inside at the top of the Do loop. This is different from our previous programs which employed two READ statements—one prior to the Do-While loop and one at the bottom of the Do-While loop.

The logic in Figure 5-14 also works when the file is empty (that is, when the file contains no records). If the PART.DAT file is empty, the `OPEN` statement in the partial program still opens the file for input. However, when the `DO WHILE` statement is executed, the `EOF` function immediately detects the end-of-file mark on the empty file, thereby causing control to pass to the statement following the corresponding `LOOP` statement.

SAMPLE PROGRAM 5B — PROCESSING A SEQUENTIAL DATA FILE

In this sample program we will show how to read data and generate a report using the part file (PART.DAT) built by Sample Program 5A. The display shown in Figure 5-15A instructs the user to prepare the printer to receive the report. The report shown in Figure 5-15B contains a detail line for each part number. The total cost for each part is determined by multiplying the number of on hand by the wholesale price.

As part of the end-of-job routine, the sample program prints the number of part records processed, total number of parts in inventory, and the total cost of all the parts.

A. SCREEN DISPLAY

```
Set the paper in the printer to the top of page.

Press the Enter key when the printer is ready...

End of Job
```

B. PRINTED REPORT

```
                    Part Cost Report

Part                                  Wholesale        Part
No.     Description         On Hand   Price            Cost
----    -----------         -------   ---------        ----
323     Canon PC-25              12      799.92    9,599.04
432     Timex Watch              53       27.95    1,481.35
567     12 Inch Monitor          34       50.30    1,710.20
578     Epson Printer            23      179.95    4,138.85
745     6 Inch Frying P          17        9.71      165.07
812     Mr. Coffee               39       21.90      854.10
923     4-Piece Toaster           7       17.57      122.99
                            -------               ---------
                                185               18,071.60

Total Number of Parts =====>      7

End of Job
```

FIGURE 5-15 The screen display (A) and printed report (B) generated by Sample Program 5B

A top-down chart, a program flowchart for each module, a program solution, and a discussion of the program solution follow.

Top-Down Chart and Program Flowcharts

Figure 5-16 illustrates the top-down chart and corresponding program flowcharts for each module in Sample Program 5B.

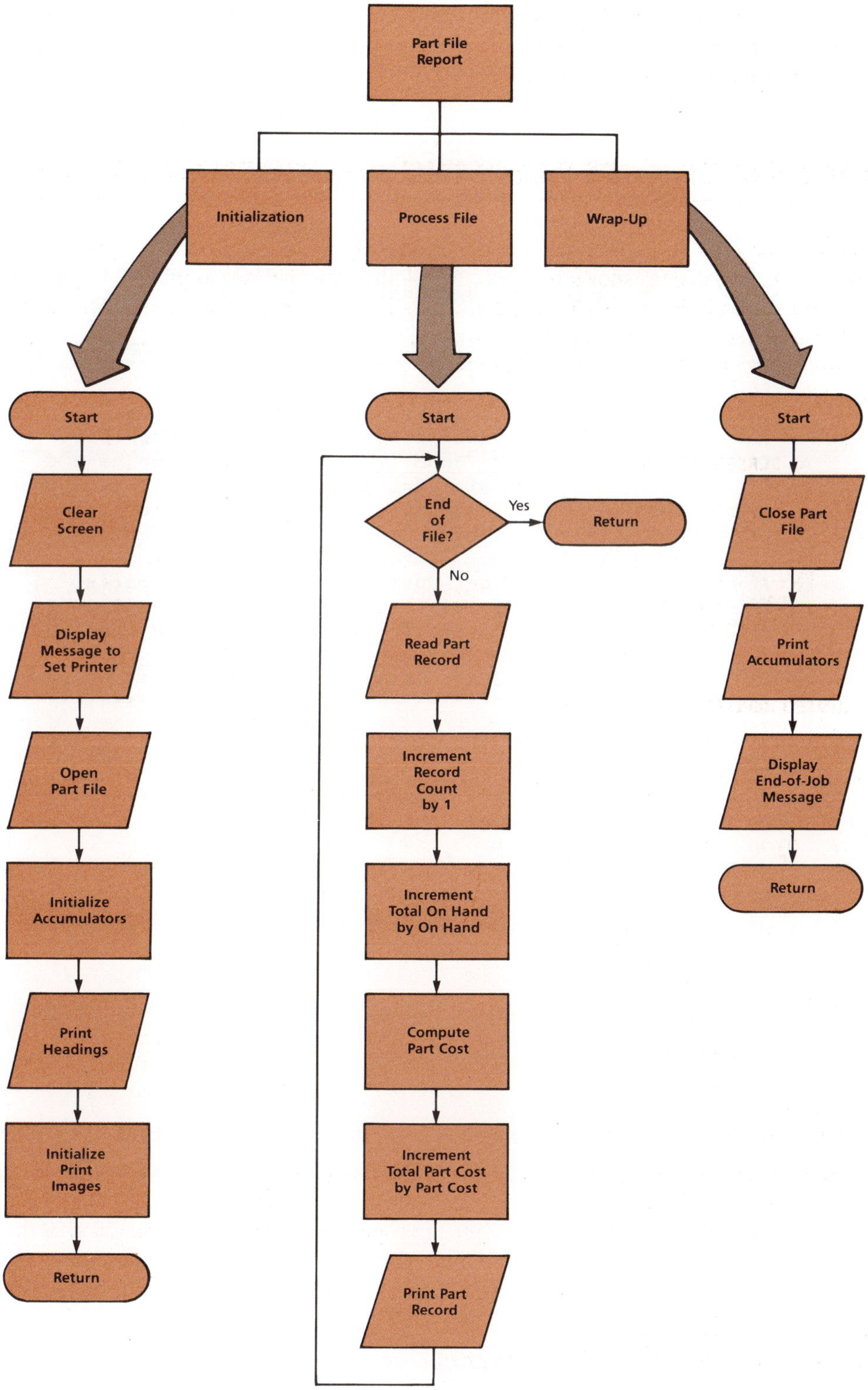

FIGURE 5-16 A top-down chart and corresponding program flowcharts for Sample Program 5B

The QuickBASIC Program

The program in Figure 5-17 corresponds to the top-down chart and program flowcharts in Figure 5-16.

FIGURE 5-17
Sample Program 5B

```
' ****************************************************************
' *  Sample Program 5B                         September 15, 1994 *
' *  Part File Report                                             *
' *  J. S. Quasney                                                *
' *                                                               *
' *  This program reads records from the data file PART.DAT       *
' *  and generates a report on the printer.                       *
' *       The number of part records processed, total pieces      *
' *  in inventory, and the total cost are printed as part of      *
' *  the Wrap-Up module.                                          *
' *                                                               *
' *  Variables:  Part.No$          -- Part number                 *
' *              Description$      -- Part description            *
' *              On.Hand           -- Number on hand              *
' *              Total.On.Hand     -- Total pieces on hand        *
' *              Wholesale         -- Wholesale price of part     *
' *              Record.Count      -- Count of records added to   *
' *                                   PART.DAT                    *
' *              Part.Cost         -- Cost of parts               *
' *              Total.Cost.Part   -- Cost of all parts           *
' *              Control$          -- Response when printer is    *
' *                                   ready                       *
' *              DL1$, TL1$, TL2$, TL3$, TL4$  -- Print Images*
' ****************************************************************

' ****************************************************************
' *                          Main Module                          *
' ****************************************************************
GOSUB Initialization
GOSUB Process.File
GOSUB Wrap.Up
END
```

FIGURE 5-17 (continued)

```
' ****************************************************************
' *                       Initialization                         *
' ****************************************************************
Initialization:
   CLS   ' Clear Screen
   LOCATE 10, 20
   PRINT "Set the paper in the printer to the top of page."
   LOCATE 12, 20
   INPUT "Press the Enter key when the printer is ready...", Control$
   OPEN "B:PART.DAT" FOR INPUT AS #1
   Record.Count = 0
   Total.On.Hand = 0
   Total.Part.Cost = 0
   LPRINT "                   Part Cost Report"
   LPRINT
   LPRINT "Part                                Wholesale      Part"
   LPRINT "No.     Description      On Hand    Price          Cost"
   LPRINT "----    -----------      -------    ---------      ----"
   DL1$ = "\ \     \             \    #,###     #,###.## ##,###.##"
   TL1$ = "                         -------           ---------"
   TL2$ = "                          ##,###          ###,###.##"
   TL3$ = "Total Number of Parts ====>#,###"
   TL4$ = "End of Job"
RETURN

' ****************************************************************
' *                        Process File                          *
' ****************************************************************
Process.File:
   DO WHILE NOT EOF(1)
      INPUT #1, Part.No$, Description$, On.Hand, Wholesale
      LET Record.Count = Record.Count + 1
      LET Total.On.Hand = Total.On.Hand + On.Hand
      LET Part.Cost = On.Hand * Wholesale
      LET Total.Part.Cost = Total.Part.Cost + Part.Cost
      LPRINT USING DL1$; Part.No$; Description$; On.Hand; Wholesale; Part.Cost
   LOOP
RETURN

' ****************************************************************
' *                           Wrap-Up                            *
' ****************************************************************
Wrap.Up:
   CLOSE #1
   LPRINT TL1$
   LPRINT USING TL2$; Total.On.Hand; Total.Part.Cost
   LPRINT
   LPRINT USING TL3$; Record.Count
   LPRINT
   LPRINT TL4$
   LOCATE 14, 20
   PRINT "End of Job"
RETURN

' ********************** End of Program **********************
```

Discussion of the Program Solution

When Sample Program 5B is executed, the screen display and printed report shown earlier in Figure 5-15 on page QB 92 are generated. The following points should be considered in the program solution represented by Sample Program 5B in Figure 5-17.

- Lines 39 through 42 in the Initialization module display on the screen instructions to the user to set the paper in the printer and press the Enter key when ready. Notice how the `INPUT` statement in line 42 temporarily halts the program until the user has prepared the printer to receive the report.
- Line 43 opens the data file PART.DAT on the B drive for input as filenumber 1. Hence, the program can read records from B:PART.DAT.
- The `DO WHILE` statement in line 63 controls the Do-While loop using a condition made up of the `EOF` function. The loop continues to execute while it is not end-of-file.
- Within the Do-While loop, the `INPUT #n` statement in line 64 reads a PART.DAT record by referencing filenumber 1 which was specified in the `OPEN` statement (line 43). After lines 65 through 68 manipulate the data and accumulate totals, line 69 prints the detail line. Line 70 returns control to the `DO WHILE` statement in line 63 which tests for the end-of-file mark.
- When the end-of-file mark is sensed in line 63, control passes to the `RETURN` statement in line 71. Line 71 returns control to line 31 in the Main module. Line 31 calls the Wrap-Up module, which prints the accumulators and displays an end-of-job message on the screen. Finally, control returns to the `END` statement in line 32 and the program terminates execution.

TRY IT YOURSELF EXERCISES

1. Fill in the blanks in the following sentences:
   a. The ____________ statement with a mode of ____________ must be executed before an `INPUT #n` statement is executed.
   b. The ____________ statement must be executed before a `WRITE #n` statement is executed.
   c. The ____________ function is used to test for the end-of-file mark with a sequential data file.
   d. When records are to be added to the end of a sequential data file, the ____________ mode is used in the `OPEN` statement.
2. Assume Cost = 15, Desc$ = Keyboard, and Code = 4. Using commas, quotation marks, and ↵ for end of record, indicate the makeup of the record written to auxiliary storage by the following `WRITE #n` statement:

   ```
   WRITE #1, Cost, Desc$, Code
   ```
3. Explain why the `EOF` function should be used in a condition controlling the loop before the `INPUT #n` statement is executed.
4. A program is to read records from one of three sequential data files: PART1.DAT, PART2.DAT, and PART3.DAT. The three files are stored on the diskette in the A drive. Write three `OPEN` statements that would allow the program to read records from any of the three sequential files.
5. Which of the following are invalid file-handling statements? Why?
   a. `OPEN Seq$ FOR OUTPUT AS #1`
   b. `INPUT #1, Cost,`
   c. `DO WHILE NOT EOF(#2)`
   d. `CLOSE #1`
   e. `WRITE #2, A,`
   f. `OPEN FOR INPUT "INV.DAT" AS #2`
   g. `WRITE #1, USING "####.##"; Cost`

STUDENT ASSIGNMENTS

STUDENT ASSIGNMENT 1: Payroll File Build

Instructions: Design and code a top-down QuickBASIC program to build the payroll file PAYROLL.DAT. Use the sample data shown under INPUT. Generate a screen to receive the data similar to the one under OUTPUT. At the end-of-job, display the number of records written to the data file.

INPUT: Use the following sample data:

EMPLOYEE NUMBER	EMPLOYEE NAME	DEPENDENTS	PAY RATE	HOURS WORKED
23A5	Linda Frat	3	6.75	40
45K8	Joe Smit	1	12.50	38.5
56T1	Lisa Ann	1	16.25	48
65R4	Jeff Max	5	17.75	42
73E6	Susan Dex	2	13.50	40
87Q2	Jeff Web	0	22.45	50
91W2	Marci Jean	3	13.45	40
92R4	Jodi Lin	9	11.50	56
94Y2	Amanda Jo	12	12.75	20
96Y7	Niki Rai	3	16.00	42.5

OUTPUT: The sequential data file PAYROLL.DAT is created in auxiliary storage. The results for the first payroll record are shown below on the left. The results below on the right are displayed prior to termination of the program.

```
Payroll File Build
------------------

Employee Number ========> 23A5

Employee Name ==========> Linda Frat

Number of Dependents ===> 3

Rate of Pay ============> 6.75

Hours Worked ===========> 40

Enter Y to add record, else N ===> y

Enter Y to add another record, else N ===> y
```

```
Creation of PAYROLL.DAT is Complete

Total Number of Records in PAYROLL.DAT ===> 10

Job Complete
```

STUDENT ASSIGNMENT 2: Processing a Payroll File

Instructions: Design and code a top-down QuickBASIC program that generates the messages shown on the screen display under OUTPUT and prints the payroll report under OUTPUT. Apply the following conditions:

1. Gross pay = hours worked × hourly rate.
   Overtime (hours worked > 40) are paid at 1.5 times the hourly rate.
2. Federal withholding tax = 0.2 × (gross pay − dependents × 38.46). Assign federal withholding tax a value of zero if the gross pay less the product of the number of dependents and $38.46 is negative.
3. Net pay = gross pay − federal withholding tax.
4. At the end-of-job, print the number of employees processed, total gross pay, total federal withholding tax, and total net pay.
5. Print the report on the printer.

INPUT: Use the sequential data file PAYROLL.DAT created in Student Assignment 1. If you did not do Student Assignment 1, ask your instructor for a copy of PAYROLL.DAT.

OUTPUT: The following screen with messages and prompts is displayed:

```
Set the paper in the printer to the top of page.

Press the Enter key when the printer is ready...

End of Job
```

The following report prints on the printer:

```
                         Payroll File List

Emp.                            Pay
No.   Name        Dep.  Hours   Rate  Gross Pay   With. Tax  Net Pay
----  ----        ----  -----   ----  ---------   ---------  -------
23A5  Linda Frat    3    40.0   6.75     270.00       30.92   239.08
45K8  Joe Smit      1    38.5  12.50     481.25       88.56   392.69
56T1  Lisa Ann      1    48.0  16.25     845.00      161.31   683.69
65R4  Jeff Max      5    42.0  17.75     763.25      114.19   649.06
73E6  Susan Dex     2    40.0  13.50     540.00       92.62   447.38
87Q2  Jeff Web      0    50.0  22.45   1,234.75      246.95   987.80
91W2  Marci Jean    3    40.0  13.45     538.00       84.52   453.48
92R4  Jodi Lin      9    56.0  11.50     736.00       77.97   658.03
94Y2  Amanda Jo    12    20.0  12.75     255.00        0.00   255.00
96Y7  Niki Rai      3    42.5  16.00     700.00      116.92   583.08

Total Employees =======>     10
Total Gross Pay =======>  6,363.25
Total Tax =============>  1,013.97
Total Net Pay =========>  5,349.28

End of Payroll Report
```

PROJECT 6

Arrays and Functions

In the previous projects we used simple variables such as Count, Emp.Name$, and Balance to store and access data in a program. In this project we discuss variables that can store more than one value under the same name. Variables that can hold more than one value at a time are called **arrays**.

An array is often used to store a **table** of organized data. Income tax tables, insurance tables, or sales tax tables are examples of tables that can be stored in an array for processing purposes. Once the table elements are assigned to an array, the array can be searched to extract the proper values.

Functions are used to handle common mathematical and string operations. For example, it is often necessary in programming to obtain the square root of a number or extract a substring from a string of characters. Without functions, these types of operations would require that you write sophisticated routines in your program. Functions clearly simplify the programming task.

Although we discuss only the most frequently used functions, you should be aware that QuickBASIC has over 70 built-in functions to aid you in your programming. For a summary of all the functions available in QuickBASIC, refer to pages R.4 and R.5 of the reference card in the back of this book.

ARRAYS

The banking application in Figure 6-1 illustrates an example of table processing. The account number, name of the account holder, and account balance of individuals who have savings are stored in arrays. When the teller enters account number 20013, the program searches the account number array to find an equal account number.

When the equal account number is found, the corresponding name (Darla Simmons) and the corresponding balance (932.49) are *pulled* from the table and displayed on the screen.

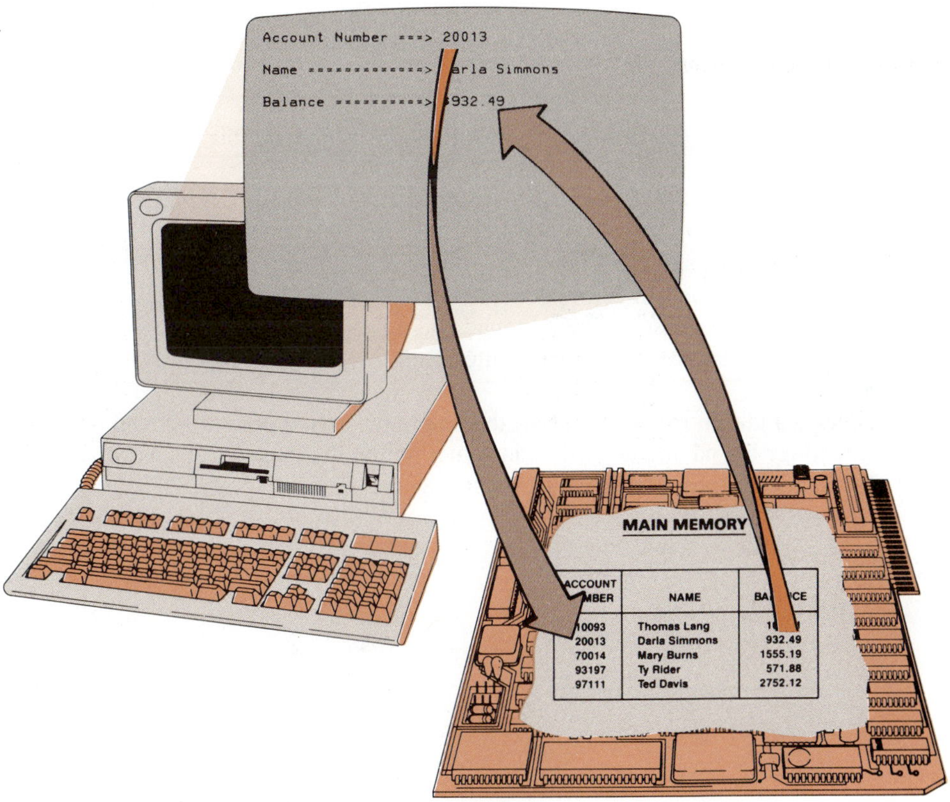

FIGURE 6-1
An example of table processing

THE DIM STATEMENT

Before arrays can be used, they must be declared in a program. This is the purpose of the DIM statement, also called the dimension statement. The general form of the DIM statement is shown in Figure 6-2.

> DIM array-name(lb_1 TO ub_1), ..., array-name(lb_1 TO ub_n)
>
> where **array-name** is a variable name, **lb_1** is a positive or negative integer or numeric variable that serves as the lower-bound value of the array, and **ub_n** is a positive or negative integer or numeric variable that serves as the upper-bound value of the array.

FIGURE 6-2 The general form of the DIM statement

Figure 6-3 illustrates several examples of declaring arrays. Example 1 reserves storage for a one-dimensional numeric array Tax, which consists of 5 elements, or storage locations. These elements—Tax(1), Tax(2), Tax(3), Tax(4), and Tax(5)—can be used in a program the same way in which a simple variable can be used. Notice that the elements of an array are distinguished from one another by **subscripts** that follow the array name within parentheses.

EXAMPLE	DIM STATEMENT
1	`DIM Tax(1 TO 5)`
2	`DIM Job.Code$(1 TO 15), Bonus(1 TO 15)`
3	`DIM Part.No$(Begin TO Fin), Des(Begin TO Fin)`
4	`DIM Function.Tax(1 TO 50, 1 TO 25)`
5	`DIM Inventory.No$(15 TO 35)`
6	`DIM X(-5 TO 10)`

FIGURE 6-3 Examples of the DIM statement

Example 2 in Figure 6-3 declares two arrays—Job.Code$ and Bonus. Both arrays are declared to have 15 elements. Thus, Job.Code$(1) through Job.Code$(15) and Bonus(1) through Bonus(15) can be referenced in the program containing the DIM statement. Job.Code$(0) and Job.Code$(16) do not exist according to the DIM statement, and therefore, should not be referenced. You may declare as many arrays in a DIM statement as required by the program.

Example 3 illustrates that the lower-bound and upper-bound values can be variables that are assigned a value prior to the execution of the DIM statement. Example 4 illustrates a two-dimensional array. QuickBASIC allows an array to have up to 60 dimensions.

Examples 5 and 6 in Figure 6-3 show that the lower-bound of an array can be a value different from 1. It is important to note that the lower-bound and upper-bound values define the range of the array. Any subscript reference that is outside the range will cause a diagnostic message to display.

SAMPLE PROGRAM 6 — CUSTOMER ACCOUNT TABLE LOOKUP

In this sample program we implement the banking application shown on page QB 99 in Figure 6-1. The account number, name of the account holder, and account balance of customers who have savings accounts are shown in Figure 6-4. The table data is stored in the sequential data file ACCOUNTS.DAT. ACCOUNTS.DAT includes a data item (5) prior to the first account record that is equal to the number of records in the data file.

ACCOUNT NUMBER	CUSTOMER NAME	BALANCE
10093	Thomas Lang	$ 100.51
20013	Darla Simmons	932.49
70014	Mary Burns	1,555.19
93197	Ty Rider	571.88
97111	Ted Davis	2,752.12

FIGURE 6-4 The table data stored in ACCOUNTS.DAT

The screen display in Figure 6-5 illustrates the output results when the user enters account number 70014. When the user enters the account number, the program should direct the PC to *look up* and display the corresponding customer name and balance. The message at the bottom of the screen in Figure 6-5 asks the user to enter the letter Y to look up another account or the letter N to terminate the program.

If the account number is not found in the table, a diagnostic error displays.

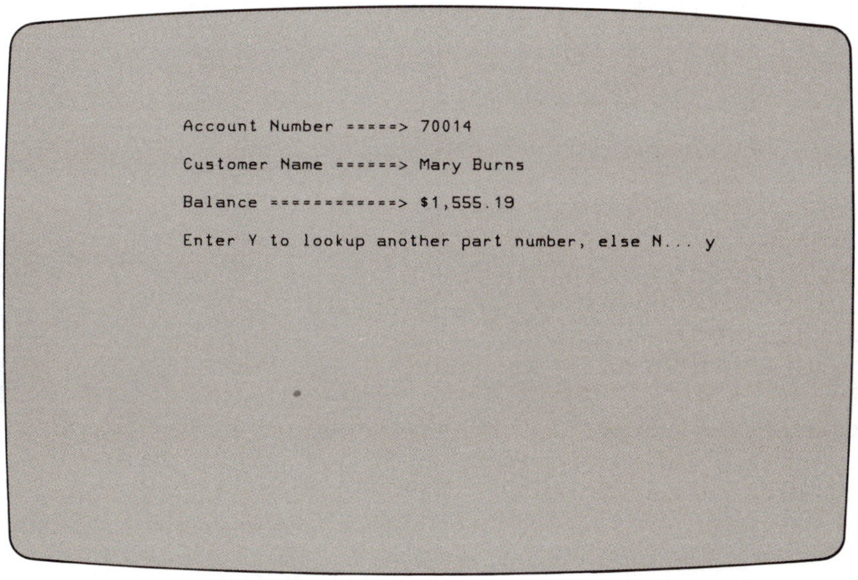

FIGURE 6-5
The display due to the execution of Sample Program 6 and the entering of account number 70014

A top-down chart, a program flowchart for each module, a program solution, and a discussion of the program solution follow.

Top-Down Chart and Program Flowcharts

The top-down chart and corresponding program flowcharts that illustrate the logic for the Sample Program 6 are shown in Figure 6-6.

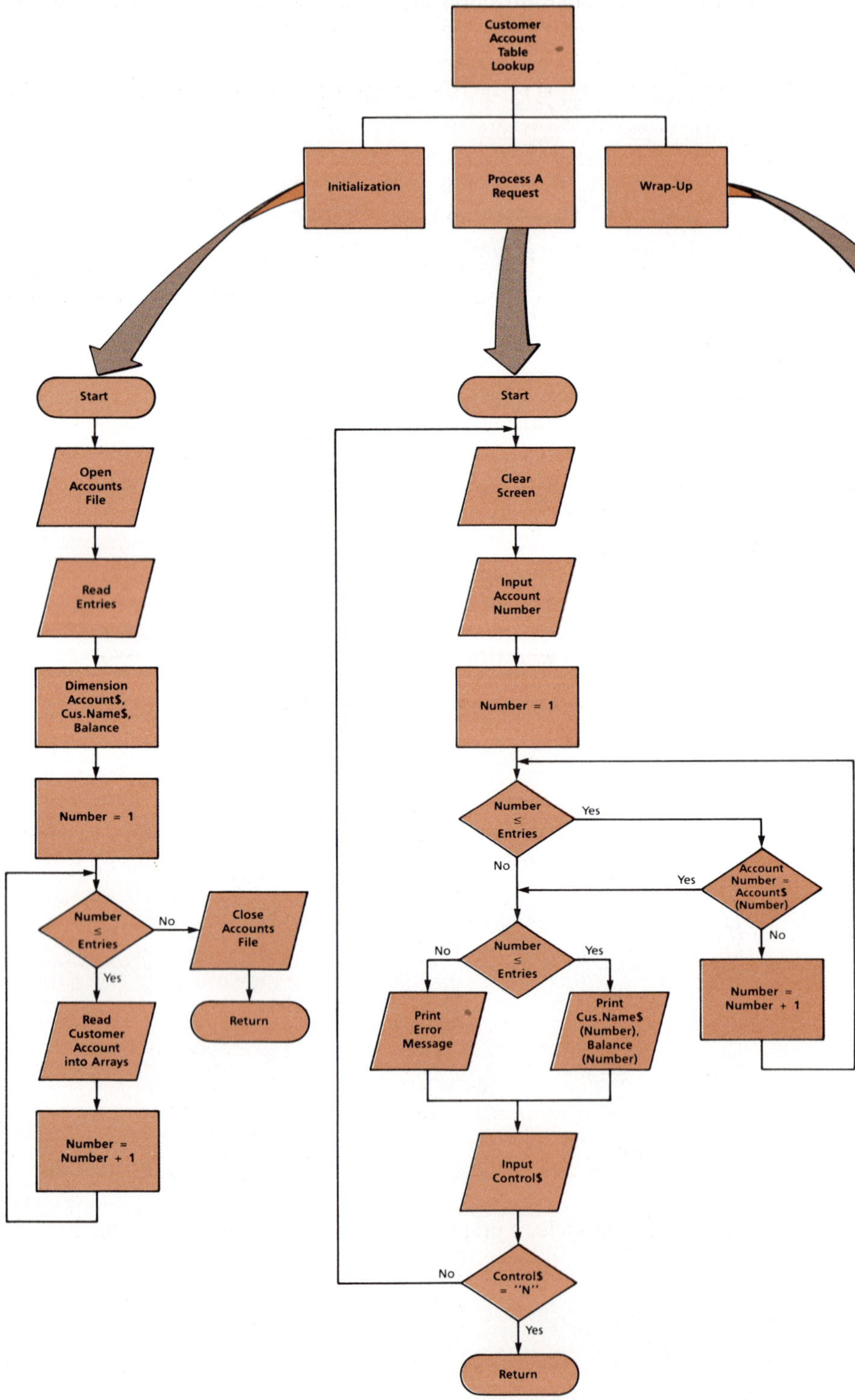

FIGURE 6-6 A top-down chart and corresponding program flowcharts for Sample Program 6

In the Initialization module in Figure 6-6, ACCOUNTS.DAT is opened and the number of records in the account file is read. This value is used to dimension the three arrays that will hold the account information. Next, the same value is used to control a Do-While loop that assigns the account information to the three arrays. After the Do-While loop is finished, ACCOUNTS.DAT is closed.

In the Process A Request module, the program accepts the account number from the user. A Do-While loop is then used to search the array that contains the account numbers. If the search is successful, the customer name and balance display. If the search is unsuccessful, a diagnostic message displays. Finally, the user is asked if he or she wants to enter another account number.

When the user enters the letter N (or n), control returns to the Main module and the Wrap-Up module displays an end-of-job message.

The QuickBASIC Program

The QuickBASIC code in Figure 6-7 corresponds to the top box in the top-down chart in Figure 6-6. The GOSUB statements call the subordinate modules. Following the return of control from the Wrap-Up module, the END statement terminates execution of the program.

```
' ****************************************************************
' *                        Main Module                           *
' ****************************************************************
GOSUB Initialization
GOSUB Process.Request
GOSUB Wrap.Up
END
```

FIGURE 6-7 The Main module for Sample Program 6

Initialization Module The Initialization module for Sample Program 6 is shown in Figure 6-8. The primary objective of this module is to load the data in ACCOUNTS.DAT into the arrays. Line 35 opens ACCOUNTS.DAT on the B drive. Line 36 assigns the first data item in ACCOUNTS.DAT to the variable Entries. Entries is then assigned the value 5. Line 37 dimensions the three arrays with an upper-bound value equal to Entries. The For loop in lines 38 through 40 reads the data in ACCOUNTS.DAT into the three arrays. Arrays Account$, Cus.Name$, and Balance, therefore contain the data in ACCOUNTS.DAT. Since each array contains data that corresponds to the other arrays, we call them **parallel arrays**. Line 41 closes ACCOUNTS.DAT before control is returned to the Main module.

```
31  ' ****************************************************************
32  ' *                          Initialization                      *
33  ' ****************************************************************
34  Initialization:
35     OPEN "B:ACCOUNTS.DAT" FOR INPUT AS #1
36     INPUT #1, Entries
37     DIM Account$(1 TO Entries), Cus.Name$(1 TO Entries), Balance(1 TO Entries)
38     FOR Number = 1 TO Entries
39        INPUT #1, Account$(Number), Cus.Name$(Number), Balance(Number)
40     NEXT Number
41     CLOSE #1
42  RETURN
```

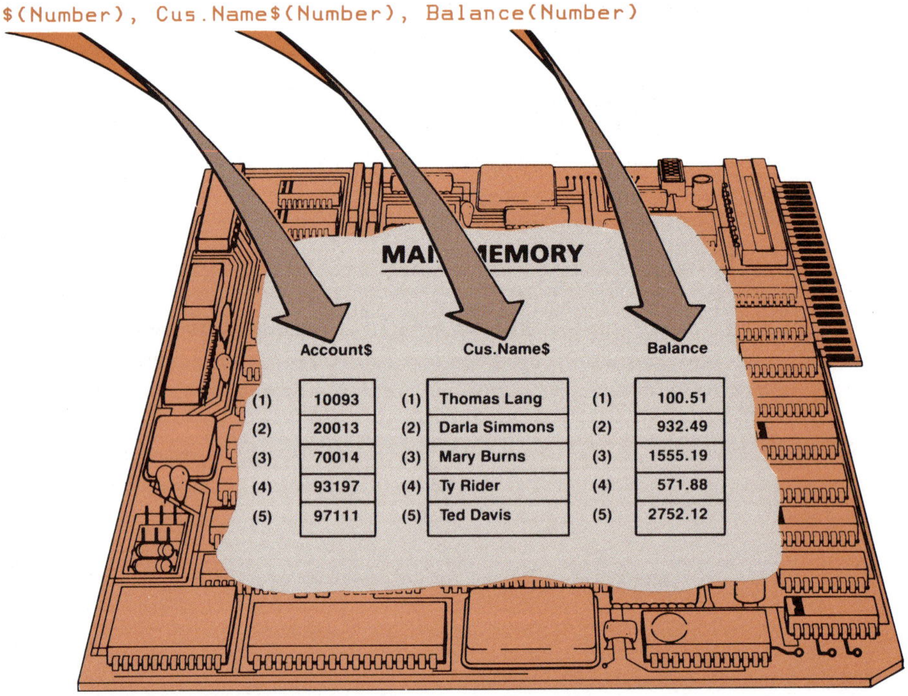

FIGURE 6-8 The Initialization module for Sample Program 6

Process A Request Module After the data in ACCOUNTS.DAT is loaded into the arrays and control passes back to the Main module, line 27 transfers control to the Process A Request module (Figure 6-9). This module begins by clearing the screen and accepting the account number from the user. The account number is assigned to the variable Search.Argument$ (line 51).

```
44  ' ***************************************************************
45  ' *                      Process A Request                     *
46  ' ***************************************************************
47  Process.Request:
48     DO
49        CLS   ' Clear Screen
50        LOCATE 5, 15
51        INPUT "Account Number =====> ", Search.Argument$
52        FOR Number = 1 TO Entries
53           IF Search.Argument$ = Account$(Number) THEN
54              EXIT FOR     ' Process a Table Hit
55           END IF
56        NEXT Number
57        IF Number <= Entries THEN
58           LOCATE 7, 15
59           PRINT "Customer Name ======> "; Cus.Name$(Number)
60           LOCATE 9, 15
61           PRINT USING "Balance ============> $$,###.##"; Balance(Number)
62        ELSE
63           LOCATE 7, 15
64           PRINT "Account Number "; Search.Argument$; " NOT FOUND"
65        END IF
66        LOCATE 11, 15
67        INPUT "Enter Y to lookup another part number, else N... ", Control$
68     LOOP UNTIL Control$ = "N" OR Control$ = "n"
69  RETURN
```

FIGURE 6-9 The Process A Request module for Sample Program 6

The For loop in lines 52 through 56 of Figure 6-9 searches the Account$ array for a match with Search.Argument$. Each time through the loop, the `IF` statement (line 53) compares Search.Argument$ to the next element in Account$ until a *hit* is made. When a *hit* occurs, the `EXIT FOR` statement in line 54 causes a premature exit from the For loop and control passes to line 57. If no *hit* occurs, a normal exit from the For loop also passes control to line 57.

Line 57 determines if the search for the account number in Account$ was successful. If the search was successful, then Number is less than or equal to Entries. In this case, the customer number and balance from the two corresponding arrays are displayed using the value of Number for the subscript. Figure 6-10 shows the display due to a successful search.

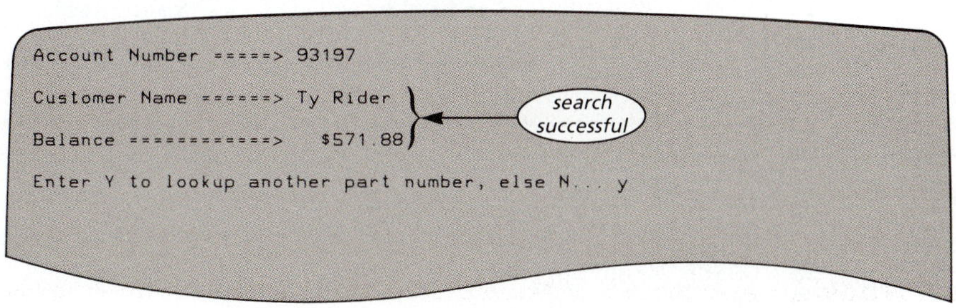

FIGURE 6-10 The display from Sample Program 6 due to entering the account number 93197

If the search is unsuccessful, then Number is greater than Entries and the diagnostic message in line 64 displays as shown in Figure 6-11. Note that if there is a premature exit from the For loop, the search is successful. If the For loop ends normally, the search is unsuccessful.

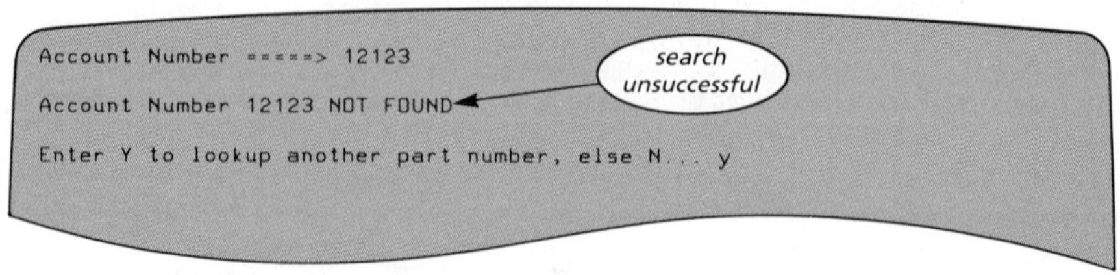

FIGURE 6-11
The display from Sample Program 6 due to entering the invalid account number 12123

After the true or false task in the `IF` statement (lines 57 through 65) is executed, line 67 requests that the user enter the letter `Y` to process another account number or the letter `N` to terminate execution of the program.

The complete QuickBASIC program is shown in Figure 6-12.

FIGURE 6-12
Sample Program 6

```
1   ' ****************************************************************
2   ' *  Sample Program 6                         September 15, 1994  *
3   ' *  Customer Account Table Lookup                                *
4   ' *  J. S. Quasney                                                *
5   ' *                                                               *
6   ' *  This program loads the data in ACCOUNTS.DAT into arrays.    *
7   ' *  The user enters the account number and the program looks    *
8   ' *  up and displays the customer number and account balance.    *
9   ' *       If the account number is not found, then a             *
10  ' *  diagnostic message is displayed.  After processing a        *
11  ' *  request, the user is asked if he or she wishes to           *
12  ' *  display information of another account or terminate the     *
13  ' *  program.                                                    *
14  ' *                                                               *
15  ' *  Variables: Account$          -- Account number array        *
16  ' *             Cus.Name$         -- Customer name array         *
17  ' *             Balance           -- Customer balance array      *
18  ' *             Search.Argument$  -- Account number requested    *
19  ' *             Control$          -- Response to continue        *
20  ' *             Entries           -- Number of customers         *
21  ' ****************************************************************
22
23  ' ****************************************************************
24  ' *                        Main Module                            *
25  ' ****************************************************************
26  GOSUB Initialization
27  GOSUB Process.Request
28  GOSUB Wrap.Up
29  END
30
```

FIGURE 6-12 (continued)

```
' **************************************************************
' *                       Initialization                        *
' **************************************************************
Initialization:
   OPEN "B:ACCOUNTS.DAT" FOR INPUT AS #1
   INPUT #1, Entries
   DIM Account$(1 TO Entries), Cus.Name$(1 TO Entries), Balance(1 TO Entries)
   FOR Number = 1 TO Entries
      INPUT #1, Account$(Number), Cus.Name$(Number), Balance(Number)
   NEXT Number
   CLOSE #1
RETURN

' **************************************************************
' *                      Process A Request                      *
' **************************************************************
Process.Request:
   DO
      CLS  ' Clear Screen
      LOCATE 5, 15
      INPUT "Account Number =====> ", Search.Argument$
      FOR Number = 1 TO Entries
         IF Search.Argument$ = Account$(Number) THEN
            EXIT FOR   ' Process a Table Hit
         END IF
      NEXT Number
      IF Number <= Entries THEN
         LOCATE 7, 15
         PRINT "Customer Name ======> "; Cus.Name$(Number)
         LOCATE 9, 15
         PRINT USING "Balance ============> $$,###.##"; Balance(Number)
      ELSE
         LOCATE 7, 15
         PRINT "Account Number "; Search.Argument$; " NOT FOUND"
      END IF
      LOCATE 11, 15
      INPUT "Enter Y to lookup another part number, else N... ", Control$
   LOOP UNTIL Control$ = "N" OR Control$ = "n"
RETURN

' **************************************************************
' *                           Wrap-Up                           *
' **************************************************************
Wrap.Up:
   LOCATE 13, 15
   PRINT "Job Complete"
RETURN
' ********************** End of Program **********************
```

FUNCTIONS

QuickBASIC includes over 70 numeric and string functions. Numeric functions are used to handle common mathematical calculations. String functions are used to manipulate strings of characters.

Numeric Functions

Three of the most frequently used numeric functions are the INT, SQR, and RND functions. The purpose of these functions is summarized in Figure 6-13.

FUNCTION	FUNCTION VALUE
INT(X)	Returns the largest integer that is less than or equal to the argument X.
SQR(X)	Returns the square root of the argument X.
RND	Returns a random number greater than or equal to zero and less than 1.

FIGURE 6-13 Frequently used numeric functions

INT Function The INT function returns a whole number that is less than or equal to the argument. Figure 6-14 shows several examples of the INT function.

VALUE OF VARIABLE	QuickBASIC STATEMENT	RESULT
X = 12.45	LET Y = INT(X)	Y = 12
H = 27.89	LET G = INT(H + 10)	G = 37
J = -15.67	LET K = INT(J)	K = -16

FIGURE 6-14 Examples of the INT function

SQR Function The SQR function computes the square root of the argument. Figure 6-15 illustrates several examples of the SQR function. Note that the argument for the SQR function must be a non-negative value.

VALUE OF VARIABLE	QuickBASIC STATEMENT	RESULT
Y = 4	LET X = SQR(Y)	X = 2
D = 27	LET P = SQR(D * 3)	P = 9
E = -16	LET U = SQR(E)	Illegal Function Call

FIGURE 6-15 Examples of the SQR function

RND Function The RND function returns an unpredictable number that is greater than or equal to zero and less than 1. The partial program in Figure 6-16 uses a For loop and the RND function to generate three random numbers — .7132002, .6291881, and .3409873.

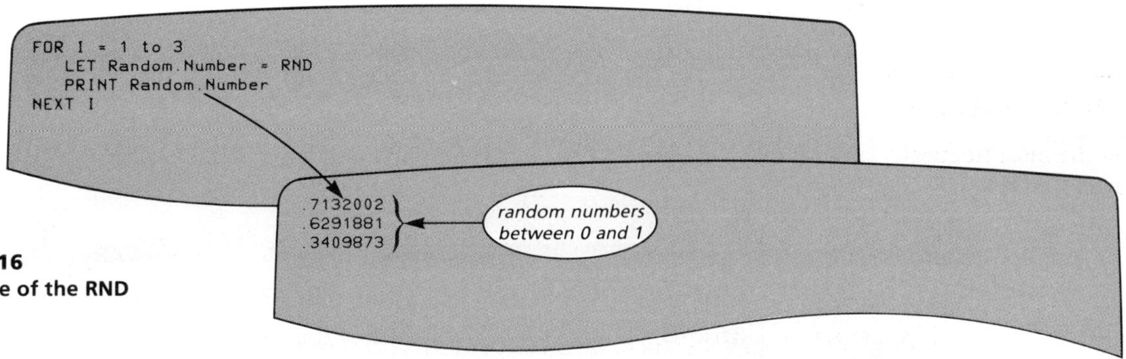

FIGURE 6-16
An example of the RND function

The INT and RND functions can be used to generate random digits over any range. The following expression generates random numbers between L and U:

```
INT((U - L + 1) * RND + L)
```

For example, to simulate the roll of a six-sided die, we can write the following:

```
LET Die = INT((6 - 1 + 1) * RND + 1)
```

or

```
LET Die = INT(6 * RND + 1)
```

In Figure 6-17, the For loop generates five rolls of two dice. The first LET statement represents the roll of one die and the second LET statement represents the roll of the second die.

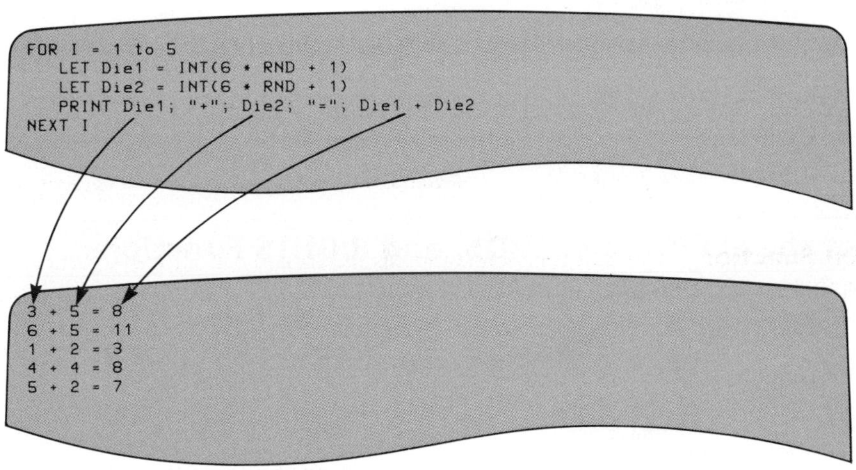

FIGURE 6-17
An example of a partial program that simulates five rolls of two dice

Each time you run the program in Figure 6-17, it generates the same sequence of random numbers. To generate a new sequence of random numbers each time you execute the program, insert the RANDOMIZE statement at the top of the program. When executed, the RANDOMIZE statement requests that you enter a number between –32768 and 32767. The value you enter is used by the PC to develop a new set of random numbers.

String Functions

The capability to process strings is important in business applications. In QuickBASIC, you can join two strings together through the use of the concatenation operator (+). For example, the following LET statement:

```
LET Join$ = "ABC" + "DEF"
```

assigns the variable Join$ the value ABCDEF. Besides the concatenation operator, QuickBASIC includes over 25 functions that allow you to manipulate string values.

The most frequently used string functions are shown in Figure 6-18.

FUNCTION	FUNCTION VALUE
DATE$	Returns the system date as a string in the form mm-dd-yyyy.
LEFT$(S$, X)	Returns the leftmost X characters of the string argument S$.
LEN(S$)	Returns the number of characters in the string argument S$.
MID$(S$, P, X)	Returns X characters from the string argument S$ beginning at position P.
RIGHT$(S$, X)	Returns the rightmost X characters of the string argument S$.
TIME$	Returns the system time of day as a string in the form HH:MM:SS.

FIGURE 6-18 Frequently used string functions

The DATE$ and TIME$ Functions The DATE$ and TIME$ functions return the DOS system date and time. For example, if the system date is initialized to September 15, 1994, then the statement PRINT "The date is "; DATE$ displays the following result:

```
The date is 09-15-1994
```

If the system time is equal to 11:44:42, then the statement PRINT "The time is "; TIME$ displays the following result:

```
The time is 11:44:42
```

The system time is maintained in 24-hour notation. That is, 1:30 P.M. displays as 13:30:00.

Use of the LEFT$, LEN, MID$, and RIGHT$ Functions

The LEN(S$) function returns the number of characters in S$. For example, the following LET statement assigns Length the value 5 because there are 5 characters in the string BASIC:

```
LET Length = LEN("BASIC")
```

The LET statement LET Number = LEN(DATE$) assigns Number the value 10 because there are 10 characters in the system date (mm/dd/yyyy).

The LEFT$, MID$, and RIGHT$ functions are used to extract substrings from a string. Figure 6-19 illustrates several examples of these functions.

VALUE OF VARIABLE	QuickBASIC STATEMENT	RESULT
Assume S$ is equal to `GOTO is a four-letter word`		
1	`LET Q$ = LEFT$(S$, 7)`	`Q$ = GOTO is`
2	`LET W$ = LEFT$(S$, 4)`	`W$ = GOTO`
3	`LET D$ = RIGHT$(S$, 11)`	`D$ = letter word`
4	`LET K$ = RIGHT$(S$, 1)`	`K$ = d`
5	`LET M$ = MID$(S$, 6, 2)`	`M$ = is`
6	`LET T$ = MID$(S$, 16, 6)`	`T$ = letter`

FIGURE 6-19 Examples of the LEFT$, RIGHT$, and MID$ functions

QuickBASIC also allows the argument to include a function. For example, if the system date is 9/15/94, then the `LET` statement `LET Day$ = MID$(DATE$, 4, 2)` assigns Day$ the string value `15`. If the system time is equal to 10:32:52, then the `LET` statement `LET Second$ = MID$(Time$, 7, 2)` assigns Second$ the string value `52`.

Consider the partial program in Figure 6-20 and the corresponding output results. Lines 1 and 2 display the system date and time. Lines 4 through 6 display on separate lines the substrings month, day, and year. Lines 8 through 10 display on separate lines the substrings hour, minute, and second.

```
1  PRINT "The date is "; DATE$
2  PRINT "The time is "; TIME$
3  PRINT
4  PRINT "The month is "; LEFT$(DATE$, 2)
5  PRINT "The day is "; MID$(DATE$, 4, 2)
6  PRINT "The year is "; RIGHT$(DATE$, 4)
7  PRINT
8  PRINT "The hour is "; LEFT$(TIME$, 2)
9  PRINT "The minute is "; MID$(TIME$, 4, 2)
10 PRINT "The second is "; RIGHT$(TIME$, 2)
```

```
The date is 09-15-1994
The time is 10:32:52

The month is 09
The day is 15
The year is 1994

The hour is 10
The minute is 32
The second is 52
```

FIGURE 6-20 An example of a partial program that uses string functions. Assume system date is 9/15/94 and system time is 10:32:52

TRY IT YOURSELF EXERCISES

1. What is displayed when the following programs are executed?

   a.
   ```
   ' Exercise 1.a
   City$ = "Los Angeles"
   PRINT LEFT$(City$, 1) + MID$(City$, 5, 1) + " LAW"
   END
   ```
   b.
   ```
   ' Exercise 1.b
   PRINT "Number", "Square", "Square Root"
   FOR I = 1 TO 10
      PRINT I, I ^ 2, SQR(I)
   NEXT I
   END
   ```

2. Assume arrays Part and Cost are dimensioned by the statement `DIM Part(1 TO 5), Cost(1 TO 5)`. Assume that the two arrays were loaded with the following values:

ARRAY PART	ARRAY COST
15	1.23
71	2.34
92	.25
94	1.37
99	5.25

   Indicate how you would reference the following values using subscripts. For example, .25 can be referenced by Cost(3).
   a. 71 b. 5.25 c. 2.34 d. 15 e. 1.37 f. 1.23 g. 99

3. Write a `DIM` statement to minimally dimension array X so that subscripts in the range 1 to 900 are valid and array Y so that subscripts in the range –5 to 22 are valid.
4. Given that array G has been declared to have 10 elements (1 to 10), assume that each element of G has a value. Write a partial program that includes a `DIM` statement to shift all the values up one location. That is, assign G(1) to G(2), G(2) to G(3), and G(10) to G(1).
5. Identify the errors, if any, in each of the following:
   a. `DIM Amt(1 TO -1)` b. `DIM Bal (1 TOO 10)`
   c. `DIM Sales` d. `DIM (1 TO 35)X`
6. Indicate what each of the following are equal to. Assume Phrase$ is equal to `Aim the arrow carefully.`
   a. `LEN(Phrase$)` b. `MID$(Phrase$, 4, 3)`
   c. `LEFT$(Phrase$, 13)` d. `RIGHT$(Phrase$, 5)`
7. Assume that the system date is equal to December 25, 1994 and the system time is equal to 11:12:15. Evaluate the following:
   a. `X$ = TIME$`
   b. `X$ = MID$(TIME$, 4, 1)`
   c. `X$ = RIGHT$(DATE$, 2)`
   d. `X$ = LEFT$(DATE$, 2)`

8. Write a LET statement that assigns Number a random value between 1 and 52.
9. Explain the purpose of the RANDOMIZE statement.
10. What does each of the following equal?

a. INT(23.46)	b. SQR(121)
c. LEN("ABC")	d. INT(-12.43)
e. SQR(SQR(81))	f. SQR(INT(36.57))

STUDENT ASSIGNMENTS

STUDENT ASSIGNMENT 1: Phone Number Lookup

Instructions: Design and code a top-down QuickBASIC program that requests a person's last name and displays the person's telephone number.

Read the data shown in the phone number table under INPUT into parallel arrays from a sequential data file or DATA statements. If you plan to use a sequential data file, ask your instructor for a copy of PHONE.DAT.

Accept a person's last name in lowercase from the user. Search the last name array. If the search is successful, display the corresponding telephone number. If the search is unsuccessful, display a diagnostic message. After the search, ask the user if he or she wants to look up another telephone number. The output results should be similar to the displayed results shown under OUTPUT.

INPUT: Use the following phone number table data. Include a value at the beginning of the file which indicates the number of elements required in the parallel arrays that will hold the names and phone numbers.

Look up the phone numbers of the following individuals: fuqua, bingle, smith, and course.

NAME	PHONE NUMBER
miller	(213) 430-2865
flaming	(213) 866-9082
fuqua	(714) 925-3391
bingle	(805) 402-3376
course	(213) 423-7765

OUTPUT: The following results are displayed for bingle and smith:

```
Person's Name =====> bingle
Phone Number ======> (805) 402-3376
Enter Y to lookup another phone number, Else N... y
```

```
Person's Name =====> smith
The Name smith NOT FOUND
Enter Y to lookup another phone number, Else N... y
```

STUDENT ASSIGNMENT 2: Weight Table Lookup

Instructions: Design and code a top-down QuickBASIC program that accepts a male or female height and displays the average weight ranges for a small-framed, medium-framed, and large-framed person. If the search is unsuccessful, display an error message. The table entries are shown in the height and weight table data under INPUT. The output results are shown under OUTPUT.

INPUT: Use the following height and weight table data. Read the table data into two separate sets of parallel arrays, one for the male weights and one for the female weights, by means of a data file or `DATA` statements. If you plan to use a sequential data file, ask your instructor for a copy of WEIGHT.DAT. Initialize a variable to nine (the number of different heights for males and for females prior to the `DIM` statement). Use this variable to dimension the arrays and control any loops that search for heights. Look up the following:

Sex – Male, Height – 72
Sex – Female, Height – 64
Sex – Male, Height – 76
Sex – Female, Height – 72
Sex – Male, Height – 70

MEN

HEIGHT	SMALL FRAME	MEDIUM FRAME	LARGE FRAME
66	124–133	130–143	138–156
67	128–136	134–147	142–161
68	132–141	138–152	147–168
69	136–145	142–156	151–170
70	140–150	146–160	155–174
71	144–154	150–165	159–179
72	148–158	154–170	164–184
73	152–162	158–175	168–189
74	156–167	162–180	173–194

WOMEN

HEIGHT	SMALL FRAME	MEDIUM FRAME	LARGE FRAME
62	102–110	107–119	115–131
63	105–113	110–122	118–134
64	108–116	113–126	121–138
65	111–119	116–130	125–142
66	114–123	120–135	129–148
67	118–127	124–139	133–150
68	122–131	128–43	137–154
69	126–135	132–147	141–158
70	130–140	136–151	145–163

OUTPUT: The following screen displays for the first set of data under INPUT:

```
Person's Sex (M or F) ========> M

Person's Height in Inches
Male 66-74, Female 62-70) ====> 72

Small Frame Weight Range =====> 148-158

Medium Frame Weight Range ====> 154-170

Large Frame Weight Range =====> 164-184

Enter a Y to lookup another weight range, else N... Y
```

APPENDIX

QuickBASIC Debugging Techniques

Although the top-down approach and structured programming techniques help minimize errors, they by no means guarantee error-free programs. Owing to carelessness or insufficient thought, program portions can be constructed which do not work as anticipated and give erroneous results. When such problems occur, you need techniques to isolate the errors and correct the erroneous program statements.

QuickBASIC can detect many different **grammatical errors** and display appropriate diagnostic messages. However, there is no BASIC system that can detect all errors. Some of these errors can go undetected by QuickBASIC until either an abnormal end occurs during execution or the program terminates with the results in error.

There are several techniques you can use for attempting to discover the portion of the program that is in error. These methods are **debugging techniques**. The errors themselves are **bugs**, and the activity involved in their detection is **debugging**. QuickBASIC has a fully integrated debugger which pinpoints errors by tracing, or highlighting, through the QuickBASIC source code. The QuickBASIC debugging features include the following:

- Examining values through the immediate window
- Executing one statement at a time
- Breakpoints
- Tracing
- Set next statement
- Recording
- Watch variables and watchpoints

EXAMINING VALUES THROUGH THE IMMEDIATE WINDOW

Following the termination of execution of a program, the program's variables remain equal to the latest values assigned. Through the immediate window, you can examine their values. This is an easy-to-use, and yet, powerful debugging tool.

To activate the immediate window, press F6. You may then display the value of any variables in the program by using the `PRINT` statement and the names of the variables. Recall that when a statement is entered in the immediate window, it is executed immediately. After viewing the values, press F6 to deactivate the immediate window and activate the view window.

If you have a mouse, move the pointer to the inactive window and click the mouse button.

EXECUTING ONE STATEMENT AT A TIME

Another debugging tool is the Step mode. In the **Step mode**, the PC executes the program one statement at a time. To activate this mode, press the F8 key. The first time you press the F8 key, the PC displays the first executable statement in reverse video. Thereafter, each time you press the F8 key, the PC executes the statement in reverse video and displays the next executable statement in reverse video. Hence, the PC steps through the program one statement at a time as you press the F8 key.

While the PC is in the Step mode and before you press the F8 key again, you can do any of the following to better understand what the program is doing:

- Activate the immediate window and use the `PRINT` statement to display the values of variables.
- Use the F4 key to toggle between displaying the program and the output screen.
- Modify any statement in the program. If you modify the statement in reverse video, the reverse video disappears. It reappears as soon as you move the cursor off the line.

To exit the Step mode, press the F5 key. The F5 key continues normal execution of the program. If you want to halt the program again, press Ctrl + Break. To continue execution after pressing Ctrl + Break, you can do one of the following:

- Press F5 to continue normal execution
- Press Shift + F5 to start execution from the beginning of the program
- Press F8 to activate the Step mode

BREAKPOINTS

A **breakpoint** is a line in the program where you want execution to halt. Breakpoints are established by moving the cursor to the line in question, followed by pressing the F9 key or selecting the Toggle Breakpoint command in the Debug menu. When you execute the program after setting one or more breakpoints, the PC halts execution at the next breakpoint and displays it in reverse video. Once the program halts at a breakpoint, you can do one of the following:

- Press the F8 key to enter the Step mode and execute from the one statement at a time to the next breakpoint
- Display the values of variables in the immediate window
- Edit the program
- Delete or add new breakpoints
- Press F5 to continue execution of the program

To toggle off a breakpoint, move the cursor to the breakpoint and press the F9 key. An alternative method for clearing breakpoints is to select the command Clear All Breakpoints in the Debug menu. This latter method can be useful, especially when you have set a number of breakpoints and cannot remember where they are located in the program. A breakpoint only displays in reverse video when it halts execution of the program.

To save time, you should carefully select breakpoints. Commonly used breakpoints include lines immediately following input, calculations, and decision statements.

TRACING

The Trace On command in the Debug menu causes the PC to trace the program. **Tracing** means that the program will execute in slow motion. As the program executes in slow motion, the PC highlights each statement as it executes it. With the Trace On command you can quickly get an idea as to flow of control in your program. This activity must be observed to be appreciated.

The Trace On command works like a toggle switch. Select it once and the PC will trace the flow of control. Select it again, and you turn tracing off. You know that tracing is on when there is a bullet in front of the command in the Debug menu. If you are using the commercial version of QuickBASIC, note that you must toggle on Full Menus in the Option menu for the Trace On command to display in the Debug menu.

Two QuickBASIC statements that carry out the same function as the Trace On command are `TRON` and `TROFF`. The `TRON` statement turns on tracing for all future statements executed. The `TROFF` statement turns tracing off. Although most QuickBASIC programmers use the Trace On command to trace a program, some find the `TRON` and `TROFF` statements useful for tracing small sections of a program.

SET NEXT STATEMENT

The Set Next Statement command in the Debug menu allows you to establish with the cursor where execution will continue following a program halt. For example, assume that you have set a breakpoint in a program. When the PC halts execution at the statement, you can move the cursor to any line in the program and select the Set Next Statement command. When execution resumes, it will begin at the cursor rather than at the statement in reverse video. The Set Next Statement command works much like the infamous `GOTO` statement. Use caution when evaluating the program results following the use of this command since skipping over code can produce unexpected results. If you are using the commercial version of QuickBASIC, note that you must toggle on Full Menus in the Option menu for the Trace On command to display in the Debug menu.

RECORDING

The History On command in the Debug menu is often used in conjunction with breakpoints. When you select the History On command, the PC records the last 20 lines executed by the program. When the program halts at a breakpoint, you can use the Shift + F8 to go back through the last 20 lines executed. You can use the Shift + F10 to go forward through the last 20 lines executed.

Stepping through the last 20 lines can also be useful when your program halts due to a logic error. If you select History On prior to execution, then you can step through the last 20 lines executed before the program's premature termination.

To stop recording the last 20 lines, select History On. This command acts like a toggle switch. Select it once and it's on. Select it again and it's off. You know that the History On command is active when there is a bullet in front of the command in the Debug menu. (Full Menus in the Option menu must be active for the History On command to display in the Debug menu.)

WATCH VARIABLES AND WATCHPOINTS

The Add Watch command in the Debug menu allows you to enter the names of variables or expressions that you want displayed in the watch window. The **watch window** (Figure A-1) displays above the view window whenever watch variables are active. Watching a variable is often combined with the Step mode (F8) or breakpoints to track its value, thus avoiding repeated use of the `PRINT` statement in the immediate window.

FIGURE A-1
The watch window displays above the view window. Program halts on LOOP statement when Emp.Number$ = "128". Value of Emp.Hours is 38. Value of Emp.Rate is 4.6.

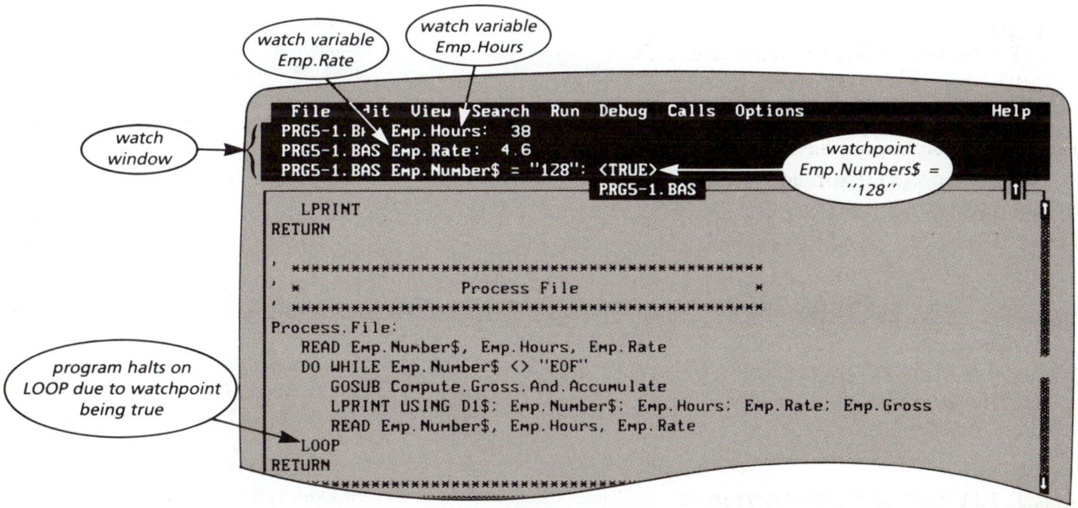

With the commercial version of QuickBASIC, you can add watch variables or conditions to the watch window by pressing Shift + F9 or selecting the Instant Watch command. The main difference between the Instant Watch and Add Watch commands is that with Instant Watch you do not have to type the variable name or condition. You simply select a watch variable by moving the cursor within the variable name in the program. To select a condition, you must use the Shift and arrow keys to highlight it before pressing Shift + F9.

The Watchpoint command in the Debug menu allows you to enter a watchpoint in the watch window. A **watchpoint** (Figure A-1) is a condition that halts program execution when it becomes true.

To delete individual watch variables or watchpoints, select the Delete Watch command in the Debug menu. To delete all watch variables and watch points, select the Delete All Watch command.

QuickBASIC Index

–A–

Accumulator, QB 28
 counter, QB 29
 running total, QB 29
Add Watch command, QB 117
Addition, QB 25
Alt key, QB 17
AND operator, QB 52
Apostrophe. *See* REM statement
APPEND mode for files, QB 83
Appending records, QB 84
Arguments in functions, QB 108
Arithmetic operators, QB 25
Array, QB 99–107
 declaring, QB 100
 lower bound of, QB 100
 name, QB 99, QB 100
 parallel, QB 104
 range of, QB 99
 upper bound of, QB 100

–B–

Backslash format symbol, QB 35, QB 36
Backspace key, QB 16
BASIC. *See* QuickBASIC
BEEP statement, QB 64
Blank, line, QB 6
Breakpoint command, QB 116
Button in dialog box, QB 15

–C–

Calling a subroutine, QB 73
CASE clause, QB 55
CASE ELSE clause, QB 55
Case structure, QB 42, QB 54, QB 55
Circumflex for exponentiation, QB 25
Clause, QB 43, QB 55
Clear
 All Breakpoints command, QB 116
 screen, QB 6, QB 65
Clipboard, QB 17
CLOSE statement, QB 83, QB 84
CLS statement, QB 6
Comma
 format symbol, QB 36
 separator, QB 37
Comparisons
 numeric, QB 9, QB 42, QB 43
 string, QB 9, QB 42, QB 43
Compound condition, QB 51, QB 54
Concatenation operator, QB 110
Condition, QB 43
 compound, QB 51, QB 54
Constant, QB 25
 numeric, QB 25
 string, QB 25
Contents command Help menu, QB 22
Context-senitive help, QB 22
Control structure
 Case, QB 42
 Do-Until, QB 66
 Do-While, QB 66
 If-Then-Else, QB 44
Counter, QB 29
Counter-controlled loop, QB 62, QB 68
Cursor, QB 16
 movement keys, QB 15
Cut and paste, QB 17

–D–

Data, QB 2, QB 25, QB 62–63
 items, QB 2
 validation, QB 65
DATA statement, QB 5, QB 30
DATE$ function, QB 110
Debugging, QB 115
 techniques, QB 115
Decimal point format symbol, QB 35, QB 36
Decision
 making, QB 42
 statement, QB 51, QB 54
 symbol in flowchart, QB 45, QB 66, QB 71
Delete
 All Watch command, QB 117
 key, QB 16
 Watch command, QB 117
Design
 program, QB 1, QB 30–32
 test, QB 1
Detail line, QB 29
Dialog box, QB 15
DIM statement, QB 100
Dimension, QB 100
Dirs/drive box, QB 20
Division, QB 25
Do loop, QB 8, QB 9, QB 31
DO statement, QB 71
DO UNTIL statement, QB 8–10
DO WHILE statement, QB 8–10
Documentation, QB 30
Do-While logic structure, QB 66

–E–

Editing a program, QB 16, QB 33, QB 116
ELSE clause, QB 47
END statement, QB 7
 IF, QB 43, QB 47
 SELECT, QB 55
End-of-file, QB 9, QB 31
 detection, QB 9, QB 91–92
 mark, QB 4, QB 91, QB 96
 routine, QB 9

EOF function, QB 91
Equal sign, QB 31, QB 35
Esc key, QB 13
EXIT FOR statement, QB 105
Expressions, QB 25–26
  match, QB 56
  numeric, QB 25
  string, QB 25

–F–

Field, QB 2
File, QB 2
  appending records to, QB 84
  creating a, QB 84
  extension, QB 20, QB 21, QB 22
  handling statements, QB 83
  name, QB 84
  opening a, QB 83–84
  organization, QB 83
  random, QB 83
  sequential, QB 83
  specification, QB 20, QB 83
Filenumber, QB 83, QB 84
Flowchart, program, QB 2–4
For loop, QB 62, QB 68
  execution of, QB 68
  flowchart representation, QB 68
  nested, QB 27
  range of, QB 68
FOR statement, QB 66, QB 68
Format field, QB 34, QB 36
  symbols, QB 35
Function, QB 108–111
  keys, QB 15
  numeric, QB 25, QB 108
  string, QB 110

–G–

GIGO, QB 65
GOSUB statement, QB 73
Grammatical errors, QB 16, QB 115

–H–

Hard-copy output, QB 18
Header lines, QB 28
Help, QB 13, QB 15, QB 22
  menu, QB 22
  QB Advisor, QB 13, QB 22
Hierarchy
  of arithmetic operations, QB 25
  of logical operators, QB 53
Hyperlinks, QB 22

–I–

IF statement, QB 42–44
  nested, QB 52
If-Then-Else
  logic structure, QB 42–43
  nested forms, QB 46–47
  simple forms, QB 44–46
Immediate window, QB 14, QB 115
Increment value, QB 68
Initialization module, QB 5, QB 30, QB 104
Initialize accumulator, QB 29, QB 30
Input
  prompt, QB 63
  prompt message, QB 63, QB 64
INPUT mode for files, QB 83
INPUT statement, QB 62
INPUT #n statement, QB 85, QB 91
Insert key, QB 16
INT function, QB 108
Interactive programming, QB 62–77

–K–

Keyword, QB 7, QB 25

–L–

Lead read, QB 2
LEFT$ function, QB 110
LEN function, QB 110
LET statement, QB 25, QB 35
Limit value, QB 68, QB 69
LOCATE statement, QB 64, QB 71
LOOP statement, QB 8, QB 62, QB 71
LOOP UNTIL statement, QB 62, QB 71
Lower-bound value, QB 100
LPRINT statement, QB 20, QB 38, QB 50
LPRINT USING statement, QB 38, QB 50

–M–

Main module, QB 73, QB 77, QB 103
Menu bar, QB 14, QB 17
Microsoft QuickBASIC, QB 1
  Advisor, QB 13, QB 22
  editor, QB 16
  functions, R.4–R.5
  help, QB 13, QB 15, QB 22
  quit, QB 16
  reserved words, R.6
  shortcut keys, QB 18
  statements, R.1–R.3
MID$ function, QB 110
Mouse unit, QB 16
  button, QB 15
  pointer, QB 15
Multiple statements per line, QB 45
Multiplication, QB 25

–N–

Nested, QB 27
New command, QB 20, QB 22
NEXT statement, QB 66, QB 68
NOT operator, QB 51
Number sign format symbol, QB 36

–O–

OPEN statement, QB 83
Open command, QB 20, QB 21, QB 22
Operators
  arithmetic, QB 25
  concatenation, QB 53
  logical, QB 50–54
  relational, QB 9, QB 44, QB 51

OR operator, QB 52–53
Order of operations, QB 26
OUTPUT mode for file, QB 83
Output screen, QB 6, QB 18

–P–

Parallel arrays, QB 104
Parentheses, QB 27, QB 54
Precedence, rules of, QB 54
 arithmetic, QB 26
 logical, QB 54
Primary read, QB 2
Print
 command, QB 19
 items, QB 6
 zones, QB 6
PRINT statement, QB 6, QB 28, QB 32, QB 38, QB 71, QB 115
PRINT USING statement, QB 28, QB 33–35, QB 71
Problem analysis, QB 1
Process File module, QB 31
Process A Request module, QB 104, QB 105

–Q–

QB Advisor, QB 13, QB 22
QuickBASIC. *See* Microsoft QuickBASIC

–R–

Raising to a power, QB 25
Random file, QB 83
Random numbers, QB 109
RANDOMIZE statement, QB 109
READ statement, QB 7, QB 52
Record, QB 2
Relational operators, QB 9, QB 44, QB 51
REM statement, QB 4, QB 5
Remark line, QB 4, QB 5
Report editing, QB 33
RETURN statement, QB 73
RIGHT$ function, QB 110
RND function, QB 108, QB 109
Run menu, QB 17
Running total, QB 29

–S–

Save As command, QB 20
SELECT CASE statement, QB 42, QB 54–56
Semicolon separator, QB 32, QB 36
Sentinel record, QB 9
Sequential file, QB 83
 creating, QB 83
 organization, QB 83
Set Next statement, QB 116
Shortcut keys, QB 118
SPC function, QB 65
SQR function, QB 108
Status line, QB 14
Step mode, QB 115
String
 comparing, QB 9
 constant, QB 35, QB 37
 expression, QB 34, QB 36, QB 43
 function, QB 25
 sub, QB 110, QB 111
 variable, QB 7, QB 34, QB 36
Subroutine, QB 73
Subscript, QB 100
Subtraction, QB 25

–T–

TAB function, QB 6
Table, QB 99
 hit, QB 105
 lookup, QB 101
 organization, QB 101
 search, QB 99
THEN clause, QB 47
TIME$ function, QB 110
TO attribute, QB 100
Top-down
 approach, QB 72, QB 73
 chart, QB 73, QB 86, QB 102
 programming, QB 62, QB 72
Total line, QB 29, QB 31
Tracing, QB 116
Trailer record, QB 2, QB 9

–U–

Upper-bound value, QB 100

–V–

Validating data, QB 65
Variable, QB 7
 initialize, QB 28, QB 29
 loop, QB 29
 names, QB 7
 numeric, QB 7
 simple, QB 7
 string, QB 7
 subscripted, QB 100
View window, QB 13

–W–

Watch
 variable, QB 117
 window, QB 117
Watchpoint, QB 117
 command, QB 117
Wrap-Up module, QB 12, QB 85, QB 90
WRITE #n statement, QB 83, QB 84–85

MICROSOFT QuickBASIC REFERENCE CARD

Legend: Uppercase letters are required keywords. You must supply items within < >'s. You must select one of the entries within { }'s. Items within [ ]'s are optional. Three ellipsis points (...) indicate that an item may be repeated as many times as you wish. The symbol ƀ represents a blank character.

Summary of BASIC Statements

STATEMENT

BEEP
Causes the speaker on the PC to beep for a fraction of a second.

CALL <name> [(argumentlist)]
Transfers control to a subprogram.

CHAIN <"filespec">
Instructs the PC to stop executing the current program, load another program from auxiliary storage and start executing it.

CHDIR <pathspecification>
Changes the current directory for the specified drive.

CIRCLE <(x, y), radius> [,color [,start,end [,shape]]]
Causes the PC to draw an ellipse, circle, arc, or wedge with center at (x, y).

CLEAR [,,stack]
Reinitializes all program variables, closes files, and sets the stack size.

CLOSE [#] [filenumber] [,[#] [filenumber]]...
Closes specified files.

CLS
Erases the information on the screen and places the cursor in the upper left corner of the screen.

COLOR [background] [,palette]
In medium-resolution graphics mode, sets the color for the background and palette of colors.

COLOR [foreground] [,background] [,border]
In the text mode, defines the color of the foreground characters, background, and border around the screen.

COM(n) {ON | OFF | STOP} Enables or disables trapping of communications activity on adaptor n.

COMMON [SHARED] <variable> [,variable]...
Passes specified variables to a chained program.

CONST <constantname> = <expression> [, constantname = expression]...
Declares symbolic constants that can be used in place of numeric or string expressions.

STATEMENT

DATA <data item> [,data item]...
Provides for the creation of a sequence of data items for use by the READ statement.

DATE$ = mm {/ | -} dd {/ | -} yy[yy] Sets the system date, where mm = month, dd = day, yy = year, yyyy = 4-digit year.

DECLARE {FUNCTION | SUB} name [(parameterlist)]
Declares references to QuickBASIC procedures and invokes argument-type checking.

DEF FN<name> [(variable, [, variable]...)] = <expression>
Defines and names a function that can be referenced in a program as often as needed. Multiline functions end with an END DEF statement.

DEFtype <letterrange> [,letterrange]...
Sets the data type for variables and functions.

DIM [SHARED] <arrayname(size)> [AS type], [arrayname(size) [AS type]]...
Reserves storage locations for arrays and declares the array type.

DO
Causes the statements between DO and LOOP to be executed repeatedly. The loop is controlled by a condition in the corresponding LOOP statement.

DO UNTIL <condition>
Causes the statements between DO UNTIL and LOOP to be executed repeatedly until the condition is true.

DO WHILE <condition>
Causes the statements between DO WHILE and LOOP to be executed repeatedly while the condition is true.

DRAW <string expression>
Causes the PC to draw the object that is defined by the value of the string expression.

END [{DEF | FUNCTION | IF | SELECT | SUB | TYPE}] Ends a QuickBASIC program, procedure, or block of code.

ERASE <arrayname> [,arrayname]...
Eliminates previously defined arrays.

ERROR <integerexpression>
Simulates the occurrence of a QuickBASIC error or allows the user to define error codes.

EXIT <statement>
Exits statement, where statement is equal to FOR, DO, DEF, FUNCTION, or SUB.

STATEMENT

FIELD <#filenumber, width AS string variable> [,width AS string variable]...
Allocates space for variables in a random file buffer.

FILES [filespecification]
Lists the names of all programs and data files in auxiliary storage on the default drive or the drive specified by file specification.

FOR <loopvariable> = <initial> TO <limit> [STEP increment]
Causes the statements between the FOR and NEXT statements to be executed until the value of loopvariable exceeds the value of the limit.

FUNCTION <name> [(parameterlist)] [STATIC]
Declares the name, the parameters, and initiates a function procedure that ends with an END FUNCTION.

GET <(x_1, y_1) – (x_2, y_2), arrayname>
Reads the colors of the points in the specified area on the screen into an array.

GET <[#]filenumber> [,record number]
Reads the specified record from a random file and transfers it to the buffer that is defined by the corresponding FIELD statement.

GOSUB {linelabel | linenumber} Causes control to transfer to a subroutine beginning at the specified line. Also retains the location of the next statement following the GOSUB statement.

GOTO {linelabel | linenumber} Transfers control to the specified line.

IF <condition> THEN [clause] [ELSE [clause]]
The single line IF statement causes execution of the THEN clause if the condition is true. If the ELSE clause is included, it causes execution of the ELSE clause if the condition is false.

IF <condition> THEN
[statementblock$_1$]
[ELSE
[statementblock$_2$]]
END IF
The block IF statement allows for multiple lines in the THEN and ELSE clauses. Causes execution of the THEN clause if the condition is true. Causes execution of the ELSE clause if the condition is false. The ELSE IF <condition> THEN clause may be used in place of the ELSE clause.

INPUT [;]["prompt message" {, | ;}] <variable> [,variable]...
Provides for the assignment of values to variables from a source external to the program, such as the keyboard.

INPUT <#filenumber, variable> [,variable]...
Provides for the assignment of values to variables from a sequential file in auxiliary storage.

(***BASIC Statements*** *continued on page R.2 in left column*)

MICROSOFT QuickBASIC REFERENCE CARD

Summary of BASIC Statements *(continued)*

STATEMENT

KEY {**n, string value** | **ON** | **OFF** | **LIST**} Assigns a string value to a function key. Also used to display the values and enable or disable the function key display line.

KEY(n) {**ON** | **OFF** | **STOP**} Activates or deactivates trapping of the specified key n.

KILL <filespecification>
Deletes a file from disk.

[LET] <variable> = <expression>
Causes the evaluation of the expression, followed by the assignment of the resulting value to the variable to the left of the equal sign.

LINE [(x_1, y_1)] <–(x_2, y_2)> [,color] [,B[F]][,Style]
Draws a line or a box on the screen.

LINE INPUT [;]["prompt message";] <string variable> or
LINE INPUT <#filenumber,><string variable>
Provides for the assignment of a line up to 255 characters from a source external to the program, such as the keyboard or a sequential file.

LOCATE [row] [,column] [,cursor] [,start] [,stop]
Positions the cursor on the screen. Can also be used to make the cursor visible or invisible and to control the size of the cursor.

LOCK <[#]filenumber>, {**record** | **[start] TO end**}
Locks all or some of the records in a file.

LOOP {**WHILE** | **UNTIL** | **ƀ**} **[condition]** Identifies the end of a loop.

LPRINT [item] [{**,** | **;** | **ƀ**} **item]...** Provides for the generation of output to the printer.

LPRINT USING <string expression;> <item> [{**,** | **;** | **ƀ**} **item]...**
Provides for the generation of formatted output to the printer.

LSET <string variable> = <string expression>
Moves string data left-justified into an area of a random file buffer that is defined by the string variable.

MID$ <(string var, start position [,number]> = <substring>
Replaces a substring within a string.

MKDIR <pathname>
Creates a new directory.

NAME <oldfilespecification> AS <newfilespecification>
Renames a file on disk.

STATEMENT

NEXT [numeric variable] [,numeric variable]...
Identifies the end of the For loop(s).

ON COM(n) GOSUB {**linelabel** | **linenumber**}
Causes control to transfer to the specified line when data is filling the communications buffer (n).

ON ERROR GOTO {**linelabel** | **linenumber**}
Enables error trapping and specifies the first line of an error-handling routine that the PC is to branch to in the event of an error. If linenumber is zero, error trapping is disabled.

ON <numeric expression> GOSUB {**linelabel-list** | **linenumber-list**}
Causes control to transfer to the subroutine represented by the selected line. Also retains the location of the next statement following the ON-GOSUB statement.

ON <numeric expression> GOTO {**linelabel-list** | **linenumber-list**}
Causes control to transfer to one of several lines according to the value of the numeric expression.

ON KEY(n) GOSUB {**linelabel** | **linenumber**}
Causes control to transfer to the specified line when the function key or cursor control key (n) is pressed.

ON PEN GOSUB {**linelabel** | **linenumber**}
Causes control to transfer to the specified line when the light pen is activated.

ON PLAY(n) GOSUB {**linelabel** | **linenumber**}
Plays continuous background music. Transfers control to the specified line when a note (n) is sensed.

ON STRIG(n) GOSUB {**linelabel** | **linenumber**}
Causes control to transfer to the specified line when one of the joystick buttons (n) is pressed.

ON TIMER(n) GOSUB {**linelabel** | **linenumber**}
Causes control to transfer to the specified line when the specified period of time (n) in seconds has elapsed.

ON UEVENT GOSUB {**linelabel** | **linenumber**}
Defines the event-handler for a user-defined event.

OPEN <filespec> FOR <mode> AS <[#]filenumber>
[LEN = record length]
Allows a program to read or write records to a file. If record length is specified, then the file is opened as a random file. If the record length is not specified, then the file is opened as a sequential file.

STATEMENT

OPTION BASE {**0** | **1**}
Assigns a lower bound of 0 or 1 to all arrays declared with only an upper-bound value.

OUT <port>, <data>
Sends a byte to a machine I/O port.

PAINT <(x, y)> [[,paint] [,boundary]]
Paints an area on the screen with the selected color.

PALETTE [attribute, color] or
PALETTE USING <arrayname> [(arrayindex)]
Changes one or more of the colors in the palette.

PCOPY <sourcepage>, <destinationpage>
Copies one screen page to another.

PEN(n) {**ON** | **OFF** | **STOP**} Enables or disables the PEN read function used to analyze light pen activity.

PLAY <string expression>
Causes the PC to play music according to the value of the string expression.

PLAY {**ON** | **OFF** | **STOP**} Enables, disables, or suspends play event trapping.

POKE <address>, <byte>
Writes a byte into a storage location.

PRESET <(x, y)> [,color]
Draws a point in the color specified at (x, y). If no color is specified, it erases the point.

{**PRINT** | **?**} **[item]** [{**,** | **;** | **ƀ**} **item]...** Provides for the generation of output to the screen.

{**PRINT** | **?**} **<#filenumber,> [item]** [{**,** | **;** | **ƀ**} **item]...**
Provides for the generation of output to a sequential file.

PRINT USING <string expression;> <item> [{**,** | **;** | **ƀ**} **item]...**
Provides for the generation of formatted output to the screen.

PRINT <#filenumber,> USING <string expression;>
<item> [{**,** | **;** | **ƀ**} **item]...** Provides for the generation of formatted output to a sequential file.

(***BASIC Statements*** *continued on page R.3 in left column*)

MICROSOFT QuickBASIC REFERENCE CARD

STATEMENT

PSET <(x, y)> [,color]
Draws a point in the color specified at (x, y).

PUT <(x_1, y_1), arrayname> [,action]
Writes the colors of the points in the array onto an area of the screen.

PUT <[#]filenumber> [,record number]
Writes a record to a random file from a buffer defined by the corresponding FIELD statement.

RANDOMIZE [numeric expression]
Reseeds the random number generator.

READ <variable> [,variable]...
Provides for the assignment of values to variables from a sequence of data items created from DATA statements.

REDIM [SHARED]<arrayname(size)> [AS type] [arrayname(size) [AS type]]...
Changes the space allocated to an array declared $DYNAMIC.

{REM | '} [comment] Provides for the insertion of comments in a program.

RESET
Closes all disk files.

RESTORE {linelabel | linenumber}
Allows the data items in DATA statements to be reread.

RESUME {linelabel | NEXT | 0 | ƀ} Continues program execution at the linelabel, or the line following that which caused the error, after an error-recovery procedure.

RETURN {linelabel | linenumber}
Causes control to transfer from a subroutine back to the statement that follows the corresponding GOSUB or ON-GOSUB statement.

RMDIR <pathname>
Removes a directory from disk after all files and subdirectories have been removed.

RSET <string variable> = <string expression>
Moves string data right-justified into an area of a random file buffer that is defined by string variable.

RUN {linenumber | linelabel | ƀ} Restarts the program in main storage.

SCREEN [mode] [,color switch] [,active page] [,visual page]
Sets the screen attributes for text mode, medium-resolution graphics, or high-resolution graphics.

SEEK <[#]filenumber>, <position>
Sets the position in a file for the next read or write.

STATEMENT

SELECT CASE <testexpression>
CASE <matchexpression$_1$>
[range of statements$_1$]
[CASE <matchexpression$_2$>
[range of statements$_2$]
.
.
.
[CASE ELSE
[range of statements$_n$]
END SELECT
Causes execution of one of several ranges of statements depending on the value of testexpression.

SHARED <variable> [AS type] [,variable [AS type]]...
Gives a SUB or FUNCTION procedure access to variables declared at the module level without passing them as parameters.

SHELL [commandstring]
Places the current QB session in a temporary wait state and returns control to MS-DOS. Can also execute another program or MS-DOS command as specified in commandstring.

SLEEP [seconds]
Suspends execution of the calling program.

SOUND <frequency>, <duration>
Causes the generation of sound through the PC speaker.

STATIC <variablelist>
Causes variables and arrays to be local to either a DEF FN, a FUNCTION, or a SUB, and maintains values between calls.

STOP
Stops execution of a program. Unlike the END statement, files are left open.

STRIG(n) {ON | OFF | STOP} Enables or disables trapping of the joystick buttons.

SUB <globalname> [(parameterlist)] [STATIC]
Establishes the beginning of a subprogram. The end of the subprogram is identified by the END SUB statement.

SWAP <variable$_1$>, <variable$_2$>
Exchanges the values of two variables or two elements of an array.

SYSTEM
Closes all open files and returns control to MS-DOS.

TIME$ = hh[:mm[:ss]]
Sets the system time, where
hh = hours, mm = minutes, and ss = seconds.

TIMER {ON | OFF | STOP} Enables or disables trapping of timed events.

STATEMENT

TROFF
Disables statement tracing.

TRON
Causes the PC to trace execution of program statements.

TYPE <labelname>
<fieldname$_1$> AS <fieldtype>
.
.
.
<fieldname$_n$> AS <fieldtype>
END TYPE
Creates user-defined data types containing one or more elements.

UEVENT {ON | OFF | STOP} Enables, disables, or suspends user-defined event trapping.

UNLOCK <[#]filenumber>, {record | [start] TO end}
Unlocks records in a file.

VIEW [[SCREEN] (x_1, y_1) – (x_2, y_2)] [,color] [,boundary]
Defines a viewport.

VIEW PRINT [topline TO bottomline]
Establishes boundaries for the screen text viewport.

WEND
Identifies the end of a While loop.

WHILE <condition>
Identifies the beginning of a While loop. Causes the statements between WHILE and WEND to be executed repeatedly while the condition is true.

WIDTH {40 | 80} Erases the information on the screen, sets the width of the line on the screen to 40 or 80 characters, and places the cursor in the upper left corner of the screen.

WIDTH LPRINT <width>
Sets the printer column width.

WINDOW <[SCREEN] (x_1, y_1) – (x_2, y_2)>
Redefines the coordinates of the viewport. Allows you to draw objects in space and not be bounded by the limits of the screen.

WRITE [expression list]
Writes data to the screen.

WRITE <#filenumber,> [item] [{, | ; | ƀ} item]...
Writes data to a sequential file. Causes the PC to insert commas between the items written to the sequential file.

MICROSOFT QuickBASIC REFERENCE CARD

Summary of BASIC Functions

FUNCTION

ABS(N)
Returns the absolute value of the argument N.

ASC(X$)
Returns a two-digit numeric value that is equivalent in ASCII code to the first character of the string argument X$.

ATN(N)
Returns the angle in radians whose tangent is the value of the argument N.

CDBL(N)
Returns N converted to a double-precision value.

CHR$(N)
Returns a single string character that is equivalent in ASCII code to the numeric argument N.

CINT(N)
Returns N converted to an integer after rounding the fractional part of N.

CLNG(N)
Returns N converted to a long integer after rounding the fractional part of N.

COMMAND$
Returns the command line used to start the program.

COS(N)
Returns the cosine of the argument N where N is in radians.

CSNG(N)
Returns N converted to a single-precision value.

CSRLIN
Returns the vertical (row) coordinate of the cursor.

CVI(X$), CVL(X$), CVS(X$), CVD(X$)
Returns the integer, long integer, single-precision, or double-precision numeric value equivalent to the string X$. Used with random files.

DATE$
Returns the current date (mm-dd-yyyy).

EOF(filenumber)
Returns −1 (true) if the end-of-file has been sensed on the sequential file associated with filenumber. Returns 0 (false) if the end-of-file has not been sensed.

ERDEV
Returns an error code from the last device that caused an error.

FUNCTION

ERDEV$
Returns a string expression containing the name of the device that generated a vital error.

ERL
Returns the line number preceding the line that caused the error. If no line numbers are used, then ERL returns a zero.

ERR
Returns the error code for the last error that occurred.

EXP(N)
Returns e(2.718281...) raised to the argument N.

FILEATTR
Returns the file mode for an open file.

FIX(N)
Returns the value of N truncated to an integer.

FRE(N)
Returns the amount of available stack space (N = −2), string space (N not equal to −1 or −2), or size in bytes of the largest array you can create (N = −1).

FREEFILE
Returns the next free QuickBASIC file number.

HEX$(N)
Returns the hexadecimal equivalent of N.

INKEY$
Returns the last character entered from the keyboard.

INP(N)
Returns the byte read from an I/O port N.

INPUT$(N)
Suspends execution of the program until a string of N characters is received from the keyboard.

INPUT$(N, [#]filenumber)
Returns a string of characters from the specified file.

INSTR(P, X$, S$)
Returns the beginning position of the substring S$ in string X$. P indicates the position at which the search begins in the string X$.

INT(N)
Returns the largest integer that is less than or equal to the argument N.

LBOUND(arrayname[,dimension])
Returns the lower-bound value for the specified dimension of arrayname.

FUNCTION

LCASE$(X$)
Returns X$ in all lowercase letters.

LEFT$(X$, N)
Returns the leftmost N characters of the string argument X$.

LEN(X$)
Returns the length of the string argument X$.

LOC(#filenumber)
With a random file, it returns the number of the last record read or written. With a sequential file, it returns the number of records read from or written to the file.

LOF(#filenumber)
Returns the number of bytes allocated to a file.

LOG(N)
Returns the natural log of the argument N where N is greater than 0.

LPOS(N)
Returns the current position of the line printer's print head within the printer buffer where N is equal to 1 for LPT1, 2 for LPT2, and so on.

LTRIM$(X$)
Returns X$ with leading spaces removed.

MID$(X$, P, N)
Returns N characters of the string argument X$ beginning at position P.

MKI$(N), MKL$(N), MKS$(N), MKD$(N)
Returns the string equivalent of an integer, long integer, single-precision, or double-precision value. Used with random files.

OCT$(N)
Returns the octal equivalent of N.

PEEK(N)
Returns the value of the byte stored at the specified storage location N.

PEN(N)
Returns light pen coordinate information. The information is dependent on the value assigned to N.

PLAY(n)
Returns the number of notes currently in the music background buffer.

PMAP (c, n)
Returns the world coordinate of the physical coordinate c or vice versa. The parameter n varies between 0 and 3, and determines whether c is an x or y coordinate, and whether the coordinate is to be mapped from the physical to the world coordinate or vice versa.

(***BASIC Functions*** *continued on page R.5 in left column*)

MICROSOFT QuickBASIC REFERENCE CARD

***Summary of BASIC Functions** (continued)*

FUNCTION

POINT {(x, y) | (n)}
With the argument (x, y), the PC returns the foreground color attribute of the point (x, y). With the argument n, the PC returns the physical or world x or y coordinate of the last point referenced. The parameter n varies in the range 0 to 3.

POS(O)
Returns the current position of the cursor on the screen.

RIGHT$(X$, N)
Returns the rightmost N characters of the string argument X$.

RND(N)
Returns a random number between 0 (inclusive) and 1 (exclusive). If N is positive or not included, the next random number is returned. If N is 0 (zero), the previous random number is returned. If N is negative, the random number generator is reseeded before a random number is returned.

RTRIM$(X$)
Returns X$ with trailing spaces removed.

SCREEN(row, column)
Returns the ASCII code for the character at the specified row (line) and column on the screen.

SEEK(filenumber)
Returns the current file position.

SGN(N)
Returns the sign of the argument N: -1 if the argument N is less than 0; 0 if the argument N is equal to 0; or +1 if the argument N is greater than 0.

SIN(N)
Returns the sine of the argument N where N is in radians.

SPACE$(N)
Returns a string of N spaces.

SPC(N)
Displays N spaces. Can be used only in an output statement such as PRINT or LPRINT.

SQR(N)
Returns the square root of the positive argument N.

STICK(N)
Returns the x and y coordinates of joystick N.

STR$(N)
Returns the string equivalent of the numeric argument N.

STRIG(n)
Returns the status of the joystick buttons.

STRING$(N, X$)
Returns N times the first character of X$.

FUNCTION

TAB(N)
Causes the PC to tab over to position N on the output device. Can be used only in an output statement such as PRINT or LPRINT.

TAN(N)
Returns the tangent of the argument N where N is in radians.

TIMER
Returns a value that is equal to the number of seconds elapsed since midnight.

TIME$
Returns the current time (hh:mm:ss).

UBOUND(arrayname[,dimension])
Returns the upper-bound value for the specified dimension of arrayname.

UCASE$(X$)
Returns X$ in all uppercase letters.

VAL(X$)
Returns the numeric equivalent of the string argument X$.

VARPTR(variablename)
Returns the storage address of variablename.

VARPTR$(variablename)
Returns a string representation of the storage address of variablename for use in DRAW and PLAY statements.

Summary of All Operators

ORDER OF PRECEDENCE	*OPERATOR*	*SYMBOL*
Highest	Arithmetic	^
		+ or − (Unary + or − sign)
		* or /
		\
		MOD
		+ or − (Binary + or − sign)
	Concatenation	+
	Relational	=, >, >=, <, <=, or <>
	Logical	NOT
		AND
		OR or XOR
		EQV
Lowest		IMP

Summary of Command Line Options

For the desired effect, append one or more of the following to the QB or QBI command when you enter QuickBASIC:

OPTION	*FUNCTION*
/ah	Permits arrays to exceed 64 KB.
/b	Designates monochrome display.
/c:size	Sets the size of the communications port buffer.
/cmd str	Passes the string str to the COMMAND$ function.
file	Loads and displays the QuickBASIC program file.
/g	Designates faster video output.
/h	Designates maximum resolution for the video device.
/l[lib]	Loads the specified library or QB.QLB if lib is omitted.
/mbf	Causes conversion functions to treat IEEE-format numbers as Microsoft binary format numbers.
/nohi	Allows monitor that does not support high intensity.
/run file	Loads and executes the QuickBASIC program file before displaying it.

Limits to QuickBASIC

	MAXIMUM	*MINIMUM*
Variable name	40 characters	1 character
String length	32,767 characters	0 characters
Array dimensions	60	1
Array subscript value	32,767	-32,768
Integers	32,767	-32,768
Long integers	2,147,483,647	-2,147,483,648
Single precision (+)	3.402823E+38	1.401298E-45
Single precision (-)	-1.401298E-45	-3.402823E+38
Double precision (+)	1.797693134862315D+308	4.940656458412465D-324
Double precision (-)	-4.940656458412465D-324	-1.797693134862315D+308

Variable Type Definition

APPEND CHARACTER	*DECLARATION*
%	Integer variable
&	Long integer variable
!	Single-precision variable
#	Double-precision variable
$	String variable

MICROSOFT QuickBASIC REFERENCE CARD

Cursor Movement Keys

KEYS	FUNCTION
←	Character left
→	Character right
↓	Down one line
↑	Up one line
Ctrl + ←	Word left
Ctrl + →	Word right
Ctrl + End	End of program
Ctrl + Enter	Beginning of next line
Ctrl + Home	Beginning of program
Ctrl + Q + E	Top of window
Ctrl + Q + S	Beginning of current line
Ctrl + Q + X	Bottom of window
End	End of line
Home	First indent of current line
Tab	Tab to next tab setting

Scroll Keys

KEYS	FUNCTION
Ctrl + ↓	Line down
Ctrl + ↑	Line up
Page Down	Page down
Page Up	Page up
Ctrl + Page Down	Left one full screen
Ctrl + Page Up	Right one full screen

Execution and Debugging Keys

KEYS	FUNCTION
F5	Continues execution from current statement.
Shift + F5	Starts execution from beginning.
F7	Executes program to cursor.
F8	Executes next program statement.
Shift + F8	Traces execution history backward.
F9	Toggles the Debug menu Breakpoint command.
Shift + F9	Instant watch.
F10	Single step, tracing around a procedure call.
Shift + F10	Traces execution history forward.

Search Keys

KEYS	FUNCTION
F3	Repeats the last find.
**Ctrl + **	Searches for selected (highlighted) text.

Help Keys

KEYS	FUNCTION
F1	Displays help on the item in which the cursor is located.
Shift + F1	Displays help on help.
Alt + F1	Displays previously requested help topic. (Repeat up to 20 times.)
Ctrl + F1	Displays next help topic in Help file.
Shift + Ctrl + F1	Displays previous help topic in Help file.
Alt + H	Displays help through Help menu commands.
Esc	Clears help from the screen.
Letter	Moves cursor to help-topic title beginning with letter entered.
Shift + letter	Moves cursor to previous help-topic title beginning with letter entered.
Tab	Moves cursor to next help-topic title in help screen.
Shift + Tab	Moves cursor to previous help-topic title in help screen.

Insert and Copy Keys

KEYS	FUNCTION
Insert	Toggles insert or overtype.
Ctrl + Insert	Copies selection to clipboard and keeps.
Shift + Insert	Inserts contents of clipboard.
Shift + Delete	Copies selection to clipboard and deletes.
Ctrl + Y	Copies current line to clipboard and deletes.
Ctrl + Q + Y	Copies from cursor to end of line to clipboard and deletes.

Delete Keys

KEYS	FUNCTION
Backspace	Deletes character to left.
Ctrl + T	Deletes rest of word.
Delete	Deletes character at cursor or selected text.
Shift + Tab	Deletes leading spaces from selected lines.

Selection (Highlight) Keys

KEYS	FUNCTION
Shift + ←	Character left
Shift + →	Character right
Shift + Ctrl + →	Word right
Shift + Ctrl + ←	Word left
Shift + ↓	Current line
Shift + ↑	Line above
Shift + Page Down	Screen down
Shift + Page Up	Screen up
Shift + Ctrl + Home	To beginning of program
Shift + Ctrl + End	To end of program

View Keys

KEYS	FUNCTION
F4	Toggles between view window and output screen.
F6	Makes next window the active one.

Reserved Words

ABS
ACCESS
ALIAS
AND
ANY
APPEND
AS
ASC
ATN
BASE
BEEP
BINARY
BLOAD
BSAVE
CALL
CALLS
CASE
CDBL
CDECL
CHAIN
CHDIR
CHR$
CINT
CIRCLE
CLEAR
CLOSE
CLS
COLOR
COM
COMMAND$
COMMON
CONST
COS
CSNG
CSRLIN
CVD
CVDMBF
CVI
CVL
CVS
CVSMBF
DATA
DATE$
DECLARE
DEF
DEFDBL
DEFINT
DEFLNG
DEFSNG
DEFSTR
DIM
DO
DOUBLE
DRAW
ELSE
ELSEIF
END
ENDIF
ENVIRON
ENVIRON$
EOF
EQV
ERASE
ERDEV
ERDEV$
ERL
ERR
ERROR
EXIT
EXP
FIELD
FILEATTR
FILES
FIX
FOR
FRE
FREEFILE
FUNCTION
GET
GOSUB
GOTO
HEX$
IF
IMP
INKEY$
INP
INPUT
INPUT$
INSTR
INT
INTEGER
IOCTL
IOCTL$
IS
KEY
KILL
LBOUND
LCASE$
LEFT$
LEN
LET
LINE
LIST
LOC
LOCAL
LOCATE
LOCK
LOF
LOG
LONG
LOOP
LPOS
LPRINT
LSET
LTRIM$
MID$
MKD$
MKDIR
MKDMBF$
MKI$
MKL$
MKS$
MKSMBF$
MOD
NAME
NEXT
NOT
OCT$
OFF
ON
OPEN
OPTION
OR
OUT
OUTPUT
PAINT
PALETTE
PCOPY
PEEK
PEN
PLAY
PMAP
POINT
POKE
POS
PRESET
PRINT
PRINT#
PSET
PUT
RANDOM
RANDOMIZE
READ
REDIM
REM
RESET
RESTORE
RESUME
RETURN
RIGHT$
RMDIR
RND
RSET
RUN
SADD
SCREEN
SEEK
SGN
SELECT
SETMEM
SGN
SHARED
SHELL
SIGNAL
SIN
SINGLE
SLEEP
SOUND
SPACE$
SPC
SQR
STATIC
STEP
STICK
STOP
STR$
STRIG
STRING
STRING$
SUB
SWAP
SYSTEM
TAB
TAN
THEN
TIME$
TIMER
TO
TROFF
TRON
TYPE
UBOUND
UCASE$
UNLOCK
UNTIL
USING
VAL
VARPTR
VARPTR$
VARSEG
VIEW
WAIT
WEND
WHILE
WIDTH
WINDOW
WRITE
WRITE#
XOR

Photo Credits

Chapter 1

Page 1.1 H. Armstrong Roberts/Camerique / **1-1** Photo Network/Michael Manheim / **1-2, 1-3** International Business Machines Corp. / **1-4** Wyse Technology / **1-8** (a) Compaq Computer Corp.; (b) NCR Corp.; (c) International Business Machines Corp.; (d) Cray Research, Inc.; (e) Paul Shambroom / **1-10** Curtis Fukuda / **1-15** Hewlett-Packard Co. / **1-16** Honeywell Bull, Inc. / **1-17** Modular Computer Systems, Inc. / **1-18** Hewlett-Packard Company / **1-19** Coin Financial Systems / **1-20** Control Data Corp. / **1-21** Racal-Milgo / **1-22** McDonnell Douglas Automation Co. / **1-23** Intertec Diversified Systems / **1-24** Racal-Milgo / **1-25** Management Science America / **Page 1.25** Top: United Press International; Bottom: (left) Carl Howard; (center) Iowa State University; (right) Princeton University / **Page 1.26** Top: U.S. Department of the Navy; Bottom: (both) / International Business Machines Corp. / **Page 1.27** Top: (left) International Business Machines Corp.; (right both) Intel Corp.; Bottom: (left) Dartmouth College News Service; (right) Digital Equipment Corp. / **Page 1.28** Top: (left both) International Business Machines Corp.; (right) Ira Wyman; Bottom: (left) The Computer Museum, Boston; (right) Apple Computer, Inc. / **Page 1.29** Top: (left) Microsoft Corp.; (right both) Lotus Development Corp.; Bottom: International Business Machines Corp. / **Page 1.30** Top: International Business Machines Corp.; Bottom: Compaq Computer Corp.

Chapter 2

Page 2.1 P. Skrivan/H. Armstrong Roberts / **2-1** (a,b,d) Curtis Fukuda; (c) Ashton-Tate / **2-2** (left) Curtis Fukuda; (right) Hewlett-Packard Co. / **2-12** (left) Curtis Fukuda; (right) Lotus Development Corp. / **2-14** International Business Machines Corp. / **2-21** Curtis Fukuda / **2-29** Compaq Computer Corp. / **2-30** Radio Shack, A Division of Tandy Corp. / **2-31** Electrohome Ltd. / **2-32** Aldus Corp. / **2-33** Claris Corp. / **2-34** Curtis Fukuda / **2-35** (top both, bottom left) Curtis Fukuda; (bottom right) TDA, Inc. / **Page 2.20** MicroPro International Corp. / **Page 2.21** (both) Ashton-Tate / **Page 2.22** Polaroid Corp.

Chapter 3

Page 3.1 Gary Gladstone/Image Bank

Chapter 4

Page 4.1 Texas Instruments, Inc. / **4-2** Curtis Fukuda / **4-3** (left) Wyse Technology; (right) Apollo Computer, Inc. / **4-4** Wyse Technology / **4-5** International Business Machines Corp. / **4-6** (top) Logitech, Inc.; (bottom) Curtis Fukuda / **4-7** Logitech, Inc. / **4-8** Compaq Computer Corp. / **4-9** Diebold, Inc. / **4-10** Adage, Inc. / **4-11** Lear Siegler, Inc. / **4-12** CalComp / **4-13** Computervision Corp. / **4-14** Texas Instruments, Inc. / **4-16** NCR Corp. / **4-17** Soricon Corp. / **4-20** Caere Corp. / **4-21** (both) Spectra Physics / **4-22** AST Research, Inc. / **4-23** Wang Laboratories, Inc. / **4-24** LXE Division of Electromagnetic Sciences, Inc. / **4-25** Motorola, Inc. / **4-33** Curtis Fukuda / **4-37** Mohawk Data Sciences Corp. / **4-44** Acme Visible Records

Chapter 5

Page 5.1 Micron Technology, Inc. / **5-18** Intel Corp. / **5-20** NCR Comten, Inc. / **Page 5.17** (1), (2), (3) Intel Corp. / **Page 5.18** (4), (5) Siltec Corp.; (6), (7), (8) Intel Corp. / **Page 5.19** (9) Intel Corp.; (10) National Semiconductor Corp.; (11) International Business Machines Corp.; (12) AT&T Bell Laboratories; (13) 3M Company

Chapter 6

Page 6.1 Eastman Kodak Co. / **6-1** Xerox Corp. / **6-6** Micrografx, Inc. / **6-7** International Business Machine Corp.; / **6-8** Micrografx, Inc. / **6-11** (left) Storage Technology Corp.; (right) Atchison, Topeka and Santa Fe Railway Co. / **6-12** Epson America, Inc. / **6-13** (both) Printronix / **6-14** DataProducts Corp. / **6-18** Okidata / **6-19** Beagle Bros. / **6-20** Radio Shack, A Division of Tandy Corp. / **6-22** International Business Machines Corp. / **6-24** Hewlett-Packard Co. / **6-26** McDonnell Douglas Automation Co. / **6-27** Dataproducts Corp. / **6-28** Xerox Corp. / **6-29** Beehive International / **6-32** Toshiba America, Inc. / **6-33** Radio Shack, A Division of Tandy Corp. / **6-36** (left) Applicon, Inc.; (right) Evans & Sutherland / **6-38** Hewlett-Packard Co. / **6-39** (both) CalComp

Chapter 7

Page 7.1 Michael Salas/Image Bank / **7-2, 7-3** Curtis Fukuda / **7-5** Kao Corp. of America / **7-12** Hewlett-Packard Co. / **7-13** (both) Plus Development Corp. / **7-14** Seagate Technology / **7-16** Plus Development Corp. / **7-17** Curtis Fukuda / **7-18** Everex Systems, Inc. / **7-19** NNC Electronics / **7-20** International Business Machines Corp. / **7-21** Lockheed Corp. / **7-24** (top) Hewlett-Packard Co.; (bottom) Curtis Fukuda / **7-27** Hewlett-Packard Co. / **7-28** Curtis Fukuda / **7-32** (left) 3M Company; (right) Drexler Technology Corp. / **7-33** Hitachi America Ltd. / **7-34, 7-35** Storage Technology Corp.

Chapter 8

Page 8.1 © Brett Froomer 1988 / **8-17** Hewlett-Packard Co.

Chapter 9

Page 9.1 Lou Jones/Image Bank / **9-2** BR Intec Corp. / **9-3** Corning Glass Works / **9-4** Siecor Corp. of America / **9-5** Gregory Heisler/Image Bank / **9-6** Hewlett-Packard Co. / **9-7** NASA / **9-16, 9-17** Hayes Microcomputer Products, Inc. / **9-18** Panasonic Industrial Co. / **9-20** International Business Machines Corp. / **9-21** Hayes Microcomputer Products, Inc. / **9-25** Bank of America

Chapter 10

Page 10.1 AT&T Archives / **10-9** UIS, Inc. / **10-11** International Business Machines Corp. / **10-12** Apple Computer, Inc.

Chapter 11

Page 11.1 American Software / **11-2** (c) Adobe Systems, Inc. All rights reserved. / **11-3** T/Maker Co. / **11-4** WordPerfect Corp. / **11-5** TOPS, A Division of Sun Microsystems, Inc. / **11-6** Computer Associates / **11-7** Ziff-Davis Publishing Co. / **11-11** InfoWorld Publishing, Inc. / **11-12—11-14** Curtis Fukuda

Chapter 12

Page 12.1 Kay Chernush/Image Bank / **12-1** Internal Revenue Service / **12-2** Hewlett-Packard Co. / **12-3** Integrated Software Systems Corp. / **12-4** Neuron Data, Inc. / **12-18** Curtis Fukuda / **12-19** American Software / **12-20** Walter Bibikow/Image Bank / **12-21** Curtis Fukuda

Chapter 13

Page 13.1 Curtis Fukuda / **13-12** U.S. Department of the Navy / **13-26, 13-27** Oracle Corp.

Chapter 14

Page 14.1 Compaq Computer Corp. / **14-1** Radio Shack, A Division of Tandy Corp. / **14-2** © 1988 Christopher Springmann / **14-4** ComputerLand / **14-5** Radio Shack, A Division of Tandy Corp. / **14-6** Cullinet Software / **14-12** Interface Group, Inc. /

Chapter 15

Page 15.1 Don Carroll/Image Bank / **15-1** (top to bottom) Radio Shack, A Division of Tandy Corp.; Claris Corp.; Lotus Development Corp.; Compaq Computer Corp.; Hewlett-Packard Co. / **15-2** Canon USA, Inc. / **15-3** NEC America, Inc. / **15-4** Apollo Computer, Inc. / **15-5** NASA / **15-6** General Motors Corp. / **15-8** (both) Broderbund Software, Inc. / **15-9** Electronic Arts / **15-11** Quicksoft, Inc.

Cover: Art direction and design by Alexander Atkins Design / **Photo(s)**: Tim Davis Photography.

Computer Concepts Index

See also:
Introduction to DOS Index, page DOS 32
WordPerfect Index, page WP 175
Lotus 1-2-3 Index, page L 239
dBASE III PLUS Index, page dB 240

Access arms: Mechanical arms that hold one or more read/write heads; used in hard disk drives.
and hard disk storage, 7.9
Access time: The time required to access and retrieve data on a floppy disk.
defined, 5.15, 7.7–8
Actuator (See Access arms)
Adding records, 8.7–8.8
Ada: A language used by the Department of Defense that is designed to be portable (usable on different computers) and easy to maintain; named after Augusta Ada Byron.
Alpha numeric, 3.4
American National Standards Institute (ANSI) and program flowcharts, 13.6
American Standard Code for Information Interchange (See ASCII)
Analog signal: A signal used on communications lines that consists of a single, continuous electrical wave. Compare with digital signal.
and data communications, 9.9
Analysis: In information system development, the separation of a system into its parts to determine how the system works, combined with the development of a proposed solution to system problems.
defined, 12.6 detailed system, 12.7–9
example of, 12.10
feasibility study, 12.9–10
preliminary investigation, 12.7
ANSI (See American National Standards Institute)
Application generators: Programs that produce other programs based on input, output, and processing specifications from the user.
and program development, 13.18
Application software package: Computer programs that perform common business or personal tasks; purchased from software vendors or stores, 1.10
commercial, 11.2
example of, 1.12–15
general, 11.3–6
microcomputer, 1.10–15, 15.11
operating system and, 10.4
purchasing guidelines, 2.18
system software vs., 10.2
types of, 1.11
Arithmetic/logic unit: The part of the CPU that performs arithmetic and logic operations.
CPU and, 5.3
instruction execution and, 5.10
Arithmetic operations: Numeric calculations such as addition, subtraction, multiplication, and division.
in CPU, 5.3
defined, 1.7
example of, 3.9–10
Arrow keys, 4.5
Artificial intelligence: Methods of simulating aspects of human reasoning with computers.
and expert systems, 12.4
ASCII (American Standard Code for Information Interchange): The most widely used computer code for representing characters.
data representation and, 5.5–6
floppy disk storage and, 7.7
Assembly language: Similar to machine language, but uses abbreviations for machine instructions called mnemonics or symbolic operation codes that are easier for humans to work with.
defined, 13.12–13
Asynchronous transmission mode: Data communication method in which individual characters (made up of bits) are transmitted at irregular intervals, for instance as they are entered by a user.
defined, 9.10
Attribute: A field in a relational database.
defined, 8.13
Automated office: Describes the use of computers, facsimile machines, and electronic communications to make office work more efficient.
information processing trends and, 15.2
summary of, 15.5
Auxiliary storage: Stores programs and data when they are not being processed; similar to a filing cabinet.
defined, 7.2
direct-access storage devices, 7.12
disk cartridges, 7.10
file organization methods, 8.3–7
floppy disks, 7.4–8
hard card, 7.9
hard disks, 1.7, 7.8–10
in information processing cycle, 3.3
magnetic disks, 7.12–14
magnetic tape, 7.14–17
mass storage devices, 7.18
on microcomputers, 7.4–12
on medium and large computers, 7.12–17
networks and, 9.15
optical, 7.17–18
solid-state devices, 7.18
types of, 1.17–18, 7.19
user needs and, 7.3
Auxiliary storage unit: Computer hardware used to store instructions and data when they are not being used in the main memory of the computer.
defined, 1.7 (See also Auxiliary storage)

Backup of data files, 3.6
disks and, 7.11–12
magnetic tape and, 1.17, 7.15
reasons for, 7.9, 7.21
sequential files and, 8.4
Bandwidth: The range of frequencies that a communications channel can carry.
and transmission rates, 9.11
Banking, and data processing, 4.10
Bar chart: A common form of graphical display of information in which data is represented by vertical or horizontal bars.
advantages of, 6.4
graphics and, 2.14
Baseband: A type of coaxial cable that carries only one signal at a time, 9.4
BASIC (Beginner's All-purpose Symbolic Instructional Code): A commonly used high-level programming language.
described, 13.15
Batch control: The technique of balancing numeric data to a predetermined total to check the accuracy of data input.
and batch processing, 4.24
Batch processing: Data is collected and at some later time, all the data that has been gathered is processed as a group or batch.
applications for, 3.16
batch control and, 4.24
combined with interactive processing, 3.18
compared with interactive processing, 3.16
data entry for, 4.23–24
defined, 3.16
example of, 3.16–17
offline data entry and, 4.24
source documents and, 4.24
Baud rate: The number of times per second that a data communications signal changes; with each change, one or more bits can be transmitted.
and data transmission, 9.12
Benchmark test: A test that measures the time it takes for particular software or hardware to process a set of transactions.
and software evaluation, 11.10
Bidirectional printing: A form of printing in which the print head can print both when moving left to right and when moving right to left.
and printer features, 6.8
Binary number system bit representation and, 5.5
described, 5.8–9
Bit: An element of a byte that can represent either of two values, "on" or "off".
defined, 5.5
Bit-mapped display: A type of screen used for graphics in which the number of addressable locations corresponds to the number of dots (pixels) that can be illuminated. Also called dot-addressable display.
and display methods, 6.17
Bits per inch (bpi): A measure of the recording density of a disk.
and floppy disk storage, 7.7
Bits per second (bps): A measure of the speed of data transmission; the number of bits transmitted in one second.
and transmission rate, 9.12
Blocked records: A method of organizing records on magnetic tape into groups called blocks for easier access.
and storage, 7.16
Bold: Bold characters are displayed on a screen with greater brightness than the surrounding text.
defined, 6.15
Booting: The process of loading the operating system into main memory of the computer.
described, 10.3–4
Bottom-up design: Design approach that focuses on the data, particularly the output, of a system.
and information system development, 12.11
Broadband: Describes coaxial cable that can carry multiple signals at one time.
defined, 9.4
Bucket: The location where a record is stored in a direct file.
and direct file organization, 8.6
Buffer: A reserved area of memory that the operating system uses to temporarily store data that has just been read or is about to be output.
and memory management, 10.7
Bugs: A name for programming errors.
and program testing, 13.10
Bulletin board systems (BBS): Computer systems that allow users to communicate with each other and share data.
data communications and, 9.18
entertainment and, 15.10
Bus: A path along which bits are transmitted from one part of the computer to another.
and processor speeds, 5.12
Bus network: A network in which all devices share and are connected to a single cable.
advantages of, 9.17
Byron, Augusta Ada, 13.17

Byte: A unit of storage, equal to 8 bits; each storage location in main memory consists of a byte.
defined, 5.4

C: A language originally developed for writing systems software but now among the most widely used general-purpose programming languages.
described, 13.16
CAD (See Computer-Aided Design)
Careers
computer servicing, 14.5
professional organizations and, 14.8
salaries in, 14.6 (See also Information processing careers; Personnel)
Cartridge tape drive: A device commonly used to make backup copies of data on hard disks on personal computers.
defined, 7.12
for medium and large computers, 7.16
Cathode ray tube (See Screen(s))
CDROM (Compact Disk Read-Only Memory): A relatively small optical disk that uses the same technology as audio compact disks.
described, 7.18
Cell: The intersection where a row and column of an electronic spreadsheet meet.
defined, 2.9
naming, 2.21
Centralized data entry: A specialized data entry operation within an information systems department in which trained operators enter data from source documents.
procedures for, 4.29
Central processing unit (See CPU)
Certificate in Data Processing (CDP): A certificate awarded to those who pass examinations that cover computers (hardware and software), management, and systems analysis.
and career development, 14.9
CGA (Color Graphics Adapter), and graphics displays, 6.18
Change management: Procedures for implementing and tracking changes made to an information system.
and information system development, 12.18
Characters: The elements that comprise data, including alphabetic characters (A–Z), numeric characters (0–9), and special characters (such as punctuation).
blinking, 6.15
display methods, 6.15, 6.16–18
storage, 5.4–6
types of, 3.4
Charts
bar, 2.14, 6.4
flowcharts, 12,12–13, 13.6–7
line, 6.5
pie, 2.14, 6.4
structure, 13.4
Child record: A record that is the descendant lower in the hierarchical tree than a parent record; it is also directly linked to the parent.
and hierarchical databases, 8.14
Chips (See Microcomputer chips; Integrated circuit)
Clip art, and desktop publishing, 11.4
Coaxial cable: A high-quality communication line consisting of a wire or central conductor surrounded by a nonconducting insulator that is in turn surrounded by a woven metal shielding layer and a plastic coating.
baseband, 9.4
broadband, 9.4
COBOL (COmmon Business Oriented Language): A high-level language developed in 1960 and used for business applications.
described, 13.15
Coding: The process of writing the program instructions that will process the data and produce the output specified in the program design.
and program development, 13.9

Collision: When different keys in a hashing scheme lead to the same record location.
defined, 8.6
Color Graphics Adapter (See CGA)
Color screens: Screens that are capable of displaying several colors. Compare with monochrome screens.
defined, 6.14
types of, 6.16, 6.18
graphics and, 6.18
Column, in spreadsheets, 2.9, 2.21
COMDEX (COMputer Dealer EXchange): A large, annual computer trade show.
and education, 14.9
Commands: Instructions issued by the user to operate software.
defined, 2.2
as input, 4.3
Commercial application software: Software that has already been written and is available for purchase.
acquisition of, 11.7–10
custom software and, 11.6–7
defined, 11.2
desktop publishing, 11.3–4
evaluating requirements for, 11.8
functional applications, 11.5–6
general applications, 11.3–5
summary of, 11.11
training and, 11.12
vendors of, 11.9
Communication channel: A link or path that data follows as it is transmitted form the sending to the receiving equipment in a data communications system.
characteristics of, 9.9–12
coaxial cable and, 9.4
example of, 9.6
fiber optics and, 9.4
microwaves, 9.4
satellites as, 9.5
signal types, 9.9
transmission and, 9.10–11
twisted pair wire, 9.3
types of, 9.3 (See also Data communications)
Communication equipment front-end processors, 9.13
modems, 9.12–13
multiplexors, 9.13
types of, 9.12–13
Communication network (See Network)
Communication satellites: Satellites that receive signals from Earth, amplify the signals, then retransmit them back to Earth.
as communication channels, 9.5
earth stations and, 9.5
Communication software, types of, 9.14
Compiler: A program that converts a program written in a high-level language into machine language that can be processed by a computer.
and programming languages, 13.13
Composite video monitor: A type of graphics display that uses a single electron beam to activate the color phosphors within a pixel.
defined, 6.18
Computer: An electronic device, operating under the control of instructions stored in its own memory unit, that can accept data (input), process data arithmetically and logically, produce output from the processing, and store the results for future use.
auxiliary storage, 7.1–21
calculating ability of, 1.14
careers in, 14.1–10
categories of, 1.8–9
components of, 1.6–7
criteria for classifying, 1.8
databases, 8.11–18
data communications, 9.1–19
defined, 1.3
file organization, 8.3–11
hardware
(See Hardware information system development life cycle), 12.1–20
information processing and, 1.4–6, 3.1–21
input to, 4.1–32
microcomputers (See Microcomputers)
operating systems, 10.3–12
operations of, 1.3–4
output from, 1.3, 6.1–24
power of, 1.4
processor unit, 5.1–21
program development, 13.1–21
social issues, 15.12–16
software (See Software)
speed of, 5.11–12
trends, 15.2–12
users of, 1.3 (See also specific issues)
Computer-Aided Design (CAD): The use of a computer and special graphics software to design products instead of using manual drafting.
and automated factory, 15.6
Computer-Aided Engineering (CAE): The use of computer simulations to test product designs.
and automated factory, 15.6
Computer-Aided Instruction (CAI): The use of personal computers for education.
and home computers, 15.8
Computer-Aided Manufacturing: The use of computers to control factory production equipment, including robots.
and automated factory, 15.6
Computer-assisted retrieval: A technique in which microfilm readers controlled by a computer perform automatic data lookup.
and microfilm, 6.21
Computer crime: The use of a computer to commit an illegal act.
computer security and, 15.12–13
databases and, 8.20
malicious damage and, 15.13
Computer engineering: Deals with the design and manufacturing of electronic computer components and computer hardware.
defined, 14.7
Computer information systems (CIS): The use of computers in business.
defined, 14.7
Computer-Integrated Manufacturing (CIM): The total integration of the manufacturing process using computers.
and automated factory, 15.6
Computer literacy: Understanding of computers and how they are used.
computer purchasing and, 15.11
defined, 2.2
Computer output microfilm (COM): An output technique in which output from a computer is recorded as microscopic images on film.
and output methods, 6.20–21
Computer program (See Program)
Computer science: The study of technical aspects of computers such as hardware operations and systems software.
defined, 14.7
Computer security: Procedures and safeguards established to detect and prevent unauthorized use and deliberate or accidental damage to computer systems and data.
and computer crimes, 15.12–13 (See also Security)
Computer service technician: Good position for people who have a strong background in electronics and who like to solve problems.
career, 14.5
Conditions, in logical operations, 3.11, 13.5
Consultants: People with technical skills in computers and information processing that advise organizations and individuals.
and computer careers, 14.10
software, 11.9, 11.12
Control program (See Kernel)

Control structures: In structured programming, control structures are used to form the logic of a program.
and program development, 13.4–5
Control unit: That part of the CPU that controls the fetching, decoding, execution, and storage of program instructions.
defined, 5.3 (See also CPU)
Conversion: During the implementation phase of system development, the process of changing from the old system to the new one.
types of, 12.17
Coprocessor: A special microprocessor chip or circuit board that speeds up a particular task, such as numeric calculations.
and CPU design, 5.14
Copy protection for software, 15.13
Cost/benefit analysis: In the design of an information system, the cost/benefit analysis identifies the estimated costs of the proposed system and the expected benefits (including potential cost savings).
and system analysis, 12.9
CPU (central processing unit): Computer component consisting of a control unit and an arithmetic/logic unit that controls all computer operations. Sometimes called simply processor.
architecture of, 5.13–14
arithmetic operations, 5.3
control unit, 5.3
coprocessor and, 5.14
defined, 1.7
described, 5.3
design of, 5.16
logical operations, 5.3
machine cycle and, 5.11
machine language instructions and, 5.10, 13.12
memory addressing and, 5.10
multiprocessing and, 5.14, 10.5
number systems and, 5.7–9
operating system management of, 10.6
parallel processing and, 5.14
parity and, 5.7
program execution and, 5.10–11
screen display and, 6.16
speed of, 5.11–12
storage and, 5.4–7
CPU utilization: The proportion of time that a CPU is doing useful work, not idle waiting for data to process.
and system performance, 10.9
Crime, using computers, 8.20, 15.12–13
CRT (cathode ray tube) (See Screen(s))
Cursor: A symbol, such as a highlighted rectangle or an underline character, that indicates where on the screen the next character will be entered.
control keys, 4.5
defined, 4.5
moving, 2.20
positioning in menus, 4.18
screen and, 6.15
Custom software: Special software that is developed by the user or at the user's request to meet a particular need.
and commercial software, 11.7
example of, 11.7
reasons for using, 11.6
Cylinder: A group of tracks on a floppy disk (or hard drive) all having the same number; for example, cylinder 0 on a floppy disk consists of track 0 on side 1 and track 0 on side 2.
and storage, 7.6
Cylinder method: A method for physically organizing data on disks in which all the tracks with the same number are treated as part of the same group, called a cylinder.
and hard disk storage, 7.14

Data: Raw facts, including numbers and words, that are processed by a computer.
access time, 5.15, 7.7–8
accuracy of, 1.15, 8.10
ASCII format, 5.5–6
attributes, 3.6
communication of (See Data communication)
defined, 1.3
in information systems department, 1.18, 14.4
input of (See Input)
integrity of, 3.6, 8.12
maintenance, 3.7, 8.7–11
management of, 3.5–7, 8.11–18
in memory, 5.3–6
moving, 3.8
organization of, 3.4–5
output (See Output)
protecting, 7.11–12
representation of, 5.5–6
security, 3.6, 8.12–13
sorting, 2.13
storage of (See Storage)
timeliness, 4.29
transmission of, 9.12
validation of (See Data editing)
Database: A collection of data that is usually organized in multiple files.
administration of, 1.20, 8.17, 12.12
advantages of, 8.11–13
commercial, 9.17–18
computer crime and, 8.20
data communications and, 9.17–18
data management and, 8.11–18
data organization and, 3.5
defined, 2.12, 8.11
design of, 12.12
example of, 2.12–13
field, 2.12
file, 2.12
hierarchical, 8.14
indexed, 2.22
network, 8.14–15
privacy and, 8.20, 15.14
query languages and, 8.15–16
record, 2.12
relational (See Relational database)
summary of, 8.18
types of, 8.13–15 (See also Database management system)
Database administrator (DBA): A person who coordinates all database activities in an organization.
database design and, 12.12
responsibilities of, 1.20, 8.17
Database design: In information system design, the specification of the most efficient configuration of data files needed to solve a particular problem.
described, 12.12
Database management system (DBMS)
data dictionary and, 8.15, 12.8
data integrity and, 8.12
data security and, 8.12–13
defined, 8.11
features of, 8.15–16
file management system vs., 2.12, 8.11–12
security and, 8.15
users' responsibilities in, 8.17
Database software: Allows user to enter, retrieve, and update data efficiently.
defined, 1.12
described, 2.12–14
file management software vs., 2.12
tips, 2.21–22
Data bus (See Bus)
Data collection devices: Equipment designed and used for obtaining data at the site where the transaction or event being reported takes place.
described, 4.14
Data communications: The transmission of data over a communication channel, such as a standard telephone line, between one computer (or a terminal) and another computer.
analog signals and, 9.9
banking and, 9.17
bulletin board systems (BBS) and, 9.18
database and, 9.17–18
defined, 9.2
efficiency of, 9.13
electronic commuting and, 9.20
electronic mail, 11.5, 15.4
encryption and, 9.14
equipment for, 9.12–13
error correction in, 9.10
hackers and, 9.20
line configurations, 9.6–9
microcomputers and, 9.17–18
networks, 9.14–17
satellites, 9.5
shopping and, 9.17
software for, 2.16, 9.14
speed of, 9.12
summary of, 9.18
system of, 9.3
transmission direction, 9.10–11
transmission modes, 9.10 (See also Communication channels)
Data communications software: Allows you to transmit data from one computer to another.
described, 2.16, 9.14
Data dictionary: In a DBMS, the data dictionary contains descriptions of the fields, files, and the relationships among them. Also used in system design and analysis.
DBMS and, 8.15
system analysis and, 12.8
Data editing: Used to check input data for proper format and acceptable values.
defined, 4.17
Data encryption: In data communications, the conversion of data at the sending end into an unrecognizable string of characters or bits and the reconversion of the data at the receiving end.
described, 9.14
Data entry
arrow keys and, 4.5
batch processing (See Batch processing)
centralized, 4.29
default values and, 4.29
distributed, 4.29
ergonomics and, 4.30
error handling and, 4.29–30
example of, 3.7–8
interactive processing and, 4.22–23
offline, 4.24
online, 4.24–28
personnel, 1.19, 4.30
procedures for, 4.28–30
reliability of, 3.6
security and, 4.30
transcription errors and, 4.30
Data flow diagrams: Graphic diagrams that illustrate the flow of information through a system.
and system analysis, 12.8
Data integrity: The "quality" of data, comprising data accuracy, reliable data entry, and timeliness.
DBMS and, 8.12
defined, 3.6
Data library: Stores the disk packs and tapes associated with a large computer system when they are not in use.
defined, 1.18
Data management: The techniques, methods, and procedures that ensure that the data required for an application will be available in the correct form and at the proper time for processing.
database and, 8.11–18
data integrity and, 3.6
data security and, 3.6
data maintenance and, 3.7
defined, 3.5
on microcomputers, 8.18

Data processing
banking industry and, 4.10
magnetic ink character recognition and, 4.10
methods of, 3.14–19 (See also Information processing)
Data security: Methods of protecting data to keep it from being misused or lost.
and DBMS, 8.12–13
defined, 3.6 (See also Security)
Data transfer rate: The rate at which a disk drive transfers data from the disk to main memory.
and floppy disk storage, 7.8
DBMS (See Database management system)
Debugging: The process of locating and correcting program errors (bugs).
and program testing, 13.10
Decimal number system, 5.8
Decision support system: A system designed to help someone reach a decision by summarizing and comparing relevant data.
described, 12.4
Decision table: Identifies the actions that should be taken under various conditions in an information system.
and system analysis, 12.9
Decision tree: Identifies the actions that should be taken under various conditions in an information system.
and system analysis, 12.9
Decoding: The second step in the machine cycle, in which the control unit of the CPU translates the program instruction into commands the computer can process.
in CPU, 5.3
and instruction execution, 5.10
Dedicated line: In a data communications system, a point-to-point line between sending and receiving devices that is always connected.
and line configurations, 9.7–8
Default values: In data entry, data that is displayed automatically for the user to cut down input time, but that can be changed if necessary.
defined, 4.26
Design review: In the development of an information system, a review by management at the end of the design phase to determine whether it's worth proceeding with development.
described, 12.14–15
Desk checking: Reading a program and mentally reviewing its logic.
and program development, 13.9
Desktop publishing (DTP): Software that allows users to design and produce professional-looking documents that contain both text and graphics.
advantages of, 11.3
automated office and, 15.4
clip art in, 11.4
described, 2.16
general applications software and, 11.3–4
graphics and, 11.3–4
laser printers and, 11.4
page composition in, 11.4
scanner used in, 11.4
word processing and, 11.4
Development: The phase in the information system development life cycle when program development and equipment acquisition occurs.
example of, 12.16
Dialogue: On an interactive system, the sequence of user inputs and computer responses that occur when a user enters data.
and information system development, 12.12
Digital signals: A type of signal for computer processing in which individual electronic pulses represent bits that in turn represent characters.
and communications channels, 9.9
Digitizer, as input device, 4.9
Direct-access storage devices (DASD): A term sometimes applied to disk devices for medium and large computers.
and auxiliary storage, 7.12
Direct conversion: In information system development, direct conversion means immediately discarding the old system and beginning to use the new one.
and system implementation, 12.17
Direct file: A file that contains records that are stored and retrieved according to either their disk address or their position within a file. Also called a relative file.
bucket, 8.6
file organization and, 8.6–7
hashing and, 8.6
retrieval methods, 8.7
Disk
backup of, 7.11–12
fixed, 1.17, 7.9, 7.13
magnetic, 1.17, 7.12–14
removable, 1.17, 7.13 (See also Floppy disks; Hard disks)
Disk addresses, and indexed file organization, 8.5
Disk cartridge: A variety of removable hard disk storage sometimes used with personal computers.
as auxiliary storage, 7.10
Diskette (See Floppy disks)
Disk I/O (Input/Output), 10.9
Disk pack: A storage device with removable disks, used on medium and large computers.
and auxiliary storage, 7.13
Display, of characters, 6.15–18
Display terminals (See Screen(s); Terminals)
Distributed data entry: Describes a situation where data entry is performed at various locations in an organization, rather than in one central office.
and data entry procedures, 4.29
Document(s)
appearance of, 2.20
desktop publishing and, 2.16, 11.3–4
naming, 2.20
saving, 2.21
source, 1.18, 4.24, 12.14 (See also Word processing software)
Documentation
change management and, 12.18
importance of, 1.15
in information systems, 1.21, 12.6
maintenance and, 13.10
program development and, 13.3, 13.10
for software, 2.18
of spreadsheets, 2.21
Document template, 2.20
Domain: In database terminology, the name of an attribute in a relational database.
and relational databases, 8.13
Dot-addressable display: A screen used for graphics in which the number of addressable locations corresponds to the number of dots (or pixels) that can be illuminated.
and display methods, 6.17
Dot matrix printers: Impact printers in which the print head consists of a series of small tubes containing wires that, when struck against a ribbon and paper, print a pattern of small dots.
graphics and, 6.10
output for small and medium computers, 6.8–1
printing methods of, 6.9
Do-until structure: A looping structure in which processing continues until a given condition is met.
and structured programming, 13.5
Do-while structure: A type of looping structure in which first a condition is tested and then, if the condition is true, a process is performed.
and structured programming, 13.5
Downlink: The link from the satellite down to the ground.
and satellite communications, 9.5
Downloading: Transferring data or programs from a data communications link to a computer. Compare with uploading.
and electronic bulletin boards, 9.18
Dynamic RAM: A small and relatively inexpensive form of RAM in which the current or charge on the chip is periodically refreshed by special electronic circuits in order for the chip to retain stored data.
and processor design, 5.15
Earth stations: Communication facilities that use large dish-shaped antennas to transmit and receive data from satellites.
and communications satellites, 9.5
EBCDIC (Extended Binary Coded Decimal Interchange Code): A computer code for representing characters that is sometimes used on mainframes.
data representation and, 5.5–6
magnetic tape storage and, 7.16
Editor: A common operating system utility that allows programmers to make direct changes in programs and data.
and operating systems, 10.9
Education
career development and, 14.7–8, 14.10
computer careers in, 14.5
information processing, 14.7–8
microcomputers used for, 15.8
system implementation and, 12.17
EEPROM (Electronically Erasable Programmable Read-Only Memory): A form of ROM in which the contents can be electronically erased without removing it from the computer.
and processor unit design, 5.16
EGA (Enhanced Graphics Adapter), 6.18
Electronic banking, and data communications, 9.17
Electronic bulletin boards (See Bulletin board systems) (BBS)
Electronic commuting, 9.20
Electronic mail: Software that provides the ability for users to communicate directly with other users by sending text messages electronically over communication channels.
automated office and, 15.4
example of, 11.5
Electronic office (See Automated office)
Electronic shopping, and data communications, 9.17
Electronic spreadsheet software: Allows user to perform both standard arithmetic calculations and user-defined calculations on rows and columns of numbers.
advantages of, 1.12
automatic recalculation in, 2.9–10
described, 1.12, 2.9
documentation and, 2.21
example of, 1.12–15, 2.10–11
importance to management, 2.10
input to, 1.13
output from, 1.14
processing in, 1.14
tips, 2.21
Electrostatic plotter: Type of plotter in which the paper moves under a row of wires that creates an electrostatic charge at places on the paper where images will appear after the paper passes through a developer.
described, 6.19–20
Engineering
computer-aided, 15.6
of computers, 14.7
Enhanced Graphics Display (See EGA)
Entertainment software, 15.9–10
EPROM (Erasable Programmable Read-Only Memory): A form of ROM in which the contents of memory can be erased (using a special ultraviolet light device) and replaced.
and processor unit design, 5.16
Equipment (See Hardware)

Ergonomics: The study of the design and arrangement of equipment so that people will interact with the equipment in a healthy, comfortable, and efficient manner.
and data entry, 4.30
Error(s)
data entry and, 4.29–30
information system design and, 12.14, 12.19
program design, 13.9
transcription, 4.30
transposition, 4.30
user interface and, 4.21
Error correction: In the maintenance phase of information system development, error correction consists of dealing with problems caused by programming and design errors in the system.
in data communications, 9.10
information system design and, 12.19
parity and, 5.7
program testing, 13.10
Excel, 2.10
Exception report: A report that contains information that is outside of "normal" user-specified values or conditions and is thus an exception to the majority of the data.
defined, 6.4
and quality of information, 3.20
Executing: The third step in the machine cycle, in which the control unit of the CPU actually processes the computer commands.
in CPU, 5.3, 5.10
Executive, operating system (See Kernel)
Expert systems: Systems that combine the knowledge on a particular subject of one or more human experts into a computerized system that simulates some aspects of human reasoning.
defined, 12.4
Extended Binary Coded Decimal Interchange Code (See EBCDIC)
External report: A report that is primarily used outside of the organization that prepares it.
defined, 6.3

Facsimile (Fax): Machine that transmits an image of a document over standard phone lines.
and automated office, 15.4
Factory automated, 15.6–7
Fault tolerance: The ability of a system to continue processing when a major component fails.
and multiprocessing operating systems, 10.5
Feasibility study: In the design of an information system, the feasibility study discusses whether the proposed system is practical and capable of being implemented.
and system analysis, 12.9
Feed mechanism, of printers, 6.7
Fetching: The first step in the machine cycle, in which the control unit within the CPU obtains the next program instruction from main memory.
in CPU, 5.3
and instruction execution, 5.10
Fiber optics: A type of communications line that uses hair-thin strands of material to conduct light with high efficiency.
and communications channels, 9.4
Field: A specific item of information, such as a name or social security number, in a record of a database file.
database, 2.12
defined, 8.3
types of, 3.4
File: A collection of related data records that is usually stored on an auxiliary storage device.
data, 3.5
database, 2.12
defined, 8.3
direct, 8.6–7
indexed, 8.4
naming, 2.21
organization methods, 8.3–7
random, 3.5
sequential, 3.5, 8.3–4 (See also File organization)
File maintenance
backup and, 3.6
changing records and, 8.8–9
File management system: Software that allows a user to create, maintain, and access a single file at a time.
DBMS vs., 2.12, 8.11–12
defined, 8.11
File organization auxiliary storage and, 8.3–7
data maintenance and, 8.7–11
direct, 8.6–7
indexed, 8.4–5
keys and, 8.3
random retrieval and, 8.5
relative, 8.6–7
sequential, 8.3–4
types of, 8.3–7
File-oriented system (See File management system)
Firmware: Program instructions that are stored in ROM.
and processor unit design, 5.16
Fixed disks (See Hard disks)
Flat panel display: Screens such as plasma or LCD types that do not use a cathode ray tube, and are thus relatively thin and flat.
display method of, 6.18
and types of screens, 6.16
Flicker, of CRT, 6.16–17
Floppy disks: The principal auxiliary storage medium for personal computers. A floppy disk consists of a disk of mylar coated with a magnetic medium, enclosed in a square, flexible plastic jacket.
access time and, 7.7–8
as auxiliary storage, 1.7, 7.4–8
care of, 7.8
cylinders and, 7.6
data transfer rate, 7.8
double-sided, 7.6
format of, 7.5–6
hard-sectored, 7.6
latency, 7.7
read/write head and, 7.7
recording density of, 7.7
seek time, 7.7
settling time, 7.8
single-sided, 7.6
size of, 7.4
soft-sectored, 7.6
storage capacity of, 7.6–7
storage method, 7.7
types of, 7.4
write-protect notch, 7.11
Flowchart
ANSI and, 13.6
system, 12.12–13
Formatting
documents, 2.8
floppy disks, 7.5–6
hard disks, 7.14
Formula, in electronic spreadsheet, 2.9
FORTRAN (FORmula TRANslator): A language developed in the 1950s for engineering, scientific, and mathematical applications.
defined, 13.16
Fourth-generation languages: Programming languages that are easy to use, both for programmers and non-programmers, because the user specifies only what problem is to be solved rather than how to solve it.
Front-end processor: A computer that is dedicated to handling the data communication requirements of a larger computer.
and communications equipment, 9.13
Full-duplex transmission: Transmission method in which data can flow on a communications line in both directions at the same time.
and data communications, 9.11
Functional application software: Software that is developed to perform a specific task or function. Compare with general application software.
defined, 11.5–6
Function keys: Special keys on a keyboard that can be programmed to perform tasks that assist the user.
defined, 4.5
user interface and, 2.3

GB (See Gigabyte)
General application software
common, 2.4
desktop publishing, 11.3–4
microcomputers, 2.2, 15.11
types of, 11.3–6
General microcomputer applications software: Software that is useful to a broad range of users.
advantages of, 2.2
Geosynchronous orbit, and satellite communications, 9.5
Gigabyte (GB): A measurement of memory space, approximately equal to one billion bytes.
defined, 5.4
GIGO: An acronymn that stands for "Garbage in, garbage out."
and quality of information, 3.20
Grammar checker software: Identifies possible grammar, writing style, and sentence structure errors.
described, 2.6
Graphic(s): Information presented in the form of a graph or chart.
analytical, 2.14–15
CGA, 6.18
clarity of, 2.22
daisy wheel printers and, 6.11
described, 2.14–15
desktop publishing and, 11.3–4
dot matrix printers and, 6.10
EGA, 6.18
importance of, 2.14
input devices, 4.9
output and, 6.4–5
presentation, 2.15
projected, 2.22
resolution of, 6.17–18
screen display and, 6.17–18
software, 1.12
tips, 2.22
VGA, 6.18
Graphics software: Provides the ability to transform numbers and text into a graphic format.
defined, 1.12
Graphics tablet, 4.9

Hackers
computer security and, 15.13
data communications and, 9.20
Half-duplex transmission: Data transmission method in which data can flow in both directions on the transmission line, but only one direction at a time.
and data communications, 9.10
Hard card: A special kind of hard disk drive sometimes used on personal computers, consisting of a hard disk mounted on a circuit board.
and hard disks, 7.9
Hard copy: Output in printed form.
defined, 6.2
Hard disks: Auxiliary storage devices consisting of one or more rigid metal platters coated with a magnetic storage medium, and one or more read/write heads.
access arms, 7.9
advantages of, 7.10
as auxiliary storage, 1.7, 7.8–10
cylinders of, 7.14
defined, 1.17

hard card, 7.9
head crash, 7.9
medium and large computers, 7.13
microcomputers, 7.19
storage methods, 7.9–10, 7.14
Hardware: Computer equipment such as input devices, the processor unit, output devices, and auxiliary storage units.
data communications, 9.12–13
defined, 1.6
in information systems department, 1.16–18
manufacturers of, 14.3
Hardware resource sharing: One of the benefits of local area networks: each computer on the network can access and use devices such as a laser printer that would be too expensive to provide for each user.
and local area networks, 9.14–15
Hashing: A method of file organization in which the location of a particular record can be found with a mathematical formula based on a key field value in the record.
and collisions, 8.6
Head crash: An event in which a contaminant or particle on the surface of a hard disk platter causes the read/write head to crash into the platter, damaging the disk and often destroying data.
and hard disk storage, 7.9
Health, of users, 4.30
Hexadecimal number system: A number system often used with computers because it can represent binary numbers in a compact form.
and computers, 5.9
Hierarchical databases: A database that is organized in the form of a family tree, in which records are either child records (the descendant of a record higher in the tree), parent records (the ancestor of one or more child records), or both.
described, 8.14
Hierarchy chart (See Structure charts)
High-level languages: Computer languages that contain nouns, verbs, and mathematical, relational, and logical operators that can be grouped together in what appear to be sentences. Compare with low-level languages such as assembly and machine language.
defined, 13.13
High-speed laser printers: Laser printers that print output at rates of over 400 pages per minute.
and output for large computers, 6.14
High-speed printers: Printers that print at rates of 600–3000 lines per minute.
and paperwork, 6.25
Home computers, 15.7–10 (See also Microcomputers)
Home systems, computer control of, 15.8
Hopper, Grace M., 13.15
Horizontal application software: Software that can be used by many different organizations, for instance accounting software. Compare with vertical application software.
defined, 11.6
vendors of, 11.9
Host computer: In a data communications system using a multidrop line, a main computer that several devices (such as terminals or personal computers) communicate with over a single line.
defined, 9.8

IC (See Integrated circuit)
Icon: Screen symbols or pictures that are used instead of words to list program options.
defined, 2.4, 4.19
If-then-else structure: A control structure used to represent conditional logic in a program. Also called a selection structure.
and structured programming, 13.5
Image processing
automated office and, 15.5
described, 4.13
Impact printer: Printers that transfer an image onto paper by some type of printing mechanism striking the paper, ribbon, and character together.
band, 6.13
chain, 6.13
daisy wheel, 6.11
described, 6.6
dot matrix, 6.8–10
Implementation: The phase of system development when people actually begin using the new system.
example of, 12.17–18
information system development and, 12.16–18
Index: In database terminology, a file containing a list of the values of the key field and the corresponding disk address of each record in a file.
in database, 2.22
file organization and, 8.4
Indexed file organization: A file that contains an index that lists the disk address of each record in a file, so that records can be retrieved at random. Compare with sequential file organization.
described, 8.4–5
disk addresses and, 8.5
Inference rules: Logical rules used by an expert system that determine how knowledge is used to reach a decision.
and expert systems, 12.4
Information: Data that has been processed into a form that has meaning and is useful.
cost of, 3.20
defined, 1.3
qualities of, 3.20
Information age
automated factory, 15.6–7
automated office, 15.4–5
business systems in, 15.2–7
home use and, 15.7–12
social issues, 15.12–15
Information processing: The production of information by processing data on a computer.
careers in, 14.4–5
cycle of (See Information processing cycle)
data management, 3.5–7
data organization, 3.4–5
defined, 1.3
education and, 14.7–8
home, 15.7–10
processing methods, 3.14–19
trends in, 15.16
Information processing careers
certification for, 14.9
consultants, 11.9, 11.12, 14.10
continuing education for, 14.9
education and training, 14.10
preparing for, 14.7–8
professional organizations, 14.8–9
salaries in, 14.6
service and repair, 14.10
skill development, 14.8–9
summary of, 14.10
Information processing cycle: The sequence of input, process, output, and storage operations performed by a computer.
arithmetic operations, 3.9–10
data in, 3.7–13
defined, 1.3–6
input, 3.7–8
logical operations, 3.10–11
overview of, 3.2–3
processing, 3.8–11
storage, 3.3, 3.13
Information resource sharing: A benefit of LANs: anyone using a computer on the network has access to unrestricted data stored on any other computer on the network.
described, 9.15
Information system: A collection of elements including equipment, software, data, personnel, users, and procedures that provides accurate, timely, and useful information.
analysis of, 12.6–10
in business, 15.2–7
change management, 12.18
defined, 12.2–3
documentation in, 1.21
elements of, 1.15–21
evaluation of, 12.17
expert systems and, 12.4
for management, 12.3
integration of, 12.4
operational, 12.3
types of, 12.3–5
Information system development life cycle: An organized series of steps for developing and maintaining an information system.
analysis and, 12.6–10
conversion to, 12.17
cost/benefit analysis, 12.9
database design and, 12.12
defined, 12.5
design, 12.11–15
development, 12.16
documentation and, 12.6
implementation, 12.16–18
maintenance, 12.18–19
personnel and, 12.6
summary of, 12.19
Information systems department
career opportunities in, 14.4
data in, 1.18
described, 1.16–21
equipment in, 1.16–18
management personnel in, 1.20
personnel in, 1.18–20
software in, 1.18
users in, 1.21
Input
of data, 3.7–8
data collection and, 4.14
data editing and, 4.17
defined, 4.3
devices (See Input devices)
types of, 4.3
user interface and, 4.15–22
voice, 4.10
Input controls: Procedures that assure the accurate conversion of source document data to machine-processable form.
and information system development, 12.14
Input design: A description of what data a system needs and how it will be entered.
and information system development, 12.12
Input devices: Used to enter data into a computer.
defined, 1.6
digitizer, 4.9
ergonomics and, 4.30
function of, 3.3
graphics and, 4.9
graphics tablet, 4.9
image processing and, 4.13
keyboards, 4.4–5
keypunch, 4.2
light pen, 4.9
MICR and, 4.10
mouse, 4.7–8
optical mark reader, 4.12
scanners, 4.11–13
summary of, 4.15
terminals, 4.5–7
touch screens, 4.8
UPC and, 4.13
Instruction cycle: The first part of the machine cycle: fetching the instruction and decoding it.
and CPU, 5.11
Instruction register: A special area within the memory of the control unit of the CPU that can store a single instruction at a time.
and machine language instructions, 5.10

Instruction set: The collection of commands that a particular CPU is capable of executing.
and CPU, 5.10
Integrated circuit (IC): A complete electronic circuit that has been etched on a small chip of nonconducting material such as silicon.
CPU design and, 5.13
manufacturing process, 5.17–19
microcomputers, 1.2, 1.4
Integrated services digital network (ISDN): An international standard for the digital transmission of data using different channels and communication companies.
and wide area networks, 9.16
Integrated software: Combines several applications such as word processing, electronic spreadsheet, database, graphics, and data communications in one package that allows data to be shared between applications.
described, 2.17
Interactive processing: Processing in which data is processed upon input and output is produced immediately.
combined with batch processing, 3.18
compared with batch processing, 3.16
data entry for, 4.22–23
defined, 3.14
dialogue and, 12.12
types of, 3.14–16
Interblock gaps (IBG): Spaces between records on magnetic tape to allow for starting and stopping.
and magnetic tape storage, 7.16
Interpreter: Translates a program in a high-level language one statement at a time into machine language. Compare with compiler.
advantages and disadvantages of, 13.14
programming languages and, 13.13–14
Interrecord gaps (IRG): Gaps between records on magnetic tape to allow for stopping and starting.
and magnetic tape storage, 7.16
I/O (Input/Output) disk, 10.9
Iteration: A control structure in which one or more processes continue so long as a specified condition holds.
and structured programming, 13.5

KB (See Kilobyte)
Kemeny, John, 1.2, 13.15
Kernel: The essential and most frequently used instructions in an operating system, always kept in main memory. Also called the supervisor, executive, monitor, master program, or control program.
of operating system, 10.3
Key: In database terminology, a special field that contains information that is used to sequence the records in a file.
in file organization, 8.3
Keyboard
and ergonomics, 4.30
as input device, 4.4–5
Keyboard template: Plastic sheet that fits around portion of keyboard and has a list of keyboard commands.
as software learning aid, 2.20
Key field: A field in a database file that is used to arrange records in a specific order.
defined, 3.5
Keypunch as input device, 4.2
Kilobyte (KB): A measurement of storage space in memory, equal to approximately 1000 bytes.
defined, 5.4
Knowledge base: The combined knowledge on a particular subject of human experts, used as data for an expert system.
defined, 12.4
Kurtz, Thomas, 13.15

Label, in spreadsheet cell, 2.9
Languages (See Programming languages)
Large computers, printers for, 6.13–14
Laser printer: A nonimpact printer that operates in a manner similar to a copying machine.
in desktop publishing, 11.4
for small and medium computers, 6.12
Laser scanner, 4.13
Latency: The time it takes for the sector on a disk containing desired data to rotate under the read/write head.
and floppy disk storage, 7.7
LCD (Liquid crystal display): A flat panel display often used on portable computers, as well as on calculators and digital watches.
method of, 6.18
types of screens and, 6.16
Learning aids
software, 2.19 (See also Education)
Leased line: In a data communications system, a dedicated line that is provided by an outside organization. Also called a private line.
line configurations and, 9.7
multidrop configurations and, 9.8–9
Letter quality: A description of printed output of high enough quality to use for business or legal correspondence.
defined, 6.11
Licenses
site, 9.15
software, 11.10
Light pen, as input device, 4.9
Line charts: A form of graphical display of information in which continuous lines across the chart represent data relationships.
defined, 6.5
Line configurations: Types of line connections in a data communications system.
multidrop, 9.8–9
types of, 9.6–9
Line diagrams, 2.14
Line printer: A medium- or high-speed printer capable of printing multiple characters on a single line at the same time.
described, 6.7
Liquid crystal display (See LCD)
Loading
operating system, 10.3–4
programs, 1.13
Local area network (LAN): A communications network that is privately owned and that covers a limited geographic area, such as an office, a building, or a group of buildings.
data communications and, 9.14–15
information resource sharing, 9.15
Logic: A program's logic is a step-by-step solution to a programming problem.
conditional, 13.5
program design and, 13.4
Logical design: In system analysis, a design that offers a solution to an existing problem without specifying details such as the specific programming language or particular computer that will be used. Compare with physical design.
and information system development, 12.11
Logical operations: Ccomparisons of data in the processor to see if one value is greater than, equal to, or less than another value.
comparisons in, 3.11
conditions in, 3.11, 13.5
in CPU, 5.3
described, 1.7, 3.10–11
types of, 3.10–11
Logical records: A logical record is the amount of data that a program actually uses when it processes one record. Compare with physical record.
and magnetic tape storage, 7.16
Logic testing: Testing the sequence of program instructions to make sure they provide correct results.
and program development, 13.9
Logon code: On a multiuser system, the user enters a logon code to indicate the desired application.
and system security, 10.9
Looping: A control structure in which one or more processes continue to occur so long as a given condition holds.
and structured programming, 13.5
Lotus 1-2-3, 2.10
Low-level languages: Languages such as machine language or assembler language that are closely dependent on the design of a particular computer.
assembly language as, 13.13
defined, 13.12–13
Low-speed printers: Printers that print one character at a time; can print 15–600 characters per second.
described, 6.7
Machine cycle: The four steps which the CPU carries out for each machine language instruction: fetch, decode, execute, and store.
CPU operations and, 5.10–11
decoding, 5.3, 5.10
executing, 5.3, 5.10
fetching, 5.3, 5.10
storing, 5.3
Machine language: The fundamental language of a computer's processor, consisting of instructions that perform basic operations such as adding, moving, and reading data. Also called low-level language.
as compiler output, 13.13
described, 13.12
Machine language instruction: An instruction that the electronic circuits in the CPU can interpret and convert into one or more of the commands in the computer's instruction set.
and CPU, 5.10, 13.12
Macintosh operating system, 10.11
Macroinstruction: An assembly language instruction that generates more than one machine language instruction.
and assembly language, 13.12
Magnetic disk: An auxiliary storage device often used on large computers.
auxiliary storage and, 7.12–14
described, 1.17
Magnetic ink character recognition (MICR): A machine-readable data processing technique used almost exclusively in the banking industry.
described, 4.10
Magnetic tape: A thin ribbon of plastic coated on one side with a material that can be magnetized to record the bit patterns that represent data.
as auxiliary storage, 7.14–17
backup and, 1.17, 7.15
data storage methods, 7.16–17
tape density and, 7.16
Mainframe: Large, powerful computer system that serves numerous users simultaneously.
defined, 1.9
Main memory: A part of the processor unit that electronically stores data and program instructions when they are being processed.
data transfer rate and, 7.8
defined, 1.7
organization of, 5.3–4 (See also RAM; Memory)
Maintenance: The process of supporting an information system after it is implemented, including performance monitoring, change management, and error correction.
Ada and, 13.17
documentation and, 13.10
example of, 12.19
information system development and, 12.18–19
program, 13.11
structured programming and, 13.6
Management
of data, 3.5–7, 8.18
of information systems department, 1.20

information systems for, 12.3
of memory, 10.6–8
project, 11.5, 12.5–6 (See also Database management system)
Management information systems (MIS): Information systems that provide timely and accurate information for the top, middle, and lower levels of management in an organization.
defined, 12.3
Manufacturing, computer-aided, 15.6
Mass storage devices: Electromechanical systems that provide automated retrieval of data from a "library" of storage media such as tape cartridges or floppy disks.
and auxiliary storage, 7.18
Master program (See Kernel)
MB (See Megabyte)
Medium-speed printers: Printers that print from 300–600 lines per minute.
described, 6.7
Megabyte (MB): A measurement of memory space, approximately equal to one million bytes.
defined, 5.4
Megahertz: A measurement used to describe the speed of the system clock; it is equal to one million cycles (or pulses) per second.
and processor speeds, 5.11
Member: A child record in a network database.
defined, 8.14–15
Memory
access time, 5.15
buffer, 10.7
data in, 5.4–6
EEPROM, 5.6
evolution of, 5.14–15
main, 1.7, 5.3–4
management of, 10.6–8
operating systems and, 10.6–8
PROM, 5.16
RAM, 5.15
ROM, 5.16, 10.4
segmentation and, 10.7
semiconductor and, 5.14–15
swapping in, 10.8
types of, 5.14–16
volatility of, 7.2
Memory address: Just as a street number gives the location of a particular house on a street, this number gives the location of a particular byte of storage in main memory.
CPU and, 5.10
main memory and, 5.4
Menu: A special kind of screen prompt used in applications to provide a list of processing options.
advantages and disadvantages of, 4.20
defined, 2.4, 4.18
icons and, 4.19
selection methods, 4.18–19
types of, 4.18–19
Menu generator: Software that lets the user specify a menu (list) of processing options and then automatically generates a program that displays the menu on the screen.
and program development, 13.18
MICR (See Magnetic ink character recognition)
Microchips (See Microcomputer chips)
Microcode: Program instructions that are stored in ROM (also called firmware).
and processor unit design, 5.16
Microcomputer(s): Small, desktop-sized computer systems; also including laptop, portable, and supermicro computers.
applications for, 2.1–23, 15.11
auxiliary storage for, 1.7
chips, 1.2, 1.4
compatibility of, 15.12
databases, 2.12–14, 2.21–22
data communications, 2.16, 9.17–18
data maintenance and, 8.18
defined, 1.8
desktop publishing, 2.16
electronic spreadsheets, 2.9–11, 2.21
general application software for, 2.2, 15.11
graphics, 2.14–15, 2.22
hardware selection, 15.10–12
integrated software, 2.17
learning aids, 2.19–20
software selection, 2.18, 15.11
vendors, 15.12
word processing, 2.4–9, 2.20–21
Microcomputer chips
data processing and, 1.4
function of, 1.2 (See also Integrated circuit)
Microfiche: A sheet of film sometimes used for computer output.
defined, 6.20
Microfilm, as output, 6.20–21
Microprocessor: A single integrated circuit that contains the CPU and sometimes memory.
and CPU design, 5.13
Microsecond: A millionth of a second; a measurement of time once used to measure memory access time.
and memory access time, 5.15
Microwaves: A type of radio waves that can be used to provide high-speed transmission of both voice and data.
as communications channel, 9.4
Minicomputers: Computers with more processing power than microcomputers, and which can simultaneously serve a number of users performing different tasks.
defined, 1.9
MIPS: Acronymn for millions of instructions per second, a measurement of processor speed.
defined, 5.11
Mnemonic: A simple, easily remembered abbreviation used in assembly language programming to represent a machine operation code. Also called symbolic operation code.
and assembly language, 13.12
Model, and decision support systems, 12.4
Modem (MOdulate/DEModulate: An electronic device that converts the digital signals of a terminal or computer to analog signals that can be transmitted over phone lines.
computer service and, 14.5
fax machine and, 15.4
transmission rates of, 9.13
types of, 9.12–13
Module: In structured program design, a module (also called a subroutine) is a part of a larger program that performs one specific task.
and program development, 13.4
Monitor, operating system (See Kernel)
Monitor (See Screen(s))
Monochrome screen: Screens that display white, green, or amber characters on a black background.
and types of screens, 6.16
Mouse: A small input device used to control the movement of the cursor and to select options displayed on the screen.
advantages and disadvantages of, 4.8
described, 4.7–8
MS-DOS: A popular operating system for personal computers developed by Microsoft Corporation. IBM Version called PC-DOS.
use of, 10.10–11
Multidrop lines: In a data communications system, a single line with multiple connections for devices that communicate with a main (or host) computer.
design of, 9.8
line configurations and, 9.8–9
Multiplexor: An electronic device that converts multiple input signals into a single stream of data that can be cheaply transmitted over a communication channel.
defined, 9.13
Multiprocessing operating system: A system that controls the operations of a computer with multiple CPUs.
advantages of, 10.5
Multiprocessor: A type of computer with more than one CPU.
and operating systems, 10.5
Multiprogramming operating systems: Systems that allow more than one program to be run at the same time on the same computer, by rapidly switching the CPU between various programs.
CPU management in, 10.6
defined, 10.4–5
Multiuser computers: Computers that concurrently process requests from more than one user.
defined, 1.16
Multiuser-multiprogramming operating systems: Systems that allow multiple users to run multiple programs simultaneously.
described, 10.5

Nanosecond: A billionth of a second; the most common unit of time used to measure memory access time.
and memory access time, 5.15
Natural language: A type of query language that allows a user to make queries in ordinary English rather than special computer syntax.
defined, 13.14–15
Network(s): In data communications, a network is a collection of terminals, computers, and other equipment that use communication channels to share data.
auxiliary storage and, 9.15
bus, 9.17
communication, 9.14–17
configurations of, 9.16–17
defined, 9.14
area, 9.14–16
ring, 9.17
star, 9.16
topology of, 9.16
Network control unit: A computer dedicated to handling the communications needs of other computers on a network.
and local area networks, 9.15
Network databases: Similar to a hierarchical database except that each child record can have more than one parent.
advantages and disadvantages of, 8.15
file organization and, 8.14–15
Nonimpact printers: Printers that transfer an image to paper without using a mechanism that strikes against the sheet.
described, 6.6
ink jet, 6.12
laser, 6.12, 6.14, 11.4
page, 6.14
thermal, 6.12
Nonprocedural: Said of fourth-generation languages, because the programmer does not specify the actual procedures that the program must use to solve a problem.
defined, 13.14
Nonvolatile: Data and programs are retained in auxiliary storage even when power is turned off.
defined, 7.2
Number systems
binary, 5.8–9
decimal, 5.8
for computers, 5.7–9
hexadecimal, 5.9
summary of, 5.9
Numeric calculations (See Arithmetic operations)
Numeric keypad, and data input, 4.4

Object code (See Object program)
Object program: The machine instructions produced by a compiler from a program originally written in a high-level language.
and high-level languages, 13.13

OCR (See Optical character recognition)
Office, automated, 15.2, 15.5
Offline data entry: The device from which data is being entered is not connected to the computer that will process it; data is stored on disk or tape for later transfer.
 and batch processing, 4.24
Online data entry: The device from which data is being entered is connected directly to the computer that processes it.
 example of, 4.24–28
 and interactive processing, 4.22
Online help, 2.19
Operating system (OS): A program or set of programs that manage the operations of a computer. The operating system functions as an interface between the user, the applications programs, and the computer hardware.
 common, 10.10–11
 CPU management in, 10.6
 defined, 10.3
 evolution of, 10.10
 functions of, 10.3, 10.5–9
 kernel, 10.3
 loading, 10.3–4
 Macintosh, 10.11
 memory management in, 10.6–8
 MS-DOS, 10.10–11
 multiprogramming, 10.4–5
 multiuser–multiprogramming, 10.4–5
 OS/2, 10.11
 PICK, 10.11
 portable, 10.10
 ProDos, 10.11
 proprietary, 10.10
 resource allocation in, 10.6–8
 services of, 10.5–9
 single program, 10.4
 summary of, 10.12
 types of, 10.4–5
 UNIX, 10.10
 utilities, 10.9
Operational system: An information system that is designed to process data generated by day-to-day business activities.
 defined, 12.3
Operation code: The first part of a machine language instruction; it indicates what operation the CPU is to perform.
 and machine language instructions, 5.10
Operations personnel, in information systems department, 14.4
Optical character recognition (OCR): OCR devices are scanners that read typewritten, computer-printed, and in some cases hand-printed characters from ordinary documents.
 applications for, 4.12
 described, 4.11–12
Optical disks: Hard plastic disks on which data is recorded by a laser beam that etches microscopic holes in the surface of the disk to represent data.
 as auxiliary storage, 7.17–18
 computer-aided instruction and, 15.8
 storage capacity of, 7.18
Optical mark reader (OMR): Scanning device that can read carefully placed pencil marks on specially designed documents.
 described, 4.12
OS/2 (Operating System/2): A multi-programming, single-user operating system for personal computers developed by Microsoft Corporation and IBM.
 described, 10.11
Output: Data that has been processed into a useful form called information that can be used by a person or a machine.
 defined, 6.2
 examples of, 1.3, 1.5
 graphics, 6.4–5
 hard copy, 6.2
 information processing and, 1.4, 3.3
 microfilm, 6.20–21
 plotters, 6.19–20
 printers, 6.6–14
 reports, 6.3–4
 screens, 6.14–18
 soft copy, 6.2
 summary of methods, 6.22
 types of, 3.12, 6.2–5
 voice, 6.21
Output design: The design of specific screen and report layouts that will be used to display or report information on a new system.
 and information system development, 12.11
Owner: A parent record in a network database.
 defined, 8.14–15

Page composition in desktop publishing, 11.4
Page printer: A very high-speed printer capable of printing an entire page at once.
 described, 6.7
Page scanner, 4.13
Paging: A memory management method in which a fixed amount of data (a "page") is transferred from disk to memory each time new data is required. Also, in screen displays a method of moving lines displayed on a screen in which an entire new "page" or screen of data is displayed instantly. Compare with scrolling.
 memory management and, 10.7
 screens and, 6.15
Parallel conversion: In information system development, continuing to process data on the old system and simultaneously processing some or all of the data on the new system.
 and system implementation, 12.17
Parallel processing: A method of processing in which several CPUs within the same computer divide up a task, each works simultaneously on its portion of the job, and finally the results are combined.
 and CPU design, 5.14
Parent record: A record that has one or more descendants.
 and hierarchical databases, 8.14
Parity bit: An extra bit associated with each byte that is used for error checking.
 data communications and, 9.10
 error correction and, 5.7
Partitions, and memory management, 10.7
Pascal: A high-level language that stresses the use of structured programming techniques.
 programming language, 13.16
Password: Unique user identification codes that are used on multiuser systems to allow only authorized users access to the computer; entered during the login procedure.
 security and, 10.9, 15.13
 user interface and, 4.21
PC-DOS (See MS-DOS)
Pen plotters: Plotters that create images on a sheet of paper by moving one or more pens over the surface.
 described, 6.19
Performance monitoring: Comparing response times, file size, and other system performance measures against the values that were estimated when the system was designed.
 and information system development, 12.18
Peripheral devices: Computer hardware that surrounds the processing unit, such as input devices, output devices, and auxiliary storage units.
 defined, 1.7
Personal computers (See Microcomputers)
Personnel
 data entry, 1.19, 4.30
 information system development and, 12.6
 in information systems department, 1.18–20 (See also Careers)
Phased conversion: A method for implementing large systems in which individual modules are brought into use at different times.
 and information system development, 12.17
Phosphor coating, of screen, 6.16
Physical design: In information system development, a design that identifies actual procedures to be automated, and specifies a programming language and hardware to be used. Compare with logical design.
 and information system development, 12.11
Physical records: The amount of data that is physically transferred from tape to memory when a record is being processed.
 and magnetic tape storage, 7.16
PICK operating systems, 10.11
Picture element (See Pixel)
Pie chart: A form of graphic display in which the relative proportions of parts of a whole are depicted by the relative sizes of "slices" of a "pie".
 advantages of, 6.4
 graphics and, 2.14
Pilot conversion: Implementation of a new information system by only part of an organization.
 and information system development, 12.17
Pins, and dot matrix printer, 6.9
Pixel (picture element): On a graphics display, an addressable dot that can be illuminated.
 and graphics displays, 6.17
Plasma screens: A flat panel display that produces a bright, clear image with no flicker.
 defined, 6.16
 display method of, 6.18
Platter: A rigid metal disk coated with a magnetic storage medium; part of a hard disk drive.
 defined, 7.8
Plotters: An output device used to produce high-quality line drawings such as building plans, charts, or circuit diagrams.
 cost of, 6.20
 drum, 6.19
 electrostatic, 6.19–20
 flatbed, 6.19
 pen, 6.19
 resolution of, 6.20
 speed of, 6.20
Point of sale terminal: A special cash register, connected to a computer, that gathers data about sales transactions.
 described, 3.18, 4.7
 source data collection and, 4.29
Point-to-point line: In a data communications system, a direct line between the sending and receiving devices.
 and line configurations, 9.7–8
Polling: In data communications, the process of checking connected terminals or computers to see if they have data to send.
 and communication equipment, 9.13
Portable operating systems: Operating systems that will run on a wide variety of computers. Compare with proprietary operating systems.
 defined, 10.10
Portable programming languages, 13.19
Postimplementation evaluation: The process of evaluating the performance of a new information system after it has been installed.
 and information system design, 12.17
Preliminary investigation: Process in which it is determined whether a request for the development or modification of an information system justifies further detailed investigation and analysis.
 information system development and, 12.7
Primary storage (See Main memory)
Prime number: A number that is divisible only by itself and 1.
 and hashing, 8.6
Printers band, 6.13

bidirectional, 6.8
carriage size, 6.7
chain, 6.13
classification of, 6.6–7
daisy wheel, 6.11
dot matrix, 6.8–10
features of, 6.7–8
feed mechanisms, 6.7
high-speed, 6.13
impact, 6.6, 6.8–11
for large computers, 6.13–14
ink jet, 6.12
laser, 6.14
letter quality, 6.11
low-speed, 6.7
medium-speed, 6.7
non-impact, 6.6, 6.12–14
as output devices, 6.6–14
page, 6.7, 6.14
for small and medium computers, 6.8–12
speed of, 6.7, 6.11, 6.13
spooling, 10.8
thermal, 6.12
very-high-speed, 6.7
wide carriage, 6.7

Print spool: The current list of reports or data on disk waiting to be printed.
input/output management and, 10.8

Priorities, in multiprogramming systems, 10.6

Privacy
computer threats to, 15.14
databases and, 8.20, 15.14 (See also Security)

Private line (See Leased line)

Procedures (See Documentation)

Process design: In an information system design, the specification of exactly what actions will be taken on the input data to create output information.
described, 12.12–14

Processing, of data, 3.8–11 (See also Information processing)

Processing controls: Procedures that determine the accuracy of information after it has been input to the information system.
and information system development, 12.14

Processor unit (See CPU)

Process specifications: In information system analysis and design, process specification describe what actions are taken on data that flow through the system.
described, 12.9

ProDos operating systems, 10.11

Professional organizations, and information processing careers, 14.8

Program: A detailed set of instructions that directs a computer to perform the tasks necessary to process data into information.
compiler, 13.13
as controller of processing, 3.7–13
defined, 1.4, 13.2–3
design of, 13.4–9
development of (See Program development)
errors in, 13.10
firmware, 5.16
as input, 4.3
interpreter, 13.13
loading, 1.13
logic, 13.4, 13.5
processor execution of, 3.3
source, 13.13
storage in main memory, 5.4–6
testing of, 13.9–10 (See also Software)

Program design: The phase in program development when a logical solution to the programming task is developed and documented.
control structures and, 13.4–5
defined, 13.4
desk checking, 13.9
flow charts and, 13.6–7
principles of, 13.4–6
pseudocode and, 13.8
structured walkthroughs, 13.8–9
tools for, 13.6–9

Program development: An organized process of five steps—reviewing, designing, coding, testing, and finalizing documentation—used to produce one or more programs to perform one or more specific tasks on a computer.
application generators in, 13.18
coding, 13.9
defined, 13.3
design, 13.4–9
documentation, 13.3, 13.10
and information systems, 12.16
maintenance, 13.11
review of program specifications, 13.3
screen generators and, 13.18
steps in, 13.3–10
testing, 13.9–10

Program flowchart: A diagram in which all the logical steps of a program are represented by a combination of symbols and text.
and program design, 13.6–7

Program generators (See Application generators)

Program maintenance: All changes, including error corrections and improvements, that are made to a program after it is implemented and processing real transactions.
program development and, 13.11
standards for, 13.11

Programmer: Designs, writes, tests, and implements programs that process data on a computer.
in information systems department, 1.19, 14.4
program specifications and, 13.3

Programming language(s): A set of written words or symbols and a grammar that allow the programmer or user to communicate with the computer.
Ada, 13.17
application generators and, 13.18
assembly, 13.12–13
BASIC, 13.15
C, 13.16
categories of, 13.11–15
choosing, 13.19
COBOL, 13.15
common, 13.15–17
compatibility considerations, 13.19
compiler and, 13.13
defined, 13.11
FORTRAN, 13.16
fourth-generation, 13.14–15
high-level, 13.13–14
interpreter and, 13.13–14
low-level, 13.12–13
machine, 13.12
maintenance and, 13.19
natural, 13.14–15
Pascal, 13.16
portability of, 13.19
query, 8.15–16, 13.14
RPG, 13.17
selecting, 13.19
summary of, 13.19

Program specifications: Program development documents including data flow diagrams, system flowcharts, process specifications, a data dictionary, screen formats, and report layouts.
described, 13.3

Program statements: The "sentences" of a high-level programming language.
defined, 13.13

Project management: Planning, scheduling, reporting, and controlling the activities that are part of large projects such as the development of an information system.
information system development and, 12.5–6
software for, 12.6

Project management software: Allows users to plan, schedule, track, and analyze the events, resources, and costs of a project.
function of, 11.5

Project plan: A week-by-week listing of start and finish dates and estimated completion times of all activities involved in a large project.
and project management, 12.5

PROM (Programmable Read-Only Memory): A type of memory that is similar to ROM when it is in the computer (its contents can only be read, not modified), but which can be loaded with data immediately before it is installed in the computer.
and processor unit design, 5.16

Prompt: A message to the user that displays on the screen and provides helpful information or instructions regarding some entry to be made or action to be taken.
defined, 2.4, 4.17

Proprietary operating systems: Operating systems specifically designed to run on only a single manufacturer's machine. Compare with portable operating systems.
defined, 10.10

Protection, of data, 7.11–12

Prototyping: Building a working model of a proposed system.
and information system development, 12.15

Pseudocode: A structured design process in which the logical steps in the solution of a program are written as English statements, and indentation is used to represent control structures.
and program design, 13.8

Public domain software: Software that is not copyrighted and may be freely distributed.
and personal computers, 15.11

Query language: A simple English-like language that allows users to tell the computer what data they want to see on a report or screen display.
DBMS and, 8.15–16
example of, 8.16 (See also Structured Query Language)

RAM (Random Access Memory): The name given to the integrated circuits or chips that make up main memory.
and processor unit design, 5.15

Random access memory (See RAM)

Random file: File in which the records are not arranged in any sequence or order.
defined, 3.5

Random retrieval: A retrieval method in which any record can be directly accessed regardless of its position in the file. Compare with sequential retrieval.
and file organization, 8.5

Read-only memory (See ROM)

Read/write head: A device that is part of the floppy disk drive. It rests on the surface of the rotating disk, generating electronic impulses to record bits, or reading bits previously recorded.
and floppy disk storage, 7.7

Record(s): A collection of related data items (or fields).
adding, 8.7–8
changing, 8.8–9
data, 3.4
database, 2.12
defined, 8.3
deleting, 8.9–11
logical, 7.16
updating, 8.7–11

Recording density: The number of bits that can be recorded on one inch of the innermost track of a disk.
and floppy disk storage, 7.7

Relational database(s): A database that is organized in tables that in database terminology are called relations.
database design and, 12.12
described, 8.13
increased use of, 15.2

structured query language and, 8.16
Relational operations: In database terminology, operations (such as select, join, or project) that may be performed on a relational database.
and query languages, 8.16
Relative file (See Direct file)
Removable disks
described, 1.17
on medium and large computers, 7.13
Report: Data or information presented in an organized form.
detail, 6.3
exception, 3.20, 6.4
external, 6.3
internal, 6.3
summary, 6.3
Request For Proposal (RFP): A written list of an organization's software requirements that is given to prospective software vendors to help the vendors determine if they have a product that is a possible software solution.
and software evaluation, 11.8
Resolution
graphics displays and, 6.17–18
of plotters, 6.20
of screens, 6.14
Resource allocation, and operating systems, 10.6–8
Response time: The elapsed time between the instant a user enters data and the instant the computer responds.
operating systems and, 10.8–9
user interface and, 4.21
Retrieval
file organization and, 8.5
hashing and, 8.6
Reverse video: The process of reversing the normal background and foreground colors of a screen in order to highlight particular characters.
in menus, 4.18
screen features and, 6.15
RFP (See Request for proposal)
RGB monitor: A type of color monitor that uses three signals, one for each of the colors red, green, and blue, to activate the required screen phosphors.
and graphics displays, 6.18
Ring network: A network without a central computer; instead, a series of computers communicate with each other on a ring of cable.
and local communications, 9.17
RISC (Reduced Instruction Set Computing): A method to speed up computers by reducing the instruction set to those that are executed most frequently.
and processor design, 5.14
Ritchie, Dennis, 13.16
Robotics, 15.6
ROM (Read-only memory): A form of memory in which the data or programs are written to it once at the time of manufacture and always retained thereafter, even if the computer's power is turned off.
operating system and, 10.4
processor unit design and, 5.16
Root: In a hierarchical databases, the root is the original parent record at the top of the tree; it may have children, but does not have a parent itself.
and hierarchical databases, 8.14
Row, in spreadsheets, 2.9, 2.21
RPG (Report Program Generator): A language developed by IBM specifically to generate reports quickly and easily.
described, 13.17

Salaries, in computer careers, 14.6
Satellites (See Communication satellites)
Scanner(s): Devices that read printed codes, characters, or images and convert them into a form that can be processed by the computer.
in desktop publishing, 11.4
fax machine and, 15.4
as input devices, 4.11–13
laser, 4.13
page, 4.13
Screen(s): Also called a monitor, CRT, or VDT, a screen is one of the most common output devices.
bit-mapped, 6.17
brightness of, 6.17
CGA, 6.18
character display, 6.15
color, 6.14
composite video, 6.18
CPU and, 6.16
dot-addressable display, 6.17
EGA, 6.18
ergonomics and, 4.30
features of, 6.14–15
flat panel, 6.18
graphics, 6.17–18
monochrome, 6.16
as output device, 1.7, 6.14–18
paging and, 6.15
phosphor coated, 6.16
plasma, 6.18
refreshing of, 6.16
resolution of, 6.14
reverse video, 4.8, 6.15
RGB, 6.18
scrolling and, 6.15
size of, 6.14
touch, 4.8
user interface, 4.21
VGA, 6.18
windows in, 2.17
Screen generator: Software that allows the user to design an input or output screen by entering the names and descriptions of input and output data directly on the screen.
and program development, 13.18
Scrolling: A method of moving lines displayed on a screen up or down one line at a time.
and screen features, 6.15
Secondary storage (See Auxiliary storage)
Sector: A section of a track; the basic storage unit of floppy disks.
and floppy disk format, 7.5
Sector method: A method for organizing data on disks in which each track is divided into individual storage areas called sectors.
and hard disk storage, 7.14
Security
computer, 15.12–13
computer viruses and, 15.13
and database administrator, 8.17
and data entry procedures, 4.30
and DBMS, 8.15
of disk data, 7.11–12
hackers and, 15.13
passwords and, 10.9, 15.3
system, 4.21, 10.9
user interface and, 4.21
Seek time: The amount of time it takes for a floppy disk drive to position the read/write head over the appropriate track.
and floppy disk storage, 7.7
Segmentation: A memory management scheme in which programs are divided into segments that are brought into main memory from disk only when needed.
and memory management, 10.7
Selection structure: A control structure used to represent conditional logic in a program. Also called if-then-else structure.
and structured programming, 13.5
Semiconductor memory: The most common form of computer memory, consisting of integrated circuits that contain thousands of transistors.
and evolution of computer memory, 5.14–15
Sequence structure: A control structure used in programming in which one process occurs immediately after another.
and structured development, 13.4–5
Sequential access (See Sequential retrieval)
Sequential file: Records are arranged in alphabetic or numeric order by a key field.
described, 3.5
Sequential file organization: A method of data file organization in which records are stored one after another, usually in ascending or descending order.
backup and, 8.4
data storage methods and, 8.3–4
Sequential retrieval: Retrieval method used on sequential files in which records are retrieved one after another in the same order that the records are stored.
and file organization, 8.4
Sequential storage: Magnetic tape is considered a sequential storage medium because the tape drive must read records one at a time in sequence until it finds the one it wants. Compare with direct-access storage devices.
and magnetic tape, 7.16
Serial processing: The most common processing method, in which a single CPU executes instructions sequentially, one at a time.
and CPU design, 5.14
Server: In local area networks, a computer dedicated to handling the communications needs of other computers on the network.
defined, 9.15
Settling time: The time required for the read/write head to be placed in contact with the disk.
and floppy disk storage, 7.8
Shareware: Software that users may try out on their own system before paying a fee.
and personal computers, 15.11
Significant identification numbers, in database files, 2.21
Simplex transmission: Data transmission method in which data flows in only one direction.
defined, 9.10
Simulation software: Educational software that teaches a user by creating a model of real situations.
personal computers and, 15.9
Single entry/single exit: An approach to programming that specifies that each programming control structure will have exactly one entry point and exactly one exit point for processing.
and structured programming, 13.6
Single-sided disk: Disks on which data can be recorded on one side only.
and floppy disk storage, 7.6
Site license: A special agreement that allows a purchaser of software to use the software on all the machines in a network.
networks and, 9.15
software piracy and, 15.3
Social issues, and computers, 15.12–16
Soft copy: Output that is displayed on the screen rather than printed.
defined, 6.2
Soft-sectored disk: A diskette on which the number of sectors is determined by software at the time of formatting. Compare with hard-sectored disk.
and floppy disk format, 7.6
Software: Another name for computer programs.
commands, 2.2, 4.3
commercial application (See Commercial application software)
compatibility of, 11.8
consultants, 11.12
copy protection for, 15.13
custom, 11.6, 11.7
database (See Database software)
data communications, 2.16, 9.14
data management, 8.18

defined, 1.9
desktop publishing, 2.16, 11.3–4, 15.4
documentation, 2.18
drill and practice, 15.8
ease of use, 4.16
educational, 15.8
electronic spreadsheet (See Electronic spreadsheet software)
employment opportunities in, 14.3
entertainment, 15.9–10
examples of, 1.10–15
evaluation of, 11.9
file management, 2.12, 8.11
function of, 1.9
functional application, 11.5–6
general application (See General application software)
grammar checker, 2.6
horizontal application, 11.6, 11.9
importance of, 1.10
in information systems department, 1.18
installation of, 11.10
integrated, 2.17
learning aids, 2.19–20
maintenance of, 13.6
public domain, 15.11
purchasing, 2.18, 11.10
selecting, 11.6, 11.7
site licenses for, 9.15
support of, 2.18
system, 10.2–12
thesaurus, 2.5
tutorial, 2.19, 15.8
vendors, 11.9
vertical application, 11.6, 11.9 (See also Program)
Software houses: Businesses that specialize in developing software for sale.
and commercial application software, 11.9
Software license: A license from the software manufacturer to the buyer that describes certain limits on how the software may be used.
and software purchasing, 11.10
Software piracy: Illegal copying of commercial software packages.
and computer crime, 15.13
Solid-state storage devices: Groups of RAM chips that provide high-speed access to data.
and auxiliary storage, 7.18
Sorting data, 2.13
Source data collection: A procedure in which data is entered immediately as the event or transaction is occurring and at the location where it is occurring.
and data entry procedures, 4.29
Source documents: Original documents, such as sales invoices, from which data can be entered.
batch processing and, 4.24
controls for, 12.14
in information systems department, 1.18
Source program: A program written in a high-level language, and later converted by a compiler to machine language.
and high-level languages, 13.13
Spelling checker software: Allows you to check individual words or entire documents for correct spelling.
described, 2.5
Spooling: A technique in which data that is to be output on a printer is first written to disk or memory, until the printer is ready to process it.
input and output management and, 10.8
Spreadsheet (See Electronic spreadsheet software)
Star network: A network with one central computer and one or more computers or terminals connected to it, forming a star.
advantages and disadvantages of, 9.16
Static RAM: A large and relatively expensive form of RAM that does not require periodic refreshing in order to retain stored data; compare with dynamic RAM.
and processor unit design, 5.15
Storage
and access time, 7.7–8
auxiliary (See Auxiliary storage)
of characters, 5.4–6
costs of, 7.21
disk cartridges, 7.10
floppy disks, 7.6–7
hard disks and, 7.8–10, 7.14
in information processing cycle, 3.13
main memory, 5.3–4
microfilm, 6.20–21
recording density and, 7.7
sequential, 7.16
types of, 7.2 (See also Backup storage; Memory)
Storing: The fourth step in the machine cycle, in which the result of processing is written to main memory.
in CPU, 5.3
Structure charts: Charts that show the relationship of different modules within a program.
and program development, 13.4
Structured analysis: The use of analysis and design tools such as data flow diagrams, data dictionaries, structured English, and decision tables and trees to document the specifications of an information system.
defined, 12.7
Structured design: A design approach that concentrates on the major functions of an information system, and keeps breaking them down into smaller and smaller activities (modules) that can be programmed.
and information system development, 12.11
Structured program design: A methodology that uses the program design concepts of modules, control structures, and single entry/single exit to create programs that are easy to write, test, and modify.
control structures, 13.4–5
modules, 13.4
Pascal language and, 13.16
and program development, 13.4
single entry/single exit, 13.6 (See also Program design)
Structured Query Language (SQL): A widely used query language for relational databases developed and promoted by IBM.
on personal computers, 8.18
relational databases and, 8.16
Structured walkthrough: In information system design, a step-by-step review of the process design by the people involved with the development of an information system. In programming, a meeting between programmer(s) and the systems analyst to review program logic after the program has been designed.
information system design and, 12.14
program design and, 13.8–9
Submenu, and user interface, 4.20
Subroutine (See Module)
Supercomputer: Very powerful computer designed to perform a large volume of numerical calculations quickly.
defined, 1.9
Superminicomputer, 1.9
Supervisor, operating system (See Kernel)
Swapping: When using paging or segmentation, the operating system sometimes needs to "swap" data in memory with new data on disk.
and memory management, 10.8
Switched line: In a data communications system, a point-to-point line that uses a regular telephone line to establish a communications link.
advantages and disadvantages of, 9.7
Symbolic addressing: The ability to address a specific location in memory by a symbolic name (such as TOTAL) rather than by its actual machine address.
and assembly language, 13.12
Symbolic operation code (See Mnemonic)
Synchronous transmission mode: Data communications method in which large blocks of data are transmitted at regular intervals. Compare with asynchronous transmission.
described, 9.10
Synonyms: In hashing, identical record locations generated from different keys.
and hashing, 8.6
Syntax errors: Common programming errors that involve violations of the grammar and spelling rules of a programming language.
and program testing, 13.9
System analysis (See Information system development life cycle)
System clock: An electronic "pulse generator" that the control unit of the CPU uses to synchronize all computer operations.
and processor speed, 5.11
System controls: Procedures that ensure that only valid data is accepted and processed by an information system.
and information system development, 12.14
System flowchart: A graphical depiction of the major processes, reports, data files, and types of input devices that provide data to the system.
and information system development, 12.12–13
System houses: Businesses that specialize in developing and selling combined software/hardware systems.
and commercial application software, 11.9
System monitoring, as operating system function, 10.8–9
System performance
CPU utilization and, 10.9
measurements of, 10.8–9
thrashing and, 10.9
Systems analyst
database design and, 12.12
input design and, 12.12
output design and, 12.11
program specifications and, 13.3
role of, 1.19–20
System security (See Security)
System software: All programs including the operating system that are used in controlling the operations of computer equipment.
application software vs., 10.2
defined, 10.2

Tape
cartridge, 7.12, 7.16
magnetic, 1.17, 7.14–17
streaming mode, 7.12
Tape density: The number of characters or bytes that can be stored on an inch of tape.
defined, 7.16
Telecommuting, and home computers, 15.8
Teleconferencing: The use of computers and television cameras to transmit video images and sounds of a conference to other participants with similar equipment at a remote site.
and automated office, 15.5
Terminal: Consisting of a keyboard and a screen, is the most commonly used input device for a large computer.
defined, 1.16
described, 4.5–7
dumb, 4.6
intelligent, 4.6
point of sale (See Point of sale terminal)
types of, 4.6–7
(See also Screen(s))
Terminal emulation software: Software that allows a personal computer to imitate or appear to be a specific type of terminal so that the computer can connect to another computer.
and data communications, 9.14

Test data: Data that simulates the type of data a program will process when it is implemented.
and program development, 13.9–10
Testing design information system analysis and, 12.14
program development and, 13.9–10
Thesaurus software: Allows you to look up synonyms for words in a document while you are using your word processor.
described, 2.5
Thrashing: A condition where the operating system is spending more time swapping pages to and from the disk than processing data.
and system performance, 10.9
Time slice: In a multiprogramming operating system, the CPU is switched rapidly among several programs all running simultaneously; the amount of time it spends on each program (usually measured in milleseconds) is called a time slice.
and CPU management, 10.6
Top-down design: A design approach that concentrates on the major functions of an information system and keeps breaking them down into smaller and smaller activities that can be programmed.
and information system development, 12.11
Topology: The actual physical layout or pattern of a network; common network topologies include star, bus, and ring.
defined, 9.16
Touch screen: Allows user to interact with computer by touching the screen.
described, 4.8
Track: A narrow recording band forming a full circle around the disk.
and floppy disk format, 7.5
Tracks per inch (tpi): Then number of tracks that can be stored per radial inch on a disk.
and floppy disk storage, 7.7
Transaction processing: A type of interactive processing in which the user enters all the data pertaining to a complete transaction and the program immediately performs all the processing required for that particular transaction.
defined, 3.14
example of, 3.14–15
Transistor: An electronic component that can be either on or off and represents a bit in memory.
and computer memory, 5.14
Transmission
asynchronous, 9.10
direction of, 9.10–11
full-duplex, 9.11
half-duplex, 9.10
media, 9.6
modes, 9.10
rates, 9.11–12
synchronous, 9.10
(See also Data communications)
Tuple: A row in a relational database table.
defined, 8.13
Turn-around document: Documents such as utility bills that are returned by the customer and read by OCR
devices.
defined, 4.12
Tutorial software: Software that uses text, graphics, and sometimes sound to teach a user about subjects such as chemistry or music theory.
education and, 15.8
as learning aid, 2.19
Twisted pair wire: A communication medium consisting of pairs of copper wire twisted together and insulated with a thin plastic covering, as in standard telephone line.
advantages and disadvantages of, 9.3

Universal Product Code (UPC), and input, 4.13
UNIX: A popular multiuser operating system first developed by scientists at Bell Laboratories in the 1970s.
described, 10.10
UPC (See Universal Product Code)
Uplink: The transmission link from the ground to the satellite.
and satellite communications, 9.5
Uploading: Transferring programs or data from a computer to a data communications network.
electronic bulletin boards and, 9.18
intelligent terminals and, 4.6
User(s)
auxiliary storage needs of, 7.3
of computers, 1.3
DBMS and, 8.17
health considerations, 4.30
importance of, 1.15
in information systems department, 1.21
input design and, 12.12
interface with (See User interface)
output design and, 12.11
priority, 10.6
program specifications and, 13.3
software evaluation and, 11.10
User ID: A unique identifier, such as first name, last name, or initials, that the user enters as part of a login procedure. The user ID is public.
and system security, 10.9
User interface: The combination of hardware and software that allows the user to interact with the computer.
data editing and, 4.17
defined, 2.3, 4.15
design of, 4.21–22
evolution of, 4.15–19
features of, 4.21–22
function keys and, 2.3
icons and, 4.19
prompts and, 4.17
response time and, 4.21
screen design and, 4.21
security and, 4.21
submenus and, 4.20
Utilities: Operating system programs that perform common functions such as file management, sorting, and editing.
and operating system functions, 10.9

VDT (video display terminal) (See Terminals)
Vertical application software: Software developed for a particular use within a specific industry, such as application packages developed for construction, real estate, or food service. Compare with horizontal application software.
defined, 11.6
vendors of, 11.9
Very high-level languages (See Fourth-generation languages)
Very high-speed printers:
Print in excess of 3000 lines per minute; often called page printers.
described, 6.7
VGA (Video Graphics Array), 6.18
Video display terminals (See Terminals)
Video Graphics Array (See VGA)
Virtual machine operating systems: A system available on some large computers that allows a single computer to run two or more operating systems.
advantages of, 10.5
Virtual memory management: Increases the effective ("virtual") amount of memory by making it appear as if main memory is expanded to include all available disk space.
advantages of, 10.7
Virus: A computer program designed to copy itself into other software and spread through multiple computer systems.
and computer security, 15.13
Voice input: Allows user to enter data and issue commands to a computer with spoken words.
described, 4.10
Voice mail: Similar to an answering machine; callers can leave voice messages, but the messages are digitized and stored on disk for later replay or editing.
and automated office, 15.4
Voice output: Computer output in the form of spoken words.
described, 6.21
Voice synthesizer: A device that transforms words stored in a computer to sounds that imitate human speech.
and output methods, 6.21
Volatility: Dynamic RAM is said to be volatile because programs and data stored in it disappear when the computer's power is turned off.
and memory, 5.16

Warnier-Orr: A program design technique in which the programmer analyzes output to be produced from an application and develops processing modules that are needed to produce the output.
defined, 13.8
Wide area network (WAN): A communications network that is geographic in scope and that uses phone lines, microwaves, satellites, or a combination of communication channels. Compare with local area network.
and data communications, 9.16
Window: A rectangular portion of the screen that displays information.
in integrated software, 2.17
Wirth, Niklaus, 13.16
Word processing software: Used to create and print documents.
advantages of, 1.12, 2.4
automated office and, 15.4
defined, 1.12
desktop publishing and, 11.4
editing in, 2.6–7
example of, 2.6–8
features summary of, 2.8
formatting in, 2.8
replace operations, 2.6
support software, 2.5–6
tips, 2.20–21
Word size: The number of bits that the CPU can process at one time.
and processor speeds, 5.12
WORM (Write Once, Read Many): Unlike most optical disks, which contain only pre-recorded information, WORM disks can be written once by the user.
described, 7.18
Write-protect notch, and floppy disk storage, 7.11
WYSIWYG (What You See Is What You Get):
Desktop publishing software that displays a page on screen exactly as it will appear when printed.
and page composition, 11.4